Harry Bridges

THE WORKING CLASS IN AMERICAN HISTORY

Editorial Advisors
James R. Barrett, Thavolia Glymph, Julie Greene, William P. Jones,
Alice Kessler-Harris, and Nelson Lichtenstein

A list of books in the series appears at the end of this book.

Harry Bridges

Labor Radical, Labor Legend

ROBERT W. CHERNY

UNIVERSITY OF
ILLINOIS PRESS
Urbana, Chicago, and Springfield

Harry Bridges/Ballad of Harry Bridges (aka Song For Bridges)
Words and Music by Pete Seeger, Lee Hays and Millard Lampell
Copyright © 1941 Stormking Music, Inc. and Howard Beach Music, Inc.
Copyright Renewed
All Rights for Stormking Music, Inc. Administered by Figs. D Music
    c/o Concord Music Publishing
All Rights for Howard Beach Music, Inc. Administered by Kohaw Music, Inc.
    c/o Concord Music Publishing
All Rights Reserved Used by Permission
Reprinted by Permission of Hal Leonard LLC

The Library of Congress cataloged the cloth edition as follows:
Names: Cherny, Robert W., author.
Title: Harry Bridges : labor radical, labor legend / Robert W. Cherny.
Description: Urbana : University of Illinois Press, [2022] | Series:
    The working class in american history | Includes bibliographical
    references and index.
Identifiers: LCCN 2022013431 (print) | LCCN 2022013432 (ebook) |
    ISBN 9780252044748 (cloth) | ISBN 9780252053795 (ebook)
Subjects: LCSH: Bridges, Harry, 1901–1990. | Labor movement—United
    States. | Stevedores—Labor unions—United States. | International
    Longshore and Warehouse Union—History.
Classification: LCC HD8073.B7 C44 2022 (print) | LCC HD8073.B7
    (ebook) | DDC 331.88092 [B]—dc23/eng/20220321
LC record available at https://lccn.loc.gov/2022013431
LC ebook record available at https://lccn.loc.gov/2022013432

Paperback ISBN 978-0-252-08802-5

To Sarah

Contents

Preface

There is more than one story about Harry Bridges. One story, told many times, is that he was a member of the Communist Party and that that is the most important thing to know about him. Another story, also told many times, is that he was the victim of an elaborate frame-up to prove that he was a Communist and therefore liable for deportation, that he was the victim of repeated federal prosecutions that had as their intent the elimination of an effective labor leader, and that those are the most important things to know about him. Both stories have elements of truth in them, but neither is the most important story about Harry Bridges. The most important story is that he was a remarkably effective leader of a remarkable union. This book tells all those stories, but I hope that I have centered my story in a way that both recognizes Bridges's many accomplishments and acknowledges his limitations and foibles.

To tell Bridges's history is also to tell the history of the Pacific Coast longshore workers, whose union Bridges was instrumental in creating and which he led for more than forty years. That union, now the International Longshore and Warehouse Union (ILWU), began on the docks of Pacific Coast ports. In the 1930s, it moved inland, organizing warehousemen. In the 1940s, it organized sugar- and pineapple-field workers in Hawai'i. In the 1950s, it absorbed locals in other fields. Its members now range from hotel workers in Hawai'i to borax miners and cotton compress workers in Southern California, from tugboat workers in Alaska and craft-beer workers in San Francisco to bookstore workers in Portland. Throughout that long history, longshore workers have remained at the center of the union. It was from them that Bridges came, it was they who remained his constant touchstone, and the relationship between them was synergistic. There have been other books written about the ILWU's warehouse division and about Local 142, the Hawaiian local that now includes not only longshore, warehouse, and field workers, but also workers in tourism, hospitality, and other fields. To have given all those groups the space they deserve in this book would have added hundreds more pages to what is already a very long book. All those are topics for books by other historians.

So this book centers on Harry Bridges and longshore workers. Other units of the ILWU appear but cannot be treated at the length appropriate to their own histories. Some readers may conclude that I have ignored, overlooked, or slighted important information. Like all historians, I have had to winnow a huge amount of information to focus on what I understand to be central to the story, and I have had to trim some three hundred pages from my first draft. I shall contribute all the research material I have accumulated to the Labor Archives and Research Center at San Francisco State University (LARC), where subsequent researchers—and those who will inevitably criticize the decisions I have made about what is important—can conduct their own research and come to their own conclusions.

Was Bridges a member of the Communist Party? He always denied having been a member but was always equally open about his commitment to a Marxist view of the economy, his close relations with Communists, and his high regard for the Soviet Union. I found no simple answer to what turns out to be a very complex question about Bridges's relationship to the party. I also concluded, very early in this project, that focusing centrally on that question would not be productive. For me, the most important questions have been: How effective was Bridges as a union leader? And how was Bridges effective as a union leader? A subsidiary question, to which I return in the final chapter, is: Did Bridges's relationship to the Communist Party affect his effectiveness as a union leader?

As the title of this book indicates, Harry Bridges has long since achieved iconic status. Those who complicate that story have experienced not just polite criticism but sometimes harsh words, as witness the reception of Charles Larrowe's 1970 biography or the 1992 documentary by Minott-Weinacht Productions. I received some of the same after I appeared in a documentary and mentioned information from the files of the Communist Party of the United States (CPUSA) in the Russian State Archive for Socio-Political History. I was present when ILWU president Brian McWilliams denounced any use of those archives as red-baiting, and I am grateful to the late Albert Vitere Lannon—a former student of mine—for coming to my defense. Nonetheless, when I began this work, it was with the condition that I would tell the full story as I understood it, "warts and all." I would not have begun with any other understanding. I am also grateful to Harry and Noriko for accepting that condition.

Acknowledgments

Since beginning this book more than thirty-five years ago, I have accumulated many debts, more than I can list here. The first is, of course, to Harry and Noriko Sawada Bridges, who invited me to undertake this project, welcomed me into their home, made themselves available for interviews, and provided access to their personal papers and Rolodex. Over the following twelve years, I visited many libraries and archives, from Harvard to Honolulu, from Moscow to Melbourne, accumulating more than four large filing cabinets of material. Then other university responsibilities intervened. I never lost sight of the Bridges biography, but returning to it in a serious way had to wait until I retired.

I was fortunate that Bridges's four children agreed to interviews, as did many who knew Bridges or worked with him. I plan to give all those interviews to the Labor Archives and Research Center at San Francisco State University. The late Archie Green, David Selvin, and Don Watson were all consistently supportive, encouraging, and helpful, as have been Robert Bridges, Harry's son, and Marie Shell, Harry's granddaughter. Jim Barrett, Peter Cole, Bill Issel, the late Albert Vitere Lannon, Harvey Schwartz, the late Jules Tygiel, and an anonymous reviewer all read drafts and provided helpful comments.

The ILWU maintains a remarkable library and archive, and I have benefited greatly from the assistance of the ILWU librarians since 1985: Carol Cuénod, Sarah Stewart, Gene Vrana, and Robin Walker. Robin Walker has been especially helpful in the past few years. I am similarly grateful to the directors of the Labor Archives and Research Center at San Francisco State University: Lynn Bonfield, Susan Sherwood, Catherine Powell, and interim director Tanya Hollis, and to LARC staff members, especially the late Carol Cuénod. I also benefited from the assistance of Sarah Cooper and Mary Tyler of the Southern California Library, Los Angeles; the staff of the Walter Reuther Library at Wayne State University, especially the late Philip Mason; the staff of the Library of Congress manuscript division; Waverly Lowell, Kathleen O'Connor, Richard Boyden, and Lisa Miller at the National Archives, San Bruno, California; and the National Archives staff in Washington, DC, especially Jerry Hess, who provided a sympathetic ear when I told him of the theft of a bag with all the copies I had made days before and did everything he could to assist me in replacing the missing materials in the shortest possible time.

My initial research in Moscow was possible because of appointment as a Distinguished Fulbright Lecturer at Lomonosov Moscow State University. John Haynes, then at the Library of Congress, was very helpful in preparing me for research at what is now the Russian State Archives of Socio-Political History in Moscow. I must also thank Datia Lotareva who was my research assistant and translator there in 1996 and 2003, the attendants in reading room 413, and my colleagues and students at Moscow State University who assisted me in various ways.

For opening their archives to me, I am grateful to the officers and staff of ILWU Local 8 (Portland); the officers and staff of Local 142 (Honolulu), especially Betty Yanagawa; and Gunnar Lundeberg of the Sailors' Union of the Pacific (SUP).

The late Ottilie Markholt generously shared her large personal collection of materials on the history of Pacific Coast maritime workers and her manuscript (since published) on their history; she also provided conversation, coffee, and copying assistance during the several days I spent in her living room reviewing her collection. Her collection has since been deposited with the Labor Archives, University of Washington, Seattle. The late Stanley Kutler, University of Wisconsin, Madison, generously gave me research materials he had collected in the course of his own research. The late Ron Magden, of Tacoma, Washington, also shared aspects of his research.

During the first dozen years of my research, I benefited from several very capable research assistants: Marie Bolton, Sarah Cherny, Gretchen Lemke Santangelo, Cynthia Taylor, David Vaught, Jennifer Choi, and Michelle Kleehammer, all in San Francisco; David Wells, in New Orleans; Andrew Brown, John James Feeny, and John Steel, in Australia; and, recently, Kyle Pruitt, in Washington, DC. Barbi Marshall, Helen Harvey, and Silia Tahlvi transcribed interviews.

I am grateful for financial assistance from the National Endowment for the Humanities for a summer stipend and a yearlong fellowship, the American Council of Learned Societies for a research grant, the Henry J. Kaiser Family Foundation for a grant to study at the Walter P. Reuther Library, the American Philosophical Society for a grant to assist in acquiring Bridges's Federal Bureau of Investigation (FBI) file, and the California State University Emeritus and Retired Faculty and Staff Association for a grant toward the cost of securing photographs and permissions for this publication. I owe thanks to Patricia Grimshaw and Alan Mayne, who facilitated my appointment as a visiting scholar at the University of Melbourne, permitting my research in Australian libraries and archives. San Francisco State University provided two summer stipends, two yearlong sabbaticals, and funds for research assistants, travel to collections, and transcription of interviews.

Thanks also must go to Laurie Matheson, James Engelhardt, Alison K. Syring Bassford, and Ellie Hinton at the University of Illinois Press who have provided advice, moral support, and understanding.

And, of course, all errors are my own.

Finally, thanks have to go to my family for their support and encouragement. Rebecca, my wife and partner, and Sarah, our daughter, have lived with this project since Sarah was in middle school. Our granddaughters, Cerys and Sabina, have lived with it since they were born. This book is dedicated to Sarah. Throughout much of 2017, while working on this book, I was facing a major medical issue, and none of the specialists at the world-famous medical center near my home could diagnose the cause. Sarah, who is a pathologist at Kaiser San Francisco, asked her colleague Dr. Marc Lee, a radiologist, to review my scans, and he correctly diagnosed a serious bone infection. In early 2018, Sarah found a new medical team for me, at the other world-famous medical center not far away. I am very grateful to Drs. David Lowenberg, Gina Suh, and Eila Skinner whose skills led to a successful resolution. At one point during all that, Sarah recognized that I was likely going into sepsis and got me to medical care in time. So, in a very real sense, Sarah saved my life and made this book possible.

The following publishers have kindly granted permission for my previously published works to be incorporated into this book, most in significantly revised form:

"Harry Bridges, Labor Radicalism, and the State." Occasional Paper Series, no. 1, Center for Labor Studies, University of Washington, 1994.

"The Making of a Labor Radical: Harry Bridges, 1901–1934." *Pacific Historical Review* 64 (1995): 363–88.

"Longshoremen of San Francisco Bay, 1849–1960." In *Dock Workers: International Explorations in Comparative Labor History, 1790–1970*, edited by Sam Davies et al. 2 vols. Aldershot, Hampshire: Ashgate, 2000.

"Constructing a Radical Identity: History, Memory, and the Seafaring Stories of Harry Bridges." *Pacific Historical Review* 70 (2001): 571–600.

"Prelude to the Popular Front: The Communist Party in California, 1931–1935." *American Communist History* 1 (2002): 5–37.

"The Longshoremen of San Francisco: An Exception in the American Labor Movement?" In *Environnements Portuaires/Port Environments*, edited by John Barzman and Eric Barré. Dieppe: Publications des Universités de Rouen et du Havre, 2003.

"Anticommunist Networks and Labor: The Pacific Coast in the 1930s." In *Labor's Cold War: Local Politics in a Global Context*, edited by Shelton Stromquist. Urbana: University of Illinois Press, 2008.

"The Communist Party in California, 1935–1940: From the Political Margins to the Mainstream and Back." *American Communist History* 9 (2010): 3–33.

"Harry Bridges's Australia, Australia's Harry Bridges." In *Frontiers of Labor: Comparative Histories of the United States and Australia*, edited by Greg Passmore and Shelton Stromquist. Urbana: University of Illinois Press, 2018.

Abbreviations

Some of these abbreviations are also used in the notes. See also the list of abbreviations used only in the notes, preceding the notes.

ACA	American Communications Association
ACLU	American Civil Liberties Union
AFL	American Federation of Labor
ALP	Australian Labor Party
ARA	American Radio Association
ARTA	American Radio Telegraphists Association
CI	Communist International
CIO	Committee on Industrial Organization, later Congress of Industrial Organizations
CLF	California Labor Federation
CLRC	Coast Labor Relations Committee
Comintern	Communist International
CP	Communist Party of the United States, unless otherwise indicated
CPA	Communist Political Association
CPUSA	Communist Party of the United States
ECCI	Executive Committee of the Communist International
FBI	Federal Bureau of Investigation
HUAC	House Committee on Un-American Activities
IBL	International Brotherhood of Longshoremen
IBT	International Brotherhood of Teamsters
IBU	Inland Boatmen's Union
ILA	International Longshoremen's Association

ILA-PCD	International Longshoremen's Association, Pacific Coast District (Local 38)
ILWU	International Longshoremen's and Warehousemen's Union (now International Longshore and Warehouse Union)
INS	Immigration and Naturalization Service
ISU	International Seamen's Union of America
IUE	International Union of Electrical Workers
IWW	Industrial Workers of the World
LNPL	Labor's Non-Partisan League
M&M	Mechanization and Modernization Agreement (first in 1961, second in 1966)
MC&S	Marine Cooks and Stewards Union, part of the ISU, AFL
MC&S-AFL	Marine Cooks and Stewards Union, part of the SIU, AFL
MEBA	Marine Engineers' Beneficial Association
MFOW	Marine Firemen, Oilers, Watertenders, and Wipers Association
MFP	Maritime Federation of the Pacific Coast
MFW	Maritime Federation of the World, part of the WFTU
MM&P	International Organization of Masters, Mates, and Pilots
MWIU	Marine Workers Industrial Union
NMU	National Maritime Union
NRA	National Recovery Administration
NUMCS	National Union of Marine Cooks and Stewards, CIO
PCMIB	Pacific Coast Maritime Industry Board
PMA	Pacific Maritime Association
PolBuro	Political Bureau, the highest level of decision-making in the U.S. Communist Party
R&S	Riggers' and Stevedores' Union
SAC	Special Agent in Charge of an FBI field office
SIU	Seafarers International Union
SUA	Seamen's Union of Australia
SUP	Sailors' Union of the Pacific
SWOC	Steel Workers Organizing Committee
TUUL	Trade Union Unity League
UAW	United Automobile Workers
UE	United Electrical, Radio, and Machine Workers
ULP	Union Labor Party
USW	United Steel Workers
WEA	Waterfront Employers' Association
WEU	Waterfront Employers' Union
WFTU	World Federation of Trade Unions

Harry Bridges

From Australia to the
San Francisco Docks

Alfred Renton Bridges, able seaman, age eighteen, preferred to be called Harry. In late 1919, he walked out of his parents' home in Australia, never to return. In early 1978, Harry Bridges, age seventy-six, recently retired after forty-four years of union leadership, spoke about his life at the National Gallery of Art in Washington, DC. His title, "Up from Down Under," invoked his childhood and youth in Australia as the source of his understanding of labor and politics, a theme he had repeated many times before, even though some of the seafaring experiences he related could not have happened as he described them.[1] Bridges's youth in Australia and early seafaring provided him with varied influences. Some of them he embraced, some he rejected, and some took time to mature into adult commitments.

His father was Alfred Bridges, whose parents were English and chose a civil marriage. Alfred married Julia Dorgan, Irish and Catholic, in 1894, in St. George's Catholic Church, in Carlton, a suburb of Melbourne, the capital of the Colony (later State) of Victoria. Their first child, Lucy, was born in 1895. Eileen followed in 1898. By 1901 they lived in Kensington, another Melbourne suburb, where Julia gave birth to their first son on July 28, 1901. They christened him Alfred Renton Bridges. Alice was born in 1904, followed by Thomas Lester in 1906.[2]

The year of young Alfred's birth, 1901, also marked the birth of the Australian nation, and Melbourne was temporarily its capital. Despite stereotypes of Australia as a land of sheep and desert, Melbourne counted a half-million people, and its residents took pride in its new five- and ten-story commercial buildings and modern cable-driven tram (streetcar) system.[3]

Young Alfred grew up not amid the bustle of downtown Melbourne but in Melbourne's more relaxed northwestern suburbs. Much of Kensington was working class, close to the railroad yards, abattoirs, and mills where many of its residents worked. The family remained there for the next nine years, living behind and above two shops, one occupied by the senior Alfred Bridges's enterprises and the other usually by Julia's dry-goods business.[4] Despite declaring insolvency in 1901, Alfred rebounded quickly, becoming a pioneer developer for the area, subdividing country estates, selling real estate, and acquiring inexpensive cottages that he rented to working-class tenants.[5]

Around 1910 the family moved a half block away to the "Bridges Block," a large brick corner building across from the train station. Alfred's real-estate office occupied the prime corner location, and the family lived above it. As Alfred's business prospered, the family moved to substantial houses—a different one every year or two, all relatively near each other.[6]

Just under six feet tall, with a dapper handlebar mustache, Alfred was, his son recalled, "a great bushman" and a crack shot with a rifle, skills he taught his son. Alfred also taught the children to swim. Young Alfred developed into a good swimmer and served as captain of a swimming team. Largely self-educated, the senior Alfred filled their home with energy, creativity, and enthusiasm for new projects, including a vaudeville revue in which his children were actors.[7]

Alfred sometimes spent Sunday morning playing the piano, ranging from Mozart to popular pieces. He and Julia took their children to see opera, light opera, and musical comedies. Other family members also contributed to young Alfred's musical education. Phil Munro, Julia's cousin, a seaman, lived in West Melbourne, near the Bridges family's home. Munro's mandolin playing so fascinated young Alfred that he persuaded Munro to teach him to play. When Alfred, Lucy, or Eileen played the piano, young Alfred joined with his mandolin. The family all sang, including songs composed by Alfred.[8]

Julia Bridges and her sisters, Ellen and Beatrice, were devout Catholics, and Julia and Ellen considered themselves friends of the coadjutor-archbishop, later archbishop, Daniel Mannix. Bridges always remembered Mannix as "a great hero to my family." Formerly president of Maynooth College in Ireland, Mannix arrived in Melbourne in March 1913 and served St. Mary's Star of the Sea parish, a heavily Catholic, working-class neighborhood near Ellen Dorgan's rooming house. Ellen and Julia likely met Mannix during his tenure as parish priest. Mannix was a committed Irish nationalist and defender of working-class organizations, many of which were filled and led by Irish Catholics. Alfred's father never attended church, but young Alfred followed his mother's example, attended church regularly, and served as an altar boy.[9]

Julia also gave young Alfred lessons in Irish nationalism. He later enjoyed telling how his mother had him use only penny stamps—twelve or more—when he mailed her letters to her family in Britain. He complained that he had to paste the stamps everywhere on the front and put some on the back and that the glue left a bad taste in his mouth. Julia explained that penny stamps featured a kangaroo, but larger denominations pictured the king, and she did not want her son licking the king's backside. Julia probably didn't invent the lesson. A memoir from the era recorded, "A Labor politician said that he would rather lick the backside of a kangaroo than that of a king."[10]

Young Alfred first attended the Kensington State School, then changed to St. Brendan's School, attached to their parish church. Victoria's school laws required attendance for ages six through fourteen, and most students completed tenth grade. Melbourne schools reflected the city's class structure. Private schools (as in England, called public schools) prepared children of the largely Protestant elite for the university. State schools and Catholic schools taught mostly middle-class and working-class students.[11]

In May 1912, young Alfred, almost eleven years old, was enrolled at Christian Brothers' College in West Melbourne, far enough from home that he took the train. The college, a secondary school, prepared Catholic youth for careers in business or civil service. Bridges earned good marks, but little in the curriculum fired his interest. History came closest, especially accounts of Captain James Cook's voyages. School sports also drew his attention, especially football and cricket. His name appeared on the register as Renton, reflecting his preference for his middle name. Though other family members and childhood friends called him Renton throughout his life, his father continued to call him "Alf." Around age fifteen or sixteen, however, he began to call himself Harry, in emulation of his favorite uncle.[12]

Henry Renton "Harry" Bridges, Alfred's brother, had married Julia's sister Beatrice. They lived on a small farm near Yea, eighty miles north of Melbourne. Bridges remembered his uncle as a union member and strong supporter of unions. Uncle Renton worked as a woolpresser, compressing bales of wool during shearing season, and belonged to the Australian Workers' Union, major support for the Australian Labor Party (ALP) in rural areas. Whenever Uncle Renton visited the family in Melbourne, his young namesake couldn't bear to let him out of sight. Uncle Renton loved horse racing and came to Melbourne for the annual Melbourne Cup. Young Alf was fascinated by horse racing and loved to listen when his father and uncle swapped horse stories.[13]

Among the stories Bridges remembered about Uncle Renton was that he had served in South Africa during the Boer War and had become disillusioned with the British cause. Bridges also recalled him speaking of Australian troops in South Africa going over to the Boers. He misunderstood those stories, for Uncle Renton never served in South Africa, nor did any Australian troops go over to the Boer side.[14] Regardless, the stories remained in young Bridges's memory, raising doubts about his father's portrayals of the glories of the British Empire.

Bridges's father and uncle also talked about politics and unions. The Yea newspaper described "Harry Bridges" as "the local organizer for the Labor

Party," and noted, "Whilst holding that position he took a most prominent part in electioneering. . . . He was a fearless speaker at all times, and a fair fighter." Charles, brother of Alfred and Renton, also participated actively in the ALP, later serving as a member in the state legislature of New South Wales and as a Sydney alderman.[15] Bridges's memories of family discussions of politics included only his father and uncles, not the female members of his extended family, even though women gained voting rights when Bridges was a child.

By 1914 Australia was the most unionized nation in the world, with 106 union members per 1,000 inhabitants. By comparison, the United Kingdom counted 86 union members per 1,000 and the United States 27. Like their English models, most Australian unions organized along the lines of skill, with separate organizations for each trade. Like their counterparts in Britain and the United States, early Australian unions focused on the eight-hour day and better wages. Like early labor organizations in California, they strongly opposed Chinese immigration.[16]

The ALP advocated nationalization of monopolies, social-welfare measures, Australian nationalism (rather than identity with Britain), and trade-union issues. The party benefited from the growth of unions, which was encouraged by a system of industrial arbitration adopted in 1904. All major parties, including the ALP, also supported the "White Australia" policy, intended to prevent immigration from Asia. The Naturalization Act in 1903 barred naturalization of non-European peoples. Some states placed additional restrictions on Chinese or Asians.[17]

Young Alfred's Laborite relatives had cause for rejoicing in 1910 when the ALP became the first social-democratic party in the world to win a solid national electoral majority and clear majorities in both houses of Parliament. The victorious Laborites extended the jurisdiction of industrial arbitration courts, established a graduated tax on land intended to break up large estates, and created a commonwealth bank to compete with privately owned banks. Harry's father supported the ALP and waxed especially enthusiastic about William Morris Hughes, a founder of the Waterside Workers (dockworkers) union, who became prime minister in 1915.[18]

On young Harry's thirteenth birthday, July 28, 1914, Austria-Hungary declared war on neighboring Serbia. Soon most of Europe was at war. Australians greeted the war with naive excitement and cheerful optimism and joined other parts of the British Empire in sending troops. Some feared a German victory might have serious consequences for them, as the German colony in nearby New Guinea could serve as the base for an invasion of Australia. Others looked greedily toward German possessions in the Pacific.[19]

The senior Alfred Bridges mirrored early enthusiasm for the war and the empire. New patriotic songs burst forth, and Alfred contributed "When

Britannia Wants a Soldier," a song dripping with sentimental patriotism. Singers delivered "When Britannia Wants a Soldier" from theater stages during intermission, while the Bridges children hawked copies in the lobby.[20]

Male Australians rushed to volunteer, eventually including two-fifths of eligible men. Uncle Renton enlisted in February 1915, saw action amid the staggering Australian losses at Gallipoli, then went to France as a company sergeant major. He was seriously wounded on July 28, 1916—young Harry's fifteenth birthday—and died twelve days later. Flags were at half-staff throughout Yea, and the local newspaper eulogized him. Harry's father composed a patriotic poem, "Our Valiant Dead," which was published in the *Melbourne Age* and the *Yea Chronicle*. Renton was one of many Australian war casualties—more proportionately than from any other part of the empire.[21]

Young Harry had readily absorbed lessons in school that reinforced his father's patriotism and pride in the British Empire. Now he wanted to emulate Uncle Renton and a cousin who also volunteered. Harry, however, chose the navy. He tried to volunteer but required his parents' consent because of his age. They refused. Instead, Harry worked for his father when not in school, riding his bicycle to the working-class cottages his father owned, collecting rent, delivering eviction notices, and posting "To Let" signs. He disliked that work, especially when it brought him into contact with his classmates' families. Harry left the Christian Brothers' school in February 1915. His father wanted him to join the family business. Instead, Harry worked briefly in a clothing factory with his friend Mick Turner, then became a "junior clerk" with Sands and McDougall, a stationery firm, where he worked until July 1917.[22]

Harry devoured adventure novels, especially sea stories. Jack London's *The Sea Wolf* and *Martin Eden* were favorites. When off work, he frequented the Melbourne docks, talked with seamen, took odd jobs aboard ships, and dreamed of going to sea. A half century later, his sister Lucy recalled, "Our brother was a real devil as a child. We were always fetching him off the waterfront to eat his tea."[23]

Harry could not ignore the war in Europe. Campaigns for volunteers played a constant counterpoint to news from the front. High casualty rates produced ever more insistent demands for additional Australian troops. In the spring of 1916, as Australian troops dug in along the western front, English troops suppressed the Easter Rising in Ireland and began to execute its leaders. Archbishop Mannix spoke out publicly against the executions. In Victoria, Irish nationalism became increasingly coupled with criticism of the war. Uncle Renton's death pained the family all the more because of the staunch Irish nationalism of Julia, Beatrice, and Ellen.[24]

By late 1916, the need for additional troops led Prime Minister Hughes to endorse conscription. Most unions and most of the ALP opposed conscription, so Hughes called for a national referendum instead of a parliamentary vote. His plan backfired. Proponents of conscription condemned him for failing to ram a measure through Parliament, and labor spokesmen damned him as a class traitor. The Waterside Workers expelled him. The conscription referendum aroused intense emotions. Major opposition came from labor and the Left, but Mannix emerged as the most prominent opponent, blaming conscription for the "disastrous proportions" the war had assumed. Mannix found strong support among the many Australians who traced their roots to Ireland. Harry's mother and aunt Ellen opposed conscription and disliked the war more generally.[25]

The referendum resulted in a small margin against conscription. The ALP then voted no-confidence in Hughes. He left the ALP, and he and other former Laborites joined with the Liberal Party to form the Nationalist Party. Alfred Bridges followed Hughes out of the ALP and became, according to his nephew George Bridges, "a very strong Tory."[26]

While Harry worked as junior clerk in 1916 and 1917, the war continued to dominate the lives of most Australians. Inflation prompted some unions to seek wage increases, and a few strikes demonstrated labor militancy in the face of governmental opposition. The press and the Hughes administration blamed the Industrial Workers of the World for fomenting opposition to the war. Formed in the United States in 1905, the IWW appeared in Australia a few years later. The Australian IWW spoke out early and loudly against conscription. Authorities arrested IWW leaders, charged them with treason, and accused other IWW members of sabotage. In late 1917, Prime Minister Hughes blamed the IWW and Irish nationalists for the increasing difficulties in finding volunteers to fill the insatiable need for additional troops. By then membership in the IWW had been outlawed, some hundred members were in prison, and the organization had been largely suppressed.[27]

Harry took little interest in the IWW, but dramatic events in 1917 began to shape his evolving political understanding. In mid-1917, the Melbourne Waterside Workers cited high food prices and a food shortage when they resolved to load food supplies only onto ships bound for Britain and Allied ports. Sydney dockworkers soon joined. In mid-August, Melbourne dockworkers closed the port. Government railway shop workers in New South Wales struck over what they condemned as a speedup. Coal miners, seamen, and others soon joined what came to be called the "Great Strike." Much of the strike centered in New South Wales, but workers in Queensland and Victoria swelled the number of strikers to ninety-seven thousand. The Hughes government blamed enemy agents and the IWW. Newspapers vied with government spokesmen in discerning in the walkout the specter of the IWW's "general strike," in which all workers struck to destroy capitalism and the state.[28]

In Melbourne carters and drivers, seamen, iron molders, and waitresses all joined the striking Watersiders. Throughout the Great Strike, political and civic leaders and the daily press maintained a steady drumbeat of attacks on the loyalty of the strikers, likening the strike to mutiny or insurrection. When civic and business leaders sought volunteers to replace the strikers, thousands of men responded. The army set up a camp a short distance outside the city where strikebreakers slept in army tents, protected by guards. The strikes largely collapsed by late September.[29]

Bridges later said he paid little attention to the strikers' arguments because he was too young and too imbued with his father's pro-Hughes and antiunion attitudes. Though Harry felt little involvement in the Great Strike, he recalled joining a demonstration, a march to an army camp outside Melbourne—perhaps the camp established for strikebreakers. But he also remembered that he had marched primarily for the excitement and felt little stake in the strike. Fifty years later, the significance of the Great Strike loomed much larger for him: "I did not know what it was all about then, but later on I could look back and I could remember. . . . No [labor movement] since 1917 has ever organized the power to shut down industry as Australian unions shut down this whole country in 1917, no nation before 1917 did it, no nation since has managed it." And, he concluded, it "began my real working class education."[30]

With the Great Strike under way, Adela Pankhurst launched a series of demonstrations. Daughter of the British suffrage leader Emmeline Pankhurst, and herself a member of the Socialist Party of Australia and an activist in the Women's Peace Army, Pankhurst campaigned against conscription and high food prices. In September women carrying red flags (banned by the Hughes government) and singing "songs of revolt" marched through Melbourne. On September 19, demonstrators smashed the windows of shops and offices. In late September, Pankhurst married Thomas Walsh, leader of the Seamen's Union of Australia (SUA), a socialist and early leader in the anticonscription effort. Shortly after, she was imprisoned at Pentridge Gaol, until late January 1918. Harry's aunt Ellen was governess of the women's section of Pentridge and likely told her sister's family about the excitement at the prison.[31]

During November 1917, a second conscription referendum campaign was under way, more rancorous than the first—one Australian remembered it as "bitter hatred" with potential for "local civil war." That acrimony was most intense in Victoria where Mannix escalated his criticism of conscription. In return, Hughes, the Protestant clergy, the largely Protestant press, and other conscription advocates intensified their criticism of Mannix. Given Mannix's leadership of the anticonscription cause, Ellen and Julia probably sympathized with Adela Pankhurst's anticonscription views, if not her socialist leanings. Ellen arranged for Harry to meet and talk with her famous prisoner. The second conscription referendum lost by a larger margin than the first.[32]

Throughout his life, Harry loved to talk about the Great Strike, the conscription campaigns, and his introduction to Pankhurst. Their influence on his political views seems to have come slowly, as they became integrated with later experiences. If he read newspaper accounts of events in Petrograd in November 1917, they had no particular effect on him. He probably didn't know that Thomas Walsh and Adela Pankhurst Walsh supported the Communist Party of Australia from the time of its founding. Eventually, Bridges read John Reed's *Ten Days That Shook the World* and gained some understanding of the Bolshevik seizure of power. Sometime after he left Australia, he bought Marx's *Capital* but—like many others—gave up before making his way through it.[33]

The war brought financial stress to the Bridges household. Alfred owned rental housing and loaned money on real estate. The war affected both. One law limited evictions, and another permitted mortgagors to postpone payments. Investment in housing fell dramatically. Commodity prices soared. The moratorium on mortgage payments, decline in investment in dwellings, and inflation brought Alfred close to financial disaster. Julia opened a confectionery shop. The family's financial problems may have prompted the family's many moves, almost one each year during the war.[34]

Harry remembered relations between Julia and Alfred as often strained, with frequent noisy arguments, perhaps due to financial problems and the frequent moves. Harry himself contributed to some arguments. When he ran off to the docks to talk with seamen, his father punished him physically, and his mother, though not condoning his behavior, tried to prevent the discipline. In 1920 (after Harry left home), Julia was living at Ellen's house, not with Alfred. Harry also remembered living at Aunt Ellen's boardinghouse for a time.[35]

Family tensions may have pushed young Harry further in the direction pointed by his visits to the Melbourne waterfront, his love of sea stories, and the tales of his seafaring cousin, Phil Munro. Harry sought out the Ancient Mariners' Club, retired seamen who instructed boys in seafaring. Alan Villiers, another participant, described the lessons: "We learned to pull an oar; to handle a boat under sail or oars; to worm, parcel, and serve both wire and rope; to do simple splices, the usual knots, and some fancy-work; to use the lead, read the log, box the compass; and signal by lamp, semaphore, and with the flags of the international code." Harry's father was not pleased. He visited Captain Corbett Suffern, leader of the Ancient Mariners, and, as Harry recalled, "raised hell with him for wanting to ship me out." Suffern replied only that "if he has his mind set on going, he's going to go."[36] Suffern's response proved accurate.

Unable to enlist in the navy, Harry fantasized about serving on a merchant ship and being attacked by a German raider or U-boat—an acceptable alternative to combat duty. His father set out to discourage Harry. Alfred regularly played poker with F. Olsen, the Norwegian-born master of a small ketch, the *Daisy Knights*. Alfred arranged for Harry to serve on the *Daisy Knights* for a trip to Tasmania. Harry left in early December 1917 and returned a month later.

Alfred urged Olsen to be harsh with the boy in the hope of curing his romantic infatuation with the sea. Alfred's plan backfired. Harry recalled, "They gave me all kinds of rotten jobs, worked my ass off, and I just loved it." For the next five years, Harry worked aboard ships, first as a cook, then an ordinary seaman (OS), and soon an able seaman (AB).[37]

From mid-February 1918 until mid-January 1919, Harry shipped on the *Lialeeta*, a two-masted ketch with a crew of five, sailing between Melbourne and Tasmania, carrying a mixed cargo to Tasmania and lumber on the return. The Tasmanian port of Smithton had no longshoremen for small vessels, so Harry also learned loading and unloading and the importance of packing cargo tightly to prevent it from shifting in a storm and endangering the ship.[38]

Throughout 1918 and early 1919, Harry shipped on ketches, small sailing vessels with a crew of four or five: master, mate, one or two ABs, and a cook. He found a Tasmanian girlfriend, Honor Farnham, who taught school outside Smithton. Harry recalled being "crazy about her" and wanting to marry her. On Sundays they took long walks or rode horses in the countryside. Honor was somewhat older than Harry, but he had already begun to add a year or two to his age. After mid-1919, he routinely cited July 28, 1899, as his birth date. He later claimed he did not rediscover the actual date until the FBI provided his birth certificate in 1941.[39]

Dreaming of becoming an officer, Harry adjusted to the routine of a seaman's life. Each seaman took a two-hour turn at the wheel one or more times, day and night, scrubbed the deck, and maintained the sails and lines. When the weather changed, they went aloft to trim the rigging. Aboard ship, experienced seamen taught new hands the skills of their trade and also taught that a competent sailor should do what was expected but no more and should always keep his self-respect and dignity when dealing with an officer. The master's word was not always law, and working conditions could be negotiated by individual crews as well as by unions.

In his free time, Harry filled the hours with his mandolin and added a camera and developing apparatus. He also read voraciously—all the works of Jack London and scores of sea stories, ranging from those by unknown writers to those by Joseph Conrad, Herman Melville, and William Clark Russell. Though Harry heard his share of sailors' tall tales, especially from the South Seas, he recalled no talk about politics.[40]

Tales of cruel captains, sadistic mates, and harsh discipline filled the novels and magazines that Harry loved, but he recalled no personal experience with cruelty or undue harshness—in part, he later concluded, because of the power of Australian unions to prevent such abuses. While he may have been correct in attributing the situation to union power, it is also clear that Harry quickly left crews where he felt uncomfortable and stayed with those he liked.[41]

For more than a year, Bridges sailed across the Bass Strait between Victoria and Tasmania. The Bass Strait was notorious for severe storms, hidden reefs, and small islands. Once a storm caused the *Lialeeta* to run aground on a small deserted island. Packing their gear into their seabags, they abandoned ship. Harry worried about his mandolin but floated it safely ashore in his seabag—the source of a story, published years later, that he had once floated to safety on his mandolin. When the skies cleared, they got the ketch afloat. It is a striking indication of the dangers of the Bass Strait that every one of the five vessels on which Bridges sailed between 1917 and 1919 had sunk or been stranded and abandoned by 1925.[42]

Throughout most of 1919, Bridges sailed the Tasman Sea between Australia and New Zealand. In February 1919, he joined the *Valmarie*, a new three-masted schooner with a crew of ten. Bridges's recollections of his seafaring included no mention of the strike by the Seamen's Union of Australia in mid-1919. He did recall, accurately, that the *Valmarie* and the other small vessels on which he worked were not covered by the union's arbitration award that defined wages and conditions, so they were presumably not part of the strike. He remembered that he had joined the SUA, but the union's dues registers do not list anyone named Bridges during the years 1917, 1918, or 1919—perhaps mute testimony to his memory that the SUA was not very important for the small sailing ships on which he worked. At some point, he learned the basics of developing photographic film and bought a small developing kit.[43]

As the *Valmarie* was returning to Melbourne in September 1919, Harry had the watch in the bow. Around three thirty on the morning of September 30, the ship beached in ten feet of water, offshore from Ninety-Mile Beach, along the southeast coast of Victoria. When their efforts to refloat the *Valmarie* failed, the crew took the train to Melbourne. Harry testified to a Court of Marine Inquiry regarding charges of misconduct against Charles Harris, master of the *Valmarie*. The court found Harris guilty of misconduct and suspended his master's certificate for three months. In 1966 Harry described those events: "I was on lookout one night—or supposed to be. . . . Ran aground on the beach while trying to go about. It was the second mate's watch, and . . . he was in the galley drinking coffee and I happened to be with him. We had to lie like hell in the inquiry to wave [save?] his and the skipper's tickets."[44]

After a salvage crew refloated the *Valmarie*, Harry signed on again. When Harry bid good-bye to his family and boarded the *Valmarie* bound for New Zealand in late December 1919, the leave-taking was no different from other times during the previous two years. As the *Valmarie* slipped out of the Melbourne harbor, neither Harry nor his family expected that almost forty-seven years were to pass before he saw Australia again.[45]

In Auckland Harry signed on the *Ysabel*, a barkentine (four-masted sailing vessel) bound for San Francisco, because he could not resist the opportunity

Harry Bridges about eighteen or nineteen years old, at the helm of a small sailing vessel, one of the vessels on which he shipped when he first went to sea, ca. 1919. Bridges had a camera and developing apparatus, so it's likely that he developed and printed this picture. (Photo courtesy of Anne Rand Library, ILWU)

to visit the region he had read about in the novels of Jack London. After taking on cargo in the Cook Islands, the captain then set a course for San Francisco, more than four thousand nautical miles away. Against an intransigent captain, the crew demanded a day off following Easter, when they proposed to stand watch as usual but be exempted from the usual scrubbing and other routine daily tasks.[46]

The *Ysabel* arrived in San Francisco on April 12, 1920. George Maynard, an American crew member, had become friends with Bridges during the long voyage. Maynard later stated that, in San Francisco, "Bridges on the spur of the moment decided that he would go ashore with me," but that Bridges had no intention of leaving Australia permanently. Harry gathered his mandolin, books, photographic equipment, rifle, and seabag, and he and Maynard shared a hotel room for a week or so while Maynard showed Bridges around the city. On April 21, Bridges applied for an American certificate as an able seaman and joined the Sailors' Union of the Pacific, receiving card 2869. Having decided to remain for more than a few days, Harry also paid the immigration permit fee of eight dollars, even though some of his erstwhile crewmates laughed at him for wasting enough money for four trips to a brothel.[47]

San Francisco was the major Pacific Coast port for cargo to and from the western part of the United States. Harry knew of San Francisco's storied Barbary Coast, reputed to contain every conceivable form of pleasure and vice, but he found his pleasures in reading, playing his mandolin, and dabbling with his photographic equipment. Having come to San Francisco for sightseeing, Bridges explored the Valley of the Moon, where London had established his ranch, and then traveled up the Sacramento River, which he recalled from another book. He then signed onto the *Silver Shell*, an oil tanker, en route to a refinery on the northern extension of San Francisco Bay. He found the accommodations so attractive that the *Ysabel* was his last voyage under sail. Back in San Francisco, Harry signed onto the *Delisle*, a year-old steamship.[48]

Since boarding the *Daisy Knights* three years before, Harry had learned the trade of seaman, how to behave toward officers, and something of the role of unions. He had abandoned his goal to become a ship's officer and begun to question the dogma of British imperial grandeur propounded by his father and teachers. He frequented skating rinks and dance halls and stayed away from brothels. He drank very little but had begun smoking cigarettes and a pipe. The onetime altar boy had also come to question his mother's faith and had stopped attending church.[49] He had also been exposed to events that were yet to show their full effect, especially the potential power of organized workers.

As the *Delisle* slipped out through the Golden Gate on May 29, 1920, Harry Bridges began a new phase in his evolving understanding of labor and politics. In Australia he had accepted without thinking the presence and role of unions, the ALP, and the Australian system of industrial arbitration that gave unions a protected legal status. He was about to discover that, in the United States, few employers acknowledged the legitimacy of unions and that government—local, state, and federal—often supported employers in labor disputes, sometimes stayed neutral, but rarely sided with labor.

For most of the preceding twenty years, San Francisco had departed from prevailing patterns of labor relations and labor politics elsewhere in the United

States, and Harry's new union, the Sailors' Union of the Pacific, had been central in forging those patterns. Dating to 1885, the SUP was one of the three largely autonomous districts of the International Seamen's Union of America (ISU). In 1901 the SUP had joined other waterfront unions in the City Front (waterfront) Federation, a central body for maritime unions. Soon after, Teamsters Local 85, led by Michael Casey, found themselves in a life-or-death struggle with the Employers' Association. The City Front Federation voted to strike in support of Local 85, shutting down the port. The long, violent strike earned Casey the sobriquet "Bloody Mike" and ended only when the governor intervened. At the same time Australian unionists were organizing the ALP, angry San Francisco unionists created the Union Labor Party (ULP). Andrew Furuseth, head of the SUP, supported this demarche, observing, "Inasmuch as we are to have a class government, I most emphatically prefer a working class government." However, in 1911 Furuseth and a few other union leaders broke with the ULP and backed James Rolph Jr., a popular shipowner and builder who employed only union labor. Repeatedly reelected, Rolph usually remained neutral in labor disputes and sometimes sided with labor.[50]

After World War I, many unions hoped to recover purchasing power that had been lost to inflation, but many employers wanted to roll back the union tide. The nation was soon racked by strikes, nearly all of which failed, including a strike by San Francisco longshoremen, which Harry learned about later, after beginning to work on the docks. In September 1919, members of the left wing of the American Socialist Party joined with some IWW members and other Bolshevik sympathizers to form two, competing, American communist parties, each pledged to overthrow capitalism.[51]

Those strikes ended before Harry Bridges arrived in San Francisco in early 1920, but talk about them went on in SUP halls and ships' forecastles. Harry countered with glowing accounts of the ALP and Australian unions. As a result, the SUP members on the *Delisle* elected him ship's delegate, an unpaid position comparable to a shop steward. The trip saw few "beefs," so Bridges found no occasion to challenge the authority of the officers. Discharged in Philadelphia, Harry returned to the Pacific Coast by train. He then shipped out of San Pedro, the Port of Los Angeles, on small vessels in the coastal trade, including steam schooners plying the lumber trade between California and the Northwest. As in the small Tasmanian ports, the small lumber ports of the Northwest had no longshoremen, so Bridges again found himself loading and unloading cargo. In 1907 Samuel Gompers, president of the American Federation of Labor (AFL), had arbitrated a jurisdictional dispute between the SUP and the International Longshoremen's Association (ILA) regarding the steam schooners, giving the SUP some rights to unload steam schooners even where there were longshoremen.[52] Bridges's first experience with steam schooners was not his last, as jurisdictional disputes over steam schooners persisted nearly as long the last steam schooner operated.

Bridges rejoined the *Delisle* in late December 1920, bound for Boston. In Boston he found severe unemployment and recalled a demonstration by jobless men auctioning themselves off on the Boston Common. Ordered to rig down the ship in the freezing weather, Harry instead drew his pay and got himself to New Orleans. One day he heard music in the street and discovered a jazz band playing for a funeral procession—the beginning of his lifelong love for jazz. He registered and paid his union dues at the ISU's Eastern and Gulf district hall and then hung around the hall to talk and look for a ship to Australia, but found none. The unemployed seamen in the hall attracted IWW organizers. Harry joined. He had heard talk about the IWW throughout his seafaring years, especially on the Pacific Coast. In the lumber ports of Washington and Oregon, many lumber workers and longshoremen supported the IWW, and the IWW maintained halls in Seattle and San Pedro.[53]

The IWW dated to 1905, when it included nearly all the leading figures on the American Left, who saw it as the socialist alternative to the American Federation of Labor. Like most Australian unions, AFL unions defined themselves according to the skill (or craft) of their members and limited membership to skilled workers. Some AFL unions also limited their membership to whites, or males, or white male citizens. The IWW was one union for all workers, regardless of skill, race, sex, or national origin, organized by industries, not skill. All maritime workers—deckhands, engine crew, cooks and stewards, and longshoremen—could join the IWW's Marine Transport Workers Industrial Union.

By 1910 many IWW members, often called Wobblies, had embraced syndicalism. Syndicalists emphasized direct action at the point of production, the individual work site, typically by shutting down a job to seek better conditions. Syndicalists argued that governments existed to protect property owners and bosses against their workers. They looked on electoral politics as corrupt and unproductive and instead embraced the concept that organized and class-conscious workers, through a great nationwide general strike, could take control of their work sites, destroy capitalism, and operate the economy themselves without political parties or governments. With a reputation as militant and uncompromising, Wobblies became targets for official and vigilante action during World War I. By 1921 the IWW had lost most of its members and former leaders.[54]

Harry's decision to join the IWW marked a significant step in his political evolution. Growing up in Melbourne, he had hated to collect rent from poor families and absorbed his uncles' admiration for the ALP. He had marched in support of the Great Strike, admired the commitment of Adela Pankhurst, and fallen away from the church. He had served as a union representative, been dismayed at unemployment in Boston, and found himself unemployed in New Orleans. He may have known of the danger posed by criminal syndicalism laws (state laws making it a crime to advocate for syndicalism), but the government typically deported foreigners rather than imprisoning them for IWW membership—and Harry had been trying to get back to Australia anyway. His IWW membership signified that these experiences had come together to produce identification with a militant, class-conscious organization that rejected capitalism. Harry, son of a music composer, had only one problem with the Wobblies: they borrowed the tunes for their songs from the popular music of the day, something Alfred Bridges had raged about as a violation of copyright and theft of an individual's creative effort.[55]

The IWW expected every member to be an organizer. Wherever they might be, Bridges later recalled, committed Wobblies tried to educate their fellow workers, organize them, and agitate against the bosses. Bridges and his new friends soon put those concepts into action. An employment agency sent him and three other Wobblies, all Scots, to work on a levee on the southernmost tip of the Mississippi delta. There, several hundred levee workers lived in bunkhouses and ate at a common mess, for which the company deducted half or more of their pay. Harry and the three Wobblies organized their fellow workers and took them out on strike against the miserable accommodations and high prices. The sheriff of Plaquemines Parish quickly arrived and identified the four Wobblies as the strike leaders. Years later, Harry mimicked the sheriff: "Well, well, well. If Ah were you boys, Ah wouldn't let the sun set on me aroun' heah. We don't go for this kind of stuff. We'ah nice peaceful people heah." The four caught a mail boat across the river and then walked back to New Orleans.[56]

Bridges and the three Scots stayed at the Seamen's Institute, a few blocks from the riverfront docks. They attended Wobbly meetings where they discussed racial segregation and agreed to challenge it. This was something new for Harry, who had been raised with the "White Australia" policy. The SUP also excluded those of Asian or African descent and had long inveighed against Asian immigration. The IWW's stress on class solidarity across the lines of race was new to the young Australian, but he seems to have taken to it as quickly as to the constant organizing and worksite job actions. New Orleans IWW members took direct action to oppose segregation. When Harry and his fellow Wobblies rode a streetcar, they sat in the back. If the conductor told them to move because they were white, they replied that they were colored. They did the same in movie theaters, sitting in the Jim Crow section.[57]

In early 1921, shipowners demanded a large wage cut and an increase in hours from fifty-four to eighty-four per week and no preference in hiring for union members. The proposals affected all ISU members nationwide: seamen, marine firemen (engine crews), and cooks and stewards. When negotiations failed, the federal government, through the U.S. Shipping Board, endorsed the owners' proposals.[58]

As those negotiations were proceeding, Bridges shipped out aboard the *James Timson*, bound for Central America. On May 1, while Bridges was at sea, the ISU and the recently formed Marine Engineers' Beneficial Association (MEBA, licensed officers) voted to strike. In New Orleans, union members picketed the waterfront, urging that no one accept the new conditions and attacking strikebreakers. On May 7, a federal judge issued a restraining order and then an injunction. Picketing and demonstrations brought police action. Conflict raged along the waterfront. Arrests of pickets or demonstrators reached nearly twelve hundred by May 24, when Guy Molony, the police superintendent, ordered the arrest of every man on or near the riverfront who was not working.[59]

Harry's ship returned to New Orleans in late May. After paying his ISU dues, Harry reported for picket duty. Bridges and other Wobblies also tried to build support among New Orleans longshoremen. In early June, while Bridges was attempting to recruit some Black longshoremen, police arrested him and charged him with loitering—a common charge against pickets. He spent a night in jail but was released without a court hearing.[60]

By then shipowners sensed victory, one crowing, "We are done with unions." Newspaper headlines announced that strikers should choose between "Work or Prison" after a police captain said, "They've got to work or go to jail." The press added another option: leave town. The strikers seized on this, even though Molony denied that "Work, leave the city, or go to jail" was an appropriate interpretation of his order. Years later, Bridges recalled the edict as "Go to work, get out of town, or go to jail," though he attributed it to the mayor. "Work, leave town, or go to jail" became the strikers' rallying cry as they tried to involve other unions in their struggle.[61]

Shipowners felt they could easily replace striking seamen, firemen, and cooks and stewards but knew they could not operate without MEBA, the licensed engineers. On June 4, under the headline "General Strike Is New Threat Here," the *New Orleans States* reported that the local MEBA representative planned to request a sympathy strike of all AFL maritime workers, including longshoremen, unless shipowners restored the 1920 wage scale and work conditions. Others, especially Wobblies, also talked about a general strike. Bridges joined with descriptions of the Great Strike in Australia.[62]

By then the strike was unraveling. MEBA accepted a settlement on June 13. The local ISU representative cited a "one for all and all for one" compact binding all the unions to stay on strike until they all settled, but to no effect. MEBA's return to work ended the strike that had already become a lost cause. From 1934 through 1948, Bridges repeatedly insisted that all unions on strike must settle before any returned to work. On June 21, ISU's Eastern and Gulf district voted to return to work on any terms available. The SUP held out until July 29 and then voted the same. New Orleans newspapers called it "one of the most crushing [defeats] ever suffered by a labor organization." ISU membership stood at 115,000 before the strike but fell to 16,000 by 1923.[63] It was just one of a series of crushing defeats suffered by unions after World War I.

Harry did not remain in New Orleans until the vote to return to work. When it became clear the strike was lost, Harry and the three Wobblies decided to go to Mexico. They had heard of opportunities for skilled riggers in the Mexican oil fields, so they walked and bummed rides to Tampico. Finding no oil-field jobs, the group broke up. Harry tramped and bummed rides south, eventually all the way to Bluefields in Nicaragua, where he caught a ship for New Orleans. He had contracted malaria during his trek and spent the entire voyage sick in his bunk. In New Orleans, he went into the Marine Hospital until he recovered. (Marine Hospitals were federal agencies for the treatment of merchant seamen.)[64]

Recovered, Harry found that, as an alien, he could no longer work on a U.S.-flagged ship. On July 13, he filed a declaration of intention to become an American citizen, identifying himself as twenty-one years old (he was actually nineteen), five foot eleven, weighing 165 pounds. He soon found a ship and remained on it until October 7 and then signed onto the *El Dorado*, bound for San Francisco. He joined the crew as a standby at twenty-five cents a month plus room and board but was needed during the voyage, so he received OS wages when the ship reached San Pedro. He then signed on at AB wages and remained on the *El Dorado* until late February 1922.[65]

After the disastrous 1921 strike, ISU leaders launched an all-out drive to persuade members to drop IWW memberships and expel all remaining Wobblies. The SUP newspaper printed the California criminal syndicalism law and warned of the legal liabilities of IWW membership. SUP officials also claimed to have proof that shipowners paid the IWW. The IWW retorted in kind, labeling Furuseth a "reactionary" and a "grafter." Harry left the Wobblies in 1922 or 1923.[66]

While on the *El Dorado*, Bridges nearly lost his life in San Francisco. The ship was docked in the Third Street Channel, known to maritime workers as "Shit Creek" because of its industrial and human waste. Bridges and another seaman were repainting the numerals on the bow, working on a punt, a flat-bottomed platform hung alongside the ship. As the tide ran out, the ship's lines parted and it began to slip out. The second mate released the anchor, not realizing the two men were directly below. Bridges and the other seaman heard a warning noise, and both jumped into the channel. Longshoremen on the dock lowered a rope and pulled them up, hooting at their dunking in the sewage. The second mate brought them moonshine whiskey to apologize.[67]

In late February 1922, Bridges left the *El Dorado* in San Francisco, hoping to find a ship to Australia, but instead signed on the *Lydonia* as quartermaster. A former yacht, the *Lydonia* was operated by the Coast and Geodetic Survey to map the Pacific Coast. On March 30, before the *Lydonia* left San Francisco, Bridges came down with what he thought was a recurrence of malaria. Unconscious, he was taken to the San Francisco Marine Hospital, where doctors diagnosed meningitis. The *Lydonia*'s crew started a collection for funeral flowers, Bridges later learned, because they considered meningitis inevitably fatal. However, researchers had recently succeeded in treating meningitis with a spinal injection, and an injection was promptly dispatched from Chicago. Long afterward, Harry remembered how the painful the injection was. He remembered too how the doctors seemed unusually interested in him: not only was he their first meningitis patient to receive the spinal injection, but he was also the first Australian seaman they had treated who did not have venereal disease.[68]

Discharged on May 15, Harry rejoined the *Lydonia*, then surveying Humboldt Bay in Northern California. Harry got along well with the other crew members and enjoyed the duties of quartermaster: checking those coming aboard and going ashore, maintaining and mounting signal flags, and operating the sounding machine used to map the bottom of the bay. Their next survey was of Coos

Harry Bridges, in his impressive Coast and Geodetic Survey uniform, with Agnes Brown, aboard the *Lydonia*, 1922. Bridges may have developed and printed this picture. (Photo courtesy of Anne Rand Library, ILWU)

Bay, Oregon. The young crew in their snappy uniforms took the area by storm. Local women came aboard to parties. Harry met Agnes Brown, a waitress. Agnes had rejected her father's strict morality at an early age. When only fifteen, she gave birth to a son, Kenneth McClay. A year later, she married Walter Moore, a sawmill worker, and had another child. Separated but not divorced, she rented space on a houseboat, and her children lived elsewhere.[69]

Harry and Agnes quickly became intimate, but he wanted no permanent commitment. He planned to return to Australia and knew his parents would not approve of Agnes or their relationship. When the *Lydonia* returned to San Francisco, Bridges planned a temporary stay in San Francisco. He thought of himself as an Australian seaman but considered San Francisco a good place to find a ship home when he tired of the city. Agnes came to San Francisco to live with him. To pay the rent, he accompanied an acquaintance to work at the Matson dock. Harry Bridges became a San Francisco longshoreman.[70]

2

San Francisco Longshoreman

1922–1929

By going "on the beach" as a longshoreman, Harry Bridges followed many other Pacific Coast seamen. He understood longshore work—he had loaded and unloaded cargo in Tasmania and in the "dogleg" ports along the West Coast. But the small ships for which he had worked cargo were very different from the ships that lined the San Francisco waterfront. Bridges still had much to learn, both about longshoring work in San Francisco and, importantly, about power relations on the waterfront and in the city more generally.[1]

On the San Francisco waterfront, longshoremen worked in gangs, one gang per hatch. Each hatch opened into the hold. The hold of a general cargo ship was an open space as much as forty feet deep, usually containing a variety of cargo. Twelve to eighteen men made up most gangs in San Francisco during the 1920s. The gang boss directed the work of the gang, and a walking boss supervised the work of all the gangs on a ship. Every gang included an experienced winch driver who operated the cargo winch, powered by the ship's steam, that lifted the cargo. The hatch tender on each gang guided the cargo as it was moved through the hatches and over the side of the ship. Other gang members worked in the hold or on the pier. Large items might be taken up one at a time. Break-bulk cargo consisted of boxes, barrels, sacks, or other containers that were packed into slings for lifting. Hold men unloaded sling loads of cargo and stowed it during loading or broke out cargo and packed it into sling loads when unloading. Pier men moved the cargo to the ship's side, then loaded it into slings for lifting into the hold, or they unpacked slings, piled and sorted the cargo, and transferred it to hand trucks that they pushed elsewhere on the pier, to a waiting railroad car, or to a teamster's rig. Each gang worked with a ship's clerk who kept the paperwork involved in loading and unloading. Ships' clerks were not attached to longshore gangs and, before 1919, belonged to a separate union.

Bridges probably spent more time in the hold than at any other task, although he worked as a hatch tender in the early 1930s.[2]

In the hold, dunnage—wood used to create temporary floors—separated types of cargo, helped to stabilize the cargo, and provided footing for the longshoremen as they packed or unpacked the hold. Stowing and breaking out cargo required both expertise and muscle. Knowledgeable hold men broke out goods without damage and avoided endangering themselves and others by falling cargo. Experienced hold men knew how to build floors of dunnage between types of cargo and how to attach the winch hook to move large heavy items stowed at an angle to the hatch opening.[3]

Bridges, like other longshoremen, used an iron hook, a foot or so long, usually with a wooden handle, to seize cargo and move it. Pier men and hold men handled and often lifted 100 pounds or more. A bag of flour weighed 100 to 150 pounds, a bag of coffee 135 to 200, a bag of sugar 250 to 330. A bale of San Joaquin Valley cotton weighed 500 pounds, about the same as a barrel of lubricating oil from the refineries across the bay. In 1930 the Bureau of Labor Statistics stressed brawn: "The essential requirements for the job of a longshoreman are a mighty arm, a hard muscle, and a large, strong back." Herb Mills, who began working on the San Francisco waterfront before containerization, emphasized that longshore work also required "initiative, ingenuity, a willingness to cooperatively innovate, and a wide range of skills and experience."[4]

The weight of a sling load varied, depending on the cargo, from 1,000 pounds up to 3 tons; 3,000 to 4,000 pounds was typical during the 1920s and early 1930s. A poorly loaded sling or a mistake by the winch driver or hatch tender could bring a sling load down on top of an unwary hold man or pier man or knock a hatch tender into the hold or over the side. By the early 1930s, pallets had replaced slings for some cargoes.[5]

Harry soon learned that San Francisco shipping companies insisted that "the hook never hangs," meaning the winches were always moving. Work rules specified that if work stopped for more than an hour, the gang received half pay until work resumed or the boss dismissed them. An experienced gang could move upwards of 20 tons in an hour. A hundred men could load a 3,000-ton steamer in two days and a night, stowing enough cargo to fill a train of freight cars five miles long.[6]

During the mid- and late 1920s, the waterfront hummed with activity. The Board of State Harbor Commissioners, the state agency that controlled the waterfront, declared San Francisco "the great American hub of trade on the Pacific." In the mid-1920s, 118 steamship lines called at the port. Fifty were engaged in foreign commerce, and 28 sailed only to other American ports, including Hawai'i and Alaska. Processed food and petroleum products dominated shipping to the East Coast; half of all cargo arriving from the East Coast

Ship-loading activities at the Matson dock, Pier 31, probably late 1920s, showing crates of Del Monte products being winched onto a ship. Although this photo is dated as ca. 1920, it shows pallet boards rather than slings, and pallet boards became widespread in the late 1920s. Bridges worked at the Matson dock at times, and the Matson dock was later the site of crucial job actions. (Photo by Ralph Young and Haryden Lothers, Lothers and Young Studio Collection, courtesy of Sonoma County Library)

consisted of metal products. Raw sugar and canned pineapple from Hawai'i accounted for nearly half the goods coming from outside the continental United States.[7]

Harry quickly learned the layout of the port. A wide street, the Embarcadero, ran in front of most of the piers. The symbolic center of the port was the Ferry Building, at the foot of Market Street, the city's main thoroughfare. North of the Ferry Building, twenty finger piers carried the odd numbers from 3 through 43 (except for 13), serving foreign lines and riverboats bringing agricultural products from the interior to the produce district, across from the first several piers. The seventeen piers south of the Ferry Building, with even numbers from 14 through 46, included those used by the major steamship lines with offices in San Francisco, including the Pacific Steamship Company, Matson Navigation, and Dollar Lines, as well as several smaller companies. Several coffee-roasting plants stood near the southern piers, and the aroma of roasting coffee usually hung in the air. Inland from the waterfront lay warehouses, lumberyards, and light manufacturing, especially food processing. The commercial blocks south of Market Street catered to waterfront workers with saloons, restaurants, poolrooms, cheap hotels, pawn shops, bookmakers, a mission, a YMCA, and the few surviving waterfront unions.[8]

China Basin marked the south end of the Embarcadero. Inland from China Basin ran the Mission Creek or Third Street Channel (into which Harry was dunked), lined by railroad tracks, terminals, and lumberyards. South of China Basin stretched the vast Southern Pacific railway yards, with their own pier. Farther south, oil companies and lumber companies had their wharves, as did Union Iron Works, the largest shipyard and metal-working plant in the city. Still farther south was the Western Pacific Railroad freight slip and the Islais Creek Channel, site of a grain terminal and wharf for grain, oil, and lumber, nearly six miles distant from the army transport docks at Fort Mason, at the far northern end of the waterfront. Between China Basin and Fort Mason, tracks of the state-owned Belt Line railroad ran along the center of the Embarcadero, connecting piers to warehouses and to the Southern Pacific and Santa Fe rail yards near the southern waterfront.[9]

San Francisco in the 1920s had one of the most cost-efficient longshore workforces in the country. In the years 1927–31, the American-Hawaiian Steamship Company averaged $0.99–$1.03 per ton for loading in San Francisco, $1.85–$1.99 in New York, and $2.17–$2.43 in Boston. In discharging bags of raw sugar, San Francisco longshore workers averaged 3.45 tons per man-hour, compared to 2.72 in New York, 1.61 in Philadelphia, and 1.35 in Galveston. In discharging lumber, San Francisco longshoremen averaged 1,650 board feet per man-hour, compared to 1,050 in New York and 710 in Philadelphia.[10]

Bridges quickly learned that such efficiency had its costs. In the late 1920s, San Francisco longshoremen experienced two hundred to four hundred disabling injuries for every million hours worked, equivalent to about one disabling injury every hour among the port's three thousand longshoremen. The largest number of injuries resulted from falling objects. Official data significantly underestimate the number of injuries. Men rarely reported minor injuries because making a claim could lead to blacklisting for increasing the company's costs. Bridges later recalled, "You had to report if you got injured. If you got two serious injuries while working, regardless of how they occurred—it didn't necessarily have to be your own fault—you were generally through on the waterfront." He had his own experiences with injuries. In 1923 a load of steel fell into the hold where he was working, injuring his shoulder and leg. No bones were broken, but he lost a week's work. In 1929 his foot was crushed.[11]

Bridges blamed his crushed foot on a speedup. Longshoremen often attributed accidents on efforts to speed up the work, especially when bosses raced one gang against another to see which could move the most cargo in the least time. Harry told how bosses once set up a race between two hatch gangs loading copper slabs, and a poorly loaded sling of copper slabs fell into the hold, killing one man and severely injuring another. In late 1931 or early 1932, Bridges remembered, his gang was unloading pipe, and the bosses were "storming around with their watches in their hands and rushing things along." One man did not get clear before the winch began to move a load, and his foot was broken.[12]

Just as longshore work was hard and dangerous, so longshore labor relations often proved difficult and sometimes violent. Shortly before Bridges first landed in San Francisco, dockworkers had carried out a strike that shaped working conditions throughout the 1920s and early 1930s. Harry recalled that, after he became actively involved in the union, he studied the 1919 strike and a related strike in 1916.[13]

Bridges may have learned that unions had come to the San Francisco waterfront during the gold rush. The Riggers' and Stevedores' Union (R&S), dating to 1853, included the riggers, who maintained ships' riggings, and the stevedores, who packed and unpacked cargo. To move cargo on the docks, the stevedore foremen hired less skilled men—men along the shore, called longshoremen by the late 1880s, perhaps earlier. By 1910 *stevedore* usually designated a person or, more typically, a company that contracted with shipping companies to unload or load ships and was applied only occasionally to the men who did the actual work. *Longshoremen* meant the men who loaded and unloaded ships, both in the hold and on the pier.[14]

Bridges may also have learned that, in 1893, the AFL chartered the International Longshoremen's Association, which then recognized four locals in San Francisco, including the R&S. He likely learned about the origin of the Pacific Coast District (ILA-PCD). A jurisdictional battle in the early twentieth century led the Pacific Coast longshoremen to disaffiliate. The ILA secured their return only by chartering the separate and autonomous Pacific Coast District, with its own officers and jurisdiction over all Pacific Coast ports. In 1915 shipping and stevedoring companies formed the Waterfront Employers' Union, in order, they said, to meet "the increasing and often unreasonable demands of Union Labor." The WEU signed a contract with the ILA-PCD in 1915, but the district called a coastwise strike soon after. The ILA-PCD survived the strike with their contract intact, but the R&S settled separately from the ILA-PCD, lost control over gang size and sling weights, and withdrew from the ILA.[15]

Harry likely heard stories on the docks about how World War I had seriously affected the R&S. New members flooded in, and some existing members left for other jobs or military service. The federal War Shipping Board and the R&S negotiated a contract separate from that of the ILA-PCD. Sling-load sizes increased, justified as patriotic duty. Late in 1918, the influenza pandemic produced high levels of absenteeism at union meetings and killed scores of R&S members.[16]

Harry learned that working conditions in the 1920s had been determined by a strike during the tumultuous summer of 1919. At the time, critics of the R&S

in other unions, especially the SUP and Teamsters, claimed that syndicalists controlled the R&S, and most subsequent historians have accepted that view. However, Sam Kagel, writing in 1930 and drawing on conversations with participants, characterized the R&S leadership as "vigorously active trade unionists . . . not connected with any radical groups." The R&S minute books provide no evidence of radical control. However, because the R&S conducted two open membership meetings each month, vocal radicals attracted attention out of proportion to their numbers.[17]

In 1919, at an R&S membership meeting, radicals pushed through a resolution that proclaimed, "The only way to keep this country from running red with revolution . . . is to adopt an economic and industrial policy that will give to the workers an ownership and dividend interest in the industries of the country." The resolution directed R&S negotiators to seek a quarter of future profits, a 10 percent share in ownership, and seats on the board of directors. Although this demand played no role in negotiations, it appeared repeatedly in attacks on the R&S by employers and leaders of other unions.[18]

In bargaining the R&S sought a dollar an hour, a forty-four-hour week (down from forty-eight), new overtime rules, a minimum gang size of sixteen, and a maximum sling-load weight of twelve hundred pounds. They called the limit on sling-load weight a "return to normal conditions" after higher weights were "imposed" during the war. Negotiations deadlocked over gang size and sling-load weight. In September the R&S voted to strike. Given the longshoremen's reputation for radicalism, Labor Council support was tepid and other waterfront unions disassociated themselves from the strike.[19]

Shipping and stevedoring companies imported strikebreakers, especially Mexican immigrants and African Americans. Violence flared. The WEU refused to negotiate, claiming they could not rely on the radicals who, they insisted, dominated the union. (Later versions of the WEU made similar claims repeatedly, most notably in 1948.) The union eventually chose a committee acceptable to the employers, but the WEU then made such extreme demands as to suggest they had no real desire to bargain. The strike collapsed.[20]

In early December, several gang bosses created the Longshoremen's Association of the Port of San Francisco and Bay Districts, claiming the same jurisdiction as the R&S and asserting support from a thousand longshoremen. The new union immediately signed a five-year contract with the WEU at ninety cents per hour and no mention of gang size or sling-load weight. To work a longshoreman usually had to display an up-to-date dues book in the new union, called the "Blue Book" because its dues book was blue.[21]

Bridges quickly learned that the Blue Book did little more than collect dues. Its opponents routinely called it a company union. In 1937 Paul Eliel, a Stanford faculty member and former official of the city's leading open-shop association, specified that the Blue Book failed to meet the definition of a company union because it was not organized, controlled, or funded by the WEU. But Eliel also noted that the Blue Book was very solicitous of the companies. Many longshoremen in the 1920s simply considered the Blue Book a racket—they had to pay Blue Book dues to work, but the Blue Book provided no protection in return.[22]

The experience of San Francisco longshoremen was replicated up and down the Pacific Coast. Longshoremen lost strikes and lost their unions in Seattle in 1920, Portland in 1922, and San Pedro in 1923. Only in Tacoma did the ILA hold on. By default the ILA Pacific Coast District became synonymous with Tacoma.[23]

In 1921, shortly after the disastrous seamen's strike that Harry experienced in New Orleans, San Francisco business leaders took the first steps toward creating a powerful antiunion organization. When the San Francisco Building Trades Council went on strike, the Chamber of Commerce gave full support to construction industry employers, collecting a million-dollar fund, a third of which came from only thirty firms—nearly every bank, the Southern Pacific Company (the state's dominant railroad and largest landowner), the Santa Fe Railroad, Standard Oil of California and other large oil companies, C&H Sugar, and Pacific Gas and Electric. None of these companies was directly involved in construction. That committee soon evolved into the Industrial Association of San Francisco. From 1921 onward, the Industrial Association closely governed much of the city's labor relations and promoted the American Plan—their name for the open shop. Declaring itself committed to "the public interest" and "the welfare of the city," the Industrial Association proclaimed that unions no longer served any useful purpose.[24]

By the time Harry Bridges landed in San Francisco in 1922, nearly all the city's manufacturing and construction operated under the American Plan, and longshore work was controlled by the Blue Book. He briefly worked on the Matson docks, then as a lumber longshoreman. Told to join the Blue Book if he wanted to continue working, Harry refused, and the Blue Book business agent ordered him discharged. He tried to dodge the Blue Book business agent, but found it impossible to work because the business agent always appeared and had him fired. He finally joined in early 1923 but often lost positions for failure to pay his dues.[25]

Paying Blue Book dues was no guarantee of a job. Men who wanted to work gathered on the sidewalks across from the Ferry Building before seven in the morning. Anyone could come to the shape-up—unemployed men, men seeking extra income on their day off, college students during summer break, sailors between voyages. With some three thousand longshoremen as of 1930, the shape-up also attracted street peddlers, religious proselytizers, politicians at election time, agitators for left-wing causes, and bootleggers.[26]

Gang bosses shaped first, but separately. Walking bosses, in charge of an entire ship, first hired their gang bosses, and then gang bosses chose their gang. If a gang boss approved of a man's work, he usually rehired him, making him part of a steady gang. "Every [steady] gang more or less hangs around in a certain spot," Harry later explained, "waiting for the gang boss to come and give them an order." Some men bought drinks for gang bosses or otherwise tried to curry favor with them. Some bosses solicited kickbacks, but Harry never personally experienced that. Being in a steady gang did not guarantee job stability. A walking boss, company representative, or Blue Book business agent could blacklist a man. The shape-up abetted exploitative work practices by denying work to anyone who protested a speedup, challenged unsafe practices, disputed a refusal to pay overtime, reported an injury, or confronted the Blue Book. As John Olsen later said, "If you complained, then you weren't . . . picked next morning, no matter how long you'd been working."[27]

The Blue Book was central to this arbitrary and exploitative system. In 1937 Paul Eliel, an erstwhile official of the Industrial Association, described the Blue Book's contracts as meeting "reasonable standards as to hours and wages." "However," Eliel continued, "general working conditions of equal or greater importance were not the subject of collective bargaining or negotiation between employers and Blue Book Union officials. This failure to control these conditions resulted in what might be termed secondary exploitation." The Blue Book, Eliel acknowledged, "made no effort to protect its members," so longshoremen had no recourse against working conditions that were "little short of barbarous. . . . [O]vertime was not paid for brief periods at the end of the normal day, and demands for increased output caused workers to feel that they were being made the victims of the 'speed-up.'"[28]

This casual labor market had some benefits. Casual laborers had some control over their work lives. A man might occasionally choose not to attend the shape-up and return a day or two later, although too many absences could endanger his position in a steady gang. If a gang boss earned a reputation as a tyrant, he might find that capable men refused to work for him, and if he could not present an efficient gang, he might find that the walking bosses passed him by. Longshoremen worked in pairs, often staying with the same partner over long periods of time, and the casual labor market permitted and even encouraged such partnering.[29]

Once the gang boss had his assignment and picked or filled out his gang, he ordered them to report to a particular pier at a certain time, usually 8:00 a.m. If he had no assignment, he told the gang to stand by. A gang could remain on unpaid standby all day. If they were lucky, they might be paid just to relieve another gang during lunch. Men whose usual gang boss had no work might seek work in other gangs still shaping. Men who were not a part of a steady gang sought work in incomplete gangs. By 7:30, as commuters began to pour out of the Ferry Building, the shape-up was over. Those not chosen in the shape-up could try "prospecting," walking from pier to pier to seek work. At the end of the day, gang bosses told their gang either to report to a particular pier the next morning if they already had a work assignment or to "ferry in the morning," meaning to attend the shape-up.[30]

Longshoremen were paid by the job with a small numbered brass disk with a hole so it could be strung on a key chain. Such brass checks varied in value by the length of the job. Longshoremen cashed them at the stevedoring company or at waterfront poolrooms, bookmakers, and bootleggers. Harry once borrowed money from a bootlegger and repaid that loan by cashing his checks with the bootlegger. Wage levels changed little: ninety cents per hour from December 1920 through 1921, eighty cents from 1922 through most of 1923, and ninety cents from late 1923 through 1930.[31]

Bridges's status an immigrant was not unusual on the docks. Of 2,732 longshoremen counted by the 1920 Census, 4 of every 5 were either foreign born or of foreign parentage, and that changed little over the next decade. Bridges, in 1939, guessed that "possibly 65 per cent of the men are Irish Catholics," but he was seriously overestimating the Irish presence on the waterfront. In 1920 Irish accounted for about a quarter of the foreign-born longshore workers, followed by Scandinavians and Germans. Many longshore gangs were predominantly of one ethnic group. Bridges recalled that in the late 1920s, the star gangs (steady gangs that got first choice of jobs) seemed to be largely Scandinavian, especially the bosses and skilled men, and that the Irish and Portuguese gangs fell toward the bottom of the waterfront ethnic hierarchy. During Harry's early years on the waterfront, he often worked with an Irish gang.[32]

The 1930 Census counted 57 Black longshoremen (1.6 percent). Black men, including experienced longshoremen from the Gulf Coast, had worked as strikebreakers in 1916 and 1919. Recruiters had promised permanent jobs, but only Pacific Mail and Luckenbach kept their promises. Those who remained formed separate Black gangs. By the late 1920s, only two Black gangs worked on the waterfront. Given the widely prevalent racial attitudes of the time, virtually anyone darker than average might find himself classed with the Black gangs. The R&S had limited membership to white males and required either citizenship or declaration of intent. The Blue Book did not admit Black members. Similar practices were typical of most San Francisco unions.[33]

Regardless of race or ethnicity, men who lifted bags and barrels weighing more than a hundred pounds often saw "their occupation as a proof of virility," according to William Pilcher in his study of Portland longshoremen. Herb Mills, describing San Francisco longshoremen from the mid-1930s to the 1960s, made a similar point: longshoring was "man's work." The job attracted large men, and the work gave them a physique that made them seem even larger. Pilcher noted, "Confidence in one's physical abilities and the ability to remain calm in the presence of some degree of danger are absolutely essential in the longshore workplace, and the longshoremen do not leave this confidence behind when they leave their workplace. They often seem swaggering and overbearing to outsiders." And, Pilcher added, "their willingness to battle with their fists is often impressive and sometimes alarming to outsiders." A typical longshoreman refused to accept intimidation but looked with contempt on a bully. "Related to these attitudes," Pilcher continued, "is the belief that force is a legitimate and sometimes the only means of settling some disputes. Violence in the form of fighting with the fists is thought to be the most appropriate response to an offense to one's dignity or integrity." Honorable men fought only with their fists, considering a weapon unfair and cowardly. Harry did not fit the pattern that Pilcher describes: he was tall but wiry, and he avoided waterfront fisticuffs, partly because he felt it accomplished nothing and partly because so many of the longshoremen outweighed him by fifty pounds or more.[34]

Nicknames were part of the waterfront culture. Pilcher observed, "Nicknames are seldom given to persons who are not generally well liked." Bridges fitted these patterns. His nicknames, "Limo" or "the Limey" (referring to his background as a British seafarer) and "the Nose," clearly fitted the pattern of labeling a man by a distinguishing feature: his accent and his physiognomy.[35]

Waterfront labor relations periodically seethed through the 1920s. Harry likely heard about the Portland ILA strike in 1922, when the ILA accused Wobblies of being strikebreakers. The SUP had made similar claims in its campaign against the IWW in 1921. Harry later recalled that a Wobbly program to "scab the [AFL] unions out of existence" had contributed to his disaffection. He knew that Wobblies struck on the San Pedro waterfront in 1923. They called a strike on the San Francisco waterfront in mid-July, but few responded.[36] By then Harry had broken his ties to the IWW.

Harry was receptive to efforts to revive the R&S. Limping along with a handful of members, the R&S launched organizing drives in 1923, 1924, and 1925. In June 1923, the Riggers' Organization Committee claimed "nearly three thousand members," but the WEU short-circuited the organizing drive by granting a ten-cent-per-hour wage increase to the Blue Book. The R&S tried a new organizing drive in mid-1924. Harry joined, paid dues, and marched in the Labor Day parade with some four hundred other longshoremen. Blue Book officials recorded their names for blacklisting. Blacklisted, Harry lost his car when he couldn't make the payments. Lee Holman, also blacklisted in 1924, organized a third effort in June 1925. Like previous efforts, that of 1925 failed.[37]

Harry took little part in the 1925 effort, perhaps because of his experience in 1924 and perhaps because of an increasingly demanding home life. At first Agnes worked as a waitress, and they managed to live comfortably, if modestly. Harry liked to dance, and Agnes liked to drink, and they went dancing and drinking regularly; Prohibition was the law but never the reality. Harry had expected that his relationship with Agnes was temporary and that he'd be returning to Australia. That began to change some eight months after they moved in together, when eight-year-old Kenneth McClay arrived. Agnes had not told Harry about Kenneth, nor had she informed Harry that her son was coming to live with them. Harry was furious. He felt trapped: "I'm trying to avoid having a family and I'm trapped with one. . . . I could have taken off and sailed away. . . . I can distinctly remember considering that." Agnes took Kenneth to the Protestant Orphanage. The admission record noted, "This is an illegitimate child. The mother . . . is compelled to work and so had no place to keep the child." No mention of Bridges appears in the orphanage's records. Sixteen months later, in August 1924, Agnes took Kenneth out of the orphanage, explaining that she had not been working—she was, at the time, five months pregnant.[38]

On December 26, 1924, Agnes gave birth to a daughter, Betty Jacqueline. Harry did not welcome fatherhood. Agnes had previously had an abortion, and she later claimed Bridges encouraged her to do the same when she was pregnant with Betty Jacqueline. "But," she claimed, "I cried so hard when I went to see the doctor that he told me to go home and have the baby." A psychiatric evaluation of Betty Jacqueline—Jackie—in 1949 noted, "In early childhood she had witnessed frequent parental quarrels and had often felt that she was the cause of them. Her mother, an alcoholic, had tried to alienate her from her father by telling her that he had never wanted her."[39]

Now father to a newborn and stepfather to a nine-year-old, Harry took his unwanted family responsibilities seriously. Once Kenny drove a needle into his knee while crawling on the carpet. Harry, dressed in work clothes and with little cash, carried the boy from hospital to hospital trying to get treatment. Turned away because he couldn't pay, he finally found help at a city emergency hospital. He recalled it later as a "terrible" experience, in which a child suffered because of Harry's working-class appearance and lack of funds. Kenneth later told the FBI about that injury and also that "he could not have been better treated by his own father, and that there was never any occasion when he was mistreated by HARRY BRIDGES."[40]

Harry stopped writing to his parents. He couldn't ignore his living situation in letters to them, but neither could he find the words to tell them about it. Agnes's divorce became effective on June 20, 1923, but Harry's devoutly Catholic mother would never approve of a divorced woman even if Harry had wanted to marry her. Eventually, his parents began circulating a flyer among seamen in Melbourne, seeking information on Harry: "Seamen from San Francisco, America, are asked if they can kindly supply any information of the whereabouts of Alfred Renton Bridges, better known by shipmates as 'Bill' or 'Harry' Bridges, who mysteriously disappeared about July 1924 . . . well educated, good writer and of very tidy habits. Was radical and outspoken in his labour views. . . . [I]nformation concerning the above named . . . will be gladly welcomed by his anxious Father and Mother." On July 10, 1925, the acting British vice consul in San Francisco notified Alfred Bridges that Harry was working there as a longshoreman, but Harry did not resume writing.[41]

Harry remembered 1925 and 1926 as years with a lot of work. He worked his way onto steady gangs and, at times, a star gang. A star gang received preferences: for example, if one hatch required a full day's work and one required only a few hours, the star gang got the "long" hatch or "big hatch." For several years, beginning in 1927 or 1928, he worked in Rasmus Karlson's gang unloading steel. Karlson remembered Bridges as "a good worker" and "happy-go-lucky in those days. A good mixer." Bridges believed in being a good worker and took pride in the ability of the gangs in which he worked.[42]

By 1928 Harry was earning enough that the family could move to a small house near the southern boundary of the city and buy a used car. He was working such long hours that he sometimes caught the streetcar near midnight, fell asleep, and woke up at the end of the line. He once worked for twenty-eight hours with only meal breaks. Such a long stint was neither typical nor unusual. Henry Schmidt, who started working on the docks about the same time as Bridges, recalled one shift of thirty-six hours and one of fourteen hours without a meal break.[43]

Harry failed to complete his naturalization in 1928. After filing his declaration of intent in New Orleans in 1921, he needed to submit final papers seven years later. He filled out the preliminary form on June 28, listing "Agnes Bridges" as his wife and giving December 2, 1923, as their wedding date. He received a postcard telling him to appear with his witnesses on August 3. When they arrived, Bridges was told that his papers had expired on July 13 and he had to file a new declaration of intent. He did so on August 9, 1928, including the statement that "I am married; the name of my wife is Agnes, she was born in Scotland, and now resides with me."[44]

Harry repeatedly clashed with the Blue Book. He tried to evade the business agents, who, he recalled, were often too busy with card games or racketeering to enforce the blacklist. Discharged from a gang in July 1925 because his Blue Book dues were fourteen months behind, he paid them and returned to the gang. He then kept his dues paid for a while because he was working regularly and didn't want to face discharge. He later lost his position in a steady gang after complaining about being underpaid. He attended one Blue Book meeting, enough to convince him that members were not welcome. He later recalled, "If any ordinary working longshoreman raised a protest at the union meeting—we tried it once—why, we got thrown down the stairs."[45]

Pilferage provided one way to strike back at this exploitative system. Petty pilferage—some bananas, a bottle of Scotch whiskey—was considered almost routine, part of longshoremen's prerogatives. Harry, in 1945, acknowledged that he and the gang he worked on had been "good at pilfering." He recalled that they "looked upon getting away with some stuff as a part of the bonus—as . . . they used to call it—also as making up for all the time they were chiseled out of as well as in the many other ways the employers used to cheat them." Waterfront storytellers repeated tales of dramatic though unlikely coups: the disappearance of an entire shipment of grand pianos (and the longshoreman who had a grand piano for each member of his family) or the man who assembled an entire Model T Ford by pilfering one piece at a time from shipments to the Ford assembly plant. Profanity provided another release for work-related tension and hostility. Longshoremen routinely attached blasphemous, obscene, or insulting adjectives to ships, tools, machinery (especially winches), and the employer.[46]

While Harry and others pilfered bananas and swore at the Blue Book, some labor leaders—unknown to the men working on the docks—plotted a different approach. As early as 1923, Emil Stein, Blue Book secretary, approached T. V. O'Connor, ILA international president, about affiliation. Paul Scharrenberg, secretary-treasurer of the California Labor Federation (CLF) and a leader in the SUP, later introduced Stein to Anthony Chlopek, O'Connor's successor. In 1926 Scharrenberg informed Chlopek of the "unanimous opinion" among himself, Michael Casey of Teamsters Local 85, the officers of the San Francisco Labor Council, and "several of the former officers of the Riggers and Stevedores" that they welcomed Blue Book affiliation with the Labor Council and state federation. Affiliation, Scharrenberg argued, would "enable us to educate them to the point where they will also want to affiliate with the I.L.A."[47]

Scharrenberg and Casey came from unions that worked closely with longshoremen, and both deplored what they considered irresponsible radicalism among longshoremen. If longshoremen were to strike and close down the waterfront, Scharrenberg's Sailors and Casey's Teamsters could not work. If waterfront employers tried to break a strike, Sailors and Teamsters faced a dilemma: support the strikers and endanger their own relations with employers, or ignore the strikers and destroy labor solidarity. Scharrenberg pointed to the 1916 and 1919 longshore strikes as proof "that an active and organized radical minority can dominate and ultimately destroy a 100 per cent labor union." Casey, too, repeatedly expressed concern about longshore radicals and the damage they could do. His local's contract pledged that the union "will do everything they can to avoid" sympathy strikes. In 1916 Casey worried whether the officers of Local 85 could "control our own members" during the longshoremen's strike. In 1919, when the longshoremen struck, Casey reported that he and other officers of Local 85 "advised the men to continue doing their own work," but "the men simply told us to go to hell." John O'Connell, secretary of the Labor Council and associated with Casey in the leadership of Local 85, considered the 1919 strike to have been precipitated by "irresponsibles," "radicals," and "adventurers."[48]

Anxious about labor radicals, sympathy strikes, and a strike-prone union of longshoremen, Scharrenberg, O'Connell, and Casey likely found the Blue Book attractive for its undemanding posture vis-à-vis waterfront employers and its tight internal control. Throughout the mid-1920s, they sought to arrange affiliation with the ILA. In November 1927, they and the new ILA president, Joseph P. Ryan, agreed that the Blue Book Union might affiliate with the Labor Council and the state federation. Bridges recalled that he and others went to a Labor Council meeting to protest against affiliation "because it kept the same constitution, the same officials, and we knew the same tie-up with the employers. That was just another move to gloss it over with a veneer of bona fide unionism." What remained of the R&S also protested. Given the protest, the Labor Council delayed action. When Ryan added stipulations unacceptable to the Blue Book, the organization withdrew its application to the Labor Council. Scharrenberg did admit them to the state federation, continued his efforts to bring them into the Labor Council, and succeeded in February 1929. Ryan continued to push for the Blue Book to affiliate with the ILA.[49]

Finally, in April 1931, Blue Book members voted on ILA affiliation. Bridges recalled that he and some friends campaigned to get others to pay their Blue Book dues so they could vote. That vote lost by 939–88. Ryan feared the upcoming ILA convention might "censure myself and others of our International Executive Council severely" over the situation. He asked William Green, president of the AFL, to direct the CLF and San Francisco Labor Council to disaffiliate the Blue Book. Green complied, as did the two central bodies. Ryan later claimed his ultimatum had been intended to force the Blue Book to apply for an ILA charter. Affiliation failed, Ryan acknowledged, due to opposition from some Blue Book officers and from a few company representatives.[50]

Bridges, his friends, and others who worked on the docks knew little of these maneuverings among high-ranking labor officials. They knew the result: the Blue Book's affiliation with the Labor Council and the proposal to affiliate the Blue Book with the ILA. At the time, Bridges remembered, he was always just "struggling to make it."[51]

On April 10, 1929, Bridges was seriously injured. He was working in the hold unloading a boiler. He hooked onto the boiler and then scrambled out of the way as the winch driver began to pull. The boiler jammed against some packing cases, crushing Harry's foot. He continued working, but his foot became swollen and painful. The gang boss assigned him as hatch tender, but even that became impossible. Reporting an injury meant a workman's compensation claim, and Harry feared that a claim might cost him future work. Nonetheless, unable to work, he saw a doctor, filed for workman's compensation, and received twenty-five dollars per week for sixty-eight days—probably more money than he would have made on the waterfront. When his doctor told him to return to work before the foot fully healed, his gang boss assigned him to work on the pier, where the footing was less risky.[52]

Bridges's injury came a few months before the stock-market crash in October 1929. Finding work on the waterfront soon became more difficult. Wages fell, to eighty-five cents per hour in 1931 and seventy-five cents just before Christmas in 1932. Harry and Agnes found themselves unable to afford their little house. He sold his car as scrap, but that delayed matters only briefly. In 1930 Harry moved his family to a twenty-five-dollar-per-month flat at the end of Harrison Street. John Larsen, a one-eyed longshoreman nicknamed "Pirate" for his eye patch, showed Harry how to rig the gas meter so that it didn't show the full amount. Thirteen-year-old Kenny, listed in the 1930 Census as a lodger, got a job at a nearby doughnut shop, earning four dollars per week, but the family still found it difficult to feed four mouths and pay the rent. They moved next door, to an attic apartment, where they paid only fifteen dollars per month.[53]

The 1920s were unusual in American labor history. Until then, unions usually made gains when the economy expanded, and employers needed labor and could afford improvements in wages and conditions. Unions usually declined when the economy contracted, unemployment drove down wages, and employers found themselves hard-pressed. The 1920s were different. In a period of prosperity, American unions retreated in the face of a well-organized and multifaceted open-shop drive. For Harry Bridges, the 1920s brought family responsibilities despite his aversion to becoming a husband or father, and he withdrew from the radical activism of 1921. From 1922 to 1932, he touched upon union matters only occasionally and burned his fingers when he did. Instead, in flush times, he went dancing with Agnes, socialized with other couples over bootleg liquor, or played pinochle in a waterfront poolroom.[54] In lean times, he kept fully occupied providing for his family. Just as the prosperous 1920s witnessed a decline in organized labor contrary to previous patterns, so the Depression years of the 1930s soon witnessed a dramatic surge of unionization, one that picked Harry out of anonymity and made him a national figure.

3

San Francisco Longshoremen Organize
1929–May 9, 1934

In the early 1930s, Harry Bridges struggled to keep his family housed, fed, and clothed. After the stock-market crash in October 1929, unemployment increased steadily. Fewer ships arrived on the waterfront. Unemployment brought more men to the shape-up to compete for fewer jobs. In early 1932, Harry lost his place in Ras Karlson's gang. As he remembered it, one morning the gang was sent to a different pier in midday. When Harry and another man arrived later than other gang members, the walking boss told Karlson to fire them. Harry believed that he was actually fired because he had recently testified for a man seeking overtime pay.[1]

Bridges applied for work relief in March 1932. By then their rent, $15 per month, was three months in arrears. One week's work provided a three-week supply of groceries, including milk for the children, and payment of utilities, but no cash. The relief worker described Bridges as "a young neat appearing man" who "gets an occasional days [sic] work on the waterfront, but has had nothing for a month." Harry worked demolishing dilapidated stables and building a new road. He found some work on Pier 26 between early May and September 1932, and occasionally through the end of 1932, but the work was not full-time, and he averaged less than $25 per week and sometimes as little as $2.10 per week ($1.00 in 1932 had equivalent purchasing power to nearly $21 in mid-2022).[2]

In December 1932 or January 1933, Bridges found a place in a steady gang. The family's food relief was discontinued on February 1, 1933, but there were still days with no work. When he could find no work, Harry sometimes spent the day in the public library. Other times he took Jackie (Betty Jacqueline) with him, checked out a stack of books, and went to the park to read while Jackie played nearby. His reading ranged from shipping-industry trade journals and the *Wall Street Journal* to socialist publications. He concluded that the existing economic system held no prospect for shaking off the Depression.[3]

Amid this crisis, two small groups began to organize longshoremen. Lee Holman, who had led ILA organizing efforts in 1924 and 1925, headed one group. Communist Party members made up the other small group. Bridges's relation to the Communist organizing eventually became a subject for courtroom arguments and remains a source of disagreement among historians. This chapter details Holman's efforts, the work of CP activists, and Bridges's activities, based in part on sources not used by most previous historians.[4] Chapter 8 reviews all relevant evidence about Bridges's relation to the CP in the 1930s.

In September 1931, Lee Holman gathered a small group of ILA veterans who elected him temporary president and business manager. In March John Bjorklund, secretary of the ILA Pacific Coast District, refused to give Holman financial support, blaming financial difficulties, but Bjorklund may have also recalled Holman's earlier failures.[5]

Also in March 1932, a small number of CP activists turned their attention to the waterfront. The key figure was Samuel Adams Darcy, district organizer for California (District 13). Twenty-five years old, Darcy had spent nearly two years at party work in Moscow and served briefly as editor of the *Daily Worker*. When he arrived in San Francisco late in 1930, Darcy found a tiny organization, divided, demoralized, penniless, and with a history of serious factional conflict and failed district organizers. The district sold only 323 membership books statewide in mid-1930. Party headquarters in San Francisco had become a flophouse for drunkards and hobos. During 1931 and 1932, Darcy worked to revitalize the party and to support the struggling Cannery and Agricultural Workers' International Union, the party's union.[6]

In its publications, speeches, and schools for members, the CP condemned the economic system that produced poverty in the midst of plenty, claimed that history demonstrated that capitalism was doomed and communism inevitable, and argued that workers should unite as a class, ignoring race, ethnicity, religion, and gender, to bring "the end of all exploitation." The party's model for success was the Soviet Union, and the CPUSA was part of the Communist International (CI, or Comintern), headquartered in Moscow, linking Communist Parties around the world. Individual party members were expected to accept party decisions, just as leaders of the CPUSA accepted the leadership of the Comintern, expressed in occasional World Congresses but usually through its executive committee.[7]

In 1928 the Comintern's Sixth World Congress had endorsed Joseph Stalin's analysis that capitalism had entered a Third Period in its post–World War I development, a time when the collapse of capitalism was imminent and all capitalist nations were preparing for war against the Soviet Union. The duty of Communists was to prepare for the collapse of capitalism and prevent war against the Soviet Union. Communists argued that capitalists were using fascism to maintain their power in this time of crisis. Claiming to be the only genuine working-class party, the CP presented itself as the only true enemy of fascism. Other parties on the Left and existing trade unions, the CP insisted, misled workers and thereby abetted fascism. Communists labeled AFL union leaders as social fascists or sometimes just fascists.[8]

In 1986 Harry Bridges remembered he had attended some meetings sponsored by the Trade Union Educational League (TUEL) or Trade Union Unity League (TUUL), but recalled nothing more about them. Before 1928 CPUSA members worked through the TUEL to "bore from within" AFL unions, challenging existing leaders and trying to move members to a militant and class-conscious posture. With the Third Period line, the Communist Trade Union International, a Comintern affiliate, informed CPUSA leaders that American workers required a revolutionary alternative to the "reformist" AFL. In response, the CPUSA converted the TUEL into the TUUL, dedicated to creating new red unions to challenge AFL unions.[9]

In early 1930, the CPUSA created the Marine Workers Industrial Union to contest all the AFL's maritime unions. Committed to "establishment of a revolutionary workers' government," MWIU officials also stressed maritime workers' crucial role in defending the Soviet Union. When initial organizing produced few results, directives from Moscow insisted on improvement: "The TUUL must especially concentrate its attention on organizing the seamen and dockers . . . to prevent the transportation of munitions." MWIU organizing remained sluggish. Darcy later acknowledged that, when District 13 began to focus on the maritime industry in early 1932, "We were compelled to do so particularly because of the fact that the danger of war on the Pacific makes the west coast of the united states [sic] a key vantage point of struggle."[10]

Early in 1932, the MWIU sought to bolster organizing in San Francisco by sending Harold "Harry" Hynes, who had helped found the MWIU and served as its first secretary. When he arrived in San Francisco, the local MWIU organization had not remitted enough dues even to cover its postage. In March 1932, district officers met with Hynes and resolved to "organize the water-front unit" and "immediately to begin to issue the West Coast Bulletin for the marine workers." To "organize the water-front unit," Darcy and three other men were to attend the shape-up and recruit longshoremen. One was Elmer (Efrim) "Pop" Hanoff. Born in Russia, Hanoff had worked most recently as a steelworker; he joined the CP in 1919 and held several leadership positions in the California party. He had been ordered to be deported to Russia in 1930, but, since the Soviet Union would not accept him, he had remained in the city and remained active in the CP. One of the others was almost certainly Mitchell Slobodek, a seaman and the party's waterfront section organizer throughout most of 1933. Bruce B. "Ben" Jones later claimed to have been involved; he was a party member and onetime seaman but recently an unemployed railroad fireman. By attending the shape-up, Darcy got to know John "Pirate" Larsen, who introduced him to Harry Bridges. Years later, Bridges remembered Larsen as "a party man" and remembered Darcy as "a great man," "one of the best men I ever knew."[11]

Darcy was soon complaining to party headquarters that Hynes and other MWIU cadres were ineffective: "There is absolute chaos in their methods of work. At the present time there is a Shore Organizational Committee here consisting of five comrades, all of them depending upon support for a livelihood on the union. These five comrades constitute the top fraction, the leadership of the union, and with the exception of two or three, the rank and file of the union. They are unable to even raise rent or any of their small expenses." Hynes also complained, but to MWIU headquarters, claiming Darcy and the district leadership knew nothing about the waterfront. Darcy later blamed "serious sectarian errors" for the MWIU's failure, but sectarianism was inherent in the party's Third Period policies, which isolated Communists, prevented cooperation with the non-Communist left or mainstream labor, and led party activists into rhetorical excesses.[12]

In late 1932, as Holman sought ILA funds, Darcy and Hynes exchanged complaints, and Bridges labored in the city's work-relief program, Americans held a presidential election. The seeming paralysis of Herbert Hoover's administration in the face of depression, massive unemployment, and widespread destitution guaranteed his defeat. Franklin D. Roosevelt swept to victory, winning almost two-thirds of San Francisco voters. Upon taking office in March 1933, he responded to an impending banking crisis by ordering the banks closed and summoning Congress into special session. Bridges recalled that Roosevelt's "bank holiday" meant that waterfront bootleggers had no cash available to exchange for longshoremen's brass checks. Within a hundred days, Roosevelt and Congress wrote into law the first New Deal, designed to resolve the banking crisis, reverse the economic paralysis, initiate economic reforms, provide relief for the unemployed, and end Prohibition. Under the New Deal's vehicle for recovery of manufacturing and commerce, the National Recovery Administration (NRA), each industry was to create a "code" of fair competition that would encourage economic recovery. Section 7a of the act required that each code include a guarantee that "employees shall have the right to organize and bargain collectively through representatives of their own choosing, and shall be free from the interference, restraint, or coercion of employers of labor, or their agents, in the designation of such representation."[13]

Hynes's most important project in San Francisco had been to launch the *Waterfront Worker*, part of the plan adopted in March 1932: "Immediately . . . issue the West Coast Bulletin for the marine workers." The first issue was less than immediate, perhaps one source of Darcy's complaints. The *Waterfront Worker*, a mimeographed newsletter, finally appeared in December 1932, aimed at San Francisco longshoremen. That first issue announced that it was "issued by a group of longshoremen for longshoremen." In fact, it seems to have been issued by Hynes with assistance from a few others. The second and third issues, in February and March 1933, apparently also by Hynes, hinted at some new organization but provided no further information.[14]

Articles in these early issues treated waterfront issues, provided accounts of the 1916 and 1919 longshore strikes, criticized Andrew Furuseth of the ISU and "Sharenburg" for "playing the shipowners' game," and appealed for support of leftist causes, especially freedom for Tom Mooney. (A left-wing union organizer, Mooney was convicted of planting a bomb during the San Francisco Preparedness Day parade in 1916; Mooney had since languished in San Quentin prison, even though key witnesses against him were revealed as perjurers shortly after his conviction.) Jones collected information and cranked the mimeograph machine. Slobodek went to the shape-up to hear the soapbox orators, especially Fred West of the Proletarian Party, who, Slobodek thought, had the best approach to issues. Slobodek then wrote up what West had said for the *Waterfront Worker*—without crediting West, of course. In the fourth issue, in April 1933, the *Waterfront Worker* finally acknowledged its connection to the MWIU. The fifth issue, in May 1933, cited the MWIU as the only viable organization for longshoremen and called for a "United Front" of seamen, teamsters, and stevedores. (In Third Period analysis, "United Front" meant not a negotiated common front but the "United Front from below," in which CP organizers led members of other organizations to support the CP and depose their "reformist" leaders.) The same issue carried a letter from Roy Hudson, head of the MWIU, and a long article on the refusal of Seattle longshoremen to load military supplies going to Siberia in 1919, concluding that "the longshoremen hold a strategic position in the struggle." The June issue criticized Holman and promoted the MWIU. Other articles described abusive gang bosses, the Blue Book, dangers on particular docks, injuries and deaths on the job—and encouraged longshoremen to share their experiences through the *Waterfront Worker*.[15]

In March 1933, the ever-persistent Lee Holman again sought ILA financial support. This time, ILA president Joseph Ryan told Holman to consult with Clyde Deal, head of the Ferryboatmen's Union, who advised Holman to sign up members and seek an ILA charter. In late June 1933, as Ryan prepared the charter for Holman's group, Paul Scharrenberg, head of the California Labor Federation, blasted Ryan for not giving the charter to the Blue Book; Ryan responded with equal venom. Soon Holman had a flyer circulating along the waterfront: "The organizing of Longshoremen on the San Francisco waterfront into the International Longshoremen's Association (I.L.A.) is meeting with the approval and support of all Longshoremen who are tired of Communistic Rot, tired of silly and senseless Soap Box Ravings and sick of Blue Book Misrepresentation."[16]

By then Harry Bridges was involved in these efforts. He and others had long traded talk of unions and strikes, with Harry always ready to expand upon the power of unions in Australia and his experiences in New Orleans. "We had no organization," he later recalled. "We used to hang around the waterfront, in the bootleg joints, and just talk." Jones recalled that longshoremen turned more and more to Bridges for advice: "He had a lot of good ideas, he was always there when meetings were called, and most important, he'd had more experience than any of the rest of us had. . . . [W]e just naturally turned to Harry. He always had an answer." Jones added, "Sometimes the Party was too sharp, . . . too dogmatic. Harry could take that and switch it around, and say the same thing but it'd come out in a beautiful way. . . . Harry is a very practical man. Pragmatic, very pragmatic."[17]

As pragmatic as Bridges was, his political views were moving well to the left, the result, apparently, of the combined influence of Australian labor politics, his IWW experience, the working conditions on the docks, the exploitative and authoritarian rule of the Blue Book, and the willingness of local AFL leaders to accept the Blue Book as the legitimate union for longshoremen. In many ways, the San Francisco docks exactly fitted the CP's description of American workers as exploited and oppressed by both their employers and their union leaders.[18]

By mid-1933, the friction between Hynes and Darcy became even more serious. They had disagreed from the beginning over the best way to organize maritime workers, with Hynes committed to the revolutionary mission of the MWIU and contemptuous of the unemployed comrades Darcy had organized into a waterfront section. Darcy found Hynes sectarian in his pronouncements and elitist in his insistence that only maritime workers could organize other maritime workers. In mid-May 1933, Darcy wrote to CPUSA headquarters, "Comrade Hynes has really not moved with events. . . . [W]e decided that since Comrade Hynes had been asking to be taken out from this territory for a long time, that we grant his request and have him replaced." As if in confirmation of Darcy's analysis of the MWIU's "sectarian errors," unnamed MWIU officials, at about that same time, developed a plan for organizing Pacific Coast maritime workers that specified, "The anti-imperialist war campaign is the outstanding task in all our work," and the "outstanding" slogans "must be against imperialist war, for the defense of the Chinese people and the Soviet Union." Similarly, the California convention of the TUUL in August 1933 reported that, during the previous year, the MWIU had placed first emphasis upon the "strategic position of marine workers particularly in view of war danger."[19]

With Hynes gone by late July 1933, Harry Jackson was assigned to become MWIU organizer in San Francisco. He arrived around mid-September. Jackson had been an ironworker in San Francisco before becoming a full-time party functionary. He had taken a leading role in San Francisco during the CP's factional struggles of 1929, when he had a led a group who seized District 13 headquarters from the "majority" faction and claimed to be acting on behalf of the rightful leaders of the party. He was later sent to the South as an organizer, then to the MWIU in New York. Jones remembered him as a demanding party leader with little toleration for error. Slobodek disdained Jackson and most other party "reps"—except Hynes—as bureaucrats rather than maritime workers. Darcy also had little use for Jackson, dismissing him as a "freak" and "an agent of Browder."[20]

In early July 1933, the CPUSA held an Extraordinary Party Conference in New York City. Party secretary Earl Browder berated the delegates for the party's failures in organizing workers. He condemned the New Deal as "brutal oppression" and "industrial slavery," called AFL support for 7a "the sharpest American example of . . . the role of social-fascism as the bearers among the masses of the program of fascism," but nonetheless pointed to 7a as a potent organizing device. In places where TUUL unions had not taken root—virtually everywhere—party members were now told to work within AFL unions and use discussions of NRA codes to "crystalize the left opposition."[21] Without disavowing Third Period analysis, Browder pointed the party in the same direction already taken by large numbers of American workers: joining AFL unions and drafting NRA codes.

This new legitimacy for working within AFL unions came nearly two weeks *after* the District 13 comrades had made exactly that decision. Darcy later claimed credit for encouraging CP members and sympathizers to join the ILA and form a militant, but not exclusively CP, caucus there. Jones, however, later characterized the situation as "like a person standing on the ocean shore and a big wave comes and carries you along. . . . We were carried along with this big wave of ILA."[22]

On June 28, 1933, the District Secretariat adopted a six-point program:

1) That we get as many comrades as possible to join ILA
2) Special issue of the Waterfront Worker.
3) Emergency meeting of all our longshore contacts to be held Friday [June 30].
4) Membership meeting of waterfront section.
5) Wire NY to ask that Hy. [Hynes] be allowed to stay here during this situation.
6) Call mass meeting on waterfront under auspices of "Waterfront Worker."[23]

The District Secretariat was *not* scrapping the MWIU. On July 2, the *Waterfront Worker* called a meeting—likely the "mass meeting" approved on June 28. Both the *Waterfront Worker* and the *Western Worker*, the CP's weekly newspaper, reported that about a hundred men attended and listened to speeches urging them to form "fighting groups" within the ILA. The *Western Worker*, overseen by Darcy, added that the meeting was cosponsored by the MWIU and included recruiting for the MWIU. In District Secretariat meetings as late as September 1933, some members were still expecting to move longshoremen into the MWIU.[24]

Thus, midway through 1933, these separate events converged. On June 28, the District Secretariat approved its six-point plan, including "get as many comrades as possible to join ILA." On July 5, the ILA office in New York issued a charter for Local 38-79. On July 7, Harry Bridges joined Local 38-79 as member 2569.[25]

Bridges and a dozen or so ILA members then began to meet informally on Sunday mornings. Eugene "Dutch" Dietrich, a founding member, later explained, "We would formulate a program that we were going to introduce on the floor [of the local membership meeting] the following Monday." He continued, "We thought we were doing the right thing" by opposing "the reactionary officials that we had in office at the time." Bridges later described the group as "more or less under the direction of the MWIU, not [Roy] Hudson but Jackson and some others." Party members, he recalled, "were very active. Very active as a part of the waterfront, like Schomaker, Schmidt, and others. We had a rank and file group, and primarily it was directed by the Communist Party.... That did not mean that all members of the group were members of the party.... Everybody was pulling together then. We had across-the-board unity of all kinds of guys that later on turned vicious and red-baiting."[26]

As Bridges recalled, the group was politically heterogeneous, although all were militants and critical of Holman. About half of the original members later identified with other factions within the union, including Dietrich, Ralph "Red" Mallen, Albin Kullberg, and Roger "Fats" McKenna. Within the Albion Hall group, according to Jones and Dietrich, was a smaller caucus of CP members. In 1939 Dietrich named John "Pirate" Larsen, John Schomaker, Bjorne Halling, Henry Schmidt, and a few others as the CP caucus. Schomaker, the most open CP member in the group, was a latecomer. Jones and Dietrich agreed that CP members caucused prior to the larger group's meetings. Bridges remembered Harry Jackson coming to his home to discuss strategy and tactics, but nothing more about Jackson's role in the CP caucus. Some of the group stopped attending when they realized the existence of the CP caucus.[27]

Henry Schmidt later described the group as meeting in a small room upstairs from a beer hall on Valencia Street. The Workmen's Educational Association—English name of the Arbeiter Bildungs Verein, a German working-class organization—operated a two-building complex, with Equality Hall at 141–143 Albion Street and other facilities at 540a Valencia Street. The group was always referred to as the Albion Hall group. Schmidt, active in German social organizations, knew about the meeting room because he went there to sing *Lieder*. Dietrich, in 1939, added, "As soon as we got through with the meeting we chipped in and would buy beer and that was the rent for the hall."[28]

The Albion Hall group met every week or two. They never had bylaws and never elected a chair, but Bridges usually led its discussions and activities. He later described the discussions as "pretty informal." Schmidt bluntly called them "bullshitting around." Others, however, recalled planning for the next membership meeting. The group was never large. The room wouldn't hold more than a dozen or so people, and participants changed from session to session, depending on who could attend. In 1941 Schmidt named twelve participants. Dietrich claimed they started with "about 15 or 16" and included as many as "25 or 40," but never at any one time.[29]

The party's approach, as defined on June 28, initially meant that the *Western Worker* continued to recruit for the MWIU and to criticize ILA leaders, but also urged working within the ILA "to fight for the election of honest officials and compel a policy of militant struggle." The July 1933 issue of the *Waterfront Worker*, prepared around July 15, made clear this shift of emphasis. "Like the rest of the stevedores," it proclaimed, "we have signed up in the I.L.A." Aside from endorsing ILA membership, most of the earlier tenor remained, including an attack on the "self elected" Holman leadership, criticism of the NRA as "Anti-working class," and acknowledgment that the MWIU helped in issuing the paper. That acknowledgment soon disappeared.[30]

The District Secretariat's decisions on June 28, the departure of Hynes in July, and the expulsion of Slobodek in September likely prompted Darcy to hand control of the *Waterfront Worker* to a new group, including some who attended the Albion Hall meetings. In September the District Secretariat approved a "line" for its "opposition group" within the ILA: "to create distinct TUUL group as soon as possible, which group to issue the 'Waterfront Worker.'" The Albion Hall group was too politically diverse to be considered a "distinct TUUL group," but some members of it, including Bridges, now found themselves responsible for the *Waterfront Worker*. Beginning with the issue of September 15, the paper described itself as issued by "a rank and file group in the ILA."[31]

Darcy later described the new group publishing the *Waterfront Worker* as including a minority of Communists and claimed his objective in turning the paper over to them was to develop "a united militant group (not limited to Communists alone)." Bridges did some of the writing, as did Schmidt and Jones. After Schomaker came into the group, he spent a good deal of time on the paper, and his wife typed many of the stencils. Jones often turned the crank of the antiquated and sometimes balky mimeograph machine that had belonged to the MWIU. A young woman, a party member, did the cartoons, which showed considerable ability. The group recruited youngsters from the South-of-Market neighborhood to hawk the papers on the waterfront for a cent or two per copy,

The *Waterfront Worker* was mimeographed, stapled, and sold for a penny a copy. It was a significant organizing device for Bridges and the Albion Hall group in their struggles with both Lee Holman and the Blue Book. (Photo courtesy of Anne Rand Library, ILWU)

reasoning that the men were more likely to keep and read something they paid for. Bridges later recalled that some paid more and that a voluntary collection once netted $500.[32]

Bridges and the Albion Hall group aimed for local leadership, but Holman refused to call elections. Deal became convinced that Holman "wanted to change one dictatorship for another," and quoted Holman, "The longshoremen, why, look, you can't trust them." Shocked, Deal insisted that Holman and his committee adopt a democratic constitution, hold regular membership meetings, and elect officers.[33]

In July 1933, the Blue Book began to enforce its rule that only Blue Book members could work on the docks. On July 17, a Blue Book business agent told a gang boss to discharge four men who had not paid their dues. Holman fired off telegrams to William Green, Joseph Ryan, and NRA officials. Calling the Blue Book a company union, Holman requested NRA intervention, claiming the discharges violated Section 7a, which prohibited compulsory company union membership. There was little immediate response. The Blue Book offensive continued into August, especially on the Matson docks.[34]

In reporting on the Blue Book offensive, the *Waterfront Worker* blamed Holman: "The Blue Book is getting a grip on the waterfront again. This is made possible by Holman and Co. who are preaching passivity and inaction and by covering up this treachery to the longshoremen by crying, 'Communists and fanatics' at every worker who proposes to take militant action to smash the Blue Book." The *Waterfront Worker* encouraged workers on each dock to elect a dock chairman, who would notify the *Waterfront Worker* in event of a discharge, so the *Waterfront Worker* could dispatch a speaker "to mobilize the stevedores for a stoppage of work or any other action that the men themselves decide upon."[35]

At the same time, in late July and early August, Bridges and the Albion Hall group were focusing on election of officers. They anticipated elections at the July 27 membership meeting in the Labor Temple, the San Francisco Labor Council's building. Holman, however, defined the meeting as "educational" and presented an agenda of speakers and reports. Schmidt recalled, "Harry got up and said, 'When are you going to initiate us and when are you going to give us the obligation?'" The new members were initiated, but Holman then ended the meeting.[36]

The next membership meeting was scheduled for August 15. That day the *Waterfront Worker* condemned Holman for inaction against the Blue Book and urged longshoremen to "take the organization into our own hands" and elect local officers and an executive board "of about 24, so that the organization will remain in our own hands." Soon after, Deal informed Bjorklund that Holman "didn't want any meetings, didn't want the members to elect permanent officers, didn't want to turn the money into the Union's account but wanted to keep it in a Safe Deposit Box." Bjorklund then explicitly directed Holman: "Arrange meeting as soon as possible [for] the purpose of nominating permanent officers."[37]

Bjorklund also sent representatives to San Francisco to demand that Holman adopt a constitution and hold elections. Holman finally drafted a constitution that gave full power to a board of directors and largely eliminated membership meetings. Deal and Kullberg prepared a minority report for a more democratic organization. Holman declared his version adopted, adjourned the meeting, and left the room. Deal then grabbed the gavel, declared the adjournment out of order, and persuaded the group to approve the constitution that he and Kullberg had prepared. Local elections were finally scheduled for September 1 and 2.[38]

At the time of the election, several members of the Albion Hall group laid out their views on local leadership and policies in an anonymous article in the *Western Worker*:

1. [Leaders of the local] will devote their time and energies to fighting the Blue Book and for higher wages, shorter hours, and better conditions, and not fighting us, your fellow stevedores.
2. They will not start splits among the workers by trying to eliminate them for political beliefs, whether they are Communist, Republican or anything else.
3. Let no official hold office for more than a year. There are plenty of good men on the docks so that we can rotate our officials.
4. No official should get higher pay than longshoremen.
5. Elect a big Executive Committee, representative of all nationalities and militant opinions who will fight to improve conditions, not sit around looking important in some office, drawing fancy salaries.
6. Keep the power of immediate referendum and recall in your own hands—so that you can remove any official who doesn't serve you right at any time.
7. Get a large Executive committee—of at least 20 to 24 men. This will help prevent a small clique getting control.
8. Don't allow any discrimination. Instead of resisting the militants give them a place where they can serve you. Unite against the shipowners— not against other workers. The only condition for unity should be the fight for better conditions, not political, religious or any other beliefs or racial (or national) origin.[39]

Several items reflect a distrust of long-term, entrenched union leaders, stemming perhaps from experience with Holman, the Blue Book, and the cautious and conservative union leaders of the 1920s. Rotation in office may have owed as much to the IWW (which enacted such a rule in 1919)[40] as to experience with the Blue Book; the principle was adopted by the San Francisco local and remains in its constitution. Opposition to ethnic, racial, or religious discrimination reflected a long-standing emphasis within the Left—the CP, the IWW, and often socialist organizations—on class unity despite ethnic and racial diversity. In all, these principles derived both from the experience of dockworkers in the 1920s and from the influence of the Left. The list reflects two priorities above all: the unity of all workers and the maximum degree of membership control. These two principles remained central for Harry Bridges.

Elections finally took place on September 1 and 2. At least three groups presented slates, including the "Committee of 500 Bona Fide Longshoremen Now Working on the S.F. Waterfront," the grandiose name adopted by the Albion Hall group. Their slate included some Albion Hall members along with others who opposed Holman's leadership. They endorsed Kullberg for president. For business agents, they choose William Lewis, a twenty-five-year longshore veteran and former R&S member, well known on the docks and with a significant following of his own; Ralph "Red" Mallen, an Albion Hall member and friend of Bridges whose nickname described his hair rather than his politics; and Lynn Harvey Hockensmith, who had been discharged for wearing his ILA membership button. None of those endorsees were party members. Their slate presented twenty-five candidates for the executive committee, including Bridges, identified as "Limo." Given waterfront ethnic patterns, the slate was reasonably well balanced: ten Scandinavian names (including Bjorne Halling), seven Irish, six German (including Schmidt), and a scattering of others. The slate did very well. Lewis was elected as business agent, as were eighteen of the committee's executive committee candidates, including Bridges, Schmidt, and Halling. Holman won the presidency with 865 votes to 447 for Kullberg and 87 for a third candidate.[41]

On September 7, W. T. "Paddy" Morris, Bjorklund's representative, wired Bjorklund that Local 38-79 had met, installed officers, and affiliated with the Labor Council. He added, "Men determined not to submit to domination of Blue Book Union believe they mean business."[42]

The new officers—including Harry Bridges—meant business but faced serious challenges: to break the domination of the Blue Book, protect ILA members from retaliation by employers, develop a close working relationship with other locals in the ILA-PCD, work out demands to be made on employers, write their demands into the NRA code, and, perhaps most important, build confidence and unity among Local 38-79 members such that they could defy and defeat the inevitable opposition from employers. They approached these daunting tasks amid a nationwide strike wave. NRA Section 7a had spurred an organizing flurry, but disappointment with the NRA codes soon produced strikes. Most strikes failed. The few successful strikes of 1933 nearly all grew from a previous organizational base.[43]

Amid this strike wave, Bridges and his allies began to serve as officers of Local 38-79. Their actions—and those of others—over the next several months proved crucial for that organization to develop into a militant union, able to carry out one of the most significant strikes of the early 1930s. However, Bridges and the other successful candidates endorsed by the Committee of 500 did not became a smoothly functioning majority. The newly elected executive committee, like the local, contained several loosely defined factions, one led by Holman, another by Kullberg, and a third by Lewis, as well as the Albion Hall caucus led by Bridges and Schmidt. No one seemed to command the consistent loyalty of more than a relatively small group. On September 25, for example, at its fourth meeting, the executive committee elected Bridges as the second of six members to meet with delegates from the ILA-PCD meeting in Portland in July (see below); he was the only member of the Albion Hall group so chosen. Later that same day, the committee elected a permanent chairman. The nominees were Bridges and Harry Curtis, both from the Committee of 500 slate. Curtis, not part of the Albion Hall caucus, won.[44]

The same day that Local 38-79 elected officers, the NRA Board of Adjustment ruled on the ILA's claim that the Blue Book was a company union. After hearing representatives of Local 38-79, the Blue Book, and the Waterfront Employers' Union, the board specified that, in the absence of an NRA code, its rulings were only advisory but then ruled that the Blue Book was not a company union and its existing contract was valid, including the requirement that longshoremen have their Blue Book dues paid to work. However, the board also advised the Blue Book to "be tolerant," not to discharge men "who are delinquent in dues because of lack of work or other sufficient reason," and not to blacklist ILA members.[45]

Bridges and others set out to test the Blue Book. The *Waterfront Worker*—now under their control—reported, "On Thursday, Sept. 14th, the stevedores working on the Matson Dock, decided amongst themselves that the B.B. [Blue Book] had ruled them long enough." Told to present their dues books, "the men refused and walked off the dock 100%, and after a little discussion outside proceeded to tear up their B.B.s, and dump them in a pile on the sidewalk." After consulting Blue Book business agents, Matson officials hired several gangs without regard for Blue Books.[46]

Bridges and the Albion Hall group were centrally involved in organizing the Matson action. They targeted Matson because Matson's discharge of four men had triggered the NRA board decision and because Matson was known to be the most antiunion employer on the waterfront. The NRA board had given Local 38-79 a shred of legitimacy. By taking the issue to the work site, the men were applying a lesson that Bridges learned in the IWW and that he argued repeatedly: "solidarity of the rank and file"—an organization strong enough to shut down the work site could prove more powerful than board hearings.[47]

The September action established that longshoremen no longer had to pay Blue Book dues to work at Matson. However, many places, including Matson, still discriminated against ILA members. On October 7, proclaiming "All for One, One for All," the *Waterfront Worker* declared, "The discrimination on the Matson against union men is . . . the concern of all of us on the waterfront." On October 11, discharge of four men from the Matson docks for wearing ILA pins produced a spontaneous strike against Matson by 150 men, according to a company estimate, and 500 according to Holman. When Matson brought in nonunion workers, Local 38-79 threatened to strike the entire waterfront. Bjorklund threatened to stop work on Matson ships in the Northwest and informed Ryan that he "may be obliged to pull the District." George Creel,

NRA regional administrator, appointed an arbitration board that found for the discharged men. Persuaded either by the NRA or, more likely, by Bjorklund's threat, Matson reinstated the men. Now Local 38-79 had twice proved it could protect its members. In September the target had been the Blue Book and Matson only indirectly, and the Blue Book then faded rapidly. In October the target was Matson directly, one of the most powerful waterfront employers.[48]

The actions against Matson built confidence among ILA members. The newly elected officers also needed to build unity and commitment—other key components of militancy. Shortly after the first Matson action, the men on Pier 26, the American-Hawaiian Steamship dock, where Harry worked, agreed on a day when they would all come in with union buttons on their caps. Bridges described the consequence, "The company didn't say boo. They didn't dare to."[49] By making decisions, taking risks, and winning encounters with the Blue Book and employers, the men developed confidence in themselves and their union as they also increased their commitment to each other, to their organization, and to their leaders.

Bridges and his allies also began to address issues of race within Local 38-79. Throughout the ILA Pacific Coast District, only the Tacoma and Seattle locals admitted Black members. On October 3, 1933, the *Waterfront Worker* confronted this racism: "Many of us fail to grasp the importance of uniting with the Negro stevedores in the coming struggle with the shipowners to break the B.B. and win humane working conditions for every stevedore on the front." After surveying the use of Black strikebreakers in 1916 and 1919, the article concluded, "Negroes must not be discriminated against. They must be mixed with the white gangs, and be given the same opportunities. They must be organized with the white stevedores or else we shall see another 1919 fiasco." The *Waterfront Worker* on October 7 called for "no discrimination against any stevedore because of creed, color or political beliefs."[50]

On October 9, the local's executive committee listened to what the minutes described as "a very descriptive account of the part that the colored boys have played in our business" and responded by issuing credentials to a Black member of the local to work "with the colored boys." Despite the racist terminology, the action constituted the local's first step toward bridging the eighty-year racial divide on the San Francisco docks. The constant advocacy in the *Waterfront Worker* for the integration of work gangs points to CP influence. From its beginnings, the CP opposed segregation and discrimination, energetically recruited Black members, made certain that they held positions of prominence within party organizations, and worked to keep the Scottsboro case in the national eye.[51]

In February 1934, the membership meeting heard a report from Titus Humphrey, "colored representative of Local 38-79," who explained that "the colored brothers have been made fool[s] of in the past" and "the employers tried to round up the colored men" (the minutes no longer used "boys") as strikebreakers during the Matson strike. Humphrey claimed they failed because the Black longshoremen "were 100% behind the I.L.A." As tensions mounted between the union and the employers, Humphrey spoke again at a membership meeting on March 6, 1934, reporting that "the colored men were going to stick by the I.L.A."[52]

A third issue facing Local 38-79 in late 1933 revolved around the NRA code. Codes emerged from hearings in which representatives of companies and unions presented arguments regarding code language, with an NRA administrator presiding. Two months after creation of the NRA, nearly seven hundred industry codes had been drafted.[53]

In late July 1933, before the election in Local 38-79, representatives from all ILA-PCD locals had met in Portland to finalize a code proposal. Their work defined the district's demands over the following year: recognition of the ILA as bargaining agent; the six-hour day and thirty-hour week; wages of $1.00 per hour and $1.50 for overtime; a coastwise code, with the same wages, hours, and working conditions at every port; and preference of employment for ILA members and job assignments on a rotational basis, to spread available work evenly among registered longshoremen, through hiring halls operated by each local.[54]

Code hearings were slow to get under way. In September ILA president Ryan proposed wages of 75–85 cents per hour and $1.10–$1.30 for overtime—well below the ILA-PCD demands. The *Waterfront Worker* immediately belittled Ryan's proposal, called for election of "our own representative to Washington," and demanded a membership vote on any code or agreement. Bridges and others held fast to the demand for a membership vote over the following year, and a full membership vote on any contract became a principle of the ILA-PCD and later the ILWU.[55]

The Local 38-79 executive committee voted to hire Henry Melnikow of the Pacific Coast Labor Bureau to represent them at the code hearings. *Business Week* later called Melnikow "exceedingly well educated, keen as a razor and an indefatigable worker." Small in stature and soft-spoken, he had studied labor relations with John R. Commons at the University of Wisconsin, served with army intelligence in World War I, studied law in night school, and in 1920 opened the Pacific Coast Labor Bureau. The bureau had a small office in the Ferry Building where it provided unions with economic data and advice and helped with negotiations. By the early 1930s, Melnikow had attracted a group of bright young University of California graduates, including Sam Kagel and David Selvin, devoted to the cause of unionism and willing to work long hours for low pay.[56] Melnikow became the most significant consultant for the Pacific Coast longshore union throughout the 1930s.

Code hearings for all maritime workers finally began in Washington on November 9. Melnikow filed the material requested by Local 38-79 but said nothing about longshoremen in his testimony because his primary clients were the licensed seagoing unions: the International Organization of Masters, Mates, and Pilots (MM&P) and the Marine Engineers Beneficial Association. John R. Owens, from ILA headquarters in New York, followed Melnikow, presented a written statement of ILA objections to the code proposals, and advocated uniform wages and working conditions within each of the ILA's four districts (Pacific Coast, North Atlantic, South Atlantic and Gulf, and Great Lakes). Though unproductive, the November hearings fleshed out the ILA-PCD position formulated in July. A. H. Petersen, from the San Pedro local, represented the ILA-PCD. He presented the points from the July conference and added one for settlement of disputes through port arbitration boards consisting of equal numbers of employee and employer representatives, with an impartial chairman and a board to oversee safety improvements.[57]

The demand for a hiring hall brought differing approaches. F. P. Foisie of the Seattle Waterfront Employers promoted their employer-operated hall and specified that a hiring hall should distribute work "according to the needs of the men equally with the employers." Boris Stern, of the U.S. Bureau of Labor Statistics, proposed that a National Decasualization Board organize and administer hiring halls; he also proposed that employers hire permanent gangs to be guaranteed work equivalent to two-thirds of the maximum weekly hours but that other gangs have no guarantee of work. By contrast, the ILA-PCD's proposal for rotary dispatching specified that every registered longshoreman would receive assignments on a rotating basis, so all shared equally in available work. An employer-administered hall, the ILA-PCD argued, would make it possible to blacklist individuals or even lock out the union. Only with union-elected dispatchers in a union-controlled hall would it be possible to end discrimination and distribute work equitably.[58] The ILA-PCD position on union control of dispatching and rotation defined key issues not only then but for years to come. Bridges and his caucus were not involved in formulating any of these demands.

In late November, ILA-PCD locals sent representatives to Portland to discuss the initial code hearings. No one from the Albion Hall group was present. The conference condemned the Stern plan, opposed government involvement in hiring halls, affirmed the July demands, and emphasized coastwise negotiations. The conference also directed Bjorklund, the district secretary, to proceed to a strike vote if the companies did not reply to a request for coastwise negotiations by December 10.[59]

Bridges recalled he and his group had sneered at the code hearings and argued that the union needed solid organization based on rank-and-file participation and, when organization was solid, a strike for recognition and a contract. By December the failure of the code hearings and the refusal of the employers to recognize the ILA-PCD pushed activists everywhere on the coast to much the same conclusion. In early December, the Northwest ports voted to seek strike sanctions, the first step toward a strike vote. On December 18, Local 38-79 took up Bjorklund's request that locals seek strike sanctions. Some twenty-five hundred men attended and voted unanimously in favor. San Francisco was one of the last locals to seek strike sanctions.[60]

Also in December, the Albion Hall militants proposed a special coastwise meeting of rank-and-file representatives chosen by each local as a means of bypassing such dominant ILA-PCD officers as Bjorklund and Petersen. So far as the San Francisco militants were concerned, the existing district leaders had proved themselves incompetent, and the *Waterfront Worker* pilloried them mercilessly. The cautious approach taken by such leaders seemed to correspond with the CP's portrayal of timid "misleaders of labor" and scheming "fakers." Bridges later recalled that he and Harry Jackson had devised the proposal for a coastwise conference of rank-and-file representatives. In late December, the Local 38-79 executive committee requested that future ILA-PCD meetings "relative to agreements with employers, or subject matter pertaining thereto," be held in San Francisco and asked Bjorklund to call a conference in San Francisco in January "for the purpose of uniting the whole coast."[61]

The San Francisco local sent Bridges, Dietrich, and Hockensmith to the San Pedro local (Port of Los Angeles) to build support for meeting in San Francisco. Dietrich eventually became identified with the most conservative element in the local but in early 1934 was apparently still part of the Albion Hall caucus and a friend of Bridges. Hockensmith was not part of the Albion Hall caucus. On January 16 in San Pedro, Hockensmith took the lead in explaining the reasons for meeting in San Francisco. Dietrich warned against having a code forced on the ILA-PCD, and Bridges focused on the Blue Book. The San Pedro local endorsed most of what they asked.[62]

On January 31, another NRA hearing in Washington took up a revised proposal for maritime workers that bore not even a remote resemblance to the ILA-PCD's demands. It called for a forty-eight-hour week (most codes specified thirty-five or forty) and wages at the levels of July 1, 1933 (less than current wages for most Pacific Coast longshoremen), but with a guaranteed minimum of fifty cents per hour for the Pacific Coast—far below current wages. It called for a study of decasualization but said nothing about eliminating the shape-up. Disputes were to be settled through arbitration by a port board of four members, two from labor appointed by the code administrator and two from the industry chosen by the companies.[63]

John Owens, for the ILA national office, condemned the proposal, but his alternatives—a forty-hour week for all longshoremen and ninety cents per hour for the ILA-PCD and less for all other districts—also fell far short of the ILA-PCD demands. He said nothing about hiring halls, in keeping with Ryan's commitment to the shape-up as an effective means for controlling the New York locals; as was true with the Blue Book, the shape-up permitted Ryan loyalists to blacklist those who challenged his regime. Action on the proposed code was again delayed.[64]

The militants in Local 38-79 now shifted from their proposal for a coastwise conference of rank-and-file representatives to arguing for rescheduling the district convention. At a special membership meeting on January 17, members voted that the district convention should be held in San Francisco sooner than May and that delegates should be elected by the membership of each local—this last, an effort to make it a "rank-and-file" convention. To drum up support, the members voted to dispatch Bridges and Dietrich to the Northwest locals.[65] Bridges, by then, was well known as an outspoken member of the executive committee and leader of the Matson job actions. That the membership chose Bridges to represent them to other locals testifies to his standing with the membership and his advocacy regarding the coast conference. It meant, too, that Bridges was to meet with members of other Pacific Coast locals, hear their concerns, and give them a sample of his abilities to persuade. Dietrich was more centrist but highly critical of Holman and apparently still associated with the Albion Hall caucus.

In Portland Bridges and Dietrich addressed a membership meeting and secured the local's endorsement of the change in the conference schedule. In Tacoma they talked with Morris, Bjorklund's representative. In Seattle they spoke at a local meeting and won some important support, then returned to Tacoma, where Morris agreed to move the district convention to late February.[66]

The call for the annual convention soon appeared. Local 38-79, at a membership meeting, elected twenty delegates. The twenty delegates included at least seven Albion Hall members: Bridges, Dietrich, Halling, Larsen, Mallen, Schomaker, and Schmidt. Larsen and Schomaker were CP members; Bridges, Halling, and Schmidt were, at the very least, close to the party. Dietrich and Mallen were not. Neither, so far as I can determine, were any of the other delegates.[67]

The convention met from February 25 to March 6. On the first day, the body elected a temporary chairman. Bridges was nominated but not elected. The early days of the convention focused on organizational matters, resolutions, and a new constitution and bylaws. Melnikow reported on the code hearings and quoted shipowners as claiming they "couldn't deal with the ILA in the port of San Francisco [because] it was not a well organized or well disciplined body. . . . [I]t was dominated by radicals and was irresponsible"—a refrain employers were to repeat for the next fourteen years. On March 5, a delegation met with WEU representatives. Thomas G. Plant, president of the Waterfront Employers' Union, claimed the WEU could negotiate only for the San Francisco Bay Area and voiced concerns about "16 Communists" among convention delegates. Bjorklund responded that "the employers . . . were solely responsible for . . .

the 'Communists,' for they were in a position to exploit the workers at will and did so."[68]

The seven Albion Hall members did not vote as a bloc. On a procedural vote on March 4, the group split five to two, but the entire Local 38-79 delegation split ten to eight. Schmidt and Lewis were among the three nominees for district president; Dietrich nominated Lewis. The Local 38-79 delegation split ten to ten between Lewis and Schmidt. Lewis was elected, and Schmidt placed third. Bjorklund was reelected as district secretary by acclamation.[69]

Though failing to elect any of the district officers, the Local 38-79 militants claimed another success. On Monday, March 5, the San Francisco delegation, less three, presented a four-point resolution:

1. That we negotiate and deal with the shipowners only as a district.
2. Recognition of the ILA, embodying our original demands.
3. That we will not arbitrate these demands on the grounds that we have nothing to arbitrate.
4. If a favorable consideration is not given these demands by March 7, a date shall be set, not later than 10 days after the convention, to take a strike vote by the Pacific Coast District.

The first two points simply reiterated the district's long-standing positions, but the third and fourth points were new. Voted on seriatim, the first three each passed unanimously. The fourth was debated at length but also passed unanimously with an amendment regarding the date and an understanding about how a strike vote was to be called.[70] Thus, at the urging of the San Francisco militants, the ILA-PCD tried to remove key issues from arbitration and set a timetable for a strike vote.

The demand for a coastwise contract, harking back to the 1915 coastwise agreement, formed the logical extension of the district's organizational structure and reflected its members' experience with port-by-port determination of wages and conditions. The ILA-PCD sought to unite all longshore workers at every port from Bellingham, Washington, twenty miles south of Canada, to San Diego, California, ten miles north of Mexico. For those who remembered the coastwise strike of 1916, the San Francisco strike of 1919, the Portland strike of 1922, or the San Pedro strike in 1923, the unity of the coast was crucial to success. If locals struck separately, companies could divert ships to an open port. With wages determined port by port, companies could shift traffic to low-wage ports, playing off the longshoremen of one port against those of another to keep wages at the lowest common denominator.

The hundred or so steamship lines and the several stevedoring companies of the Port of San Francisco, most of them part of the WEU, claimed to have no connections to their counterparts in other Pacific Coast ports, although several lines were, in fact, involved primarily in trade with other Pacific Coast ports. Some stevedoring companies operated at several ports, others at only one. The organizational charts of shipping and stevedoring companies rarely ran parallel to the ILA-PCD's structure, but records of the Seattle Waterfront Employers make clear both the frequent communication among the employer associations in the major ports and the role of San Francisco as the lead port.[71] However, the WEU continued to maintain that they could not bargain with the ILA-PCD because they did not represent all the companies on the Pacific Coast.

In mid-March, both sides prepared for a strike. The ILA-PCD locals voted to strike. Local 38-79, one of the last to vote, was 96 percent in favor. Coastwise, the vote was 92 percent in favor. On March 19, Bjorklund advised all locals, "Immediately select a strike committee." Local 38-79 did so on March 21, when a packed membership meeting created a strike committee of seventy-five members, drawn from gangs that worked regularly at every dock with additional members at large. The WEU stepped up its strike preparations. Plant threatened, "The employers will make every effort to keep the commerce of the port moving normally." A newspaper advertisement aimed at longshoremen similarly threatened: "If you strike, it is . . . your own livelihood that you give up. The ships will be kept working." Plant declared that the WEU had a full force of strikebreakers ready to work and "will depend on the police for the protection of lives and property." Police Chief William Quinn announced arrangements to add more officers at Harbor Station and warned, "If trouble starts they'll find us ready to handle it."[72]

On March 21, George Creel, the regional NRA administrator, wired President Roosevelt, described the imminent strike, and predicted the "inevitable result is bound to be industrial war." The employers, Creel continued, were "actually eager for conflict[,] feeling loss of millions [will be] amply compensated by destruction of union." He added, "Longshoremen equally confident."[73]

On March 22, the day before the strike was to begin, Roosevelt wired Lewis, ILA-PCD president, asking him to wait "until an investigation of all matters in controversy can be made by impartial board which I will name." Lewis agreed. For his fact-finding committee, Roosevelt appointed the heads of the Regional Labor Boards from Seattle, San Francisco, and Los Angeles, with Henry Grady of the San Francisco board as chairman. Hearings began on March 28.[74]

Also on March 22, the Local 38-79 strike committee met for the first time. The first motion was "That Brother Bridges be chairman temporarily." It was seconded and carried. The minutes do not indicate consideration of any other candidate. Halling moved, "That we instruct our Dist Pres & Dis Exec. board to give a time limit of 15 days to the investigation committee, to reach a decision." It was carried unanimously. The strike committee was already flexing its muscle.

Later in the meeting, Bridges spoke on "the different angles of arbitration." The full membership concurred in those decisions at its next meeting.[75]

During the delay, Michael Casey, of Teamsters Local 85, wrote to Daniel Tobin, president of the International Brotherhood of Teamsters, that he had little hope for a solution, "for the reason that most all the officers of the Longshoremen are radicals of the worst type." He predicted trouble: "We will be in a tough spot, with our membership driving in on the docks, where nigger strikebreakers will be unloading and loading ships." Tobin reproduced parts of Casey's letter and sent it to Roosevelt's secretary, commending Casey's analysis. A San Francisco Labor Council official wrote to Ryan on March 28 and cited Holman as the source for a claim that "the present officials who are conducting the negotiations"—that is, Lewis, Bjorklund, and other district officials—"are communistically inclined," and urged Ryan to come west to take charge.[76]

The mediation board reported on April 1. Los Angeles employers refused to take part. The board accepted the WEU's arguments that they could not negotiate for other ports and that the ILA-PCD could not demonstrate that it was the sole representative of Pacific Coast longshoremen. The board recommended that negotiating bodies in each port deal with matters unique to that port and a coastwise negotiating body determine matters common to all ports. The WEU presented a counterproposal for bargaining just for the Port of San Francisco.[77]

ILA-PCD representatives accepted the WEU proposal as a basis for discussions, but meetings on April 4–6 failed to reach agreement. When ILA-PCD representatives insisted that wages be uniform for all ports, Henry Grady, the Regional Labor Board chairman, ruled that negotiations were to deal only with the Port of San Francisco. The ILA-PCD negotiating committee then disbanded, and Local 38-79 members chose a negotiating committee to meet with the WEU. This bargaining was clearly in conflict with the principles adopted in July and repeatedly endorsed by the district. However, negotiations quickly broke down over wages, with Local 38-79 representatives insisting on uniform wages and hours at all ports. The WEU then proposed to turn all unresolved matters over to mediation. The Local 38-79 representatives refused and broke off the talks. Lewis called for the strike to begin on May 9. Locals voted their assent. Local 38-79 was among the last to act, but did so by a unanimous vote at a membership meeting attended by some two thousand.[78]

Amid all this, Local 38-79 removed Lee Holman as president. He had sometimes been absent from meetings. He claimed to have pneumonia in August 1933 when being pressured to hold elections. During the Matson strike, he wrote that he was considering "going to a sanitarium . . . to regain my health." On March 22, the day before the strike was to begin, he claimed, "I was taken ill today from overwork." Holman had also repeatedly undercut the ILA-PCD officers, urging Ryan on March 20 to oppose the pending strike and arguing for port-by-port settlements. On March 22, he asserted he could obtain "mostly everything" the local sought if the local were to settle separately. He predicted that Local 38-79 would soon begin to lose members and that "likely a new organization independent of the I.L.A. will spring up"—a repetition of the events in 1919. He told Labor Council secretary John O'Connell that the ILA-PCD negotiators were "communistically inclined."[79]

Local 38-79's executive committee, on March 28, passed a resolution charging Holman with insubordination and malfeasance and recommending he be suspended without pay. Vice president Joseph Johnson took over as the local's business manager. Holman blamed "radicals," asked Ryan to intervene, and claimed—despite the overwhelming strike vote—that the majority of local members opposed striking and only "want to hire officials and expect them to care for their affairs." He bemoaned the ability of militants to sway the local by attending meetings: "The only solution . . . is to have no meetings, except on very rare occasions."[80]

On April 9, Local 38-79 members voted to set up a trial committee to hear the charges. Holman was told the trial would proceed whether he attended or not. Holman produced a physician's excuse for not attending, a long letter defending himself, and a threat of legal action to secure his salary. The trial began with Holman absent. Larsen, one of eleven trial committee members, was one of the few leftists in prominent roles. Curtis, Dietrich, and Herman Hellwig led the prosecution. Curtis announced that the ILA-PCD officers favored removal of Holman. Holman's defenders did little except request delays. The trial committee deliberated briefly, then, by a vote of nine to two, found Holman guilty and, by ten to one, removed him from office and prohibited him from holding local office for a year.[81]

Holman's contempt for democratic procedures, his red-baiting, and his view of union leadership as primarily a well-paying job all combined with his opposition to striking to make him a severe liability for the local. In all, his behavior provided fodder for the Left, who could point to Holman when painting established union leaders as "misleaders of labor" and "fakers," interested only in protecting their well-paid jobs, opposed to militant action, and willing to sell out the workers.

The large strike committee elected on March 21 was reconstituted and met on May 8, the day before the strike was to begin. Bridges was again nominated for chairman, and again there were no other nominations. Three subcommittees were appointed: Publicity, Relief, and Defense. The Strike Committee created a Picketing Committee the next day and a Finance Committee on May 12. A Women's Auxiliary was organized on June 5.[82]

By May 8, 1934, the eve of the strike, Bridges and his allies on Local 38-79's executive committee had come a long way since the election eight months before.

The actions on the Matson Docks in September effectively ended the Blue Book's closed shop and reduced the Blue Book to a meaningless shell. Actions at the same site in October demonstrated the power of the local to protect its members against employer blacklists. Bridges and others had worked to promote unity and confidence, and the executive committee had addressed the potentially divisive issues of race and political opinion. The local had confronted Holman's failed leadership and dealt with it.

The removal of Holman pointed up continuing problems with the local's leadership. Johnson, now acting president, had little following within the local. Curtis, chairman of the executive committee, spoke frequently at committee meetings but "wasn't very effective," according to Schmidt.[83] Given this vacuum in local leadership, decision making could flow up to district and national officers or down to lower-ranking local officers and the membership. Both happened simultaneously. In the end, the key figure in the 1934 strike turned out to be not a district or national officer but instead the militant, uncompromising chairman of Local 38-79's strike committee: Harry Bridges.

Seven weeks shy of his thirty-third birthday, Harry Bridges stood well prepared for the leadership role that was about to fall upon him. His Australian education had developed his native intelligence so that he was more capable than most longshoremen in writing and public speaking. His flowing script and competence in composition distinguished him from Holman and Ivan Cox, the local's secretary. His speaking ability guaranteed him an audience. His experience with unions in Australia and as a seaman, despite its brevity, provided him with examples that caused longshoremen to look to him for answers. His experiences during twelve years working on the waterfront gave him a deep understanding of the work, the men, and the issues, as well as a wide acquaintance among the men. His teenage commitment to his uncle's labor party views, deepened and broadened under the influence first of the IWW and then of Sam Darcy and Harry Jackson, gave him an analytical framework that went beyond particular issues to class interests. All this gave him a sense of self confidence—even cockiness—that suggested he could stand up to a boss without flinching. That, in turn, inspired confidence in others. Only under fire would that confidence deepen to respect for his commitment to unity and rank-and-file control and for his integrity and courage.

4

The Big Strike

May 9–July 4, 1934

In 1934 a torrent of strikes broke all across the country. The strike by ten to fifteen thousand Pacific Coast longshoremen proved to be one of the most significant. From beginning to end, the striking longshoremen adamantly refused any compromise over a union hiring hall and a district-wide contract. Five weeks into the strike, they raucously rejected their national president for compromising those issues. The strike proved centrally important for Pacific Coast longshore workers and also for Harry Bridges, who emerged as the de facto leader of the San Francisco local and one of the most important leaders on the entire coast.[1]

When the longshoremen walked out on May 9, they surely expected strong resistance from employers and local officials. During the last six months of 1933, the American Civil Liberties Union counted fifteen strikers killed, two hundred injured, hundreds arrested, and a half-dozen deployments by the National Guard. "Labor's rights to meet, organize and strike have been widely violated," the ACLU concluded, and identified five states as "the worst areas of repression." California led the list.[2]

San Francisco employers were long experienced in the use of labor spies, strikebreakers, and private armed guards. The Senate investigating committee chaired by Robert La Follette Jr. later described the Industrial Association of San Francisco as "an example par excellence of local association success in denying labor its collective bargaining rights" and in exercising "complete dominance of organized labor." It was, the committee concluded, "a model of militant employer tactics." The Industrial Association destroyed nearly all its records shortly before receiving a subpoena from the Senate investigators, but investigators did secure the contribution list for 1936. Companies and individuals from every part of the city's economy were on the list. All the city's banks, except only the Bank of America, provided the largest share—14.5 percent—of the association's income.

Utilities—railroad, transit, gas and electric, and telephone companies—came next, with 13 percent. Oil companies contributed 9 percent. Hawaiian interests—C&H Sugar, Matson Navigation, and others—supplied 6 percent. The Hawaiian companies and nearly all the oil companies relied on maritime transportation to move their goods. Other waterfront companies—steamship companies, importers, and the Waterfront Employers Union—all contributed, and the association's board of directors consistently included representatives from leading waterfront employers.[3] In 1934, however, this "model of militant employer tactics" was about to confront bitter and angry strikers whose militancy became the model for other workers.

At first the Industrial Association stood back as the WEU and city police prepared for the strike. On May 9, two hundred policemen—soon increased to three hundred and then to five hundred—patrolled the waterfront on foot, horses, and motorcycles and in cars. An armored car carried strikebreakers along the waterfront. The WEU had fitted out the *Diana Dollar*, a freighter, as a floating hotel for hundreds of strikebreakers so that they would not have to cross the Embarcadero to get to the piers. One strikebreaker later described his fellows as "pasty-faced clerks, house-to-house salesmen, college students and a motley array of unemployed." One strikebreaker had served several terms in the San Quentin penitentiary.[4]

On May 12, some five hundred longshoremen tried to stop the hiring of strikebreakers at the WEU office near the Embarcadero. Herbert Resner interviewed witnesses and summarized events: A group of strikers approached the office from across the street, shouting "scab" and "fink," and then "a dozen police with drawn clubs advanced on the men with the order to move on. One of the strikers cried out, 'Stand your ground men! This is a public street! We have a right to stand here!' Immediately he was seized upon by several police and clubbed."[5] The WEU moved its recruiting, eventually to Oakland, where a launch could transport strikebreakers to the water end of the San Francisco piers.[6]

Strikers in the Northwest were generally successful in blocking strikebreakers from the docks. On May 10, Portland strikers prevented strikebreakers from reaching the docks and repeated their success the next day. On May 12, in Seattle, strikers from Tacoma and Everett joined Seattle strikers to storm aboard ships being worked by strikebreakers, beat them, and drive them off the docks. In some places, however, such efforts met with gunfire. On May 15, police in Wilmington (Port of Los Angeles) fired into strikers charging a hotel ship for strikebreakers; twenty-three strikers were wounded, two fatally. On May 23, three strikers were wounded by gunfire outside the Oakland home of a man whose company was recruiting strikebreakers.[7]

Strikers dealt with scabs in their own ways. One strikebreaker reported that if the strikers captured a strikebreaker, they would "put his leg across the curb and jump on it. Or kick his teeth out." The ship where the strikebreakers lived had a full-time doctor, to treat both job-related injuries and those resulting from encounters with pickets. On June 8, the Local 38-79 Strike Committee addressed one such situation gone bad. Bridges accompanied the victim, a seaman and not a strikebreaker, to his ship; the Strike Committee agreed to pay for work on the man's teeth and to make the ILA doctor available for his other injuries.[8]

Trying to recruit Black strikebreakers, the companies painted the union as lily-white and racist. Sam Darcy mobilized CP auxiliaries, especially the Scottsboro Action Committee and the International Labor Defense (ILD), to counter such claims in the Black community. The *Waterfront Worker* called on all longshoremen to "appeal to the Negro workers," and Local 38-79 issued an appeal "TO ALL NEGRO PEOPLE," stressing that the ILA "is for the workers 100% regardless of race, creed or color or nationality" and that the local accorded Black longshoremen full equality. During the strike, Bridges spent some Sundays at Black churches; a Black newspaper later reported, "He had only one sermon he used—he implored Blacks to join him on the picket line and when the strike was settled, Blacks would work as union members on every dock in the Bay Area and the West Coast."[9] Nonetheless, some Black men signed on as strikebreakers.

The strike spread rapidly. From the outset, the *Waterfront Worker* urged the rapid broadening of the strike to include all maritime workers. The MWIU immediately announced that its seafaring members were abandoning ships when they entered port and joining the picket lines. Other seamen did the same, and their unions soon followed. On May 15 and 16, the three Pacific coast divisions of the ISU—the Sailors' Union of the Pacific; Marine Firemen, Oilers, Watertenders, and Wipers Association (MFOW); and Marine Cooks and Stewards Union (MC&S)—numbering some forty-seven hundred men, joined the strike with their own issues. Within another week, the licensed officers—MM&P Local 90 and MEBA Locals 79 and 97—also struck. On May 15, the *Examiner* noted, "For the first time in history not a freighter left a Pacific Coast port."[10]

Support from the International Brotherhood of Teamsters was crucial. The Strike Committee worked to keep IBT officers informed, providing reinforcement for thousands of individual friendships and acquaintances among the residents of San Francisco's working-class neighborhoods and parishes. On May 14, Michael Casey wrote to Daniel Tobin, IBT national president, that, on the second day of the strike, "Local Eighty Five held its regular meeting and let me say for the thirty four years I have been president of this union I never experienced such an insane mob[.] I could do nothing with them[.]" The officers persuaded the members to agree to a special meeting the next Sunday, when fifteen hundred members voted to "haul no freight in or out of the strike bound docks" and also "to uphold our agreement with the Draymen." In a transparent effort to avoid confrontation with the Draymen, Casey claimed that the Teamsters' action was a matter of safety, not a violation of their contract. At the same time, he told a reporter, "We are determined . . . to back the longshoremen here and in every other port, 100 per cent." Some Teamsters joined picket lines. Teamsters in Seattle, Oakland, and Los Angeles followed the lead of Local 85 and agreed not to haul goods to or from the waterfront. Other waterfront unions also voted their support.[11]

Soon a thousand strikebreakers were working in San Francisco, but loading and unloading ships proved less significant than being able to move goods onto and off the piers. With the Teamsters' refusal to enter the docks, the state-owned Belt Line railroad became centrally important. Belt Line workers—state employees—refused to respect the strike, so strikers parked cars on the tracks or stood or lay down in front of trains. They gave up when the head of the harbor commissioners announced that he would request National Guard intervention. The Belt Line, however, could not move the volume of goods that strikebreakers could unload, and goods accumulated on the piers. A week into the strike, the Pacific Steamship Company had ten thousand tons of cargo on its docks, with no way to move most of it and perishable goods spoiling. Matson Navigation announced, on May 18, that it had shifted many operations from San Francisco to Los Angeles, where the Teamsters were less powerful.[12]

San Francisco mayor Angelo Rossi requested that Edward F. McGrady, assistant secretary of labor, try to settle the strike. When McGrady arrived, he asked unions and employers to give full authority to their committees to act on their behalf. Other ILA locals agreed, but a membership meeting of Local 38-79 approved only with conditions presented by Henry Schmidt: coastwise bargaining and "exclusive control and management of the dispatching hall" were not negotiable, wages and hours could be submitted to arbitration, any agreement must be approved by the entire ILA-PCD membership, and settlement of the seamen's strikes had to accompany any longshore agreement. This was the first time the ILA had tied settlement to the success of other striking unions.[13]

On May 19, at McGrady's urging, representatives of the waterfront employers from Seattle and Portland came to San Francisco to join their San Francisco counterparts. That morning ILA-PCD representatives, including Bridges, met with McGrady and the presidential committee and specified that a signed agreement recognizing ILA control of hiring halls and the closed shop was the prerequisite to negotiations on other issues. Employer representatives from Los Angeles joined those from the other three cities on May 20. At that point, negotiations became coastwise, but the employers remained adamant that a closed shop and union control of hiring halls "cannot be acceded to."[14] The presence of Bridges in the May 19 meeting demonstrates both his status as an important leader of Local 38-79 and the growing significance of the Strike Committee, as that body more and more filled the vacuum left by the ineffective local officers.

On May 21, John W. Mailliard Jr., president of the San Francisco Chamber of Commerce, claimed that Communists controlled the ILA-PCD. Mailliard, president of an importing firm and director of a dozen companies, including some in shipping, was also among the leaders of the Industrial Association. He declared the strike had become "a conflict . . . between American principles and un-American radicalism," and claimed, "There can be no hope for industrial peace until Communistic agitators are removed as the official spokesmen of labor and American leaders are chosen to settle their differences along American lines."[15] The Industrial Association had long insisted that labor leaders came in only two varieties: the racketeer and the Communist. If Mailliard believed the rhetoric of the organization he had so long helped to lead, that labor leaders who were not corrupt were Reds, he may have expected that, once the "radicals" were removed, their "American," that is, corrupt, successors would quickly settle. Twenty-some years later, J. Paul St. Sure, a longtime corporate representative, reflected on such rhetoric: a "nonresponsible union leader" was "the union leader who asked the employer for something the employer wasn't ready and willing to give upon being asked."[16]

Mailliard and John Forbes, president of the Industrial Association, met with sixty business leaders and created a committee of seven to "act on behalf of the business community." That committee then met with McGrady, Henry Grady of the president's committee, and representatives of shipping companies. Paul Eliel, an officer of the Industrial Association, used the passive voice to describe this shift in control of the employers' side of the strike: "About the middle of May . . . the Industrial Association . . . was brought into the picture and . . . it played a more and more prominent part in connection with all activities relating to the controversy."[17] Who made the decision to "bring in" the Industrial Association? The leaderships of the Industrial Association, the Chamber of Commerce, major shipping companies, and the conservative wing of the Republican Party were so intertwined that one suspects the decision was made by a few men sitting in the Pacific Union Club.

The public relations firm retained by the Industrial Association suggested that, if the organization wished to present itself as an independent force representing the community, it should meet with the unions as well as the shipping companies and government officials. Their client refused.[18]

A. H. Petersen, speaking for the ILA-PCD, dismissed Maillard's allegations of Communist influence as "a typical propaganda effort," and insisted, "The executive board of the I.L.A. and members of the I.L.A. are a true cross section of Americanism." Local 38-79's Publicity Committee issued a similar statement: "All leaders of the International Longshoremen's Association are conservative American Federation of Labor men. . . . [A] great majority of the striking long-shoremen are adherents of conservative political parties. . . . [A]ll of them are agreed upon one thing, and that is, conditions as they have prevailed upon the water front cannot be tolerated in the future." "The bosses with their 'Red Scare' hope to divide us up," the *Waterfront Worker* explained and urged, "Pay no attention to their lies."[19]

Unfortunately for such denials, claims of Communist influence within the ILA-PCD leadership were repeated by CP spokesmen, especially Sam Darcy. In an article written in mid-June and published in the July issue of the *Communist*, the CP's theoretical journal, Darcy (and those who edited his draft) stopped only slightly short of claiming credit for every aspect of the strike from the organization of the ILA to the prominence of the Strike Committee. Darcy's article may be read narrowly as describing CP support for the strike (and there was significant support) but may also be read as a claim that Darcy had directed much of the strike itself. In a subsequent article published in October 1934, Darcy (or his editor) was more direct: "There would have been no maritime or general strike except for the work of our Party." In 1994 Darcy told me that his articles were edited for adherence to the party line and that one of the articles had a conclusion significantly different from the one he provided. In a two-part article published in 1982, however, Darcy reiterated his claim to have created the ILA on the docks, established the demands, and been responsible for recruiting Black longshoremen into the ILA.[20] I discuss this matter further in chapter 8.

Darcy's claims of Communist influence and control, like those of Mailliard, far exceed what the evidence indicates. Darcy himself, in an interview in 1979, acknowledged that there were only six or eight CP members among the seventy-some members of the Strike Committee.[21] The Strike Committee also showed considerable ambivalence about accepting aid from Communists. On the first day of the strike, May 9, a representative from the CP's *Western Worker* offered the Strike Committee the full support of the paper, and the committee accepted. The result, the "Baby Western," was a small separate page, consisting of material provided by Local 38-79's Publicity Committee. At the Strike Committee meeting on May 13, however, it was moved to sever connections with the *Western Worker*. The motion was amended to specify instead that the Publicity Committee had authority to censor all ILA news in the *Western Worker*, and it then passed. On May 23, a motion to continue the connection narrowly passed: nineteen yes, thirteen no, four not voting.[22]

On May 14, the Strike Committee accepted a twenty-five-dollar donation from the Communist Party, just as it accepted all donations. That day the committee also agreed that the International Labor Defense, a CP auxiliary, could use the union hall to assist the Defense Committee. On May 30, Elaine Black, local head of the ILD, asked the Strike Committee to appoint delegates to a meeting at 121 Haight Street, CP headquarters, and the committee granted the request. The next day, however, the Defense Committee reported it had lifted the credentials of a "defense man" in Oakland because "too much ILD injected," that is, too much CP content. A motion to sever connections with any organizations not affiliated with the AFL then carried but was immediately rescinded.[23] That ambivalence continued.

Just as Elaine Black, a CP member, attached herself to the Defense Committee, so Norma Perry, a secret CP member, volunteered—or, more likely, the party directed her to volunteer—as typist for the Publicity Committee. Perry then was living with Arthur Kent, also a CP member, and Kent later told the FBI that Perry's party assignment was "to see that all publicity sent out by the strike committee was in accordance with the Communist party and policies, but not to let the non-Communists know that this was being done." Kent proved himself a liar on many occasions, however, so it is impossible to know whether to credit his statement or to know to what extent Perry was successful if Kent was accurate.[24]

In the midst of these discussions within Local 38-79 over the role of the CP and its auxiliaries, the presidential fact-finding committee suggested on May 23 that the federal government operate longshore hiring halls. Such a compromise was contrary to the long-standing positions of both the ILA-PCD and the WEU. One committee member even predicted it would fail. Bridges opposed it. Local 38-79 rejected it on the grounds that government halls would actually be controlled by the shipping companies. The employers rejected the proposal, claiming it would lead to the closed shop.[25]

Joseph Ryan, ILA president, arrived from New York on May 24. He immediately claimed "the only vital point at issue" was recognition and collective bargaining. He did not even mention the hiring hall. The WEU disputed Ryan's claim and specified that the only issues were the closed shop and a union hiring hall. At the same time, Mailliard threatened that, if negotiations failed, "the merchants will open the port of San Francisco." Local 38-79 responded with its own ultimatum: failure to achieve the closed shop and union-controlled hiring halls would precipitate a "fight to the finish."[26] Thus, the WEU and Local 38-79 agreed that Ryan did not understand the central issues.

McGrady continued to seek middle ground on the hiring-hall issue. He reported to Secretary of Labor Frances Perkins on the twenty-sixth that the employers would accept joint control, the ILA insisted on exclusive control, and he hoped to persuade both for "triple control": union, employers, and the U.S. Employment Service. Likely drawing on his prior experience as an AFL union official, McGrady also expressed concern that "the workers are getting away from the strike leaders." At a membership meeting of Local 38-79 on May 26, Ryan proposed preferential hiring (that is, union members would have preference) rather than a closed shop. Bridges, identified by the *Examiner* as leader of "a radical group of workers" and "an alien," rejected Ryan's proposal: "The workers are going to hold out for nothing less than a closed shop." The membership voted to reject Ryan's efforts to dilute their proposals, reiterated their commitment to a closed shop and union hiring hall, and pledged solidarity with the other striking maritime unions.[27]

On May 28, police and pickets collided violently. Until then there had been many scuffles, but no major clash. Pickets had been meeting daily on the vacant lot opposite the local's headquarters to hear reports on negotiations and receive instructions. Afterward, the picket line, some two thousand strong, marched four abreast down the Embarcadero, led by the American flag, the ILA banner, and drums, before dispersing to areas across the Embarcadero from the piers.[28]

On May 28, militants planned to occupy Pier 38 in a sit-down; they were toward the front of the line of march and planned to rush the doors when the line moved past. When the parade leaders reached the front of Pier 18, however, mounted police intercepted the column. One newspaper reported that "strong details of police had been posted there." John Schomaker, near the head of the

Early each day of the strike, pickets met in the vacant lot across from the union office to get instructions for the day. They then paraded the length of the Embarcadero before taking up their positions opposite the piers. This photo was taken on Friday, May 10, 1934, the second day of the strike. (Photo courtesy of the Bancroft Library, University of California, Berkeley)

procession, sent word back to Bridges, who was closer to the middle, asking for instructions. Bridges said to move forward peacefully. When the line kept moving, police attacked with clubs, tear gas, and at least one shotgun. Some thirty plainclothes police who had been circulating among the strikers, posing as ILA members, pinned on their badges and joined in the clubbing. Schomaker was beaten on the head with a police baton, resulting in scalp lacerations; hit in the mouth, loosening several teeth; and arrested. Two others had head wounds, and one man was shot in the back, not fatally. A police inspector, two patrolmen, and a reporter were hit by rocks, and two patrolmen were overcome by tear gas. Local 38-79 issued a press release presenting themselves as victims of an "attack . . . provoked and carried out by the police."[29]

Later that day, May 28, McGrady joined ILA-PCD district officers and employer representatives to announce a tentative agreement: recognition of the ILA-PCD as bargaining agent; establishment of hiring halls in each port, with no discrimination against union or nonunion workers, employers free to select any workers, and workers free to select any jobs; arbitration of wages and hours; and approval of the settlement by the union membership. Though accepting the principle of the hiring hall, the proposed agreement did not provide for the closed shop or even preferential hiring, did not give the ILA control of the halls, implicitly rejected rotational hiring, and could be read as retaining the most objectionable features of the shape-up—employers free to select any workers, union or nonunion. The agreement said nothing about the other striking unions. Ryan, however, claimed that it "gives us exactly what the longshoremen have fought for and is all we want."[30]

Bridges and Mallen immediately condemned the proposed agreement. The Strike Committee dismissed it as "futile even to discuss" and then criticized nearly every aspect of it: strikebreakers were allowed to continue to work, hiring halls were to be controlled by the employers, and sole recognition was not granted. The Strike Committee promised solidarity with other striking unions and proclaimed, "The strike has just started, and will probably involve other unions which have no connection with the marine industry. The possibility of a general strike along the Pacific Coast is almost a certainty." A special membership meeting the next evening reviewed the proposal, and, according to the minutes, "THE TWENTY FIVE HUNDRED MEMBERS PRESENT WITH ONE ACCORD SHOUTED NO." After the membership meeting, the Strike Committee unanimously voted to prepare a request to the San Francisco Labor Council and the Building Trades Council for a twenty-four-hour sympathy strike of all unions.[31] Again, the Strike Committee was acting in the absence of other local leadership.

McGrady warned, "If the proposal is rejected the employers are bound to take the offensive and bloodshed and violence will result." He wanted a secret mail ballot, but some locals refused to comply and instead took standing votes or voice votes. May 31, Memorial Day, was chosen for voting in those locals that had agreed to secret ballots. Ryan, in Portland, appealed to the northwestern locals to "vote down San Francisco and save that local from itself," but the Portland local rejected it by acclamation.[32]

As members of Local 38-79 prepared to vote, the police stationed two policemen outside the local's headquarters and five mounted policemen nearby. The local denounced the police presence as a "deliberate attempt to intimidate the strikers." The strikers were not intimidated: the vote was 78 in favor and 2,401 opposed. By the same margin, the men supported staying on strike until all maritime unions secured settlements.[33]

Before announcement of the vote on the proposal, Local 38-79 members witnessed another example of police brutality. The Young Communist League had called a meeting on the waterfront for noon, Memorial Day, May 30, to demonstrate against war and fascism and support the strikers. Although the YCL distributed leaflets widely, the police refused a permit. Party officials tried to call off the meeting, but 250–300 young people gathered, milling in confusion when no speakers appeared. One version of events was that a YCL leader was hoisted to another's shoulders to explain that the meeting had been canceled. When he spoke, police attacked the crowd with nightsticks and blackjacks. The police version was that they were pelted with rocks before they attacked the crowd. All this took place on Steuart Street, in front of the ILA's second-story headquarters, and in the vacant block across the street. "I've been a seaman," said one longshoreman who watched from the ILA office, "and you get to see plenty of things like that. . . . I have never seen anything like that attack upon those kids. . . . Those cops just slugged and beat everybody." Local 38-79 protested "the insane brutality of San Francisco police." A committee representing twenty-two organizations, headed by a Presbyterian minister, interviewed witnesses before calling it a "riot planned in advance by the police," one of the first usages of the concept of a police riot.[34]

After the police attacks of May 28 and 30, the Strike Committee scheduled a march on Sunday, June 3, to protest "police brutality." Some five thousand strikers, family members, and strike supporters marched from ILA headquarters near Steuart and Mission, up Market Street to the Civic Center, two miles away, where they listened to speakers, including Joseph Johnson, acting president of the local, who announced that it might be necessary to seek a general strike if negotiations failed.[35]

Across the country, others were also talking about a general strike. In Toledo the same week, the central labor council threatened a general strike unless a strike were settled within forty-eight hours. In Minneapolis the previous week, a strike by Teamsters had brought building-trades unions on strike in support of both the Teamsters and their own issues.[36]

The same day as the protest march, June 3, the *New York Times* presented a long analysis by George P. West. Calling the strike "a startling demonstration of labor's fighting spirit," West noted that the longshoremen had gone on strike against the advice of "seasoned labor leaders" who had predicted a "quick and decisive" defeat because so many unemployed men were willing to be strikebreakers. The strike had been successful everywhere but Los Angeles, which West attributed to the Teamsters' refusal to enter the docks in the other ports. West correctly identified the "crux of the dispute" as the hiring hall. He claimed public opinion had not initially favored the strikers but that many had been impressed by the "all but unanimous withdrawal of labor" as indicating "a genuine sense of grievance and a solidarity that was not expected in this time of depression." Employers, he claimed, had been alarmed both by the success of the strikers and by the support from other labor organizations. "Threats of a general strike are flying," West continued, and "the employers are preparing for a finish fight." West's conclusions were ominous: "Moderates on both sides are losing their influence," and "indications are for greater violence."[37]

Also on June 3, someone mailed a handwritten letter to Bridges: "Listen Bridges: You dirty rotten foreigner—Meet me at 4th and Folsom Tuesday night at 9 pm. If you are not there you'll not live the week out. because I and my 'gang' are out to kill you. Save us the trouble—kill yourself at once."[38]

After four weeks, the strike had cost the life of Richard Parker, shot in San Pedro on May 14. Another San Pedro striker, John Knudson, died of his wounds three years later. The strike had seriously disrupted shipping. Some 150 ships were idled in San Francisco Bay. One estimate suggested that the first month of the strike cost $2.75 million in San Francisco. The success of the strikers in closing the Northwest ports had caused cargoes bound for those ports to come to San Francisco to be unloaded by strikebreakers and then transferred to the Belt Line and finally to northbound railroad cars. On June 7, several hundred longshoremen quit work in Brooklyn and Jersey City, in support of the Pacific Coast strikers, but Ryan ordered them back to work.[39]

The strike affected other industries. C&H Sugar and Western Sugar closed their refineries. The lumber industry of the Pacific Northwest slowed, and many plants closed. Construction on the Bay Bridge slowed, as steel could not be unloaded until ship's crews unloaded it directly on the bridge piers.[40]

Since mid-May, the Industrial Association had sponsored meetings of "representative business men" to discuss the strikes. Eliel reported that, at a June 5 meeting of some one hundred "representative persons in the community," a "decision was reached . . . to place the full responsibility for the conduct of the waterfront strike in the hands of the Industrial Association in cooperation with the shipowners." That same day, the WEU informed McGrady, "Unless men go back to work promptly . . . steps [will] be taken to move cargo by other means and this may well precipitate . . . violence and perhaps bloodshed." As a gesture, they accepted McGrady's suggestion for government supervision of hiring halls, something the ILA had repeatedly rejected.[41]

Though IBT Local 85 had decided not to enter the docks, Teamsters had hauled cargo taken from Belt Line railroad cars pulled to sidings away from the docks. A Local 85 leader told Eliel, "The men were winking at the arrangement with the longshoremen." However, Local 38-79 members began to follow Belt Line railroad cars and railroad cars loaded by strikebreakers in Los Angeles and sent to San Francisco for unloading. When Teamsters appeared, the strikers tried to persuade them not to accept the freight. On June 7, after vigorous discussion, Local 85 members voted to boycott all cargo handled by strikebreakers. Local 38-79's Strike Committee then recommended that "pickets investigate before swinging on teamsters," suggesting the nature of previous "persuasion." The next day, Industrial Association officials informed Casey that Teamsters' "refusal to handle this freight would precipitate a crisis and necessitate the hauling of freight by other means." Eliel concluded that the Teamsters' action "changed the whole course of the strike and led directly to the general strike in July."[42]

Casey's inability to control Local 85 members exemplifies a more general shift in decision making away from longtime officers accustomed to working with their business counterparts and toward unpredictable members. Eliel later wrote, "Union leaders privately admitted that while in the past they had been able to direct the destinies of their organizations they were now unable to lead them." George West reported, "The rank and file have gotten out of hand and are leading their leaders," specifically Casey and Scharrenberg.[43]

The actions of June 5 and 7—the waterfront employers' decision to give responsibility to the Industrial Association and a significant increase in the effectiveness of the unions' cordon on the port—changed the nature of the strike. Until then it had been a dispute between the longshore and maritime unions and their employers. Both sides looked for allies, but both carried their side of the struggle and kept control over decision making. Now, the Industrial Association became as central as the WEU. Ironically, those business and civic leaders who had fretted over the prospects for the strike moving beyond the maritime unions now moved the employers' side of the strike away from the waterfront employers. The repeated claims of Communist influences among the strikers motivated anti-Communist groups to become involved. Eliel and Albert Boynton, director of the Industrial Association, cautioned against overemphasizing the Communist issue, but John Forbes, the association's president, agreed with other business leaders who saw the strike as an opportunity "to drive the Communists out of the State of California."[44]

Roger Lapham, president of American-Hawaiian Steamship Company and a key figure on the employers' side, argued that raising the issue of communism was not an antiunion tactic but instead addressed a genuine danger to the nation. On June 8, in a letter to Postmaster General James Farley, Lapham stressed, "This is not a mere longshore strike, or a strike of seamen, firemen, etc., but is really a communistic move." "We have actual proof," he claimed, "that many of the strikers' committee here are leading members of the communist party, and take orders from communist leaders, and are being supported by communist money." (Such proof was never released.) The Communist threat extended to fruit harvesters, oil-field workers, and the railroad brotherhoods. "Unless the President does act," Lapham predicted, "I am afraid we are in for a change in our form of government." Lapham noted that he had "continually stressed" the danger of communism to McGrady and pushed McGrady to convince AFL leaders to unite with employers to "stamp it out." Lapham also indicated that the employers were more committed to a hiring hall than was Ryan, who clearly preferred the shape-up. Lapham, like other business leaders and also like McGrady, Ryan, and some other AFL leaders, clearly expected that the proper role of union leaders was controlling their members.[45]

On June 8, Ryan brokered an arrangement in the Northwest to allow shipments to Alaska, where matters were reaching a stage of desperation. On June 10, Grady left for Washington, to confer with McGrady, Perkins, and Senator Robert Wagner of the National Labor Board. Grady thought the only possible resolution of the hiring-hall issue was for both sides to accept government control. Ryan accepted government-supervised hiring halls but, according Perkins's sources, attached such "impossible conditions to his acceptance" as to amount to rejecting it. Ryan also suggested a separate agreement for the Northwest ports, which could then be used to "force the San Francisco employers and strikers to accept them." The Local 38-79 Strike Committee had "got[ten] out of hand," Ryan claimed, and something was needed to "force the hands of strikers and employers in San Francisco." The Strike Committee responded with a unanimous vote of censure and asked Ryan to come to their next meeting to explain himself.[46]

On June 12, Mailliard, as president of the Chamber of Commerce, released a letter to the Industrial Association, charging that "the strike was out of hand" and control of Local 38-79 had passed to "an irresponsible group of radicals who do not want a settlement" and were conspiring "to promote a general strike." Mailliard proclaimed, "The time has now come for the citizens of San Francisco to settle this strike" and called upon the Industrial Association "immediately [to] assume the responsibility of determining a method of ending this intolerable condition."[47]

The next day, Forbes, for the Industrial Association, accepted the responsibility for "ending the intolerable conditions." He presented a narrative of the strike that emphasized the toleration, patience, and generosity of the WEU and the violent, capricious, and arbitrary behavior of the ILA. The Industrial Association's public relations firm, however, revealed a very different attitude in internal correspondence on June 15: "There is unquestionably a great deal of feeling on both sides that this would be a swell time for a complete showdown."[48] From mid-June on, regardless of the state of negotiations, the Industrial Association moved ahead to open the port with nonunion labor by renting nonunion warehouse space, forming a nonunion trucking company, buying trucks, and finding nonunion drivers.

Hoping to head off the looming violence, Mayor Rossi continued to push for a negotiated settlement. On June 14, Ryan presented a proposal to Rossi, based on the ILA's Eastern Seaboard agreement but including preferential hiring and joint operation of hiring halls. Bridges declined to comment, but the *News* quoted members of the Strike Committee as saying that the ILA-PCD would insist on union control over any hiring hall. The next day, Ryan, Casey, John McLaughlin (secretary of Teamsters Local 85), and Dave Beck of the Seattle Teamsters met with officers, directors, and staff of the Industrial Association. Ryan insisted that a settlement acceptable to him and the Teamsters would be accepted by the ILA membership. Casey and Beck promised that if Ryan agreed to a settlement, the Teamsters would resume hauling freight to and from the docks. Ryan, Plant, and Boynton then went to city hall, where Rossi announced that an agreement seemed possible.[49] Discussions stretched over the next few days involving Ryan and three ILA-PCD officers (Lewis, Petersen, and J. J. Finnegan, a member of the district committee from the San Francisco ship clerks' local); Casey, McLaughlin, and Beck, for the Teamsters; Plant and Herman Phleger for the WEU; and Forbes and Boynton for the Industrial Association.

While Rossi worked toward a settlement, the mayors of Seattle and Portland announced they intended to open their ports, and a citizens' committee in Tacoma made a similar threat. On June 12, the *Waterfront Worker* appealed for a general strike. On June 15, the Industrial Association wired Roosevelt, Perkins, and McGrady, urgently requesting presidential intervention to enforce the previous agreement. Machinists Lodge 68 announced that members would vote on June 20 regarding participation in a general strike. The ILA Auxiliary began distributing a flyer headlined, "Forward to a General Strike!"[50]

On June 16, all those who had been negotiating came to the mayor's office for the formal signing. The key features of the agreement were: it was coastwise; the employers recognized the ILA as bargaining agent; the hiring halls would be under "joint and equal control," the two parties would share equally in hiring-hall expenses, neither party would discriminate in hiring on the basis of union membership or nonmembership, employers could select their employees from any registered longshoremen available, and longshoremen could select from any jobs available; each port would have a labor relations committee of three employers and three longshoremen to determine wages, hours, and work rules; and registration would be limited to men who had worked on the waterfront on or before December 31, 1933. Compared to the previous agreement, the new agreement added equal and joint control of the hiring halls; port-by-port determination of wages, hours, and work rules; and exclusion of strikebreakers from registration. To equalize earnings, the labor relations committee in each port was to set maximum work hours for each man in a given period of time. Employers could pick and choose whom they hired. Ryan and Finnegan signed. Lewis and Petersen did not sign, because, as Lewis explained, the agreement required membership approval. Plant signed four times, once for the waterfront employers' organization of each of the four ports. Casey, McLaughlin, and Beck signed as guaranteeing the observance of the agreement by the ILA. Forbes signed as a guarantee of observance by the WEU. The nature of these guarantees was not specified. No one even mentioned the striking maritime unions.[51]

Plant later acknowledged that the negotiators knew their agreement would not be approved by the ILA-PCD members in a referendum vote. "It was suggested," Plant said, not identifying who had done the suggesting, that he and Ryan should "exercise such authority as we held" and work out an agreement that would be binding on both sides. "Ryan," Plant added, "considered that he had the necessary authority." Lewis and Petersen made clear that they did not agree. "Mr. Ryan told us," Plant continued, "that when he returned to his room in the Whitcomb Hotel he was confronted by Mr. Bridges, who advised him that he may have thought he had executed an agreement, but he would find out that he had no control, at all over the situation, and that the thing would not stick. Ryan told us specifically that he had never been talked to in his life as Bridges talked to him at that time."[52]

Banner headlines in all four daily newspapers announced the end of the strike, proclaimed major gains for the ILA, and carried editorials—most on the front page—proclaiming the need to implement the agreement to prevent violence. The *San Francisco Chronicle*'s photograph of the signing showed Finnegan, Petersen, and Lewis in back and Ryan in the front row with Rossi, Plant, and Forbes.[53] This press unanimity resulted from work by the Industrial Association and, especially, by John Francis Neylan, éminence grise of the local Republican Party and general counsel to the Hearst papers. The *San Francisco News*, a Scripps-Howard publication, apparently beyond Neylan's influence, sounded the only discordant note: its banner headline specified that the agreement would have to be approved by ILA members. San Francisco's business leaders congratulated themselves for having bypassed the Local 38-79 militants and congratulated John Francis Neylan for his "swell job of getting the papers together."[54]

Their congratulations were premature. Bridges, the Local 38-79 Strike Committee, and their counterparts in the Northwestern ports were not about to accept Ryan's compromises. The Strike Committee met the morning of June 17, unanimously rejected the agreement, pledged continued solidarity with the striking seamen, and suggested the local elect its own negotiating committee, including Lewis and Finnegan. The full membership of the local met at 2:00 p.m. Ryan later claimed Bridges's supporters sent out more than a hundred men as messengers, to contact every radical in the local and urge them to attend and oppose ratification and also to arrive early to occupy the available seats and deprive conservatives of space in the hall; there's no way to evaluate such a claim.[55]

At the membership meeting, a motion to conduct a referendum on the agreement lost by a standing vote. Amid jeers and boos, Ryan defended the settlement as "virtually the same as a closed shop." Representatives from other striking unions urged rejection. Henry Schmidt, just returned from the Northwest, reported that those locals were certain to reject. A motion to repudiate the agreement carried with no dissenting vote. At the end of the meeting, the members elected five representatives to a new Joint Marine Strike Committee. Bridges was elected first, by acclamation. The other four were Schmidt, Schomaker, Charles Cutright, and John MacLalan. Only MacLalan was voted on; the others were chosen by acclamation. The same day, locals in Portland, San Diego, and Tacoma rejected the agreement. Los Angeles voted in favor, by 638–584. The Seattle local did not act.[56]

Ryan then announced he would "let someone else take a hand in settling it." Ryan himself, after rejection of the June 16 agreement, encouraged all the striking unions to "get your proposals together and present your demands jointly." Participants from the striking unions agreed on a Joint Maritime Strike Committee of five members from each striking union. It was, Sam Kagel assured me, the first time that licensed officers (MEBA and MM&P) had ever sat down with unlicensed unions.[57]

After the actions by the ILA locals, Michael Casey reconsidered his earlier statement that Teamsters would be at the docks on Monday, "regardless of what action is taken by the longshoremen." On Monday, he said, "Sending teamsters to the waterfront today would only result in confusion and possibly worse."[58]

Plant charged Ryan and the ILA with bad faith, claimed no membership ratification had been anticipated despite Lewis's and Petersen's statement to the contrary, and claimed Casey and Beck had agreed to stand behind the agreement. Plant also proclaimed that rejection of the agreement proved that "the Longshoremen's Association is dominated by the radical element and Communists" whose "avowed purpose is to provoke class hatred and bloodshed and to undermine the government." Finally, he called upon the Industrial Association "to bring this strike to an end."[59]

While Plant was acting the wounded innocent and accusing the ILA of class hatred and a desire for bloodshed, the Industrial Association's public relations representatives informed their New York office that their client now had a useful justification for the all-out fight planned well before the ILA rejected the agreement: "The Mayor, the head of the Teamsters' Union, and a couple of Federal mediators [sic] guaranteed that the Longshoremen's Union would perform, all of which is in a way rather ridiculous but seems now to serve the purpose. . . . [There is] little sincere determination to settle the strike without violence."[60] The Industrial Association had created Atlas Trucking, hired nonunion drivers, bought trucks and equipment, rented warehouse space, and hired armed guards. Frank Merriam, who had become governor when James Rolph died on June 2, confirmed to the Industrial Association that the National Guard would be available. The San Francisco Police Department laid in $13,000 (equivalent to more than $275,000 in mid-2022) worth of tear-gas supplies, paid for by Lapham's American-Hawaiian Steamship Company.[61]

Similar efforts were under way in the Northwest. On June 16, the Seattle Chamber of Commerce ordered ten twelve-gauge shotguns, shotgun shells, and a variety of tear-gas equipment for delivery to the Seattle Police Department. On June 19, the mayor of Portland announced that his city's port "will be opened" and that the city "stands ready to use force." Perkins's source reported that the Portland Chamber of Commerce had pledged $50,000 "to start a civil war to open the port."[62]

On June 19, for the first time in forty-five years, no ship entered the Golden Gate. The new Joint Marine Strike Committee met with Rossi, then held a mass rally in Civic Auditorium. The *Chronicle* estimated attendance at ten thousand. The *Western Worker* estimated fifteen thousand. Schmidt spoke first, followed by other union representatives. Then Bridges spoke. Greeted by the most thunderous applause of the evening, he spoke of the abuses of the Blue Book, the inhuman nature of the shape-up, the dangerous and exhausting work, the organization of the ILA, and the failure of the presidential mediation board. He especially pleaded for the hiring hall, "one of the basic things the union is built on." As the audience responded with shouts of "That's no lie," "Damn right," and "You tell 'em, Harry," he closed by stressing the national significance of the strike: "[This strike] is probably the turning point in the struggle of labor and capital. . . . [I]f we are successful other unions will demand better conditions all over the country."[63]

The audience's response to Bridges provided convincing demonstration that his eloquence, militancy, and refusal to compromise had made him the focal point of the strikers' cause. As Bridges concluded, Mayor Rossi entered the hall, escorted by police, and was greeted by boos and hisses. Rossi tried to speak about his and Roosevelt's efforts to end the strike but was drowned out by jeers and boos. After several other speakers, Humphrey proclaimed the loyalty of Black longshoremen to the union and the strike and then told the other striking unions, several of which barred Black members, that "every union should organize the black worker." The final, unscheduled, speaker was Harry Jackson, who concluded his address by leading three rousing cheers for a general strike.[64]

Sentiment for a general strike was growing. On June 20, Machinists Lodge 68 voted to participate in a general strike in support of the waterfront unions. Oakland Teamsters voted for a full-scale sympathy strike. Alarmed by preparations by the Industrial Association and the growing sentiment for a general strike, Edward Vandeleur, president of the San Francisco Labor Council, and John O'Connell, the secretary, wired Roosevelt on June 21: "Strongly urge that you act quickly to prevent outbreak of violence, bloodshed, property destruction in waterfront strike here. Employers preparing to move goods to and from docks under police or military convoy which possibly will lead to general strike. . . . [W]e have deadlock that can be broken only by action of strong authority such as only you personally can exert."[65]

Also on the twenty-first, Perkins urged the WEU to agree to arbitration of "the one point still in dispute," control of the hiring halls. Plant immediately responded, rejecting Perkins's view of the crucial issue. Just as the Industrial Association's public relations people had indicated, he claimed the rejection of the June 16 agreement was due to Communists, and he pointed to the unanimity of newspaper opinion as evidence for the fairness of the agreement. That day the Industrial Association brought Michael Casey to its office and persuaded him to call William Green, AFL president, to convince Green that the only issue preventing a longshore agreement was the ILA demand for simultaneous settlement of all the maritime strikes. Green agreed to convey those sentiments to Perkins. Beck, too, sent a similar message to Green.[66]

Also on the twenty-first, armed Seattle police protected strikebreakers loading a ship, leading the ILA-PCD to abrogate the agreement permitting loading of ships to Alaska. Rossi issued a proclamation opening American Legion Week, decrying "the poison of communism," celebrating the Legion's anticommunism, and urging everyone to enlist "for the duration of the war" on behalf of Americanism and against communism.[67]

The next day, June 22, efforts to secure presidential intervention multiplied. The Strike Committee telegraphed Perkins to assure her of their willingness to arbitrate wages and hours but only after agreement on ILA control of hiring halls, preference for ILA members, and no discrimination against ILA members for strike activities. Twenty minutes after the ILA Strike Committee's telegram was received in Washington, Casey spoke on the telephone with Charles Wyzanski, solicitor of the Department of Labor, and claimed, "The chief difficulties do not now revolve around the question of hiring halls." Casey's description of the key issues, however, included all those in the ILA telegram except the hiring hall: recognition and preference in hiring, no discrimination against strikers, dismissal of strikebreakers, and settlement of the other maritime strikes.[68]

Wyzanski spoke with Rossi, then summarized the situation for Perkins. He recounted Rossi's continued support for the June 16 agreement, adding, "The reasonable labor leaders [probably Casey and his fellow Teamsters] were of the same opinion, although the radical element among the longshoremen were, of course, unwilling to accept it, being stimulated partly, in the opinion of the Mayor, by Communists and by an alien leader [undoubtedly Bridges] whose name he did not give to me." Rossi told Wyzanski that the Industrial Association intended to open the port the following Monday, June 25, "even though that involved the possibility, which he recognized, of bloodshed." Wyzanski strongly urged Rossi to seek postponement of the port opening until at least Wednesday and sounded out Rossi on prospects for a new presidential board. Rossi agreed to try to delay opening the port, to give Roosevelt time to act.[69]

Later that day, Perkins summarized matters for Roosevelt, including her preparation of an executive order for his signature to appoint a special board. She accurately summarized the two key issues: "the demand of both sides for exclusive control of the hiring halls" and "the Longshoremen feel they must stay out until the Marine workers grievances are adjusted." Senator Hiram Johnson joined the chorus demanding a new committee and assured Roosevelt that the alternative was "horrors and possible blood shed."[70]

Still later on the twenty-second, at its regular Friday-evening meeting, the Labor Council reacted to Jackson's participation in the June 19 rally with a resolution repudiating and denouncing "all communist organizations, especially the so-called Marine Workers Industrial Union" and calling upon the ILA to "disavow all connections with the communist element on the waterfront." The resolution passed by 129 to 22, clearly indicating the sentiment of the large majority of the city's unions. A few days later, members of Local 38-79 cited the Labor Council's advice "to disavow all connections with the Communist element" and resolved, "any member of Local 38-79, International Longshore-men's Association, who refuses to abide by this advice shall be held to trial on charges of insubordination and if found guilty shall be expelled from Local 38-79."[71]

On Saturday, June 23, John Forbes, president of the Industrial Association, seized banner headlines by announcing the association intended "to open the port within a few days." Rossi stressed, "The police department is not going to be used to open up anything." However, Police Chief Quinn and the head of the Police Commission were part of Forbes's press conference (Rossi was not), and Quinn announced, "If necessary, every police officer in San Francisco will be detailed to the waterfront to give necessary protection and prevent violence." Bridges told the press, "The citizens of San Francisco will not stand for this; it would incite riots and jeopardize life and limb." Mallen was more cynical: "The Industrial Association has been threatening to open the port every Monday for the last three weeks. Well, seeing is believing."[72]

Later on the twenty-third, the WEU wired Perkins, claiming that ILA capitulation was the only alternative to bloodshed and violence: "From the beginning, a powerful faction of employers has condemned compromise and concession and has used all its influence to force a show-down, regardless of the bitterness, violence and loss.... Just one thing can win the day for moderation and peace as against violence, bloodshed and disaster. That is for the longshoremen to settle the strike at once on the basis of the agreement arrived at last Saturday." Also that day, Governor Merriam threatened to use the National Guard to open the port if negotiations failed.[73]

The next day, Sunday, the twenty-fourth, McGrady returned from Washington. Bridges and a delegation met him. "We wanted to be sure that you talked to the right people this time," Bridges told him. The delegation arranged to meet McGrady the next morning and promised to return for more meetings at his call. The Industrial Association offered to assist McGrady only "to get the members of the I.L.A. to return to the docks under the agreement signed in Mayor Rossi's office." On the evening of Monday, the twenty-fifth, a Local 38-79 membership meeting gave a vote of confidence to Bridges and the other ILA members of the Joint Marine Strike Committee.[74]

On Tuesday, the twenty-sixth, Rossi met with twenty-nine leaders of commerce and finance, including several current or former directors of the Industrial Association. "We have no control over the longshoremen's union," Rossi announced. "Their demands are unreasonable and cannot be met," he added, but he then urged that the port not be forced open and the militia not be called out. Instead, he recommended that McGrady be given "a chance to complete his job." The group's spokesman, Leland Cutler, insisted that "our patience will be at an end" if McGrady failed to show prompt results.[75]

That day McGrady met with Plant and Boynton, who expressed interest only in implementation of the June 16 agreement. Boynton confirmed that the Industrial Association was ready to open the port "when they [unclear antecedent] say the word." McGrady met later with an ILA delegation that included Ryan and Lewis. Late that day, Andrew Furuseth, the eighty-year-old leader of the International Seamen's Union, arrived in San Francisco. The same evening, the American Legion announced formation of "an advisory committee of citizens and American Legion members ... to oppose communism in San Francisco."[76]

On Wednesday, the twenty-seventh, President Roosevelt appointed a National Longshoremen's Board (NLB): Edward J. Hanna, Oscar K. Cushing, and McGrady. Hanna, archbishop of San Francisco, seventy-three years old, was to chair the board. Though widely respected in the city, Hanna had served on the arbitration board that, in 1921, cut wages in the building trades, precipitating the strike that brought the open shop in the construction industry and the organization of the Industrial Association; he had also served on the Industrial

Association's "Impartial Wage Boards" in 1922 and 1926. Under that regime, wages for building-trades workers fell from among the highest in the nation to among the lowest. Hanna refused to participate after 1926. Cushing, nearly as old as Hanna, a lawyer, and a Democrat, was known primarily for his charity and relief work. Roosevelt charged the NLB to investigate, hold hearings, make findings of fact, and act as arbitrator if requested.[77]

The NLB was well received by nearly everyone but the strikers. Hanna and Cushing had reputations as solid members of the community with well-known sympathies for the less fortunate. Rossi called the announcement "the best news we have had in weeks." Forbes pledged "complete cooperation" by the Industrial Association. Casey and Ryan thought the board "splendid." Bridges refused to comment. Hanna's past cooperation with the Industrial Association made him suspect in the eyes of some ILA members, as did Cushing's relations with business leaders and McGrady's proposal for government-controlled hiring halls. Bridges thought that Roosevelt had been pressured into appointing a board favorable to the employers. Forbes postponed the Industrial Association's plans to open the port until noon, Thursday, the twenty-eighth, and McGrady appealed to the strikers to return to work before then. Rossi pleaded with strikers to "go back to work and trust the board."[78]

Still on June 27, the Joint Marine Strike Committee passed a unanimous vote of confidence in Bridges. The committee also approved a mass meeting, sponsored by the Joint Strike Committee, on the following Saturday, to discuss a general strike with members of other unions.[79]

The next day, June 28, saw a flurry of activity, all raising hopes for a peaceful solution. At Hanna's request, the Industrial Association postponed the opening of the port until Monday, July 2. Furuseth proposed that strikers return to work pending arbitration. Ryan suggested a compromise on hiring halls: control by a joint board of three ILA members and three employer representatives, but with the dispatcher chosen by the ILA and no preference in hiring between members and nonmembers. Bridges was skeptical but terse: "The majority shall rule."[80]

On Friday, the twenty-ninth, the Joint Marine Strike Committee wrote to Roosevelt over Bridges's signature, insisting on ILA control of hiring halls and preferential hiring. The same day, most striking seagoing unions agreed to submit their issues to arbitration and return to work when the longshoremen's strike was settled.[81] By then nearly all the strikers were looking to Bridges as their leader.

That day ILA officials and employers vied in denouncing Bridges. Boynton focused on the ILA leadership. "Who represents the men?" Boynton asked. "Does Joseph Ryan, as international president, or W. J. Lewis, as district president, or Harry Bridges, as chairman of the strike committee?" Lewis responded, "Harry Bridges does not speak for the I.L.A." Ryan, just before leaving for the

East, issued a similar blast: "Bridges doesn't want the strike settled. . . . [H]e is acting for the Communists."[82]

In response, Bridges denied he was a Communist, challenged his accusers to prove it, and rejected Ryan's assertion that he didn't want the strike to end. He insisted that he, like everyone on the waterfront, wanted the strike settled. The difference, he insisted, was that he "wanted it settled on a basis favorable to the men." And, he specified, any settlement that did not include a closed shop had to be voted on by the members. That evening the regular Labor Council reacted coolly when Cutright advocated for a general strike.[83]

The next day, Saturday, June 30, the NLB met with both sides to consider a vote by the strikers on the question of submitting all outstanding issues—including the hiring hall—to arbitration. Lewis, Petersen, and Bridges represented the ILA. Afterward, Bridges supported the proposed referendum: "I'm willing the men should vote on anything that they see fit to." The employers again raised the issue of the reliability of the union's negotiators. When asked if he would support an election among the strikers on their bargaining representatives, Bridges was equally amenable: "I am going to ask the San Francisco longshoremen to vote." When employers raised the prospect of having the strikers vote on the rejected June 16 agreement, Lewis and Petersen opposed, but Bridges again indicated his willingness that the men vote.[84]

Newspaper stories about Bridges began to appear in Australia. On June 29, the Australian Press Association issued a release based on a telegram from an Australian in San Francisco, who stated that Bridges "heads the strike" and described him as "a forceful speaker" who "has established leadership which the strikers accept, in the belief that he is incorruptible," adding, "They have lost their faith in other leaders." That weekend a reporter startled Julia Bridges when he rang her doorbell and asked if she were the mother of Harry Bridges. Bridges's family had received no letters from him for several years and knew nothing of his union activities, so his mother's first reaction was to ask if he were dead. The reporter replied that Bridges was very much alive and explained his prominence in the strike.[85]

On Sunday, July 1, the NLB met with the employers, then with union representatives, and again with employers and the Industrial Association, but found little change. Pressed to postpone the deadline for opening the port, the Industrial Association representatives announced they would give their decision the next day. On the evening of July 1, Local 38-79 held a special membership meeting, called by the Strike Committee. Bridges was clearly in charge, introducing the meeting by reporting on rumors and the growing support for a general strike. At the close of the meeting, Bridges reported on the employers' suggestion of a referendum vote to determine whether he could represent and speak for the local and that he "wanted this question settled to-night." Lewis reacted defensively and at length; he defended arbitration and pledged to carry out the policies of the district. The members passed a motion instructing Bridges, MacLalan, and Cutright "to sit in on all negotiations, entered into by the Pacific Coast District, I.L.A."[86]

The next day, Monday, July 2, newspapers reported the death of Shelby Daffron, member of the Seattle ILA local, shot in the back by a guard the day before in Everett, Washington. John O'Connell, Labor Council secretary, wrote a long letter to William Green, AFL president, reporting on the growing agitation for a general strike and seeking advice. At 10:00 a.m. that day, at the NLB meeting, Forbes announced that the Industrial Association would open the port at 3:00 p.m. Rossi urged another postponement, but crowds gathered along the southern waterfront, where thousands of strikers silently faced hundreds of police. At 2:42 p.m., Rossi announced that the opening had been delayed until the next day. Eliel later revealed that the delay came only because the Industrial Association had not yet completed "arrangements with the municipal authorities."[87]

Ryan, back in New York, wired Bjorklund in Tacoma: "Majority of S. Ship Interests . . . are willing to concede dispatchers shall be members of our International"—a key change in those employers' position—however, "Industrial Association of San Francisco and Merchants and Manufacturers of Los Angeles [counterpart to the Industrial Association] are bringing strong pressure to bear on S. Ship Companies not to recognize our International."[88] On the employers' side, decision making had moved from the waterfront employers to organizations funded by and led by banks, insurance companies, manufacturers, merchants, and railroads, as well as shipping companies. Corporate executives who bemoaned the prospect of class warfare now stood ready to launch it.

In the morning on Tuesday, July 3, the NLB met and submitted to both sides a proposal to submit everything to arbitration and requested that they all respond before midnight, July 5. Bridges responded that he did not think that the longshore union would agree to arbitration because there was no guarantee that they could secure a union hiring hall.[89]

That day the edginess of the previous day was repeated and compounded. Thousands of strikers and strike supporters—including many members of other unions—gathered at dawn opposite the southern piers, especially Pier 38. Police created a barricade of police cars, blocking off an eight-block area, from Pier 38 to the Garcia and Maggini Warehouse (now city landmark 229) two and a half blocks away. Noon—announced time for the opening—came and went. Tension mounted. Police officers hefted nightsticks and riot guns. Some on the other side collected bricks and rocks, even as police tried to keep them away from piles of bricks at construction sites.[90]

Shortly before 1:30 p.m., the steel doors of Pier 38 opened. Two trucks came out, under heavy police escort, to loud jeers from the thousands facing the piers.

Thousands more gathered along the police barricades and near the warehouse. The barricades held, and the trucks moved unhindered. Three more trucks soon left the pier, and the five trucks moved goods for the rest of the afternoon. Outside the barricades, chaos reigned. Furious strikers attacked six trucks driven by nonunion drivers in the vicinity of the warehouse, mistaking them for the trucks used by the Industrial Association, overturning three trucks and beating several of the drivers. Police responded with clubs and tear gas. Some strikers replied with bricks or lobbed tear-gas canisters back at the police. Police asked firemen to turn a fire hose on the protesters. When the firemen refused, police laid down a barrage of tear gas and fired over the heads of the strikers, hitting a striking seaman in the ankle. A bank teller was cut by glass shards when a bullet shattered a window. Tear gas wafted throughout the area. A brick shattered the window of the police car in which the chief of police was riding. At 5:00 p.m., the pier doors closed, ending the battle. The Industrial Association announced no work would be conducted the next day, July 4. That afternoon the Joint Marine Strike Committee called for a conference of all AFL unions on July 7 "to discuss and prepare for a general strike."[91]

An affidavit by Jack MacLalan in 1939 describes other events beginning on July 3. That afternoon he was contacted by a former prizefighter, Joe Miller, who asked MacLalan to tell Bridges that "these people at the Palace Hotel" (where Neylan and other corporate and civic leaders were in constant conferences) were willing to give Bridges $50,000 (equivalent to nearly $1.06 million in mid-2022) to end the strike. MacLalan continued, Bridges "immediately said, I couldn't do that, you know that, Jack." Nonetheless, Bridges, MacLalan, and two other longshoremen met Miller that evening, and Miller repeated his offer of $50,000 or "maybe more." Bridges stalled before saying no, fearing that MacLalan and the others might be in danger if he refused. Later, one of Bridges's opponents claimed the narrative was concocted to enhance Bridges's reputation. In 1964, however, Randolph Sevier, then president of Matson, told Charles Larrowe that the bribery attempt was real and that the funds had been put up by an officer of Matson. If Industrial Association leaders believed their oft-repeated claim that all labor leaders were either corrupt or Communist, Bridges's refusal of a large bribe may have provided their final proof that he was a Communist.[92]

All parties spent July 4 preparing. Rossi issued a Fourth of July address on the dangers of communism: "The communists made rapid headway during the past year. . . . This has been abundantly demonstrated by the activities of some of their members in the strike which has paralyzed the business of San Francisco's port." The American Legion took a quarter-page ad in the daily papers to declare: "Our Country is in the midst of the greatest battle in our history. It is the Argonne of 1934. The principles of Life, Liberty and the pursuit of Happiness must continue today through the endorsement of Law and Order by duly constituted authorities."[93]

On July 4, 1934, the city of San Francisco stood on the brink of class warfare. The longshore strike had grown to include all seagoing unions, and Harry Bridges had emerged as the leader of the strikers. The waterfront and maritime employers had given carte blanche to the Industrial Association, the "model of militant employer tactics," which had enlisted the police to force open the port and break the strike. Some long-established union leaders, notably Mike Casey, had tried to straddle the conflict. On July 5, they had to decide which side they were on.

5

The Big Strike: Bloody Thursday and After

July 5 to the End of 1934

Two months into the strike, the San Francisco business community united to smash Local 38-79 and intimidate the reviving labor movement. Instead, brutal police tactics strengthened union solidarity and brought additional support to the strike, including a general strike that shut down most of San Francisco. Business leaders were both frightened and impressed by the unions' ability to shut down most of the city. During the general strike, business leaders pushed the waterfront employers to agree to arbitration, and Labor Council leaders pushed the maritime unions to do the same. Both sides claimed victory when the men returned to work. In retrospect, the 1934 strike stands as *the* watershed in the history of Pacific Coast longshore unionism: it firmly entrenched the union and its hiring hall, established coastwise collective bargaining, initiated a system of arbitration, indelibly stamped Pacific Coast longshoremen as militant, and gave them a leader to match.

That outcome was far from obvious on July 5, when McGrady notified Perkins that mediation had failed, the longshoremen would not arbitrate until the companies agreed to hiring halls with union members as dispatchers, and the companies would not agree to anything but joint control. "We will try once more today," he explained, "but we have not much hope." He added, "The unions are talking general strike if the governor calls out the troops." He concluded, "Both sides profess confidence in your committee but they refuse to arbitrate what they call fundamental rights."[1]

By the time McGrady sent his telegram, strikers and supporters were gathering along the Embarcadero. Police faced them, armed with riot clubs, revolvers, tear-gas guns, and riot guns (short-barreled shotguns loaded with buckshot). Mounted police, police on motorcycles, and police in radio cars patrolled the wide street. At 8:00 a.m., the Belt Line began to move freight cars into the Matson docks (Piers 30 and 32), and police began to force all strikers off the Embarcadero to prevent interference with the train. Strikers fought back with bricks and rocks and surrounded the freight cars, which caught fire. Police attacked the strikers with tear gas and riot clubs. Some strikers retreated to construction sites on nearby Rincon Hill. When the Industrial Association's trucks began to leave Pier 38, headed to the same warehouse as before, skirmishes broke out all along that route. Some five hundred strikers rushed down Rincon Hill toward police lines. Police responded with tear gas and gunshots. Mounted police rode into the crowds, clubs flailing. The *News* reported that Bridges "tried vainly to get orders to strikers to retreat and offer no violence after the first shootings," but "so great was the confusion he could not get the order spread."[2]

George Hedley, a theologian and sometime faculty member at the Pacific School of Religion, was with the strikers. Two weeks later, he said, "During the morning I retreated a total of seven blocks under police attack; in no case did I see any violence initiated by the strikers. . . . I have seen no retaliation but that of the throwing of bricks and rocks; and each time that has happened, I have heard the older strikers order their young comrades to desist." Strikers provided similar descriptions of the events.[3]

After a lunchtime truce, strikers tried to block another Belt Line train moving freight cars, and police responded with gunshots and tear gas. Police then began to clear the entire southern Embarcadero, using tear gas to push strikers and strike supporters northward. Observers agreed that police often waited to act until motion-picture camera crews were in place.[4]

Once the Embarcadero was cleared, police pushed more and more strikers into the streets and vacant lots near Local 38-79's headquarters on Steuart Street, near Mission. About 1:30 p.m., an unmarked police car drove into the center of the intersection of Steuart and Mission, forty feet or so from the stairs leading to the local's second-story office. A plainclothes officer stepped out of the car, armed with a riot gun and revolver. The many witnesses differed in what happened. Some said the strikers—perhaps 100 or 150—began calling the officer names. Several witnesses, not all strikers, testified that the officer cried out, "Now any of you sons of bitches want trouble, come on." Some witnesses said rocks were thrown at the officer before he fired. Others, including several who were not strikers, agreed that rocks were thrown only after he began shooting. Most witnesses specified that he shot deliberately and repeatedly at groups of men, not over their heads. When he stopped shooting and walked away, two men, Howard Sperry and Carl Olsen, lay on the sidewalk, blood pouring from their wounds as other men scattered in all directions. Sperry had been stuck in the arm, shoulder, chest, and abdomen. Olsen was shot in the body and the face. Police drove the strikers away from the wounded men and loaded them into an ambulance. Sperry died an hour later; Olsen survived. Shortly before

4:00 p.m., another man, Nicholas Bordoise (George Counderakis), was found dead a block away, killed by a shot from a riot gun.[5]

Sperry was fifty years old, unmarried, a registered Republican, and a World War I veteran who had risen to the rank of sergeant. He lived on Third Street, a working-class area with cheap rooms. He and Olsen had been working in the strike kitchen and dining room during the noon meal and were on their way to the union office to get their picket cards certified. Counderakis, about forty-three years old, was a CP member, born in Greece, married, a member of Cooks' Local 44. Though recovering from appendicitis, he had been volunteering in the strike kitchen.[6]

Several of the wounded were carried into the Local 38-79 hall, where a doctor treated those suffering from gas or lacerations. The hall was on the second floor, and police shot tear-gas canisters up the stairs. Henry Schmidt ran up the stairs and into the hall just before the door was closed and locked. Schmidt later recalled that, a few minutes later, someone rattled the doorknob and could be seen through the opaque glass of the door. Those inside refused to open it. Schmidt recalled, "All of a sudden, this individual out there gave us his profile. Then everybody recognized the long nose. . . . Everybody said simultaneously, 'Let him in, it's the "Limey."' Here was Harry, crying like a kid [from the] tear gas." Hedley later quoted someone in the hall during the gas attack: "The headquarters telephone rang. 'Are you willing to arbitrate now?' said the voice on the wire."[7]

The press claimed 109 were injured, but did not include those treated by doctors in the union office or those who went home to recuperate. The *Chronicle* listed 73 of the injured by name, injury, and relation to the conflict. Of 10 injured police officers, 3 were treated for tear gas, 4 for being hit by rocks, 1 for both, 1 for abrasions, and a mounted policeman for lacerations from being thrown from his horse. Five bystanders were shot, including 2 in passing streetcars, 1 was gassed, and 1 was clubbed. Two strikebreakers and a newspaper photographer were beaten. Of 46 injured strikers, 23 had been shot (4 in the back, 10 in the legs, 5 in the head, 4 elsewhere), 10 clubbed, 2 beaten, and 4 gassed in the eyes. The unions' own list added another 9, 4 of them with gunshot wounds. Given the amount of shooting, it seems remarkable that only 34 of the several thousand strikers and bystanders had been shot. Revolvers, to be certain, are inaccurate at a distance, and, the union reported, "nearly all the men wounded were injured at long range."[8] Perhaps many of the police—neighbors, fellow parishioners, relatives of the strikers—were purposely shooting over the strikers' heads or, given the number wounded in the feet and legs, at the ground. Nonetheless, what emerges from the many accounts is a police riot—a riot that the police instigated or escalated, characterized by widespread police brutality.

After the first shots, Bridges and members of the Joint Strike Committee went to city hall, barged into Mayor Rossi's office, and protested what they called "police brutality." Rossi replied that the police were protecting life and property and declared, "There are only two ways to settle this strike. One is mediation. The other is force." He said that they had been warned that blood would be shed unless they accepted a peaceful settlement.[9] Rossi's statement, together with the many threats of bloodshed from the Industrial Association, suggests that police had been instructed to be unsparing in their attacks.

The Joint Strike Committee wired President Roosevelt: "Reign of terror inaugurated at the behest of Industrial Association. . . . As American citizens we urge that you take the necessary action to eliminate this terrorism." To William Green of the AFL, the committee said, "Police are gassing bombing and shooting American working men," and described it as "a fight between organized labor and organized capital."[10]

At 3:00 p.m., Governor Merriam issued an executive proclamation in which he cited "tumultuous, riotous and unlawful assemblies with intent to do violence to persons and property" in San Francisco and directed the National Guard to take over the port. His order was broad, permitting the National Guard to act throughout the entire city. The next day, he cited "communist and subversive influences" among the longshoremen and appealed to "independent, sincere labor leaders" and "saner, clear-thinking workers" to oppose "any effort to involve other groups of labor" in the controversy. By dawn on July 6, two thousand National Guardsmen were in place. Observers and marksmen with

Howard Sperry and Carl Olsen were shot by the police in the intersection of Steuart and Mission Streets on Thursday, July 5. Olsen recovered. Sperry did not. Nicholas Bordoise (George Counderakis) was found dead a block away. Strikers created this ad hoc memorial on the site where Sperry's and Olsen's bodies lay. The chalked signs read, "Police Murder" on both sides and "2 ILA Men killed shot in the back" at the front. (Photo AAD-5196 courtesy of the San Francisco History Center, San Francisco Public Library)

rifles took positions on top of piers. Sentries with bayoneted rifles marched in front of the piers. Machine-gun nests guarded key locations. Tanks prowled the Embarcadero. The Industrial Association opened a second warehouse, and the Belt Line began to move goods from several piers.[11]

Teamsters Local 85 held its regular membership meeting the evening of July 5 and voted that they could not work under such conditions. A special membership meeting was set for July 8 to vote on "whether they wish to continue to work." Mike Casey was shaken by the work of his friends in the Industrial Association. He told IBT headquarters in Indianapolis: "Press reports fall far short of describing the blood curdling condition on the San Francisco waterfront."[12]

The evening of July 5, the Waterfront Employers told the NLB they would arbitrate but not on hiring halls. McGrady summed up for Perkins: "Neither side will agree to arbitrate on terms that would be acceptable to the other side. Your committee will proceed at once to hold public hearings and arrange for elections [for the maritime workers]. . . . Because militia is called out maritime unions want a general strike called."[13]

On July 6, the *News* described July 5 as "Bloody Thursday," the name that has persisted ever since among Pacific Coast longshore workers. On July 8, Bridges moved, Schmidt seconded, and the Strike Committee resolved, "As long as the I.L.A. exists—no I.L.A. member shall perform any work on the waterfront of S.F. on July 5th in memory of our brothers who were killed on that day at the orders of the S.F. Industrial Association."[14] Bloody Thursday, July 5, later became a contractual paid holiday for all Pacific longshore workers—an annual reminder to employers of the consequences of their resort to violence.

On July 6, the labor movement began to move toward common action in support of the striking unions. At the Labor Council's regular Friday meeting, everyone talked about a general strike. Fourteen unions had already voted in favor, and Local 85 was to vote on July 8. Bridges secured unanimous support for the ILA's position that the hiring hall could not be submitted to arbitration. Leaders of the council presented a motion to establish a Strike Strategy Committee to consult with and advise striking unions and to refute "the continual charges made by irresponsible propaganda agencies" that the longshore and maritime unions "are directed by people not in sympathy with the aims and objects of the American Federation of Labor." Vandeleur appointed himself, John O'Connell (the Labor Council secretary), and five of the most prominent labor leaders in the city, but not any member of a striking union. Among the five was George Kidwell, president of the Bakery Wagon Drivers, a onetime Socialist turned Democrat.[15]

Kidwell became the Labor Council's chief strategist and tactician for the crisis. Henry Melnikow later called Kidwell "the brain of the Labor Council during the 'twenties' and 'thirties.'" Kidwell reasoned that, rather than trying to halt the burgeoning sentiment for a general strike, the Labor Council had to take it over and direct it. He told Melnikow, "If you called a General Strike and had a General Strike Committee, then you could control the situation and you could work out a solution. . . . The whole idea was to get it out of the hands of the individual unions, particularly the longshore and get it into the hands of the Labor Council." Kidwell was well aware of events in Seattle in 1919, when a general strike "blew up"—his term—and destroyed much of the city's union movement. He also assured Sam Kagel, "In a general strike situation, you've got to end it fast."[16]

Described in the press as the city's "conservative" labor leaders' move to block a general strike, the Strike Strategy Committee was in fact a serious effort both to resolve the longshore and maritime strikes and to direct any general strike. After meeting secretly with that committee on Friday evening, Bridges agreed not to call for a general strike at the mass meeting of the city's unions called by the Joint Maritime Strike Committee for the next day and instead to await the next regular meeting of the Labor Council.[17] At the mass meeting, on July 7, Bridges was the principal speaker. "The longshoremen have retreated to the wall," he declared. "All issues except control of hiring halls have been relegated to the background." He insisted, "This is no longer the I.L.A.'s fight alone," and explained that the mass meeting had been called before the Labor Council had created its Strike Strategy Committee. Bridges did not call for those present to vote on a general strike but instead urged them to return to their locals and press for a vote on a general strike. Fifteen unions reported that they had already voted in favor.[18]

On July 8, Ed Vandeleur, president of the Labor Council, perhaps with coaching from Kidwell, strongly defended Local 38-79: "The longshoremen themselves are a reasonable and orderly group and there are no agitators among them. . . . All references to an extreme group are made by parties unfamiliar with the general character of the men on strike." Vandeleur explained that seeking to resolve the strike "in a cool headed and deliberate manner" did not preclude "the most drastic steps." "We are ready," he warned, "to unleash the full strength of organized labor in San Francisco."[19]

That same day, July 8, 1,500 members of Teamsters Local 85 met. Afterward, Casey told the IBT national office that the men were "frenzied" and "became well-nigh unmanageable and demanded to vote." Paper ballots were distributed with the question: "Are you willing to continue to work under present conditions?" The tally was 1,220 no and 271 yes. Nonetheless, Casey managed to delay final action until another meeting of the entire local, on Wednesday, July 11.[20]

All day on July 8, mourners filed past the two caskets in the union hall, many stopping to cross themselves and pray, a few stopping to raise a fist in the communist salute. On Monday, July 9, a brief eulogy was delivered inside the union hall: "You have been killed because of your activity in the labor movement. . . .

July 9 was the funeral for the slain men, held in the union hall, the second floor of the light-colored building in the center. The intersection at the lower right is where the fatal shooting took place. At 12:30 p.m., a brief eulogy was given inside the union hall, followed by a prayer by a priest. The proceedings were carried by loudspeakers to the thousands outside. The flowers, union banners, and caskets were then carried down the narrow staircase and placed on trucks: several for the flowers, one for Sperry's casket covered by a U.S. flag, and another for Counderakis's casket with a spray of flowers. (Photo courtesy of Bancroft Library, University of California, Berkeley)

Your killing was inspired by the Industrial Association and the Chamber of Commerce. . . . [O]rganized labor will answer that deed many-fold." Bridges declined to speak. A priest offered a prayer. The proceedings were carried by loudspeakers to thousands standing outside.

The caskets along with flowers and union banners were carried down the narrow staircase and placed on flatbed trucks: one for Sperry's casket covered by a U.S. flag, another for Counderakis's casket with a spray of flowers, and several for the flowers. ILA members who were veterans, wearing their military uniforms or veterans' organization caps, marched alongside the trucks. Then came members of the Musicians' Union playing a solemn funeral dirge. Next came a few cars with Julia Bordoise, the mother of Tom Mooney, and other friends or family members of the two martyrs. Next in line came a U.S. flag and the ILA flag, followed by marchers: first Lewis and Bridges, the local's executive board, and the strike committee, then, eight abreast, the members of Local 38-79 followed by the striking maritime unions and the city's other unions, all led by their union banners and U.S. flags. Then came strike supporters and sympathizers, followed by cars carrying the wives and children of the marchers. The *News* estimated seven thousand marchers; the *Chronicle* thought fifteen thousand. Strike supporters estimated as many as forty to fifty thousand. More silent thousands lined the sidewalks, either to pay their respects or to gawk. The cortege stretched for a mile and took an hour to pass any point. Even the usually hostile *Chronicle* was awed: "They came as far as you could see in a silent orderly file of march, a mass demonstration of protest which transcended anything of the like San Francisco has seen." And, in boldface: "**Any who doubted the solid sympathy of the labor movement with the striking unions were shamed by that demonstration.**"

The ILA's funeral arrangements committee had told Police Chief Quinn that they wanted all police off the route of the funeral procession, from the union hall to Market Street, 2.2 miles down Market to Valencia, and another mile down Valencia to Duggan's funeral parlor. Quinn reluctantly agreed but specified that there were to be no Communists involved. In response, the funeral arrangements committee placed Sam Darcy in the first open car next to Julia Bordoise. Police stayed out of sight, a block away from Market, directing traffic away from the route of the funeral procession. The funeral committee specified there were to be no placards, and the rule was enforced—when a few CP members tried to hawk the *Western Worker*, they were shooed away. The procession ended at Duggan's funeral parlor, which was providing services without charge. Sperry's casket remained there, waiting for a family service; as a veteran, he was buried the next day in the National Cemetery at the Presidio of San Francisco. Counderakis was taken to Cypress Lawn Cemetery, south of the city, where Darcy delivered a stirring funeral address.[21]

Noting that the funeral procession "created a temporary but tremendous wave of sympathy for the workers," Eliel added, "Only after two or three days had passed did San Francisco awaken to the fact that its sympathies had been aroused by a brilliant and theatric piece of propaganda." However cynical, Eliel was accurate in his appraisal that the funeral procession had moved a general strike from possibility to certainty.[22]

The Industrial Association, the Chamber of Commerce, and Mayor Rossi, having concluded that "force" and "bloodshed" would send the longshoremen docilely back to work, must have been sorely disappointed that their actions had, instead, provoked such resentment and anger that they accomplished what the striking longshore and maritime workers had failed to do on their own—they created the most dramatic demonstration of labor solidarity in twentieth-century U.S. history.

On the morning of July 9, the day of the funeral, the NLB began its public hearings. After hearing from a half-dozen witnesses, Archbishop Hanna recessed the hearing so union members could attend the funeral. The next day, the board heard from Petersen and Bridges, representing the ILA. Petersen explained that the ILA had agreed to arbitrate hours, wages, and working conditions, but specified that "the hiring halls should belong to us." Bridges began by making clear that the ILA wanted a district-wide settlement. He reiterated the ILA demands, argued that joint hiring halls would in fact be dominated by employers, and compared the shape-up to "a slave market." Eliel described the scene: "Bridges made an extraordinary presentation before the Board speaking without notes and extemporaneously. He showed not only unusual command of the subject matter but of the English language as well. Employers were able for the first time to understand something of the hold which he had been able to establish over the strikers both in his own union and in the other maritime crafts." After the funeral and the dramatic procession down Market Street, the NLB met far into the evening, in closed session, with the Strike Strategy Committee and representatives of waterfront employers and shipping companies. NLB members urged both sides to agree to arbitration. "Let us settle this controversy by intelligent, civilized means," McGrady pleaded. Vandeleur then met with the Joint Maritime Strike Committee until two in the morning.[23]

On July 11, much of the NLB hearing was taken up by T. G. Plant—now known to the strikers as "Tear Gas" Plant—a spokesman for the waterfront employers, who read a long statement reviewing all events from the employers' standpoint. Then, to the surprise of the union members in the room, he announced that the four waterfront employers' associations were willing to arbitrate every aspect of the strike and that forty-one steamship, lumber, and oil companies were willing to engage in collective bargaining with the seagoing unions. Lewis announced that the ILA-PCD would conduct a referendum of all members to determine if they agreed to submit all matters to arbitration. Petersen specified two caveats: the referendum would not be conducted until the employers of the maritime unions agreed to arbitration, and the request to arbitrate might be rejected if ILA-PCD members refused to arbitrate the hiring hall because "the strength of the union is entirely dependent upon control of the hiring hall."[24]

That evening Teamsters Local 85 met. Vandeleur and Kidwell, on behalf of the Strike Strategy Committee, urged that any strike be delayed. Casey and McLaughlin, too, strongly recommended delay. Bridges and a group of ILA members waited outside until a cry went up: "Bridges, Bridges, get Bridges in here!" Bridges was brought in. Casey introduced him as "the man of the hour." Bridges spoke with restraint, explaining that defeat of the maritime strikers would challenge the entire labor movement and that a Teamster strike would double the power of the current strikers. He took questions, which Casey required to be written out. Asked if he had been a red in Australia, he explained that, if that were true, it would have been long since revealed and that "if anything could have been pinned on me to associate me with Communism, it would have been found out long ago." Casey wrote to IBT headquarters the next day that "our entire membership was the victim of an unrestrained rage" over Bloody Thursday and the Industrial Association's use of nonunion drivers. He explained the situation of Local 85's leaders: "When you see an avalanche coming, don't stand in front of it." The next day, four thousand Teamsters in San Francisco and Oakland stopped work. Pickets turned back trucks on roads leading into the city. Oil and gasoline deliveries ceased. Fresh produce began to disappear from stores.[25]

After the Teamsters' decision, the only questions about a general strike were of timing and leadership. On Friday, July 13, a reporter asked Vandeleur if there would be a general strike. He replied, "Do you fellows have to see a haystack in the air before you can see the way the straws are blowing?" Kidwell told Melnikow the only ones against the general strike were "those who didn't understand his [Kidwell's] strategy and those who . . . saw through it." More and more unions were voting to strike or follow the lead of the Labor Council. However, the long Labor Council meeting on Friday, the thirteenth, was inconclusive. In the meeting, Bridges advocated for a general strike and a large strike committee, chosen by the rank and file of all participating unions. Kidwell and Labor Council leaders outmaneuvered Bridges and his supporters. The council voted to have a committee of five members from each local meet the next morning, "for the purpose of maintaining a united policy in this great emergency." Vandeleur explained that the committee would be empowered to recommend a general strike but not call one, since AFL county labor councils were not authorized to call strikes by their affiliated unions.[26]

The General Strike Committee (GSC), the large committee approved on the thirteenth, met the next day. After three hours of discussion and by a vote of 315 delegates (sixty-three unions) in favor, 15 (three unions) against, and 245 (forty-five unions) not authorized to vote, the committee resolved that unions that had already approved strike action should go out on Monday, July 16, at 8:00 a.m. and that unions that had not approved action should vote immediately. Bridges made that motion. The delegates next established an executive committee. Vandeleur was named chairman by acclamation. Bridges was defeated for vice chairman. Kidwell was chosen secretary by acclamation. Vandeleur appointed the remaining 25 members (including Casey and McLaughlin from Local 85), officers of the Building Trades Council, the Bay Area Council of Carpenters, and the Iron Trades Council. Ten of the 25 were Teamsters. Bridges was the lone representative from the striking maritime unions. Kidwell and the council's leaders had again outmaneuvered Bridges and his supporters. The

Alameda County Labor Council, across the bay, also set a time for its unions to go on strike.[27]

Also on July 14, Local 38-79 held a special membership meeting to discuss the proposed referendum on submitting all issues to arbitration. Lewis reported that National Guard troops and strikebreakers would remain on the docks unless the ILA agreed to arbitrate. Bridges reported on the Labor Council's discussion on arbitration, during which he had announced the ILA would not arbitrate the question of the hiring hall. The members resolved, "That Local 38-79 goes on record as refusing to submit the question of the hiring hall and a closed shop to arbitration." Bridges emphasized that "the heat is on us, and that it all depended on whether or not the other locals will take a referendum vote on the question of arbitration."[28]

The decision for a general strike changed many dynamics of the longshore and maritime strikes. Labor Council officials both directed the general strike and pushed the striking longshore and maritime unions to accept arbitration. Federal officials intensified their efforts to bring an arbitrated solution. Key members of the city's elite also worked to promote arbitration. And Harry Bridges often found himself on the sidelines.

The few days preceding the general strike were busy ones. So many families were stockpiling groceries that stores began rationing their stock. Some among the city's elite sent their wives and children out of town as the adult males hunkered down at home or at their club. On July 14, Kenneth Kingsbury, president of Standard Oil of California, from inside the Pacific Union Club, assured a friend, "With the character of the men, who are red and Communists, . . . the guardsmen plus the police will not be able to cope with the situation," and he complained that pickets were even outside his club! The next day, Senator Hiram Johnson wired his old friend Harold Ickes, secretary of the interior, "Here is revolution not only in the making but with the initial actuality." Bay Area district attorneys and federal attorneys assured Attorney General Homer Cummings that the general strike was for "overthrow of the government." J. Paul St. Sure later recalled, "In those days, militant unionism, radical unionism, communism, these were synonymous terms in the language of the businessman."[29]

Some among the city's elite viewed the general strike differently—as a prime opportunity to crush unions once and for all. William H. Crocker, president of Crocker Bank, director of major corporations, and prominent in the conservative wing of the Republican Party, told a reporter: "This strike is the best thing that ever happened to San Francisco. . . . We've lost millions on the waterfront in the last few months. But it's a good investment, a marvelous investment. It is solving the labor problem for years to come, perhaps forever." He continued, "When this nonsense is out of the way and the men have been driven back to their jobs, we won't have to worry about them any more. They'll have learned their lesson. Not only do I believe we'll never have another general strike but I don't think we'll have a strike of any kind in San Francisco during this generation. Labor is licked." The reporter, however, described the strike as "class warfare, a bitter, relentless battle between those who have money and those who earn wages."[30]

On July 15, Roger Lapham, president of the American Hawaiian Steamship Company, phoned Secretary of Labor Frances Perkins to explain how to accomplish Crocker's objective: "We can cure this thing best by bloodshed. We have got to have bloodshed to stop it. It is the best thing to do . . . the best thing that could happen." The next day, less bloodthirsty, Lapham wired Perkins his proposals for driving the men back to work. Claiming "the present movement is largely led and directed by the Communist Party and its members, most of whom are aliens," Lapham demanded they all be quickly deported. Perhaps harking back to the Pullman Strike of 1894, he urged that the attorney general immediately enjoin all striking unions for having "openly conspired to restrain . . . trade and commerce" and punish their officers "by fine and imprisonment." Finally, he recommended immediate approval of a shipping code for seamen and arbitration of the longshoremen's strike based on the June 16 agreement.[31]

That same day, Mayor Angelo Rossi spoke to a nationwide radio audience. He began by praising organized labor but concluded by condemning those "who willfully seek to prolong strife, either for their own selfish ends or for the disturbance or overthrow of the government." Rossi proclaimed an emergency, effectively suspending the city charter (presumably to prevent it from being overthrown). "Acts of violence will not be tolerated," he announced. And he urged, "Let there be no hysterical action." The next day, Perkins wired to President Roosevelt, "Only danger San Francisco strike is that mayor is badly frightened and his fear has infected entire city." Other prominent San Franciscans soon used Rossi's term, *hysteria,* to describe the state of mind of the city's leaders.[32]

Monday, July 16, first day of the general strike, dawned fair but cool. The Market Street Railway (privately owned streetcar lines) was not running. Workers on the Municipal Railway (city-owned streetcar lines) were also respecting the strike, but the GSC quickly advised them to return to work because, as civil service employees, they risked losing their jobs. No taxis or trucks moved on the streets. Movie theaters, barbershops, dry cleaners, bars, auto-repair shops, and most gas stations were closed. Many small businesses in working-class neighborhoods also closed. The GSC authorized nineteen unionized restaurants to open and was issuing permits to delivery drivers for unionized bakeries and dairies. Newspapers continued to publish. Pacific Gas and Electric workers stayed on the job.[33]

John Francis Neylan again marshaled the press to speak with one voice. The *Chronicle*'s headline blared, "Labor Acts to Rule City." Front-page editorials defined the situation as "no longer a strike" but "a challenge to all the rights of all the people." The *Examiner* and *Chronicle* carried front-page accounts about "aroused citizens" ending the 1926 general strike in Britain. The *News* again declined to follow Neylan's lead, provided less sensationalist coverage, and announced that the Municipal Railway was operating, the GSC was approving food deliveries, and more restaurants would soon open.[34]

In reaction to the press claims, the GSC adopted a statement of purpose drafted by Henry Melnikow and Ray McClung, a newspaper reporter. Melnikow later described their intent: "We were going to make sure that the world knew that this was not a political general strike but an economic general strike, which was called purely for enforcement of trade union policy. . . . The newspapers and the powers that be in San Francisco did not want the world to know that this was an economic general strike. They wanted the world to believe that this was a political revolution." Melnikow continued, "The program that McClung and I drafted was adopted by the entire General Strike Committee as *the* program . . . the official statement of what the strike was all about. Merely to gain the right to collective bargaining, to designate their own representatives and to dispose of disputes by voluntary arbitration."[35]

Though couching the statement in conservative terms, Melnikow, given his studies with John R. Commons, would have been well aware just how bold, how significant, the Labor Council's step was. They were shutting down the city to protest police violence and the use of the National Guard to protect strikebreakers. It was not a "political revolution," but it was definitely a political act, designed to demonstrate the solidarity of organized labor in support of the striking maritime unions.

On July 15, Secretary Perkins accurately informed Roosevelt that the only impediments to arbitration were longshore strikers' refusal to arbitrate the hiring hall and shipowners' refusal to arbitrate with seafaring unions. Louis Howe told the president, "Strike so far proceeding in very business like and orderly way with no violence up to tonight and a singular absence of hot temper on either side." He added, "I have feeling that both sides would like to compromise before it is too late," and advised Roosevelt, "So long as public thinks you are not worried there is no danger of general panic."[36]

Other federal officials agreed there was no danger. Robert Hinckley, of the Federal Emergency Relief Administration, talked with Oscar Cushing of the NLB and Dan Murphy, a longtime labor official now a vice president of the Bank of America. Hinkley reported, "Everything is all right," and advised against Roosevelt's coming.[37]

Such on-the-ground observations by New Deal officials dramatically contrasted with the behavior of local and state officials. On July 14, Police Chief Quinn created a new division within the police department, the Anti-radical and Crime Prevention Bureau, giving the city its own Red Squad. Police horses were fitted with goggles and gas masks. Rossi called on citizens to stand with him so "that those who seek the destruction of this government shall find no comfort." On July 16, Governor Merriam more than doubled the number of National Guard troops in the city, stood ready to impose martial law over the entire city, and called upon "workers" to undertake "a more active and intensified drive to rid this state and nation of alien radical agitators."[38]

On the second day, July 17, the *Call-Bulletin* claimed, "The Communist party today is out in the open as directing the strike" and cited a *Daily Worker* article in which Earl Browder played directly into the hands of the Industrial Association and its allies by claiming credit for the general strike and declaring that twelve hundred Communists were "directing the workers of San Francisco."[39]

That day, as tanks cruised the Embarcadero and the National Guard extended its operations, the GSC issued more permits for bakeries, dairies, and restaurants to open, and the GSC executive committee considered a resolution from George Kidwell recommending that the striking longshore and maritime unions submit all issues to arbitration. Bridges moved to exempt the hiring hall from arbitration but lost by 28 to 9 with 1 abstention. The full GSC approved the motion by 207 to 180. Kidwell's plan to move decision-making from the maritime unions to the Labor Council remained on track, but by a thin majority.[40]

On July 18, William Randolph Hearst wired instructions to the editors of the *Examiner*s in both San Francisco and Los Angeles for editorials denouncing the general strike as "political revolution," an attempt to overthrow the government "by force and violence," and a "treasonable attempt to destroy democracy and install communism." "If forces of democracy are too feeble," he continued, "there will be nothing left to combat communism but facism [*sic*]."[41]

Since early May, Hearst's *Examiner* had been foremost in sounding the alarm over the Communist threat. The longer the longshore strike lasted, the louder grew the press's claims of Communist control, claims repeated by business leaders, civic leaders, and some labor leaders. With the general strike, such alarms ratcheted to full volume. The statements by Rossi, Kingsbury, Hiram Johnson, and others suggest that the constant claims of Communist control of the strikes and of an imminent, Communist-led revolution may have persuaded many business and civic leaders that their city really did face revolution. The Red Scare now escalated, apparently with approval by city leaders.[42]

On July 16, first day of the general strike, Oakland police raided that city's CP office and beat and arrested those inside. Fifty unidentified men attacked the CP office in Hayward, beat its occupants, and burned its furnishings. One hundred and fifty men attacked a Communist meeting in Oakland. On July 17, San Francisco police backed by National Guardsmen with machine guns raided the MWIU office and arrested everyone in the vicinity—85 in all. That same day, anonymous vigilantes described as 30–40 "roughly dressed men," armed with rocks and clubs and wearing heavy leather jackets, attacked the office of the *Western Worker*, broke up the printing press, then attacked CP headquarters. In each case, a car drove past, and men hurled bricks through the windows. Next more cars arrived, and men rushed into the building, broke up furniture and equipment, beat up anyone inside, and quickly departed. Police then arrived and arrested all those who had just been beaten. Seven locations were raided on July 17. The *News* reported, "The campaign had apparently been carefully prepared." Total arrests that day numbered 350. More raids followed. On the eighteenth, Captain John O'Meara, head of the new Red Squad, specified, "Those Communist hangouts raided today and yesterday must not be reopened. . . . Anyone attempting to reopen them will be jailed."[43]

The identity of the vigilantes was never definitively established. Eliel claimed they were "representatives of conservative labor organizations." The press sometimes pointed to the Teamsters, but IBT officials denied any involvement. Ella Winter reported, "A Legionnaire has told me he has proof of the legionnaires the police employed, [and] gave workers['] clothes and Union buttons to break up the workers' centers in SF." Others suggested the raiders were strikebreakers hired by the Industrial Association, businessmen, or police officers out of uniform. A later FBI report claimed, "The raids were made by vigilante committee composed possibly of a few members of the Police Department and several members of the Teamsters' Union."[44]

A vice president of a steamship company told a noontime meeting on July 17 (before the first raid in San Francisco) that raids would start soon and implied official approval. Industrial Association files indicate advance knowledge of some raids. The close cooperation between the vigilantes and police also points to some level of official approval, perhaps reaching to the mayor's office.[45] Vigilante and police raids continued through the rest of July.

The strikes had increased local CP membership, but the vigilante actions brought a sharp drop. Darcy later reported that, between 1932 and 1934, membership had increased from 285 to 3,000, but "about 800 dropped out during the period of the terror."[46]

On the second day of the general strike, Hugh Johnson arrived in the city. A brigadier general in World War I, Johnson headed the NRA. His invective and public drunkenness led Roosevelt to order him to take a long vacation, so Johnson ostensibly arrived only to speak in Berkeley at the University of California. However, upon arriving in San Francisco, Johnson first met with newspaper publishers who tried to convince him to side with the employers. Neylan recalled that Johnson, though inebriated, announced he planned to broker a compromise. Neylan insisted, "You couldn't compromise with civil war," and persuaded Johnson to rewrite his university speech. The speech, broadcast over local radio, dealt largely with the strikes. Johnson defended labor and criticized the shipping companies, but then equated the general strike with "civil war" and "bloody insurrection" and finally called on "responsible labor organizations" to drive out "subversive influences."[47] As he spoke, vigilante raids were taking place.

San Francisco's civic leaders were receiving mixed messages from federal authorities. On the same day Johnson was encouraging vigilantism, Marvin McIntyre, FDR's secretary, asked Herbert Fleishhacker, a prominent and politically well-connected banker, to "warn authorities to prevent troops guards or armed citizens committee starting any trouble."[48]

Also on the seventeenth, Johnson, perhaps influenced by Neylan, addressed Kidwell and praised the GSC's resolution "to put everything up to an impartial board." Johnson promised, "If you will . . . call off the general strike, I have sufficient assurance from the employers to warrant me in saying that I believe I can have this whole matter in arbitration before the President's Board at once."[49] Despite the qualifiers, it was a bold promise.

The next day, July 18, the third day of the general strike, the NLB presented a seven-point proposal calling on all sides to agree to arbitration, call off the strikes, and return to work pending the NLB's decision. That morning Johnson met with Vandeleur, Kidwell, Casey, and others, but no members of the striking maritime unions. Johnson again insisted they call off the general strike as a precondition to any further federal efforts to settle the strikes. That same day, McIntyre assured Roosevelt he was "using all sources here [to] bring operators to arbitrate."[50] McIntyre's efforts were private. Johnson, not reflecting the administration's position, spoke publicly to the GSC officers.

Labor Council leaders continued toward Kidwell's two goals: resolving the waterfront and maritime strikes through arbitration and closing down the general strike. Their resolution on arbitration was not well received. Although Plant reiterated that the WEU was willing to arbitrate everything, Lapham refused arbitration with the seamen's unions. Bridges and others insisted the ILA would never arbitrate control of hiring halls. In the GSC, Bridges moved, on behalf of the Joint Marine Strike Committee, to endorse the Labor Council's position on exempting the hiring hall from arbitration. Vandeleur ruled Bridges's motion out of order and was sustained on appeal. Regarding Kidwell's second goal, closing down the general strike, the GSC executive committee authorized all union restaurants and butcher shops to open and approved more bakeries for deliveries. When a delegate to the GSC challenged the authority of the executive committee to do so, Vandeleur ruled him out of order; on appeal the chair was upheld 198–180.[51] The council leaders' majority was getting thinner.

The next morning, July 19, the GSC met, and Kidwell moved a long, complex motion that cited the threat of martial law, the resolution on arbitration, and the

NLB's proposal, then concluded with two resolved clauses: first, upon acceptance by the employers of the NLB's proposal, the GSC "will accept such basis for the immediate termination of the [general] strike"; second, the GSC asks all those striking in sympathy with the longshore and maritime workers to return to work and pledges "every resource, moral and financial, for the continued prosecution for the successful termination of the maritime workers' and longshoremen's strikes." The motion generated intense debate, especially on whether there were, in fact, assurances from the employers. Vandeleur responded, as Johnson had insisted, that the general strike had to be called off before federal or city officials would pressure employers to accept arbitration. Vandeleur also stated, "The delegates can take it for what it is worth that all government agencies including the President's Longshoremen's Board . . . will do everything in their power to compel the employers of the maritime workers and the longshoremen to accept the terms for arbitration that this General Strike Committee has proposed." The GSC voted by the same thin majority, 191–174, to end the general strike, then unanimously approved motions that the GSC not be dissolved and the chairman be empowered to call it back if necessary and that state troops be immediately removed from the city.[52]

The resolution ending the general strike stated explicitly that the longshore and maritime strikes continued. To banish any doubt, Bridges assured the press, "We can run our own strike. . . . The resolution has no effect on us," and he announced meetings of the Joint Marine Strike Committee and the Local 38-79 membership for the purpose of continuing strike operations. Johnson, too, announced that he did not expect the longshore and maritime unions to call off their strikes and that he would try to bring about arbitration of their issues. He then left town.[53]

The two questions posed by Perkins on July 15 continued to block solutions to the longshore and maritime strikes: Were ILA-PCD members willing to arbitrate everything, including control of the hiring hall? Were employers of maritime labor willing to agree to arbitration? Both were decided on Friday, July 20. That day Teamsters' Local 85 voted, by 1,138 to 285, to return to work, putting heavy pressure on the ILA to arbitrate. That same day, Neylan held what he later called "an ice-water lunch, no cocktails," at his home in an elite suburb. Neylan invited shipping executives, WEU representatives, Industrial Association officials, and newspaper publishers. He later described events: "I took them down in the open air where all the orators could blow off steam and so on, and we read the riot act to them: that the waterfront had been badly handled; that they had played right into the hands of the radicals by their atrocious neglect of the legitimate interests of labor down there; that they had to . . . get in line and help us out of this thing. That went on all afternoon." One source later claimed that Neylan flatly informed Herman Pfleger, attorney for major shipping companies and the WEU, that the press would announce that the shipowners *had* agreed to arbitrate and let them try to deny it. Those present finally agreed that steamship owners "should" arbitrate.[54]

Neylan, in San Francisco, and McIntyre, in Washington, were not the only ones pressuring the shipowners. On July 19, Ryan assured Bjorklund that he was continually impressing upon the shipowners "that they must give our men on the Pacific Coast a real say in the management of the hiring halls." On July 20, the Roosevelt administration announced an inquiry into the sizable federal subsidy that shipowners received for carrying mail. Perhaps not coincidentally, Postmaster General James Farley arrived in San Francisco. He denied any intention to pressure the shipowners, but his very presence underlined the significance of the mail subsidy.[55]

On July 21, the city's newspapers announced that the WEU had agreed to arbitrate all issues if the ILA-PCD agreed and that forty-two steamship companies had agreed to arbitration with the maritime unions. That placed the ILA-PCD under heavy pressure to arbitrate everything, including the hiring hall. One ILA-PCD officer summarized their situation: "A refusal to . . . arbitrate will leave us in a position where organized labor[,] the general public[,] and the government will class us as outlaws. . . . Shippers have agreed to arbitrate all issues with maritime unions who have also agreed to arbitration provided the Longshoremen agree to arbitrate[.] That leaves Longshoremen in position where they will carry the blame for nonsettlement of the whole strike if arbitration is defeated."[56]

On July 21, the NLB announced a referendum among longshoremen. The same day, the Strike Committee dissolved itself. Bridges was again just a member of Local 38-79's executive committee, but he continued to exercise significant influence.

On July 23, voting began in all ILA-PCD locals, supervised by NLB staff. The ballot asked if the longshoremen should submit all issues to arbitration and be bound by the board's decision. More than twenty-seven hundred voted in San Francisco, more than eighty-two hundred in the entire district. Local 38-79 voted three to one in favor, and the total vote was more than four to one in favor. Only two small ports in Washington rejected arbitration. Results were announced on July 25.[57]

Members of Local 38-79 met on July 23, before the referendum results were known. Lewis and Bridges made reports. Bridges described the GSC executive committee as "wrecking" the general strike. The members then discussed creation of a union hiring hall and scheduled a meeting of gang bosses for that purpose. Titus Humphrey requested that "the colored members be distributed in the various gangs of the waterfront," thereby ending racial segregation, a measure implemented not long afterward.[58]

Discussions now turned to when and how the men would return to work. The Joint Marine Strike Committee, on July 23, resolved, "Under no circumstances shall any one of the striking groups be left alone, but return to work shall be by all simultaneously at an agreed time and conditions." Local 38-79 met the next day to discuss whether the local should return to work without the seamen. Bridges discussed that question in detail but apparently made no recommendation other than "if we were to go back we should do in a body and not straggle back one by one." Paddy Morris was present and strongly concurred in Bridges's remarks.[59]

Longshore workers were ready to return, but on their own terms. The ILA-PCD proposed to the NLB that there be no hiring from the sidewalks or docks and that all hiring be through union halls or jointly operated halls. The employers' associations argued to return to prestrike hiring procedures. The NLB ruled that hiring in ports that formerly had employer-operated hiring halls would be through those halls, with NLB and ILA representatives present to guard against discrimination, and that hiring in San Francisco would be through the shape-up.[60] Local 38-79 members refused.

At a membership meeting on Sunday, July 29, members first voted that everyone return to work at 8:00 a.m., July 31. Bridges then presented the conditions under which they would return: men were to return as part of their regular gangs under conditions prevailing before the strike, all men employed since May 9 (strikebreakers) were to be discharged, no one was to work more than fifteen hours without an eight-hour break, gangs were to work no more than forty-eight hours a week, and there was to be no discrimination because of union membership or strike activities. A follow-up motion specified that men not part of regular gangs were to report to the union hall to receive work assignments and that anyone soliciting jobs at the docks was to be fined.[61] By creating their own hiring hall and defining basic work conditions, members of Local 38-79 set out to test whether the solidarity of the strike could extend to control of hiring and working conditions.

Just as the Teamsters' vote to return had pushed the ILA-PCD to accept arbitration and return to work, so the ILA's decision pushed the maritime unions to do the same. However, many ISU members refused to return under the continuous discharge book—the "fink book"—created by shipping companies. Seamen had to present their book when signing onto a ship and received it back at the end of the voyage with comments—making it a tool for blacklisting. Furuseth proposed a solution: burn all fink books. On July 30, Furuseth, eighty years old, presided over a gigantic bonfire near the Embarcadero, as fink books were dumped into the flames. Similar book burnings took place in Portland and San Pedro.[62]

As the striking unions returned to work, many questions remained. A Local 38-79 bulletin on August 10 specified, "Working conditions are made on the job," then outlined a system of gang stewards, to meet once or twice a month on how "to improve working conditions." Stewards were to make certain no one worked more than forty-eight hours in one week or more than fifteen hours in one stretch, to verify that every gang member belonged to the union, to remind men to pay their dues, and to inform gang members about "what action is to be taken to bring about improvement on the front." The bulletin was issued over the names of Bridges, Cutright, and MacLalan, but Bridges and Cutright denied any role in creating it. Lewis, Morris, and Petersen, on behalf of the ILA-PCD officers, repudiated it.[63] Nonetheless, the system of gang stewards and efforts to "improve working conditions on our own initiative" were soon under way.

The NLB opened hearings in San Francisco on August 8. Melnikow represented the ILA-PCD, Pfleger the WEU. Melnikow later described Pfleger as "a star football player . . . [who] carried some of those tactics into the arbitration"; he thought Pfleger's arrogance and condescension led him into errors. Lewis was the first witness. Bridges testified on August 13. After reading a prepared statement summarizing his work as a seaman and longshoreman, Bridges demonstrated his wide-ranging knowledge of longshore work in response to questions from Melnikow. Sam Kagel had carefully coached Bridges on what to expect: load size, loading and unloading of various commodities, gang size, dangers, accidents he'd witnessed, and the shape-up. Pfleger asked Bridges about his duties as Strike Committee chairman, specifically, "Did you run the affair?" Bridges responded, "I acted at all times in conjunction with the committee and the local. . . . The duties were the same as chairman of any committee." Other ILA-PCD witnesses included MacLalan, Schmidt, Curtis, and Morris. When Pfleger asked Schmidt, "Are you a member of the Communist Party?" Schmidt responded, "Is it compulsory to answer that?" Melnikow objected, and Cushing sustained the objection.[64]

Then came Pfleger's turn to call witnesses. An early one, J. P. Gribbin, manager of the Seaboard Stevedoring Corporation, testified, "We don't work them [longshoremen] beyond physical endurance," which he defined as twenty-four hours, though he also explained, "a 15-hour shift is plenty long enough for a man to work." Gribbin acknowledged, "There may have been one or two instances where we worked [men] beyond the 24-hour period, say for two or three hours," but he emphasized that longshoremen averaged only one twenty-four-hour shift per week. "If a gang is working for three or four days and working until nine or ten o'clock every night [13–14-hour shifts]," he said, "then you hit them with a 24-hour shift, I don't think it is doing right by the men." The transcript does not reveal the reaction of NLB members to Gribbin's concern for his employees.[65] After concluding in San Francisco, the NLB traveled to Portland, Seattle, and Los Angeles for further hearings.

On September 15, as arbitration proceedings were winding down, Local 38-79 elected officers for the coming year. For president, Bridges defeated Joe Johnson, the acting president, by two to one. Cutright, Dietrich, and MacLalan were elected as business agents. Two days later, at the membership meeting for installation of officers, Bridges's opponents within the local challenged his eligibility because he was not a citizen. Johnson nonetheless installed Bridges as president.[66]

On September 24, the NLB returned to San Francisco to take closing arguments. Melnikow spoke first, focusing on wages, hours, and hiring, the last of which he called "the most fundamental problem" and "the most important point" facing the board. Hiring and dispatching, he argued, should be done through each local ILA hall with a five-person labor relations committee to adjust disagreements, two appointed by local ILA, two by employers, and "an impartial chairman." Anticipating Pfleger's argument that ILA leaders were irresponsible radicals, Melnikow pointed to the work of his mentor, John Commons: "It has been the history of the American labor movement that responsibility made for conservatism."[67]

Pfleger, in closing, laid out four issues: the definition of longshore labor (that is, which workers were covered by the award), wages, hours, and hiring. He denied any need for changes in wages or hours. The hiring hall, he argued, "would deprive the employer of his fundamental right to select his employees; would destroy all incentive on the part of the men to be efficient and competent; . . . would turn over to union officials the distribution of work and the filling of jobs and would constitute a closed union shop." "If it were granted," he continued, "the I.L.A. would have such control over the situation that it could enforce any demand upon the employer." In closing, Pfleger presented the argument that Melnikow had anticipated: "An unanswerable argument against the I.L.A. demand is the thoroughly demonstrated lack of responsibility of its officers and lack of discipline among its membership," as evidenced most recently by the election of Bridges as president of Local 38-79, which, Pfleger claimed, violated the ILA constitution that required officers to be citizens.[68]

Melnikow later thought, "The piling up from port to port of all these petty despotisms and tyrannies and inequities, some people earning $80–$90 a week and others starving, did get under the skin of both Archbishop Hanna and Mr. Cushing, and . . . was the most influential" part of the hearings for them. Melnikow saw McGrady as "more interested in working out a peaceful solution."[69]

The board's award, on October 12, covered all major issues: a definition of longshore work; a six-hour day and thirty-hour week; base pay of $0.95 per hour with $1.40 for overtime; hiring through jointly operated halls, with the dispatcher selected by the ILA; dispatching without discrimination between union and nonunion longshoremen; and labor relations committees (LRC) in each port of three ILA representatives and three employer representatives to supervise hiring halls and resolve questions regarding implementation of the award. The report was signed by Hanna and McGrady; Cushing concurred in everything except wage levels, which he thought too high. The press described the hiring-hall decision as a victory for the employers. Bridges initially agreed, but that view was seriously shortsighted.[70]

In retrospect, the ILA scored a smashing victory: the six-hour day and thirty-hour week (which remained in Pacific Coast longshore contracts until 1987), a modest increase in wages, and, most important, control over dispatching, which proved nearly as detrimental to employers' authority as Pfleger had predicted. And, over the long run, the experience of the ILA in general and of Bridges in particular bore out Melnikow's prediction that "responsibility made for conservatism"—at least with regard to observing contracts.

Results for the maritime unions were more ambiguous. Voting to designate bargaining agents began after maritime workers returned to sea and was staggered over several months, so all could vote. Not until late October did voting close and bargaining begin. The six maritime unions (three divisions of unlicensed personnel in the ISU and three unions of licensed officers) *each* bargained with several separate corporations and associations. When bargaining broke down, the parties submitted to arbitration by the NLB. Awards for were finally announced between February and April 1935.[71]

Almost immediately after announcement of their award, ILA-PCD members began implementing their hiring halls and seeking control over working conditions. In San Francisco, gangs refused to work under what they considered unsafe working conditions. As work stoppages multiplied, the six-person LRC for San Francisco frequently deadlocked between the ILA and WEU members. On November 14, Charles Wyzanski, solicitor for the Labor Department, informed Perkins about work stoppages in San Francisco: "The men insist on going out first and thereafter bringing their cases to the arbitration boards. . . . The men are entirely out of control, and a 10% radical group is defying all agreements and actually indulging in physical violence beating up those workers who are reluctant to join the movement." Melnikow later described those events differently: "[Bridges] was testing the employer's strength. . . . The union did engage in job action, and sometimes in violation of the agreement, but if they followed my advice, they always went back immediately when the arbitrator said to."[72]

On November 16, Bridges, now president of Local 38-79, wired Perkins, urging that she appoint an additional member of the San Francisco LRC to act as arbitrator, something anticipated in the arbitration award. The same day, McGrady spoke on the phone with Cushing and a federal official who both described the situation as "very tense," with a hundred police assigned to the waterfront. They, too, urged appointment of an arbitrator and added, "In addition to the arbitrator in each port . . . there should be one arbitrator appointed for the entire Coast" to decide questions that affected all ports. Perkins appointed Marcus C. Sloss, a widely respected lawyer and member of the city's social and civic elite, as longshore arbitrator for San Francisco and, in early December, also for the entire Pacific Coast.[73] Though the process for selecting port arbitrators and coast arbitrator changed over time, the positions themselves became central for Pacific Coast longshore labor relations.

The strike proved to be *the* watershed for Pacific Coast longshore workers. What came after was significantly and permanently different from what had come before. Two central, long-term elements for Pacific Coast longshore labor relations had been established: union control of dispatching and a system of port and coast arbitrators. More fleeting was the prospect for continued unity of the striking unions, a possibility of that took form as the Maritime Federation of the Pacific Coast (MFP) in early 1935. And, of course, the strike also gave Pacific Coast longshore workers their leader for the next forty-three years.

6

Pursuing Maritime Unity

October 1934–January 1937

The events that catapulted Bridges to leadership also brought greater unity among longshore and seagoing unions than had existed since the San Francisco strike of 1901. Much of the unity of mid-1934 was spontaneous and informal, with no central organization until creation of the Joint Maritime Strike Committee halfway through the strikes. Unity among Pacific Coast maritime unions reached its apex with the creation of the Maritime Federation of the Pacific in April 1935. That unity began to unravel almost immediately, due especially to job actions and boycotts that strained not only relations between unions and employers but also relations between unions, strains compounded by conflict between Harry Bridges and Harry Lundeberg, leaders of the two largest unions in the MFP. Those strains on unity were magnified during the MFP strike from early November 1936 until late January 1937.

Efforts for maritime unity came amid a redefinition of the role of the federal government in labor relations and the emergence of significant disunity within the AFL. An important new law in 1935, the Wagner Act—the National Labor Relations Act—used regulation to accomplish a significant redistribution of economic power. It incorporated the old 7(a) and parts of other legislation, added definitions of unfair employer practices, and authorized the National Labor Relations Board (NLRB) to implement and enforce the new regulations. The new law spurred further union organizing and protected existing organizations. The number of union members more than doubled between 1935 and 1941, and unions emerged as a powerful political force in the 1936 elections.[1]

The Wagner Act came as the AFL grappled with increasing internal disarray. When AFL officialdom did little toward creating industrial unions in unorganized industries, John L. Lewis, president of the United Mine Workers (UMW), created the Committee on Industrial Organizations (CIO) to bring together unions committed to an industrial model of organizing. Those efforts brought him and his committee into increasing conflict with the AFL leadership.[2]

In some Pacific Coast ports, new ILA locals were expanding from the docks to related groups of workers. Warehouse workers in San Francisco resurrected Local 38-44, originally chartered in 1919, and set out to organize warehouses and related facilities near the waterfront. In San Francisco, the ILA added two new locals, Local 38-100 for ship scalers, who scraped and painted ships, and Local 38-101 for barge workers.[3] In the Northwest, ILA locals were organizing ships' clerks (also called checkers) and others who worked with longshoremen.

One obstacle to maritime unity was removed in late 1934, when the Pacific Coast MWIU was dissolved. That change was prompted in part by events in San Francisco. At the PolBuro (Political Bureau, the highest level of decision making in the CPUSA) meeting of October 25, 1934, Jack Stachel reported on union organizing. After a perfunctory nod toward the TUUL, he emphasized, "At this moment the main task is to work in the AFL." "What will happen," Stachel asked, "if we will really elect not only one Bridges, but hundreds of Bridges in Section and district leadership, not to talk of national leadership. . . . [I]f we are on the inside, we will have thousands of Bridges, and because we will be on the inside, we will have more influence since the workers are becoming radicalized." The PolBuro unanimously approved "the line of the report."[4] The "line of the report" was to abandon the TUUL in all but name, and even that relic was soon dissolved. The PolBuro, pushed by events in San Francisco, was taking its first step toward what would become the Popular Front and the high point of CP influence in the United States.

Even before the new line became public, Sam Darcy and the District 13 comrades were moving to dissolve the Pacific Coast MWIU. Bridges explained later that, after the 1934 strikes, the "reactionary officials" of the ISU "started a drive to purge every former M.W.I.U. member off the ships." Bridges continued, "Three or four months after [the strike, that is, October–November 1934] I was advocating—and more than advocating, practically insisting" that the seamen get out of the MWIU. The decision to dissolve the MWIU on the Pacific Coast took place in a meeting in October or November 1934 in Grants Pass, Oregon, a small town roughly midway between San Francisco and Seattle. Bridges was there along with leaders from CP Districts 12 (Washington and Oregon) and 13 (California) and perhaps a few others. Darcy, long critical of the MWIU, informed Stachel on November 21, "We are instructing all comrades who are threatened with elimination from the industry under this discrimination, to join the I.S.U." That decision attracted opposition, especially from Harry Jackson, who was so outspoken that he was removed as a party functionary. Later, in June 1935, a SUP membership meeting approved opening membership to all seamen with "clear" strike records, and at least twenty-one MWIU members joined the SUP. Party documents referred to this as a merger.[5]

Bridges was soon involved in the organization of the Maritime Federation of the Pacific Coast. After the 1934 strike, the Northwest Joint Strike Committee earmarked $1,500 of its remaining strike funds for creation of a Maritime Federation. In mid-January 1935, Paddy Morris, ILA-PCD secretary, and Bill Lewis, ILA-PCD president, invited all Pacific Coast maritime unions to send delegates to a planning meeting. Henry Melnikow recalled, "There was some doubt in the minds of those left of center as to whether this wasn't a move from the right wingers to control the situation," and "Bridges was afraid that this was a movement to overwhelm him." Lewis and Morris's initiative brought sharp self-criticism within the CP: "For three months after the strike not one goddamn thing was done and nothing would have been done if the reactionary elements had not stepped into the situation and taken the initiative."[6]

The initial meeting, in February, in the San Francisco Labor Temple, brought delegates from most ILA locals and the seagoing unions—SUP, MFOW, MC&S, MEBA, MM&P, the American Radio Telegraphists Association (ARTA), and the Ferryboatmen's Union (the last of which was not on strike in 1934). Among the founding unions, the ILA-PCD and ISU (SUP, MFOW, MC&S, and Ferryboatmen) both claimed about fifteen thousand members, by far the two largest organizations, but both were divided into autonomous units (ILA locals and individual ISU unions) that sometimes disagreed. Bridges chaired the constitution committee. Delegates approved a draft constitution and set April 15 in Seattle for the founding conference. The delegates also resolved that July 5 should be a "legally recognized maritime workers holiday" in memory of the martyrs of 1934.[7]

In March Paul Scharrenberg, testifying in the seamen's arbitration proceedings as an officer of the ISU and the California State Federation of Labor, said, "I wish we would have a war with Japan because then the seamen would get everything they wanted, as in the World War we had everything we wanted." Bridges quickly submitted a resolution to the Labor Council to condemn the statement and censure Scharrenberg, setting off what the *News* called a "wild verbal display." Scharrenberg denounced Bridges as an alien, Communist, and "louse." Albin Kullberg of Local 38-79 defended Bridges and vehemently attacked Scharrenberg. Vandeleur tried unsuccessfully to gavel Kullberg into silence, then ordered the sergeant-at-arms to throw him out. At that, the *News* reported, "husky stevedores stirred in their chairs," and Kullberg continued to speak. The matter was referred to the executive committee. "The climax was capped," the *News* concluded, "when Secy. O'Connell likened the belligerents to a bunch of back-biting women. . . . Then the women delegates to the council protested Mr. O'Connell's remarks, and another row almost started." The executive committee subsequently ruled the resolution out of order.[8] The fracas was just one round in a longer conflict between Bridges and Scharrenberg.

By then arbitration awards for the seagoing unions were being finalized. ISU affiliates wanted a hiring hall with rotation of union members, but the awards specified preference of employment with hiring from the docks. "The chairman [Hanna] was prepared to give them the hiring hall," Melnikow recalled, but "Scharrenberg went to the chairman and said that he was opposed to it." Scharrenberg, Melnikow explained, controlled the SUP through a small group of union members who never went to sea and were therefore always available to support Scharrenberg in union meetings. Rotation through a hiring hall would have destroyed Scharrenberg's machine. After the arbitration award, the seagoing unions, especially the SUP, turned to direct action to drive strikebreakers and nonunion workers off the ships, to enforce their awards, to enforce their hiring halls, and to seek better working conditions.[9] That use of direct action soon brought problems for Bridges and his union.

The founding conference of the Maritime Federation met in April. Bridges again chaired the constitution committee. Many roll-call votes showed Local 38-79 at odds with the other longshore locals. Bridges strongly defended a section of the proposed constitution committing the MFP to "work toward the formation and establishment of a Union Labor Party," generally understood as endorsing the CP's advocacy for a Farmer-Labor Party. He failed, 58.73 to 94.95 (each union's vote was based on the number of its dues-paying members, which was then divided among that union's delegates, sometimes with awkward decimals). Bridges's support was limited to Local 38-79, a few ILA delegates from other locals, ARTA, the Alaska Fishermen, and a few SUP delegates. A motion for MFP locals to participate in May Day events produced a similar alignment and an even more lopsided outcome.[10] A large majority of the delegates were clearly opposed to what were understood to be CP positions.

Newspapers reported that Bridges hoped to be president, but the votes were not there. Instead, Local 38-79 delegates joined four other ILA delegates, ARTA, the Alaska Fishermen, all SUP delegates, and a scattering of others in supporting Harry Lundeberg of the SUP. The other ILA delegates, most MFOW delegates, and some from MC&S supported Paddy Morris's nominee, an ILA member from Seattle. Lundeberg won narrowly, 78.31 to 76.69. A similar alignment with only a few shifts elected the vice president and secretary-treasurer, but Bridges's choices lost.[11]

The new MFP had four districts: Puget Sound (District 1), Northern California (District 2), Columbia River (District 3), and Southern California (District 4). Delegates from each district elected district officers. District 2 delegates elected Bridges as president and Mervyn Rathborne, ARTA, as secretary. In the end, Bridges's supporters managed to elect only the District 2 officers and Lundeberg.

The press referred to Lundeberg as Bridges's "lieutenant" and claimed the MFP was "controlled" by Bridges, but events soon demonstrated the contrary.[12]

Largely unknown before the April convention, Lundeberg had taken a prominent role there. Born in Norway in 1901, he left home in 1918, worked as a merchant seaman, joined the SUP, and became an American citizen. Late in the 1934 strike, he was elected SUP patrolman (similar to a business agent) for Seattle. Lundeberg had an extended exposure to syndicalism while at sea and in Seattle, where IWW and syndicalist influences were strong. Syndicalists argued that workers should take direct action at the work site to improve their immediate working conditions.[13]

Bridges and members of Local 38-79 were no strangers to direct action. Beginning in August 1934, they refused to work when confronted by larger sling loads or smaller gangs than they considered safe, job actions whose success hinged on the union's control of dispatching. Though other ILA-PCD locals had good success in operating their hiring halls, Local 38-79 led the way in addressing issues of load and gang size.[14]

The ILA-PCD annual convention met in mid-May 1935. Delegates approved resolutions from Local 38-79 to establish a uniform load limit for all Pacific Coast ports and that all locals should establish "dock and gang stewards." They also instructed their delegates to the ILA national convention to seek to remove

This photo from March 1935 shows San Francisco longshoremen checking in with the dispatcher to be assigned to work. (Photo AAD-5366 courtesy of the San Francisco History Center, San Francisco Public Library)

Joseph Ryan as president. The convention approved an important constitutional change: beginning in 1936, all members, district-wide, were to elect district officers. For 1935, however, election of district officers remained with the convention. Bridges sought the presidency but lost to Bill Lewis by 69.8–50.2. Paddy Morris was reelected as secretary-treasurer by 79.2–39.8.[15]

Soon after, on Saturday evening, May 25, while in a meeting in the apartment of Norma Perry, his secretary, Bridges was stricken by acute abdominal pains. Rushed to a hospital, he was treated for a perforated stomach ulcer. The press described Bridges's condition as "grave" and quoted his doctor: "The majority of such cases are fatal." Bridges rallied but remained hospitalized until June 8.[16]

While Bridges was hospitalized, Lundeberg brought charges against Scharrenberg. Scharrenberg blamed Lundeberg's actions on "an alien Communist, the notorious Harry Bridges," but on June 3 the SUP membership voted 322–54 to expel Scharrenberg—vice president of the ISU, longtime editor of the SUP's newspaper, and executive officer of the state labor federation. In a second membership meeting in mid-July, 450 SUP members reaffirmed the expulsion, branding Scharrenberg "an enemy of the labor movement." Melnikow claimed that Scharrenberg was actually expelled because of his opposition to the hiring hall. Scharrenberg was, however, quickly reinstated as a member by the ISU's national officers.[17]

During the SUP's June vote, Bridges was still recuperating. The *Chronicle* nonetheless reported, "The anti-Scharrenberg maneuvers were mapped by Bridges, personally, from his sick bed and were carried out, it was ascertained, by Harry Lundeberg, a Bridges lieutenant."[18] The *Chronicle* never revealed its source, but the tone sounds much like Scharrenberg. Though Lundeberg may have discussed tactics with Bridges, he was not and never had been Bridges's lieutenant.

The ILA national convention met in mid-July 1935 in New York City, Joseph Ryan's base. The CP's Trade Union Commission reported that, after a major campaign to elect delegates, "out of 350 delegates we have 9 that are definitely lined up with the left wing groups, six from the East Coast and 3 from the West." Bridges was one of five ILA-PCD delegates. Though the ILA-PCD convention instructed its delegates to seek to oust Ryan from the presidency, Ryan announced, "I won't be ousted," and challenged Bridges to run against him. The next day, Bridges was the only "no" vote on a motion "indorsing" Ryan's role in the 1934 strike. In the convention, Ryan, from the podium, read telegrams and letters attacking Bridges as a Communist. Bridges replied, "If it is communistic . . . to condemn [police] officers who shot down men, to advocate that officers of the organization be elected by referendum, to demand that all agreements be submitted to the union membership for ratification—then, the whole West Coast is communistic." In the vote for president, Bridges received only four votes, all from ILA-PCD delegates.[19]

During the convention, on July 12, Bridges spoke at a mass meeting organized by a CP group and criticized AFL leaders for a "lack of aggressiveness." The next day, still in New York, Bridges met with the PolBuro. He criticized the decision to hold the mass meeting because such an event "makes our people a part of everything but the convention itself." "We cannot isolate ourselves from the rank and file of the convention," he continued. "It is a question in my mind whether it is not best to go into the activities the delegates do, sound them out and find out who they are." A senior PolBuro member, Alexander Bittelman, stated his pride in "Comrade Harry," then dismissed Bridges's criticism of party tactics.[20]

On July 13, the same day Bridges met with the PolBuro, the ILA convention was read a long document, supposedly issued by the CP, outlining an organizational structure for the Pacific Coast that included both Bridges and Lundeberg. It was a clumsy forgery: Morris Rappaport, district organizer for Washington and Oregon, described it as "stupid" and specified "with the exception of leading Comrades' names, the rest of them are either openly expelled members of the Party or non-Party members." Bridges dismissed it as a "tissue of lies" and "a joke." The *Chronicle* printed it in full the next day.[21]

By mid-1935, as union organizing surged across the country, pressures on MFP affiliates grew to support other unions' strikes. A strike by longshoremen in British Columbia led the ILA to refuse to unload vessels loaded there by strikebreakers. Late in 1935 and early in 1936, a strike by the ILA in the Gulf of Mexico produced similar requests. Strikes by other unions brought requests that cargoes produced by strikebreakers be declared "hot." The SUP picketed two ships, demanding that Filipinos be discharged from the crews. By mid-1935, hot-cargo boycotts together with job actions were producing more and more resistance from shipping companies and their business allies.[22]

Amid this tension, many longshore and maritime workers refused to work the morning of July 5, 1935, the first anniversary of Bloody Thursday. In San Francisco, Local 38-79's dispatchers were open as usual, but not one longshoreman came to be dispatched during the morning. An honor guard was posted among banks of floral tributes at Steuart and Mission Streets, where an impromptu memorial had been established the year before, and members of MFP unions marched up Market Street as a reminder of their martyrs and of police brutality on Bloody Thursday.[23]

A few weeks later, on July 21, Bridges was robbed when he pulled his car into his garage. The *Chronicle* reported one man held a gun on Bridges and told him to "come through with whatever dough" he had, and another man waited just outside. The newspaper article did not mention Jackie, then nine years old, but she remembered events differently: "We pulled into the garage, and this guy had a gun and said for me to get upstairs. I said, 'No, I'm not leaving my dad. I'm staying with my dad.' So the guy says, 'OK, Harry, you got it on your side.'

And he took off." Jackie's version calls into question whether the event was a robbery or an assassination attempt called off because a child was present. Six months later, in January 1936, a man reported to the police that he had overheard a discussion about murdering Bridges, but police discounted his claim.[24]

By late July 1935, as more ships with hot cargo were tied up in Pacific Coast ports, the WEU suggested that renewal of the arbitration award would depend on a guarantee by the ILA-PCD to halt such work stoppages. Michael Casey informed Daniel Tobin, "The Ship-owners have employed one of the most noted strike-breakers on this Coast and are quietly making all arrangements to fight it out with the Longshoremen." Tobin had earlier specified that the maritime unions should not count on Teamster support. In August Patrick Donoghue of the NLRB West Coast office informed Secretary of Labor Perkins, "The Employers Association has stated that the Longshoremen's Local at San Francisco is controlled by persons whom they choose to call 'radicals' and 'Communists,' and that the agreement . . . will not be renewed unless those persons are removed and a more 'responsible' group put in control." In response, Paddy Morris, district secretary, strongly affirmed that all ILA locals "have the right to elect and retain the officers that its membership elects."[25]

In the end, however, hot-cargo boycotts, and not Bridges, became the sticking point for renewal of the agreement. McGrady asked the ILA-PCD and SUP to send delegations to confer in Washington. The ILA-PCD board designated Morris, Bridges, and Cliff Thurston of Portland, and the SUP's three representatives included Lundeberg. The shipowners insisted on meeting the SUP and ILA separately. When the three ILA-PCD delegates met with McGrady and ten company representatives, both sides accused the other of violating the agreement. They finally agreed that the ILA-PCD delegates should wire the ILA-PCD locals and recommended releasing the five boycotted ships from British Columbia and "all others" if the SUP agreed to do so. "Employers insist," the telegram read, "that unless we rescind our action on Vancouver [British Columbia] cargo they will refuse to consider renewal of the award. All points now in dispute between longshoremen and employers will be taken up here in Washington and if not settled during our short stay, will be further considered on coast and without delay."[26]

Shortly after, "P. T.," a CP functionary, submitted a long report to the PolBuro on the Washington conference based partly on talking with Bridges. Critical of Bridges, P. T.'s report nonetheless makes clear Bridges's understanding that "hot cargo" situations endangered maritime unions' ability to maintain working relationships with their employers, endangered maritime solidarity, and endangered his own leadership.[27]

While Bridges was in Washington, the deadline passed for him to complete the naturalization process that he had begun in 1928. He waited until May 2,

1936, to file his third declaration of intent to become a citizen.[28] At that point, Bridges seems to have been still rather indifferent about becoming a citizen.

Upon the delegates' return from Washington, the ILA-PCD board met. Morris reported, "The employers insisted that if the award is to be renewed, there must be absolutely no violation of same on our part. . . . [A]ny stoppage of work under any circumstances would constitute a violation of the award. . . . [T]he longshoremen had no right to refuse to handle loads regardless of the size or weight of same, that if the men considered them unsafe, the matter should be taken up through the [local labor] relations committee." Load sizes had come up repeatedly in the discussions, and the employers insisted, "Under the award they had a right to establish the size of loads [and] that the men should perform work as directed." After Morris concluded, Bridges added only, "There had been harmony in the committee while in Washington." All locals favored renewing the award.[29]

During the period August 19–23, 1935, ILA-PCD members voted on ending the boycott of ships from British Columbia and on renewing the agreement. The first failed, due to a lopsided negative vote in Local 38-79. Portland also voted no, but by a much narrower margin. By large margins, the other large ports voted to end the boycott. The second question, on renewing the agreement, carried, 8,468–1,329. All the large ports were in favor, and by larger margins than San Francisco.[30]

In September 1935, the award was renewed for another year. The waterfront employers' organizations had earlier predicated renewal on correction of "intolerable conditions" in San Francisco, but in the end they informed Morris they would neither terminate the awards nor agree to any changes.[31]

The annual election of officers in Local 38-79 in mid-September 1935 brought a strong endorsement of Bridges from those who knew him best: reelection as president by 2,318–286. However, no "Bridges machine" appeared in the election results. Henry Schrimpf, a CP member and apparently still part of the Bridges group, lost for vice president by 1827–305. The incumbent recording secretary, Ivan Cox, received 1005 votes to 902 for Henry Schmidt, Bridges's closest associate, and 309 for another candidate; Cox won the runoff. John Schomaker lost big for financial secretary-treasurer, 1221–313. Bridges's supporters did win the delegate positions to the Labor Council and state federation convention.[32]

Soon after, the California State Federation of Labor annual convention met in San Diego. CP District 13 had an acting district organizer, Jack Johnstone. He reported, "There were some 25 party members" among the delegates and another "70 to 90 delegates that supported major points in the rank and file program." A caucus of some forty on the evening of the first day decided to concentrate on resolutions opposing red-baiting and favoring a labor party and on defeating Scharrenberg. They lost on all three. The convention passed, by nearly four to one, a resolution condemning communism and urging expulsion of Communists from unions. By similar margins, delegates reelected Scharrenberg, defeated Bridges for vice president, and defeated the resolution for a labor party.[33]

Hot-cargo issues continued to strain relations between ILA-PCD locals and waterfront employers, and between MFP affiliates. By late September 1935, seventeen ships, most from British Columbia, were tied up in San Francisco due to hot-cargo boycotts, and fourteen hundred longshoremen had been blacklisted for refusing to work those ships. On September 28, Marcus Sloss, port and district arbitrator, ruled that longshoremen did not have the right to refuse to handle hot cargo. Bridges and Lewis pointed to Referendum 1 to explain that they had no power to lift the boycott, that only ILA-PCD members could do so. Bridges and Lewis pointed to each other as the proper person to initiate another referendum. Soon, more than thirty ships stood idle, due to the employers' blacklist and the union's enforcement of a 120-hour-month. When the Canadian longshore union finally released all Canadian cargo, Bridges immediately announced that gangs would work those ships.[34]

Hot-cargo issues and job actions produced a special MFP convention on November 12, 1935. The meeting centered on a proposal by Bridges, Resolution 47, to define job action narrowly and place limits on job actions affecting other unions. His goal was to rein in the seagoing unions, especially the SUP, from undisciplined job actions that were endangering other unions' agreements. Lundeberg led efforts to rewrite Resolution 47, which passed in a substantially weakened form.[35] The lines drawn between the ILA and SUP, between Bridges and Lundeberg, over job actions grew more pronounced as job actions and hot-cargo boycotts continued to roil Pacific Coast waterfronts.

In December the SUP elected Lundeberg as secretary-treasurer (the union's executive officer), and he resigned as MFP president. The ISU's sclerotic and remote national leaders responded in late January 1936, at the first ISU convention since 1930. The convention, securely controlled by the national leaders, ordered all ISU affiliates to dissolve their affiliation with the MFP. The MFOW and MC&S formally withdrew but afterward sent fraternal (nonvoting) delegates. The convention also lifted the charter of the SUP. Lundeberg's response was, "We'll fight to the last ditch." Thousands of SUP members signed pledges to stay with the existing organization. Lundeberg hired Aaron Sapiro, a nationally prominent attorney, to represent the SUP in a legal battle over bank accounts and real estate.[36] Lundeberg did not change his views on job actions.

Bridges, however, continued to seek some resolution for the continuing problems created by job actions. On February 16, 1936, a *New York Times* headline read, "Coast Is Hopeful of Peace on Docks: Harry Bridges's Shift from Militant to Moderate Leader Is Factor." Apparently drawing on an interview with Bridges, the reporter, George West, claimed that Bridges "began to think more than six months ago [amid the hot-cargo and job-action crises of mid-1935] that the maritime unions were losing the sympathy of the public, and forging solidarity among shipowners for a finish fight, by what their opponents called violations of arbitration awards to force minor concessions not called for in the agreement." Calling Bridges "among the shrewdest leaders developed by labor on this coast," West pointed to Bridges's success in ending the hot-cargo issues of the previous fall and claimed that Bridges hoped to resolve the issue of sling-load weights not through job actions but through changes in the agreement.[37] West's prediction of prospective peace to the docks was soon proved wrong, as hot-cargo issues again disrupted relations between the ILA and SUP and between Local 38-79 and the Waterfront Employers Association, the recently organized umbrella group for the employers in all Pacific Coast ports.

In April 1936, disarray within the East Coast ISU reached San Francisco over the liner *Santa Rosa*, which sailed from New York with an ISU crew drawn from the Great Lakes to replace members of a striking rank-and-file group led by Joe Curran. The SUP, supporting Curran's group, declared the *Santa Rosa* unfair. Local 38-79 and MFP District 2 (Northern California) did the same.[38] Shipping companies prepared for confrontation over the *Santa Rosa*. The company president flew to San Francisco to take charge. When the *Santa Rosa* arrived in San Francisco on April 14, SUP pickets let gangs from Local 38-79 unload mail and passengers' baggage but not cargo. When Curran informed Bridges that his group's strike was failing, Bridges asked the MFP's District 2 council to declare the ship fair. SUP pickets were withdrawn. By then, however, the WEA had suspended relations with Local 38-79, specifying, "This is an action taken solely against radical and subversive leadership of San Francisco longshoremen." The WEA also claimed to be willing to resume relations with the ILA when "causes of the violations have been removed." The implication was that ILA-PCD officials should take control of Local 38-79's hiring hall. The press was rife with rumors that the local's charter would be lifted. Local 38-79 faced its greatest crisis since the strike in 1934.[39]

The next day, six gangs from Local 38-79 showed up to work the *Santa Rosa*, but WEA officials told them they could work only as individuals and not as having been dispatched from the hiring hall. The men refused. In response to the WEA having made Bridges the issue for resumption of relations, four thousand members of Local 38-79 voted unanimously that they stood by their elected officers and would refuse any employment not through the hiring hall. E. H. FitzGerald and F. P Marsh, Labor Department conciliators, wired McGrady, "Results of meeting indicate Bridges and his policy in absolute control Local membership."[40]

Outraged that employers dared to designate employees' representatives, Mike Casey steered a strong resolution to that effect through the IBT Joint Council. At its regular meeting on April 17, the San Francisco Labor Council approved a resolution from Bridges in support of Local 38-79's position. Nonetheless, on April 18, FitzGerald wrote that employers "will not have anything to do with Bridges under any circumstances." WEA representatives then met with ILA-PCD officers and Local 38-79's Labor Relations Committee, producing a "peace pact," in which both sides promised to abide by the 1934 award and agreed that "all questions, disputes and grievances of a local nature" were to be submitted to the local LRC and to Sloss, as arbitrator, in the event of deadlock. Not part of the conference, Bridges repudiated the agreement. The LRC members from Local 38-79 then also repudiated it as being in conflict with their instructions from the local.[41]

FitzGerald, Marsh, Labor Council leaders, and the ILA-PCD officers pressured Bridges and the LRC members to reconsider. They agreed to give the final word to Local 38-79 members, who then ratified the "peace pact" in a near-unanimous vote. Almost simultaneously, a membership meeting of the Teamsters voted their support for the longshoremen. The affair marked a significant step toward the unique system of arbitration that eventually developed on Pacific Coast docks. Bridges's agreement marked a similarly significant step toward his developing embrace of arbitration as a viable, contractual alternative to job actions and embargoes. Lundeberg, however, fumed because the peace pact meant "no more job actions" for the SUP, and he consistently connected Bridges to "the comrades," that is, the CP. Further, Lundeberg growled, Bridges is a "low down son of a bitch" who "hates my guts."[42]

The peace pact was soon tested. In October 1935, the CP's Trade Union Commission had told its marine fractions and coastal districts to work together to "develop a concrete plan of action" for "stopping the shipment of all goods and materials to Italy." Months later, on May 1, 1936, San Francisco longshoremen cited the Neutrality Act of 1935 in refusing to load scrap iron on a ship bound for Italy because Italy's invasion of Ethiopia meant that the cargo was "contraband of war." Bridges had wired Secretary of State Cordell Hull to ask about such cargoes; Hull replied that scrap metal was not enumerated in the Neutrality Act. Bridges then wired Secretary Perkins asking the same question. Perkins referred Bridges to Hull's earlier telegram. When Sloss ruled that longshoremen were required to load the scrap iron, they did so.[43]

On May 4, 1936, the ILA-PCD annual convention opened in San Pedro. It was tumultuous. Lewis initially announced that he would seek reelection as district president. At the end of the convention, however, Lewis and Morris surprised the delegates by refusing to be nominated and resigned effective upon election of their successors. Two slates were nominated, one headed by Bridges for president and Matt Meehan of Portland for secretary, and the other by Cliff Thurston of Portland for president and Elmer Brudge of San Pedro for secretary. For the first time, all ILA members were to elect the officers.[44]

Morris later wrote to Joseph Ryan to explain their decisions not to run: "For the past year neither Brother Lewis, Petersen or myself have had any active support from our friends. . . . [W]e decided that something should be done to jar them up, so we decided not to run for re-election." "Bridges," Morris claimed, "is scared to death of Judge Sloss and the employers and they have his number. He will, if elected District President, . . . be forced to do a lot of backing up," which, Morris anticipated, will "be the end of him as a leader." He urged Ryan, "You should not do anything that will give them the chance to blame the International." When the ballots were counted, Bridges won by 7150 to 2550, and Meehan won by nearly as much, 6400 to 3001.[45] The lopsided election results suggest Morris and Lewis may have declined to run because they had figured out that they were unlikely to win. Regardless, Ryan initially followed Morris's advice about giving Bridges and the new officers a free hand.

Before the balloting, the second annual MFP convention took place. Bridges's supporters commanded the ILA caucus. One resolution called on the entire labor movement to support an embargo on all war materials to "aggressor nations." When Bridges tried again to limit job actions, Lundeberg moved a weaker substitute. After disposing of the substitute and several amendments, the body approved Bridges's motion, with Lundeberg voting no. It was one of Bridges's few victories and one of Lundeberg's few defeats. In the election of officers, Lundeberg's choices swept all positions. In voting for officers, Henry Schrimpf broke with the other Local 38-79 delegates, voted with Lundeberg, and was rewarded when Lundeberg nominated him for trustee.[46]

With election as ILA-PCD president, Bridges resigned as president of Local 38-79 and was succeeded by the vice president, William Marlowe, who did not seek a full term. In the election, Henry Schrimpf lost to Henry Schmidt for president by a vote of 1,679 to 977. Ivan Cox—never close to Bridges or Schmidt—was reelected as financial secretary. Schomaker again lost.[47] Again, the election results do not suggest a "Bridges machine."

The MFP convention had defeated a resolution endorsing a Farmer-Labor Party, the early position of the CP regarding the approaching presidential election. However, the CP then changed course and nominated Earl Browder to run against Roosevelt. Bridges ignored the CP line and urged Local 38-79 "to support such groups as the Labor's Non-Partisan League, which has endorsed President Roosevelt for reelection." Local 38-79 members voted to endorse Roosevelt and donated $750 (equivalent to $15,200 in mid-2022) to his campaign.[48]

In retrospect, it is difficult to imagine how uncertain the outcome of the presidential election was throughout September and October. The most widely known poll was that of the *Literary Digest*, which had accurately predicted the previous five presidential elections. *Literary Digest* polls buoyed many Republicans with the projection Roosevelt would lose, giving shipping executives reason to anticipate an end to federal support for unions and collective bargaining.[49]

In August shipping interests announced that they wished to negotiate changes in the 1934 agreements with most MFP affiliates. Several observers concluded that the companies really intended to humiliate the administration with a strike at the height of the election campaign. On September 8, John R. Steelman, special assistant to Labor Secretary Perkins, wrote that Matson, Dollar, and American-Hawaiian executives "would go to any extent and any cost to embarrass the administration." On September 9, Bill McCarthy, San Francisco postmaster, wrote to Jim Farley, FDR's political adviser, that the employers intended "to discredit the Roosevelt Administration and to make it responsible for all the suffering, loss and; [sic] perhaps, bloodshed, that may come." On September 20, Edward McGrady sent FDR a long analysis, concluding that shipowners were determined "to destroy the maritime unions" and "would also like to defeat the present Administration."[50]

At the same time, tensions were surging between AFL leaders and John L. Lewis's CIO. William Green, AFL executive officer, denounced it as a dual union. Undeterred, Lewis and his colleagues launched organizing drives among steel-, auto-, and rubber workers. For months, Green and Lewis engaged in a war of words. In August, as the WEA and ILA-PCD were launching their own war of words, the AFL ordered the CIO unions to either leave the CIO or be suspended from the AFL. Lewis ignored the threat. He committed $600,000 (equivalent to more than $12 million in 2022) of UMW funds to Roosevelt's reelection, an unprecedented expenditure, and Lewis personally campaigned for Roosevelt.[51]

As tensions between the MFP unions and their employers ratcheted up during the three months preceding Election Day, so did tensions between the ILA-PCD and the SUP and between Harry Bridges and Harry Lundeberg. A letter to Perkins, probably from Steelman, in September, surveyed causes for the rift, beyond disputes over job actions and hot cargo. He noted, first, that the ILA "got pretty much what it wanted from the 1934 settlement," but "the Seamen got very little." This asymmetry meant that "Bridges has become the *status quo* leader, eager to consolidate his gains, to play ball—and politics—with the official labor leaders." Lundeberg's union, however, had been expelled from the ISU and therefore the AFL. Steelman also pointed to the role of the CP: "The revolt against Bridges among the maritime unions . . . is a revolt against what the men consider CP domination and its use of the [Maritime] Federation for political ends. This is the fault of the CP, and in a sense of Bridges, because he could have made the CP keep out of the controversy." As an example, Steelman pointed to the "ferocious campaign" by the *Western Worker* against Lundeberg, the SUP, and the *Voice of the Federation*, the MFP's newspaper, then edited by Lundeberg's appointees.

Steelman also pointed to personality differences. "Bridges is abler, shrewder, and probably more intelligent [but] he is playing a rather Machiavellian game within the labor movement." Lundeberg "is slower, more stubborn, less flexible ... definitely less political-minded ... the most completely 'proletarian' union official I have ever met [which] makes him somewhat more difficult to negotiate with. ... He has no diplomacy, but his intelligence should not be under-rated." Steelman added that Lundeberg "is being shrewdly advised, possibly by Sapiro."[52]

Steelman concluded with a comment about Lundeberg's secretary, Norma Perry. After serving as a secretary for Local 38-79's publicity committee during the 1934 strike, she had become Bridges's secretary. In 1935 Perry became secretary to Lundeberg, for which she was expelled from the CP. Bridges later claimed that he fired her because she was a company spy. Vilified by the CP, Perry was defended by the SUP as a loyal unionist who had "seen the light" and abandoned Bridges and the CP. Waterfront gossip inevitably added a sexual dimension to Perry's change of employment.[53]

George West, in the *New York Times*, provided an analysis similar to Steelman's. Describing Bridges as "wary, self-assured, suspicious, pugnacious, a lightning thinker," West claimed he makes "the shrewdest of corporation lawyers ... seem soft and a little helpless in contrast." Emphasizing Bridges's commitment to internal union democracy, West stated, "The longshoremen who know him best follow him with loyalty and affection." "Shipowners hate and fear Bridges," West specified, but acknowledged, "A few companies, including two of the largest, have operated efficiently under his regime and have had very little trouble with him or his longshoremen." West claimed that, ironically, the waterfront was moving toward a strike "at a time when Bridges ... had been working for months to discipline the longshoremen to prevent irresponsible stoppages, to improve work standards and thereby to remove those legitimate causes of resentment that would jeopardize public and trades-union sympathy and goad employers to a finish fight." West called Lundeberg "the opposite of Bridges," who criticized Bridges for any concessions.[54]

Steelman and West agreed that the conflict between Bridges and Lundeberg, between the ILA and SUP, was at base a conflict between two approaches to union leadership. Lundeberg embraced the syndicalist vision of job actions as the prerogative of any group of workers at any time and encouraged the SUP to act accordingly. Bridges had quickly realized that unrestricted job actions not only threatened relations with employers but also drove wedges between unions. He had initially endorsed job actions to define longshore working conditions, but he soon backed off from the syndicalist approach and came to see negotiations as the way to define working conditions and arbitration as the way to enforce them.

When the WEA requested changes to the agreement, either through bargaining or arbitration, Bridges set up a membership referendum to determine whether to seek renewal of the existing award or to seek modifications, especially a wage increase. Bridges encouraged a vote for changes and cooperation with other maritime unions seeking improvements; the referendum was strongly in favor of changes in the agreement.[55]

The WEA insisted on a commitment to arbitration prior to any bargaining, but Bridges instead demanded a meeting to outline their differences. Bridges and Henry Melnikow represented the ILA-PCD, with Melnikow the spokesman. When the parties first met, T. G. Plant, the WEA spokesman, arranged for reporters to be present and dared the union to deny them access. Melnikow acquiesced but acidly, and accurately, noted, "We shall probably find ourselves talking for the press rather than to each other." Talking to the press instead of the ILA remained the approach of the WEA until nearly the end of the strike.[56]

Plant insisted that the prerequisite for negotiations was agreement that anything not resolved be submitted to arbitration by a three-person panel, one each chosen by the union, the employers, and the president of the United States, thus tying arbitration to the ongoing presidential campaign. The ILA-PCD refused, since any such agreement could mean arbitrating matters already settled through the previous arbitration. Steelman agreed, telling Perkins, "The operators have been unfair and obtuse as to their arbitration proposals." The ILA-PCD asked for a wage increase, a revised definition of overtime, uniform working conditions (especially load weights and gang sizes) in all ports, preference of employment, and the right of longshoremen to refuse to cross other unions' picket lines. The WEA demanded penalties for violations of the award, a neutral dispatcher, continuation of arbitration, revision of the six-hour day, a direct link between productivity and wages, and no interference with work "as ordered by the employer," that is, no maximum load weights and minimum gang sizes. Control of the hiring hall was at the center of several of these issues. Arthur Caylor, editor of the *San Francisco News*, informed McGrady, "The unions can't concede . . . without laying themselves open to gradual disintegration." The two sides last met on August 28.[57]

On Labor Day, September 7, some ten thousand ILA marchers strode down Market Street, the men in black jeans, hickory shirts, and white caps and the women's auxiliary similarly dressed but wearing black denim skirts. As Henry Schmidt reported, "The shipowners had a good opportunity to watch us march by the Matson building, and we presume they did. Ten thousand men in uniform clothing and uniform thought—SOLIDARITY." That solidarity was mirrored in a membership referendum on the employers' proposal for prior commitment to arbitration: 95 percent voted no. ILA president Joseph Ryan seemed to be on board, responding to a telegram from Plant with a lecture on the intent of the Wagner Act to promote bargaining rather than arbitration. Ryan agreed to Bridges's request to meet in New York with representatives from all ILA districts to hear proposals for a uniform contract expiration date and a national maritime federation, but Ryan opposed the ILA-PCD's proposals on hiring, wages, hours, and load weights.[58]

By September 20, with ILA-WEA bargaining stalled and little or no negotiating taking place with the other MFP unions, McGrady wrote to President Roosevelt suggesting ways to prevent a strike, but acknowledging "a determination on the part of each side to smash the other." That same day, as if confirming McGrady's claim, Plant announced conditions once the agreement expired on September 30: a small increase in wages, an eight-hour day and forty-four-hour week, all hiring at the piers, and all work (load weights and gang sizes) as directed by the employers. Plant added that negotiations could resume anytime the ILA-PCD agreed to arbitrate anything unresolved in negotiations. The ILA-PCD offered to arbitrate wages and hours but not the hiring hall, blacklisting of union members, or safety rules.[59]

Other MFP affiliates encountered similar refusals to negotiate. McGrady spoke to the MFP's Joint Negotiating Committee on September 29 to support an extension of the existing agreements requested by the recently created Federal Maritime Commission. Bridges suggested an extension of thirty days, but Lundeberg refused more than fifteen. The committee compromised, agreeing to fifteen but holding out the possibility for fifteen more. On September 30, McGrady and Labor Department conciliators E. H. FitzGerald and F. P. Marsh brokered what the press called a "truce." The employers accepted the unions' proposal of a fifteen-day extension.[60]

The Maritime Commission then entered the situation. Congress had created the commission the previous summer, but Roosevelt delayed making appointments until September, when he named a temporary three-person commission of two retired navy admirals and a Treasury Department official, none experienced with collective bargaining or even with unions. Rear Admiral Harry Hamlet of the Coast Guard was designated to advise the commission. The legislation directed the commission to investigate working conditions in ocean shipping and to establish wage, manning, and other standards for federally owned or chartered shipping. The commission was also authorized to subsidize U.S.-flag shipping. The legislation said nothing about authority over labor on shore or on privately owned ships, something Lundeberg repeatedly raised in the Joint Negotiating Committee.[61]

Despite the fifteen-day extension, the new commission did nothing for two weeks, during which business leaders pressured commissioners to force the unions to accept binding arbitration. Finally, on October 14, the commission chair announced that Hamlet would go to San Francisco to investigate. McGrady urged the unions to extend the truce; they did so, until October 26. Hamlet arrived October 18. Assuming he was there to mediate, he met first with Lundeberg and then other union representatives, employer representatives, and Sloss. Bridges described the Maritime Commission as having "little understanding of the situation" and having adopted "the employers' sentiments."[62]

On October 19, Hamlet persuaded the major shipping companies to extend the existing agreements for a year. Bridges and Melnikow met with Hamlet and specified any extension must include "present practice" as part of the agreement. Bridges also made clear he could not make a commitment by himself. Lundeberg reacted similarly and also specified "present practice." The employers acquiesced to "present practice" pending future investigation by the Maritime Commission. Hamlet thought he resolved everything but seems to have misunderstood either what the union leaders told him or the nature of union democracy, for the union leaders were clear they could not make a commitment without consent of their fellow officers. As Melnikow later recalled, Hamlet "didn't understand what it was all about."[63]

On October 20, the Joint Negotiating Committee adopted conditions for an extension. The ILA asked only continuation of the six-hour day and the hiring halls. The seagoing unions specified employment through hiring halls, overtime paid in cash rather than time off, and an eight-hour day. Bridges specified that any extension required "a referendum vote of the members of all the unions." The employers turned down the seagoing unions' demands but accepted the ILA's conditions. Bridges decried this as an effort to split the MFP.[64]

On October 23, twenty-seven steamship companies broke with the WEA to offer the ILA-PCD an extension of the agreement, increased wages, and preference of employment. Those companies, nearly all headquartered in New York and representing a small fraction of dock work in San Francisco, specified that they made their offer because ILA president Ryan threatened a strike by the East Coast ILA in support of the ILA-PCD unless the companies made that offer. By making the offer, whether accepted or not, those companies—and Ryan—were precluding any sympathy strike by East Coast longshore workers. Bridges responded, "We cannot and will not break off from the other unions."[65]

On October 24, as the clock ticked down to the October 26 deadline, the Joint Negotiating Committee presented Hamlet with a proposal to extend the agreements for a year and avoid a strike; it restated earlier positions but added that the Maritime Commission could determine increases in pay retroactive to October 1. Failure to agree by the twenty-eighth would bring a strike on the twenty-ninth. Two days later, on October 26, Hamlet withdrew from mediation and announced a thorough investigation into wages and conditions of seagoing workers, an investigation likely to take six months to a year.[66]

McGrady, Marsh, and FitzGerald then resumed their efforts at mediation, seeking to bring the sides together before the strike deadline. On October 28, the WEA rejected an offer from the ILA-PCD contingent upon not being "called upon to work with strikebreakers." Plant, the companies' spokesman, correctly observed that the proposal was "valueless unless we satisfied the demands of all other maritime unions." Strike preparations advanced on both sides. In the early hours of October 29, Bridges, seeking to prevent a strike, favored a twenty-four-hour postponement. Lundeberg opposed, and employers proved intransigent. McGrady explained to Roosevelt's assistant, "Not one of those shipowners we depended upon came through. . . . Everything humanly possible was done but when our alleged friends fail us we have not much chance to succeed." Michael Casey posed a more political explanation: the shipowners hoped by the strike "to undermine the possibility of re-election of the present national administration," and the best efforts of McGrady and Hamlet—and, he might have added, Bridges—to secure postponements past election day had failed. Some thirty-seven thousand maritime workers walked off the job on October 30.[67]

Four days later, Roosevelt took 61 percent of the popular vote and carried all but two states. California gave Roosevelt 67 percent, and he took 74 percent in San Francisco. Democrats gained a 334–88 majority in the House and a similarly lopsided majority in the Senate. The election shredded any hope of maritime employers for a more favorable administration, but they remained adamant in their determination to roll back the union tide.

Unlike 1934, the companies made no effort to work the ships with strikebreakers. Local 38-79's picketing records suggest that one of that committee's major activities was dealing with drunks. Wallace Wharton, executive secretary to the governor of Oregon, reported that, by completely closing the port, shipowners expected to maximize support from merchants and farmers who relied on waterborne shipping.[68] That, and the new regulatory regime of the Wagner Act, made for a much less violent strike than in 1934. Like the 1934 strike, however, that in 1936–37 went on, and on, and on—for ninety-nine days, longer by two weeks than in 1934.

On October 31, some one thousand seamen in New York City voted unanimously to strike in support of the West Coast strikers. The meeting took place following an official ISU meeting. ISU officers had barred Joe Curran and his closest supporters, but they came inside and took control of the meeting when the ISU officers left. Curran and the Seamen's Defense Committee worked to spread the strike, over objections from ISU national leaders. By November 8, seven thousand men were out on the East Coast. As the East Coast seamen's strike developed, the Seamen's Defense Committee developed its own strike demands. Pacific Coast strikers and those on the Atlantic and Gulf Coasts were in constant communication, offering support for each other's goals. On November 23, the MM&P and MEBA ordered their members to stop work at Atlantic and Gulf ports. ARTA followed on November 30. However, on Ryan's orders, Atlantic and Gulf ILA locals refused to recognize the East Coast seamen's strike.[69]

Before the MFP strike began, Steelman had warned the president, "Strong pressure would come for intervention . . . but [it] must not be done." Roosevelt chose a "hands off" policy and, according to Perkins, told her "to do the best that I could."[70]

From the beginning of the MFP strike, the maritime unions wanted more significant changes than the ILA-PCD, reflecting their less successful experiences after the 1934 strike. Bridges was clear: the ILA "will be striking in support of the other unions."[71]

Before the strike, the MFP unions agreed to employers' demands to negotiate with each union individually, rather than with the Joint Negotiating Committee, which then became the Joint Policy Committee. Where the ILA-PCD was dealing with one agreement and one employer representative, the maritime unions were dealing with several separate agreements—six unions each negotiating separate contracts for steam schooners, oceangoing ships, and the Alaska trade, for a total of eighteen agreements. Throughout November, negotiations lagged despite McGrady's efforts to mediate. Melnikow recalled that the Dollar Lines, Matson, American-Hawaiian, and Swayne Hoyt were adamantly opposed to settling because they wanted to maintain control of hiring and were "afraid of rotation on the jobs for seamen."[72]

The companies seem to have been playing a waiting game, to see if their resources were greater than those of the unions. The MFP unions had resources of their own and received significant support from other AFL unions and some donations from small waterfront businesses, organizations (most on the Left), and individuals (most on the Left). Several waterfront cafés and restaurants set special prices for strikers. The strike fund, however, worked out to only a few dollars per striker in the Bay Area. Some strikers found work elsewhere, and the ILA-PCD shared the little work available on the few docks not being struck.[73]

When Curran's organization informed Bridges that East Coast ILA locals were working West Coast ships, Bridges and the ILA-PCD sought to persuade Ryan to stop such work. When that failed, Bridges, on behalf of the ILA-PCD Executive Board, wrote an open letter to Ryan, called his stance "regrettable and nauseating," accused Ryan of employing "gangsters and thugs" to attack striking East Coast seamen, and urged him to desist from "strike breaking."[74] Though Ryan had generally followed Morris's advice up to the time of the strike, his orders to work West Coast ships, his efforts in support of the ISU leadership, and Bridges's scathing denunciation of him brought that truce to an end.

In early December, McGrady proposed that the seagoing unions' settlements include three-person port committees to settle disputes over interpretation of agreements, with one member chosen by the union, one by the employers, and a neutral third member chosen by the Labor Department, an arrangement modeled on what existed for longshoring. The Joint Policy Committee approved the concept, and similar committees, variously composed, became part of the settlements. However, there was no immediate move toward settlement for any union.[75]

The 1936–37 strike was a war of words. Both sides issued press releases and sought to persuade the public. Employers frequently took full-page newspaper ads to press their case and attack the unions and, especially, Bridges. Both sides took to the radio to inform their members and to sway the public. A mass meeting in Seattle included not only union leaders but also the mayor, John F. Dore. The MFP sponsored mass meetings open to union members and the general public, as a way of building public support. One such, in Oakland Civic Auditorium, was cosponsored by the East Bay Council of the National Negro Congress and featured Bridges as the chief speaker. The same two organizations distributed a pamphlet titled *Negroes and the Maritime Strike*.[76]

The war of words took on a new, and surprisingly civil, character on December 8, when Bridges debated Roger Lapham, a leading spokesman for the employers, in San Francisco's Civic Auditorium. The press reported that nearly twenty thousand attended, filling all seats and all standing room, with others outside. The audience included many union supporters but almost as many members of the public. Lapham spoke first and received a respectful hearing. Bridges then spoke, calmly and thoughtfully, blaming the companies for the prolongation of the strike and arguing they intended not only to defeat the striking unions but also to injure the union movement more generally. The next day, the *Chronicle* editorialized that the event "should mark a new era in the settlement of such affairs."[77] Though other such meetings were held later, they did not materially contribute to a settlement. They may have helped to counteract Bridges's reputation as a radical firebrand.

During the strike, the Joint Policy Committee became the forum in which the striking unions reported on their negotiations and developed advice for the Joint Strike Committees in each port. In the absence of negotiations for most unions throughout November and December, however, the committee members fell to fighting one another over strike operations, especially whether to unload or protect perishables. Melnikow later reminisced, "The struggles within the Maritime Federation were enough to wear out anybody."[78]

A major conflict erupted over articles in the *Voice of the Federation*, the official newspaper of the MFP. The editor was Barney Mayes, a former CP member who had become a Trotskyist and outspoken opponent of the CP. Lundeberg had appointed him as editor on the advice of Norma Perry, who also worked on the *Voice*.[79] Bridges and his allies criticized Mayes for focusing most *Voice* coverage on the SUP and downplaying the ILA-PCD. Eventually, the editorial board suspended Mayes but specified that the charges against him were "groundless and of too small importance to be raised at a time when it is necessary to present a solid front against the Shipowners." The board committed itself to appoint a "neutral" editor.[80]

Amid these intra-MFP struggles, Bridges flew to New York to speak at a mass rally on December 14, followed by trips to Boston, Baltimore, and Philadelphia. He stressed throughout that his goal was to persuade East Coast longshore workers not to work West Coast ships. The press, however, suggested that he was trying to bring East Coast longshoremen out on strike. Bridges met with Ryan, who refused to support any strikers except the longshoremen, denounced Bridges as a disrupter and a Communist, and ousted him as ILA international representative on the West Coast.[81]

Bridges and Curran spoke in Boston on the fifteenth and at Madison Square Garden on the sixteenth, where they were joined by several local labor leaders, Congressman Vito Marcantonio, and Adam Clayton Powell, pastor of the Abyssinian Baptist Church in Harlem. Sixteen thousand East Coast maritime strikers and their supporters packed the Garden. Louis Adamic, in the *Nation*, called the rally "inadequately advertised and poorly handled," but said of Bridges, "I have never heard a better organized, more effective, more intelligent or more sincere speech than Bridges made." He added, Bridges is "an extraordinary man—intelligent, honest, potentially capable of handling almost any situation, physically slight and perhaps not in perfect health, but strong and tough, driven on a straight course by a great passion."[82]

On December 17 and 18, Pacific Coast newspapers announced, "Sailors Near Vote on Peace Terms, Says Lundeberg." On December 21, Lundeberg and the employers agreed on terms for the offshore (seagoing) and Alaska companies, including prohibition of work stoppages "for any cause." A similar agreement was worked out with MFOW. However, John Steelman reported to Perkins that MM&P leaders were critical of the settlements, "thinking the operators might be planning to leave them until last, and then 'squeeze them into an agreement.'" When the SUP and MFOW did not immediately ratify the agreements, Plant angrily accused Bridges and "a few of his close associates" with sabotaging the agreements in an effort to force settlement of the East Coast seamen's strike at the same time as that on the West Coast. The ILA-PCD immediately issued "an emphatic denial," but Plant's complaint was echoed by McGrady and Steelman.[83]

Meeting minutes tell a different story. The ILA-PCD Executive Board met on December 19. Bridges reported on his East Coast meetings and Ryan's refusal to support the East Coast seamen, then stated bluntly, "The indications are such that the East Coast strike is now washed up; and . . . it will be necessary for the West coast to give some support otherwise they are sunk," and "the only thing that the East Coast seamen could get out of this strike was possibly the right to vote" on representation. The minutes say nothing regarding what support Bridges thought the Pacific Coast unions might offer, any specific action he proposed, or any proposal to tie a Pacific Coast settlement to one on the Atlantic and Gulf. In the next board meeting, Bridges indicated that "matters are quiet [sic] complicated for us in considering matters of a settlement, due to the east Coast Seamen, B. C. [British Columbia], and Honolulu longshoremen, and S. F. Machinists," but he again proposed no action.[84]

On December 21, the Joint Policy Committee took up the reports that the SUP was preparing to ratify an agreement. Bridges pointed out that SUP ratification "would create an open split in our ranks" and moved that the committee "request the S.U.P. to hold in abeyance the actual voting on any agreement reached until all organizations are ready to take a referendum," and the motion carried.[85]

After the motion on SUP ratification, Bridges reported on his trip and the East Coast strike. He announced that he had reached a tentative agreement with the East Coast strikers' strategy committee. The proposal was for the MFP to stay on strike until East Coast strikers on intercoastal ships received an agreement for West Coast wages and conditions, or until there was a federally supervised election for a bargaining agent for East Coast seamen. Stating, "If the strike is settled on the West Coast without regard to the situation of the East Coast seamen the rank and file movement on the East Coast will be broken," Bridges moved that the MFP remain on strike until one of the conditions he had specified was obtained. His motion failed and was replaced by a motion deferring any such action until all the unions could caucus. No further action was taken.[86] Thus, Bridges failed to delay MFP settlements in support of the East Coast strikers. Continuation of the MFP strike was not due to Bridges's efforts on behalf of the East Coast strikers.

Bridges spoke at a mass meeting of members of all striking unions on December 23 and depicted the SUP's tentative agreement as a ploy by the companies to get the unlicensed unions back to work so the companies could tell the licensed unions, "Take what we give you." He strongly supported a resolution drafted by the ILA-PCD Executive Board that endorsed the Joint Policy Committee's stand that all unions should submit agreements for ratification at the same time. It was adopted "almost unanimously."[87]

On December 26, Bridges was in Long Beach, driving to a mass meeting of union members to report on prospects for settlements. Suddenly, an eight-year-old boy on his new bicycle appeared out of the darkness, headed toward Bridges's car. Bridges braked and swerved but hit the boy, who was pronounced dead at the hospital. Long Beach police held Bridges for several hours, but all witnesses agreed that the accident was unavoidable. A coroner's jury agreed, finding it "accidental and unavoidable."[88]

The next day, December 27, Bridges—described as grief stricken—and Lapham again met in debate, this time at Olympic Auditorium in Los Angeles. The event was carried on three Los Angeles radio stations and one in San Francisco. Lundeberg was expected but failed to show up.[89]

Lundeberg's failure to appear coincided with his and his union's increasing attacks on Bridges. An article in the SUP's newspaper, *West Coast Sailors*, decried "disruptive, factional and unprincipled attacks" by Bridges and others, accused Bridges and the ILA of seeking to undermine Lundeberg and the SUP, and proclaimed, "They have asked for this fight! And now they're going to get it!" Internal SUP communications called Bridges's supporters "phoneys," "comrades," and "bastards," and complained, "Their class colaboration [*sic*] policy and strike policy is so god damn phoney that it jibes perfectly with the reactionaries."[90]

At the end of December, negotiations were still stalled for all unions except the SUP. McGrady informed Perkins, "We are tied up just as tight as we have been on the question of licensed personnel" and left for Washington. The press reported that the only way of breaking the negotiating logjam seemed to be presidential intervention or legislation. Mayor Rossi also called for presidential intervention.[91]

Marsh and FitzGerald met with the Joint Policy Committee on January 11. Marsh stressed that Roosevelt and Perkins were under "plenty of pressure," claimed "some kind of legislation" was likely to come out of Congress," and emphasized that "if the unions can settle the strike by negotiation . . . it will be a far better settlement than we can get from any board." Soon after, Lundeberg phoned from Washington with similar news. "We are in a legal hot spot," he reported, because at worst "the Government would take entire charge of the situation, would dump overboard all tentative agreements arrived at so far; throw everything back to the beginning; and have every claim submitted to arbitration, including the hiring halls."[92]

The reports from Marsh and Lundeberg may have focused the unions on wrapping up the strike, one way or another. However, several unions continued to report only tentative or partial agreements. ILA-PCD negotiations continued to be deadlocked, and MC&S and MFOW negotiations remained unproductive. By the twenty-first, Marsh and FitzGerald concluded only federal intervention would bring a settlement. That same day, Curran led the East Coast seamen to vote to end their strike. On January 23, Plant claimed to have tentative agreements with all the seagoing unions except MC&S.[93]

By then the ILA was also very close to agreement. At an initial meeting on January 5, the employers had asked only for continuation of the 1934 award, and the ILA asked for continuation with pay increases and preference of employment. Subsequent meetings produced no change. By January 18, the ILA was the last union without a tentative agreement, and the employers began taking out full-page newspaper ads with the purpose, as Bridges viewed it, "to squeeze them and force them back to work under the same conditions as prevailed before the strike." Once the WEA offered some concessions, Bridges pushed hard to wrap things up. On January 29, the Joint Policy Committee approved his motion, "to inform the Mayor that they are ready and willing to mediate or arbitrate points still in dispute." Bridges also moved to bring the strike to an end: "If the employers do not agree by noon tomorrow to negotiate further concessions or agree to arbitrate our remaining point at issue with those unions that are not satisfied with tentative agreements, the Policy Committee meets at noon tomorrow to prepare a ballot for a referendum to ratify the agreements and end the strike." The motion passed unanimously.[94]

The next day, Bridges moved "that the Policy Committee immediately recommend that all Unions take a vote on the ratification of their agreement and upon ratification of agreement by majority membership of the Federation, the strike will be automatically terminated." It carried unanimously. Henry Schmidt then moved, "After termination of the strike no organization shall indiscriminately declare any ship 'hot' until a thorough investigation has been made by the District Council." That motion passed with only one SUP delegate voting nay. On February 4, a motion to end the strike at 8:00 a.m. the next day carried unanimously, and the committee was dissolved. After ninety-nine days, the strike was finally over. Perkins congratulated Bridges on his part in ending the strikes and hoped the settlements would bring "a new day in maritime labor relationships" and "a finer relationship in the future."[95]

Throughout, Bridges had tried to get settlements for all MFP unions before any one of them held a ratification. According to Melnikow, once Lundeberg got what he thought was the best deal he was likely to get, "he told the other organizations, 'You'll just have to take what you can get.' . . . He was always looking out, first of all for Lundeberg, secondly for the sailors, thirdly for the other seamen. But he was always willing to tell the licensed people, who of course depended greatly on him, that they would have to take what they could get. And of course he was always ready to tell that to Bridges."[96]

Though ILA-PCD spokesmen said repeatedly that all they wanted was to continue the 1934 award with past practice, they did somewhat better. The hiring hall was unchanged, with the dispatcher elected by union members. ILA members were now to have preference for employment. The six-hour day was maintained, and wages were unchanged at $0.95 per hour and $1.40 for overtime, with the understanding that gangs would typically work eight-hour days, that is, a day's earnings would be $8.50, 50 cents more than the East Coast ILA.

Port Labor Relations Committees were little changed: six members, three chosen by employers and three by the ILA, with the possibility of an arbitrator designated by the secretary of labor. However, the LRCs gained specific responsibility for dealing with job actions: "In case a dispute arises, work shall be continued pending the settlement of same . . . ; in case they are unable to settle the matter involved within twenty-four (24) hours, then upon request of either party, the matter shall be referred to the Labor Relations Committee." This was the contractual beginning of what evolved into a unique system of instant arbitration for work-site disputes.

The right of the employer "to introduce labor saving devices and to institute such methods of discharging and loading cargo as he considers best suited to the conduct of his business" was now subject to agreed-upon health and safety standards and agreed-upon load weights. Two joint committees were created, one to negotiate a safety code to be incorporated into the agreement and the other to investigate, negotiate, and adopt maximum loads for standard commodities. The two sides agreed on maximum load weights on April 26, 1937. Henceforth, the employers' ability to require "work as ordered" was limited by the safety code and the mutually agreed-upon load weights. With these provisions, together with the expanded role of the LRCs and arbitrators in providing immediate arbitration of job actions, the ILA had achieved what later scholars have termed "contractually sanctioned job action."[97]

The MFP strike overlapped with other significant events for Bridges and the ILA-PCD. One was a strike by San Francisco warehouse workers, organized as ILA 38-44. They had secured an agreement in 1934, but negotiations deadlocked over the union's request for a hiring hall, forty-hour week, and wage increases. As Thanksgiving approached and food supplies were tied up by the strike, pressures mounted to reach a settlement. Mayor Rossi announced on November 15 that settlement of the grocery warehouse strike was a victory for mediation and thanked McGrady and FitzGerald. Negotiations for the other warehouses dragged on through late November and into December. Final agreements were a victory for the union, and the strike ended on January 5.[98]

As the MFP strikes were entering their final days, on January 30, the San Francisco Labor Council held its annual election of officers, and the ILA scored two more victories. After Vandeleur announced he would not run for another term as president, speculation immediately focused on John Shelley, a young law-school graduate who had chosen to work as a bakery delivery driver and IBT member. A protégé of Kidwell, Shelley was nominated with wide support. The election was held on January 30, following a vote to reinstate the SUP with two delegates, despite the SUP remaining outside the AFL. Shelley was elected; Henry Schmidt made it into a runoff for vice president but lost. John O'Connell, longtime secretary, was easily reelected over Louis Goldblatt from the warehouse local. Bridges was narrowly elected to the executive committee. Michael Casey wrote to Daniel Tobin that the longtime leaders of the council had "lost complete control of the situation."[99]

Though the San Francisco Bay Area warehouse strikes ended successfully, a potential obstacle appeared in a letter from William Green, president of the AFL, to Daniel Tobin, IBT president, in response to ILA warehouse organizing.

Green specified the ILA had no "jurisdiction over warehousemen . . . inland, away from the waterfront, anywhere or any place," and those "jurisdictional rights" belonged to the IBT "and other organizations." Green cited Ryan as not approving of the "march inland" and as not claiming jurisdiction over inland warehouse workers. Green also encouraged Tobin to resist "this encroachment on the jurisdiction of bona fide organizations associated with the American Federation of Labor by leaders of the Maritime Federation of the Pacific Coast."[100] The ILA-PCD (and ILWU later) and the IBT were to contest those jurisdictions for more than twenty years.

Throughout 1936 the ILA-PCD had sought charters for longshore workers in Hawai'i, but Ryan had refused. William Craft, Ryan's appointee to replace Bridges as district organizer, was in Hawai'i in early November. Craft and Bridges kept in close contact. Craft informed Bridges that Hilo longshoremen were "100% organized" and Honolulu was more than 80 percent. Hawaiian longshore workers wrote to Ryan directly, requesting "immediate release of the Charters." The ILA-PCD Executive Board pressed the issue in February, after the strike. Ryan again refused. Like the issue of warehouse jurisdiction, the issue of the Hawaiian longshore charters remained unresolved.[101]

Throughout the strike, the Communist Party was much less visible than in 1934—less visible (but clearly present) within the ranks of the strikers, less visible in the publicity produced by the companies, less visible in the daily press—even less visible in its own newspaper, the *Western Worker*. In the weeks leading up to the strike, CP publications mirrored Bridges's reluctance to strike. The party's relatively low profile may have been tactical: keeping a low profile may have helped to avoid charges of CP influence on the strike leaders. Accusations that Bridges and other strike leaders were Communists appeared mostly in ads paid for by companies or articles from conservative or patriotic publications or organizations—and from the SUP. There was no repetition of the Red Scare that seized the city in 1934, although the Hearst press continued its vitriolic attacks on Bridges.[102]

With the end of the long strike, Bridges, the ILA-PCD, and the other MFP unions faced questions that surfaced during the strike: How would they relate to the conflict within the AFL over industrial unionism? How would they relate to the emergence of the CIO as a separate labor federation? And, as they faced those questions, was it possible to mend the badly frayed relations within the MFP, especially the conflict between the SUP and the ILA-PCD?

7

Founding the ILWU

1937–1940

After the MFP strike, Bridges and his union faced a rapidly changing national context for unions in general and for their organization specifically. John L. Lewis's Committee on Industrial Organization was expelled from the AFL, but also made major gains in organizing auto- and steelworkers, and soon launched a new national labor federation, the Congress of Industrial Organizations. By August 1937, CIO unions counted more members than all AFL affiliates.[1] Bridges and the ILA-PCD were soon caught up in those developments, emerging as a separate CIO-chartered union, the International Longshoremen's and Warehousemen's Union, with Bridges as its president and also as CIO western regional director. The central role of Bridges and the ILWU in the CIO on the Pacific Coast immediately made them prominent targets in struggles between the AFL and CIO. At the same time, the ILWU annually bargained with the Waterfront Employers' Association, helping to establish collective bargaining as the norm in longshore labor relations and further evolving their unique system of arbitration. Though relations with the WEA improved somewhat, Bridges continued to face questions and challenges regarding his relationship with the Communist Party.

Communist Party leaders had rushed to analyze the rapid rise and success of CIO unions. In September 1936 in Moscow, Clarence Hathaway informed the Comintern's Anglo-American Secretariat (AAS, the intermediary body between the CPUSA and the Executive Committee of the Comintern) of the CPUSA's difficulty in reconciling support for CIO organizing with the party's commitment to the unity of the AFL. In March 1937, the AAS logged a confidential memorandum on the most important issues facing the CPUSA, focused especially on the party line regarding the CIO. The previous line was to prevent any split in the AFL, but the memorandum acknowledged that "our influence" was unable "to hold back the C.I.O." from becoming a separate federation. The conclusion was that the CP should give full support and "guidance" to the CIO as a separate federation while still looking for "eventual re-unification of the whole labor movement." AFL unions under "progressive" leadership were to be encouraged to come into the CIO, but the party was to discourage "splitting any existing union."[2]

When Earl Browder met with the AAS in Moscow in April 1937, he glowingly described the CIO as "the first large-scale movement towards the crystallization of the American working class as a class" and argued that "the success of the CIO" was necessary for "preservation of democracy in America, for the defeat of reaction, fascism and war." But, he emphasized, the party opposed taking a union into the CIO "where it means a split." The executive committee of the Comintern approved the new line for the U.S. party, which it summarized as "giving every support to the industrial union movement (CIO) while combatting the criminal attempts of the reactionary leaders of the AF of L to split the trade union organizations."[3]

While the CP was reassessing its position vis-à-vis the CIO, the New Deal coalition in Congress was unraveling. Conservative Democrats, mostly from the South, increasingly joined most Republicans to oppose extensions of the New Deal. This conservative coalition also declared war on the Left, creating a special House committee to investigate "un-American propaganda." The new committee soon targeted communism in general, the CIO in particular, and Harry Bridges specifically.[4]

Bridges was temporarily removed from these events. He had been in noticeably poor health during much of the MFP strike, and soon after, on February 13, 1937, he was again admitted to St. Luke's Hospital in San Francisco for treatment of "aggravated stomach ulcers." He remained hospitalized for three weeks, until March 6.[5] By late March, he was back in the thick of things. As a state federation vice president, he led opposition to Edward Vandeleur's plan to deny an industrial charter to farmworkers and instead to charter several separate unions. Bridges denounced the plan as carrying "craft distinctions into an industry," but he and one other vice president were alone in arguing for an industrial charter. Bridges and other ILA-PCD officers also took the lead in defending CIO locals against expulsion from AFL central bodies: "We favor a program of unity between A.F. of L. and C.I.O. unions for the purpose of organizing the unorganized."[6]

At the same time, Bridges had to deal with thorny problems with the WEA. In late March 1937, East Coast seamen threw up a picket line in San Francisco in a jurisdictional dispute. When Local 38-79 members refused to cross the picket line, the WEA threatened to break off relations with the union. Joe Curran, leader of the East Coast seamen in New York, and Bridges and Henry Schmidt in San Francisco persuaded the East Coast seamen to withdraw their pickets. The WEA then refused to accept longshore gangs because they reported at noon, after the pickets were withdrawn, instead of in the morning when they had been requested. Almon Roth, new head of the local WEA, met with Bridges, and they agreed that "stoppages of work would not occur because of disputes arising on issues outside the agreement." Work on the waterfront resumed.[7]

On May 2, 1937, Mike Casey, founding president of Teamsters Local 85, died. Casey and Bridges had developed a mutually respectful relationship. Casey was a close friend of Henry Melnikow, and Bridges and Casey had sometimes met for discussion in Melnikow's office even though, as Melnikow put it, "the mere name of Harry Bridges was anathema to a great many people." Among the mourners at Casey's funeral was one who swiftly moved into the power vacuum Casey left—Dave Beck, the Teamster boss from Seattle, whom Bridges had encountered in conflicts over warehouse organizing in the Northwest, and who soon took a large role in the IBT in California.[8]

The ILA-PCD's 1937 convention met on May 3. Within Local 38-79, Bridges had been elected as a delegate by nearly 90 percent of the vote. Breaking with precedent, Bridges on March 20 sent all district locals a detailed president's report, laying out issues to be discussed in each local before the convention. Noting that the "program of the C.I.O. is against splitting the A.F.L. . . . and against C.I.O. affiliation of local or district groups," he recommended that the district both reaffirm its position of support for the CIO and demand a referendum of all ILA members, nationwide, on affiliation with the CIO. He next recommended that the district "actively participate" in Labor's Non-Partisan League (LNPL), the CIO's political arm. Regarding warehouse jurisdictional issues, he recommended, "We must maintain our organization as at present constituted and move to extend it in all ports." He proposed more democratic election procedures for the district executive board and complained that salaries of the district president and secretary were "far more than any rank and file I.L.A. member earns," a first step toward his later position that officers should be paid no more than the highest-paid longshore worker. Regarding longshore organizing in British Columbia and Hawai'i, he encouraged more organizational work in the former and full integration of the latter into the district.[9]

The district convention opened with Seattle mayor John Dore praising Bridges as "the greatest leader labor has ever seen in this country" but warning against abusing the goodwill of the public with unrealistic demands and jurisdictional disputes. Delegates engaged in lengthy discussions about the previous year and the strike and adopted resolutions endorsing the LNPL, reaffirming support for the CIO and a national maritime federation, and approving three additional warehouse organizers. Bridges was again nominated for district president.[10]

The press speculated that the convention would vote on joining the CIO, but that was not on the agenda. As the convention met, tensions continued to grow between the AFL and CIO, and between the ILA-PCD and IBT. Halfway through the convention, Curran, in New York, announced agreements between the recently organized National Maritime Union (NMU) and shipping companies and claimed that all seamen in the Port of New York were now shipping through the NMU hiring hall, a major defeat for the ISU. That same week, the ISU executive board considered restoring the SUP's charter. On May 19, MEBA opened talks about affiliation with the CIO. Still during the ILA-PCD convention, on May 20, the Seattle labor council, on orders from AFL president William Green, unseated the ILA warehouse union for violating the IBT's jurisdiction. The Portland labor council, under similar orders, took the same action. Harold Pritchett, head of the Federation of Woodworkers—lumber workers in the Pacific Northwest affiliated with the Carpenters' union—announced a referendum on joining the CIO.[11]

On May 14, Bridges spoke to some two hundred students and faculty members at the University of Washington. The next day, the *Seattle Post-Intelligencer* quoted him as saying, "Our policy is one of class struggle," and "we have nothing in common with our employers. There'll be a time when there aren't any employing classes any more, and we subscribe and look forward to that day." The paper also quoted him as saying, "The C.I.O. must turn from economic power to political power. . . . We must move into politics. . . . There are forces who are attempting to chisel away our economic gains and we must fight them on a political front."[12] Bridges often repeated his arguments about the necessity for unions to be involved in political action, but his purported comments—he later denied he had been quoted accurately—about "class struggle" and the end of "any employing classes" dogged him for years to come.

Shortly after the district convention, Bridges flew to Washington, DC, where he and other maritime union leaders conferred with John L. Lewis. Bridges summarized Lewis's comments: "If the ILA membership wished a charter for . . . the Pacific Coast, they [the CIO] would be glad to grant it." Lewis also proposed that Bridges "take charge of the Pacific Coast situation for the CIO." Bridges said later that he "didn't consider it" because he would first need "to find out what the wishes of the men are, and if they favor the CIO definitely by referendum." Bridges then put the AFL on notice: if it did not change its course on industrial organization, "there is no doubt what action the West Coast I.L.A. will take. No other course will be open to the West Coast I.L.A. than to join forces with the C.I.O."[13]

Bridges's announcement on May 30 that the Pacific Coast ILA might "join forces with the C.I.O." was contrary to the CP's position at that time, which remained opposed to splitting national unions. On June 3, however, the PolBuro adopted a new position, noting that "the opinion of the people with whom we discussed" the issue—likely including Bridges—was that "the time was ripe and the situation justified immediate affiliation on a District scale." The minutes also indicate, "The main question . . . hinges around the Pacific Coast ILA." After discussion of various options, the PolBuro decided that the Pacific Coast ILA should propose that all unions affiliated with the Maritime Federation of the Pacific conduct a referendum on the question, again, likely reflecting Bridges's views.[14]

The annual MFP convention opened in Portland on June 7, with the CIO the major topic. Delegates heard from John Brophy, Lewis's chief lieutenant. Harry Lundeberg and Bob Dombroff of the SUP closely questioned Brophy about whether the SUP could immediately receive a charter, since Brophy had intimated that might be possible for the ILA-PCD. Brophy answered that chartering a seafarers' union would be taken up at a conference. Lundeberg did not want to be in the same CIO union with the much larger NMU, some of the leaders of which were close to the CP. Bridges sought a convention vote on CIO affiliation, but SUP delegates insisted the matter go to committee and come up in the regular order. In response, ILA delegates caucused and called for a referendum of ILA-PCD members on CIO affiliation.[15] The SUP had recently carried out such a referendum, but the results had not been announced.

Lundeberg was keeping his options open. On June 11, four days into the MFP convention, he wrote to Lewis, asking "whether the CIO will issue a charter to the Sailors Union of the Pacific." Lewis immediately replied, welcomed the SUP to the CIO, but added, "No charters have been issued by the CIO in maritime industry and none will be issued until a conference can be held of representatives of various interested groups including yourself." Lundeberg replied that he "heartily" endorsed a conference and stated, regarding the recent SUP referendum, "Needless to tell you how we voted although memberships instructions are to seal ballot boxes until after your conference." The next day, the seventeenth, Lundeberg cabled Lewis, insisted he "immediately state definitely whether we can get a charter," and added, "Sentiment of our membership is strong for CIO." With no answer by June 22, E. R. Stowell, the SUP representative in Washington, demanded of Lewis: "Either yes or no." Lewis repeated that the CIO "is glad to welcome the Sailors' Union of the Pacific. . . . [C]harters cannot be issued, however, until after we have a conference on the maritime situation."[16]

The Lundeberg-Lewis exchange took place during the MFP convention, and Lewis's refusal of an immediate charter for the SUP likely determined Lundeberg's convention strategy. On June 12, Bridges and other ILA delegates sought a special order of business on the question of affiliating with the CIO. After prolonged discussion, the motion got a majority, 88.771–80.560, but not the necessary two-thirds for a special order. On June 14, a resolution drafted in the Committee of the Whole and unanimously adopted by the body specified that each MFP affiliate should separately conduct a referendum on CIO affiliation and that CIO affiliation should be the "first order of business" of the convention.[17]

That didn't happen, although the convention went on and on. On June 22, the convention took up charges that, on June 20 (the thirteenth day of the projected ten-day convention), Bridges had accused the SUP of needlessly prolonging the MFP convention. Schmidt then stated that he, not Bridges, had said the convention was so long because of disruptive tactics by unlicensed groups. Lundeberg, in return, accused "certain revolutionary fakers" of "disrupt[ing] the working classes" and told "all these phoney politicians" to "go to hell." That tenor characterized the latter part of the convention. William Fisher, MFP president, called Bridges "a dirty rat." Henry Schrimpf condemned Bridges and Schmidt as "slimy, lousy politicians." The convention majority opposed political action by the MFP. On June 24, the day after Lewis definitively rejected a CIO charter for the SUP, Lundeberg led the opposition to endorsing LNPL, making the syndicalist argument that "the strike and the threat of a strike . . . is sufficient. No political action is necessary to gain our ends."[18]

Throughout the long MFP convention, Bridges and his supporters were usually outvoted. They did succeed in pushing through a resolution strictly limiting job actions, although the SUP voted no. Lundeberg again argued that the decision to strike and picket could not be delegated to elected officials, and another SUP delegate reiterated the syndicalist mantra, "The right to strike and to picket is vested entirely in the workers at the point of production."[19]

John Brost, the CIO field representative who attended the convention, later told the FBI, "It was the practice . . . of the right-wing element in the convention to hold meetings . . . [to] discuss the strategy and plans for combatting the movements and activities of the left-wing or Communist element." He added that the right-wing delegates knew that the left-wing delegates were similarly caucusing and that Bridges caucused with them.[20]

Bridges and his supporters lost nearly all votes. When electing a delegate to represent the MFP at John L. Lewis's maritime conference, Bridges's candidate lost to Lundeberg's candidate. However, Bridges's candidate for president, James Engstrom, a member of the MFOW, won with support from nearly all ILA delegates, most MC&S delegates, and all MFOW delegates. A report by the Portland Police Red Squad claimed that the majority had permitted the election of Engstrom so that the Communists would not break up the federation. For other offices, however, most seafaring union delegates voted with the SUP. Late in the convention, delegates also voted to fire the editor of the *Voice*, James O'Neil, apparently because he was a Communist. The convention finally adjourned on day thirty-four.[21]

A Portland newspaper claimed that Bridges's "tremendous loss in prestige" at the convention had been due to his, and John L. Lewis's, support for political action by unions. The Portland Red Squad's analysis was that the majority formed around opposition to Communist control of the MFP and CIO.

Manipulation also seems to have been involved. In 1950 James Stewart, a former MFOW official under the name John Ferguson, claimed that, in April 1937, a shipping company executive gave him $2,000 (equivalent to nearly $40,000 in mid-2022) for his and Lundeberg's use in organizing the MFP convention against Bridges. Like the Portland Red Squad, Stewart claimed that the election of Engstrom was the result of deeply secret work by the anti-Bridges forces.[22]

Before the long MFP convention adjourned, most ILA-PCD members had voted on CIO affiliation, with 77 percent in favor. On June 26, Bridges wired Lewis to confirm that a CIO charter should be issued for the West Coast long-shoremen. Lewis's conference of maritime unions began in Washington July 7. Bridges attended as head of the ILA-PCD. He also had a preconference personal meeting with Lewis, leading *Time* magazine to claim, "Thus unofficially Harry Bridges was admitted to the C.I.O. high command." Lewis proposed that the licensed unions (MM&P, MEBA, ARTA) receive separate CIO charters and that the unlicensed organizations (SUP, MFOW, MC&S, NMU) form one organization.[23]

The conference delegated a subcommittee of Bridges, Mervyn Rathborne (ARTA), and Curran to meet Joseph Ryan and propose both a referendum of all ILA members on CIO affiliation and a democratic restructuring of the ILA. If Ryan refused—they surely did not have even the slightest doubt—they were to deliver an ultimatum: the CIO would charter the ILA-PCD with jurisdiction over all longshore and warehouse workers nationwide in direct competition with the ILA. Arthur Eggleston, labor reporter for the *Chronicle*, suggested that Lewis "had confidence that Ryan's longshoremen could be taken away from him." Ryan refused even to meet the subcommittee. The subcommittee then asked Lewis to issue a CIO charter for the Pacific Coast ILA.[24]

On July 15, the PolBuro jumped on the rapidly departing train when it voted "to affiliate the West Coast District of the ILA to the CIO"[25]—that is, the PolBuro resolved to do what the members of the ILA-PCD had voted to do three weeks before and what the CIO's maritime conference had decided the week before!

Lewis also named Bridges as the CIO's western regional director. George West in the *New York Times* characterized that decision as certain to bring accusations that the CIO was "ultra-radical" and "communistic." West also described Bridges as a "shrewd and aggressive fighter" and declared, "The longshoremen out on this coast believe in him implicitly." Robert Zieger, in his history of the CIO, concluded that Lewis had "no real alternative to Bridges" as West Coast director.[26]

Time put Bridges on its July 19 cover with the peculiar subtitle, "A Trotsky to Lewis' Stalin?" The cover photo was also peculiar—Bridges, in his undershirt, bent over a sink, and looking at the camera over his shoulder. The news story sounded many of the same themes as George West. Some information clearly came from Bridges himself. The article provides insight into the way that Bridges both presented himself and was seen by an important part of the national media as of mid-1937. A few excerpts: "the most conspicuous maritime labor leader in the U. S. today . . . the principal threat to A. F. of L. power on the Pacific Coast . . . damned as a communist, an alien agitator, a ruthless doctrinaire, an unscrupulous wrecker with a lust for power . . . Nervous, quick, wary, intolerant . . . a masterful hand with the rank & file . . . though Bridges is no revolutionist, millions of people think he is. . . . a stickler for union democracy . . . Incorruptible by cash, favors or flattery . . . has an almost fanatic following." The *Time* article also noted that Bridges "lives very modestly . . . is behind on the installments on a two-year-old Ford, has about finished paying off $600 of hospital and doctor bills," information that could only have come from Bridges.

The *Time* article reviewed the Bridges-Lundeberg conflict, dismissed the Norma Perry story, and concluded, "Bridges believes in unity at all costs, being willing to sacrifice the interest of one group for the benefit of the whole. Lundeberg is intensely loyal to his sailors, and Bridges suspects him of trying to gain advantages for them at the expense of other unions," again a perspective likely from Bridges. The article claimed, "Harry Bridges and John Lewis are working for Labor, both believe in political action by Labor. But their thinking processes are as different as those of Trotsky and Stalin." The article provided no further explanation of its opaque claim that Bridges thought like Trotsky and Lewis like Stalin.[27]

Many details had to be worked out within the CIO's new union. The ILA-PCD executive board met in Seattle on July 18. Bridges reported on his Washington meetings and answered questions. Schmidt's motion to endorse the CIO's maritime program carried with one negative vote. Nearly all the votes had been counted in the referendum on CIO affiliation, but Schmidt moved that, upon receiving the final vote count, "we officially apply for a CIO charter." The motion carried, with one dissent. After long discussion on a name, board members agreed on the International Longshoremen's Transportation and Distribution Workers' Association. Two days later, Bridges informed board members that the long name might infringe on other CIO jurisdictions and suggested "International Longshoremen's and Warehousemen's Union." The board approved. The final vote on CIO affiliation, announced on July 26, was 11,721 to 3,353, nearly 78 percent in favor. Only in Tacoma and a few small northwestern ports had a majority opposed. The CIO issued the charter on August 11, 1937. ILWU locals were immediately expelled from their local labor councils and state federations.[28]

Joining the CIO set off nearly a year of legal arguments over the ILWU's right to succeed to the contractual and property rights of the ILA-PCD. Most important was the ILWU's ownership of the agreement with the WEA. Other issues were local, such as ownership of the San Pedro local's bank account. That issue, however, led Bridges to his first trial before the U.S. Supreme Court. The case began when the president of ILA Local 38-82 (San Pedro) filed suit to block the president of ILWU Local 13 (San Pedro) from the local's bank account. A state judge found for the ILA loyalists, represented by Aaron Sapiro, the SUP's lawyer, and named a receiver for the bank account and other property. The ILWU appealed. By February Bridges was threatening to tie up shipping on the entire coast over the issue. On appeal the judge decided for the ILWU, but cited Bridges and other CIO leaders for contempt of court, charging Bridges with having pressured the judge by giving the press a telegram he sent to Secretary Perkins. Bridges appealed, eventually all the way to the U.S. Supreme Court, which by 5–4 decided in his favor, citing freedom of speech. The decision in *Bridges v. California* was only the second time the Court had invoked the Fourteenth Amendment as limiting the ability of state government to infringe upon the liberties in the First Amendment, but more such decisions followed.[29]

The most significant challenge facing the ILWU was settled by the National Labor Relations Board. Small groups of ILA loyalists in several ports, including San Francisco, claimed to be the legitimate parties to the contract with the WEA. The WEA stood apart, refusing to endorse either side but continuing to deal with the ILWU everywhere but the ports that had voted to remain in the ILA.[30]

The ILWU asked the NLRB to determine the collective-bargaining representative for Pacific Coast longshoremen. ILA loyalists rejected NLRB involvement, arguing that the contract between the employers and ILA-PCD deprived the NLRB of jurisdiction. Other AFL unions were also arguing that existing contracts or the AFL's determinations of jurisdiction took precedence over NLRB decisions. The ILA loyalists also argued that the board could not designate a bargaining unit larger than the individual employer, an argument that came, ironically, from veterans of the ILA-PCD leadership of 1933–34, when the district had demanded a single contract covering all ports and all employers on the coast. The ILWU countered that more than nine thousand Pacific Coast longshoremen had signed cards designating the ILWU as their bargaining representative. The NLRB decided that the appropriate unit consisted of all longshore workers in all ports in the three Pacific Coast states and that the ILWU had representational rights to all those workers—including in ports that voted to remain in the ILA. Having designated the ILWU as bargaining representative for all Pacific Coast longshore workers, the NLRB refused to comment further on ownership of the contract. The ILWU executive board and the WEA had both agreed not to reopen the agreement and thereby to renew it.[31]

News of the contract renewal on September 1, 1937, was overshadowed by the announcement that the Teamsters were refusing to handle cargo onto or from the San Francisco docks because of a seemingly minor warehouse dispute. John Steelman wrote to Secretary Perkins to make clear it was not a minor matter:

"There is a lineup between the Teamsters, AFL, shippers, and business organizations in general, to crush Bridges. . . . [S]hippers intimated to us that they do not care if they are tied up for a while. . . . The entire community here—organized labor, business and political organizations—are out to get Bridges and the CIO." Steelman added that Bridges had offered to settle the issue by an NLRB vote of all warehousemen involved, but the IBT refused because the AFL had given that jurisdiction to the IBT. Melnikow recalled that he and Bridges were convinced that the embargo was planned by Dave Beck, who had taken charge of IBT strategy and tactics on the Pacific Coast after the death of Mike Casey. The *Chronicle* called it a "CIO-AFL War."[32]

Henry Schmidt, president of ILWU Local 10, addressing a crowd of ILWU members and Teamsters, September 24, 1937. Schmidt tried to persuade the Teamsters to permit ILWU members to enter the piers without a fight. The next day, when Teamster pickets refused to let the longshoremen through, ILWU members formed a flying wedge and broke through the Teamsters' line. (Photo AAD-5409 courtesy of the San Francisco History Center, San Francisco Public Library)

In 1937 J. Paul St. Sure was legal counsel for the California Processors' and Growers' Association, which included the company that owned the warehouse where the war began. St. Sure later recalled that the WEA had worked out a deal "whereby the AF of L would agree to man a single dock with AF of L longshoremen. The Teamsters, in turn, would start moving cargo over that dock. The sailors [SUP], in turn, would handle the cargo for the AF of L longshoremen but refuse to handle cargo on ships if it was put on by ILWU." "It was," St. Sure confirmed, "a program to break the ILWU."[33]

The war reached into the annual convention of the California Labor Federation, when George Kidwell introduced a resolution calling on President Roosevelt to intervene in the AFL-CIO dispute, only to be denounced as "an agent of Communism." John Shelley, president of the San Francisco Labor Council and a Teamster, defended the NLRB. Later he was seriously beaten. A Machinist official identified the assailants as Shelley's "own brother members" and added, "The A. F. of L. group are perfectly satisfied with what happened."[34]

Though Teamsters refused to drive onto the San Francisco piers, ILWU members continued to work, loading and unloading ships and loading and unloading the boxcars of the Belt Railway. Three weeks into the embargo, IBT officials directed their members to prevent ILWU members from entering the piers because "the workers on the waterfront are led by communists." When Teamsters attempted to block access to a pier, ILWU members formed a flying wedge and forced their way in. After four weeks, the operation seemed only to be embarrassing the Teamsters and financially damaging the businesses. John Francis Neylan held a meeting to find some way to save face for the Teamsters. St. Sure recalled, "The best thing that could be thought about at the time was that the Associated Farmers [a viciously antiunion organization partly funded by the Industrial Association] should request the Teamsters to resume operation," which St. Sure termed "very lame." St. Sure also recalled that John McLaughlin, longtime secretary of Local 85, considered that his union had been burned by the employers. The IBT ended its embargo on September 28.[35]

The San Francisco Teamsters had done little previously to organize warehouse workers, apparently fearing that doing so might threaten their relations with the business community. That changed after Mike Casey's death and with pressure from outside IBT officials. Joe Casey, Mike's son, informed Daniel Tobin, IBT international president, about the difficulties in organizing warehouse workers: "Under the most difficult circumstances, we have been obliged simply to bring warehousemen's locals into existence in San Francisco and Oakland. There were no demands whatever from any groups for these locals." Casey complained about the costs involved in maintaining the ghost locals. All that maneuvering, Casey made clear, was to preserve the IBT's claimed jurisdiction in warehousing. By then, however, the ILWU had organized some eight thousand warehouse workers.[36]

Within nine months of the ILWU's charter, all but four of the former ILA-PCD locals had joined the ILWU, leaving only Tacoma and three small Puget Sound locals where ILA loyalists were the majority. Bridges repeatedly specified that the ILWU represented and supported *all* longshoremen, whether ILA or ILWU. The ILWU made no effort to invade the four ILA ports and even invited those locals to send fraternal delegates to the founding convention of the ILWU. Although Ryan threatened to lift the charter of any ILA local that accepted, the Tacoma local nonetheless split on the issue, 149 in favor of accepting the invitation to 188 against.[37]

That founding convention took place in April 1938, in Aberdeen, Washington. Routine reports and resolutions occupied most of the meeting, which was free of the clashes that had characterized the ILA-PCD's annual conventions. Bridges and Matt Meehan, the secretary, reported on organizing efforts outside the Pacific Coast, focused in part on what Bridges called "getting some sort of democratic, rank and file movement into the ILA locals." Bridges had traveled to the East Coast in late February and remained for most of March, meeting with ILWU organizers and ILA members from Boston to New Orleans. The ILWU had chartered longshore locals in Mobile and New Orleans, coal-handler locals in Providence and Norfolk, and a banana-handler local in Philadelphia.[38]

The convention approved several constitutional amendments, including one for recall of officers by a petition signed by 15 percent of the members, a provision Bridges often cited. One resolution opposed introduction of labor-saving devices without "compensation to the workers involved" and stated any introduction of labor-saving devices should be subject to negotiation. Other resolutions reaffirmed the union's policy of "no discrimination against workers on account of race, color or creed" and gave "full and unqualified support to the present administration and our President, Franklin Delano Roosevelt."[39]

At the time the convention was meeting, the Seattle and Portland locals were caught in a jurisdictional dispute between the NMU and SUP. At issue were two Shepard Line ships, the *Sea Thrush* and *Timber Rush*. The SUP had an old contract with the Shepard Line, but the two ships' crews had voted for the NMU in an NLRB election. The SUP argued that the contract took precedence over federal regulations. When the *Timber Rush* arrived in Seattle and the *Sea Thrush* docked in Portland, the SUP threw up picket lines. The ILWU convention, nearby in Aberdeen, called on the Seattle and Portland ILWU locals to go through the SUP picket lines and work the ships. The Portland longshoremen went through the picket line, but the Seattle men refused until Bridges personally led some five hundred men through the SUP picket line.[40]

The *Sea Thrush* arrived in San Francisco on April 17, greeted by a mass SUP picket line and a promise by the officers of Local 10 (formerly Local 38-79) that longshoremen would work the ship. The SUP picket line did not give way. Fists flew. Blood flowed. Longshoremen accused sailors of swinging baseball bats.

Sailors claimed longshoremen were using cargo hooks. Lundeberg took pride in having struck the first blow. Twenty police struggled to maintain order. Two men were hospitalized. After fifteen minutes of fighting, police assisted the longshoremen in entering the pier. The MFP district council, with no delegates present from the SUP or MM&P, condemned the jurisdictional picketing as threatening to both the MFP and the Wagner Act.[41]

On May 10, John Steelman wrote to Secretary Perkins to report on a consequence of the battles over the two ships: "There is now a definite move for the Sailors' Union of the Pacific to reaffiliate with the AFL. While this development has been 'in the mill' for some time, the psychological moment for it has developed during the past 2 weeks." Steelman concluded, "When and if the Sailors' Union votes AFL, there will doubtless be even more trouble than at present."[42]

Steelman was well informed. SUP members voted two to one in favor of AFL affiliation. The AFL then chartered the Seafarers International Union, a new international union, replacing the ISU and challenging the jurisdiction of the NMU. Lundeberg was president and empowered to issue SIU charters to seamen on the Gulf and East Coasts and the Great Lakes. Now the maritime industry was divided between the AFL and CIO: ILWU versus the ILA on the docks, SIU versus the NMU on the water. Of the unlicensed West Coast ISU affiliates, the MC&S, Alaska Fishermen, and IBU went to the CIO, and the MFOW became independent. Of the licensed unions, MEBA and ARTA were CIO, and MM&P remained AFL.[43]

The bloody fight between the ILWU and SUP over the *Sea Thrush* in April 1938 had demonstrated the MFP's inability to mediate jurisdictional conflicts. Soon after, at the MFP annual convention, the few ILA locals insisted on separate seating from the ILWU. The ILWU opposed, and the convention voted to deny the request. The ILA delegates walked out, followed by the SUP, MFOW, and MM&P. The MFOW returned, but not the SUP and MM&P. That convention marked the de facto end of the MFP, although it was not officially dissolved until June 1941.[44]

ILWU-WEA bargaining in 1938 produced few changes in the agreement. It continued the provision for the secretary of labor to appoint a "Standing Coast Arbitrator" and "a Standing Local Arbitrator in each of the four Regional Districts." The agreement set wages, hours, and working conditions for all Pacific Coast ports, but the ILWU waived its rights to preference of employment in the four ILA ports until a majority of the registered longshore workers there were ILWU members.[45]

The bitter AFL-CIO conflicts were somewhat tempered in 1937 and 1938 by the need for labor unity in politics. In San Francisco in March 1937, most unions—AFL and CIO—joined with New Deal Democrats, CP members, and several civic organizations to repeal the city's twenty-year-old antipicketing ordinance. The same coalition defeated an initiative that fall for a new anti-picketing ordinance. In the 1938 general election in California, business and conservative groups backed Proposition 1, a statewide initiative to restrict unions by limiting picketing, prohibiting secondary boycotts, and making unions liable for damages caused by members. Backed by the Industrial Association of San Francisco, the Associated Farmers, the Merchants and Manufacturers Association of Los Angeles, the Los Angeles Chamber of Commerce, and similar groups, Prop 1 supporters launched the most expensive political campaign for a proposition up to that time. They also supported the two leading Republican candidates, Frank Merriam, the incumbent governor who had sent the National Guard into San Francisco in 1934, and Philip Bancroft, candidate for U.S. Senate, who had close ties to the Associated Farmers.[46]

Bridges joined with leaders of CIO unions, AFL unions (though the state federation refused to endorse candidates), and the railway brotherhoods to create the Organized Labor Democratic Committee, a joint campaign committee "for the election of Democratic New Deal candidates and the defeat of the anti-labor Proposition 1." The committee focused especially on the election of Culbert Olson as governor and Ellis Patterson as lieutenant governor. (Patterson was close to the CP, and rumors swirled that he was a party member.) Germain Bulcke, president of Local 10 and close to the CP, served as the committee's vice chairman. AFL president Green endorsed Merriam, claiming that "the enemies of the AFL" were supporting Olson, but AFL leaders and members across the state indignantly repudiated his action. The president of the state federation and the head of the Los Angeles county labor council urged Green to withdraw his endorsement. Almost everything, it seemed, was coming together to promote the unity of labor and the Left. Many on the Left now concluded that a broadly based coalition of nearly all organized labor (except the IBT and some building trades unions), some small-scale farmers, and liberals was coming to birth inside the California Democratic Party.[47]

The result was a sweep for labor and New Deal Democrats. Olson, Patterson, and Sheridan Downey, Democratic candidate for the U.S. Senate, all won, and Democrats took a majority in the assembly. Bridges proclaimed, "We have a strong and powerful California Labor's Non-Partisan League which speaks with political power and is committed to a progressive program for labor. We established unity with the AFL membership and many local officers." Conservatives had given organized labor an external threat much greater than the AFL and CIO posed for each other, and the large majority of labor leaders worked hard to achieve the broadest possible labor unity and to minimize potential discord.[48]

Defeat of Proposition 1 and election of Olson and the others initiated a few heady months for labor and the Left in California. Olson, in one of his first official actions, freed Tom Mooney, something labor and the Left had been seeking for nearly two decades. Upon arriving in San Francisco, Mooney led a huge parade down Market Street. Bridges greeted him, briefly walked with him, then dropped back with those following Mooney. Olson, Downey, and several legislators had even felt comfortable meeting with William Schneiderman, head of CP District 13, and other CP leaders to discuss the campaign and legislative initiatives. Schneiderman later said, "A certain euphoria was prevalent in Party ranks."[49]

Olson acknowledged his debt to unions through several appointments, including Bulcke for the State Harbor Commission. New Deal Democrats in the state legislature introduced a raft of proposed legislation, including a bill for a state health insurance program, a "Little Wagner" bill, and bills protecting picketing, restricting injunctions, improving unemployment compensation, repealing the criminal syndicalism law, and establishing minimum wages and maximum hours. Issues that progressives had been pushing for years now seemed to have a chance of passage. Contrary portents soon appeared. In early March, the Republican-controlled state senate rejected Bulcke as harbor commissioner. By the end of the legislative session, most labor and liberal bills had met defeat. The state senate even considered, but defeated, a bill that would have prevented aliens from holding union office in California, a measure aimed at Bridges.[50]

The 1938 elections and 1939 legislative session took place amid international crisis. Civil war raged in Spain, where the republican government tried to resist the forces of Francisco Franco, who had support from Nazi Germany and fascist Italy. Japanese forces occupied large parts of China. Both conflicts received significant attention from the CP and its allies in the unions. The Left sent funds and volunteers to Spain, including members of MFP affiliates, but American volunteers began to return in late 1938, as the republican government teetered toward collapse.

In December 1938, organizations in San Francisco's Chinatown formed a picket line at Pier 45, where a ship was waiting to load scrap iron for shipment to Japan. Over the next few days, the two hundred initial pickets swelled to five thousand and extended to another ship, also at Pier 45, also ready to load scrap iron for Japan. Local 10 members refused to cross the picket lines. Over the next eight months, ILWU members from the Puget Sound to Southern California refused to cross picket lines of Chinese Americans—including children with their grandmothers. Longshoremen who had charged through Teamster and SUP picket lines now told the press it was not safe to cross lines staffed by elderly women and children. The boycotts ended after intervention by U.S. marshals in Seattle in July and an August ruling by the new coast arbitrator, Wayne Morse, dean of the University of Oregon Law School. In the end, the Chinese American demonstrators and ILWU members who honored their picket lines helped to create a national embargo on such shipments in 1941.[51]

In April 1938, Nazi Germany absorbed Austria. In September Neville Chamberlain, the British prime minister, agreed for Germany to dismember Czechoslovakia. Germany invaded Czechoslovakia in mid-March 1939. In late March, Franco captured the Spanish capital. In early April, Italy invaded Albania. In early May, Germany made demands on Poland. In late August, Germany and the Soviet Union negotiated a nonaggression pact, the Molotov-Ribbentrop Pact. In mid-September, Germany and the Soviet Union invaded Poland and divided it between them. Much of Europe and the world was soon at war.[52]

Given the long-standing opposition of the CP to fascism, many CP members and sympathizers were shocked by the Soviet Union's bargain with Hitler. Al Richmond, managing editor of the *People's World*, remembered he was personally confused and that the newspaper staff was "unprepared, knocked off balance by this abrupt turn." Bridges recalled that Schneiderman called a meeting at party headquarters, to explain the logic of the pact.[53]

From mid-1935 until mid-1939, the CP had stressed coalitions to oppose fascism. The People's Front, often called the Popular Front, lasted from 1935 to 1939. The CP dropped its criticism of Roosevelt and the New Deal, tried to join with other Left groups, and depicted communism as "Twentieth-century Americanism." By 1938, in a few places, notably California and Washington, this led the CP further into the political mainstream than ever before. In 1939, however, the CP interpreted the Molotov-Ribbentrop Pact as an entente, and the CP line changed to keep out of "the imperialist war." This cost the CP credibility, and it lost some of the gains from recent years.[54] This turn in the party line coincided with increased criticism from within the CIO of Bridges's ties to the CP and the role of the CP in the CIO more generally.

Amid all this, the ILWU-WEA agreement was set to expire on September 30, 1939. Negotiations stalled over the San Francisco ship clerks (Local 34), who had not been covered by the previous agreements for longshore workers. The longshore negotiating committee found no support for a coastwise strike on behalf of Local 34, and the WEA adamantly refused concessions. Bridges feared that the WEA was setting up the union for a strike that ILWU members did not want and might not support. In the end, Local 34 voted to strike despite efforts by a federal mediator and against the wishes of Bridges and other ILWU officers. Local 10 voted to respect the picket lines, shutting down most of the port. However, the ILWU declared that the strike was not against the ships, so the other maritime unions were not affected. Shipping companies diverted freight to other Pacific Coast ports, apparently hoping that it would create "hot cargo" and close all Pacific Coast ports. Instead, the ILWU offered members of Locals 10 and 34 work at other, now very busy, ports. Bridges later explained, "The union moved in every direction possible to narrow the strike down to the smallest number of men possible and the smallest possible area." With the

Harry Bridges led the ILWU contingent in the 1939 Labor Day Parade on Market Street in San Francisco. (Photo courtesy of Anne Rand Library, ILWU)

WEA's failure to shut the entire Pacific Coast and with assistance from federal mediators and Governor Olson, the strike ended successfully.[55]

In late 1940, a new contract was approved by two-thirds of the members. A new and very important arbitration provision was voted on separately and approved by an even larger margin. It provided for a Coast Labor Relations Committee of six members, three from each side. The CLRC was to interpret the agreement, decide disputes arising under it, and choose the coast arbitrator to decide disputes that the CLRC could not. Only if the parties could not agree would the coast arbitrator be chosen by the secretary of labor. The parties were also to select four arbitrator's agents (later called port arbitrators), one for each district (Puget Sound, Columbia River, Northern California, Southern California). In disputes over working conditions deemed dangerous to the health or safety of longshore workers, the arbitrator's agent was to be immediately dispatched to the scene to make an on-the-spot decision so that work could resume as quickly as possible. Thus, over the preceding six years, the system of arbitration in Pacific Coast ports had evolved into one intended to produce immediate settlement of disputes over working conditions, a development that became a fixture in ILWU longshore contracts. The results quickly appeared:

throughout 1941, according to Almon Roth, president of the San Francisco Employers' Council, "Quickie strikes . . . have been entirely eliminated." Sam Kagel told me, toward the end of his long career as an arbitrator, that there was nothing like this system of arbitration anywhere else.[56]

In early 1941, Bridges gave a long and frank interview to David Wills of the *News-Chronicle* of London. The new contract, Bridges said, represented "a fundamental change in attitude." He was pleased that the contract strengthened arbitration and permitted employers to introduce labor-saving devices, but also protected longshore workers' wages and specified that total employees would not decrease. Wills quoted Bridges as depicting this arrangement as "the solution of technological unemployment." The contract, Bridges declared, meant that "the profits of labor-saving devices must be shared with labour."[57]

As these important developments were taking place with the ILWU's longshore contract, the CIO was changing its views on the role of Communists in CIO unions. Though most AFL leaders had long been anti-Communist, the CIO was a different story. Clarence Hathaway, in Moscow in September 1936, reported that Lewis and Sidney Hillman "have shown a readiness to consult with us and make known their policy." Lewis had reinstated Communists and militants who had been expelled from the UMW and had hired forty to fifty Communists as organizers. "They have brought our people in everywhere," Hathaway concluded. In April 1937, Earl Browder, in Moscow, assured the AAS, "With the CIO and its leadership we have the closest cooperative relations." By December 1938, the CP seemed to feel they had a pledge that the CIO would not discriminate against party members.[58]

Nonetheless, by mid-1938, some CIO leaders were launching efforts to reduce the influence of Communists in general and of Bridges in particular. Most historians have looked only at the CIO purge of the Cold War period and have not recognized that the acceptance of the CP within the CIO was always tenuous at best. Almost from the beginning, some West Coast CIO leaders chafed at the CP members or sympathizers in their organizations and councils.

In July 1938, William Dalrymple, field director for the Steel Workers Organizing Committee in California, wrote to Philip Murray, national head of SWOC, to recommend that charters be lifted from SWOC lodges in San Francisco and Oakland because they were controlled by Communists. In early August 1938, the *San Francisco Examiner* revealed "a move to crush Communist party influences that have developed within the CIO on the Pacific Coast," a revolt organized by leaders of several Southern California CIO unions, especially SWOC and the United Automobile Workers (UAW). The *Los Angeles Examiner*, the next day, reported on efforts to oust Bridges as regional director. Leaders of five Southern California CIO unions, claiming one-fifth of all CIO members on the West Coast, announced they were withdrawing from local and state Industrial

Union Councils and blasted Bridges for running a "Communist dictatorship" and controlling IUCs through "paper locals." Bridges dismissed them as "a few conspiring officials," and Lewis sent John Brophy to quash the rebellion. Paul Scharrenberg, then legislative representative for the AFL in Washington, DC, assured William Green, "We have quietly, but I think effectively encouraged the revolt among C.I.O. unions in Southern California."[59]

The next year, CIO officials in Oregon and Washington—Bridges's territory as western regional director—began a mini-purge. In September 1939, a month after the Molotov-Ribbentrop Pact, Richard Francis, president of the Washington State Industrial Union Council and secretary-treasurer of UMW District 10, reported to Lewis that the state IUC was "in constant turmoil and disruption" caused by delegates from the ILWU, the Woodworkers' union, and city or county Industrial Union Councils. These groups, Francis charged, "are not out to build the CIO organized labor movement in this State but to further the interests of the Communist Party."[60]

In late 1939, Lewis limited Bridges's authority as CIO regional director to California and appointed separate directors for Oregon and Washington. Lewis made clear that the purpose was to reduce Communist influence but said nothing specific about Bridges. The two new West Coast regional directors were Francis, in Washington, and Dalrymple, in Oregon. Both of them, Lewis knew, were strongly anti-Communist.[61]

In March 1940, Francis urged, "We cannot much longer delay cleaning house of these subversive elements." Later he dismissed the entire Washington State CIO council. In preparing for a meeting to reconstitute the council, Francis used UMW funds to assist some locals "who are in favor of the correct CIO program and not that of the Communist Party." Left-wing delegates bolted, and an anti-Communist resolution then carried. The meeting elected state IUC officers who, according to CIO national representative H. C. Fremming, "are all known to be 'white'"—that is, not red.[62]

Dalrymple conducted similar operations in Oregon. "The CIO is NOT a Communist Party," he proclaimed in August 1940, and added that CP members "must refrain from interfering with our affairs." He garnered support from several CIO locals across the state. Some CIO unions in the Northwest followed Francis's and Dalrymple's lead including the Seattle Newspaper Guild, which voted out the CP sympathizers in its leadership and passed an anti-Communist resolution. As late as February 1942, Bridges and his followers hoped to purge both Dalrymple and Francis, but any further purges seem to have been set aside for the duration of the war.[63]

The CIO's mini-purge of Communists in the Northwest played out against the efforts by the CP and its supporters within CIO unions to demand American neutrality. During the 1940 presidential campaign, the CP and its allies condemned Roosevelt as a warmonger and pulled out all stops first to deny him renomination and then to deny endorsement by CIO affiliates. Bridges followed the lead of both John L. Lewis and the CP to oppose the reelection of Roosevelt and condemn the "betrayals and sellouts of the New Deal," a 180-degree reversal of the position taken by the 1938 annual convention. The 1940 ILWU convention opposed any involvement of American men, money, or material in foreign wars. Less than two weeks before Election Day, Lewis escalated his attacks on Roosevelt; endorsed the Republican candidate, Wendell Willkie; and promised—or threatened—to resign from the CIO presidency if Roosevelt were reelected. Bridges flew to Washington to consult with Lewis. Upon returning, he met with the state Industrial Union Council, endorsed everything Lewis had said, refused to endorse any candidate for president, and ripped Roosevelt as a betrayer of labor. He received both cheers and boos.[64]

Bridges's attacks on Roosevelt brought rebukes from ILWU members. When Bridges spoke out against Roosevelt in Local 10, he received boos as well as applause, and one reporter described Bridges's attack on Roosevelt as "out of line with the overwhelmingly pro-Roosevelt sentiment among his men." In Local 10's last membership meeting before the election, members voted to endorse Roosevelt. The Seattle ILWU local went further, demanding that Bridges resign as ILWU president.[65] Not even Harry Bridges could persuade rank-and-file longshoremen to oppose Roosevelt.

From the mid-1930s until mid-1939, Bridges and the ILWU had enthusiastically embraced Roosevelt and New Deal and especially the NLRB. They took the position that unions must be deeply involved in the political process to maintain their gains from political intervention. In jurisdictional battles with the IBT, the ILWU consistently called for NLRB elections as the democratic way to determine unions' jurisdictions. The IBT, SUP, and AFL usually took the contrary position, defending the AFL's long-standing role in determining union jurisdictions and arguing that existing contracts took precedence over NLRB elections. For them, the new enemy became the NLRB in particular and sometimes the New Deal in general. Bridges and the ILWU had quickly understood and benefited from the new role of the federal government in regulating labor relations. Other unions too, sooner or later, came to understand that the old way of determining jurisdictions had become obsolete and that the Wagner Act meant that jurisdictions were now determined by a vote of the workers. In 1939, however, the Molotov-Ribbentrop Pact and the CP's "Yanks Are Not Coming" line deterred Bridges and other ILWU leaders from the path they had laid out at the height of the Popular Front and led them into a political dead-end.

8

Harry Bridges and the Communist Party in the 1930s

Evidence from the Russian Archives

The claims during the CIO's mini-purge that Harry Bridges was a Communist were not new. The first such accusations came less than two weeks into the 1934 strike. Such claims were widespread in the press thereafter, became central in legal proceedings over seventeen years, and have appeared in works by journalists and scholars. In public statements in the 1930s, Bridges often, but not always, took the same position as the CP on national politics and foreign affairs. In this chapter, I address claims that the Communist Party controlled the 1934 strikes and controlled Bridges and the longshore union afterward. At base, the question must be, is there reliable evidence for such claims? In this chapter, I shall present the relevant evidence, especially material I discovered in Russian archives, regarding Bridges's relation to the CP in the mid-1930s and the relation of the CP to the Pacific Coast strikes and the longshore union.

Though scholars and journalists have generated an extensive historiography on Bridges and the ILWU, surprisingly few have undertaken serious research into his relation to the CPUSA. The earliest treatment by a journalist was Estolv Ward's *Harry Bridges on Trial* (1940), an account of Bridges's 1939 Immigration and Naturalization Service (INS) hearing. Ward was, at the time, the head of Bridges's defense committee and also a CP member. Ward assumes that Bridges was not a CP member and that the hearing was a transparent effort to frame Bridges, an evaluation much like the conclusions of several subsequent scholars. *The Big Strike* (1949) by Mike Quin, the name that Paul William Ryan used as a journalist, is a popular account of the 1934 strikes that does not address Bridges's relationship to the CP; Sam Darcy privately criticized Quin's initial draft for minimizing the role of the CP.[1]

The 1950s saw several works that, in passing, claimed Bridges was a Communist or that the ILWU was Communist controlled, based almost entirely on the same evidence as in his legal proceedings or on even less reliable sources.[2] After the post–World War II Red Scare faded in the late 1950s, scholars focused on other matters. Charles Larrowe, a labor economist, produced the first scholarly biography of Bridges in 1972; Larrowe studied Bridges as a union leader and examined his legal battles but did not challenge the view that Bridges had been falsely accused of being a Communist. In 1980 Harvey Schwartz surveyed the existing historiography and concluded, "Historians miss the point even if they describe the unionist [Bridges] as a 'fellow traveler.' In fact, the party appears to have been *Bridges'* fellow traveler," that is, the party more often followed Bridges's lead than vice versa. Schwartz emphasized that Bridges's accomplishments as a union leader were more relevant for evaluating him than speculations about his relationship to the CP. Five detailed studies of the 1934 strikes or of Pacific Coast longshore workers appeared between 1981 and 1996. For all but one of the authors, Bridges's relationship to the CP was not a major concern. Howard Kimeldorf (1988) described Bridges as a syndicalist whose views moved close to the CP over time. Bruce Nelson (1988) concluded, "Bridges's stubborn (but not absolute) adherence to the Party line . . . cost him and his union dearly." The exception is Ottilie Markholt's *Maritime Solidarity* (1998); Markholt strongly defended Lundeberg and the SUP and argued that Bridges was a Communist and was used by Communists. None of those authors used the files on Bridges created by the INS or FBI. Stanley Kutler was the first to examine Bridges's INS files; he produced an excellent summary and analysis of the legal history. Ann Fagan Ginger's biography of Carol King thoroughly treats one of Bridges's lawyers, based in part on King's FBI file but not that of Bridges.[3]

In 1992 major Russian archives opened to American researchers for the first time. What is now the Russian State Archive for Socio-Political History (usually identified by its Russian acronym, RGASPI) contains thousands of files from the CPUSA, the Anglo-American Secretariat, and the Red International of Labor Unions (RILU or Profintern). The AAS was the intermediary body between the Comintern and the CPUSA in the 1930s; it regularly received reports from CPUSA leaders and prepared directives to the CPUSA.[4] John Haynes, the first American researcher there, and Harvey Klehr produced several works based on those archives, notably *The Secret World of American Communism* (1995), emphasizing espionage, and *The Soviet World of American Communism* (1998), emphasizing Soviet control of the CPUSA.[5] Their early revelations included new information about Harry Bridges, so in the spring of 1996 I spent several days each week at RGASPI during my semester as a Fulbright lecturer at Moscow State University, and I returned for several weeks in the summer of 2003.

Material from RGASPI does *not* appear in several recent works on legal history. Peter Afrasiabi's *Burning Bridges* burns with indignation but fails to make good on his claim that he was using new sources. Colin Wark and John

F. Galliher drew on FBI files to survey the lawyers who defended Bridges; after reviewing two small parts of Bridges's massive FBI file, but not RGASPI material, they conclude, "The available evidence demonstrates that Harry Bridges was not a Communist." Most recently, Amanda Frost's study of citizenship stripping addresses an aspect of Bridges's legal battles that does not involve evaluating RGASPI or FBI evidence.[6]

Vernon Pedersen's *The Communist Party on the American Waterfront* (2019) does draw on RGASPI documents to make extensive claims that Bridges was a member of the CPUSA and that the Communist Party controlled waterfront events in 1934 and later. Even more extreme claims about Bridges's and Communists' control of the 1934 strike appear in an article by Michael John in *American Communist History* in 2014.[7] A point-by-point examination of Pedersen's and John's claims would take a chapter by itself. What I offer instead is my understanding of Bridges's relation to the CP in 1934, the role of the CP in the 1934 strikes, and Bridges's and his union's relation to the CP from 1934 through 1938, based on my own research in all the available evidence, especially the RGASPI files.

Regarding the 1934 strikes, the issues raised by Pedersen, John, and their predecessors may be broken down into five specific questions:

- How significant were Communists in creating Local 38-79, the demands of the ILA-PCD, and the timetable for striking?
- How significant were Communists in determining strike tactics and strategy and in supporting the strike more generally, especially in Local 38-79?
- Did Communists initiate or direct the general strike?
- How significant were Communists in determining the outcome of the longshore strike?
- What was the relationship between Bridges and the CP in 1934?

A final question is, what was the relationship between Bridges and the CP after the 1934 strikes and until about 1940?

First, how significant were Communists in creating Local 38-79, the demands of the ILA-PCD, and the timetable for striking? My summary of events in chapter 3 makes clear that Communists played no role in creating Local 38-79. When CP leaders encouraged party members and party sympathizers to join Local 38-79, they did so because they recognized that the large majority of San Francisco longshoremen were already joining. Chapter 3 also establishes that the ILA-PCD's basic demands were developed in late July 1933 and that neither Bridges, other Local 38-79 militants, nor any known CP members had any role in those events. The six-hour-day demand directly contradicted the party line, which called for a seven-hour day and was highly critical of the six-hour day.[8]

In January 1934, Roy Hudson claimed that "our group" was responsible for a "rank and file convention in San Francisco Calif., with no paid officials as delegates." Many others—including Bridges himself—also credited Bridges and the Albion Hall group with responsibility for a "rank-and-file convention" in 1934. However, as chapter 3 indicates, the proposal for a rank-and-file convention *failed*, and the February convention was, in fact, the regular annual convention of the ILA-PCD with many "paid officials" as delegates.[9] Hudson's claim and all those subsequently must be understood as conflating the *demand* for a rank-and-file convention with the *rescheduling* of the regular annual convention that included both rank-and-file union members and "paid officials." As I indicate in chapter 3, the accomplishments of Bridges and the Local 38-79 militants during that convention were limited to one resolution, passed unanimously, that disavowed arbitration and set the timetable for a strike vote.

Second, were Communists significant in the strike itself, in determining strike strategy and tactics, and in supporting the strike more generally, especially in Local 38-79? I make clear in chapters 4 and 5 that ILA-PCD officers, none of them Communists, and sometimes ILA president Joseph Ryan represented the ILA-PCD in negotiations and also in the arbitration proceedings. Participation by others, including Bridges, was with permission of the district officers. ILA-PCD officers determined overall strike strategy including the San Francisco local's insistence on membership ratification of any agreement. Control of the hiring hall and a coastwise contract, the two central and nonnegotiable issues, dated to July 1933. Bridges and the militants in Local 38-79 gave strong support to those two positions, but they did not create them and they were never alone in holding fast to those two positions. The locals in the Northwest Strike Committee, which was securely under the control of Bjorklund and Morris, gave similarly strong support to those positions and sometimes did so in advance of Local 38-79.

There was significant CP *support* for the strikes in San Francisco and elsewhere. CP members in San Francisco and elsewhere were among the most militant and committed strikers, devoting enormous amounts of time and energy to supporting the strike. Some were on the front lines of militant actions. Some served on the various committees. Darcy participated in discussions of tactics in San Francisco. In 1937 he wrote privately to Mike Quin, also a CP member, and described himself and a few other Communists as "strike advisors." In 1971, many years after Darcy had been expelled from the CP, he expanded on his involvement, explaining that he and strike leaders sometimes met late at night at the beach to discuss tactics. "We'd stand around and discuss the day's work and what the strategy should be for the next day," Darcy said, confounding strategy and tactics. "They could say no to me. . . . I had no authority. . . . I was an accepted consultant," he added.[10]

It is an error to equate Communists and militants, as so many business leaders did. Communists did not have a monopoly on militancy. Several of the most militant strike leaders in Local 38-79—Mallen and Dietrich, for example—were never Communists. The actions by Bjorklund and Morris on May 12 in leading ILA members from Tacoma (which had few if any CP members) and Everett (a small port that had a fair number of CP members) to eject and beat strike-breakers on the Seattle docks was as militant—and violent—as any actions by longshore strikers anywhere.[11]

Third, did Communists initiate the general strike, and were they significant in carrying it out? The evidence does not allow for a simple yes-or-no answer, but Communists were not the primary agents in creating and shaping this important event. Communists early on called for a general strike, but they were not alone. Talk of a general strike, by Communists and others, began in mid-May, when newspapers were reporting on general strikes in Toledo and Minneapolis, neither led by Communists. On May 29, the Local 38-79 Strike Committee called for a twenty-four-hour sympathy strike by the city's unions, and on June 3 acting president Joseph Johnson—never accused of being a Communist—raised the prospect of a general strike. Charles Cutright, also never accused of being a Communist, did the same in the Labor Council meeting of June 29. By late June, support for a general strike was coming from other non-Communist militants—for example, Machinists Lodge 68. The final surge of support for a general strike came from thousands of union members across the city outraged by the police riot of July 5 and the protection of strikebreakers by the National Guard. No one has ever suggested that Communists dominated Teamsters Local 85, but their membership vote was both crucial and overwhelming. There is no way to know if the demand for a general strike would have taken such a hold without the early and continuing efforts by Communists. Established union leaders, none of them Communists, maintained tight control over the general strike, from when they realized it was inevitable until they shut it down. Communists had prominently and loudly called for a general strike, but they were deeply dissatisfied with the general strike they got.

Fourth, how significant were Communists in determining the outcome of the longshore strike? In general, the CP opposed arbitration. The decision for arbitration was by a vote of the strikers and by an overwhelming majority. The militancy of the strikers and their insistence on control of the hiring hall and a coastwise contract, and the dramatic demonstration of union solidarity through the general strike, undoubtedly affected the arbitration board. One of the broader outcomes of the longshore strike—the long-term development of arbitration—came through federal intervention along lines forecast in the award itself. Another broad outcome of the strike—the use of work-site actions to determine working conditions—involved both Communists and non-Communist militants. The SUP engaged in similar, and sometimes much more extreme, job actions, led by *anti-Communist* syndicalists.

Though there is no evidence that Communists *controlled* the 1934 strikes, I do not minimize the *influence* of the CP and others on the Left. Several recommendations from the *Western Worker* in September 1933 were later adopted by the San Francisco longshore local: no consecutive terms in office; no discrimination based on politics, religion, race, or national origin; and the right of referendum and recall. Another constant CP position, albeit never limited to the CP, was the emphasis on the central position of the rank and file in decision making, including approval of contracts. With the exception of term limits, these all became central first to the ILA-PCD and then the ILWU, although racial discrimination long remained a problem at some ports. Bridges was a strong proponent for all these positions through his many years as president.

Finally, and perhaps most centrally, what was the relationship between Harry Bridges and the Communist Party in 1934 and after? Within days of the beginning of the strike, Bridges was accused of being a Communist, and claims continue to appear that Bridges was a Communist or was controlled by Communists. My reading of the evidence for the period through July 1934 is that his relationship to the CP was ambiguous. Chapter 3 presents my understanding of the Albion Hall group and Bridges's involvement with the *Waterfront Worker*, based on all the sources I have found. Bridges always denied having ever been a party member, but he often acknowledged that he was a Marxist and received support and advice from Communists. For example, in 1982, in writing privately to Darcy about a memoir Darcy had published about the strikes, Bridges acknowledged "the great contribution you made in helping organize the Strike as well as the critical organizing preceding it," but he then admonished Darcy for taking too much credit for himself and not giving sufficient attention to "the overwhelming force exerted when all the workers and their leaders got together."[12]

In RGASPI documents, the first appearance of Bridges's name, chronologically, comes in correspondence from Harrison George, a CP functionary so deep underground in San Francisco that he did not use his own name even in party meetings. Beginning in 1929 when he arrived in San Francisco, George was the eyes and ears—and factional partisan—for his former brother-in-law, Earl Browder. Browder and Darcy were never allies, and George continued his factional role in 1934, writing repeatedly to Browder, complaining about Darcy's handling of the CP role in the longshore and maritime strikes. On May 26, seventeen days after the longshore strike began, George sent Browder a long letter. "Now, if half what I hear is true, the strike—from a Party viewpoint—is in such condition that . . . I simply must say something to you, since I cannot say anything to swell-head [Darcy]," George began. He specified: "1. The Party face has been hidden, much to the injury of the Party and equally to the injury of the strike. 2. A policy of 'Tailism' is being carried out, and Economism; with almost no politicalization of the strike." George continued in that vein, then concluded by asking for "something forceful in the line of orders to the DC [District Committee] to bring the Party into the picture in its rightful place, and to politicalize the strike."[13]

George's opening, "If half what I hear is true," is his admission he was not directly involved in local CP decision making. He called himself an "outsider," states that no one from the district or the MWIU called on him during the strike, and that he "gathered such information as was available from events, from the Party press and bourgeois press, and any comrades whom I chanced to meet and who talked about the strike." He nonetheless identified "the Chairman of the Strike Committee [Bridges], and several of its most influen[tial] members," as "'new comrades . . . scared to death" that they might be revealed as party members. George especially criticized "Comrade Bridges" for ordering a party member to leave the union hall. "Day-to-day strike policy," George claimed, was being made "practically by conversations between Comrade Darcy and Comrade Bridges," who behaved as if "the strike is their property." Roy Hudson, after visiting San Francisco, stated, "Many of the criticisms made by G were incorrect and were a result of a lack of direct contact with the situation as a whole." There's no way to establish whether George was in a position to know that Bridges was a party member or whether he was accepting the claims in the press.[14]

George's reference to Bridges as "Comrade" differs from the internal correspondence of both Darcy and Morris Rappaport, the district organizer for Washington and Oregon, neither of whom ever referred to Bridges as "Comrade."[15] Roy Hudson, however, in a report to the TUUL Buro on May 21, 1934, stated, "On the central strike committee in San Francisco, one-third of the members are members of our group, the chairman is a member of the P." However, this conflicts sharply with Darcy's later statement that there were only six or eight CP members among the seventy-some members of the Strike Committee.[16]

As a longtime, high-level party functionary, George was familiar with the party line. "Hiding the face of the party" meant concealing the role of the party. "Tailism" meant that the party was following the workers rather than leading them. "Economism," closely related to tailism, referred to a primary focus on economic issues, whereas "politicalization" meant turning the workers from economic issues toward recognition of the repressive role of the state and acceptance of the leadership of the party in the struggle against the state. George also complained, "Exceptionalism of the rankest sort is expressed by both the comrades on the Strike Committee, (which we might understand) and by the comrades around the Dist[rict] Office. . . . An opportunist and syndicalist line is followed."[17] "Exceptionalism" referred to the argument, rejected by the Comintern, that the United States was an exception to Marxist theories of economic development; I found no discussion in the Strike Committee minutes on that issue or any indication that it was an issue anywhere. Syndicalism had also been condemned by the party. The party condemned various forms of "Opportunism," but all involved ignoring or misunderstanding the party line. The key point in George's letters is that the local CP leadership and the strike leaders had seriously and repeatedly violated the party line: they were allowing union members to define the issues, were focused solely on economic issues, and were failing to politicize the strike.

In response, Browder wired Darcy with pointed questions regarding the party's activities. George continued to write his long, long letters to Browder, including one outlining the response to Browder's telegram: "The policy remains the same as before."[18]

Because George was not involved in party decision making in San Francisco, it is impossible to know whether he had firsthand knowledge regarding Bridges or the role of the party in the strike. However, one must accept his conclusion that the strike was *not* reflecting the party line. Indeed, his charges of "tailism" sound very much like the complaints by Mike Casey and many others that established union leaders were not able to control their own members.

After the strikes, Communists subjected them to repeated analysis.[19] On July 31, Browder presented to the PolBuro, the U.S. party's highest level of decision making, a long report on his visit to San Francisco. Similar to George, Browder claimed that much of the policy of Local 38-79 was being written in party fraction meetings. (A party fraction was the organized group of party members within a nonparty organization.) He also noted, however, that on one important occasion during his visit, when it came time to implement fraction decisions at a local membership meeting, "our leading comrades, instead of carrying through the policy that had been adopted, considered that they faced an entirely new situation" and ignored the party line. Roy Hudson, secretary of the MWIU, also reported on San Francisco. While generally supportive of local leaders, he indicated that Bridges (he did not say Comrade Bridges) had not carried out a party decision during a Labor Council meeting.[20]

Similar comments about Bridges appear elsewhere. Joseph Zack, a CP functionary in Cleveland in 1934 who was later expelled, told an FBI agent in 1940 that Browder stopped in Cleveland while returning to New York in mid-1934. According to Zack, Browder said about Bridges, "in substance, 'Yes, he's our Number One Man'" and "that he was a headstrong individual, not so easy to get along with, 'but we have to get along with him.'" Similarly, in 1937, Aaron Sapiro, an avowed anti-Communist, told Gerard Reilly, Labor Department solicitor, that Browder had earlier told him that "the party could not control Bridges," and "he [Bridges] was not willing to take any orders from his party superiors, saying that on the west coast 'he was the party.'" In 1971, long after Darcy had been expelled from the CP, he said about Bridges in 1934, "There was no question of bringing him into the party. . . . There was no need for it."[21]

All this suggests that, in the mid-1930s, Bridges's relationship to the CP was like that described later by Joseph Starobin, an important party functionary until 1954; in 1972 Starobin described Bridges as "never a Communist" but instead an "influential" who "enjoyed intimate ties with the Party, usually on his own terms," and "cooperated closely" with CP officials. Such influentials may or may not have been formal party members. They were listened to, consulted with, offered advice, and asked for advice, but were not given directions and were not under party discipline. Understanding Bridges's relationship with the CP requires appreciation of these complications. However, such a complex relation to the CP is incompatible with the depiction of communism as a vast, powerful, tightly disciplined, and espionage-oriented conspiracy, a view shared by the FBI, the House Committee on Un-American Activities, Senator Joseph McCarthy, and many others, including some historians.[22]

In 1934 Darcy seems to have moved a few ILA leaders into positions of leadership in District 13. On June 16, 1934, the District Buro assigned "Comrade Schmidt," apparently Henry Schmidt, as "Chairman of A.F.L. opposition work," but the minutes have no further mention of Schmidt in that position. The minutes of the District Committee for August 20, 1934, record appointment of several new members to the District Buro, including "HB." Bridges once told me he had been "co-opted" onto CP committees—that Darcy had arranged that Bridges could participate in CP activities without being a CP member because of the dangers involved with being a member. In CP usage, the term co-opted usually referred to a person placed on a party committee without having been elected. Minutes of subsequent District Buro meetings fail to mention "HB," as either attending or being given assignments. On October 13, 1934, the District Buro decided, "We meet immediately with the longshoremen to make the final decisions and take up with them the question of a West Coast conference," suggesting not that directions were being given to the longshoremen but instead that the expectation was of working with them.[23]

RGASPI files contain some information after 1934 regarding the CP's relation to waterfront affairs and the relationship between Bridges and the CP. Throughout 1935 the minutes of District 13 Buro meetings suggest that Bridges was not a Buro member because other people were consistently identified as reporting on waterfront matters and because a few minutes refer to "HB" as being invited, requested, or agreeing—but never directed—to undertake something. Further, the District Buro fretted about the need for "closer relations between waterfront and district buro." The District Buro in September 1935 adopted a long list of decisions about the waterfront, but the final one indicated that the entire list was to be sent to the party fraction in the MFP District Council for discussion and approval; the Buro later accepted what may have been a counterproposal from the waterfront fraction. In September 1935, Jack Johnstone, the acting district organizer, described the "party comrades in marine" as "an excellent bunch" and "young in the party," but complained that it was "difficult to get the units to meet" and that "political discussions are infrequent and very inadequate." An unsigned report from CP District 12 (Washington and Oregon), dated July 13, 1935, complained that Bridges and others in San Francisco had been urged to "repudiate" Melnikow and the Pacific Coast Labor Bureau but that they ignored the message.[24] As chapters 6, 7, and 11 make clear, Bridges maintained a close working relationship with Melnikow throughout the late 1930s and early 1940s.

There is a similar pattern at the national level. In July 1935, the CPUSA's Trade Union Commission wondered if Bridges was planning to attend the ILA national convention in New York but there is nothing in the minutes that even implies that body had any authority to direct him to attend. Later that month, the same body recommended that the PolBuro "instruct the California and Seattle districts to establish strong trade union commissions whose main work shall be to advise and work with our fraction on the waterfront," implying that this was not the case. But, note too, that those party bodies were to "advise and work with," not direct, the waterfront fractions.[25] All in all, the correspondence does *not* suggest any sort of smoothly functioning, much less a highly disciplined, organization.

The national CPUSA office and its various committees paid careful attention to San Francisco and the Pacific Coast more generally. As of early 1936, the strength of the CP in San Francisco unions was clearly on the waterfront. Of some 264 CP members in San Francisco AFL unions, 180 were in the waterfront unions—where they made up much less than 5 percent of the total.[26] In January 1936, the PolBuro heard a long report on maritime, probably by Roy Hudson. Though accepting the appropriateness of job actions, the report specified, "job action has been misinterpreted by Lundberg [*sic*] out there to mean actions started by one craft only on the ship," which the report characterized as "the tactic of a madman." "Our policy," the report continued, "is against job action." Nearly two months *before*, Bridges had pushed the adoption of Resolution 47 to limit job actions, that is, the CP was *following* Bridges and the ILA-PCD, not directing or controlling them.[27]

Throughout 1936, much the same pattern appeared: the CPUSA offices in New York reported on events on the Pacific Coast, acknowledged the work of local comrades, but did not send directives. In April, for example, regarding a situation on the San Francisco waterfront, Stachel told the Trade Union Commission, "We informed our comrades to use their own judgment. . . . We have to leave it to the judgment of the comrades." Regarding the *Santa Rosa* affair later that month, the report to the PolBuro, probably by Hudson, acknowledged "the correct tactics and splendid leadership of the comrades there."[28]

National CPUSA officers maintained their distance during the MFP strike. On November 5, 1936, the PolBuro received a long "Report on Marine" that focused on the East Coast seamen. The discussion revealed that the CP was also not in control of the East Coast situation—that there was going to be a strike "whether we like it or not." Of the MFP strike, the report said little other than that the "comrades of the West Coast" were opposed to linking their strike with that of the East Coast and that "the Pacific Coast will have to inform us officially on their policy." That is, the PolBuro was not even making recommendations, much less issuing directives, to its members in the MFP unions. On December 17, the PolBuro received a report on the MFP strikes that began, "We lack information," even though Bridges had been in New York the day before. The report bluntly stated, "We are not dealing with the West Coast strike." In January a report to the PolBuro noted, "It is the opinion of the Party on the [West] Coast that the quicker the strike in the East is settled the better," that is, the Pacific Coast comrades were suggesting action by the PolBuro, not vice versa. A report in the AAS files, dated March 26, 1937, mentions the MFP strike briefly but says little beyond crediting the party for "preventing the West Coast strike from being smashed."[29]

A PolBuro report on April 22, 1937, suggests how little control the CP had over their members on the Pacific Coast: "One of our people, before the Party had any time to finally discuss the question, made a recommendation . . . that the District Convention of the ILA go on record there demanding a national referendum on the question of whether or not to affiliate with the CIO. . . . [I]t was an incorrect proposal."[30] As discussed in chapter 7, once the ILA-PCD voted to join the CIO, the party line was adjusted *after* thousands of ILA members had voted to do so.

In October 1937, the CIO held its first national conference. In November the AAS logged a report on that conference that claimed, "The CPUSA has decisive political influence in the national leadership and district bodies" of a long list of CIO unions and "has an important influence" in those on another long list. The ILWU was absent from both lists. A different view appeared in a an unsigned AAS report in early 1941; though dealing mostly with antiwar activities, the report claimed that "our Party is the decisive political factor" in a list of CIO unions that included "the Longshoremen" and the San Francisco Industrial Union Council.[31]

From 1934 through 1938, the documents in RGASPI that relate to the Pacific Coast unions demonstrate that CP members or influentials (including Bridges) held significant positions in the San Francisco longshore union and in some other maritime unions. Chapter 6 makes clear that they never controlled the

MFP, although they had significant influence in District 2 (Northern California). The Pacific Coast comrades in the maritime unions provided information to the national CP and its various subsidiaries, and occasionally they made requests, but the national CP did not send directives. Nor, so far as the documents demonstrate, did the CP District 13 Buro direct the waterfront fractions. This conclusion does not fit with the claim that, in the CP, decisions were made at the highest levels and transmitted to and carried out without question by lower levels, but it is the pattern revealed by the documents preserved in RGASPI.

The files in RGASPI also contain documents regarding Bridges's role in the CPUSA as of 1936–38. The minutes of the meeting of the CPUSA's Ninth National Convention, held in New York City on June 24–28, 1936, do not record the names of those elected to the Central Committee, but, in April 1937, Earl Browder reported to the AAS, "The Pacific Coast Marine Workers' Federation is under a left leadership. Its chief leader is a member of our Central Committee." The reference is clearly intended to refer to Bridges, although Bridges was *not* the "chief leader" of the MFP, as chapters 6 and 7 indicate. In January 1938, Browder and William Z. Foster were in Moscow and provided the AAS with a list of the Central Committee members first elected in 1936. On the list of twenty-four, number twenty-one was "Rossi." Browder and Foster provided this biography for "Rossi": "ROSSI (Bridges)—CP USA CC member. President of the Longshoremen's and Warehousemen's Union. A strong trade union leader and grass-roots worker but thus far has limited party expertise and experience."[32] A third document in the AAS files, "Note sur les candidatures au B.P. du C.C. du P.C. Etats-Unis" (note on the candidates for the PolBuro of the Central Committee of the CP of the USA), dated "8.2.36" and marked "strictement confidential," presents a list of proposed PolBuro members with brief biographies, followed by several pages of notes in Darcy's handwriting. (Darcy was then the CPUSA representative on the AAS.) On one page, the name *Bridges* appears at the bottom of a list of alternative possibilities for membership. He was not approved.[33]

The RGASPI files and other sources suggest that Bridges's relation with the party was that of an "influential" from 1934 onward, *except* that he was elected to the Central Committee in 1936, a very important exception. Even so, it seems that holding a formal party position did not change Bridges's practice of acting contrary to the party line of the moment when it came to his union. I am guessing that any formal party membership for Bridges—if there ever was a formal membership—likely ended by 1938 both because the AAS as early as March 1936 was warning of the danger that noncitizen members might be deported and because Bridges and the party had become highly aware of exactly that danger for Bridges by early January 1938.[34]

Does Bridges's membership on the Central Committee and perhaps other party committees mean that he was lying all those years when he denied being a party member? One party loyalist did insist to me that Bridges could have served on those committees without being a party member, but that argument strains the meaning of membership almost beyond recognition.[35] Once Bridges initially denied his party ties, any later admission of them could lead to a serious embarrassment for both himself and the Left more generally, as well as potential charges of perjury. Once the "face of the party was hidden," it could not easily be revealed. Of course, the simple answer to the question about lying can only be *yes*, but a simple *yes* is not a complete answer. In the files of the AAS for 1938, there is a critique of the response of party members called before the Dies Committee: "The only thing they were concerned with was to discredit Dies and show how ridiculous was the charge that they were Communists.... But the impression left in the minds of a great many people was that if you can prove somebody a Communist then you are proving something very serious."[36] Given Bridges's status as an alien subject to deportation, proving him to be a member of the Communist Party was, in fact, "something very serious"—so serious as to lead to perjury charges and the possibility of deportation and even imprisonment. And, in fact, those charges were lodged.

In all the later charges that Bridges was a Communist, the events of the mid-1930s were often central. This survey of the relevant evidence, including from RGASPI files, suggests that if Bridges was ever a formal party member, it was likely for only a brief period, but that he was an influential throughout those years and later. Similarly, the evidence indicates that CP members or influentials held significant positions in the San Francisco longshore union and in other maritime unions. This evidence also indicates that those Pacific Coast comrades were largely autonomous, that is, they were not given directives from either the District 13 Buro, the PolBuro in New York, or other party officials. Thus, the picture that emerges is much the same as what the anti-Communist Aaron Sapiro told Gerard Reilly in 1937, "The party could not control Bridges," and Bridges "was not willing to take any orders from his party superiors.'"

Chapters 9, 10, 12–14, and 16 summarize the evidence that the FBI and the Immigration and Naturalization Service separately collected on Bridges's relation to the Communist Party, none of which indicates he was ever under party discipline and none of which suggests that he was ever given orders by the party.

9

Deport Bridges!

1934–1941

Bridges's union activism produced enemies in high places. Since he was not a U.S. citizen, they repeatedly accused him of being a member of the Communist Party as a way to deport him. He found himself repeatedly investigated, charged, and tried from the mid-1930s until the mid-1950s. Failing to find reliable evidence, some of Bridges's opponents in the 1930s resorted to falsification and perjury.

Several published studies have presented Bridges's legal proceedings, but none provide a complete picture. The first scholarly treatment came in Charles Larrowe's *Harry Bridges* (1972); Larrowe did not cite sources, except for short chapter-end essays, and lacked access to important archival information. Stanley I. Kutler, in *The American Inquisition* (1982), drew on Bridges's INS file for a chapter that provides an excellent summary of all the Bridges cases. Ann Fagan Ginger's *Carol Weiss King* (1993) gives several chapters to Bridges's defense, drawing on King's FBI file. Peter Afrasiabi, in *Burning Bridges* (2016), covered much the same ground as Kutler by drawing on Bridges's INS file but added more context. Amanda Frost, in *You Are Not American* (2021), views Bridges's cases as examples of citizenship stripping. None of these researchers used the papers of Richard Gladstein, Norman Leonard, or Telford Taylor, Bridges's lawyers, and none used Bridges's enormous FBI file.[1]

The first phase of these proceedings lasted from 1934 to 1940, when the Immigration and Naturalization Service was part of the Department of Labor, under Secretary Frances Perkins. In May 1934, two weeks after Bridges first came to public attention, the White House received an INS report on his status as an alien. This initial investigation produced no evidence against Bridges, but demands for his deportation soon swelled to a torrent, from business leaders, political figures, and ordinary citizens, including the governors of California and Oregon and the head of the Los Angeles Chamber of Commerce, ultimately leading to an INS hearing in 1939.[2]

Harper "Moke" Knowles served as chairman of the antiradical division of the California branch of the American Legion, which was formed to collect and analyze information on radicals. The FBI later concluded that Knowles, in investigating Bridges, "had probably been engaged in tactics which would not be considered ethical in obtaining affidavits and evidence. . . . [H]e worked in conjunction with various employer groups to such an extent that his operations might be considered to border on anti-unionism." The FBI also reported that, during Bridges's 1939 hearing, Knowles lied or "conveniently forgot" information.[3]

Knowles's committee counted law-enforcement officers among its members and claimed widespread cooperation by police, federal agencies, and business, including the Los Angeles Police Department's Red Squad, Military Intelligence at the Presidio of San Francisco, and Henry Sanborn, an army reserve lieutenant colonel who published the *American Citizen*, an anti-Communist tabloid. The Portland chief of police, Harry M. Niles, directed his officers to work with Knowles, and William Browne, a Portland police detective, was Knowles's counterpart in the Oregon American Legion. Knowles's activities earned him plaudits from the Legion's National Americanism Committee in 1936 for "success in co-ordinating the activities of your Commission with those of various groups in California which seek to expose the Communist activities which have been detrimental to coast payrolls."[4]

Stanley Doyle, nicknamed "Larry," was among the most active in investigating Bridges in the mid- and late 1930s. An Irish American lawyer with a melodramatic flair and a strong anti-Semitic streak, Doyle served as a prosecutor in Oregon before Governor Charles Martin commissioned him as an Oregon special agent. Seeking evidence against Bridges, Doyle ranged up and down the Pacific Coast, worked closely with Knowles and briefly with Sanborn, and reported to Wallace "Buck" Wharton, Martin's executive secretary. FBI investigators determined that Doyle "worked closely with employers' groups," was probably "in the employ of the Waterfront Employers to whom he was selling false information," and had an "unsavory reputation and shady methods of operating."[5]

Sanborn and Doyle hired, as an informant, Arthur Kent, alias Arthur Scott, alias Arthur Margolis. In the late 1920s, Kent served time in San Quentin for burglary. After release from prison, he undertook various CP activities in San Francisco, including a membership drive in 1936–37. In early 1936, Kent offered his services to Sanborn, who introduced him to Doyle. Doyle agreed to pay Kent, who continued his party activities and made weekly reports, which went into Knowles's files. The May 8, 1936, report quotes Kent: "In connection with stamps and book for HD, . . . it would be difficult task to secure larger denominations necessary, i.e. 40¢ stamps. Small ones were easy matter to secure." The "stamps and book for HD" apparently referred to plans to secure a CP membership book and dues stamps for "HD"; the need to secure stamps in large denominations indicates that the dues were for someone receiving a regular income.[6]

In June 1937, Kent, Doyle, and Sanborn went to Portland for the MFP convention. Doyle rented the hotel room next to that of Bridges and had Bridges's room wired with a listening and recording device. Doyle soon dashed off a note to Knowles: "Honestly believe we have Bridges nailed. This prowl netted his C.P. card." Over the next twelve years, several versions appeared regarding who did what to produce the "C.P. card," agreeing only that the Portland INS ended up with a CP membership book in the name of Harry Dorgan. In one version, Doyle gave the membership book to the Portland police chief; in a different version, Kent gave the book to the Portland INS.[7]

What is to be made of this? First, the "HD" for whom Kent was securing a membership book and stamps almost certainly stands for Harry Dorgan. As CP membership director, Kent had access to books and dues stamps, although he noted that it was difficult to secure stamps in large denominations. In January 1937, the date on the book, Kent was directing the CP's membership drive. The dues stamps were ten-cent unemployed stamps, not the larger ones for someone with a steady income. Newspaper photographs of the Dorgan book led William Schneiderman, California CP secretary, to brand it an obvious forgery. Sanborn himself later told an INS officer that the membership book was "phoney." In 1941 the FBI confirmed, "It was not a genuine book issued to Harry Bridges" and speculated that Doyle had created the fake. Kent later said that he had given eleven blank signed party membership cards to Sanborn, including the "Harry Dorgan" card. Regardless of its origin, within twelve months of the Portland MFP convention, two congressional committees received photostatic copies of the membership book, and reference to it or to "Harry Dorgan" pursued Bridges until as late as 1959.[8]

Doyle's activities were not limited to Kent and to wiring hotel rooms. On June 28, 1937, Doyle was present when Roy Norene of the Portland INS took a statement from Herbert Mills, an SUP officer, in which Mills claimed he had been a CP member and attended meetings of the party's "Top Fraction" at which Bridges had been present; he said that Bridges was known in the CP as Canfield or "something similar to Drydan or Dorgan." Asked if Bridges could have attended Top Fraction meetings without being a party member, Mills replied, "Possible but not likely." Five months later, in a subsequent deposition, Mills flatly stated, "I have heard Bridges referred to as Comrade Canfield, Comrade Rossi and also Comrade Dorgan," and "no others were permitted to sit in these [Top Fraction] sessions unless they were bonafide Communists." Shortly before, Doyle wrote to Knowles, "Sanborn and [Captain J. J.] Keegan [of the

Portland Police Department] are attempting to improve a piece of testimony that is already perfect and are on the perjury borderline in their attempt."[9] Doyle was unclear whose testimony was being improved to the point of perjury, but the possibilities are limited to Mills or John Leech, who was also in Portland for the purpose of testifying against Bridges.

Leech, a housepainter, had been active in the CP in Los Angeles but had been expelled. He provided an affidavit on December 8, 1937, the day before Mills's revised statement. Leech's statement, notarized by Keegan, identified Bridges as a CP member and claimed they had both been present at party meetings. Leech swore that Bridges was known by the name Rossi and that he, Leech, was present when Bridges was elected to the Central Committee under that name in 1936. "Rossi" did not appear in Mills's June affidavit but did appear in December.[10]

James Stewart, alias John Ferguson, provided the Portland Red hunters with an affidavit, assisted them in various ways, and testified before the Dies Committee in 1938. Later, in 1950, he contacted Bridges's defense attorneys and offered to help them. Elinor Kahn was dispatched to Britain to interview Stewart. He told Kahn that his testimony in 1937 and 1938 had been "completely untrue" and gave her a long affidavit outlining his activities on behalf of Doyle and others.[11]

Born in Britain, Stewart had been a marine fireman in the early 1930s. In the mid-1930s, he was elected to MFOW office and moved to San Francisco. He joined the CP but soon left. In early 1937, Aaron Sapiro, the SUP's attorney, introduced Stewart to a Portland police officer. Soon after, Doyle confronted Stewart with evidence of insurance fraud, bad checks, and Mann Act violations. Stewart consulted a lawyer, learned his past criminal activities could send him to prison, and then offered Doyle his complete cooperation, which included organizing the 1937 MFP convention against Bridges and securing information on Bridges.[12]

Doyle then used Stewart's past criminal activities to pressure him into making an affidavit. Stewart claimed that Rafael Bonham, of the Portland INS office, "told me that unless I made a statement that Harry Bridges was a Communist the Immigration Service would obtain my deportation." Stewart also claimed that he received $1,500 (equivalent to more than $29,000 in 2022) from Bonham and that Edward Vandeleur of the California State Federation of Labor and various Teamster officials had provided funds to individuals and to the Portland Red Squad. Stewart remained in Portland until mid-1939, assisting the INS and Portland Police. He was eventually deported.[13]

Doyle was centrally involved in devising a lawsuit filed by attorney A. L. Crawford on behalf of Ivan Cox, former secretary of Local 38-79. Filed in December 1937, the suit named as defendants CP District 13, William Schneiderman, Harry Bridges, thirteen other named individuals, and five thousand John and Jane Does. The suit contained dozens of charges against individuals, ranging from the accusation that Bridges had scabbed during the 1921 seamen's strike to the claim that Fredric March, the actor, had contributed funds "to further the cause, teachings and advocacy of communism." Cox, the plaintiff, scarcely appears in the first twenty-five pages of the suit. The suit claimed that an elaborate conspiracy by the CP had caused a shortage in the funds in Local 38-79, for which Cox was responsible. The suit requested damages in the amount of $5.1 million.[14]

Cox subsequently testified that he had heard a rumor that the CP would cause a shortage in the local's funds as a way to discredit him. When a shortage occurred, Cox went to the Secret Service to report the rumor and request assistance. They referred him to Naval Intelligence, which sent him to Army Intelligence, which sent him to the American Legion. Shortly after Cox contacted the American Legion, Doyle called and identified himself as an Oregon agent connected with the FBI. Doyle introduced Cox to Knowles and claimed they had agents who would secure the evidence to prove CP involvement in the shortage of funds. Doyle later claimed to have verified the rumor. Doyle introduced Cox to Bonham and Keegan, who took a statement. Soon Doyle was writing speeches for Cox and sending letters to the editor of the *San Francisco Examiner* in Cox's name. In late November, Doyle exulted, "I have the witness Cox that has a perfect slander and libel suit against the COMMUNIST PARTY and its leaders and wherein we can show the ENTIRE TIE-UP of the subsidiary groups, and expose a lot of left-wing Big Shots." Doyle continued, "This man can also ALLEGE AND PROVE that the N.L.R.B. is a C.P. outfit from Madame Rossiter [NLRB director in San Francisco] down the list to the cheapest stenographer. Also the activities of the Party in the WPA, in our armed forces, in the veterans groups, the grade, high and collegiate schools." Doyle then complained, "I am going to have to give him money for this Thanksgiving dinner for himself and family out of my own pocket."[15]

Doyle never permitted Cox to read the conspiracy complaint. When Cox protested that he didn't know anything about all the people cited as defendants, Doyle responded, "This is a government case, and you're doing a patriotic deed in cooperating," and said that Cox would get $100,000 out of the case. Doyle arranged with Vandeleur to put Cox on the state federation payroll, with no duties, for six months, for a total of $400. In early January 1938, Doyle released five thousand copies of the suit and sent copies of it to all members of Congress, in the expectation that it would "steam the case up a bit." The suit never went to trial, but Cox's affidavit did go to the Dies Committee (see below). Soon after, Cox wrote to Secretary Perkins, "I have learned from bitter experience that Mr. Doyle, Mr. Knowles, and an attorney named A. L. Crawford have been using me as a dupe for their schemes, and have tricked me into making statements and signing my name to documents that are not true."[16]

Bonham tried to secure testimony from Earl King, a former MFOW official. In 1936 King, Ernest Ramsey, and Frank Connor had been convicted of murder on dubious evidence. For the Left and labor in the San Francisco area, the King-Ramsey-Connor case became a cause to rival that of Tom Mooney until the three were paroled in 1939. In early 1938, at Bonham's request, an INS official approached King's brother, Garfield King, a barrister in Vancouver, British Columbia, and read a letter from Bonham. King paraphrased the letter, "If Garfield A. King would advise his brother Earl to furnish the Department with evidence proving that Bridges was a member of the Party, he, Bonham, could possibly use his influence to obtain a pardon for King." Garfield King refused and immediately described the entire episode in a letter to Bridges. Earl King and Ramsey later testified that Doyle had visited them in prison and asked them to testify against Bridges in return for freedom. San Quentin visitor records confirm that Doyle visited King and that Doyle and Stewart (alias Ferguson) visited Ramsey twice.[17]

Doyle claimed not to receive a salary from the state of Oregon, but he received enough funds to support himself and, as he once complained, "a lot of hungry witness [sic] scattered from Seattle to Los Angeles." He also said that A. C. Mattei was providing funds for Sanborn and Keegan. A pillar of the San Francisco business community, a friend and political confidant of Herbert Hoover, Mattei was a vice president of Honolulu Consolidated Oil, a company dependent on ocean shipping and closely linked through interlocking directorates with other Hawaiian interests. J. Edgar Hoover described Mattei as "well known to the San Francisco office" of the FBI. Doyle later claimed that Mattei had reneged on a promise to provide $200 per month to Keegan to maintain the witnesses. Doyle also reported that Keegan obtained $1,200 in San Francisco, source unidentified, for the testimony of Ferguson. Doyle's reference to "certain demands made by the Portland Police on officials of the Brotherhood of Teamsters" was later confirmed when Thomas Lockhart, a Portland attorney, told an FBI agent of "payments" by Teamsters' officials to the Portland Police Department.[18]

Stewart's affidavit in 1950 claimed that efforts against Bridges received financial support from several shipping company executives and AFL unions, especially the IBT and the California State Federation, and that Mattei had paid him more than $5,000 to cooperate with the INS and Portland Police. Stewart also quoted Doyle as saying that Pacific Bell had provided the recording equipment in Portland.[19]

By early 1938, Knowles, Doyle, Sanborn, and Keegan et al. had produced affidavits and the Harry Dorgan membership book as evidence to justify a deportation hearing. Up until this time, the INS and Department of Labor had regularly received demands to deport Bridges but no evidence to justify doing so.[20]

The INS was then part of the Labor Department. In her oral history, Frances Perkins stated that, when she became secretary of labor, she knew "the Immigration Service had been used improperly to get rid of certain militant and effective labor people." She resolved that nothing of that sort would happen in her administration. When the Portland INS office forwarded copies of the affidavits and Dorgan membership book and requested a warrant for Bridges, Perkins consulted with President Roosevelt. She recalled that they agreed that the Labor Department should carry out the law, "but not . . . let our imagination run away with us."[21]

Perkins sent Gerard Reilly to the West Coast to evaluate the evidence, because, Reilly flatly stated, "the Department itself suspected that some of the evidence was manufactured." In mid-October 1937, Reilly prepared a full report, identifying Doyle as "apparently on the payroll of some employer's association or the legion" and giving him credit for the Mills and Leech depositions. Reilly did not know of Kent's ties to Doyle or Sanborn but reported on Kent's deposition. Reilly fully described a deposition by Lawrence Milner, an undercover agent of the Oregon National Guard, who claimed that he had served as chauffeur for CP figures in Oregon and Washington and identified Bridges as a party member. In addition, Reilly reported, "Sapiro has come forward and offered in behalf of Lundeberg to fill in all the missing chinks in the prosecution's case."[22]

Reilly described Bonham as "an official of considerable force and ability," but "his mental outlook is that of a retired Army officer." Reilly considered that Keegan's "ability is very latent," but reported that Keegan considered Doyle "a racketeer and blackmailer." Reilly agreed that Doyle's "activities indicate he might be quite capable of framing witnesses." Reilly described Governor Charles Martin as "a charming and colorful figure, but frankly fascistic in his conversation," who was "out to make political capital of the case." Doyle refused to meet Reilly. In 1940 J. Edgar Hoover confidentially informed Attorney General Robert Jackson that Bonham "has had a rather stormy career," that "a certain faction has called him a 'red baiter,'" and that he was considered "a hard man to handle."[23]

Reilly analyzed the witnesses, beginning with Sapiro. Noting that Sapiro was counsel for the SUP, Reilly indicated he had come forward "at Lundberg's [sic] suggestion, although he said that Lundberg did not want to be brought into the case, as he feared that any deposition against Bridges may be regarded as working class prosecution, and hence a boomerang, unless Bridges was first discredited in the public mind." Reilly reported on Sapiro at length, apparently accepted his account of communist manipulation in the maritime unions, and suggested that "Sapiro's best source of information is Norma Perry."[24]

Reilly was critical of the testimony of Mills, Leech, and Milner. The Mills deposition, Reilly thought, had likely come through "some tie-up" with Sapiro. Leech was "open to reproach of being bought" and had probably testified "due largely to police intimidation." Bonham considered Milner the cornerstone of the case. Reilly disagreed, suggesting that his testimony could be readily discredited and listed the reasons: "(a) he was paid to do it, (b) his [undercover] job was precarious as it had been manufactured just to keep him on a public payroll, and hence he would try to build himself up (1) by exaggerating his acquaintance with prominent labor leaders and the extent of their radicalism, (2) by giving Martin and his military stooges the sort of information they welcomed; and (c) he is too stupid to stand up well if questioned on matters of C.P. doctrines and policy."[25]

Reilly personally interviewed Bridges in New York, on October 18, 1937. The examination was short. Asked if he was then or ever had been a member of the Communist Party, Bridges replied, "No." Asked if he had ever been known as Rossi, Harry Dorgan, or Canfield, Bridges repeated "No" each time. In a series of questions, Reilly explored the information from the Mills, Leech, and Stewart affidavits. Bridges readily admitted to meeting, sometimes secretly, with a wide range of union leaders and CP members but consistently denied attending party meetings, being a party member, or taking part in party activities. He indicated that he knew who Doyle was, that Doyle had been responsible for wiring his room in Portland, and that Doyle worked for one or more employer associations.[26]

Perkins summarized this way: "Milner was the only witness who was not either being subsidized by the Red Squad of the Portland police or who was not obviously an ally of Lundberg [sic], who had already emerged at that time as a bitter rival of Bridges in the Maritime Federation of the Pacific. . . . [A]ny testimony Milner might give would probably be impeached since he had committed perjury at the Dirk de Jonge trial." She discounted the testimony of Sapiro, because he had been disbarred in New York after conviction in the federal courts and subsequently been disbarred in Illinois. Overall, she concluded, "Because of the dubious character of these witnesses, the fact that their stories did not corroborate, and because of the complete absence of documentary evidence, I was advised by the Solicitor [Reilly] not to issue a warrant of arrest without further investigation."[27]

Those who wanted charges brought against Bridges did not share Reilly's assessment. In January 1938, James L. Houghteling, commissioner of the INS, outlined plans for a hearing. When news of those preparations reached the press, Bridges wrote to Perkins, denied a hearing was necessary, and urged none be held. In response, Perkins sent Bridges a disclaimer, drafted by Reilly, stating, "Should the Department proceed with hearings, it does not mean that it has adopted the view that the evidence . . . is necessarily trustworthy."[28] At this juncture, it would seem, Perkins saw a hearing as a way to clear the air rather than as justified on the basis of reliable evidence. Years later, she stated that she "did not believe that Bridges was a Communist."[29]

Powerful members of Congress joined the chorus demanding that Bridges be deported. On January 25, 1938, the Senate Committees on Commerce and on Education and Labor, in joint session, voted to request that Perkins provide them with the complete file on Bridges. Perkins's reply stated there had been no evidence against Bridges until the materials produced from the Portland INS office, recounted Reilly's work, and concluded that she was unwilling to send the file, given the likelihood of a formal INS hearing. Senator Royal Copeland (D-NY), chairman of the Commerce Committee and longtime political ally of Joseph Ryan, again requested the full file, promising complete confidentiality and an executive session for Perkins to testify. Perkins accordingly sent the file, stressing in her covering statement the need for confidentiality to protect potential witnesses. Four days later, Copeland announced that his committee had proof that Bridges was a Communist and subject to deportation; the proof he described included the Dorgan membership book and an affidavit linking Bridges to Communist leaders.[30]

On February 10, in a closed session with Copeland's committee, Reilly summarized his analysis of the case, noting the lack of documentary evidence and the lack of corroboration among the witnesses. The newspaper version of his testimony, however, stated only that the INS had recommended deportation and that early action was anticipated. As headlines blared these charges, Bridges telegraphed Copeland, called him a "mouthpiece of shipowners and reactionary interests," demanded to appear before the committee to respond to the charges, and claimed that Copeland would "dare not have me appear as you know we possess evidence that will force you to retract your statements." The committee voted unanimously not to hear Bridges.[31]

Bridges's repeated demands to respond to the charges against him and to present refutation were not empty rhetoric. His supporters and attorneys had collected material that indicated much about the Knowles-Sanborn-Doyle-Keegan effort. A janitor in the Veterans' Building in San Francisco, which housed American Legion officers, including that of Knowles, was sympathetic to Bridges and, during the night, brought material from Knowles's files to Bridges's attorneys, which they photocopied so the janitor could replace them before morning. Bridges's attorneys' files include some ninety items apparently from Knowles's files or his trash between late 1935 and early 1938. In addition to their knowledge of Knowles's activities, Bridges and his attorneys may have had information from La Follette Committee investigators.[32]

In addition to Garfield King's letter, Bridges's attorneys had other affidavits pointing to subornation of perjury. In one, dated before his statement in Portland, Leech stated, "To my best knowledge and belief Harry Bridges is not a Communist or a member of the Communist Party, nor was he at any such meetings where I was present," and that he had been offered as much as $10,000 to swear to the contrary.[33]

When the Copeland committee denied Bridges the possibility of testifying, he wired Perkins to request an INS hearing: "Copelands obvious attempt to prejudice my case requires immediate hearing."[34] Preparations for a hearing were already under way. A warrant was served in Baltimore on March 2, 1938, and the hearing was set for San Francisco in late April. Carol King, a New York attorney, close to the CP, and a leading immigration law specialist, joined Bridges's San

Francisco lawyers. She remained with the Bridges defense through 1945, and she developed a close, if sometimes prickly, working relationship with Richard Gladstein and Aubrey Grossman. Gladstein and Grossman were in their early thirties, but King was in her midforties and far more experienced in immigration law, a difference that she drew upon when she sometimes signed her letters as "Mother" or "Mama" and, after the birth of Richard and Carolyn Gladstein's first child, as "Grandma."[35]

A decision in another case, in which Joseph Strecker admitted CP membership but was found not to be subject to deportation, brought a delay in the Bridges hearing until an appeal could clarify appropriate grounds for deportation. However, the delay brought a storm of criticism. Keegan wrote to Sapiro, "The Madame [Perkins] has slipped another one over." The mayor of Portland demanded that the hearing proceed, and the American Legion national executive committee joined in the chorus. Joseph Ryan claimed that the delay proved Perkins was protecting Bridges and had suppressed the evidence.[36]

On August 12, 1938, the new House Special Committee on Un-American Activities under chairman Martin Dies held its first hearing. The next day, the committee moved to the topic that was to be its raison d'être over the next several decades—the danger of domestic communism. John Frey, vice president of the AFL, denounced the CIO as part of a CP conspiracy, proclaimed that Bridges was a Communist, and presented the committee with a photostatic copy of the Dorgan membership book. Soon after, a committee investigator charged that Bridges was being advised, instructed, and protected by "an outstanding official" in the Department of Labor. At the end of August, Dies demanded that deportation proceedings begin immediately.[37]

Bridges denounced the Dies Committee charges as "lies" and part of a "conspiracy of reactionary employers and A. F. of L. leaders to smash the new labor movement and the New Deal on the Pacific Coast." He argued that the attack on him was motivated by "my respect for, and loyalty to, President Roosevelt and the principles of the New Deal" and part of efforts to defeat New Deal supporters in the 1938 congressional elections. However, at the same time, Bridges added fuel to Dies's fire by refusing to denounce the CP or reject its support, describing party members as "friends of the working class and the small business men and farmers."[38]

Dies called Keegan to testify, who identified Bridges as a Communist and offered the affidavits of Stewart, Mills, Leech, and Kent. Next to the witness stand came Stewart, under the name John E. Ferguson.[39]

In December 1938, amid growing pressures for a hearing, Robert Wohlforth, executive secretary of the La Follette Committee, told Reilly, "Sanborn, Doyle, Harper Knowles and [others] . . . are really undercover agents of the Industrial Association of San Francisco and the Committee has evidence of their being on its payroll." By then Reilly had learned of similar connections for Kent and

Norma Perry and of Bonham's efforts to suborn King. Perkins continued to insist that there was little reliable evidence against Bridges and that the Strecker case appeal prevented them from holding a hearing to examine what evidence there was.[40]

On January 7, 1939, Roosevelt's cabinet discussed the Bridges case. Harold Ickes, secretary of the interior, confided to his diary, "Miss Perkins is under a great attack. . . . There are actually members of the House of Representatives who are talking about impeaching her, and she has been greatly worried." Perkins told the cabinet the evidence against Bridges was unreliable, but James Farley, postmaster general and key political adviser to Roosevelt, suggested, "Failure to deport him was going [doing?] great harm to the Democratic party. . . . [W]hether he was deportable or not, Bridges ought to be sent out of the country for the sake of the Democratic party." Roosevelt overruled Farley, however, and, according to Ickes, "made it clear that Bridges ought not to be deported unless there was legal justification."[41]

On January 24, Parnell Thomas, a conservative Republican from New Jersey, introduced a resolution to impeach Perkins, Reilly, and Houghteling. Drew Pearson, the nationally syndicated newspaper columnist, reported that Dies had put Thomas up to the ploy and that Republican congressional leaders opposed the move. Headlines nonetheless blared the charges against Perkins, and the House Judiciary Committee held hearings before voting unanimously that there was insufficient evidence to proceed. On March 24, the House tabled the Thomas resolution.[42]

While the impeachment case was pending, Bridges met privately with Perkins when she was in San Francisco and told her not to hold back on his account and to do what was necessary to save herself politically. Shortly afterward, in Washington, Bridges told Ickes that "he was ready for the hearing and he welcomed it. He predicted that the hearing would disclose facts which would be very uncomfortable to some other people." Bridges's confidence seemed well placed. On March 10, 1939, Reilly again reviewed the situation for Perkins and noted the only direct evidence that Bridges had even mentioned the use of force and violence against the government came from the Milner deposition, which "even if believed (and it is sure to be contradicted) merely shows prophecy and not advocacy."[43]

The Strecker case was decided in April 1939. A hearing for Bridges was scheduled for July 10. Perkins chose James Landis, dean of the Harvard Law School, as the hearing officer. The hearing was to be in an INS facility on Angel Island in San Francisco Bay, accessible only by ferry. Earlier, Aubrey Grossman, representing Bridges, had requested that the hearing be closed to the press, and Bonham had expressed concerns that the hearing might be "open indiscriminately to mass picketing . . . communist demonstrations, intimidation of witnesses." Angel Island was apparently chosen as a way to control attendance and prevent people from gathering outside, but the press was not barred. Every day of the hearing, the prosecution attorneys, Bridges, and his attorneys, Carol King, Richard Gladstein, Aubrey Grossman, and Ben Margolis, boarded a special boat that took them to Angel Island. Betty Jacqueline, fourteen years old, accompanied her father every day. Agnes did not. She and Harry had periodically separated over the previous several years. Bridges's attorney brought an enormous collection of documents regarding possible witnesses, since they were not given an advance list of witnesses. Their files took up a steamer trunk, two suitcases, and several card files, including an index. Though open to the press and the public, the hearing's location limited the number who could attend.[44]

The INS led with Milner, Leech, and Sapiro, all of whom Reilly considered unreliable. Bridges's defense attorneys quickly destroyed the credibility of each witness. The Dorgan membership book was introduced not as evidence but for identification. Other government witnesses proved less effective than the first three, for they had less evidence to offer. The defense revealed much of the Doyle-Knowles efforts to produce evidence, though Doyle refused to testify.[45]

Among those who had worked with the Portland INS officers, Mills could not be located. Stewart (alias Ferguson) later claimed he had expected to be called as a witness but was told by Bonham that "the defense had enough on me," and that he and James Engstrom, former MFP president and another potential witness, should "get out of town." The FBI later reported that Ferguson was not called "because of his unsavory reputation" and because "it was known he had falsely testified before a Congressional Committee." Kent was not called as a witness. He had been convicted of burglary in Los Angeles, but, through interventions by Keegan, Knowles, Sanborn, and others, Governor Frank Merriam had commuted his sentence.[46]

The hearing lasted from July 10 to September 14, with forty-five days of testimony. The INS called thirty-two witnesses, the defense twenty-seven. The high point came toward the end, with testimony by Bridges, cross-examination by the INS attorneys, and a colloquy between Landis and Bridges. Bridges responded to some of the previous testimony, denying or explaining some of what previous witnesses had said. He discussed his family and youth in Australia, emphasizing the Australian Labor Party as a source of his own views on politics and emphasizing he had already come to those conclusions before the CP existed. He spoke of his experiences on the docks, the need for union organizing, and the 1934 strikes. He acknowledged accepting help from any source, including the CP, and meeting with and discussing issues with CP members and leaders. He emphasized that the CP was more focused on theory but that he and members of his union were concerned with workplace issues. He acknowledged being a Marxist. Asked about the University of Washington speech, he replied that he had been misquoted. Throughout, he was clearly in command, sometimes giving answers that brought chuckles from Landis and laughter from some in the

All the participants in the INS hearing had to take the ferry to Angel Island. This photo, on July 10, 1939, shows Bridges, nattily dressed as always, with his daughter, Betty Jacqueline, holding his hand, and Carol King, one of his attorneys. Betty Jacqueline, age fourteen, attended every day of the hearing. (*News Call Bulletin* photo, AAA-5795, courtesy of San Francisco History Center, San Francisco Public Library)

audience. At times, Landis and Bridges held their own conversation about the matters raised by the lawyers. Bridges's testimony took three days. The transcript for the entire hearing came to nearly eight thousand pages.

Given the doubts Reilly had expressed and the effectiveness with which Bridges's defense attorneys destroyed the government case, questions immediately arose as to the seriousness of the government's case. Doyle, as early as November 1937, claimed that Reilly was revealing evidence. The Dies Committee repeated that charge and claimed that Bridges had been shown his complete INS file.

Bridges denied he was ever shown his file, although the examination by Reilly in October 1937 had ranged over nearly all the material collected up to that point, and the Dies Committee hearings themselves revealed even more of it. Aubrey Grossman told me that Bridges's attorneys knew Reilly was friendly but nothing more and that some information came from Carol King who, through contacts in New York and Washington, knew things she didn't share with the other defense attorneys. Bridges's attorneys were not provided a list of the witnesses, but the Copeland and Dies hearings, the material from Knowles's office, and their own investigations gave them a good sense of the possibilities.[47] Thus, the defense knew a good deal about the evidence against Bridges, but Bridges and his attorneys always insisted that the Department of Labor did not help them.

However, documents in the Bridges case files do indicate that the attorneys had some access to INS records. An unsigned "Memo Re Ferguson," for example, includes information from Ferguson/Stewart's statements to Norene on November 22, 1937, and April 13, 1938.[48] More significantly, one document in those files suggests, at the very least, that someone, perhaps Carol King or some source in Washington, had access to Reilly's memorandum analyzing the Portland evidence. An unsigned, unattributed, and undated five-page statement titled simply "Re: Harry Bridges," apparently prepared before the 1939 hearing, closely paraphrases the Reilly memorandum.[49] In a number of places, the two documents are virtually identical, for example:

Re: Harry Bridges

"Sapiro suing Bridges for libel stated that Lundberg [sic] did not want to be brought into the case for fear of being regarded as a labor union leader who was splitting the labor movement, i.e., working class prosecution, unless Bridges was first discredited."

"Sapiro's best source of information is Norma Perry now secretary to Lundberg, formerly sec to Bridges."

"Possibility of destroying [Milner's] testimony (1) He was paid for it; (2) his job was precarious as it was manufactured just to keep him on the public payroll; (3) He is to establish [blank space, apparently indicating missing material] did keep him if questioned on Communist Party doctrines and policies."

Reilly's Memorandum

Sapiro "said that Lundberg did not want to be brought into the case, as he feared that any deportation against Bridges may be regarded as working class prosecution, and hence a boomerang, unless Bridges was first discredited in the public mind."

"Sapiro's best source of information is Norma Perry."

Milner "could be readily discredited in the public mind at least because (a) he was paid to do it, (b) his job was precarious as it had been manufactured just to keep him on a public payroll . . . and (c) he is too stupid to stand up well if questioned on matters of C.P. doctrines and policy."

"Re: Harry Bridges" is a draft, apparently dictated, perhaps over the phone. It contains a number of blank spaces, some filled in by hand, and a number of handwritten corrections. While its source remains a mystery, it is nonetheless clear that Bridges's attorneys knew nearly all of what the Labor Department knew regarding the key witnesses. In March 1938, they received documents regarding Sapiro's disbarment in New York.[50]

Sometime before the hearing, they also received a great deal of information from an anonymous telephone informant, including comments regarding Mattei's funding for Keegan's activities and accurate predictions that Kent would not testify and that Doyle could not be made to testify. The only significant information they did not have in advance was Milner's prior perjury. Caroline Decker was then secretary to Richard Gladstein; she told me it was not until the day of Milner's testimony that she thought of the possibility that Milner had perjured himself in the De Jonge trial and that the defense then made strenuous efforts to secure the necessary evidence on time.[51]

Landis took until late December to prepare his report. In 150 pages, he thoroughly reviewed the testimony, made clear he did not believe the government's witnesses, but did find evidence for the defense lawyers' arguments for a conspiracy by Knowles, Doyle, and others. Landis thought Bridges, as witness, had shown "candor." He considered Bridges "radical" in his views, but concluded that the government had failed to prove that Bridges was or ever had been a member of the Communist Party. Perkins accepted the report and dismissed the charges against Bridges.

All were unprepared for the storm the decision generated. Landis was deluged by hate mail. Any hopes that the hearing would end calls for Bridges's deportation were soon dashed. On June 13, 1940, the House voted 330–42 for a bill by A. Leonard Allen (D-LA) that directed the attorney general to arrest and deport Bridges, "notwithstanding any other provision of law." Attorney General Robert Jackson considered the bill an unconstitutional bill of attainder, and the White House staff fretted about political damage in the midst of what promised to be a close reelection campaign, regardless of whether Roosevelt signed or vetoed. Jackson was assigned to prevent passage of the Allen bill in the Senate. With assistance from Senator Richard Russell of Georgia, Jackson secured a compromise as a result of which the Allen bill was killed. Russell was acting purely from constitutional considerations, not from any desire to protect Bridges, whom he had previously referred to as "undoubtedly a Communist who believes and teaches the overthrow of our Government by force and violence."[52]

Soon after the Allen bill died in the Senate, and as part of the compromise that produced that result, the INS was transferred from Labor to Justice, the grounds for deportation were modified from party membership to party "affiliation," and Jackson ordered the FBI to investigate Bridges, beginning a second round of investigations, hearings, and trials. By the early 1940s, the scattered, sometimes competing, sometimes amateurish anti-Communist efforts of the American Legion, local red squads, the National Guard, Military Intelligence, and INS during the 1930s had largely given way to the FBI—more centralized, better funded, and often more professional.[53]

For Harry Bridges, the results soon appeared. Beginning with the 1939 hearing and, especially, the political furor that followed it, Bridges's life and work proceeded along two tracks. One was his work as a union leader and his private life as a husband and father. The other consisted of FBI and INS investigations, legal charges, more hearings, and appeals—a seemingly never-ending process lasting with minor interruptions from 1939 until 1955.

If at First You Don't Succeed: Deportation

1940–1945

As the nation moved toward greater involvement in the wars raging in Europe and Asia, officials in Washington moved toward another effort to deport Bridges, one that lasted throughout the entire period of U.S. involvement in World War II. The 1939 INS hearing relied on evidence produced by Portland police, INS officials, and a posse of no-holds-barred anticommunists. The next stage was informed by exhaustive FBI investigations and carried out with the close involvement of the attorney general and his handpicked subordinates. Previous efforts to secure evidence had involved forgery and suborning of perjury. Now the FBI engaged in illegal wiretapping and burglaries. Bridges, in turn, required a robust defense, both public and legal, to mobilize nationwide support and persuade the Supreme Court.

Attorney General Robert Jackson's political maneuvers to kill the Allen bill led directly to a new INS hearing for Bridges, this time based on the Alien Registration Act—often called the Smith Act—which Congress approved in June 1940. Instead of being charged with *currently* being a Communist Party *member*, Bridges could now be charged with having been *affiliated at some time* with the IWW, MWIU, or CP, each of which was alleged to violate the Smith Act. According to Jackson, the change was specifically intended "to reach Bridges." Jackson recalled that Roosevelt had become "very anti-Communist—militantly so," after the CPUSA's response to the Molotov-Ribbentrop Pact had made it "all too obvious that they were Kremlin controlled." Roosevelt, Jackson said, "was fed up with Bridges and with all those people" and "wanted the deportation accomplished."[1]

In June 1940, Roosevelt moved the INS from the Labor Department to the Justice Department. Jackson then directed the FBI to investigate Bridges, fulfilling commitments he had made to block the Allen bill. J. Edgar Hoover had long since made up his mind about Bridges. In August 1936, shortly after Bridges became ILA-PCD president, Hoover assured Roosevelt that the union "was practically controlled by Communists." However, the FBI opened a file on Bridges only in 1940. On August 27, 1940, Matthew Maguire, assistant to Jackson, sent Hoover six specific questions for the FBI to address to demonstrate that Bridges was ever affiliated with an organization that "believes in, advises, advocates, or teaches the overthrow of Government by force or violence." Maguire's sixth question stressed the need for proof that Bridges was not only so affiliated but also aware of the organization's position on overthrowing the government. The enormous file created by the FBI contains nothing indicating that FBI officials were guided by Maguire's sixth question, and that issue was never raised in Bridges's various hearings and trials.[2]

Hoover flew to San Francisco to demonstrate his "personal command" of the Bridges investigation. There he explained to the press that the investigation would pursue three questions: whether Bridges is or had ever been a CP member, what the CP is and what its activities are, and what Bridges's "general activities" have been. Hoover then placed Assistant Director E. J. Connelley in charge and returned to Washington. The investigation received the code name HARBIM (*Har*ry *B*ridges *Im*migration *M*atter).[3]

Hoover often choose Connelley for difficult assignments. A small man with a pencil mustache, Connelley began with a thorough review of the 1939 INS hearing. Noting that "practically all the witnesses . . . were vulnerable as to some situation in their background," he faulted the INS for not investigating more carefully. Nearly all potential witnesses interviewed by the FBI were asked about previous convictions, previous interviews about Bridges, and other situations that might affect their credibility. Connelley was also critical of evidence provided by an "outside agency"—presumably the American Legion and Larry Doyle—and described some of it as "definitive, deliberate fraud." He criticized the INS for accepting witnesses' statements "at their face value" and failing to corroborate informants' statements.[4] Ironically, those very criticisms apply to the two key witnesses the prosecution relied on for the second Bridges hearing.

As part of Connelley's exhaustive investigation into the witnesses and evidence from the 1939 hearing, agents interviewed and sometimes reinterviewed all the witnesses, nearly everyone whose name appeared in the original testimony or subsequent interviews, and sometimes people mentioned in those secondary interviews. Many interviewees said they thought Bridges was a Communist but had no evidence. One had been told Bridges joined in 1936; another swore that Norma Perry had recruited him in 1934. Connelley concluded that none of the previous witnesses had sufficient credibility to be used again. Agents also undertook an issue-by-issue analysis of the *Waterfront Worker* and related publications.[5]

All FBI field offices submitted detailed responses to Connelley's initial request for information on Bridges and the legal status of the CP. Many reported no information on Bridges. Some provided many pages detailing Bridges's visits to various cities without connecting him to the CP.[6] Hundreds of pages on the legal status of the CP contained nothing about Bridges. The FBI apparently found nothing of interest in Bridges's tax returns.[7]

FBI agents had difficulty interviewing Joseph Ryan, who had repeatedly called Bridges a Communist. B. K. Sackett of the New York FBI office reported that, "for approximately two and a half weeks," Ryan had been "on a 'real bender' and his office was having considerable difficulty in trying to straighten him out." Ryan finally told the FBI agents that he had "absolutely no information" that Bridges was a Communist.[8] Paul Scharrenberg, equally prominent in calling Bridges a Communist, also "could offer no proof." Edward Vandeleur, John McLaughlin, John O'Connor, A. H. Petersen, Paddy Morris, and Selim Silver (a former ISU officer) all agreed that Bridges was a Communist but could offer no evidence.[9]

In mid-October, Connelly reported that things were "progressing satisfactorily" but acknowledged difficulty obtaining "fairly substantial people who are able to testify." On October 31, he told Hoover, "It is believed that we have more or less conclusively shown that HARRY BRIDGES is a member of the Communist Party," but he subsequently admitted there was "no documentary evidence listing Bridges as a member of the Communist Party" and that the case therefore hinged on "former Communists" who could testify that Bridges attended CP meetings and associated with "some sixty-nine well-known Communists." The FBI's report to Jackson, however, admitted of no doubts: "HARRY BRIDGES has been a member of and/or affiliated with the Communist Party. . . . He has participated in and has been an integral part of the activities of the Communist Party . . . and in such capacity has furthered the activities, ambitions, and policies of such Communist Party."[10]

Connelley delivered the massive report—more than 4,000 pages—to Jackson in November 1940. Bridges's attorneys were denied a copy. Part I, 1,059 pages, dealt with Bridges's membership in or affiliation with the Communist Party. The remainder provided either "information as to the illegal status of the Communist Party," including extensive quotations from CP publications, or detailed interviewees considered unreliable or irrelevant.[11]

Jackson appointed Clarence N. Goodwin as a special assistant attorney general for the Bridges case. A former justice of the Illinois Appellate Court and a constitutional law expert, Goodwin spent two months studying the FBI's long report. He concluded that it offered sufficient new evidence to justify another hearing but also flatly stated, "There is no direct evidence that the alien was ever a member of the Communist Party." Goodwin characterized the report as indicating that Bridges held a "privileged status" with the CP, with access to party leaders and meetings, which he thought might demonstrate "affiliation within the meaning of the statute."[12] Those reservations and uncertainties soon disappeared from the prosecution, even from Goodwin's own statements.

When Jackson had not acted by December 16, Hoover assured the press, "Our report confirms the belief that Bridges is a Communist and that the Communist party advocates overthrow of the United States government." On January 28, the House Immigration Committee again took up the Allen bill. Jackson was told, "Many members of the House are becoming very restive" over delays in the Bridges case. On February 12, 1941, although Goodwin had not yet completed his detailed analysis, Jackson announced he was ordering a new hearing for Bridges. The hearing was set for March 31, in San Francisco.[13]

Jackson designated Goodwin as senior counsel for the INS and Albert Del Guercio as lead prosecutor. Connelley, Goodwin, Del Guercio, and other special assistants to the attorney general developed a general strategy for the hearing: first call Bridges to establish basic facts regarding his immigration status, next call Benjamin Gitlow to explain CP ideology, and then bring witnesses to establish Bridges's relation to the CP. They wanted Bruce Hannon as an early witness, expecting he would repeat his testimony from 1939; they would then bring witnesses rebutting Hannon so they could charge him with perjury. By charging Hannon with perjury early in the hearing, they hoped to deter other witnesses from testifying falsely and persuade "important witnesses . . . to testify fully." The plan failed because Hannon had enlisted in the Canadian Air Force and was not available, but perjury charges were brought against a witness late in the hearing.[14]

Jackson's choice for hearing officer was Charles Sears, a Republican and retired judge from New York's state court system. The hearing began on March 31, in the San Francisco Federal Building, blanketed by U.S. marshals and INS security officials. Bridges's attorneys, as before, were Carol King, Richard Gladstein, and Aubrey Grossman. Goodwin's opening statement bore little resemblance to his previous analysis—he claimed flatly that Bridges had been a member of the IWW, was a member of and affiliated with the CP, and had been affiliated with the MWIU. Del Guercio, pugnacious, even bullying, throughout the trial, delighted in accusing Bridges's attorneys of being Communists. Connelley observed, "While Albert Del Guercio may not be the best trial lawyer in the world, he certainly does not let the defense attorneys push him around."[15]

The FBI had accumulated an enormous body of material issued by the CP or its affiliates, beginning with the "Communist Manifesto," to establish that the CP advocated, in the words of the Smith Act, "the overthrow or destruction" of the government "by force or violence." Agents interviewed former CP leaders and members, including Benjamin Gitlow and Jay Lovestone, both once highly placed CP leaders, both expelled in 1929. According to Gitlow, the party concluded, early in the 1920s, that the overthrow of the government would come when "most of the people wanted a change" and that "capital would resist," leading to violence. Lovestone differed: "The Party had recognized the historic inevitability [of violence], but that this had been the thought for but a short time. He did not say that in a legal sense they had advocated the overthrow of the Government by force and violence." Lovestone was not called as a witness. After Gitlow's initial interview, the FBI purchased his books and papers for $1,000, hired him "to analyze and supplement" his books and papers, and paid him as an expert witness, with the total exceeding $2,000 (equivalent to more than $38,000 in mid-2022).[16]

Hoover and Connelley talked with Gitlow "at some length" regarding "the testimony expected from him." Unlike Gitlow's initial interview, his testimony left no doubt that the CP had always been committed to overthrowing the government by force or violence. Bridges's attorneys did not cross-examine Gitlow, deeming his evidence irrelevant since Bridges had not been a CP member. Connelley was very pleased with Gitlow's testimony.[17] Thus, Gitlow launched his career as a professional witness.

A long list of witnesses then sought to establish Bridges's affiliation with the IWW, MWIU, and especially the CP. Bridges's attorneys thoroughly cross-examined all the witnesses, raising doubts about nearly all. The only other evidence consisted of issues of the *Waterfront Worker*, presented as proof of Bridges's affiliation with the MWIU and hence the CP. Bridges's attorneys disputed those claims, arguing that Bridges and the others had taken over the paper only in September 1933 (see chapter 3). The defense then presented a long list of witnesses, which INS attorneys worked to discredit.[18]

Sears denied requests by Bridges's defense attorneys to call Frances Perkins and Gerard Reilly, presumably to discuss their earlier findings, and refused to allow defense witnesses to testify to Bridges's good character. Wayne Morse did testify that Bridges was "a good trade unionist" who never said or did anything to suggest he was a Communist, but the INS argued that Morse's testimony was irrelevant. Bridges testified in his own defense, as he had in 1939, when his testimony had been almost a friendly conversation between Bridges and Landis. In 1941 Bridges appeared nervous when facing Del Guercio's pugnacious grilling, but he held up well. The hearing concluded on June 12, having produced more than seventy-five hundred pages of testimony. In the end, Sears based his decision primarily on Bridges's involvement with the *Waterfront Worker* and on the testimony of James O'Neil and Harry Lundeberg.[19]

O'Neil had become editor of the MFP's newspaper, the *Voice of the Federation*, late in 1936. Fired by the MFP annual convention in 1937, he became publicity director for Bridges and the CIO for a year. FBI agents interviewed O'Neil repeatedly. They reported that, during the second interview, O'Neil said that he had once seen Bridges pasting dues stamps into a CP membership book and had taken part in meetings with Bridges and CP officials, but that "BRIDGES never at any time attended any Communist Party meetings." A stenographer recorded that interview. O'Neil declined to sign anything and refused to testify. He ignored subpoenas but was taken into custody by U.S. marshals and sentenced to sixty days in prison for contempt of court. On the witness stand on April 28, O'Neil refused to acknowledge his previous statements. He was followed to the witness stand by the stenographer for his second interview, who read her transcription into the record. Del Guercio declared it "the most crucial in the case."[20]

Connelley recommended immediate perjury charges against O'Neil. Attorney General Jackson, however, denied permission because immediate charges "may well create the unintended impression that the Government is attempting to intimidate witnesses." That impression was not unintended. Connelly and INS commissioner Lemuel Schofield were "very anxious to go ahead" specifically because of "the psychological effect . . . on the other witnesses." The Justice Department reversed itself, and a grand jury indicted O'Neil on June 3. The U.S. attorney in San Francisco told one of Bridges's supporters that "he would not have prosecuted [O'Neil] except that the FBI insisted on it." The Bridges defense committee helped pay for O'Neil's defense, but he was convicted of perjury and sentenced to three years in prison.[21]

Very late in the hearing, Harry Lundeberg was called as a witness. He and Norma Perry had previously given long interviews to FBI agents. Perry told them, "LUNDEBERG knows that HARRY BRIDGES is a Communist but can't prove it. . . . LUNDEBERG has no absolute proof to back up any of the statements that he made." Lundeberg told FBI agents that he would never "take the witness stand" in a deportation proceeding against Bridges but also stated flatly that "he knew HARRY BRIDGES was a Communist but that he couldn't prove it." The agents concluded that Lundeberg should be subpoenaed.[22]

On April 18, the Washington INS office sent Schofield a message from former INS commissioner James Houghteling: Lundeberg had once told Houghteling that " [Lundeberg] did not know at that time whether Bridges was a member of the Party but he did know that on one occasion Bridges had asked him, Lundeberg, to join the Communist Party." Lundeberg, whose courtroom attire of sweatshirt and work jacket contrasted with Bridges's stylish suit and tie, testified he had been invited to dinner at Bridges's home in 1935, sometime after Bridges's release from the hospital. He claimed that Agnes Bridges, Norma Perry, and Sam Darcy were present and that Darcy (not Bridges) had solicited Lundeberg to join the CP. After repeated questioning by Del Guercio, Lundeberg finally added that Bridges stated he was a party member. Lundeberg also said that, soon after, at the campaign headquarters of the United Labor Party, he had been accosted by CP members, including a high-ranking official named Johnson (whom the FBI identified as Jack Johnstone) regarding his refusal to join. Under cross-examination, Lundeberg acknowledged that the first time he revealed that information to the government was the previous evening.[23]

Bridges acknowledged that Lundeberg had come to his house for dinner once. He was unclear on the date, placing it between his release from the hospital in mid-June and September. Bridges's attorneys did not attempt to fix a more precise date. Had they done so, they might have demonstrated that the event probably could not have taken place as Lundeberg described it, because Darcy left San Francisco sometime in mid- or late June. Lundeberg lived in Seattle and was in San Francisco only periodically in 1935. Johnstone did not arrive in San Francisco until mid- or late August. Assuming that Lundeberg accurately recalled his meeting with Johnstone at the ULP campaign office, it could not have occurred "soon" after the meeting Lundeberg described with Darcy. Connelly had criticized the INS for failing to corroborate dates by checking records for travel and lodging, but the FBI did not do so for Lundeberg's claim about dinner with Bridges. Nor did the FBI attempt to corroborate Darcy's presence in San Francisco at the same time that Lundeberg was there, nor did they seek to establish a date for Lundeberg's account of a meeting in the ULP campaign office. CP records, however, establish that Lundeberg was in San Francisco in late May, that some leading CP members had planned to meet with him and Bridges, but that Bridges went into the hospital *before* the planned meeting. The *San Francisco Chronicle*, *Los Angeles Times*, and *Voice of the Federation* do not mention Lundeberg's presence in San Francisco anytime between June 14, when Bridges was still in the hospital, and June 22, when Darcy was in New Jersey.[24]

Ironically, during the final stages of the hearing, two witnesses in different federal proceedings elsewhere in the country presented views of Bridges more in keeping with Goodwin's initial conclusion that Bridges held a "privileged status" with the CP. On May 27, in Little Rock, Arkansas, Joseph Zack, a former CP official, testified that Earl Browder in mid-1934 called Bridges "our No. 1 man out there," but did not call Bridges a comrade or party member, and acknowledged "having some difficulty because he [Bridges] is so headstrong." Sixteen days later, on June 12, 1941, the same day Bridges's hearing concluded, the Dies Committee in Washington took testimony from Claire Cowan, a former CP organizer; Cowan claimed the CP sent him to San Francisco in June 1934 and warned him "to be very careful in his contacts with him [Bridges] because he was then considered to be more or less unreliable."[25]

After the Sears hearing ended on June 12, the two sides prepared briefs for Sears, then prepared briefs answering the other side's brief. Most of the government brief was written by the FBI.[26] Sears took three months to write his 187-page decision. On September 29, 1941, Sears found against Bridges.

In 1939 a modest Bridges Defense Committee had raised funds for legal fees and other expenses. In 1941 there were several defense committees: the Harry

Bridges Defense Committee, successor to the earlier committee, now led by George Wilson in San Francisco; a National CIO Bridges Committee; and a California CIO Bridges defense committee. A fourth committee, the Citizens Committee for Harry Bridges, led by Virginia Gardner, a journalist, with an office in New York City, featured a long list of celebrity supporters, including Orson Welles, Stella Adler, Lillian Hellman, and Clifford Odets, as well as a host of professors and clergy members. Murray asked all CIO affiliates to contribute one cent per member to the national CIO committee. During a break in the hearing, Bridges and Wilson went to New York to raise funds and garnered $20,000 from Lewis's United Mine Workers and $20,000 from Murray's Steel Workers. The FBI compiled extensive reports on the defense committees, including any connections to the CP. The FBI's analysis, based on bank records, was that the defense committees received just over $270,000 and had disbursed more than $261,000 as of June 1, 1945.[27] (One dollar in mid-1943 was equivalent to more than $16 in mid-2022.)

The Bridges defense acquired its own song, "Song for Bridges," written by Lee Hays, Millard Lampell, and Pete Seeger and recorded by the Almanac Singers with Seeger as lead and Hays, Lampell, and Woody Guthrie as the chorus. It was released as a 78-rpm single in July 1941[28]:

Let me tell you of a sailor, Harry Bridges is his name,
An honest union leader who the bosses tried to frame.
He left home in Australia to sail the seas around,
He sailed across the ocean to land in 'Frisco town.

There was only a company union, the bosses had their way.
A worker had to stand in line for a lousy dollar a day.
When up spoke Harry Bridges, "Us workers got to get wise,
Our wives and kids will starve to death if we don't get organized."

Chorus: Oh, the FBI is worried, the bosses they are scared,
They can't deport six million men, they know.
And we're not going to let them send Harry over the sea,
We'll fight for Harry Bridges and build the C.I O.

They built a big bonfire by the Matson lines that night,
They threw their fink books in it and they said, "We're gonna fight!
You've got to pay a livin' wage or we're gonna take a walk."
They told it to the bosses, but the bosses wouldn't talk.

They said, "There's only one way left to get that contract signed!"
And all around the waterfront they threw their picket line.
They called it Bloody Thursday, the fifth day of July,
For a hundred men were wounded and two were left to die!

Chorus

Now that was seven years ago, and in the time since then
Harry's organized thousands more and made them union men.
"We must try to bribe him," the shipping bosses said.
And if he won't accept a bribe, we'll say that he's a red!"

The bosses brought a trial to deport him over the sea,
But the judge said, "He's an honest man, I got to set him free."
Then they brought another trial to frame him if they can,
But right by Harry Bridges stands every working man!

Chorus

The FBI soon received its copy, along with an informant's report that the Almanac Singers were "extremely untidy, ragged, and dirty." The FBI initiated a "very discreet inquiry" into the recording company.[29]

"Song for Bridges" summarized the leading arguments of the defense committees: Bridges was an effective union leader, the deportation proceedings were devised by "the bosses" and the FBI to destroy the union, and working people could prevent a miscarriage of justice. A similar message appeared in publications by prominent Left authors, including Leo Huberman's *Storm over Bridges* (1941), with illustrations by Giacomo Patri, and Dalton Trumbo's *Harry Bridges* (1941). Huberman was a well-known socialist (but not Communist) journalist. Trumbo was a prominent novelist and highly paid Hollywood screenwriter.[30]

Bridges joked about the FBI listening to his phone calls. In June 1941, Herb Caen reported in the *Chronicle* that when Bridges had come into a bookie joint to make a bet on a horse, the bookie told Bridges he could have called, and Bridges replied, "Think I want the FBI to get a tip on THIS horse?"[31]

Nothing in Bridges's FBI file indicates the FBI had tapped his phone in June 1941. However, a month later, while Bridges was staying at the Edison Hotel in New York, the FBI arranged with hotel management first to listen to Bridges's telephone calls, then installed a microphone in his hotel room. From the room next to Bridges's, FBI agents listened to and recorded conversations in Bridges's room. Bridges became suspicious. He told his suspicions to Virginia Gardner and Lawrence Kammet of the city's Industrial Union Council, then took them across the street to another hotel where he had rented a room with a view of the windows of both rooms in the Edison. From there, Gardner and Kammet watched the two rooms. When Bridges was out of his room, the lights were usually on in the next room and a man was often typing. When Bridges entered his room, the lights next door went out, and the man ceased typing and put on earphones. Bridges and his colleagues opened the telephone box in Bridges's room and found a microphone with a wire leading into the next room. They called in a *PM* reporter and cameraman. (*PM* was a left-leaning daily newspaper in New York City.) They also called in the hotel manager, who refused to let

Bridges into the next room. The police refused to get involved. Among those present at various points was Congressman Vito Marcantonio.[32]

Once the FBI agents realized that Bridges and others knew about their surveillance, they hurriedly cleared the room of their equipment by renting the room directly above it and hoisting everything up the outside of the building. The last agent in the room left at three in the morning, dashing down the hall to the fire escape, then up to the floor above, timed to a food cart blocking the door to Bridges's room. Later that day, the hotel management let Bridges and his colleagues into that room. It was empty except for a long wire grounded to the radiator, some electrical tape, and two used sheets of carbon paper, one of which carried the name "Evelle J. Younger, Special Agent." The hotel manager hurriedly collected those items and gave them to the FBI. Bridges's and his colleagues' accounts were published in late August in *PM* and in October in the *New Yorker*, titled "Some Fun with the F.B.I."[33]

The original surveillance generated a significant volume of FBI reports, but the newspaper stories brought more and lengthier FBI reports, culminating with a ninety-eight-page overview on September 18, complete with an index and thirty-two attached exhibits—its quantity alone suggesting the level of Hoover's anger over the FBI being held up to ridicule. The mockery was not limited to the press. Francis Biddle recalled accompanying Hoover to report the incident to Roosevelt. FDR laughed, slapped Hoover on the back, and said, "By God, Edgar, that's the first time you've been caught with your pants down!" A former FBI agent confirmed Hoover's wrath about that incident and Bridges more generally: "Just the mention of the name Harry Bridges was enough to turn the director's face livid. . . . Lots of careers began and ended with that case. It was one of Hoover's biggest failures, and he blamed everyone but himself."[34]

Marcantonio urged Bridges to charge the FBI with illegal wiretapping. Between August 28 and September 2, Bridges, Gardner, Kammet, and the *PM* reporter filed sworn statements describing the events. Bridges and Carol King formally requested the U.S. attorney for the Southern District of New York to prosecute the FBI for illegal wiretapping. On September 3, Gardner, Kammet, and the *PM* reporter testified to a Senate committee considering the appointment of Francis Biddle as attorney general. Because Biddle had been acting attorney general during the events in New York, the three witnesses charged him with violating federal law. Biddle denied any knowledge, and the committee unanimously approved his appointment. Gladstein filed for a rehearing of the proceedings before Sears on the grounds that some evidence may have been procured illegally. Hoover and Connelley signed affidavits swearing that "no telephone wire tap or microphone surveillance of any kind" had been used in investigating Bridges between August 28, 1940, and June 21, 1941, and Sears denied the motion to rehear the case.[35]

In November 1941, the FBI added Bridges to its Custodial Detention Index. Just as Hoover's agents had engaged in illegal wiretapping without permission of the attorney general, so Hoover had also created the Custodial Detention Index without authorizing legislation and without informing the attorney general. The index was a card file, begun in 1939, of persons of "German, Italian, and Communist sympathies" who, in the FBI's views, should be subject to detention in time of war or national emergency. In 1943 Biddle thoroughly reviewed the program; he determined that it served "no useful purpose" and should be discontinued. Hoover then changed its name to the Security Index. Anyone who publicly supported Bridges was added to the index.[36]

The FBI took advantage of the wartime American Censorship program to request copies of all communications sent by or received by Bridges to or from locations outside the forty-eight states. That brought the FBI copies of cablegrams of support and advice to Bridges from James Healy, head of the Waterside Workers Federation in Australia, and copies of ILWU correspondence to union members and officers in the territories of Alaska and Hawaii.[37]

After Sears released his decision, Bridges and his attorneys appealed, first to the Board of Immigration Appeals. In the BIA hearing in early 1942, Gladstein and Del Guercio rehashed their earlier arguments, and Del Guercio asked the board to deny Bridges bail. All the BIA members taking part (one was recused) rejected Sears's conclusions, especially the key ones about the *Waterfront Worker* and the testimonies of O'Neil and Lundeberg. Carol King said the decision "is so better than our brief that it is just a waste of time to read the brief." Schofield, Hoover, and other INS and FBI officials were less pleased. Schofield prepared an 88-page memorandum for the attorney general refuting the board's decision. Representative Allen demanded that the Senate vote on his bill to deport Bridges. Another representative demanded a congressional investigation of "the powerful friends . . . protecting Bridges in Washington."[38]

The unanimous opinion of INS and FBI leaders was that Biddle should uphold Sears's decision. Bridges's attorneys submitted a 248-page brief reviewing and critiquing the testimony of the government's witnesses and, finally, addressing the date of Lundeberg's alleged meeting with Darcy. Biddle took nearly five months to prepare his 7,500-word decision. Released on May 28, 1942, the decision closely followed a long memo from Schofield and concluded that Bridges should be deported. Biddle told a press conference, "We want the Court to pass on this whole proceedings, as to procedure and other mechanisms because it is a test case"—a test case for future Smith Act prosecutions, something clearly on the minds of Hoover, Connelley, and others.[39]

Secretary of the Interior Harold Ickes learned from Robert Jackson, by then a member of the Supreme Court, that Biddle had discussed his intent with Roosevelt who considered it "an offset" to Roosevelt's recent release of Earl Browder, head of the CPUSA, from prison, an action meant as a gesture toward the nation's Soviet ally. Ickes also learned from Jackson that an inquiry had been made of Stalin and "Stalin was not interested in what happened to Bridges." Jackson disagreed with Biddle's decision, thinking that Bridges was more important to the war effort than Browder. However, Jackson also thought there was basis in the legal record for Biddle to have decided either way.[40]

In addition to keeping their Smith Act test case on track, Biddle's order also served an immediate and important political purpose. In his press conference following release of his decision, Biddle claimed, "Even President Roosevelt cannot order a vacation or revocation of the order for deportation" and that Bridges's only recourse was the courts. James Landis recalled that, at the time, Biddle defended his decision as "politically wise." Immediately after his press conference, Biddle met with Roosevelt and later recalled that Roosevelt said, "The Supreme Court will never let him be deported," and, smiling, added, "The decision is a long way off."[41] By putting Bridges into the courts for years, Biddle undercut those seeking to deport Bridges through an act of Congress and simultaneously gave political cover to the Roosevelt administration for not taking action.

Five weeks after Biddle's announcement, Elinor Kahn reported to Bridges and defense committee leaders that the committee was in financial trouble, that "no work had been done," and that members of the Citizens Committee were asking "what the hell is going on." That was soon remedied. The defense efforts soon added Bartley Crum, a prominent San Francisco attorney, a Republican, and a leader of Wendell Willkie's campaign in 1940. In late June 1942, Crum told Gladstein that Willkie "is willing at the appropriate time to help out." However, Willkie died in October 1944. Bridges later said that, had Willkie lived, he would have been Bridges's chief defense counsel, without pay. Another important addition to the Bridges support group was Robert Kenny, a Los Angeles attorney who was elected as California attorney general in 1942. Roger Baldwin of the ACLU also advised the Bridges defense team.[42]

Early in 1943, the *New York Times* reported, "There had been no doubt that the deportation fight would eventually reach the Supreme Court." All parties—attorneys and judges alike—were writing for the Supreme Court. As Bridges's attorneys began organizing their appeal to the Circuit Court of Appeals, his legal team expanded. King, Gladstein, and Grossman now gave top billing to Lee Pressman, chief counsel to the CIO, but their correspondence demonstrates that Pressman's listing was primarily to demonstrate CIO support. On June 26, 1944, the Circuit Court of Appeals issued a 3–2 decision denying Bridges's appeal.[43]

Denial by the Circuit Court of Appeals set up their appeal to the Supreme Court. The Bridges defense now took two paths, one to draft a strong legal appeal to the Supreme Court and the other to mobilize public support for Roosevelt to call off the court case. In early January 1945, Gladstein wrote to King, "Our prize client [Bridges] had a flash of intelligence. The realization came over him that, if the Supreme Court turned down our petition, he was as good as on his way to Australia. He consulted numerous letters in his files . . . [and] noted my insistent remark that ultimate success could not be expected from the lawyers and their efforts alone, but . . . on the strength of the mass campaign. . . . On taking stock, he discovered that there was simply no mass campaign." Bridges replaced Wilson with Elinor Kahn in everything but name. Gladstein soon reported, "Since that great day, Elinor has been doing a dynamic job," and emphasized, "The only way to bring mass pressure on the Supreme Court was to bring to the Court's attention that one hell of a lot of people are excited about the case." Though the campaign could not be directed toward the Court, by urging the president to drop the case, Gladstein said, "the Court will catch the hint."[44]

The renamed Bridges Victory Committee quickly asked all CIO locals in California to pass resolutions, telegraph the president and attorney general, urge local members to write letters, raise funds, and issue press releases. Kahn's blitz mobilized celebrities, union leaders, and politicos, including five senators, sixteen members of Congress, and Washington's governor, all of whom lent their names to the cause. Supporters included prominent AFL union leaders in San Francisco, the commander of the California Veterans of Foreign Wars, the editor of the *Chronicle*, and the presidents of the San Francisco Chinese Society and National Association for the Advancement of Colored People.[45]

King, Gladstein, and Nathan Greene collaborated on the Supreme Court brief. Greene, in New York, did much of it. A favorite student of Felix Frankfurter at Harvard Law School, Greene, like King, was an active member of the International Juridical Association, Left lawyers who later became part of the National Lawyers Guild. Gladstein argued that he should be one of the two to present to the Court. For the other, he preferred Greene or King. Other views prevailed. Bridges was represented before the Supreme Court by Pressman and Gladstein, with Gladstein handling much of the presentation.[46]

The brief argued that deportation of Bridges "offends due process of law" and "due process of procedure," and "the Statute as construed and applied offends the Bill of Rights and bears no reasonable relation to the purpose for which governmental power to deport exists." The American Committee for the Protection of the Foreign Born, an organization close to the CP, submitted an amicus brief arguing that First Amendment rights of speech and association extended to aliens. The ACLU's amicus brief argued that deportation was subject to the Bill of Rights, that deportation under §23 of the Smith Act (the section used to charge Bridges) was punitive in nature and subject to constitutional restraints regarding punishment, and that §23 could not be applied to Bridges because §23 was *ad personam*, that is, written specifically for Bridges.[47]

The case was heard on April 2 and 3, 1945. Justice Jackson recused himself. In the decision, announced on June 18, the justices divided 5–3. Justice William O. Douglas wrote the decision and was joined by Hugo Black, Stanley Reed, and Wiley Rutledge. Douglas wrote a narrow decision, likely to maintain his thin majority, concluding that Bridges had "been ordered deported under a misconstruction of the term 'affiliation' . . . and by reason of an unfair hearing." He noted that *Bridges v. California* had established that an alien has First Amendment rights of speech and press but ignored other constitutional questions. Justice Frank Murphy concurred separately but went far beyond Douglas's narrow decision, stating, "The record in this case will stand forever as a monument to man's inhumanity to man. Seldom if ever in the history of this nation has there been such a concentrated and relentless crusade to deport an individual because he dared to exercise the freedom that belongs to him as a human being and that is guaranteed to him in the Constitution." Bridges's defense committees over the next ten years never tired of quoting Murphy. Murphy concluded that the Smith Act was unconstitutional as punishing guilt by association. Chief Justice Harlan Fiske Stone and Justices Owen Roberts and Felix Frankfurter dissented.[48] The constitutional issues raised by Murphy, Bridges's attorneys, and the amicus briefs were finally taken up by the Supreme Court in 1957, in *Yates v. US*, which essentially ended Smith Act prosecutions.

After the hearing and before the decision, Ickes lunched with Biddle. Biddle told him that, before the Bridges case reached the Supreme Court, Roosevelt had suggested that Biddle "talk to Bill Douglas and Bob Jackson and intimate that they vote against the Government," but Biddle did not indicate whether he had done so.[49]

When the decision was announced, Bridges released a statement emphasizing not the Court's narrow legal ruling but the way he and his defense committees had defined the issue: "the deportation proceedings furnished false whiskers for reaction to attack the rights of workers to organize into trade unions, to gather in free assembly and choose their own leaders and to speak out and collectively act against undemocratic forms and Fascist policies," and "the Court's ruling represents an important victory for all who cherish democratic traditions and institutions." He also stressed, "Credit for the victory must go to the millions of union men and women, liberal and progressive-minded people in all classes of our society" who had supported his fight.[50]

Bridges's version of the deportation proceedings as an attack on his union and on unions more generally had elements of truth to it, especially regarding the origins and early development of the case in the hands of Doyle and Knowles. The Bridges defense committees were highly effective in depicting the proceedings against Bridges as an attack on unions and in presenting Bridges as a martyr. To be certain, Bridges had accomplished significant things as a union leader, and it is completely unlikely that any charges would ever have been brought against him if he had remained a longshore worker. Now, to his accomplishments was added his near martyrdom.

Time magazine summarized the reaction of Pacific Coast employers: "Employers who would never learn to love Harry Bridges have learned how to live with him and like it. The case against him had become a nuisance and a bore."[51]

Throughout the years of appeals, the FBI maintained a high level of interest in Bridges and his associates. Shortly after the Sears hearing, Connelley approved a seventy-six-page report on Henry Schmidt's testimony, arguing that Schmidt had committed perjury in stating that he was not a CP member. Though Hoover directed the San Francisco SAC to take the report to the U.S. attorney for an opinion, nothing came of it then. FBI agents regularly reviewed the checks deposited by and written by the defense committee, with an analysis of every person who received a check of any amount.[52] Bridges's FBI file for 1943, 1944, and 1945 includes detailed reports on numerous telephone conversations. A report on a phone call between Bridges, in Washington, and Gladstein included the following exchange: "There was a noise on the wire and GLADSTEIN said it was probably the operator at the Hotel and Harry said, 'Or the FBI,' and GLADSTEIN said, 'Well they can kiss our [word redacted].'"[53]

The FBI kept Carol King under close surveillance. On March 23, 1942, Agent D. M. Ladd sent Hoover photographs of "material observed in the office of Carol King"—135 documents, primarily correspondence. The memo cautioned that the material necessarily be "treated as highly confidential," as "the manner in which the Bureau obtained the information would be very evident"—that is, FBI agents had burglarized King's office and photographed her files, an exercise called a "black-bag job," a practice the FBI began in 1940. Later memos indicate one or more subsequent burglaries of King's office. The burglaries of King's office were not the first time the FBI had carried out a black-bag job, but they seem to have been the first directed at a lawyer with cases pending before federal courts, including the Supreme Court.[54]

The Supreme Court's decision did not end the FBI's surveillance of Bridges, and the FBI also took an interest in all principal figures involved in Bridges's defense activities, his pending divorce trial, and his relationship with Nancy Berdecio. In late July 1945, for example, the San Francisco office prepared a twenty-page report on Bridges's activities over the previous five weeks, including ten pages summarizing evidence of "immoral conduct" (his relationship with Berdecio) and ten pages presenting evidence of "continued Communist affiliation and/or cooperation with Communists." The Supreme Court's decision, hinging on the definition of *affiliation*, apparently did not change the FBI's understanding of that term.[55]

During the early years of the deportation proceedings, Bridges had sometimes thought that the worst that could happen would be a free trip back to Australia, where he could work with his father and brother and perhaps go into politics.[56] That outcome was never likely. In May 1942, the *Melbourne Argus* reported, "Australian authorities do not desire Bridges's appearance in Australia." The Australian Labor Party had just won at the federal level for the first time since the split over conscription in 1916. The ALP government of John Curtin made no public announcement about Bridges, but, in June 1942, H. V. Evatt, the foreign minister, wired other foreign ministry officials and Curtin, "I saw Mr. Cordell Hull [U.S. secretary of state] and told him that having in view Bridges long residence and domicile in the United States we could not be expected to facilitate deportation to Australia. . . . Bridges would have no legal right to re-enter Australian territory."[57]

Such a situation was not unusual. As of late 1940, some two thousand individuals remained in the United States despite deportation orders because their home countries refused to accept them. According to an INS official, they were in "permanent custody."[58]

The extended legal proceedings from 1941 to 1945 served several political purposes: they provided a show trial to embarrass Bridges, block the Allen bill (which, after again passing the House, had again died in the Senate),[59] and prevent opponents of Bridges from pressuring the administration. The first of these was ineffective, since Bridges emerged with greater national prominence and an even stronger position in his union. The second purpose was meaningless, since deportation by an act of Congress would have been unconstitutional as a bill of attainder and would have had no more authority in the face of an Australian refusal to accept him. Keeping the case in the courts may have relieved the administration from dealing with anti-Bridges pressures, but it produced significant efforts on behalf of Bridges. None of those political objectives was realized, but, had Bridges been found subject to deportation, he could nonetheless have ended up in "permanent custody," indefinite detention, effectively removing him as a union leader.

11

World War, Labor Peace

1940–1945

The time from the initial FBI investigation of Harry Bridges in 1940 to the Supreme Court decision in 1945 coincided almost exactly with U.S. involvement in World War II. While Bridges and his legal team fought deportation, he also carried out the demanding duties of ILWU president, as all unions came under pressure to maximize production and deal with new federal regulations. As victory in war came into sight, Bridges and the ILWU also had to position themselves for an uncertain postwar economy.

From 1939 onward, U.S. politics focused largely on the wars in Europe and Asia. President Franklin D. Roosevelt's destroyers-for-bases trade with Great Britain in May 1940 initiated a de facto alliance. He further developed the entente in March 1941, when Congress approved the Lend-Lease Act to provide supplies and equipment to Britain and its dominions. The Atlantic Charter, issued by Roosevelt and British prime minister Winston Churchill in August 1941, publicly announced the alliance. However, until Germany invaded the Soviet Union in June 1941, the CPUSA interpreted the Molotov-Ribbentrop Pact as an entente between Germany and the Soviet Union. The CP and its allies in the CIO insisted, "The Yanks are not coming," and condemned Lend-Lease as a step toward war. Most ILWU members disagreed. When Henry Schmidt, Bridges's longtime ally in the San Francisco longshore local, proposed a resolution against Lend-Lease, Local 10 members strongly opposed the resolution.[1]

John L. Lewis made good on his threat to leave the CIO presidency if Roosevelt was reelected. The CIO convention choose Phil Murray, head of SWOC, as Lewis's successor. An informant told the FBI about a "private conference" during the CIO convention involving Lewis, Murray, Frederick "Blackie" Myers of the NMU, and others, perhaps including Bridges. The source claimed that Murray refused to become president if Bridges were one of the vice presidents but was willing if Bridges only picked a vice president, and that Bridges choose Joe Curran. When I asked Bridges about the report, he acknowledged that he was at the convention but denied taking part in such a discussion. He added that someone might have represented him in such a meeting and that "we supported Curran" but not as part of any bargain.[2]

Bridges had enjoyed mostly good relations with Lewis, but his relations with Murray had been strained. Robert Jackson recalled a conversation in early 1941 in which Murray said that "Bridges was a Communist, or at least he went along with them," and that "Bridges had made Murray a great deal of trouble in the CIO."[3] Relations between Bridges and Murray eased during the war, but that proved only a temporary, public truce.

During the Sears hearing, five months before Pearl Harbor, war preparations raised problems for Bridges when UAW members at North American Aviation, a Los Angeles plant manufacturing military aircraft, staged a wildcat strike. Richard Frankensteen, the UAW's lead for aircraft organizing, and others blamed Communists. Bridges, as CIO state director, sent the strikers a supportive message. In the Sears hearing, the prosecution presented Bridges's message as proof he followed the CP line. When called as a government witness, however, Frankensteen defended Bridges's message and blasted the INS for holding the hearing.[4]

Late in 1940, the few ILA locals in the Northwest sought a separate NLRB election, threatening the NLRB decision that all Pacific Coast longshore workers constituted one bargaining unit. Bridges asked for CIO help to block an NLRB election and asked President Roosevelt to intervene. Nonetheless, the NLRB opened a hearing in January 1941. Bridges strongly supported one bargaining unit for all West Coast ports, but the board decided, two to one, to schedule an election in the ILA ports. They gave large majorities to the ILA.[5]

The ILA-PCD and then the ILWU had benefited from federal intervention in the 1930s, but the NLRB decision benefiting the ILA locals indicated a change. Instead of criticizing the NLRB, AFL loyalists were now looking to the NLRB to resolve jurisdictional disputes. There was a clear message for the ILWU—what the NLRB gives, the NLRB can take away.

In April 1941, the deportation hearing was recessed to permit Bridges to attend the ILWU annual convention, which approved several changes in the union's constitution: the convention became biennial, officers' terms were extended to two years, and the president's and secretary-treasurer's offices were to be in San Francisco. Other changes gave the officers more authority, specified a potentially punitive procedure for any member seeking to discredit the officers, and restricted a local's ability to expel an international officer. Newspapers depicted the changes as a power grab by Bridges. In the elections, Bridges faced an opponent for the presidency, and the office of secretary-treasurer was also contested. The incumbent vice president, J. R. Robertson, was unopposed. Bridges won easily, as did Eugene Paton of Local 6 (San Francisco Bay Area warehouse) for secretary-treasurer. Paton's election marked the beginning of a sixty-two-year pattern that the president came from a longshore local and the secretary-treasurer from a warehouse local.[6]

On June 22, 1941, shortly after Sears concluded the hearing, German forces invaded the Soviet Union. Bridges told the press on June 25 that the German invasion did not change his views that the United States should stay out of the war and that U.S. ships should not enter war zones. Bridges's statement came as CPUSA leaders were awaiting instructions from Moscow before presenting a new party line. After those instructions arrived, CPUSA leaders adopted a "People's Program of Struggle for the Defeat of Hitler and Hitlerism." The new line denounced Nazi Germany as a menace to "the American people, the British people and the people of the world," demanded all possible aid to anyone fighting Hitler, reversed the party's harsh criticism of the Roosevelt administration, and called for "the broadest united front and People's Front activities."[7]

Bridges left San Francisco on June 25 to travel to Detroit, Cleveland, Pittsburgh, Washington, and New York, delivering addresses and conferring with CIO officials at every stop. FBI agents kept Bridges under close surveillance, identified everyone he called and who called him, surreptitiously searched his luggage, often booked the hotel room next to his, sought to listen to his conversations, and analyzed his trash. Bridges arrived in New York on July 3 and checked into the Edison Hotel where the FBI wired his room (see previous chapter).[8]

Addressing the NMU national convention on July 10, Bridges disclaimed any sympathy for the "Tory ruling class" of Britain but specified instead, "We are with the masses of the people of England." He hailed the Soviet Union as "the greatest anti-Fascist power in Europe," and he urged that the United States send munitions and supplies to "the liberty-loving anti-fascist people of Europe" but not "the Tories or the fascist fifth column of England." He flatly opposed sending U.S. troops.[9]

Still in New York on July 16, Bridges was asked by reporters why the CPUSA was so quick to change its position on the war. He answered dryly, "I suspect that there's a lot of sympathy between the Communist Party of this country and the Communist Party of Russia." Asked if his union followed "the party line," he replied, "We follow the trade-union line." Asked if he'd ever differed with the CP, Bridges reeled off a long list of detailed instances, including "We're against any step that would involve us directly in the war" and reiterated his opposition to "unconditional aid to England."[10]

Three days later, Roy Hudson indirectly rebuked Bridges in an article in the *Daily Worker*: "Unconditional support for every measure and force and country that seeks to defeat Hitler is the only policy that will guarantee Hitler's defeat." Bridges took another three months before pledging "full support" to FDR "even if it means war," which the *San Francisco Chronicle* characterized as "one of the most complete, unequivocal and forth-right pledges of support for the national defense and war effort yet given by any American labor leader." Syndicated columnists Drew Pearson and Robert Allen attributed Bridges's statement to having been "sharply criticized by the Communist Daily Worker . . . on the war question," but also speculated that Bridges's deportation status may have produced his new position.[11]

U.S. entry into the war in December 1941 transformed labor relations. Roosevelt established the National War Labor Board to prevent strikes that could impede the war effort. Like its World War I predecessor, the NWLB had equal representation from unions (including Murray), business (including Roger Lapham, Bridges's debate opponent during the MFP strike), and the public (mostly lawyers and academics, including Wayne Morse). Roosevelt authorized the board to mediate and, if necessary, impose settlements, and it held de facto control over wage increases. Regional War Labor Boards were added in January 1943. Other new federal agencies addressed prices, manpower (securing labor resources where they were most needed), and production of war-related materials. All had implications for unions.

Soon after the declaration of war, at FDR's request, William Green, for the AFL, and Phil Murray, for the CIO, provided no-strike pledges. Most international unions abided by the no-strike pledge. The major exception was driven by the NWLB's "Little Steel formula" significantly limiting wage increases. Most union leaders groused about the formula, but, on May 1, 1943, John L. Lewis led the UMW to strike against it. Bridges and other ILWU leaders were outraged. The ILWU's new newspaper, the *Dispatcher*, asserted, "Hitler has found a pal in John L. Lewis." ILWU officers decried Lewis as "the single most effective agent of the fascist powers within the ranks of labor," and Bridges personally denounced Lewis as "a traitor to the nation and to labor." Harry Lundeberg sent Lewis a message of support. The other major violations of the wartime no-strike pledge were strikes in 1944 by the United Retail, Wholesale, and Department Store Employees, CIO, against Montgomery Ward in Chicago and Detroit; FDR used the army to end both. The ILWU had organized several Montgomery Ward warehouses, which did not join the strikes.[12]

More than ten thousand local strikes took place during the war, most of short duration. Most were "wildcat" strikes, unauthorized by the international and often unauthorized by the local. About half the 1944 strikes were over wages. Some local wildcat strikes were by white workers protesting racial integration of workplaces. There were no strikes by ILWU locals, but individual members and individual gangs sometimes quit work and returned to the hall, requiring the dispatcher to replace them, a practice already well established during the 1930s. Richard Boyden counted thirty-four such instances on the San Francisco waterfront between early 1942 and the end of the war. The causes included being told to work shorthanded, or faster, or more than ten hours, or in dangerous conditions. Sometimes there were racial dimensions to such behavior. In some instances, the port Labor Relations Committee suspended or fined the men.[13]

Parts of the Pacific Coast were transformed through rapid development of manufacturing for aircraft, ships, and war materials. The equally rapid influx of workers from other parts of the country brought significant demographic changes to some ILWU locals. Between the 1940 and 1950 federal censuses, California's population grew by 53 percent, Oregon's by 40 percent, and Washington's by 37 percent. The African American population, bolstered by emigration from the South, rose by 272 percent in California and as much as 74 percent in Oregon and 64 percent in Washington, changes that affected some ILWU locals.[14]

At the same time, Japanese Americans were being removed from urban centers. In February 1942, Congressman John Tolan's subcommittee took testimony regarding the relocation of Japanese Americans in the Pacific Coast states. ILWU and CIO leaders decided that Bridges's pending appeal meant he should not testify, so Louis Goldblatt, secretary of the California CIO Industrial Council, addressed the Tolan Committee. Goldblatt scathingly denounced "the forces of hysteria and vigilantism" advocating relocation and predicted, "This entire episode of hysteria . . . will form a dark page of American history." Goldblatt's position—that of the ILWU and California CIO—was directly contrary not only to other unions but also to the CPUSA. Some CP activists denounced Goldblatt as "untrustworthy" and even "dangerous."[15]

The ILWU launched its own newspaper in December 1942. Bridges chose, as founding editor, Morris Watson, a veteran journalist from New York City who was fired for Newspaper Guild activity. Dubbed the *Dispatcher* in recognition of the central importance of the hiring hall and elected dispatcher, the paper featured a regular column by Bridges entitled "On the Beam." His first column blasted "appeasers, Trotskyists and other such Hitlerian fifth column elements" for sabotaging efforts to resolve labor shortages. His solution was to bring more women and African Americans into the workforce, and the column strongly opposed discrimination against African Americans, which he called "anti-labor, anti-American and anti-white."[16]

Throughout the war, Bridges's columns and the *Dispatcher* more generally opposed racial or gender discrimination. Ironically, praise for working women sometimes appeared on the same page as photos of attractive young women in bathing suits, something typical of many newspapers at the time. The paper often featured Japanese American union members, sometimes in army uniform and sometimes as victims of discrimination, and praised their loyalty. In April

1944, the coast longshore caucus, meeting in Portland, unanimously reaffirmed the union's commitment to "equal treatment for all regardless of race, creed, color or sex . . . without equivocation or qualification." Ironically, the caucus met in Portland, where the longshore local had long been—and remained—white, unlike other major Northwest longshore locals. In the 1945 biennial convention, the delegates endorsed a national wage policy that, among other principles, included the "elimination of race and sex differentials."[17]

Such statements may have been prompted by significant changes in the ethnic composition of the longshore workforce in San Francisco and San Pedro, changes not welcomed by all ILWU members. Throughout California, the number of longshore workers increased from 5,865 in 1940 to 8,481 in 1950, and the number of Black longshore workers increased from 83 to 2,051. The change was greatest in the San Francisco Bay Area, where the 1940 federal census listed 66 Black longshore workers in a workforce just under 3,400 (2 percent), and the 1950 federal census found 1,662 in a workforce of 4,900 (34 percent). The San Pedro local saw a significant increase in Latinos, mostly Mexican Americans, to perhaps 25 percent of the membership.[18]

Since 1934 ILWU longshore locals had built their identity and community around the hiring hall. During World War II, that commitment, along with the union's commitment to local autonomy, membership control over hiring and dispatching, and local democracy, sometimes thwarted the international officers' strongly held commitment to racial equality. Nancy Quam Wickham's study of Local 13 (San Pedro, the Port of Los Angeles) demonstrates the reaction of some white ILWU members to the influx of Black longshoremen, some of whom were experienced longshore workers from segregated ILA locals on the Gulf of Mexico. She concludes, "What distinguished the racist actions of many ILWU members and probably made those acts more tolerable to the International leadership is that it often was hard to distinguish among job consciousness, union pride, and flagrant racial discrimination." She provides examples of white longshore workers who refused to work alongside a Black worker by leaving that gang and returning to the hall to be dispatched elsewhere. Such behavior was often reported as due to job consciousness rather than racism—that is, the white workers claimed that Black workers were inexperienced or inefficient. However, some openly subscribed to racist stereotypes of Black workers as "shiftless and lazy."[19]

Control of the hiring hall permitted other potentially discriminatory practices. Each local had an Investigating Committee, responsible for screening applicants for union membership. Black applicants were sometimes held to a higher standard than white applicants. Local 8, the Portland longshore local, openly refused to admit one applicant solely because "he was a Negro." The situation caught Bridges between his opposition to racial discrimination and his commitment to members' control of the hiring hall. His only public response was to write to each member of Local 8 emphasizing the ILWU's opposition to racial discrimination, but he also worked with individual members of the local to effect change. Each local had a Promotions Committee, responsible for determining whether a member was qualified to become a gang boss. In the San Pedro longshore local, not one African American was promoted to gang boss during World War II. Toward the end of the war, the ILWU attempted to resolve disputes over promotions by specifying that anyone seeking to become a gang boss must have at least five years of experience, thus disqualifying *all* wartime newcomers.[20]

Local 10, the San Francisco Bay Area longshore local, had the largest number of new members and the largest number of new Black members. Local 10 also had a high rate of membership turnover—for example, between January 1 and July 23, 1943, 2,872 new men received probationary status and 1,746 probationers were dropped. In 1942 F. C. Gregory of the WEA told the FBI that the U.S. Employment Service was sending 300–400 new longshore workers each month to Local 10 and that "about sixty per cent have been Negroes and of these only about five per cent are experienced longshoremen." The report continued, "resentment" could arise because "an experienced longshoreman working in the hold of a vessel has no confidence in an inexperienced man who could endanger the lives of the entire longshore gang through acts due to inexperience." The report said nothing about white racism, only that the situation was a serious source of dissension within the local and that Bridges had spoken to Local 10 members at length on the importance of cooperative working relations between the races.[21]

Albert Vetere Lannon studied how Local 10 tried, but largely failed, to integrate its newcomers. Monthly membership meetings were a time for union business but also a time to socialize and become integrated into the local's post-1934 culture. All union members—full members and probationers—were fined for failing to attend at least one membership meeting out of four. Probationers could not vote, and many left the meetings soon after arriving. Probationers also showed a high rate of turnover. The local was accepting 100 probationers a month in 1943, but over the five months between July and November, roughly the same number—498—were dropped for not paying dues. The probationary period was reduced to six months, but problems with attendance continued, bringing an increased fine for missing meetings.[22] Lannon did not locate data indicating the racial breakdown of his data, but Black men were disproportionately represented among probationers.

Tensions within the local's membership may have contributed to the election of Jim Kearney as Local 10 president in late 1944. Since the election of Bridges in 1934, the San Francisco local had elected presidents closely aligned with Bridges—and the CP. Kearney, by contrast, belonged to the Association of Catholic Trade Unionists (ACTU), which supported unions but opposed communism. Following Kearney's election, J. Edgar Hoover asked the San Francisco SAC to "ascertain discreetly" the reasons "for the sudden success of the anti-Communist element in this Local." I found no response.[23]

Throughout the war, Bridges's ongoing legal battle over deportation hung over his union activities. In New York City in July 1942, Bridges attended a dinner for merchant seamen who had survived German torpedoes. When he arrived, the restaurant manager asked Bridges if he were a torpedoed sailor. "No," Bridges replied, "but I may become a torpedoed union leader."[24] Later that year, the FBI did sink a proposal that Bridges make a five-minute broadcast to Australia as part of a commemoration of the Statue of Liberty. Hoover asked Attorney General Francis Biddle to alert the Office of War Information to "the implications" of such a broadcast. Biddle's office soon informed Hoover that the proposed broadcast "has been squelched."[25]

By then German armies dominated most of Europe. The Red Army had been pushed far to the east. The CPUSA launched its own offensive, demanding a second front—an Allied landing in western Europe to divert German troops from Russia. U.S. and British strategists knew their forces were not yet ready, but the CP and its CIO allies maintained a steady drumroll demanding a second front. Bridges was prominent in those efforts, in major addresses to the NMU on July 28, 1942, and the UAW on August 4, after which both unions adopted resolutions calling for a second front. After Bridges's appeal, the CIO State Council in California also approved a resolution of support.[26]

In addressing the NMU, Bridges expressed his pleasure that the army was implementing his proposal to create a battalion of experienced longshoremen. When the FBI learned of this, an agent contacted the army, which responded that Bridges was not involved with creating longshore battalions. In fact, however, army officers *had* conferred with Bridges and other ILWU officers regarding recruiting longshore workers, including offering appropriate ranks from corporal to first lieutenant. The results were unimpressive—of eight hundred anticipated volunteers, only eighty signed up. By August 1942, Colonel A. J. McChrystal judged the plan "a complete failure." Always eager to challenge Bridges's claims of full support for the war effort, Hoover notified Biddle in February 1943 that "since June, 1942, Bridges has had no part in the formation of longshore battalions."[27]

The war brought greater security for most unions, including maintenance of membership, the dues check-off, and better wages and benefits, including paid vacations. Historians disagree regarding the long-term significance of such wartime measures as forced arbitration and increased dependence on federal agencies for improvements in wages and working conditions. Nelson Lichtenstein and others have argued that wartime changes undercut labor militancy and increased unions' dependence on lawyers and professional staff members, at the expense of control by rank-and-file members.[28] In many ways, however, Bridges and the ILWU had been through similar struggles in the 1930s, and they had long since come to rely on such professionals as Henry Melnikow and the Gladstein law firm. Their battles over work actions and jurisdictional conflicts had already produced a unique system of arbitration premised on the right of rank-and-file union members to stop work. Nor did the wartime experience noticeably diminish ILWU members' militancy.

In November 1941, Bridges wholeheartedly endorsed the "Murray Plan," CIO president Murray's proposal for a tripartite Industrial Council. Bridges soon developed the Bridges Plan for Pacific Coast shipping, focused on expediting production and creating a tripartite oversight body, with representatives from the ILWU, WEA, and federal government. Initially receptive, WEA officers soon rejected every part of the Bridges Plan. Bridges described Frank Foisie, president of the WEA, as claiming that "the motives behind the plan were sinister" and the plan was "a maneuver . . . to confuse issues and with an eye to a favorable deportation decision."[29]

Blocked in San Francisco, Bridges turned to Washington. In December 1941, Bjorne Halling, the Washington representative of CIO maritime unions, and George Wilson, head of the Bridges Defense Committee, met with the U.S. Maritime Commission. WEA representatives refused to take part. Halling and Wilson promoted a revised Bridges Plan for a tripartite joint council—ILWU and WEA representatives and one or more representatives of the Maritime Commission. The plan included "introduction and utilization to the fullest extent of . . . labor-saving machinery . . . [and] adopting methods in the loading and discharging of ships which will reduce the cost of such operations in the interests of national economy."[30]

In February 1942, the ILWU's Washington representatives presented a third version of the Bridges Plan, for a Pacific Coast Longshore Industry Council with Morse (then coast arbitrator) as government representative and chairman. Sam Kagel, now representing the union in Washington, reported that Admiral Emory Land, head of the Maritime Commission, had asked Roosevelt to confirm "the coastwise setup we are seeking." WEA representatives were en route to Washington to block approval, but, Kagel claimed, "they will not be able to prevail."[31]

Kagel was right. In March 1942, Roosevelt announced creation of the Pacific Coast Maritime Industrial Board consisting of two union representatives, two industry representatives, and an appointed chair. The ILWU mostly got what it wanted—but may have soon regretted their success. Morse was to chair the PCMIB but, to the surprise and dissatisfaction of the ILWU, with Paul Eliel as vice chair. Eliel had long since moved from the Industrial Association to the Stanford Business School. When Morse was appointed to the NWLB, Eliel became PCMIB chair. Eliel proved less favorable to the ILWU than the union had expected from Morse. Bridges and the ILWU tried unsuccessfully to have Eliel replaced. Throughout the war, Henry Schmidt and Cole Jackman (Local 8, Portland longshore) represented the ILWU on the PCMIB.[32]

Accounts conflict regarding the role of Bridges, other ILWU leaders, and the ILWU's longshore members in creating and maintaining maximum productivity during World War II.[33] Bridges, himself, left conflicting statements. In a personal letter to an old friend in New Zealand in October 1942, he said, "We are urging our longshoremen . . . to do more work and to relinquish certain gains that we have fought for in the past." He made similar, often stronger, public statements during the war. In 1950, however, he claimed the ILWU "gave all-out support to the War effort during World War II, yet at the same time, constantly stood guard against *all* efforts to *undermine the rights and conditions of our members*."[34]

Bridges's rhetoric usually exceeded the reality. In January 1942, for example, Bridges said that unions "will have to surrender some of their hard-won rights during this emergency" but exempted overtime pay and the right to organize. The ILWU also preserved longshoremen's six-hour day and thirty-hour week despite an Executive Order mandating a forty-hour week. Bridges and other ILWU officers worked to improve productivity but never considered doing "anything" to increase production.[35]

In February 1943, the CIO's Maritime Committee submitted *Wartime Shipping: A Plan and Memorandum*, the longshore section of which came from the ILWU. In that report, the ILWU argued that the War Shipping Administration (WSA) was inefficient due to "the pressure of peacetime commercial practices," and it failed to draw upon "the facilities, resources and personnel that could contribute much to its success." The report included a long list of recommendations for longshore management to increase efficiency and productivity. In a swipe at the ILA, the report argued that the WSA should establish centralized dispatching systems for ports where they did not exist—that is, East Coast and Gulf ILA ports.[36] Little was ever done to carry out those recommendations.

The WEA presented quite different versions of obstacles to productivity. In July 1942, Foisie, for the WEA, publicly complained about "notorious inefficiency in cargo handling" and blamed both "restrictive rules in the labor agreement" and the union for refusing to change them. In September 1942, Foisie called upon Eliel and the PCMIB to "outlaw the longshore slow-down" which he called a "form of sabotage." In early February 1943, Eliel claimed, "Production in the Port of San Francisco . . . is still pitifully below the standards that properly can be expected." In response, in April 1943, ILWU Local 10 released telegrams to FDR that, day by day and hour by hour, presented delays caused by management.[37]

In 1943, in testimony before the Senate Manpower Subcommittee on Military Affairs, chaired by Sheridan Downey (D-CA), Eliel complained that continuation of the hiring hall meant that longshoremen "can and do replace themselves [in a gang] almost whenever they care to," that "no-one need work more than 15 or 16 consecutive days [*sic*] if he does not care to," and that "the dispatching hall regularly arranges, during slack periods, for such gangs as have worked for long unbroken periods to get a day or days off as a gang." Eventually, the PCMIB ruled that any registered longshoreman must work at least twenty days out of twenty-eight (equivalent to a five-day work week) to remain registered.[38]

The WEA, testifying before the Downey committee, charged the ILWU with resistance to improving productivity: "There is a serious wastage of manpower which is willful, carried over into war conditions from peace time by job-action and organized slow-down, fostered by Union officials." The WEA charged that the union had caused a slowdown "by deliberate job action" and that ILWU members engaged in widespread pilferage. The WEA's proposals attacked nearly all the union's gains since 1934. One set of WEA proposals focused on the hiring hall, calling for some gangs to work for a specific employer rather than being dispatched by the union, letting the employer shift men on the job, and having dispatchers selected jointly by employers and union officials. The WEA proposed to reduce gang sizes, increase sling load weights, dispense with gang bosses, and have walking bosses withdraw from the union. The ILWU blocked all those proposals but agreed to increase sling load weights for cement. Even there, some gangs briefly refused to work the heavier loads.

The WEA also pointed to "four on–four off," a practice that developed in the 1930s in which half of an eight-man hold gang worked while half rested. According to the WEA, "The Union admits this practice and claims to have abandoned it. The reports of the inspector of the Maritime Industry Board are full of references to its continuance." Bridges and the ILWU officers opposed the practice. The *Dispatcher* published an account of hold men being caught playing cards while supposedly working and specified that such situations could not continue. Many stevedore companies, however, tolerated four on–four off because it padded the payroll and thereby benefited the employer under a cost-plus contract.[39]

Senator Downey, in mid-August 1943, summarized his committee's findings: "Longshoremen on the West Coast have done and are doing a very creditable job. . . . [W]orkers are not engaged in slowdown practices and are almost universally working to their capacity."[40] The next year, the ILWU endorsed Downey for reelection and provided significant support to his campaign.

Bridges privately complained that the WEA's charges about a slowdown were payback for the ILWU's proposals to improve efficiency in ways the companies considered management prerogatives. The FBI recorded Bridges during a phone call in April 1943 regarding the charges of a slowdown: "We have driven the guys along, and now all of a sudden they [WEA] start attacking us." He continued, "We were threatened that they would do it unless we laid off, trying to put a change in operations that went beyond the sphere of labor relations." His conclusion was that the WEA's complaints were part of "post war positioning."[41]

Postwar positioning was on the minds of Bridges and other ILWU officers. Their most controversial such action was a postwar no-strike pledge. The proposal first appeared in May 1944 when Local 6, which had a significant proportion of CP members in its leadership, adopted a proposal with three main points: "A pledge on the part of the union that there shall be no strikes for the duration and beyond. A guarantee on the part of the employer that basic union security will be respected for the duration and beyond. Agreement . . . to settle disputes peaceably through arbitration and other means." Bridges defended it: "This measure would defend the security of the nation now and after the war, permitting both employers and labor to concentrate on defeating . . . unemployment after the war."[42]

Other union leaders immediately objected. UAW president R. J. Thomas called it "ridiculous" and "defeatist." Murray refused to permit the CIO Executive Board even to discuss it, and "sources close to CIO headquarters" reported that "plans to supplant Bridges as CIO director are well advanced" because, among other things, of his advocacy of a postwar no-strike pledge.[43]

Bridges quickly began to clarify his proposal for a postwar no-strike pledge. In late May, he argued, "Looking forward to bigger and better strikes is not a part of the postwar planning of the International Longshoremen's and Warehousemen's Union. . . . [A]n employer-ILWU agreement not to engage in economic struggles would be similar to the Teheran [sic], Moscow and Cairo agreements." In July he further clarified: "The right to strike was never renunciated. . . . [T]he quid pro quo is no strikes for no union busting. . . . [T]here are employers, enlightened by the experience of the war, who are willing to embark with us upon a political program for federal unemployment insurance, public health, education, and—of super importance to both of us—expanded business and foreign trade along the principles laid down at Teheran, Cairo, and Moscow."[44]

Bridges's repeated references to Tehran and other wartime conferences aligned with conclusions drawn by Earl Browder, head of the CPUSA, from the wartime conferences of FDR, Churchill, and Stalin. In January 1944, two months after the Tehran conference, in a meeting of the CP National Committee, Browder reviewed the close cooperation of the Big Three at Tehran and declared, "Capitalism and Socialism have begun to find their way to peaceful coexistence and collaboration." Predicting the wartime Popular Front would continue after the war, he specified that the CP should engage in politics through cooperation with New Deal Democrats, no longer run its own candidates for office, and change its name to the Communist Political Association (CPA). A national convention ratified those changes in May 1944, the same month that Local 6 issued its proposal.[45] Browder's Teheran line lasted only a year but was highly influential among CP members and sympathizers until early 1945.

In February 1945, *Fortune* magazine featured Bridges's postwar no-strike pledge: "Labor unions have got to work with the employers, Bridges says, and with the public for the good of the community, the country, the world. Anyone who disagrees with that philosophy is a scab, a fink, a Trotskyite, or a fascist appeaser.... He wants American free enterprise, American capitalism, to work. ... The U.S., according to Bridges' philosophy, must build up other countries after the war so that there can be an enormously expanded foreign trade." According to *Fortune*, Bridges hoped that the no-strike pledge would become a part of every labor contract. *Fortune* also noted, "A.F. of L. and a few C.I.O. leaders are violent in their disagreement" and quoted Dave Beck and Harry Lundeberg. Such treatment in the press—and by subsequent historians—often omitted key parts of Bridges's qualifications of his no-strike pledge: "The quid pro quo is no strikes for no union busting" and "the right to strike is inherent in democracy."[46]

In the light of their subsequent behavior, CIO and AFL leaders' criticism of Bridges's proposal appears either hypocritical or red-baiting—or both. In March 1945, Murray, for the CIO, and William Green, for the AFL, signed a "charter" with the U.S. Chamber of Commerce, in which "business" endorsed collective bargaining and accepted the Wagner Act and "labor" agreed to respect management prerogatives and continue the wartime no-strike pledge—almost exactly what Bridges was proposing. The agreement soon fell apart, with many businesses seeking to roll back union gains and many unions seeking to regain purchasing power lost through inflation.[47]

In May 1944, the California CIO Council organized a dinner to recognize Bridges's ten years of leadership. Veterans of the 1934 strike joined current union leaders in celebrating his accomplishments. In response, he insisted that any honor belonged to the rank and file. "All I ever did," he said, "was act as spokesman." He also cited Tehran and Roosevelt's "second bill of rights"—the Four Freedoms—as the way forward.[48]

Another step toward postwar positioning came in July 1944 when representatives from all longshore locals met to formulate bargaining proposals. Their proposals reflected, in part, the wartime experience of unions in gaining fringe benefits when wage increases were blocked by the NWLB. The longshore caucus proposed wage increases of about 14 percent, a week of paid vacation per year of time worked, one day per month of sick leave with a maximum of fifteen per year, and a guaranteed work week of thirty-six hours, averaged over four weeks. The last of these reflected the expectation that the war's end would bring a reduction in shipping and hence in the demand for longshore labor. These proposals also represent the extent to which some casual elements remained in longshore work. An individual could take unpaid time off at any time for any reason and be able to return to the hiring hall, and the only guarantee of work was that available work would be shared equally among those registered. Thus, paid vacations, paid sick leave, and guaranteed workweeks were innovations. The conference also recommended a security preamble including the no-strike pledge. In roll-call voting, the security preamble was adopted by more than two-thirds, with opposition from Local 8 (Portland), a few small northwestern locals, and almost half the Local 10 delegates. The WEA refused the security preamble, restated its demands that PCMIB had denied, and refused any wage increase, claiming productivity did not warrant one. Negotiations failed and matters went to the NWLB for settlement. Eventually, in August 1945, the NWLB approved wage increases of less than 5 percent. The NWLB also approved, for the first time, creation of a vacation fund, consisting of employers' contributions to be administered by the ILWU.[49]

Throughout the war, Bridges reminded the ILWU of the importance of political action. Nearly every issue of the *Dispatcher* repeated the slogan "For a People's Victory and a People's Peace!" Bridges encouraged ILWU members not only to register and vote but also to participate actively in political campaigns. In the 1942 state elections, most AFL and CIO leaders resumed their cooperation from 1938, but California governor Culbert Olson lost badly against Earl Warren, a Republican with an antiunion reputation. Robert Kenny, national president of the Lawyers' Guild, won for attorney general. In October 1943, in his "On the Beam" column, Bridges argued that political action was "a matter of life and death," and that message was repeated by other ILWU leaders and the women's auxiliary. In a by-election in 1943, the Sacramento Industrial Union Council took the lead in uniting the AFL, CIO, and railroad brotherhoods to elect Clair Engle, a liberal Democrat, to a formerly Republican congressional seat. Bridges crowed, "It's a real victory for us. . . . He's our man right down the line." In the 1943 San Francisco election, however, Roger Lapham, the shipping executive, won the mayor's office.[50]

In 1944 Bridges strongly supported Roosevelt and other New Deal Democrats, and the ILWU worked to get out the vote. Bridges claimed that, in California, "we had practically 3,500 guys working" on Election Day. Statewide, the ILWU focused on Roosevelt, Downey, and key members of Congress. In San Francisco, they worked to return Franck Havenner to the seat in Congress he'd lost four years before in a campaign based largely on claims that Havenner was manipulated by Bridges and the ILWU. That tactic appeared again in 1944. Bridges said that it was as if "the only guy that was running for office was me." Roosevelt easily carried all three Pacific Coast states and had strong coattails: Downey and Havenner won, and Democrats held onto all their congressional seats in California. In Washington State, Bridges thought the CIO had run "too narrow" a campaign, but Democrats nonetheless held their congressional and Senate seats. Bridges griped that, in Oregon, "that phoney gang up there"—the anti-Bridges state CIO council—"got the situation pretty well confused." Oregon went solidly Republican, although the new Republican senator was Wayne Morse. Electoral success came at a price: Bridges complained, "We broke our bloody union. . . . [W]e're about a quarter of a million in this fight, we're flat broke."[51]

V-E Day, end of the war in Europe, came on May 8, 1945, amid momentous events in San Francisco. Between mid-April and late June, the city hosted the founding conference of the United Nations. Six thousand delegates, staff members, and media representatives crowded hotels and streetcars.

Another conference took place simultaneously in Oakland, where delegates representing organized labor from twelve nations, including the Soviet Union, met to create a new international labor organization. The AFL stayed away, refusing to sit down with the CIO and Soviet unions. On May 2, the conference held a mass meeting titled "World Labor and World Peace" in San Francisco's Civic Auditorium. Bridges presided, introducing Sir Walter Citrine from the British unions as well as labor leaders from the Soviet Union, France, and Latin America. Citrine spoke of the role of labor in maintaining a peaceful world. In the event of an embargo placed on an aggressor nation, Citrine asked, "Who would carry out such an embargo?" Turning to Bridges, he answered, "Your union, Mr. Chairman, the dockers, the seamen, and finally the workers in the factories," a comment that Bridges long recalled. The same labor organizations later created the World Federation of Trade Unions (WFTU).[52]

At one of the many receptions during the UN founding meetings, Bridges shook hands with Soviet foreign minister Vyacheslav Molotov. A photo of Bridges with Molotov promptly appeared in the press. Soon after, a *Chronicle* columnist quoted Bridges on his exchange with Molotov: "Bridges, grinning: 'What's cookin'?' Molotov, grinning back: 'O.K.'" The photo and the same account of the nonsensical exchange appeared in the *Dispatcher*. The *People's World*, the CP's daily newspaper, also carried the photo. The photo of Bridges and Molotov grinning at each other soon became a staple of anti-Bridges propaganda issued by the WEA and anticommunist groups. An FBI informant claimed that CP leaders were angry at Bridges for permitting himself to be photographed with Molotov.[53]

The war years brought a major reorganization of the ILWU international leadership and office. In May 1943, Secretary-Treasurer Eugene Paton was drafted and waived deferment. To replace him, Bridges and the executive board chose Louis Goldblatt. Born in 1910 in the Bronx, he moved with his family to Los Angeles, where he attended the University of California at Los Angeles. By 1931,

Harry Bridges and Soviet foreign minister Vyacheslav Molotov shared a toast during a reception on May 8, 1945, V-E Day. Versions of this photo that removed all the other people were later used to label Bridges as a Soviet tool. (Photo courtesy of Labor Archives and Research Center, San Francisco State University)

when he received his degree in economics, he had become active in the Young Communist League. He came to Berkeley to pursue graduate studies but spent his time in YCL work, including running for city council as a Communist. In San Francisco in 1934, he worked on strike-support activities, then as a warehouseman and joined Local 38-44 (later Local 6). He moved quickly into leadership, first local vice president, then Northern California CIO director and secretary of the California CIO Council, then ILWU field representative on the Atlantic Coast. For the next thirty-four years, Bridges and Goldblatt led the ILWU as president and secretary-treasurer.[54]

Between 1943, when Goldblatt became secretary-treasurer, and 1945, the headquarters staff nearly doubled in size, from twelve to twenty-three; the field staff increased from twenty-two to thirty-three; and the international office moved to larger quarters. In September 1943, the ILWU launched its own Research Department, initially headed by the highly efficient Elinor Kahn, replacing Henry Melnikow and his organization. By early 1945, the ILWU's research department had four "technical employees" for research and analysis, two stenographers, and a librarian. (Subsequent generations of researchers have been grateful for the union's commitment to a librarian, later librarian-archivist, responsible for preserving and organizing the union's voluminous collection of documents.) A research department had become a necessity for assembling, organizing, and analyzing the wide range of data and other information needed for relations with an increasingly numerous and diverse group of employers and a growing number of governmental agencies.[55]

Melnikow looked back favorably on his work with Bridges: "I liked his sincerity and his devotion to the labor movement. . . . [I]t was very refreshing to have a man so devoted to the cause of the men that he represented. He would be willing to work day and night, sit down in the chair in my office completely exhausted and sleep for 15 minutes and then go back to work completely refreshed." Drawing upon his training with John Commons, Melnikow always advocated for collective bargaining and the importance of the contract—that is, business unionism. From that perspective, he argued, "If Bridges is a Communist, then he shouldn't have listened to me. . . . He did listen to me and that's why I don't know to this day whether he ever became a party member or not. I do know that he had a great deal of contact with people who were party members." Melnikow blamed Goldblatt for pushing him out: "I felt Lou resented my being listened to by Bridges. . . . He was consistently advising Bridges in a different direction than I was. . . . [W]e were at real loggerheads . . . so I withdrew." What Melnikow did not say was that Goldblatt's changes eliminated a major source of non-CP advice, as most, if not all, of the new research staff were either party members or close to the party.[56]

Goldblatt, himself, however left the party around that time. He later explained his decision to drop out: "There's no question in my mind that while their [CP leaders'] intentions might have been good, in many respects they did not have as accurate or as careful an appraisal of the membership as its [the union's] leaders did. . . . [W]ith some of the party people the position they followed was so doctrinaire you couldn't get anywhere; it did not make any sense." He continued to maintain what he called "cordial" relations with party leaders: "We sat and chewed the fat once in a while."[57] Goldblatt, like Bridges, became an "Influential": someone not a party member who was close to the party, usually on his own terms, and who maintained close relations with CP officials.

The reorganization of the international office clarified lines of responsibility. Goldblatt was secretary of the Political Action Committee and responsible for the Research Department and all administrative departments including finances and office personnel. The first vice president, J. R. Robertson, was director of organization and responsible for regional directors everywhere except the Northwest, Alaska, and Canada. The second vice president, Michael Johnson, from Local 34 (San Francisco clerks), was responsible for organization in those three areas. Bridges was responsible for the other three executive officers, the Coast Labor Relations Committee and longshore labor relations generally, PCMIB, the *Dispatcher*, and political action.[58]

Wartime changes in key personnel extended to the coast arbitrator. Wayne Morse resigned to join the NWLB, then became U.S. senator from Oregon. The position remained vacant except for two brief interim appointments, neither of whom made any significant decisions.[59]

The war brought significant growth in areas other than longshoring. By early 1945, the ILWU had new locals in the Midwest, the South, Canada, and Puerto Rico. In recognition of the importance of ILWU organizations in Hawai'i and Canada, the 1945 convention amended the constitution to reserve executive board seats for those areas.[60]

When the ILWU received its CIO charter in 1937, it had immediately chartered the Hawaiian longshore locals. Longshore workers in Hawai'i experienced much the same conditions as longshore workers in San Francisco, and workers in Hawai'i were often divided by ethnicity and language.[61]

Union organizing in Hawai'i met stiff resistance from the Big Five factoring companies—Alexander and Baldwin, C. Brewer, Castle and Cook, American Factors, and Theo. H. Davies—that controlled the sugar industry, including plantations and mills in Hawai'i, Matson Navigation (the dominant shipping line between Hawai'i and the mainland), and the C&H Sugar refinery at Crockett, across the bay from San Francisco, where the ILWU began organizing workers in the 1930s. The Big Five's corporate headquarters in Honolulu were the most imposing office buildings in Hawai'i, and their corporate offices on the mainland were in the Matson Building, four blocks from the Embarcadero. Other Hawaiian firms also mainland headquarters in San Francisco. Wallace Alexander, of Alexander and Baldwin, exemplified connections among the Hawaiian companies and the San Francisco business community: a descendant of the founders of both Alexander and Baldwin and Castle and Cook, a vice president of Matson Navigation and Honolulu Consolidated Oil, an important leader in the Industrial Association, sometime president of the San Francisco Chamber of Commerce, trustee of Stanford University, and a power in the state Republican Party. Roger Lapham, of the American-Hawaiian Steamship Company, was another leader of the San Francisco business community and the Republican Party.[62] And, of course, San Francisco Bay Area docks were the vital transfer point for goods moving to and from the islands.

The Big Five had securely controlled the Hawaiian economy, society, and polity. John Francis Neylan, counsel to William Randolph Hearst, wrote in early 1934, "I can tell you from personal knowledge that there is no habitable place on the globe which is held more firmly in feudal despotism than Hawaii." Neylan described the factoring companies as "thoroughly selfish and short-sighted" and their labor contracts as "refined methods of peonage."[63]

Jack Kawano and Fred Kamahoahoa were important in organizing Honolulu longshoremen, and Kawano was president of Local 37 when the ILWU issued its charter. At the 1941 convention, Kamahoahoa reported that, with the territory's longshoremen almost completely organized, "our next move . . . is to be the sugar industry." Kawano, too, understood the advantages of following the chain of vertical integration. One plantation worker remembered Kawano's organizing pitch: "If you get into the ILWU, you'll get support from the railroad workers, the dock workers, and even in the refinery [at Crockett]. You will have a connecting link from the sugar producers right up to the refinery. The ILWU will organize everything from top to bottom." Goldblatt recognized the same logic. After studying the economic situation in Hawai'i, he realized that virtually all economic activity was directly or indirectly controlled by the Big Five. Goldblatt concluded that the ILWU could not win in longshore "until the heart of economic power in those islands, namely, the sugar industry had been organized."[64]

Jack Hall became ILWU regional director in 1944 and led the tidal wave of union organizing that soon struck Hawai'i. After high school, Hall had gone to sea, joined the SUP, became radicalized, went on the beach in Hawai'i, and briefly joined the CP. He focused on bringing workers together regardless of ethnicity, unlike the separate organizations for each ethnic group typical of previous organizing. "Know your class," Hall said, "and be loyal to it." To organize agricultural workers, the ILWU had to organize politically, to secure territorial legislation to protect fieldworkers' right to join unions and engage in collective bargaining. Hall, Kawano, and others focused their organizing outside Oahu (the most populated island), because the Big Five had gerrymandered the territorial legislature to give the rural islands disproportionate representation. In November 1944, a coalition of ILWU, other CIO unions, and some AFL unions scored important electoral victories on Hawai'i (the Big Island) and Maui. As a result, the ILWU secured legislation protecting fieldworkers' right to unionize. Success in organizing Hawaiian fieldworkers made the ILWU the first U.S. union to succeed long term in organizing and securing contracts for agricultural fieldworkers. The ILWU's success in organizing many facets of the Hawaiian economy soon gave Hawai'i the greatest density of ILWU members.[65]

In May 1945, events in Stockton, California, threatened ILWU efforts in Hawai'i. Members of the Stockton unit of Local 6 (warehouse) refused to work with an ILWU member who was Nisei (Japanese American). Hall telegraphed Bridges, "Action Stockton Unit on Nisei revolting to one thousand loyal ILWU members Japanese ancestry. Local 6 should suspend Stockton Unit forthwith unless constitutional violations corrected." Bridges and Richard Lynden, president of Local 6, rushed to Stockton. Bridges personally ripped the unit's charter off the wall and bluntly told the Stockton unit members: "Either you are in favor of discrimination or not in favor of it. . . . If you are in favor of it, you have no place in our union." All members of the unit received cards to sign, pledging never to discriminate. Those who wouldn't sign were suspended.[66]

The Stockton incident came amid crucial ILWU organizing in Hawai'i. In early May 1945, a hundred representatives of ILWU members in Hawai'i drafted a program for the sugar, pineapple, railroad, and longshoring industries. Goldblatt worked with the delegates and assisted with longshore negotiations. Goldblatt and James Blaisdell, president of the Hawaii Employers Council, issued a joint statement that included the vision that, in Hawai'i, "employers and employees can get together and settle their own problems by direct negotiations." By 1945 the ILWU counted twenty thousand members in Hawai'i, in longshore, railroad, sugar, pineapple, and other industries. However, Bridges could not yet go to Hawai'i, then a territory, until his citizenship status was settled.[67]

In 1943–44, despite union responsibilities and legal problems, Bridges indulged his love of jazz. San Francisco jazz lovers had brought to the city Willie "Bunk" Johnson, a legendary New Orleans trumpet player. After sessions at the Museum of Art and a theater, Johnson and his band found themselves unable to play because of racially based restrictions. Bridges offered the basement meeting hall of the CIO Building, soon renamed the "HJS Chamber" for the Hot Jazz Society, of which Bridges was a member. Johnson and his band, and sometimes other performers, held forth every Sunday afternoon, from July 1943 until July 1944. Alfred Frankenstein, arts critic of the *Chronicle*, described the "exhilarating show": the audience "stood and sat, drank and smoked, danced and clapped and stomped." The concerts attracted stellar guests, including Jimmy Dorsey, Harry James, Louis Armstrong, and Count Basie, either as performers or audience members.[68]

Amid the distractions of hot jazz and the demands of his responsibilities and legal battles, Bridges's personal life was under stress. His relationship with Agnes had been difficult for years. By the late 1930s, they were living apart. They lived together briefly around 1940, then Harry went to live with Herbert and Dorothy Resner. Herb Resner was a CP member and law partner of George Anderson, who, among the city's attorneys, was the most open about his CP membership.[69]

During Bridges's adventures at Hotel Edison in mid-1941, he was already dating Nancy Berdecio, born Nancy Feinstein and a professional dancer under the name Nancy Fenton. She was married to Roberto Berdecio, a Bolivian-born artist. Resner handled Nancy's divorce in 1943. Three weeks after her divorce, on May 26, 1943, Nancy gave birth to Julia Ellen Fenton, likely named for Bridges's mother and aunt. Julia's birth certificate listed Alfred Fenton as her father, but it was common knowledge that Bridges was.[70]

Late in 1944, Richard Gladstein initiated Harry's divorce from Agnes. The charge was "extreme cruelty," the usual charge at the time, and Bridges initially emphasized that he did not intend "any public reflection on his wife." Agnes countersued, represented by A. L. Crawford, whose long history of fighting Bridges and his union included the Ivan Cox lawsuit and assisting INS officials during the Sears hearing. The countersuit demanded $450 per month as alimony and half of all personal property. Crawford claimed, with no evidence, that Bridges earned $1,000 a month and had a large stock of savings bonds. In fact, he earned $90 a week and had almost no savings.[71]

After Agnes retained Crawford, Harry wrote to Nancy: "The divorce case is not an ordinary one, but a part of the whole citizen[ship] fight." He quoted Gladstein as saying, "The whole purpose of Crawford and his gang is to block the granting of citizenship papers" and that the divorce had become "a political matter, and must be handled as such." And, Bridges assured Nancy, Gladstein "is ready to go in slugging with everything we have."[72]

When the divorce trial opened, Bridges testified to Agnes's habitual drunkenness and violent behavior when she was inebriated. Agnes denied being a drunk and charged that, in the midst of an argument, Bridges had pushed her out a window in 1935. A witness for Bridges recalled that he had been shaving when Agnes fell while hanging laundry. The judge awarded Bridges the divorce and ordered him to pay alimony of $85 per month, to be used for rehabilitation and not alcohol.[73]

Soon after, on Labor Day, September 3, 1945, thirty thousand CIO members and their families marched down Market Street to the Civic Center, where Bridges and Robert Kenny, California attorney general, spoke. Bridges emphasized the need for jobs to maintain the level of employment during the war and avoid unemployment when those in service were mustered out. "I want to make it plain to the people of San Francisco that we wish to win jobs for all by peaceful means," he said, but added, "The CIO knows how to strike."[74]

Two weeks later, Bridges became a U.S. citizen. Prior to his appearance before Judge Thomas Foley, the INS examiner in the case told the judge, in chambers, that the INS had received an affidavit from Agnes Bridges claiming she had seen his CP membership book and witnessed CP meetings in their home. Foley advised the examiner that he could question Bridges based on information in the affidavit, that the affidavit itself could not be introduced into evidence since Agnes was not present, but that it could be given to the judge during the hearing. All that was done. The judge read it, summarized it, and asked Bridges regarding the allegations. Bridges denied them all. Gladstein stated that some of the claims in the affidavit had been proved false in the 1939 deportation hearing and that, in the divorce proceedings, Agnes had said she knew of no evidence that Bridges was a CP member. The INS examiner then declined to make a recommendation regarding citizenship. Foley announced there was no reason not to grant the petition for citizenship, and he administered the oath to make Bridges a citizen. The press related that Bridges "flushed a deep scarlet and seemed close to tears." Jackie was at his side. He said simply, "I have possibly had more opportunity and, I think, more good reason to recognize and appreciate that citizenship is a priceless possession." When Gladstein requested a copy of Agnes Bridges's affidavit, the INS refused. One official noted, "The case is closed both from immigration and naturalization. . . . [W]e are not going to keep this thing going on forever." Harry and Nancy were married a year later.[75]

By late 1945, many aspects of Bridges's complicated life seemed to point to better times ahead—he was a citizen, conflicts in his personal life seemed to have resolved, he was head of a clearly organized and competently staffed headquarters office, and the union had come out of the war well positioned for postwar challenges. He could not possibly have imagined the challenges that lay just ahead.

12

Cold War, Labor War

1945–1948

The bright promise of early 1945 soon gave way to a nation divided between FDR's political heirs and his opponents and a world divided between the erstwhile allies. Hopes for a postwar world in which nations would cooperate to rebuild shattered economies were replaced by the fears and insecurities of the Cold War. Despite Bridges's embrace of Roosevelt and New Deal Democrats in 1944, he gave lukewarm support to a quixotic third party in 1948. His relations with CIO leaders became more and more strained by his support of positions taken by the CP. Instead of the vision of union-employer cooperation in Bridges's proposed Security Preamble, there were two longshore strikes in three years.

Harry Truman was less politically adept than Franklin Roosevelt and definitely less charismatic. Some New Deal Democrats criticized Truman for his more moderate domestic and foreign policies, most prominently Henry Wallace, formerly secretary of agriculture, vice president, and secretary of commerce under FDR. Wallace left the cabinet over disagreements with Truman's tough stance toward the Soviet Union and was prominent in founding the Progressive Citizens of America (PCA), an effort to bring together liberals, the CIO, and the Left (CPA and those close to the CPA) to oppose the rightward drift of U.S. politics. Liberal anticommunists formed a competing organization, the Americans for Democratic Action (ADA).

Within the Communist Political Association, expectations for long-term cooperation with New Deal Democrats, as expressed in Browder's Teheran Line, were crushed on orders from Moscow that arrived via an article by a French CP leader, Jacques Duclos, condemning the transformation of the American CP into a political association. The *Daily Worker* carried the full article on May 24.[1]

Long CPA meetings followed. Harry Bridges and Dave Jenkins attended a meeting at which San Francisco CPA leaders explained the Duclos article. Jenkins later recalled Bridges's reaction: "What do those frogs know about the

United States?" Bridges's reaction was not typical. A special convention reconstituted the CPA as the Communist Party. Browder was expelled. William Z. Foster returned to prominence, and he and others in the new leadership immediately attacked Truman for abandoning Roosevelt's policies and claimed that Truman was engaged in a lead-up to war against the Soviet Union.[2]

As tensions between the United States and the Soviet Union grew, driven especially by Soviet control over parts of central Europe, domestic anticommunism—somewhat stifled during the war—reemerged more vigorously than before. Patriotic organizations and politicians vied in denouncing the Communist threat and labeling individuals and organizations as part of "the Communist conspiracy."

Although Bridges remained a pragmatist as a union leader, his support for the party line on national and international issues now brought increased criticism. During World War II, CIO president Phil Murray and other CIO leaders had largely avoided public criticism of CIO union leaders close to the CP. Even so, opposition to Bridges or to CP influence in the CIO had sometimes surfaced during the war years. In 1943 Oregon CIO state convention delegates tabled a resolution endorsing the national CIO's defense of Bridges, and one delegate announced, "As far as I am concerned they can deport Bridges tomorrow." In 1944 the Spokane, Washington, local of the International Woodworkers of America asked Murray to remove Bridges as CIO director for California. In February 1945, the Newspaper Guild national executive board defeated a motion of support for Bridges's defense.[3]

Murray had fully supported Bridges's defense in public, but private conflict between them was more than occasional. At the CIO executive council meeting in February 1943, Murray called Bridges "irresponsible." A few months later, Bridges complained that CIO officials in the Northwest and Los Angeles were hostile toward him and that CIO officials were trying to "keep the Reds and ILWU people" off federal agencies. In February 1944, Bridges concluded that "a real drive" against him and the ILWU was being conducted, but in such a way that Murray "knows nothing about it but the people around him are doing it."[4]

With the onset of Cold War, more CIO leaders attacked CP influence in CIO unions. However, when Murray first moved against Bridges, it was not ostensibly political. In June 1946, the Southern California district directors of the United Steel Workers (USW), UAW, Amalgamated Clothing Workers, Shipyard Workers, and Oil Workers petitioned Murray to divide the state and appoint a new regional director for Southern California. Bridges, they claimed, didn't give sufficient time to the South. One might wonder where the petition originated—with the signatories themselves, the presidents of those unions, or national CIO officers—but Murray quickly announced his decision to split California and appoint a new regional director for Southern California.[5]

The new director, Irwin DeShetler, quickly moved to limit the influence of Bridges and Left unions in CIO central bodies. (In the CIO of 1946, Left meant close to the CP, and Right meant non-CP or, more often, anti-CP.) DeShetler managed the election of the state CIO executive board so that it changed from one in which, he said, board members were "all the choice of Harry Bridges" to one in which "we have a fairly good group." He reported the voting strength of the Right and Left unions on the new board and the state council and suggested ways for the Right to take over.[6]

This came amid a postwar strike wave of unprecedented proportions, driven especially by the failure of wages to keep pace with inflation. Between August 1945 and August 1946, five million workers took part in some forty-six hundred strikes, most by the CIO. Murray accused industry of being responsible for the strikes by refusing to accept mediation and fact-finding despite huge profits.[7]

Bridges and the ILWU faced their own problems at the end of the war, as the Waterfront Employers Association (WEA) condemned ILWU leaders as Communists and as responsible for inefficiency. The longshore caucus—delegates from all Pacific Coast longshore locals—met in late summer 1945 to develop plans for the first postwar contract. Concerned that there would be less work once shipping returned to peacetime levels, they agreed on a thirty-hour week with no overtime to spread the work and an hourly wage of $1.75 to maintain members' income with fewer hours. The existing agreement, set to expire October 1, 1945, was repeatedly extended to permit negotiations.[8]

Bridges was promoting some form of amalgamation with other maritime unions. In February 1946, the leaders of the six CIO maritime unions—ILWU, NMU, MEBA, National Union of Marine Cooks and Stewards (NUMCS), American Communications Association (formerly American Radio Telegraphists Association), and Inland Boatmen's Union (IBU)—and the independent MFOW agreed "to recommend one big national union for all maritime workers" and called for a convention to develop that possibility. By then, after months of unproductive negotiations, more than 90 percent of ILWU longshore members had voted to strike if negotiations continued to stall. Given ongoing discussions with other maritime unions, however, ILWU locals postponed strike action pending federal fact-finding and coordination with other maritime unions.[9]

The maritime unity convention met in San Francisco on May 6, 1946, as headlines blared news of strikes or possible strikes in coal, railroads, and autos. By then the ILWU, NUMCS, and MFOW had authorized strikes, and NMU members were voting on strike action. Bridges declared maritime unity "the most effective means by the which the American maritime worker can oppose the shipowner politically and by the threat of economic action." However, opening day saw Bridges and Joe Curran, NMU president, clash over election of a convention secretary. Though the press speculated that merger would create the fifth-largest CIO affiliate, delegates instead discussed a joint strike. Bridges acknowledged that a joint strike date might not be possible due to unions' internal procedures but insisted, as he had in the 1930s, that the most important thing would be "that we all go back together"—a central principle for Bridges. Five of the seven unions agreed to strike on June 15, and the other two committed to support the strike—potentially the first nationwide shipping strike, affecting all coasts and the Great Lakes. Instead of a merger, the convention created the Committee for Maritime Unity (CMU), a joint-strike committee, cochaired by Bridges and Curran.[10]

In a long report for President Truman, J. Edgar Hoover summarized informants' reports on the convention. "Communists held a strong majority among the delegates," Hoover claimed, "and the conference was controlled by Communist CIO officials." Curran "cooperated in the general meetings" but "refused to collaborate directly with the Communist clique." ILWU, NMU, and NUMCS delegates were the most committed to amalgamation, but others "were cool." FBI informants claimed that Bridges offered the presidency of an amalgamated union to Curran, but Curran refused because he felt the executive committee would be Communist controlled. The convention then fell back on a joint strike instead of amalgamation. Informants also reported on a meeting of the Seaman's Branch of the CP, during the convention, during which William Schneiderman announced, "Plans for one big union . . . have been deferred."[11]

As the June 15 strike deadline approached, federal fact finders recommended that ILWU members receive twenty-two cents more per hour instead of the thirty-five cents the union was asking. On May 29, CMU leaders met with shipping executives in the office of Secretary of Labor Lewis Schwellenbach, who was determined to prevent a strike. As they met, Congress was considering antistrike legislation. On May 29, Truman received the Case bill, designed to prevent or end strikes. He vetoed it but had his own bill to end strikes through presidential seizure. The Senate passed Truman's bill on June 1. By then the WEA had accepted the fact finders' recommendation for the ILWU. Shipping companies, however, opposed the NMU's wage demands. Negotiations on individual contracts took place with all CMU unions represented, perhaps a lesson learned from the MFP strike.[12]

When Truman threatened to use the army and navy to move cargo ships, Bridges and Curran wrote directly to Louis Saillant, general secretary of the World Federation of Trade Unions, requesting that longshore workers in other countries not handle such "hot" cargo. WFTU affiliates pledged their support. CIO secretary-treasurer James Carey objected to Saillant's involvement, which Carey and the CIO leadership interpreted as an attempt to control the strike. More difficulties between the CIO and WFTU soon arose.[13]

In mid-June, the Labor Department took over the shipowners' side of the CMU negotiations because the federal War Shipping Administration owned the large majority of U.S.-flagged ships. Agreements were concluded shortly before the strike deadline. Curran claimed that the NMU had received the "greatest gains ever made." The ILWU gained almost nothing beyond the fact finders' recommendation. Bridges denounced fact-finding as "a snare, a delusion and a sell-out," and blamed "weaknesses and personal ambitions" for the other unions' failure to back a last-minute push for the ILWU.[14]

The ILWU-WEA agreement of June 15, 1946, was retroactive to October 1, 1945, and expired on September 30, 1946, only three and a half months away. A longshore caucus met in late June to determine demands. Unable to agree on a wage increase, they did agree on hours, benefits, and an expiration date to coincide with those of other CMU affiliates. ILWU members voted by more than four to one that, if negotiations failed, they would strike on September 30.[15]

Negotiations began, chaired by Clark Kerr, UC Berkeley economics professor and newly appointed coast arbitrator. Kerr recalled the opening statements: "Frank Foisie for the waterfront employers said: 'Mr. Bridges, we do not know what you are going to demand, but, by God, the answer is no.' Bridges replied: 'To tell the truth, Mr. Foisie, we have not yet finally decided on our demands but, by God, we will never take no for an answer.'" The parties nonetheless agreed on a wage review and expiration date, but negotiations bogged down over a safety code and disability benefits. With assistance from a federal mediator, agreement seemed close by August 6, with the only sticking points the process for appointing the coast arbitrator and the separate agreement for steam schooners. In mid-September, the NMU, MFOW, and NUMCS struck and gained major victories within sixteen days.[16] There was no CMU-wide strike.

On October 1, 1946, MEBA struck both coasts and the ILWU struck the Pacific Coast docks. Bridges insisted the only remaining issue was the ILWU and SUP's shared jurisdiction over the sixteen remaining steam schooners. Negotiations ended. The federal mediator returned to Washington. Bridges and Foisie blamed each other. Foisie called the situation "confused." Bridges called it "stupid." In mid-October, Bridges joined MEBA negotiations in New York. Once MEBA agreed to a settlement, on November 17, the ILWU and WEA quickly compromised all remaining issues.[17] By then Bridges must have been seriously questioning whether his commitment to maritime unity was worth holding his members out on strike for forty-eight days with little to show for it.

The year 1946 also saw a major strike in Hawai'i, a test of the ILWU's sugar organization. The ILWU asked for wages of sixty-five cents an hour, a forty-hour workweek, a union shop, and a say in employers' housing expenditures. (On sugar plantations, workers' housing was typically owned by the companies.) By mid-August, with a strike imminent, Jack Hall asked for either Bridges or Goldblatt to come to the islands. With Bridges in the midst of longshore negotiations, Goldblatt went. The day before the strike, Bridges predicted the strike "will end one hundred years of economic slavery in Hawai'i." The sugar strike lasted seventy-nine days. Federal mediators helped bring a settlement that included a large wage increase, but not a forty-hour week or union shop. Hall called it "a tremendous victory." The research director for the Hawaiian Employers' Council (HEC) agreed, "For the first time in Hawaiian history the employers had been soundly and definitely thwarted." One of the employers' negotiators also said, "When Goldblatt decided the time had come to settle, he was ingenious in finding solutions to the small problems."[18] Two years later, ILWU relations with the HEC came to play a significant role in Pacific Coast longshore labor relations.

Across the country in the 1946 elections, amid a growing national outcry against communism, liberal and New Deal Democrats lost, in both state and federal elections. Republicans gained majorities in Congress.

Shortly after, delegates to the 1946 CIO national convention unanimously approved a resolution rejecting efforts by the CP "or other political parties" to interfere in CIO affairs. Murray proclaimed, "This organization is not and must not be Communist-controlled and inspired," and the new policy "should be, and in fact must be, adhered to within the councils of the national CIO and its affiliates."[19]

A month later, Curran resigned as CMU cochair, claiming the ILWU and Pacific Coast maritime unions—and by implication the CP—were using the NMU. Curran's action set off a struggle between the NMU's Left and Right factions. Charging three NMU national officers with putting CP interests above those of the NMU, Curran set out to purge such "politicians" and bring the NMU into line with CIO policies. Soon the leaders of the remaining CMU unions voted to dissolve the organization. Days later, Vincent Malone, MFOW president, announced that his union had voted out all Left officers.[20]

The ILWU's seventh biennial convention met in April 1947. The officers cheerfully reported that, since 1945, membership had grown from 65,000 to 88,500 and that *Fortune* magazine ranked the *Dispatcher* among the most effective union newspapers. The officers also described "an experiment in labor education": a group of ILWU local leaders from Hawai'i came to San Francisco for six weeks to attend classes at the California Labor School, meet with international officers and staff, and visit Locals 6 and 10. The officers attributed some of the ILWU's success in Hawai'i to their "experiment."[21]

Soon after, Bridges testified at an Interstate Commerce Committee hearing. Shipping companies were requesting approval of higher rates based on labor costs and the cost of labor stoppages. Bridges insisted, instead, that the companies would not need higher rates if they stopped fighting unions and instead invested those funds in mechanization of dock work. Bridges admitted, "We know it means fewer jobs. But we are more concerned with safe and decent conditions than the number of jobs. Our men would like to get their work done with less hard, manual work and grow older."[22]

In June and July 1947, the ILWU faced difficult negotiations with the Hawaiian pineapple industry. The union's organization was shaky. The companies took a hard line. Bridges, Goldblatt, and Robertson joined Hall in negotiations. After a brief and poorly organized strike, they settled for less than what the companies had informally offered before negotiations. Despite the outcome, the companies' negotiators came away with respect for Bridges and Goldblatt as negotiators and individuals.[23]

As the expiration of the 1946 longshore agreement approached, the ILWU agreed to extend it, until June 15, 1948, conditional upon NUMCS, ACA, and MEBA arriving at satisfactory agreements. All the CIO maritime unions settled after a brief slowdown.[24]

By then the Republican majorities in Congress and their southern Democratic allies were busily rolling back the Wagner Act's protections for unions. A bill by Robert Taft (R-OH) passed the Senate on May 13, with support from all but three Republicans (Wayne Morse opposed) and half the Democrats, nearly all from southern states. Taft's bill, combined with the even more restrictive Hartley bill, passed in the House by a similar coalition. Bridges urged President Truman to veto it because the maritime unions had just demonstrated that they could resolve their disputes without federal involvement. Truman did veto the bill, calling it "shocking," "bad for labor, bad for management, and bad for the country," and "a dangerous challenge to free speech." Congress quickly overrode the veto.[25]

The Taft-Hartley Act authorized the president to intervene in strikes affecting the national security by ordering strikers back to work for an eighty-day "cooling off" period. The law denied NLRB protection to foremen's unions, and the WEA quickly notified the ILWU that it would no longer bargain over contracts for walking bosses (foremen, under the new law). The law prohibited jurisdictional strikes, secondary boycotts, and the closed shop. Taft was blunt that the last of these was aimed at the ILWU: "The closed shop . . . is exemplified by the so-called hiring halls on the west coast." The law also required union officers to file affidavits disavowing CP membership or sympathy; failure to comply could remove NLRB protection for their union.[26]

Bridges greeted the Taft-Hartley Act as a challenge: "If any employers attempt to deny . . . fundamental rights to our members, we serve notice now that we will fight back." Most CIO leaders initially refused to sign the non-Communist affidavits, although most Right CIO leaders soon did so. When Bridges and other ILWU officers refused the affidavits, the executive board agreed that, henceforth, the union would seek to bypass the NLRB.[27] They could not have anticipated the full consequences of such action.

At the 1947 CIO annual convention, the growing divide between Left and Right unions appeared in debate over a resolution supporting the Marshall Plan—although not by name—and in discussions of political action in 1948.[28] The Marshall Plan—officially the European Recovery Program—seemed an unlikely subject to divide the CIO. Parts of Europe, especially France and Italy, were still experiencing serious economic dislocations after the war, fueling a rising vote for Communists. Germany, divided into zones of occupation among the victorious Allies, was also slow to recover economically. In June 1947, Secretary of State George Marshall had announced that the United States was willing to provide major financial support for the economic recovery of Europe, including Germany, the Soviet Union, and the Soviet-occupied nations of Central and Eastern Europe. The Soviet Union rejected Marshall's initiative and instead organized the Cominform, consisting of the Soviet Union, its satellites in Eastern and Central Europe, and the CPs of France and Italy. At the Cominform's founding meeting, Andrei Zhdanov, Stalin's emissary, announced that the world was split into two hostile camps and denounced the "expansionist" aims of the United States The CPUSA then attacked the Marshall Plan as American capitalists' effort to control the economies of Europe. When the CP pushed its allies in the Left CIO unions to oppose the Marshall Plan, Right CIO leaders lined up to support it and Truman's foreign policy more generally.[29]

The year 1948 proved a time of major struggles for Bridges and the ILWU. Early that year, a political confrontation between Bridges and the ILWU, on the one hand, and Murray and other CIO leaders, on the other, seemed a struggle for survival. Later in 1948, a strike on the docks of the Pacific Coast quickly became an even more serious struggle for survival of the hiring hall and Bridges's survival as ILWU president.

The central issues in the conflict between Bridges and Murray were political, Bridges's opposition to the Marshall Plan and his lukewarm support for the third-party presidential candidacy of Henry Wallace. Behind those issues was always the charge that Bridges and the ILWU were following the lead of the CP rather than the CIO.

Bridges was fully on board with the CP line on the Marshall Plan. In his *Dispatcher* column in mid- and late 1947, he lambasted the "Truman-Marshall Plan" as "a program to prevent the rise of free peoples, and free peoples' governments in countries liberated by the war from Nazism, Fascism, or from reactionary regimes that had always oppressed the common people." He called it "a scheme to use money and food of the American people to purchase and turn over to Wall Street at practically no cost to the private interests the basic industries and raw materials of Germany and all western European nations." In December 1947, the ILWU Executive Board condemned the Marshall Plan as "detrimental to the economic and political security and the best interests of the American people." In March and April 1948, the *Dispatcher* published four full-page articles attacking the Marshall Plan, all under Bridges's name. (Items published in the *Dispatcher* under Bridges's name were not always—or even often—written by Bridges, but he controlled what appeared under his name.) Nearly a decade later, in 1956, Eugene Dennis, general secretary of the CPUSA, admitted that the CP's insistence that its CIO allies give unstinting opposition to the Marshall Plan was "very harmful, untenable and sectarian."[30] By then, however, serious damage had been done and could not be undone.

As attacks by Bridges and the ILWU on the Marshall Plan became sharper and more prominent, so too did the ILWU's embrace of a third party for the 1948 elections. This, too, derived from a decision within the CP. After replacing Browder, CP leaders seemed uncertain how to approach politics, and they received ambiguous signals from Moscow. By late 1947, they faced a difficult decision: continue to work with liberal Democrats or back a third party. Bolting the Democrats might mean losing such allies as Robert Kenny and Franck Havenner and dividing the CIO. Throughout much of 1947, the CP supported efforts both to nominate Henry Wallace as a Democrat and to form a third party. Only in December 1947, *after* Wallace decided to run as an independent, did CP leaders determine to back Wallace as a third-party presidential candidate.[31]

Earlier, in mid-1947, Robert Kenny was leading a group of Democrats trying to make Wallace the Democratic nominee. The ILWU executive board supported Kenny's efforts. Like the CP, the *Dispatcher* in September both defended the idea of a third party and promoted revitalizing the Democratic Party. The *Dispatcher* continued to straddle in October, reporting Wallace's efforts to win the Democratic nomination and efforts to put the Independent Progressive Party on the California ballot.[32]

At the state CIO convention in November 1947, Hugh Bryson of the NUMCS and Richard Lynden of Local 6, both close to the CP, pushed for the IPP. Bridges sought a middle ground, and the convention, with near unanimity, adopted a resolution acknowledging the right of individual unions to endorse or not endorse the IPP. A conference of Northern California ILWU locals in early December continued that ambivalence, endorsing the IPP, the Wallace Democrats, and CIO-PAC. However, in December, before Wallace's announcement and the final decision of the CP, the ILWU executive board endorsed the third-party movement.[33]

In January 1948, the CIO executive board declared a third party was "unwise" and endorsed the Marshall Plan. The resolution was hotly contested, and Bridges spoke at length in opposition. The vote was 33–11. Murray later said the resolution was not "compulsory" for union members, adding, "It is the obligation of the executive board to provide guidance to the membership. It does not necessarily follow that they will accept that advice." Bridges agreed, saying, "This resolution doesn't bind our union. . . . We are still free to take such action as we wish."[34]

In early 1948, FBI informants told of "strenuous efforts on the part of the Communist Party to get Bridges to publicly endorse the current Third Party drive" and that Bridges "had been very cool to this because of the belief that the drive could not be very successful." Bridges's initial statement, in late December, after Wallace's announcement, condemned "ruinous bipartisan domestic and foreign policies" and voiced the hope that a third party would bring out "millions" of voters who would otherwise not vote. In early February, Bridges spoke for the third party, but the FBI's informant said Bridges's speech "was brief and consisted of general remarks encouraging the circulation of additional petitions." Curtis MacDougall, author of a three-volume account of the Wallace campaign, describes Bridges's participation as limited to chairing a meeting in San Francisco and making a small financial contribution. Bridges permitted listing his name with the National Wallace for President Committee but failed to attend the committee's meetings.[35]

In late March, the ILWU executive board endorsed Wallace but specified that locals were free to go their own way. By April implications of the third-party move became clear when the California CIO council—under Left control— issued primary-election endorsements and the only Democrats they endorsed had filed in both the Democratic and IPP primaries. Liberal Democrats were under significant pressure *not* to cross-file as IPP because some AFL unions announced they would not support anyone who did that. Missing from the CIO Council's list of congressional endorsements, therefore, were such staunch supporters of labor as Franck Havenner, Helen Gahagan Douglas, and Chet Holifield. IPP candidates filed against all of them. By late August, the national Wallace campaign was denying any intent of defeating those candidates.[36] Thus, though the third-party movement had initially been promoted as a way to bring out voters to support progressive Democrats, it became an instrument for denying CIO endorsements to liberal Democrats who had perfect or near-perfect voting records on CIO issues but refused to file in the IPP primary.

If Bridges was lukewarm toward the IPP, other ILWU members were in outright opposition. In May Local 10 held a secret ballot referendum on two issues: the Wallace candidacy and the Marshall Plan. Despite the *Dispatcher*'s promotion of Wallace and attacks on the Marshall Plan, the local was split almost down the middle: 52 percent favored Wallace, and 55 percent opposed the Marshall Plan. In July Local 10 urged the IPP candidate running against Havenner to withdraw, and in September the San Francisco CIO Council endorsed Havenner. In October the Los Angeles CIO Council endorsed Douglas and Holifield.[37]

Nationwide, polls showed Wallace at 7 percent early in 1948, but he finished with 2 percent. In February Wallace polled at 11 percent in California, but he finished with 4.7 percent. He got 3.5 percent in Washington and 2.9 percent in Oregon. In California, Washington, and Oregon, Wallace did best in counties with ILWU locals.[38] In the end, IPP candidates seem not have drawn enough votes to defeat any progressive Democrat, but the real and lasting result of the election was to drive a wedge between the Left (the CP and its allies in the CIO unions) and mainstream Democrats.

Robert Kenny was a leader of the national Progressive Citizens of America and leader of the Democrats for Wallace in California. In 1953 he wrote, "From a purely California standpoint, . . . the third party movement was just part of the misplaced militancy that developed in the left after the Duclos letter." He called it "utter folly." Eugene Dennis later called it "erroneous and harmful" because it "widened the cleavage in the CIO and weakened the ties between the Left Wing and the mainstream of the labor movement." In 1964 Sam Darcy similarly wrote to Bridges: the Wallace campaign "worked to split unions in the country from the main body, to separate out from the Democratic Party many of the best people who came up in the ranks during the 30s, it created a bitterness among the middle-of-the-roaders." Darcy may have been thinking of Kenny when he added, "It destroyed some leaders and candidates of real progressive character who held great promise." Bridges agreed that the independent campaign of 1948 was a mistake and "did a lot of damage."[39]

Though Bridges was "cool" to the third-party movement at the time and later agreed it was mistake, he followed other ILWU leaders—and the CP—into support for Wallace and the IPP. Their decision to follow the CP in attacking the Marshall Plan and supporting the third party had far-reaching negative effects: immediately, a reduction of Bridges's role in the CIO and the division and disruption of the state CIO, and ultimately the isolation of the ILWU from the mainstream of organized labor.

In early 1948, Bridges tried to differentiate between his personal views, the position of his union, and his role as CIO regional director. That became almost impossible after the CIO executive committee's resolution in January. Within weeks Northern California directors for eight Right CIO unions, including the UAW, USW, Oil Workers, and Amalgamated Clothing Workers, wrote to Murray to request "a full-time regional director . . . unencumbered by other duties." The letter specifically asked for a CIO regional director who would "aid the development of effective political action in accordance with the policies and program laid down by the National CIO." The press soon reported that a "purge" was under way of state and regional CIO officials who disagreed with the January resolution and that Bridges was a major target.[40]

Herb Caen, in the *Chronicle*, clearly based on conversation with Bridges, reported, "Bridges is not objecting to a CIO indorsement of Truman, but rather to the attempt of the hierarchy to dictate voting policy to the membership. 'All I want,' he said Tuesday night, 'is the right to vote for Taft, if I feel like it!'"[41] Taft was then seeking the Republican nomination for president.

In mid-February 1948, at Bridges's urging, the CIO state executive board took the same position as the San Francisco CIO council, "by-pass completely such controversial issues as the third party, the Wallace candidacy, and the Marshall plan" and concentrate on congressional and legislative elections. By then the press was speculating that the only reason Bridges had not been sacked was that Murray could not persuade anyone to accept the job. On February 18, Allan Haywood, CIO director of organization, wrote to Bridges asking if it were true that Bridges was publicly supporting the third party and opposing the Marshall Plan and pointing to the difficulty of representing the positions of both the ILWU and the CIO. He stressed that Bridges, as regional director, was expected "to support unreservedly and forthrightly the position taken by CIO" and to advise Haywood "if you can not do so," so "appropriate steps can be taken." Haywood distributed copies to the press.[42]

Bridges notified Haywood that he had not changed his views about Wallace or the Marshall Plan but also that "as CIO Regional Director . . . I have taken no public position." He reported that he told local and state CIO councils that they need not adopt identical positions to those of the national CIO but should not take positions contrary to the national CIO. He then posed a series of questions to Haywood about what was expected of him and stated flatly that he would not campaign against Wallace or for the Marshall Plan. He concluded, "This letter should not be viewed as an expression of defiance, but rather as an attempt to follow a course that will do the most good and the least harm to the CIO in this area."[43]

On March 4, Haywood came to San Francisco and personally asked Bridges to resign as regional director. Bridges refused. Murray then announced that Bridges had been removed and Tim Flynn had been appointed in his place. Bridges issued his own press release, acknowledging Murray's authority to remove him but challenging the reasons, stating that enforcing the CIO's political position on CIO affiliates "not only went against my own conscience and principles, but it represented a change in the rules of the game." Murray gloated, "I was delighted to note the way in which the recent decision affecting Mr. Bridges has been hailed by our many friends throughout California."[44]

The *Chronicle*'s front-page report on Bridges's firing was directly followed with a report that a Justice Department investigator was collecting information for a third deportation attempt. Though the *Chronicle*'s placement of the two news items was probably not coincidental, the timing of this new INS investigation seems to have derived from two sources: Agnes Bridges's appearance before the Washington State Legislative Un-American Activities Committee the month before, when she testified to the same information she had given the INS at the time of Harry's naturalization, and Haywood's letter two weeks before putting Bridges on notice that his continuation as a CIO regional director was under serious question.[45]

Replacement of Bridges as CIO director for Northern California and the determination of national CIO leaders to enforce the January resolution on state and local CIO councils divided and disrupted the California CIO. On March 8, 1948, John Brophy, CIO director for industrial union councils, ordered local and state CIO councils to follow national CIO policy regarding the Wallace campaign and the Marshall Plan. When the state CIO-PAC split on the issue, Brophy recognized a new California CIO Political Action Committee as "the official representatives of the CIO for political action in California" and explained that it was now illegal for California CIO officials to use the name CIO PAC.[46]

The state CIO Council was still under control of the Left, as was the *Labor Herald*, the CIO Council's newspaper. In late June, Flynn attacked the *Labor Herald*, comparing it to the *People's World* and *Daily Worker*. Beginning July 1, the national CIO newspaper, the *CIO News*, began issuing a California edition, and Flynn and DeShetler encouraged CIO affiliates to discontinue the *Labor Herald* and instead subscribe their members to the California edition of the *CIO News*.[47]

By late 1947 and throughout 1948, the ILWU was also facing raiding. By refusing to sign the Taft-Hartley non-Communist affidavits, ILWU officers may not have realized they were opening the union to raids. Without its officers' affidavits, a union could not appear on a NLRB ballot for bargaining agent. AFL unions soon launched raids on ILWU locals, as did some Right CIO unions. When Bridges complained to Haywood about a raid by the Chemical Workers, Haywood replied that the Chemical Workers had refused his request that they desist. He noted that "the National CIO is opposed to raiding," but implied he and the National CIO could—or would—do nothing to stop raids. In late August 1948, claiming "companies are refusing to deal with Commie unions," DeShetler argued in favor of Right CIO raids on Left CIO locals "in order to save the workers for the CIO."[48]

The badly frayed relations between Bridges and the leadership of the CIO apparently encouraged the WEA to think they could roll back the ILWU's gains and even remove Bridges.[49] The showdown fight began in February 1948 when the WEA notified the ILWU that the Taft-Hartley Act made many provisions of their agreement illegal, including the hiring hall and dispatching system, preference of employment, and alleged restrictions on productivity. The WEA defined these as nonnegotiable, intending to use Taft-Hartley to force a vote on its "final offer." A month after Murray fired Bridges, the WEA notified the Federal Mediation and Conciliation Service (FMCS) that negotiations were unproductive and a strike was likely. By then, 92 percent of ILWU members had voted to strike if negotiations proved unsuccessful. Central to that vote was a commitment to maintain the hiring hall. The FMCS met with the parties, but neither budged on the hiring hall. From 1934 onward, the WEA had consistently opposed the hiring hall and, especially, the elected dispatcher and now intended to use the Taft-Hartley Act to destroy them.[50]

The next step under Taft-Hartley was for President Truman to appoint a fact-finding board to hold hearings. The ILWU was now restrained from striking for eighty days, between June 15 and September 2. The fact-finding panel reported in August, acknowledged that the hearings were "fruitful only in charges of bad faith and intensification of distrust and bad feelings," and evaluated prospects for settlement as "slim indeed." The WEA charged the ILWU with not bargaining in good faith because it was tying its bargaining to that of other CIO maritime unions.[51]

Midway through fact-finding, on July 10, Arthur Caylor, of the *San Francisco News*, reported, "The employers don't want a settlement" because they believe "they have a chance to unseat Bridges—along with several score other union officials who haven't declared themselves anti-Communists—and win the strike." Caylor continued, the WEA "firmly believe . . . that a solid core of anti-Bridges membership exists within the union and that it will increase in influence with each day of economic pressure. . . . [T]hey expect . . . that it won't be long before Phil Murray—national head of the C.I.O. and no Communist—makes a move. They don't expect it to help Bridges."[52] Caylor's mention of opposition to Bridges within the ILWU likely referred to the election in several locals, including Local 10, of officers who opposed the CP and were critical of Bridges, especially members of the Association of Catholic Trade Unionists. Caylor's sources were likely quite accurate with regard to the thinking of WEA leaders, but their expectations that a prolonged strike would lead ILWU members to reject Bridges and that Murray would move against Bridges proved far removed from reality.

The fact-finding board reconvened on August 10 to receive both final offers. The ILWU's list remained unchanged. The WEA offered minor concessions but accused ILWU leaders of taking bargaining positions determined by the CP. As Taft-Hartley required, the NLRB scheduled a vote by all ILWU longshore members on WEA's final offer. Delegates from all ports met on August 21 and voted to boycott the election. Bridges called the boycott "a demonstration of solidarity" that provided ILWU members "the opportunity to express their complete contempt for the shipowners' offer and the infamous Taft-Hartley slave labor act." Not a single ballot was cast, proving, as Bridges had predicted, a dramatic demonstration of solidarity. The *Chronicle* did not report the result of the NLRB balloting, but did report that eight thousand ILWU members marched in the city's Labor Day parade on September 6.[53]

Negotiations resumed. In a reversal, the WEA largely accepted the ILWU's position on the hiring hall, which was to continue current practice unless a judicial decision required changes. Other differences also seemed likely to be resolved when the ILWU's commitment to unity with other unions once again intruded. The NUMCS, MFOW, MEBA, and ACA had failed to reach agreement with the Pacific American Shipowners Association (PASA), so the ILWU went on strike with them on September 2, insisting that all unresolved issues had to be resolved before the strike could end. MEBA had been on the verge of an agreement but announced it would wait until the other unions had settled. A WEA representative stated on September 1, "It has been obvious all day that the union did not intend to sign a contract until the others sign."[54]

In their analysis of the strike, Betty V. H. Schneider and Abraham Siegel state succinctly what happened then: "If the union had started the strike without strong reason, management prolonged it in the same way." On September 2, WEA and PASA issued a joint policy statement: "To represent our employees from now on, union leadership must disavow Communism, as any real American would be proud to do." J. Paul St. Sure later described his understanding of that new policy: "The meeting at which this policy was voted was pretty much of a hoopla meeting. People got up and made speeches about 'don't let the old flag touch the ground and the time has come and we must stand up and be counted.' . . . [S]omebody else said, 'Let's make that in the form of a resolution,' whereupon they all voted on it and the strike was on that issue." Instead of negotiating, Foisie and Gregory Harrison, the WEA's attorney, now addressed business organizations to get endorsements of the new policy.[55]

The same day the WEA and PASA announced their new policy, ILWU longshore locals conducted their own secret-ballot referendum on two questions: should they accept the WEA's last offer and should ILWU officers sign the Taft-Hartley non-Communist affidavits. The first lost by 97 percent, the second by 94 percent. If the WEA expected a rebellion within the ILWU led by the ACTU, they failed to understand Catholic ILWU members' commitment to the union, the hiring hall and union dispatcher, and improving working conditions. James Kearney, president of Local 10, made clear that he and other ACTU members were committed to the union and to the Catholic principle that "where a conflict exists between private profit and human welfare, human welfare is paramount."[56]

The WEA also failed to learn from making Bridges a victim in the 1930s. By focusing on Bridges, they solidified his support within and outside the ILWU. A month into the strike, the WEA and PASA took a stronger position: "As long as the present party line leadership is in complete control of the longshoremen and stewards [NUMCS] it is impossible to do business with them." A few companies recognized the folly of such a position, believing, as the *Chronicle* reported, "it might freeze the strike situation in an unbreakable jam and line up the unions solidly behind Bridges."[57] By telling the ILWU that they would not negotiate until the union chose different leaders, the WEA not only, once again, made Bridges a martyr but also guaranteed that other CIO unions and leaders, Left and Right alike, would support the ILWU's right to choose its own leaders with no employer's dictation. Expecting that the CIO would jettison Bridges, the WEA instead brought CIO leaders into the strike on Bridges's side.

Shipping companies were losing an estimated $4 million per day of the strike. By early October, other companies were also experiencing serious problems. The *San Francisco News* called the situation "economic rigor mortis." When C&H announced layoffs at the Crockett refinery because a hundred thousand tons of raw sugar was in ships anchored in the bay, Bridges encouraged them to contract with independent stevedoring companies, not part of the WEA, to have the sugar unloaded.[58] But, of course, those same interlocked Hawaiian interests were part of the WEA.

On October 4, the Local 10 strike committee voted unanimously to invite Phil Murray to join the ILWU leaders in negotiations. WEA officials pooh-poohed the suggestion that Murray would assist the ILWU, but Murray pledged full support. Haywood, who had so recently butted heads with Bridges, along with R. J. Thomas, assistant director of organization, came to San Francisco. Bridges asked them "to make contact with the employers and attempt to prevail upon them to resume negotiations." Leaders of four shipping companies met with Haywood and Thomas but refused to resume negotiations with Bridges or anyone who had not signed the non-Communist affidavits. (Murray, Haywood, and Thomas had also refused to sign the affidavits as unwarranted interference in internal union matters.) Haywood and Thomas persuaded them to drop the affidavit requirement, but Thomas nonetheless described the meeting as "futile." Haywood and Thomas left San Francisco.[59]

Trying to resume negotiations, Bridges offered to withdraw in favor of a rank-and-file negotiating committee elected from the picket lines. The WEA refused. On October 20, Murray denounced "the direct challenge by these employers of the rights of the workers to select negotiating committees of their own choosing" and called it "a threat to every labor union in the country." Soon after, Almon Roth, then head of the San Francisco Employers' Council, talked with Murray, Haywood, and Thomas and pushed for involvement by both the CIO and the Employers' Council. Murray reiterated that the CIO respected ILWU autonomy and would enter such an arrangement only if the ILWU were a full party.[60]

Some shipping-company executives and shareholders, especially at Matson, were becoming deeply dissatisfied. Matson shareholders in Hawai'i, suffering financially from the strike, sent Randolph Sevier to look after their interests.

Sevier took the Matson seat at the shipowners' strategy meetings, but, after three days, he recalled, "I couldn't stomach any more. I just couldn't take the flag-waving speeches Harrison was making. . . . I said to [John] Cushing [Matson president], 'I'm not going to any more of those meetings. Those people just don't make any sense. Regardless of what we may think of Bridges and his crowd, the law says we've got to do business with them. Why don't we cut out the flag waving and start doing so?'" Cushing agreed.[61]

Some face-saving device had to be found to justify resuming negotiations. In early November, Haywood and Thomas returned to San Francisco and met first with Bridges and the ILWU negotiating committee. Thomas reported, "Bridges said the employers [council] had asked the CIO to come into negotiations as a face saving gesture. Vice-president Haywood and I pointed out emphatically that we had not come to San Francisco to save the face of any employer" but instead "to assist in getting the best possible agreement." All parties, including Roth for the Employers Council and Haywood and Thomas for the CIO, signed an agreement to resume negotiations with the CIO participating alongside the ILWU negotiating committee and with the provisos that the CIO would "underwrite" (left undefined) any agreement and that the final agreement would specify no strikes or lockouts. They also set a ten-day limit on negotiations.[62]

When contact negotiations began, Foisie was no longer the WEA negotiator. St. Sure recalled that Foisie "was 'retired' and sent on a long sea voyage." T. G. Plant also retired. The new WEA negotiator was Dwight Steele, brought from Hawai'i. Harrison was replaced as the WEA attorney. The irony that Foisie and Harrison had adamantly refused to negotiate with Bridges was not lost on anyone. When Mayor Elmer Robinson requested a seat at the bargaining table, he was politely refused, because, as one employer representative explained, "Elmer should know enough to let a honeymoon couple alone."[63]

The "honeymoon" proved smooth, thorough, and lengthy. Bridges led negotiations for the ILWU, with the CIO representatives and ILWU coast committee at his side. On the other side of the table sat Steele and twenty executives of shipping and stevedoring companies. A hundred or so ILWU longshore members watched from the sidelines. After ten days, the parties stopped the clock. Final agreement came late on Thanksgiving Day; one negotiator said, "Waiting for me at home was an angry wife and a cold turkey." When they finished, not cold turkey but a case of Scotch whiskey appeared on the bargaining table. The parties shook hands, shared drinks, and chatted. All agreed that waterfront labor relations had a "new look," a phrase that quickly came into wide use.[64] A quarter century passed before the next ILWU strike.

The new agreement specified that the hiring hall was to operate as it had previously unless judicial interpretation required changes. Significant changes appeared elsewhere. The agreement was to run for three years instead of one;

the many arbitration awards and side agreements that had so complicated previous labor relations were either reduced to contract language or thrown out; longshore workers were guaranteed one day off per week, usually Sunday; work stoppages were prohibited except for safety and refusal to cross a picket line; and the introduction of labor-saving devices likely to reduce the workforce was subject to negotiation or arbitration.[65] Agreements with other striking maritime unions quickly followed. The long strike was finally over.[66]

Soon after, the ILWU and WEA agreed on Sam Kagel as coast arbitrator. During the early 1930s, after earning his bachelor's degree and doing graduate work in economics at the University of California, Berkeley, Kagel had worked for Melnikow's Pacific Coast Labor Bureau and then briefly represented the ILWU in Washington. During World War II, he became Northern California director of the War Manpower Commission, then completed law school. Just as the "New Look" ushered in a quarter century of labor peace on the West Coast docks, so Kagel's appointment provided another source of stability. He held that position from 1948 until 2002, until he was ninety-four years old.[67]

In mid-1949, the WEA and PASA merged to create the Pacific Maritime Association (PMA). In 1952 J. Paul St. Sure became head of PMA and its chief negotiator and continued until shortly before his death in 1966, providing another element of long-term stability to Pacific Coast longshore labor relations.[68]

The CIO proved genuinely and significantly supportive to Bridges and the ILWU in resolving the long-drawn-out strike, even though their relations had deteriorated badly in nearly every other area. CIO unions, Left and Right, provided financial support during the strike, with the largest contribution, $10,000, from Murray's Steelworkers, nearly half of all contributions.[69]

The stressful events of the late 1940s took their toll on Bridges, as did aspects of his personal life. His father, Alfred Bridges, died in November 1946. Almost a year later, Harry's uncle Charles informed him that his mother's health had deteriorated. In the mid-1940s, Bridges's daughter Jackie had gone to live with some of Nancy's family in New York where Jackie was under psychiatric care. She returned to San Francisco in late 1946 and lived with Harry and Nancy. She began psychiatric care again in late 1947 but became so withdrawn that in early 1948 she was hospitalized. The physicians diagnosed her with what today would be called paranoid schizophrenia.[70]

In March 1948, Bridges spent three hours talking with a *Chronicle* reporter, who described him as "tall, lean, crackling with nervous energy." "Under questioning he is apt to pace impatiently around his big, paper-piled desk," the reporter noted, adding, "He thinks that his office, on Montgomery street, is wired and his phones tapped." Describing Bridges as "the most investigated man in America," the reporter stated that Bridges earned $150 per week as president of the ILWU (equivalent to an annual salary of nearly $95,000 in mid-2022), lived in a "modest modern house" in which a nursery had just been painted blue, and had a red setter.[71] Herb Caen described Bridges at about the same time:

> a sallow-faced balding man who is plagued by ulcers, recurrent revolts in his own unions, and apparently untiring efforts on the part of his enemies to label him a "Communist." Of the three, his ulcers have pained him the most, keeping him out of night clubs where he once diligently pursued his favorite indoor sport of the rumba. He now sits at home with his second wife, an ex-professional dancer, and plays chess and drinks enough milk to inspire Mrs. Bridges to join any and all organizations dedicated to the cause of lower milk prices.[72]

The home where Bridges played chess and drank milk, and where he, Nancy, Julie, and, briefly, Jackie lived, was in a quiet, middle-class residential neighborhood, away from busy streets. The nursery was painted blue to welcome Robert Alfred Renton Bridges, born in March 1948. Shortly after longshore workers returned to work in December 1948 and final details were worked out in the new contract, Harry underwent a five-hour surgery at the University of California hospital. He later said that they took out "99 percent" of his stomach.[73]

Though the 1948 strike initiated a long period of stability in Pacific Coast longshore labor relations, the political events of 1948—Bridges's and the ILWU's adherence to the CP line on the Marshall Plan and the Wallace candidacy—not only brought Bridges's ouster as regional CIO director but soon brought the expulsion of the ILWU from the CIO and more raiding. And those attacks on the ILWU coincided in time with a third effort to deport Bridges—and, failing deportation, to send him to prison.

13

Try, Try, Again: Deportation and Expulsion

1948–1953

Though the 1948 strike ended with handshakes and drinks, other events in 1948 brought serious problems for Bridges and the ILWU. The renewed INS investigation created new legal battles for Bridges. The CIO expelled the ILWU for its support of CP positions on the Marshall Plan and the Wallace campaign. Several locals faced raiding, but the longshore and Hawaiian locals remained strong, as did most warehouse locals. In national politics, HUAC and Senator Joseph McCarthy vied in overheated charges of CP influence almost everywhere in American society. In the end, however, Bridges and the ILWU weathered the storms of the McCarthy era.

At issue in both Bridges's legal battle and the CIO's "trial" of the ILWU was Bridges's relation to the CP. Dave Jenkins provided an understanding of Bridges's relation to the CP from the mid-1940s through the late 1950s. Jenkins was a CP functionary in the late 1940s—member of the county and state committees, director of the California Labor School, organizer in the Wallace campaign. He also directed fund-raising for the Bridges defense committee. He and Edith, his wife, lived near Harry and Nancy Bridges and socialized with them. Bridges and Jenkins played poker and visited the racetrack together. Jenkins assured me that, at that time, Bridges "was an independent figure inside the Left. Nobody attempted discipline with Bridges." Jenkins added, "Bridges listened to CP people" but was "more listened to than a listener," and stressed, "There was no secret compartment in the apparatus of the CP that met secretly with Bridges," and "never in that period was Bridges handled as anything but an independent figure." However, each month, Jenkins visited Bridges and other ILWU international officers to collect voluntary contributions, not membership dues, the amount determined by each individual.[1] Lou Goldblatt, the second most significant ILWU officer, had drifted away from the party by or during

World War II. He recalled that, though he opposed the CP positions on the Marshall Plan and the Wallace campaign, his relations with the CP remained much like those of Bridges.[2]

There was little nuance in the FBI's view of Bridges in these years. In 1945 an informant reported that William Schneiderman, head of the California CP, had complained that Bridges was taking actions without consulting with, much less getting permission from, the CP, which Schneiderman branded "incorrigible" behavior. Nonetheless, the FBI classified Bridges as "a top functionary of the Communist movement." In mid-1946, Hoover classified Bridges as "Internal Security—C" (C for Communist) and directed the San Francisco SAC to continue seeking "legally admissible evidence that the subject is a member of or is affiliated with the Communist Party." By 1949 the FBI was also classifying Bridges as DETCOM (*det*ain as *Com*munist in event of war).[3]

In launching its new investigation of Bridges in 1948, the INS asked the FBI for whatever information it had on a long list of possible witnesses, including several former CP members and also Henry Schmidt and J. R. Robertson, Bridges's witnesses for his naturalization. The FBI provided long reports on Schmidt and Robertson, claiming both were CP members. The FBI also forwarded to both the INS and the attorney general a transcript of the Washington State Un-American Activities Committee's testimony regarding Bridges. As part of the INS investigation, R. J. Norene of the Portland office reached out to "friend Larry"—Stanley Doyle—for any assistance he might be able to offer, but Doyle apparently did not respond. The renewed investigation in Portland included police officers centrally involved in the earlier investigations.[4]

Mervyn Rathborne and John Schomaker became key informants for the INS. During the 1930s, Rathborne had headed the San Francisco and California CIO industrial councils and worked closely with Bridges. He listed fifty-two possible witnesses and claimed Darcy had recruited Bridges into the CP in 1933. That claim was omitted from Rathborne's later testimony because Schomaker's testimony presented an entirely different scenario for Bridges's recruitment. Schomaker initially said, "He did not . . . have any knowledge of the subject's membership in the Communist Party," but later remembered things very differently.[5]

In early October 1948, INS investigators interviewed Allan Haywood, then about to assist Bridges and the ILWU with their negotiations. Haywood insisted that neither he nor any other CIO officer had any evidence that Bridges was a Communist, but did say that Bridges regularly followed the CP line. Haywood suggested possible witnesses, but refused "to bring pressure to bear upon any of his associates in the CIO to cooperate with the Government."[6]

In October Bruce Barber of the INS accompanied Rathborne to Washington to meet Attorney General Tom Clark and others. During the trial, Rathborne testified that James Carey, CIO secretary-treasurer, said that legal proceedings against Bridges would not be considered "an attack against the C.I.O." but also that the CIO preferred to handle such matters in its own way. Rathborne said that Phil Murray told him that "he wasn't for it but didn't oppose it." Joe Curran, Rathborne said, "gave the undertaking his blessing." Attorney General Clark assured Rathborne that Bridges was "dangerous to the country," that "something should be done" to remove him from his union position, and that the trial was not political and not antilabor. However, Clark also publicly announced, in mid-1949, that the trial was likely to end a strike in Hawai'i.[7]

The two previous legal proceedings had begun with an INS hearing. This time a federal grand jury considered whether Bridges, Schmidt, and Robertson had committed perjury during Bridges's naturalization hearing when he denied being a Communist and they vouched for him. If convicted, each could be fined and imprisoned. The government filed separately to deprive Bridges of his citizenship, the second step if he were convicted of perjury. If both proceedings proved successful, the final step for Bridges, after prison, would be deportation or long-term custodial detention.

Grand jury proceedings began on May 11, 1949. As lead prosecutor, Attorney General Clark designated F. Joseph "Jiggs" Donohue, prominent Washington lawyer and rising member of the Democratic Party establishment. The statute of limitations precluded a simple perjury charge, so federal attorneys relied on the Wartime Suspension of Limitations Act of 1942 to charge Bridges, Robertson, and Schmidt with criminal conspiracy "to defraud the United States" by giving perjured testimony during Bridges's naturalization hearing. The public face of the trial was that Bridges was charged with perjury and subject to deportation, but reliance on the 1942 suspension act ultimately proved the linchpin of the case. All three were indicted, and the trial was set for mid-November.[8]

When the ILWU, California CIO Council, and *People's World* referred to the indictment as "union busting" and a "frame-up," some San Francisco newspaper editors encouraged Donohue to get a statement from Murray contradicting such statements. Murray declined, but, during the trial, the prosecutors managed Rathborne's testimony so as to put the words they wanted into the mouths of top CIO officials. When I asked Arthur Goldberg, who became counsel for the CIO in 1948, about this, he told me, "I want to state to you in the most definitive terms that no one of authority in the CIO, including myself, in any way urged the Department of Justice to proceed criminally or civilly against Harry Bridges. There may have been meetings but it was the firm policy of the CIO not to be involved with any governmental action against Mr. Bridges."[9]

Bridges, Robertson, and Schmidt scrambled to find lawyers. Throughout, Norman Leonard, from the Gladstein firm, provided research, prepared briefs, and sometimes participated in court. Leonard was ably assisted by Elinor Kahn.

Richard Gladstein was in New York, representing defendants in the Smith Act trial of eleven prominent CP leaders. That trial ended in October 1949 with conviction of all eleven and contempt of court convictions of all their lawyers including Gladstein, who went to prison in Texas. Bridges asked James Landis to represent him in a motion to dismiss the indictment. Landis refused, but recommended his law partner, Telford Taylor. Taylor had other commitments. Bridges requested a delay but was refused. Two weeks before the trial was to begin, Bridges had no lead attorney.[10]

While Bridges scrambled to find a lawyer, some large ILWU locals were in revolt, influenced perhaps by the new CIO regional directors. In March 1949, Local 13 (San Pedro longshore) voted to stop paying per caps to the local and state IUCs. Local 10's executive board cut its subscriptions to the *Labor Herald*, some Local 10 members began circulating a petition to withdraw from the local IUC, and Local 10 members voted support for national CIO policies. Locals 8 (Portland longshore), 10, and 13 sent majority Right delegations to the biennial convention.[11]

The 1949 ILWU convention included a full-blown debate on the ILWU's support for the Wallace campaign and resolved, "The International Union shall only make recommendations to locals on political matters," and "locals shall have full autonomy" regarding political issues and candidates. The 1949 election of ILWU officers saw the first opponent for Bridges in eight years. Robertson also faced opposition. Bridges was easily reelected with more than 80 percent of the vote, but fell below that margin in several large locals. Hawaiian members gave Bridges 96 percent. Robertson also easily won reelection. Germain Bulcke was unopposed for second vice president, and Goldblatt was unopposed for secretary.[12]

CIO leaders were developing their own attack on Left unions in California. In early October 1949, leaders of seventeen CIO unions with locals in California asked Murray to pull the charter of the California CIO Council and issue a new one. By then only 78 of the 285 CIO locals in California remained affiliated with the existing, Left-dominated, state council. The 207 CIO locals outside the state council claimed more than 80 percent of CIO members in California. Murray revoked the state council's charter. The ILWU and other Left CIO affiliates were becoming increasingly isolated.[13]

On November 1, 1949, the CIO national convention adopted a constitutional amendment barring Communists, fascists, and members of totalitarian organizations from serving as CIO officers. Bridges was prominent in opposition, saying, "We are not going to change our ways. . . . To get rid of us you'll have to throw us out," which brought shouts of "good, good" from Right delegates. Bridges replied that he was "not a bit afraid" of the ILWU's ability to "stand alone." That day the resolutions committee approved expulsion of UE and the

Farm Equipment (FE) union as Communist-dominated. Later the convention adopted a strong anti-Communist resolution on foreign policy and committed to the new, anti-Communist World Labor Federation rather than the World Federation of Trade Unions on the grounds that the WFTU was Communist dominated. Bridges, recently elected president of the WFTU's Maritime Federation of the World (MFW), was a special target during those debates. Bridges defended the WFTU, but the vote was overwhelmingly on the other side.[14]

On the convention's last day, Murray was resoundingly reelected as president. Next came nominations for the executive board, which included one member from each CIO affiliate. During executive board nominations, the Fur Workers nominated their president, Ben Gold, an open CP member. Murray announced that Gold was ineligible to serve under the new constitutional amendment and invited another nomination from the Fur Workers. There was none. When each Left union offered its nominee, a Right delegate challenged the nominee's eligibility and encouraged Right unions not to vote for the nominee. Bridges and the others received only the votes of the remaining Left unions. By then some UE locals were already voting to affiliate with the CIO's newly chartered International Union of Electrical Workers (IUE), and some FE locals were affiliating with the UAW.[15]

The day after the convention, the CIO executive board met and directed CIO officers to sign the Taft-Hartley non-Communist affidavits but under protest that they were unconstitutional. Bridges and other ILWU officers signed the affidavits four months later, after the ILWU executive board approved their request to do so. The ILWU executive board also recommended that the next longshore caucus develop similar recommendations for officers of longshore locals. The boards of the major warehouse locals also recommended that their officers sign, and they did. Hoover directed the San Francisco FBI office to report anything that might support a case against Bridges for perjury in filing his affidavit, but charges were never brought.[16]

Also in November 1950, the CIO executive board set up committees to investigate the nine unions accused of following the CP line. In addition to the ILWU, the list included the NUMCS and Fishermen's Union. Though they were charged with having pursued policies contrary to those of the CIO, the real charge, everyone knew, was that they were following the CP line. Bridges's response was that the policies of the ILWU were set by the membership and that the CIO was trying to "rob the rank and file of ownership and control of its union."[17]

During all this, the criminal conspiracy trial was just days away, and Bridges, Robertson, and Schmidt still needed a lead attorney. With Gladstein and four other Left lawyers in prison for contempt of court, Bridges, Robertson, and Schmidt looked for attorneys not associated with the CP. Bridges chose Vincent

Hallinan, San Francisco's leading defense attorney for criminal cases. Hallinan recalled that, when the three first talked with him, they assured him they never had been CP members but expected the government to make strong cases based on their meetings with CP leaders and on witnesses' claims they had participated in CP meetings. They also suggested, based on the Smith Act trial, that the judge was likely to go after the defense attorneys. Hallinan was not dissuaded. He knew his ability to sway a jury, and, unlike the two INS hearings, this was to be a jury trial. Hallinan agreed to take the case and even predicted a quick acquittal. "I was terribly naive," he later said, adding that, during the trial, "I learned more about justice and its perversion than I did in thirty years of prior practice."[18]

The trial opened in mid-November 1949. George Harris, the judge, was a close friend of Harry Kimball, special agent in charge of the FBI's San Francisco field office. Donohue continued as lead prosecutor. The FBI gave Donohue a thirty-five-page report covering every person in the jury pool, noting those the FBI considered CP members or "friendly with Communists." Bridges's attorneys had their own investigator, Harold "Hal" Lipset, a former FBI agent turned private detective, a development that concerned the FBI.[19]

Hallinan immediately learned this was unlike his previous trials. He intended to use his opening statement to review the previous investigations and hearings, including the discrediting of previous witnesses and the ways that shipowners, AFL leaders, and American Legion members had conspired with the Portland INS office. Hallinan planned to alert the jury to expect more of the same, which he called "a noxious, fetid, horrible growth." Hallinan's opening statement went on and on. Harris cautioned him about relevance. The prosecution repeatedly objected, and Harris continued to caution Hallinan. At the end of the first day, with Hallinan's opening statement incomplete, Bridges urged him to tone it down and not antagonize Harris. Hallinan disagreed. On the second day, as Hallinan continued his opening statement, the prosecution repeatedly objected and Harris again cautioned Hallinan.[20]

As its first witness, the prosecution called a minor INS official to establish the basic facts of Bridges's naturalization. In cross-examination, however, Hallinan claimed the witness was part of an elaborate INS conspiracy that included the investigations in the 1930s, the bugging of Bridges's hotel room in 1937, and the tapping of his phone in 1941. When the witness acknowledged some familiarity with previous legal proceedings, Hallinan proposed to read the entire Landis and Murphy decisions, paragraph by paragraph, to determine which parts the witness was familiar with—a transparent subterfuge to present those decisions to the jury. The prosecution objected. Harris declared Hallinan in contempt of court, revoked his right to practice in a federal court, sentenced him to six months in prison, and ordered bailiffs to remove him. During all this, Bridges wryly commented that he was "just incidental" to events in the courtroom. Put on the witness stand, Bridges testified he would not be able to find an attorney in whom he had the same confidence he had in Hallinan. Rather than risk a mistrial, Harris permitted Hallinan to continue.[21]

Early prosecution witnesses included John Schomaker and Henry Schrimpf, former associates of Bridges and Schmidt who had failed to win elections in the San Francisco longshore local. Schrimpf had quit the CP and broken with Bridges by mid-1936. Schomaker left the CP around the same time or shortly after. Unlike his earlier INS and FBI interviews, Schomaker now testified he had joined the CP in 1931 and recruited Bridges into the CP in 1933. Both testified they had been in CP meetings with Bridges and that the CP had directed the 1934 strike. Other witnesses recounted CP meetings they had attended with Bridges and Schmidt. Hallinan and James MacInnis, his law partner, tried to establish that those were meetings of union members at which CP members were present and contested claims that Bridges ever admitted being a CP member. The defense attorneys' efforts to discredit early prosecution witnesses as perjurers were ineffective.[22]

Next the prosecution called its "professional" witnesses—former CP officials who traveled the country testifying against alleged CP members. Manning Johnson testified that Bridges, under the name Rossi, had been present at the 1936 national CP convention when he was elected to the CP national committee. Paul Crouch followed with similar testimony. In cross-examination, Hallinan carefully led each to specify exact days and times when he claimed to have seen Bridges at the 1936 CP national convention. On the next day of the trial, Hallinan dramatically demanded that Johnson and Crouch be arrested and charged with "abject, flagrant, arrant" perjury. Hallinan presented affidavits, newspaper clippings, and airline schedules establishing the dates of the 1936 CP convention as June 24–28; proving Bridges's presence in San Francisco on June 22–24, in Stockton on June 27, and in San Francisco on June 28; and demonstrating that it would have been impossible for Bridges to have flown to New York on June 25–26, attended the convention, and returned to Stockton. Then the trial recessed for the holidays. INS officials scrambled—but failed—to find evidence that Bridges had been on flights to New York City the week of June 24. They should not have been surprised—in earlier INS investigations, John Leech and Arthur Kent had agreed Bridges had been elected to the CP national committee in 1936, but Leech had expressed doubt that Bridges was present and Kent stated flatly that Bridges had not been. The INS should have been, at least, suspicious that Johnson and Crouch were committing perjury.[23] They were never prosecuted.

Before Crouch testified, the INS had asked the FBI for any "derogatory information" about him. The FBI declined. After Hallinan's revelations about perjury, the Miami SAC informed Hoover that, during previous, extensive discussions,

Crouch had said, "he had had no contact with BRIDGES and had no information to furnish concerning the subject." When Crouch returned to Florida, FBI agents again questioned him about his testimony. Crouch claimed, "His testimony was possibly distorted by inaccurate reporting," and "he had a faint impression that BRIDGES was present at the Communist Party convention in New York City in 1936 but he could not testify positively that BRIDGES was in attendance." Regarding Crouch's similar testimony about the 1938 national CP convention, he explained that "his memory was refreshed" by INS officials.[24] So, rather than suspect that Crouch was committing perjury, INS officials seem to have coached him to do so.

When the trial resumed, Lawrence Ross took the witness stand and claimed that he and Bridges had attended CP meetings during the 1930s. Ross claimed to have been born in Kentucky and attended the University of Kentucky, but MacInnis revealed that Ross had been born in Poland, was named Rosenstein, and had never attended school in Kentucky. Hallinan then charged Donohue and other prosecution lawyers with complicity in Ross's perjury. D. M. Ladd, assistant to Hoover, promptly informed Hoover that a Dies Committee investigator in 1941 had found that Ross was really "Rosenfeld" and had been born in Poland and that the FBI had told the INS there was no record of Ross in Kentucky. Ladd smirked, "This is another example of INS not properly evaluating and using the information given to them by the Bureau."[25]

The next prosecution witness, George Wilson, former head of the San Francisco CIO council and of an earlier Bridges defense committee, was clearly under great stress when he testified that he had attended CP meetings with Bridges. Bridges, seeing Wilson's stress and assuming that he was under some irresistible pressure to testify, asked his attorneys to go lightly on him.[26]

Two months into the trial, a *New York Times* reporter called it "the best drama in town." Then, to the surprise of the defense, the prosecution rested without calling Rathborne as a witness. The defense opened by denouncing the prosecution witnesses as liars. The first defense witness, B. B. Jones, had been named by Schomaker as present when Schomaker recruited Bridges into the CP. Jones adamantly denied such an event. Shipping executives involved in the 1948 strike testified to Bridges's truthfulness. Schmidt took the stand and denied ever having been a CP member. Robert Kenny testified to Bridges's honesty and integrity. In early February, MacInnis was cited for contempt. Bridges took the witness stand on February 7 and continued for nine days, telling his life story. He denied ever joining the CP, discussed each meeting referred to by the prosecution's witnesses, and denied either his presence or that it was a CP meeting.[27]

Much earlier, Donohue had called Rathborne "the foundation" of the case, and he finally called Rathborne as a rebuttal witness. Acknowledging that he had previously perjured himself, Rathborne contradicted Bridges's accounts of various meetings and recounted his meetings with Clark, Carey, Murray, and Curran.[28]

Closing arguments began on March 16, with Donohue telling the jury that the Schomaker testimony alone was enough to convict and made a point of defense attorneys' refusal to cross-examine George Wilson. Hallinan's closing statement characterized the three defendants as "good, honest, decent men, men of integrity" and called the prosecution witnesses "rogues," "liars," and "perjurers." On March 31, the case went to the jury. After four days, the jury returned a verdict of guilty. Nancy broke into tears. Harris sentenced Hallinan and MacInnis to prison terms for contempt of court, sentenced Bridges to five years in prison, and sentenced Schmidt and Robertson to two years. He later revoked Bridges's citizenship. Bridges's attorneys began appeals of the jury's verdict and the denaturalization order. Bridges and the others remained out on bail. Hallinan and MacInnis appealed their contempt citations, but both went to prison.[29]

Although the jury found against Bridges, the FBI was drawing different conclusions. In March 1949, the San Francisco SAC wrote to Hoover to recommend, "It is neither necessary nor desirable to afford BRIDGES continuous and active investigation" and that "the Bureau remove the subject from the status of top functionary to that of a key figure." The San Francisco field office later observed, "While BRIDGES continues to support the Communist Party line, any indication of his support of the Communist Party is usually a considerable time after 'the Communist Party line' has been determined from other sources." The memo also referred to Bridges's signing of the Taft-Hartley non-Communist affidavit and his testimony that he met with CP functionaries only to obtain assistance "in certain trade union matters." Hoover accepted that recommendation. Bridges was no longer DETCOM.[30]

Though the press speculated that deportation would come next, the *Washington Post* quoted a "highly placed" Australian official as saying that Australia would not accept Bridges and, "He is America's baby, not ours." Harold Holt, speaking later for the Liberal government of Robert Menzies, specified that Bridges should be regarded as a stateless person and any application for Bridges's admission to Australia would be considered "in the light of the current immigration policy," which prohibited entry to Communists.[31]

The Menzies government surely knew that Bridges had become an inspiration and his union an exemplar for Australia's Left unions, especially the Waterfront Workers Federation (WWF), led by James Healy. Healy, a member of the Australian CP, led Australian dockworkers in 1942 to wage increases and an end to the "bull" system of hiring, the Australian counterpart to the "shape-up," and its replacement by rotating gangs, similar to the ILWU's "low-man-out" rule. Healy had created and edited Melbourne's *Maritime Worker*; the third and fourth issues of that paper had presented "The Life Story of Harry Bridges."[32]

The Australian government's earlier refusal to accept Bridges had made the 1941–45 deportation proceedings both a ploy to take political pressure off the Roosevelt administration and, if successful, a way to remove Bridges from union leadership by placing him in "permanent custody." This time, however, federal authorities, if successful, intended to imprison Bridges before attempting to deport him. Though deportation seemed unlikely, federal authorities must have anticipated that imprisoning Bridges followed by permanent custody would remove him from union leadership.

In mid-May, shortly after the conclusion of the trial, the CIO put the ILWU on trial in the CIO's offices in Washington. The CIO's trials of its Left unions were not intended to evaluate evidence pro and con and arrive at a fair verdict. Paul Jacobs, CIO staff aide during the ILWU's trial, recalled that everyone knew "the decision . . . had been made months before." The trials were show trials, designed to demonstrate the adherence of Bridges and others to the party line and, thereby, perhaps, to trigger membership revolts that would remove them from power.[33]

The court trial had lasted for four months. The CIO's "trial" took three days, May 17–19, 1950. O. A. Knight, president of the Oil Workers, presided. William Steinberg, president of the American Radio Association, prosecuted, assisted by Jacobs. They charged the ILWU with following policies "consistently directed toward the achievement of the program and the purposes of the Communist Party rather than the objectives and policies set forth in the constitution of the CIO." Bridges, Robertson, and five executive board members represented the ILWU, and several other ILWU members attended. Prosecution witnesses were Mike Quill of the Transport Workers, M. Hedley Stone of the NMU, and Steinberg. Quill claimed he had never been a CP member and, paradoxically, that he and Bridges had attended meetings limited to CP members including one during the 1946 CIO national convention. Bridges proved that he had not attended that convention. Stone claimed he had met with Bridges and Robertson during CMU negotiations in Washington in 1946 to discuss CP matters. Bridges proved that Robertson had not been in Washington then, so Stone decided it had been Goldblatt. (The two men looked nothing alike.) Steinberg claimed that ILWU expansion into Hawai'i, Alaska, and British Columbia was solely to benefit the CP. The prosecution's documentary evidence consisted largely of newspaper articles, to demonstrate that the ILWU had "without deviation" followed the CP line.[34]

Bridges, now well familiar with courtroom tactics, led the defense, cross-examined the witnesses, and called seven ILWU members as witnesses, ranging from an executive board member to a rank-and-file member known as being anti-Communist. They explained the autonomy of locals on political matters and the democratic nature of the ILWU, especially how union policies were determined by the members, often through referenda. The ILWU submitted a brief that refuted all charges, point by point, and argued for remaining in the CIO on the grounds that the ILWU had entered the CIO with the understanding that it would retain its autonomy. Bridges also specified, "If any CIO union thinks they can raid us or the National CIO thinks they can raid us, and get away with it, they have a rough time ahead. . . . [W]e are damned hard to take." The trial committee sent its recommendation to the CIO executive board, which delayed for several months.[35]

Dave Jenkins later recalled being present when Al Lannon, the CP's point person for maritime matters, came to San Francisco to tell Bridges that the CP wanted the ILWU to walk out of the CIO. Bridges refused.[36]

Five weeks later, on June 25, 1950, North Korean troops invaded South Korea. On June 27, the UN Security Council asked UN members to join in repelling North Korea's aggression. U.S. troops were quickly mobilized. At a Local 10 membership meeting on June 28, Philip Sandin, local president, and other elected local leaders, part of a Right slate, presented a resolution that spoke of "doubts cast on our loyalty as American citizens by statements that the San Francisco longshoremen would try to halt or even sabotage shipments of war materials destined for Korea," condemned "the act of aggression of the Communist North Korean army," pledged support for "our government and our president," and promised that "we will load any and all cargoes destined for the war area." Bridges, speaking as a Local 10 member, encouraged the local not to "rush into anything" and proposed a substitute resolution "to support the United Nations order to cease fire . . . and have that organization settle the dispute peacefully." Bridges's substitute was defeated. A recount was requested, members began leaving, and Sandin adjourned the meeting. Two days later, U.S. troops landed in South Korea and soon engaged in heavy fighting. On July 7, the *Dispatcher* carried a front-page article criticizing the South Korean government as undemocratic and corrupt. On July 10, at the next Local 10 membership meeting, the local officers' resolution was again introduced. When Bridges sought to present his substitute, Sandin ruled him out of order because the substitute had previously been defeated. Bridges challenged Sandin's ruling and lost by a large margin. Fists began to fly. Five police cars arrived to break up the fighting and end the meeting. The resolution was again rescheduled.[37]

Two days later, members of the U.S. Senate Judiciary Committee claimed Bridges was endangering the U.S. war effort and questioned his right to remain free on bail. The next week, ILWU Local 91 (Bay Area walking bosses) called on

Bridges either to resign as president of the Maritime Federation of the World or to resign as president of the ILWU, because the MFW was encouraging its affiliates to oppose U.S. actions in Korea. The next day, Local 10 members overwhelmingly passed the anti-Communist resolution. Bridges offered no opposition, said that he knew the FBI was interested in his reasons for previously opposing the resolution, and read a prepared statement that he had sought only to emphasize the need for a UN cease-fire. He also explained that the MFW had been reorganized and he was no longer president, only honorary president. In reaction to press coverage, the Bridges-Robertson-Schmidt defense committee denounced a "deliberate and organized plot" to create the impression that Bridges had somehow sought to block shipment of supplies to Korea.[38]

By then Donohue was headed to San Francisco to revoke Bridges's bail. When Hoover learned that, he scrawled, "See that Kimball [SAC San Francisco] is not stampeded into any activity by Donohoe." Kimball sent a long Teletype to Hoover, concluding that there was no evidence that Bridges had "attempted to introduce policy of not loading vessels destined to Korea." Ladd warned the area SACs "to be very cautious in their dealings with Special Assistant Attorney General 'Jiggs' Donohue."[39]

Donohue was not cautious. He told SAC Kimball that he had met with Harris about revoking Bridges's bail, and Harris had assured him that, if what he had read about Bridges in the press were true and formally presented, "he would feel it his duty to revoke the bond." At the hearing, Donohue requested that Harris revoke Bridges's bail because Bridges was a "danger to internal security." Claiming that CP and ILWU publications proved that Bridges's position on Korea was the same as the CP, Donohue proclaimed that Bridges was a "dangerous enemy to our society, a threat to our national security," and thundered, "he IS our enemy!" Norman Leonard, from the Gladstein law firm, represented Bridges. He invoked the First Amendment and argued that Bridges was expressing his opinion. On August 5, Harris ordered Bridges to jail, calling him "dangerous to the security of this country."[40]

Bridges spent twenty days in the San Francisco County Jail. His attorneys sought unsuccessfully to get Harris to dismiss the charge on which bail was revoked, then petitioned unsuccessfully for a writ of habeas corpus. Then they asked the circuit court. That court agreed, described the government's effort to jail Bridges as "novel and startling," and declared there was no evidence that Bridges had "committed any recognizable crime or that he has himself counseled or advocated sabotage or sought to foment strikes or the establishment of picket lines on the waterfront"—the same conclusion the FBI had already reached. The court also described Harris's action as making Bridge "appear a victim of judicial tyranny." Bridges was released. He later claimed that he did not waste his time in jail, as he managed to convince the deputy sheriffs who staffed the jail to form a union.[41]

While Bridges sat in jail, the longshore caucus met and clarified the ILWU's position on several issues. Voting 63–9, the caucus acknowledged that the World Federation of Trade Unions and the MFW had directed their affiliates to oppose the U.S. and UN actions in Korea, stated that the ILWU membership had never voted to affiliate with either organization, noted however that, "in the eyes of American labor, and the government and public we are associated with and therefore affiliated with the WFTU and MFW," and concluded bluntly, "We sever our connections with the WFTU and MFW." Upon adoption of the resolution, the caucus chair ruled that Bridges's honorary presidency of the MFW was automatically dissolved. Bridges agreed. A few weeks later, he said, "My position is bound to be that of my union, whatever it may be. . . . It may not be what I'd like to do privately or personally, but that's beside the point."[42]

Also in August 1950, the CIO executive board acted on the recommendation from the committee that tried the ILWU in May. The decision, not surprisingly, was to expel the ILWU along with the NUMCS and the Fishermen (the latter of which had previously merged with the ILWU). The expulsions completed the CIO's purge of its Left unions. Murray announced that he expected either to charter a new longshore union to replace the ILWU or that the members of the ILWU would soon replace Bridges and return to the CIO.[43]

Neither happened. The CIO never made a serious effort to create a new longshore union. When CIO organizers circulated pledge cards in Local 10—which had regularly elected Right officers—all Local 10 officers but one issued a public statement condemning the effort. In the 1951 election of officers, Bridges and the other three international officers ran unopposed, although there were numerous members of the Right at the convention who could have made nominations to oppose them. The CIO did pick off a few ILWU cannery locals previously part of the Fishermen's Union.[44]

In July 1951, attorneys for Bridges, Robertson, and Schmidt filed their appeal. The brief, 281 pages long, raised twenty questions of law, beginning with the initial decision to bring the charges, and twenty-one charges of errors by Harris. From the beginning, one constant argument had been that the wartime waiver of the statute of limitations did not apply to naturalization. A panel of three circuit court judges heard the appeal in March 1952. In December, all three concurred in rejecting all grounds for appeal.[45] The next step was the Supreme Court.

Bridges sought a new lead counsel for the appeal to the Supreme Court, someone of such stature as to be immune to the treatment meted out to Gladstein, Hallinan, and others who defended accused Communists. Bridges again asked

Telford Taylor. This time Taylor was available and agreed to join the Bridges defense. An FBI informant reported that Bridges's decision for Taylor was against the recommendation of the CP, which, the informant claimed, preferred Bridges to continue with the Gladstein firm.[46]

Taylor had been a New Deal administrator, military intelligence officer during World War II, and prosecutor with the rank of brigadier general at the Nuremburg trials of German war criminals. He had never met Bridges before being asked to handle the appeal. He had a reputation as a liberal and had served as vice chairman of the New York City chapter of the liberal—and anti-Communist—Americans for Democratic Action. Landis had been one of Taylor's law professors at Harvard and later Taylor's law partner, so Taylor knew Landis's version of the 1939 INS hearing. The FBI promptly informed the attorney general of "Taylor's association with individuals with subversive backgrounds."[47]

In accepting the case, Taylor specified he would make all final decisions about legal arguments. In preparing the case, he worked closely with Norman Leonard and remembered Leonard as very capable and completely cooperative. Taylor found the case "prickly and complicated." Like Leonard's brief to the appeals court, Taylor's argument focused on the 1942 law waiving the statute of limitations, the concept of res judicata (the argument that the issue had already been decided before the current trial), and the due-process clause of the Fifth Amendment, all avoiding the particulars of the jury's decision about perjury.[48]

The appeal was argued before the Supreme Court on May 4, 1953, and the Court delivered its opinion soon after, on June 15. Justices Robert Jackson and Tom Clark recused themselves because of their prior involvement as attorneys general in directing prosecutions of Bridges. The remaining judges split 4–3, with the majority ruling for Bridges, Robertson, and Schmidt. Justice Harold Burton delivered the opinion, for himself and Hugo Black, William O. Douglas, and Felix Frankfurter. Burton's opinion was narrowly based. He said that using the 1942 law to avoid the statute of limitations was improper because that law applied only "where the fraud is of a pecuniary nature or at least of a nature concerning property" and could not be applied in a case such as that before the Court.[49]

In later years, Bridges was fond of saying that he had been "cleared" twice by the Supreme Court. It would have been more accurate to have said that the Court had twice found in his favor by avoiding the details of his convictions and deciding based on narrow interpretations of the statutes under which he was charged.

In 1941–45, the ILWU, the CIO, and CIO unions had provided most of the cost of the legal defense. In 1949–53, the CIO no longer contributed. The ILWU, some of its locals, and other Left unions contributed significantly to the sizable legal expenses, but Bridges, Robertson, and Schmidt necessarily looked beyond the ILWU and other Left unions. Dave Jenkins, in charge of fund-raising, toured the country, raising funds from some unions not on the Left, along with liberals and liberal organizations. Bridges, Hallinan, and others also traveled the country raising funds.[50]

Throughout the trials and appeals, Bridges continued to lead the union, and the ILWU continued to function effectively despite the near-constant headlines about Bridges's legal problems, the expulsion from the CIO, and raids by other unions. The "New Look" in longshore labor relations continued with little friction. The ILWU-PMA contract was opened for wage and benefits review each year. Frustrated by federal restrictions on wage increases during World War II and after the war, unions across the country turned to benefits programs to make up income lost to inflation. In 1949 the ILWU and PMA followed that lead and agreed to what the negotiating committee called "a modest life insurance policy and reasonably adequate medical and hospital benefits, as well as disability insurance." The ILWU-PMA Welfare Fund administered the new benefits programs. The fund, directed by three ILWU trustees and three from PMA, was funded initially by PMA paying three cents for every hour worked and ILWU members paying one percent of their wages. A new longshore contract was negotiated in 1951, for two years, with improvements in wages and benefits, including, for the first time, a pension plan.[51]

Among the medical benefits for ILWU members was participation in Kaiser Permanente, the pathbreaking, prepaid medical program that had grown out of Kaiser industries' health plans during the 1930s and World War II. The ILWU-PMA Trust Fund became one of the first large organizations to negotiate directly with Permanente over terms for its members. Initially centered in the San Francisco Bay Area, Kaiser Permanente expanded in Southern California and Oregon partly to accommodate ILWU members. Because Kaiser Permanente had prepaid clients and fixed salaries for its medical personnel, the American Medical Association viewed Kaiser Permanente as only a small step removed from the universal health care programs that FDR and Truman had promoted.[52]

With the ILWU outside the CIO, raiding threatened some ILWU locals, especially warehouse locals. In February 1950, a special Local 6 convention voted to remain with the ILWU rather than join the Teamsters or affiliate directly with the CIO. Einer Mohn, the IBT's general organizer for the Bay Area, chartered IBT Local 12 to challenge ILWU Local 6. The first members were 350 former Local 6 members who, Mohn recalled, were "anti-Bridges and anti-Goldblatt and . . . may have been anti-Communist, too." In June 1950, however, the NLRB brokered a mutual no-picketing agreement between the IBT and ILWU. Subsequent IBT raiding largely ended in 1953 when the Distributors Association granted Local 6 a union shop. Mohn later acknowledged that Harry Lundeberg of the SUP had given significant support to the IBT raiding but added, "Lundeberg was not too dependable, and he was very emotional, and he didn't outline in his own mind and to his own associates any definite position. . . . Bridges pretty well knows where he is going to go; he's a cold, calculating fellow; he's not very emotional; you pretty well know when you sit down with Bridges where he is going."[53]

On July 24, 1950, as Donohue was preparing to have Bridges's bail revoked, Secretary of Labor Maurice Tobin and other federal officials met with representatives of shipping companies and maritime unions, including ILWU Locals 10, 34 (Bay Area ship clerks), and 19 (Seattle longshore), each then with Right leadership. The participants agreed to help the Coast Guard with a program to screen CP members, "subversives," and "'notorious' fellow travelers" from the waterfront. Bridges was not invited, nor was Hugh Bryson of the NUMCS. All other maritime unions were represented. In September the longshore caucus resolved, "This caucus is prepared to cooperate in any security program on a coastwise basis providing such a program is not used by the enemies of this union for their own purposes."[54]

By then the MFOW and NMU had expelled members considered to be Communists. NUMCS leaders and some members were being screened from working aboard ships. Some who lost their jobs through expulsion or screening joined the ILWU. The ILWU also became a refuge for smaller Left unions and individual locals of expelled Left unions. The International Fishermen and Allied Workers—the CIO union for the fishing and fish-canning industry—merged with the ILWU and became the Fishermen's and Shoreworkers' Division within the ILWU. The NUMCS attempted something similar, as the ILWU Stewards Department, but lost an NLRB election (see next chapter). A few locals of the Food, Tobacco, Agricultural, and Allied Workers (FTA), another expelled Left union, joined the ILWU.[55]

During 1949 and 1950, there were several ILWU strikes in Hawai'i, beginning with a longshore strike in April 1949 that lasted almost six months. At issue was the wage differential between Pacific Coast and Hawaiian longshore workers. The ILWU wanted to close the differential. On the other side were many of the same companies that had just gone through the Pacific Coast longshore strike, its resolution, and the "New Look." Events in Hawai'i gave little sign of that. The companies offered twelve cents toward closing the forty-two-cent differential. The ILWU wanted at least sixteen. Alexander Budge, president of Castle and Cook, one of the Big Five, explained, "Ability of waterfront employers to pay is not issue." Instead, the issue was the effect of any significant wage increase on other workers in the islands. It was a bitter strike, in which the *Honolulu Advertiser*, Hawai'i's leading newspaper, consistently smeared the ILWU as communist. In June Territorial Governor Ingram Stainback established a fact-finding procedure, which recommended an increase of fourteen cents, which ILWU members rejected by 826–59.[56]

In late July, the territorial legislature passed the Dock Seizure Act, taking control of the docks and permitting the territorial government to hire strikebreakers. Bridges and the ILWU promised that any ships loaded by strikebreakers would not be unloaded anywhere on the Pacific Coast, including the C&H plant at Crockett. When the territorial government got a court order restraining the ILWU from picketing the docks, Bridges and Art Rutledge, head of the Hawai'i IBT, personally picketed. The government's nonunion longshore workers unloaded and loaded ships, but none bound for the West Coast. By late September, $61 million of sugar had piled up in the islands, and the stockholders for the Big Five and Matson were increasingly anxious.[57]

When some of the stockholders talked directly with Bridges, he proposed a deal. He and Dwight Steele (central in settling the strike the year before) soon reached agreement, but Steele had to sell it to the Hawaiian Employers' Council. The next morning, when Bridges's flight was ready to depart, he had not heard from Steele regarding the HEC's decision. Nonetheless, he read to the assembled reporters his understanding of the agreement: a fourteen-cent wage increase (the same as the fact-finders' report), eight cents of it retroactive, and seven cents more on February 28, 1950, for a total of twenty-one cents, half of the differential. The news flashed across the islands and into the room where the HEC was meeting. Though angry, they accepted the same deal but in different language and with a date of March 1 instead of February 28. Bridges called his announcement "merely a bit of strategy."[58]

Throughout the 1940s, Jack Hall's organizing in Hawai'i had included a political dimension, focused especially on the territorial Democratic Party. While the mainland ILWU was following the will-o'-the-wisp of the IPP, Hall's forces in the islands were working to take over the Democratic Party. Given that territorial administrators were appointed by the president, this set up a struggle within Hawai'i's Democratic Party. Governor Stainback and Democratic national committeewoman Victoria Holt charged that Hall's efforts to take over the Democratic Party were, in fact, Communist infiltration. Stainback appealed to the FBI for verification, and in late February 1950 Hoover provided President Truman with an eighteen-page report detailing the alleged CP connections of several Democratic Party activists.[59]

The 1951 ILWU convention was held in Hawai'i, the first time that any international union had met there. The *March of Labor*, a Left magazine, provided this glowing description: "Almost every racial or national group in the world was represented. . . . [W]ell over 90 per cent of the delegates were workers directly off the job, elected by their respective locals. . . . At times, delegates were lined up a dozen deep waiting their turn to speak." The ILWU's Right was present in the convention, took full part in debates, but lost on every vote. The international officers were unopposed for reelection. Despite all his legal problems, Bridges and his supporters—many of them not from the Left—remained in control. Holding the convention in Hawai'i was recognition of the important role of the islands within the ILWU. That year 44 percent of all ballots cast in the ILWU election of officers came from the islands.[60]

The year 1951 was also the time of a major ILWU strike on Lanai, much of which was pineapple plantations. After the ILWU's 1947 loss in pineapple, the industry had refused industry-wide bargaining and instead insisted on company-by-company, even plantation-by-plantation, contracts—a goal of nearly all Hawaiian companies. In 1951 ILWU members on Lanai, mostly Filipinos, went on strike without asking Hall or the ILWU. The ILWU did what it could to support the strikers. The strike lasted 201 days. When some two hundred thousand tons of pineapples were rotting in the fields, the industry came to Hall and Goldblatt and agreed to resume industry-wide bargaining and increase wages not just on Lanai but for all Hawaiian pineapple workers.[61]

The ILWU's problems in Hawai'i were moving outside collective bargaining and into legislative halls and the courts. In 1950 the House Un-American Activities Committee held a hearing in Hawai'i. Such hearings around the country, usually by a subcommittee, had become a standard committee practice, not for any obvious legislative intent but instead to accuse individuals of being part of "the Communist conspiracy" and to hold those individuals up to shaming, ridicule, or loss of livelihood. Hall was among those called to testify. He refused to answer when asked if he had ever been a CP member. Outside such an arena, he was relatively open in acknowledging he had joined the CP in 1936 but left it when he felt a conflict between CP membership and ILWU leadership. In front of HUAC, he refused to answer, fearing any answer might lead to perjury charges.[62]

The next year, 1951, Hall was among the Hawaiians arrested and charged with violating the Smith Act. After the Supreme Court confirmed the convictions from the New York Smith Act trial, more trials followed, including that in Honolulu. Conviction was the usual outcome, and it was the outcome for the Hawaiians, including Hall, the only defendant in that trial who had not been an open CP member or involved with the Left *Honolulu Record*. Convicted in 1953, Hall and the others were free on bail pending their appeals (see next chapter).[63]

Though Hawai'i occasionally posed problems for ILWU leaders, the Hawaiian ILWU rescued the international in the Juneau Spruce case. The case began when the Juneau Spruce Corporation opened a plant in Juneau, Alaska, but refused to join the collective bargaining agreement between Juneau waterfront employers and ILWU Local 16. Instead, the company's contract with the International

Woodworkers of America included loading lumber. In 1948 Local 16 launched a wildcat strike (not approved by the international) against Juneau Spruce. When IWA members loaded lumber on the company's barges, ILWU locals in the Northwest refused to unload them. The company charged the ILWU with a jurisdictional strike and secondary boycott, illegal under Taft-Hartley, and secured a judgment of $750,000 (equivalent to nearly $9 million in mid-2022) against Local 16 and the international. It was, the ILWU claimed, the largest judgment ever issued up to that time against a union in such a case. Although the Juneau plant was often closed between 1947 and 1949, and it burned and was not rebuilt in 1949, the legal case acquired a life quite separate from events in Alaska. The ILWU appealed all the way to the Supreme Court, which unanimously found against the union. By the time the ILWU had exhausted its appeals, the judgment was more than $1 million.[64]

The ILWU was always asset poor. During the Juneau Spruce case, this served the union well when the company tried to attach the union's bank accounts and real estate. The international sold its headquarters building in San Francisco to Local 142, the largest local in Hawai'i, and immediately used those funds to prepay salaries and bills. Goldblatt emptied the union's bank accounts and conducted most ILWU business by receiving per capita payments in cash and using cash to buy cashier's checks to pay bills. Since the international's only assets were its office furniture, the company sought to attach the assets of several large locals, including 142, the largest and most prosperous of the Hawaiian locals. Local 142 disaffiliated.[65]

In the meantime, Hall, in Hawai'i, had been pursuing a court case under the Fair Labor Standards Act. Hall offered to settle for $250,000, and the companies agreed. Hall then suggested to Goldblatt that he ask Juneau Spruce to settle for $250,000. The company agreed. The funds changed hands, and the Juneau Spruce case finally ended. Goldblatt later called it "one of the most brilliant things Jack Hall has ever done." Local 142 immediately reaffiliated, and Bridges and Goldblatt personally thanked the members for their help at Local 142's second biennial convention.[66]

Not learning from the 1948 debacle, the CP continued to promote the IPP in California. In 1950 and 1952, however, the IPP ran candidates only in selected races, usually those when a Republican used California's cross-filing law to win the Democratic nomination as well as the Republican. In those situations, the IPP candidate sometimes did quite well. The *Dispatcher* was uniformly critical of the Truman administration throughout 1950 but largely silent on electoral politics, reporting only on the three IPP candidates in statewide elections and on locals that had endorsed Democrats. In 1952 Vincent Hallinan was the IPP candidate for president. *Dispatcher* editorials roundly criticized the Democrats but also declared that a Republican victory would be "a disaster of first magnitude."

Though noting the IPP offered a chance to make a protest vote, the paper also questioned the value of protest votes. When Eisenhower was declared the winner, Bridges opined that the Democrats had brought that result on themselves and observed, "Labor will find out now, more than ever, that at all times it has to rely on its own economic and political strength and organizations, if it is to protect its gains and its rights."[67]

Prosecuted repeatedly by Democratic administrations, burned by events in 1948, Bridges, the strong proponent of political action by labor in the 1930s, had begun to shun party politics. His alienation persisted through several more election cycles, although he and other ILWU leaders sometimes returned to a favorite proposal from the 1930s: a labor party. The 1953 biennial convention endorsed the idea of a labor party, but, more realistically, specified that each ILWU district council and local should establish a legislative committee to track state legislation and lobby on behalf of the union.[68]

The CP, under attack on many fronts, was shedding members. By 1953 the party nationwide had lost two-thirds of its members. The decline was comparable in the three Pacific Coast states. From the 1930s on, the CP had been an important presence within some ILWU locals. By the early 1950s, Right slates regularly won elections in the San Francisco and Seattle longshore locals, the largest locals where the CP had been prominent. Though the CP was in decline by the early 1950s, Bridges's relation to the party, as described by Jenkins and others, seems to have changed very little. He remained accessible to party leaders. He often reflected the position of the party in his public pronouncements on domestic or foreign policies. The *Dispatcher* continued to criticize U.S. foreign and domestic policies from a Left perspective.[69]

The Bridges-Robertson-Schmidt case, expulsion from the CIO, the Hawai'i HUAC hearing and Smith Act trial, and the Juneau Spruce case meant that Bridges and the ILWU were going through very difficult times during the late 1940s and early 1950s. Bridges's home life, however, seemed more comfortable than anytime since the early 1920s. He, Nancy, and their children settled into a house in the Cole Valley neighborhood, near other Left families. Herb Resner's law firm paid for the house because Bridges could not afford it on his salary as ILWU president. With his ulcers under control, Bridges resumed drinking alcohol. In early 1952, Harry's sister Alice Whykes came for a visit, the first time he had seen any of his family since 1919. Despite the turmoil of his public life, his personal life finally seemed stable.[70]

And Bridges continued to poke fun at his adversaries. An FBI informant reported that Bridges told this story at a banquet in Los Angeles in late 1952: "Both Vice-President elect RICHARD NIXON and HARRY BRIDGES were passengers on [a plane en route from Hawaii]. . . . During a friendly conversation, NIXON told BRIDGES that he had met some important people in Hawaii who

Harry Bridges at home with his family, Nancy, Julie, and Robbie, ca. 1950. (Photo courtesy of Labor Archives and Research Center, San Francisco State University)

had a high regard for him because he was always a man of his word. NIXON, said BRIDGES, then made the following remark: 'BRIDGES, I think you're a Communist, but I don't think you're the dangerous kind. The dangerous kind we are trying to get are the ones like HISS, ACHESON and TRUMAN.' . . . The audience 'howled' and applauded wildly." The report continued: "The informant was carefully interrogated as to whether there was any indication that BRIDGES might have made the comment in jest."[71]

In April 1953, at the convention, Bridges and the officers took a more serious look at the union, its origins, its struggles, and the principles that had guided its development over the previous twenty years. They listed these as "ten cardinal rules"; the ten were reduced to nine statements and unanimously approved in a resolution:

> The membership is the best judge of its own welfare.
> Labor unity is the key to successful economic advancement.
> An injury to one is an injury to all.
> No union can permit internal disunity.
> Union organization must match employer organization.
> Organize the unorganized.
> Workers are workers the world over.
> Social gains are as important as wage gains.
> Jurisdictional warfare and raiding must be outlawed by labor itself.

These principles, including the officers' original third cardinal rule, "Workers are indivisible. There can be no discrimination because of race, color, creed, national origin, religious or political belief, sex," with more of the officers' original text and periodic updating, became the ILWU's Ten Guiding Principles that are still cited today.[72]

14

The Last Deportation Trial and New Beginnings

1953–1960

The late 1940s and early 1950s had been a turbulent time for Harry Bridges and the ILWU. The Bridges-Robertson-Schmidt prosecution sought to imprison those ILWU leaders. The Hawai'i Smith Act trial aimed at the same for Jack Hall, leader of a third or more of ILWU members. By expulsion the CIO tried to isolate, weaken, and even destroy the ILWU. The Juneau Spruce case threatened to bankrupt the union—and, it appeared at times, with federal connivance. When the Supreme Court overturned the Bridges-Robertson-Schmidt convictions, the INS and Justice Department immediately launched another effort to take away Bridges's citizenship.

Nonetheless, some things began to change for the better around 1953. The Korean War ended. Stalin died. The Cold War thawed a bit. The domestic Red Scare abated somewhat. Some Republicans in the U.S. Senate, including Wayne Morse, had criticized Joseph McCarthy as early as 1950, and in 1954 the Senate voted, 67–22, to censure him. The merger of the AFL and CIO in 1955 had little effect on the ILWU, though the leaders of the merged organization—George Meany and Walter Reuther—continued their antagonism toward both Bridges and the ILWU. The New Look continued to provide stability for ILWU longshore labor relations. Despite all the attacks, both Bridges and the ILWU managed to shed much of their pariah status by the late 1950s.

This chapter begins with the last deportation trial and last Smith Act cases, then addresses the ILWU's relations with other U.S. unions; new relations with unions outside the United States; and domestic politics, including the CP, the FBI, and HUAC; and concludes with Bridges's personal life. Important developments in longshore labor relations in the late 1950s will be dealt with in the next chapter.

Within two weeks of the Supreme Court's decision in the Bridges-Robertson-Schmidt case, the attorney general revived the dormant civil denaturalization suit, filed in 1949 but suspended pending the outcome of the criminal conspiracy case. Federal attorneys reopened that suit on June 7, 1954. The trial began a year later, before Judge Louis Goodman.[1]

Bridges again turned to Telford Taylor. At the time, Senator Everett Dirkson was accusing Taylor of having masterminded the Senate's censure of McCarthy. Taylor had, in fact, figured prominently in charges that McCarthy mishandled confidential documents. Although representing a defendant in a courtroom trial was new for Taylor, he agreed to do so in cooperation with Richard Gladstein and Norman Leonard. He set the same condition as before: he would make all decisions in the event of disagreements. Leonard recalled that Taylor told him, "We are not about to defend the Communist Party. . . . [T]hat's not our job. Our job is to vindicate Bridges. . . . I agreed with him, Harry agreed with him, and that is exactly what happened."[2]

In San Francisco, Taylor often ate at the Fairmont Hotel, the usual hotel for visiting Democratic Party leaders. One day, he met Senator Hubert Humphrey there. Humphrey greeted Taylor effusively and asked his business in San Francisco. Taylor replied that he was defending Harry Bridges. Muttering that he supposed someone had to do it, Humphrey turned away coldly.[3]

During the trial, Bridges, Taylor, Gladstein, Leonard, and Louis Goldblatt held daily strategy sessions. J. Paul St. Sure sometimes joined them. Bridges was central in those meetings. Taylor remembered him as highly articulate and very bright—one of the brightest clients that he had ever defended. Rather than risk another jury trial, they decided instead to accept the verdict of the trial judge.[4]

This time the prosecutors recycled some previous witnesses. Two weeks before the trial, the *Chronicle* revealed that John Schomaker, scheduled as a lead witness against Bridges, had been a paid federal "consultant" on communism. When the trial opened, on June 21, 1955, the prosecution first called one of its professional witnesses about communism, who put some observers to sleep with his convoluted explanations of CP ideology. The prosecution next called Bridges. Asked detailed questions about his testimony over the previous fifteen years, Bridges sometimes said that he could not remember but would stand by the record. He explicitly denied ever being a CP member. The next prosecution witness claimed he had collected CP dues from Bridges in the 1930s and was followed by one who swore Bridges had tried to recruit him into the CP in the 1930s. Next Schomaker embellished his previous account of recruiting Bridges into the CP and added new details about events throughout the 1930s. The prosecution then called Bruce Hannon, who had testified in defense of Bridges in 1939, to testify against him. After a few more witnesses on the nature of the CP, the prosecution rested.[5]

INS investigators credited the FBI with "breaking down" Hannon. In return for Hannon's cooperation, the FBI agreed to end an investigation of him and his brother. Hannon told me that the FBI "had some jerk come in and see me . . . [who] said, 'Well, you know, you're in real jeopardy. You can go to jail.'" Hannon said that he had never paid dues to the CP but had attended many meetings with CP members, and the FBI persuaded him that doing so meant that he had been a Communist. Regarding his testimony in 1955, he said, "I said what I thought was the truth," that he and Bridges had attended meetings where CP members were present.[6]

Julie, now thirteen, came to court each day with her dad. Bridges was the first defense witness. As previously, he recounted his entire history with the union, admitted accepting assistance and advice from CP members and leaders, and denied ever being a party member. B. B. Jones again testified that Schomaker's account of recruiting Bridges was a lie. Other ILWU members also testified in Bridges's defense, including Ralph Mallen, an original member of the Albion Hall group, who had testified against Bridges in 1939. The head of the San Francisco Building Trades Council also testified for Bridges. Both sides rested their cases. Rathborne was not called.[7]

Jones had testified that an FBI agent tried to bribe him. The prosecution did not challenge that statement, considering it "of no importance" to their case. J. Edgar Hoover, however, scrawled, "It is vitally important to the FBI." When FBI agents determined Jones had never been interviewed, they pressured prosecution attorneys to recall Jones or call an FBI agent to counter Jones's claim. The prosecutors refused because "Judge Goodman is trying to speed up this trial." Hoover scrawled, "It is apparent that Asst. U.S. Atty lacks 'guts'"—although he was clearly standing up to Hoover. In the end, Gladstein agreed not to oppose a prosecution motion to strike that part of Jones's testimony.[8]

On July 29, 1955, Judge Goodman delivered his verdict. He dismissed the testimony of former Communists on both sides as "tinged and colored with discrepancies, animosities, vituperations, hates, and above all, with lengthy speeches and declarations of viewpoints, which, it is not unfair to say, is a disease with which Communists are afflicted." Highly critical of witnesses on both sides, he dismissed other prosecution witnesses' testimony as "unacceptable," "flimsy," and "unsubstantial," and called the testimony of some defense witnesses "not worthy of belief." Goodman described Bridges as "not a good witness" who "made misstatements" and was "evasive." Nonetheless, he found Bridges's "denial of party membership and avowal of loyalty to the United States" to be "articulate and emphatic." Goodman specified he expected the government to prove its case to "an exacting standard," and it failed to do so. Bridges retained his citizenship. He, Julie, his attorneys, and his union promptly celebrated both the decision and Bridges's fifty-fourth birthday.[9]

During the trial, Taylor thought he discerned a pattern: Goodman was consistently ruling against the defense on procedural issues where there was any doubt.

Taylor was right—by ruling so consistently for the prosecution and against the defense, Goodman left the federal attorneys no grounds on which to appeal. There was no appeal. The trial marked the final attempt to deport Bridges. Taylor told me that he cherished his memory of those cases and that "it was fun."[10]

Jack Hall remained out on bail from 1953 to 1956 as appeals of his Smith Act conviction wound through the courts. During the initial trial, Gladstein had led the defense. For the appeal, the ILWU brought in Taylor, who argued Hall's case before the Ninth Circuit Court in 1956. Other Smith Act cases were also moving through appeals. In 1956 the Supreme Court heard *Yates v. US*, the appeal of the California Smith Act defendants. The Ninth Circuit Court delayed its decision on the Hawai'i case until the Supreme Court issued its *Yates* decision, which came in June 1957. The Court did not declare the Smith Act unconstitutional but did set such limits on it as to make it virtually unenforceable. The Ninth Circuit Court then grudgingly dismissed the case against all the Hawai'i Smith Act defendants.[11]

In what seemed a bad case of sour grapes, Treasury Department attorneys brought legal action against Bridges, Robertson, and Schmidt in 1958, claiming funds contributed for their legal defense represented income for which they owed income taxes amounting to $81,000. The case drug on until 1961, when the IRS offered to settle for $7,200. Bridges reluctantly agreed, but only to avoid more legal fees. Schmidt recalled that, years later, a former IRS official told him that the case "was just for the purpose of harassing you."[12]

A few months after Goodman's decision, and as an indication of improving relations between the ILWU and local AFL unions, Bridges spoke to the San Francisco Building Trades Council, long one of the city's more conservative AFL organizations. He thanked the council for having voted unanimously to permit its secretary to appear as a character witness during his trial. Bridges received a standing ovation from the council members.[13]

The ILWU's relations with the ILA improved significantly. In 1948 Malcolm Johnson wrote a Pulitzer Prize–winning exposé of corruption on the New York waterfront.[14] State investigations in 1951 were followed by hearings by a subcommittee of the U.S. Senate Committee on Interstate and Foreign Commerce in 1953. After revelations of ILA corruption and thuggery, the AFL revoked the ILA's charter, the first time an international union was expelled for corruption. Under indictment for stealing union funds, beset by a rank-and-file revolt in New York City, and a revolt by local and regional ILA officers outside New York, Ryan retired in 1953.[15]

In 1954 the NLRB organized a representational election between the independent ILA and a new union chartered by the AFL eventually named the International Brotherhood of Longshoremen (IBL). Bridges supported the ILA on the grounds a majority of New York dockworkers wanted it. When New York ILA locals requested financial assistance, eleven ILWU longshore locals contributed generously. The ILA won the election. The New York longshore workers also gained a union shop and began to be dispatched from government hiring centers, finally replacing the shape-up that Ryan had insisted on to maintain his power.[16]

The ILWU was one of only two unions to support the ILA rank-and-file members' efforts to maintain their union against Ryan's maneuvers and IBL raiding. The ILWU's relations with the ILA continued to improve. The 1955 ILWU convention even passed a resolution looking toward eventual unification, but there was no follow-up. In 1956–57, the revived ILA struck all East Coast and Gulf ports seeking a coastwise contract. The ILWU fully supported the strikers, and Bridges conferred informally with ILA leaders. Soon after, the ILA hosted a delegation of ILWU clerks gathering information for a wage arbitration. Then ILA members visited San Francisco to observe the workings of the International offices, including the research department, pension and welfare office, and the *Dispatcher*. The ILA and ILWU developed a joint legislative program for 1958. In late 1959, the AFL-CIO issued a new charter to the ILA.[17]

As relations between the ILWU and ILA improved, the few remaining ILA— now IBL—locals in the Northwest voted to affiliate with the ILWU. By 1958 the ILWU, including the autonomous ILWU Canada, represented all longshore workers from Alaska to San Diego and in Hawai'i.[18]

Relations with the Teamsters also improved. After the AFL-CIO expelled the IBT in 1957 for corruption, Einar Mohn, untouched by the corruption scandals, became head of the Western Conference of Teamsters. At the time, the Distributors' Association of Northern California (DANC) had negotiated mostly with the ILWU warehouse locals, and the Employers Council had dealt mostly with the IBT warehouse locals. Mohn later said the employers had done well for themselves by keeping "this fight going . . . between the Teamsters and the ILWU." In 1958, at Mohn's initiative, the ILWU and IBT presented "a united front" by refusing to sign with either employer group ahead of the other. The *Dispatcher* headlined the result: "ILWU-Teamster Unity Brings Warehousemen 'Real Victory.'" Similar cooperation ended most ILWU-IBT jurisdictional issues on the waterfront. In 1960 Mohn described himself and Bridges as on good terms.[19]

In Hawai'i in 1957, fifteen local unions, including the ILWU, Teamsters, building trades (AFL-CIO), and hotel and restaurant employees (AFL-CIO), planned a joint campaign to organize the unorganized. By then all the Hawaiian ILWU locals had merged into Local 142, which represented a wide range of workers, from railway workers to laundry workers and supermarket workers. The joint organizing campaign, in which AFL-CIO unions sometimes supported ILWU organizing efforts, was a prelude to the later ILWU-IBT agreement to divide the Hawaiian hotel industry between them.[20]

Though the ILWU's relations with the ILA and IBT significantly improved, relations with the SUP remained at loggerheads. Though the post–World War

II Red Scare had eased significantly by the mid-1950s, Harry Lundeberg never missed an opportunity to attack Bridges and the ILWU as "phonies" and "commies." Nonetheless, two long-running battles with the SUP ended in 1955, one over the Marine Cooks and Stewards and the other over the few remaining steam schooners.

The NUMCS, led by Hugh Bryson, was expelled from the CIO at the same time as the ILWU. NUMCS members—a few thousand—shipped out from Pacific Coast ports. They prepared and served food on freighters and provided food and housekeeping for passenger ships. The union had a reputation for being on the Left and being more diverse than any other maritime union, perhaps more any other union—it was sometimes described as "one-third red, one-third Black, and one-third queer," overlapping categories. When it was expelled, Lundeberg quickly chartered a Marine Cooks and Stewards, AFL (MC&S-AFL), to contest that jurisdiction in an NLRB election. After Bryson signed the Taft-Hartley non-Communist affidavit, he was indicted for perjury. At the same time, legal judgments bankrupted the NUMCS.[21]

Rather than merge with the bankrupt NUMCS, the ILWU created a Stewards Department in early 1953, too late to appear on the NLRB election ballot. Such elections permitted a none-of-the-above option, so the ILWU encouraged its supporters to vote for "neither." "Neither" won, 1,287–743. Lundeberg's SIU then petitioned for one bargaining unit for all unlicensed seagoing personnel on the Pacific Coast: seamen (SUP), engine crew (MFOW), and cooks and stewards. The NLRB decided in Lundeberg's favor. Bridges condemned it as "collusion," and the ILWU charged that it would likely mean discrimination against African Americans, given their exclusion from the SUP and MFOW. In April 1955, however, the SIU won by almost four to one, marking the end of the ILWU Stewards Department.[22]

The ILWU's other dispute with the SUP grew out of the long-running jurisdictional battle over steam schooners. SUP crews had long maintained rights to unload one hatch. In late October 1954, the *Pacificus*, one of the few surviving steam schooners, prepared to unload cargo in San Pedro. Past practice there was that the SUP worked hatch 3. There was no cargo to be unloaded from hatch 3, so the ship's master assigned the SUP to hatch 4. ILWU Local 13 refused, because in San Pedro hatch 4 on steam schooners had always belonged to the ILWU. MFOW members on the *Pacificus* cut the steam to the winches, preventing any unloading. Soon SIU crews on the entire Pacific Coast were not starting work, arriving late, and refusing overtime. When the stoppages continued into a third week, Lundeberg announced he intended "to hurt the shipowners a little," to persuade PMA to side with the SUP in the dispute over hatch 4. Those tactics were soon labeled "hard-timing."[23]

Three weeks into hard-timing, Bridges proposed to settle the dispute through arbitration. Lundeberg refused and insisted the PMA enforce the SUP contract, which said SUP crews worked at the direction of their supervisor. In late November, St. Sure acknowledged that PMA's contract with the SUP conflicted with that with the ILWU. Saying he wanted to find a solution, not fix blame, St. Sure urged "all parties" to "work out an immediate solution." He also predicted, "Unless such a solution can be found the very jobs in dispute will be destroyed, for American flag ships cannot continue to take the economic beating they are now experiencing." Bridges proposed that his executive board meet with its SUP counterpart to resolve the matter. Lundeberg refused, charging that "the Communist-controlled ILWU" was "only interested in the welfare of the Soviet Government." In discussions with Labor Department officials, Lundeberg referred to the PMA as "fellow travelers . . . supporting the communist cause."[24]

On December 7, Bridges, backed by members of the ILWU executive board, persuaded Local 13 members to let the SUP work hatch 4 of the *Pacificus* on a onetime basis. Lundeberg refused, insisting the ILWU could not determine which hatch the SUP worked. On December 22, St. Sure asked Secretary of Labor James Mitchell to intervene. Lundeberg refused, claiming that the dispute was between the PMA and ILWU and that the SUP was not involved in any labor dispute. On December 22, though, Mitchell sent a representative to Lundeberg to ask "what can he [Mitchell] do to help both management and Lundeberg's union settle the matter and give the Commies 'the business.'" The dispute finally ended in late January on the terms presented by the ILWU in December. Lundeberg declared victory.[25]

The *Pacificus* again became a flash point a few months later, when it returned to San Pedro and the company ordered the SUP to work hatch 4. Local 13 members refused. MFOW members cut off the steam. This time the ILWU immediately charged PMA with violating the contract, PMA countercharged, and the case went to the area arbitrator, likely a scenario worked out beforehand. The ILWU and PMA agreed to make minor changes in the contract for steam schooners. That seemed, finally, to settle the *Pacificus* affair.[26]

Lundeberg got the last word. Speaking to the Commonwealth Club in San Francisco, he denounced the ILWU as Communist dominated, accused the PMA of making "secret deals," and specifically charged that the ILWU and PMA had "a secret deal" regarding the *Pacificus*. He also assured the assembled shipping executives there would never be peace on the waterfront so long as "you treat one organization as sacred cows and the others as SOBs."[27]

Lundeberg had some basis for his characterization. St. Sure recalled how the employers had done "a complete reversal" in 1948. Previously, he said, "Lundeberg had been the favorite unionist who could get almost anything that he asked for and certainly with no trouble." With the New Look, St. Sure continued, Bridges was "the favored person with whom there would be no trouble and with whom there would be an agreement."[28]

The *Pacificus* affair proved the last episode in the half-century jurisdictional dispute over steam schooners. In 1959 the last steam schooner was rescued from a Seattle junk dealer and taken to San Francisco to become an exhibit at the Maritime Museum.[29]

There remained one violent chapter to the long-standing feud between Bridges and the SUP. Shortly before one o'clock in the morning on September 21, 1956, Bridges was at a restaurant. As the place began to close, Bridges finished his ginger ale and went to the men's room. Two SUP members, Fred Reppine and Donald Hansen, followed Bridges, grabbed him from behind, threw him to the floor, and began to beat and kick him. Bridges knocked over a metal towel container, attracting the bartender and manager, who rushed to rescue Bridges and were themselves attacked by Reppine and Hansen. Bridges suffered severe bruising, including two black eyes. Police arrested the two assailants, both of whom had extensive police records, including concealed weapons violations. Both had arrived from Southern California a few days before. Wilmington police described Reppine as an SUP organizer with a "fetish on Communism"; an FBI report listed him as a "former confidential source." Pete Moore, the ILWU's Southern California regional director, described Reppine as a "strong-arm man to Harry Lundeberg." Lundeberg denied any connection.[30]

Four months later, Lundeberg died of a heart attack at the age of fifty-five. His successor as head of the SUP was Morris Weisberger, who proved less combative than Lundeberg. Two weeks later, the *Chronicle*'s gossip reporter noted that Bridges was unavailable to testify during the trial of his assailants and claimed he had "no stomach for pressing the charges, now that his arch foe, Lundeberg, is dead." Bridges's assailants were convicted and sentenced to thirty days in jail.[31]

By 1960 the ILWU had improved relations with the three unions—ILA, IBT, and SUP—that had previously been major sources of conflict. In the late 1950s, Bridges also acted on his long-standing interest in developing and maintaining relations with unions, especially dockworkers' unions, elsewhere in the world. His first and closest such relation was with James Healy, head of the Australian Waterside Workers Federation. Beginning in 1940, Healy and Bridges regularly exchanged information on issues they faced.[32]

In early 1959, Bridges and William Glazier, his administrative assistant, undertook a seven-week tour of ports in Britain, Germany, Belgium, France, Italy, Greece, Egypt, Czechoslovakia, the Soviet Union, and Israel, where they observed longshoring operations and met with union leaders. Glazier drafted lengthy reports for the *Dispatcher*, published under Bridges's name. They discovered that some longshore workers were still hired through a shape-up and others through a central hiring process. None had a union-run rotational system like the ILWU. Nearly all union leaders they met were Socialists or Communists. Bridges was impressed that some longshore workers belonged to unions of all transportation workers. Nowhere did they find containerization comparable to that under way on the West Coast.[33]

The 1959 convention, soon after, chose delegates to the All Pacific and Asian Dockworkers Trade Union Conference set for May in Tokyo. Bridges and Healy had long discussed an exchange of delegates, but events repeatedly intervened. Their discussions eventually produced the Tokyo conference, where Healy and Bridges met in person for the only time. Despite hopes for broad attendance, only Australia, Cambodia, Japan, and the USSR joined the ILWU delegation, which included a Canadian delegate. Bridges gave the keynote address. Conference resolutions called for decasualization of dockworkers everywhere and for mitigating the negative effects of mechanization on dockworkers. Other resolutions supported unionization struggles of workers in less developed countries, disarmament, a ban on nuclear testing and atomic weapons, independence for colonialized peoples, an end to the Cold War, and development of more international trade.[34]

Bridges's international adventures in 1959 had one more chapter. In September Nikita Khrushchev, first secretary of the CP of the Soviet Union, arrived in the United States for a national tour before his UN address. After a frosty welcome by the mayor of Los Angeles, Khrushchev endured a meeting with national AFL-CIO leaders in San Francisco during which Walter Reuther aggressively needled him about working conditions and unions in the Soviet Union. The next day, September 21, Khrushchev made an unscheduled visit to Local 10's new hall, a striking geometric dome that included the hiring hall, meeting hall, and local offices. Bridges and St. Sure, on behalf of the ILWU and PMA, had invited him to visit the hiring hall, and Khrushchev added it to his schedule at the last minute.[35]

On short notice, ILWU and PMA officials gathered at the hall, along with several hundred Local 10 members, some coming off nearby ships. Harry, other ILWU officers, St. Sure, and other PMA leaders all welcomed Khrushchev. By chance the chief dispatcher was Mike Samaduroff, who explained the low-man-out dispatch system in Russian. Khrushchev extended greetings from Soviet workers and spoke of the need for peace and "enough work and a good wage." All his comments brought cheers. He later called it one of the highlights of his trip.[36]

A few days later, *Chronicle* columnist Herb Caen presented this account, undoubtedly supplied by Bridges: "Guess who said this to Khrushchev Mon.: 'The Republican party is the party of peace!' Answer: Harry Bridges. And when K. expressed surprise at Bridges' kindly words about the waterfront employers—'they're a pretty good bunch'—Harry grinned at the Russian: 'You Marxists have a term for it, after all. It's a capitalist contradiction.'"[37]

Though the politics of Khrushchev's visit to Local 10 were lost on no one, Bridges's own politics had taken a peculiar turn by then. In 1956 he changed his voter registration to Republican. Bridges explained that he did so, "not with any intention of endorsing the Republican party or its policies," but because "I have always resented the pat conclusion of most Democratic politicians and their labor movement followers that organized labor must stick with the Democrats no matter what." Vice President Richard Nixon reacted, perhaps wryly: "We should be concerned whether a Trojan horse is in our midst."[38]

If Bridges were a "Trojan horse," it was empty of troops. Throughout the mid- and late 1950s, the ILWU almost always endorsed Democrats. Bridges was less enthusiastic than his members. He commented about the 1956 presidential election between Adlai Stevenson, a liberal Democrat, and the incumbent, Dwight Eisenhower: "The Democratic party is not a labor party or just the party of Stevenson. It is also the party of [Senator James O.] Eastland," whom Bridges condemned for his support of segregation, efforts to destroy unions, and red-baiting. Bridges gave grudging support to Stevenson, but added that "the union membership will do as it pleases about the presidential election."[39]

In 1958 California and Washington voted on propositions to adopt state right-to-work laws, which outlawed union shops. Late in the campaign, Bridges again debated Roger Lapham, this time on San Francisco's public television station, regarding California proposition 18. As with Prop 1 twenty years before, Prop 18 unified unions, a unity that, for most, carried over to the election of Democrats to state and federal offices, part of a national trend fostered by recession. In California Democrats won all statewide elections but one, often by margins of three to two, and Prop 18 lost by almost the same margin.[40]

Bridges later explained he had to change his voter registration in 1956 because California's IPP had collapsed. That collapse was part of a larger deterioration of the Communist Party. Nationwide, after World War II, the CP had claimed almost seventy-five thousand members, with California second only to New York. A vibrant labor-Left culture then existed in the Bay Area and Los Angeles, with smaller versions in Seattle and elsewhere. Subscribers to the *People's World* (*PW*), the CP's daily West Coast newspaper, far outnumbered party members. Radio broadcasts presented a labor-Left perspective on current issues. The California Labor School (CLS) attracted thousands to its classes, lectures, and social events. These labor-Left institutions all came under attack in the late 1940s and early 1950s. Bridges's defense activities siphoned off energies and funds. Raiding on left-wing unions led some to reduce or eliminate their financial support for Left organizations. The radio broadcasts ended. *PW* subscriptions fell from fifteen thousand in 1947 to six thousand in the late 1950s. The CLS lost support, its curriculum and activities dwindled, and federal marshals padlocked its doors in 1957. After 1951, when Smith Act prosecutions scooped up some leaders and sent others underground, attendance fell at local CP club meetings, and some clubs lost contact with section leaders.[41]

In 1956 a double blow came from the public release of Khrushchev's speech describing Stalin's atrocities and the Soviet invasion of Hungary. Dave Jenkins said the Khrushchev speech "was like a rape, a mental and emotional rape because we were involved with hundreds of non-Party people to whom we had denied the possibility of these 'slave labor' camps, the murder of honorable and fine people." He and Edith resigned. Bill Bailey, a longtime party member, had joined Local 10 after the MFOW expelled him. For him the invasion of Hungary was "the straw that broke the camel's back." He remembered thinking, "You stupid bastards. Is this socialism at work?" A national convention in 1957 failed to bring new leadership, prompting more resignations, including twenty-six California party leaders who left as a group in early 1958. Nationwide, the party lost three-quarters of its members by 1959, shrinking to about three thousand members.[42]

During the 1950s, Bridges's relations with the CP seem to have become quite strained. In 1954 an FBI informant reported that Bridges "refused to go along with the CP even on relatively minor issues such as those surrounding the elections which were then underway." In 1955 the San Francisco SAC reported, "There is no evidence that he has been a member of the CP for over fifteen years; however . . . it was an unwritten, unstated fact that the CP considered BRIDGES to be a member on a top level and very important capacity." That "unwritten, unstated fact" was sufficient to keep Bridges on the Security Index and again be classified as DETCOM—detain as Communist in event of national security emergency.[43]

In 1956 one FBI informant described Bridges as "of the opinion that the CP should cease to function as it was a dead issue and no longer served any purpose." In the aftermath of the Soviet invasion of Hungary, Bridges asked rhetorically in the *Dispatcher* whether "the people of Hungary shouldn't have the right to do any damn thing they want with their government" and described the "Russian action in Hungary" as "harmful and destructive to world peace." He also equated that invasion with the British and French occupation of the Suez Canal. Sidney Roger remembered that Bridges's criticism of the Soviet Union in the mid- and late 1950s had brought him "a lot of hell" from CP members and others on the left. Herb Caen reported, in August 1957, that Bridges had run out of patience with CP members in Local 10, telling them, "I want you Commies to stay out of my hair!"[44]

Nonetheless, Bridges never lost his admiration for the Soviet Union, the Communist regimes of Eastern Europe, and, by the late 1950s, Cuba. That admiration, expressed in the *Dispatcher* and occasional in public addresses, provided the FBI's only evidence that Bridges was "a dangerous individual . . . expected to commit acts inimical to the national defense and public safety." The FBI kept him under at least occasional surveillance throughout the late 1950s.[45]

In August 1957, Bridges appeared on national television with Mike Wallace, an aggressive interviewer. Bridges exhaustively prepared by fielding the most aggressive and personal questions that Sid Roger, a former radio journalist, could throw at him. When Wallace asked Bridges his opinion of Russian communism, Bridges replied that he was knowledgeable about trade unionism but knew "very little about Russian Communism." After probing by Wallace, Bridges opined that the system in Russia was "up to the Russian people. If they want it, they're entitled to have it. And they're the ones to change it." Regarding Hungary, Bridges said, "I'm against the use of force and violence or troops against them [workers], in Hungary or in this country." Asked his views on Communists holding office in his union, Bridges replied, "The membership . . . have a right to select anyone they like."[46]

Wallace pushed Bridges, asking if he and the ILWU would consider it appropriate to block delivery of arms to Nationalist China. Bridges differentiated between his views and the union's: "As an individual I would; the union might think differently." Wallace then claimed Bridges was saying that the union should be able to exercise a veto power over Congress. Bridges disagreed: "We think that we would have a right as loyal American workers and citizens to express ourselves." Bridges consistently sought to differentiate between his opinion and the union, stating toward the end of the interview, "I'm going to serve the union that elects me and pays me."[47]

The FBI took a keen interest in the broadcast. An FBI agent reported, "Wallace was trying to needle Bridges" about communism, but Bridges "was prompt in limiting the questions to that particular phase that he could handle without difficulty." The agent concluded, "Wallace had stepped out of his league." However, a subsequent FBI report claimed Bridges had said, "It would be all right for the ILWU to strike in protest should the US decide to send arms and troops to Nationalist China," then concluded, "Subject might commit acts inimical to the United States in the event of a national emergency."[48]

Bridges's European travels in 1959 brought a subpoena from the House Un-American Activities Committee. Dick Arens, the committee's staff director, requested help from C. D. DeLoach, the third-ranking FBI official. DeLoach explained to Hoover that the committee "does not really expect to obtain any information" from Bridges, but wanted to put on record "that Bridges received a passport . . . to meet with members of the Italian Communist Party," part of an effort to persuade Congress to reverse a recent Supreme Court decision permitting passport applicants to ignore questions about CP membership. "The Committee was 'in a bind,'" DeLoach continued. "They had subpoenaed Harry Bridges . . . and all of a sudden, they remembered that they do not have a witness who will be able to place Bridges in the Communist Party." Without such a witness, the committee could not rebut a denial of CP membership, and the result might be "favorable publicity" for Bridges rather than HUAC. Arens asked the FBI for an appropriate witness. DeLoach suggested instead a long report summarizing Bridge's tangled legal history. Hoover wrote, "OK," and added, "It would be so much better if HCUA would build its cases first before 'popping off.'"[49]

During the hearing, Arens's first question was whether Bridges ever used the name Harry Dorgan. Bridges immediately asked the relevance of that question for passport legislation. Bridges asked if the purpose of the question were to reopen the past twenty years of litigation. Arens denied that it was. Bridges pursued the issue: Was the purpose of the question to cause him to waive his Fifth Amendment rights and thereby open up "thousands" of similar questions? Arens refused to answer directly. Bridges then refused to answer and, for the first time ever, cited the Fifth Amendment.[50]

Arens next read Agnes Bridges's statement to the Washington state Un-American Activities Committee. Bridges smiled throughout the reading, then announced, "Later on she repudiated that testimony." After some subsequent sparring, Arens asked why, on his passport application, Bridges had not answered questions regarding membership in the CP. The committee chairman, Francis Walters, intervened to ask if Bridges had not answered those questions because of a recent Supreme Court decision. Bridges acknowledged that had been one reason.

Arens then questioned Bridges's about his recent travels and the upcoming Tokyo conference. Bridges acknowledged that most of the reports from his trip had been written by Glazier because "he writes much better than I do." Arens posed a series of questions intended to put on record that Bridges had met with a number of Communist union leaders, but Bridges protested that they had met with a wide range of union leaders. Arens read a translation of a comment attributed to Bridges by an Italian publication and asked if Bridges had said it. Bridges responded, "It sure sounds like me." Arens asked Bridges whether a long list of ILWU officers were or had been CP members; Bridges refused to answer. Arens eventually turned to Bridges's comment about block-ing shipments to Nationalist China in event of a war, and Bridges stood by the answers he'd given Wallace. At one point, in discussing a hypothetical invasion of the mainland by Chiang Kai-shek's forces, Bridges said bluntly, "I would strenuously object and do what I could to oppose the United States engaging in such a suicide enterprise." He added that would change if Congress were to declare war—"which," he qualified, "Congress doesn't seem to do any more."

At one point in the long hearing, Bridges was asked if he had applied for a passport anytime before the recent Supreme Court decision prohibiting the question about CP membership. "No," he replied, then added, "There were too many people in this country trying to get me out without a passport." The FBI reviewed Bridges's testimony and found no instance of perjury.[51]

Two days after the HUAC hearing, Hoover told his top assistants that Attorney General William Rogers "had just been reading the testimony by Harry Bridges and he was wondering whether Bridges was on our pick-up list in the event of a national emergency. . . . The Attorney General thought it also might be well to check into those persons who would be in line to take over if Bridges were picked up and include them on the pick-up list so there could be no danger of our shipping facilities being paralyzed in the event of a national emergency."[52]

Amid the pressures of continued FBI surveillance, the fourth trial, and his union responsibilities, Bridges's marriage to Nancy had failed. Nancy secured a divorce in Nevada in January 1955. She told the judge that Harry worked too much and left her alone too much, which constituted "mental cruelty." Harry did not contest the divorce. Others assured me that Harry had been deeply in love with Nancy and was deeply saddened by the divorce. Bridges told me that it was his fault for spending too much time with the union and too little with his family. Though they originally agreed that she and the children would remain in California, Nancy moved to New York and took them with her in 1956. Bridges sued to bring the children back. A California court decided in his favor, but a New York state court subsequently ruled that they had become New York residents. Bridges deeply missed his children. When union matters took Bridges to Washington, he usually took a few extra days to go to New York to see them. Robbie told me that one time he left their apartment building in New York and was surprised to find Harry outside, as if he were there waiting there for a chance to see Julie or Robbie.[53]

Bridges was also dealing with medical problems. He was hospitalized in 1949, 1953, 1954, twice in 1956 including surgery for removal of a tumor and a "four-day checkup," twice in 1957 including once for bronchial pneumonia, and for fatigue in late 1959. He sometimes went into the hospital for a checkup in late December because it took his mind off being away from his children during the holidays.[54]

Some of the hospitalizations may have been alcohol related—to get him dried out. Bridges had begun drinking after his successful surgery in 1948. Alcohol was a part of the life of most union leaders, and all too often alcoholism was as well. All the ILWU's international officers enjoyed a drink or several. Harrington's Bar, near the ILWU offices, was known as the place to find ILWU officers. After the divorce, Harry's drinking increased. In the early and mid-1950s, he was drinking at noon with lunch and after work, and often to excess. Sidney Roger later said that Goldblatt sometimes covered for Bridges during crucial committee meetings. Bridges once told me that his fellow officers had helped to pull him out of his descent into alcoholism.[55]

In December 1958, Bridges surprised many of those close to him when he married Noriko "Nikki" Sawada, a secretary in the law office of Charles Garry and Barney Dreyfus, left-wing lawyers specializing in labor and civil rights issues. She had previously worked for civil rights groups and for the Gladstein law firm. She met Bridges at a fund-raiser on Halloween 1958. "Harry was there, drunk as hell," she recalled. "So my boss drags me over and Harry doesn't bother to get up but says, 'Where have you been?' and I said, 'Like all my life?'" He asked her for a date. She declined but called him back after a few weeks. They had their first date on Thanksgiving. Afterward, Noriko remembered, "We saw each other almost daily for almost a week, then we decided to marry."[56]

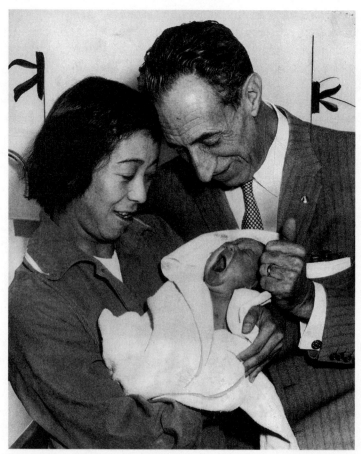

The *News Call-Bulletin* published this photo on October 6, 1959, describing it this way: "Longshore leader Harry Bridges and his wife, Noriko, pose for a typical portrait with their baby daughter . . . parents smiling and infant yowling. Miss Katherine Bridges, 7 pounds, 2 ounces, was born on Sunday." (*News Call-Bulletin* photo, AAA-6223, courtesy of San Francisco History Center, San Francisco Public Library)

They planned to go to Reno for a quiet wedding. Noriko remembered that Harry, ever tight with money, wanted to elope to avoid the cost of a big reception. They arrived on December 8, but were too late to get married that day. The next morning, the *Chronicle* had a front-page article about their impending nuptials, describing Noriko as "a pretty Nisei legal secretary," recounting how she and her family had spent World War II in a internment camp in Arizona and noting the difference in their ages. Soon after the paper appeared, the phone rang in their hotel room. Noriko answered, and, as she recalled, "My boss Charlie [Garry] says, 'Are you married?' And I said no. He said, 'Well, there's a miscegenation law in Nevada.' And I said, 'Oh Lord, give me the name of a lawyer.'" Harry and Noriko never hesitated about going through with their wedding. And, in case they were hesitating, George Anderson, part of the Gladstein firm, called and, according to Noriko, said, "remember Hawai'i"—given the ILWU's large Asian membership in Hawai'i, they had to fight Nevada's miscegenation law.[57]

They talked with the lawyer Garry recommended, told the U.S. attorney what they were going to do, then applied for a marriage license, because they had to be refused before they could file suit. Asked their nationality, Noriko replied, "American." Harry said, "She's the American, I'm the foreigner." The clerk insisted they had to identify their race, which they did. Noriko said to the reporters filling the room, "I didn't know it was so difficult for a Republican to marry a Democrat." Harry and Noriko said little else to the many reporters in the clerk's office, although Harry did say, about their marriage, "I got the better of the bargain." Denied a marriage license, they and their lawyer went to the district judge who issued a writ of mandamus. When they finally received their license, they crossed the street to a justice of the peace, who married them privately, attended only by their Reno lawyer and the justice's clerk. Bridges told a reporter that it was his last marriage, "because I'd never live through another like that."[58]

By 1960 the seemingly endless deportation hearings and trials had ended, as had the Smith Act trials and the long-running disputes with the ILA, IBT, and SUP. There were some auspicious beginnings: greater acceptance by the rest of organized labor, relations with dockworker unions elsewhere in the world, and, most important, a new marriage. For the ILWU, the most significant new beginning was the first Modernization and Mechanization (M&M) agreement, topic of the next chapter.

15

Transforming Longshoring:
The M&Ms

1955–1966

This chapter and the next cover overlapping time periods. This one deals with a transformative technological change in ocean shipping that revolutionized longshoring and brought significant changes to the ILWU. The next chapter presents other aspects of Bridges's life after 1960 along with the subsequent implications of the M&M agreements of 1960 and 1966.

The New Look in longshore labor relations that began in 1948 continued through the 1950s. Benefits steadily expanded in contract after contract: longer vacations, dental insurance, medical insurance for pensioners, dismemberment insurance (important for longshore workers given ever-present dangers), and more. In 1955 *Business Week* described the ILWU-PMA welfare fund as "always . . . an innovator," noting especially dental care and preventative medicine. In 1954 the existing longshore contract was extended to 1956, but with a wage increase negotiated during the *Pacificus* imbroglio. It was extended again, to 1958. In 1958 the contract was extended by one year, but the maximum work shift changed from nine hours (six hours' straight time, three hours' overtime) to eight hours (including two hours' overtime), the union's first reaction to the expectation that mechanization was likely to reduce the workforce.[1]

Despite agreeing to improved benefits, the PMA continued to complain about some work practices, including four on–four off, the occasional addition of an extra man to a gang (called an "unnecessary man" by PMA), and late starts and early quits. Bridges did not defend such practices, nor did many local officers, recognizing not only that they were indefensible but also that they gave the union a black eye with the public and legislators. Such practices, often called featherbedding, were prohibited by the Taft-Hartley Act and specific legislation directed at railroads. Bridges recommended, "All locals [should] take steps to eliminate these practices." However, as Bridges told a congressional committee in 1956, "Agreeing here [to eliminate the practices] is one thing. Getting people down there to do the work is another thing." That year longshore locals approved principles that tied implementation of eight-hour work shifts to elimination of late starts, early quits, four on–four off, and unnecessary men. The vote in the longshore locals was a harbinger of impending troubles: 60 percent in favor, but much closer votes in the four largest locals.[2] PMA's complaints extended to contractual rules regarding gang size and sling-load weights. Such long-standing complaints of the companies and the emerging concern within the ILWU over mechanization came together in the late 1950s.

By then Bridges, other ILWU officers, and many longshore workers were focused on a new, transformative, and potentially disruptive technology: containerization, the most important development in ocean shipping since the steam engine. Containerization permitted products to be moved vast distances more cheaply and quickly than ever before by making loading, unloading, and transferring of cargo much faster and more efficient. Containerization expanded markets abroad for U.S. agricultural products and raw materials and expanded U.S. markets for manufactured goods produced elsewhere in the world. Containerization led many U.S. firms to move manufacturing offshore, where wages were cheaper, unions largely nonexistent, and governmental regulations lax or absent. And it completely transformed ports and longshore work, beginning on the West Coast in 1958.

The ILWU was no stranger to technological innovations. During World War II, Bridges and the ILWU complained that shipping and stevedoring companies were not using more efficient technology. However, World War II did bring greater use of forklifts and pallets (replacing slings) and more powerful cranes, able to handle heavier loads. By the 1950s, forklifts and pallets had reduced the number of pier men in longshore gangs. In the Northwest during World War II, the army began to pack cargo into six-foot by four-foot wooden boxes that could be moved into and out of ships' holds by the ship's winches. In 1950 the Alaska Steamship Company adapted that technology, creating eight-foot by twelve-foot boxes, called cribs, for shipping between the Puget Sound and Alaska. A year later, Alaska Freight Lines began shipping entire semitrailers on barges from the Puget Sound to Alaska.[3] The implication was clear: when cargo comes to the piers already packed into boxes and needs only to be hoisted into the hold, fewer longshore workers are needed.

The union's earliest agreements had permitted labor-saving technology: "The employer shall be free, without interference or restraint . . . to introduce labor saving devices." However, the first ILWU convention, in 1938, had resolved "against the introduction of labor-saving devices without provisions being made for compensation to the workers involved" and instructed ILWU leaders to negotiate introduction of such devices. Accordingly, Bridges and the Coast

Labor Relations Committee announced that the 1940 agreement "constitutes recognition, for the first time, in so far as longshore contracts are concerned, of the workers' rights to share in the benefits of technological progress." In 1945 Bridges and the officers reported, "We must do nothing to hinder and must actively promote the mechanization of the industry since in the long run an increase in productivity must be the basis for an increase in the standard of living."[4]

During the 1950s, ILWU members in several fields were experiencing technological change. By 1951 mechanization had reduced the number of pineapple workers on Lanai from between thirty-five hundred and four thousand to eight hundred. By 1953 instead of shipping raw sugar in bags from Hawai'i to the C&H refinery at Crockett, Matson had converted ships to bulk cargo and installed machinery to load and unload the ships. Unloading a ship at Crockett changed from ten days to two days and required significantly fewer men. In the lumber ports of the Northwest, bundling of lumber by lumber mills reduced loading time by almost 60 percent.[5]

By 1957, as initial experiments with containers were getting under way on the East Coast, ILWU officers reported that the use of vans and cribs in longshoring was moving jobs away from the waterfront. They stressed, "The future of the longshoremen is tied up with our ability to cope with this problem." They accurately forecast, "Mechanization is developing at such a pace that it will accomplish more in the elimination of manpower in the next 10 to 20 years than has been done in the last 100 years."[6]

As of 1957, however, the ILWU had not yet grasped how transformative the technology could be. The union's initial concern was that mechanization would bring a reduction in the workforce, not the wholesale transformation of longshore work. The only relevant resolution in the 1957 convention called for reducing the workday to prevent layoffs. That resolution provoked the most discussion in the convention. Martin Callaghan, from Local 10, told the convention, "I'd like to see them install all of this machinery and equipment to do the work to make it easier for us guys around here. But let's bear in mind this: let's make these machines work for us guys, not for the employers." Robert Rohatch, also Local 10, added, "Pensions and shorter working hours are the only answer to mechanization."[7]

In October 1957, a special longshore caucus meeting discussed mechanization at length. The 114 delegates from all longshore, clerks, and walking bosses locals met for three days. The CLRC (Bridges, ex officio as president, and two members elected at large, L. B. Thomas representing California and Howard Bodine representing Oregon and Washington) presented a special report that frankly and objectively—terms used then and later by both ILWU and PMA—surveyed the situation and the position of the ILWU. The report concluded that cribs, bulk shipping, and the initial container experiments did not pose an immediate threat but stated bluntly, "It is not a good public position, whether before an arbitrator or in a strike, to be fighting to retain what the employer will label 'unnecessary men' and 'featherbedding.'" One sentence caught nearly every one's attention: "Do we want to stick with our present policy of guerilla warfare resistance or do we want to adopt a more flexible policy in order to buy specific benefits in return?" The report advocated for more flexibility.[8]

Bridges argued for trading existing work rules and practices for guarantees of work and wages. Not everyone agreed, but all agreed that the CLRC should continue informal discussions with the PMA. Lincoln Fairley, ILWU research director, later summarized the delegates' views: "The delegates, like the membership generally, were worried about the inroads on their work, were opposed to the militant position of outright refusal to accept the new methods, but were basically puzzled as to how to proceed. . . . [T]hey had confidence in the Coast leadership and were willing to wait and see what came out of the informal talks."[9]

By then two projects were forecasting the future, one in the East and the other in the West. Marc Levinson, in *The Box: How the Shipping Container Made the World Smaller and the World Economy Bigger* (2006), points out that early experiments with containers proved only slightly more cost-effective than traditional break-bulk cargo. That changed in the mid-1950s with experiments by Malcolm McLean on the Atlantic and Gulf Coasts and especially with research by Matson that proved more significant in the long run than McLean's efforts.[10]

Levinson credits McLean with the major insight that "the shipping industry's business was moving cargo not sailing ships," that not just ships but also trucks and railroad cars needed to change. His staff redesigned cargo ships and truck trailers. Their new system was given its first trial run in late 1957, between New York and Houston.[11]

By then Matson's planning was well advanced. Matson dominated shipping between Hawai'i and the mainland and had long used ships' decks for carrying such large items as locomotives. Carrying containers on deck was only a short step. In 1956 Matson created a research department to design the most efficient *system* for containerization—containers, ships, cranes, and trucks—and hired Foster Weldon, a Johns Hopkins University geophysicist, to lead the effort. Weldon assembled a staff of engineers and economists who subjected every aspect of Matson's operations to rigorous computer analysis—something new at that time. McLean's cranes were part of his ships, but Matson's researchers concluded that cranes needed to be very large and to rest on land for maximum stability and efficiency. Weldon's staff also concluded that eliminating traditional methods for transferring cargo from trucks to piers to ships to piers to trucks and eliminating existing longshore work rules would greatly speed operations and cut labor costs in half or even two-thirds. Lloyd Yates, one of Matson's engineers, told me they also forecast significant savings by sending containers to Southern California and loading them on railcars to the Midwest and East rather than sending ships to New York. (Hawai'i is closer to San Francisco than to Los Angeles, but Southern California has more efficient rail connections.) Over the next twenty years, Matson reduced its fleet from twenty-three ships to six.[12]

A front-page photo and story in the *Dispatcher* in August 1958 informed all ILWU members about Matson's container project, a key part of the preparation for an upcoming meeting of the coast longshore negotiating committee. Mechanization dominated the agenda of that meeting. Bridges announced the goal that workers "get a substantial share of the profits, and of the productivity benefits and other savings to the shipowners resulting from new operations and the increased use of modern methods of cargo handling." The *Dispatcher* followed with an illustrated report on the first Matson ship loaded with containers using existing cranes in San Francisco. By then Matson was building cranes across the bay, where there was more space for cranes and containers. From the beginning, the Port of San Francisco, with its finger piers and dense development along the waterfront, seemed an unlikely site for any significant amount of containerized shipping. Matson's giant cranes were soon in place and working at Alameda, Honolulu, and the Port of Los Angeles.[13]

Bridges and the CLRC recognized that mechanization had the potential not only to effect profound changes in longshoring but also to tear the union apart. Lincoln Fairley summarized Bridges's position, as of mid-1958: "The existing policy of putting all possible obstacles in the way of change would not work much longer and might split the Union. . . . [T]he rank and file would resist any change in policy unless something convincingly better could be worked out in negotiations."[14] Bridges and the CLRC therefore focused both on addressing mechanization and on involving the longshore membership at each step of decision making.

The Coast Negotiating Committee adopted a three-point program in early September 1958. First, Bridges and the CLRC, in informal discussions with PMA, were to maintain existing staffing despite the assumption that fewer men would be needed, to seek a share of the benefits of mechanization above and beyond normal wage increases, and to require PMA to train ILWU members on the new equipment. Second, in preparing for formal negotiations, the union was to undertake a coastwise program of discussion and education, so that all union members could understand the issues and participate in planning, with the goal of building unity in support of the negotiating committee. Third, the international officers were to seek a united approach with the ILA and IBT. Soon after, the *Dispatcher* carried two full pages on "the most sweeping revolution" in the history of the maritime industry and the union's plans to address it.[15]

Sea-Going Box Cars The freighter **Hawaiian Merchant**, with twenty large new aluminum containers on deck, departs from San Francisco for Honolulu in the first mass containerization shipment to Hawaii. The **Merchant** is one of six Matson ships which will provide container service on a weekly basis from San Francisco and Los Angeles to Honolulu. The containers—carrying everything from baby food to bleach—are 24 feet long, 8 feet wide, and 8½ feet high. They were made by Trailmobile, Inc., with aluminum furnished by the Kaiser Company and are built to fit on a truck chasis for highway shipment. Matson has ordered 350 such containers for its Hawaiian service, the first of its kind in the Pacific. In the lower panel the deck load of containers—each carrying more than 20 tons of cargo—was unloaded in Honolulu in three hours. The railroad crane in Honolulu was constructed specially for this and similar operations. On the mainland special cranes are now under construction specifically for Matson as part of the major containerization program. A new crane to be installed at Encinal Terminals, Alameda, will be 118 feet high with a boom 107 feet long and a 25-ton capacity.

Bridges and the ILWU leadership used the *Dispatcher* to inform union members about the rapid development of containerization. These photos of the first Matson ship carrying containers appeared in the issue of September 12, 1958, with the caption, "Sea Going Boxcars." (Photo courtesy of Anne Rand Library, ILWU)

The ILWU was well positioned to involve its members in the process. Since the 1930s, the longshore division had developed and institutionalized decision making involving significant numbers of union members. During the 1950s, the two elected CLRC members, L. B. Thomas, Local 13 (whose local, now with its hall and offices in Wilmington, served the Ports of Los Angeles and Long Beach), and Howard Bodine, Local 8 (Portland), were widely respected up and down the coast. Locals held regular membership meetings at which there was usually no limit on individuals' ability to speak on issues. For major issues, the contract permitted stop-work meetings, so that all local members could attend and take part. Bridges and other international officers regularly visited locals, spoke at their meetings, took questions and comments from the floor, and were used to defending their positions. The coast caucus—more than one hundred delegates elected by all longshore, clerk, and walking-boss locals—met before negotiations to thrash out the union's position and elect a large and representative negotiating committee. In 1959 the negotiating committee consisted of the four international officers (Bridges, Robertson, Bulcke, and Goldblatt), the two elected members of the CLRC (Bodine and Thomas), and ten members chosen by the caucus (six from longshore locals, four from clerks' locals). The longshore members included one from each of the large locals (San Francisco, Wilmington, Portland, and Seattle) and two from the small locals in the Northwest; the four clerks' representatives were also geographically diverse. Committee members were present for all negotiating sessions and regularly caucused over particular issues. Fairley, who held a PhD in economics from Harvard, attended all negotiations.[16]

Bridges, Bodine, Thomas, and other officers spoke at stop-work meetings of the large locals and listened to members' concerns. Members formed long lines at floor microphones to wait their turn to speak. On October 1, 1958, Locals 10 and 34 held a joint stop-work meeting at the San Francisco Civic Auditorium to discuss the three-point program. Members were required to attend and told to bring lunch. Bridges first presented the issues and the committee's program. Then members lined up at the floor microphone to speak or question the officers. The dialogue between officers and members lasted for five hours. On October 28, Local 13 held a stop-work meeting in the Long Beach City Auditorium. More than twenty-five hundred members and their families heard from Bridges, Thomas, and Local 13 officers, then took their turns at the microphone.[17]

The 1959 biennial convention, in Seattle, clearly indicated that the ILWU had lost its pariah status. The head of the Washington State Federation of Labor (AFL-CIO) welcomed the delegates and thanked the ILWU for its "fine support and cooperation" in that state. He was followed by the governor, a liberal Democrat, and by U.S. senator Warren Magnuson. The delegates heard Bridges's report on his travels in Europe and the Middle East but focused on containerization, a significant part of the officers' report. Bridges argued that "the time had come to use our union strength in order to get a share of the benefits from the new methods by cooperating in their introduction."[18]

A major issue for the convention was avoiding layoffs. Possibilities included reducing work hours with no reduction in pay, creating severance pay, and improving medical benefits for retirees. (Medicare was still in the future.) One prominent suggestion was to reduce the retirement age, so as to reduce the workforce among those most senior, rather than through layoffs of the least senior. Otherwise, if layoffs came, those with the lowest seniority would be laid off first, including many of the African Americans and other people of color who had come into the union during World War II and after, especially in Locals 10 and 13.

The convention unanimously approved Resolution 1, On Automation and Mechanization: "Wherever there is anything which can be done better or easier by a machine than by a man, it is worthwhile having the machine do it. Men can thereby be liberated for something they do better than machines. . . . [A] progressive union program for automation must include, among other things, both stimulants to the economic growth of the nation as well as concrete proposals for expanding the domestic and foreign markets for the goods of American industry." Wage increases, the resolution continued, "are absolutely essential" but not sufficient. Other solutions included reductions in the workweek, early retirements, substantial severance pay, longer paid vacations, and retraining and relocation programs. The union reiterated its long-standing efforts to expand world trade, especially by bringing China into world markets. (The United States then refused to recognize the Communist government in China, thereby preventing trade.) Jobs were clearly on the delegates' minds as they supported increasing world trade, since a significant increase in world trade might offset jobs lost through mechanization.[19]

The coast caucus met immediately following the convention and endorsed the CLRC's proposal for "a funded plan which would help provide the currently registered men with a share of the benefits of mechanization," an approach that became the center of the M&M. The idea for a fund had emerged from the informal discussions between the CLRC and PMA representatives. The CLRC also reported that data was needed for measuring the effect of mechanization on productivity so that economic gains could be apportioned to the currently registered workforce.[20]

Bridges's trips to Europe, the Middle East, and Japan came shortly before the opening of formal negotiations with the PMA. When I asked him if there was a connection between those trips and the upcoming negotiations, he answered, "God damn right!"[21] By his travels, Bridges was signaling to the shipping companies, including foreign companies, that the ILWU had excellent relations with unions in parts of the world where shipping companies needed cooperation from dockworkers.

Bridges's relationship with J. Paul St. Sure, head of the PMA, played a crucial role in negotiations. Ellen St. Sure Lifschutz, St. Sure's daughter, told me that her father and Bridges "would meet before negotiations, privately." She said that her father

> and Harry, apparently, always told each other what their bottom line was, and no one ever knew this except Harry and my father, and then they turned up at negotiations and they argued and fought and did whatever they did, but each one was aware of what the real issues were and what the absolute minimum demands were going to be on both sides. . . . They could be prepared, to know that if they went past a certain point, they were going to encounter a different kind of opposition. . . . [N]o one else was ever involved.[22]

Negotiations began in May and concluded in late July 1959. All hundred-plus members of the coast caucus attended the final sessions. Negotiators agreed on a three-year contract with wage increases and improved vacation benefits. The fully registered workforce (called A men) was to be maintained with only normal attrition and was to handle all new equipment. The PMA was to contribute a $1.5 million fund (equivalent to a $14.6 million in mid-2022) to pay A men for their increased productivity based on future data-based negotiations. These provisions reflected the prior work of Bridges, Bodine, and Thomas with St. Sure and his staff on a way to reserve funds to be apportioned to existing longshore workers based on data to be collected. The interim agreement was approved by slightly more than two to one among longshore locals and ten to one among clerks' locals. The vote was closer in the large locals other than San Francisco. Three small ports rejected the contract.[23]

The A and B categories of longshore workers had come into existence during the 1950s, replacing earlier ways of denoting the difference between full union members and others who filled in as needed. A men were fully registered, full union members. They were dispatched first. B men were probationary and were dispatched as needed. After five years, B men could advance to A status if there was sufficient work. B men were expected to attend local membership meetings but could not vote. Given the aging of A men, B men were often assigned to the more difficult or distasteful jobs, especially work in the hold.[24]

Everyone understood the 1959 agreement as interim, pending more research and further negotiations. Before the longshore caucus met in April 1960, Bridges presented his concerns and his objectives. "From its inception," he wrote, the ILWU "has put the security of the men and women as the first responsibility of the union." He emphasized, "Our first responsibility continues to be the people already working who are already members of our union," that is, the A men, and he strongly urged that no new members be added anywhere. He denied a rumor that the $1.5 million fund would simply be divided among all the A men.[25]

The caucus—102 delegates from forty-one locals—met April 4–9, 1960, one of the longest such meetings. At the outset, they reviewed the CLRC's proposal to increase the fund by an additional $3 million to guarantee a weekly income equivalent to thirty-five hours' straight time and to fund early retirements as necessary to reduce the workforce. The caucus endorsed the proposal and set out a plan: first, to shift union members from port to port and among classifications (that is, longshore workers, clerks, and walking bosses) to meet any decline in work at particular ports, at no cost to the fund; second, if that were not sufficient, to develop an early retirement program to open jobs to younger members; and third, if those were not sufficient, to use the fund to maintain a wage equivalent to thirty-five hours' straight time for registered members. The caucus also proposed to retain control over the fund if it proved unnecessary for those purposes. Benefits were to go only to registered ILWU longshore workers, clerks, and walking bosses, that is, only to the A men. B men were not included in the work guarantee or early retirement programs. The caucus also recommended that longshore workers in Alaska and Hawaiʻi be brought into the master contract with PMA.[26] It was, all in all, a remarkable proposal to adjust to mechanization at the same time that it sought to protect the existing workforce from layoffs due to mechanization. However, B men were absent in both the caucus and the benefits.

Negotiations opened on May 17, with the fourteen-member negotiating committee at the table and Fairley and Bill Glazier, the officers' administrative assistant, seated behind them. After they reached agreement on a wage increase, negotiators stopped the clock to work on mechanization. Negotiations continued through the end of July, when Bodine, on behalf of the CLRC, notified all locals that registrations were frozen for all locals: no additions were permitted to either the A or B list and no transfers between the lists. Then a dispute between Local 13 (Wilmington) and the PMA over the unloading of a fully containerized ship briefly shut down both that port and the negotiations.[27]

In early October, the entire hundred-plus members of the longshore caucus reconvened, met for one day, and then attended the negotiations—now called "fishbowl" negotiations—during which all negotiators used microphones so that the entire caucus could hear them. Caucus members had their instructions: no booing, no hissing, just take a note about whatever you want to discuss in caucus. Wayne Horvitz, part of the PMA negotiating team, told me, "the most extraordinary thing" about Bridges was how he let the negotiating team members "all have their say, never showing any impatience," nodding his head, and smoking constantly. Eventually, Horvitz continued, Bridges would "say something like, now, as I understand the proposition here," then he'd "pull it all together. . . . [H]e was a genius at that." Occasionally, the entire caucus met outside the negotiations to deal with questions or to hash out its position on some issue. All this was Bridges's way of achieving maximum unity within the ILWU.[28]

In an indication of problems to come, negotiations bogged down over four on–four off and other practices widely condemned as featherbedding. Local 13 led opposition to the CLRC proposal to end such practices and change existing gang size. In a series of negotiating committee votes on September 30, the CLRC position won, but by margins as narrow as 7.5 to 5.5. Bridges was reluctant to go into negotiations with such a split committee and took the issue to the entire caucus, which also split, 95 to 47.[29]

In the end, agreement was reached on everything but the dollar amount of the fund. According to Horvitz, St. Sure's offer was $2.5 million in addition to the previous $1.5 million, per year. Bridges called for a caucus, and it lasted through lunch and after. When they returned, Bridges said that they agreed to everything except the dollar amount. Instead of $2.5 million, he wanted $10 million per year. According to Horvitz, St. Sure asked, "Harry, where'd you get the ten? And Harry said, the same fucking place you got the two-and-a-half." And, Horvitz, acknowledged, "it was true."[30]

Horvitz's account may be completely accurate, but Fairley explained that the $10 million figure came from Local 13's representative on the negotiating committee, based on that local's studies, and that final negotiations were between the PMA's offer of $4 million and the ILWU's proposal of $5 million. Fairley also specified, "Back of the amounts proposed by the two parties were quite elaborate estimates of the costs of the benefits. The technical staffs were assisted by an actuary. . . . [E]ach side was kept fully informed of the other's estimates. . . . They were, indeed, using much the same data and most of the same assumptions." While Horvitz may have accurately related what St. Sure and Bridges *said* in negotiations, neither was pulling a figure from thin air.[31]

Final agreement was reached on October 18, 1960. The PMA agreed to contribute $5 million each year to the fund created with the original $1.5 million, for a total of $29 million ($29 million in 1960 would have had about the equivalent purchasing power as $278 million in mid-2022). The fund would guarantee against layoffs and provide minimum weekly earnings, an early retirement program or a lump sum payout for those who reached normal retirement (age sixty-five with twenty-five years of service), additional death and disability benefits, and promises of no speedup or infringement of safety rules. In return the ILWU agreed to introduction of improved methods of work and labor-displacing machinery. The ILWU and PMA announced the Mechanization and Modernization Agreement in a press release that hailed it as "epochal in the annals of industrial relations." The *Dispatcher* called it "a bold and momentous new step toward solving the problem that comes with the other blessings of improved production devices and methods."[32]

In preparation for voting on the agreement, the *Dispatcher* carried a two-page section of questions and answers about the agreement and alternative approaches to mechanization. Locals held stop-work meetings to discuss the agreement. The vote was 68 percent in favor. Only Local 13 voted against, but by 64 percent. By then Local 13 had become the largest local and continued to extend its lead over other longshore locals as the combined Ports of Los Angeles and Long Beach became the largest port on the Pacific Coast and the third largest in the country. In rejecting the M&M, George Kuvakus, president of Local 13, argued that the ILWU negotiators had settled too cheaply: "The shipping firms are going to pay us $5 million a year, but we figure mechanization will save them $50 million a year."[33]

The *San Francisco Chronicle* praised the M&M as "a significant contribution to economic history." The *New York Times* said it was "a pioneering operation that will be closely watched . . . in every industry" and described it as seeming "humane and profitable to both sides." James Mitchell, Eisenhower's secretary of labor, said, "Next only to John L. Lewis, Bridges has done the best job in American labor of coming to grips with the problems of automation." In Australia the

Otto Hagel took this photo of Bridges taking questions in the Local 10 hall in 1960. The caption, in the ILWU's publication about the M&M, *Men and Machines* (1963), was "Twice a month the membership meeting provides the forum to trash out all issues. One microphone is on the platform, three are placed on the floor. Good beefs, bum beefs, every member is entitled to his say." (Untitled photo, 1960, by Otto Hagel, © Center for Creative Photography, The University of Arizona Foundation)

Waterside Workers Federation immediately demanded a mechanization fund patterned on the ILWU-PMA agreement. By contrast, the *Wall Street Journal* called it "strangely one-sided" and proof "of the ability of monopoly unions to gain a stranglehold on any industry and enforce whatever they want in the way of a payoff" and argued that "Harry Bridges and his friends have every reason to be jubilant at the fat price they got for something that never really belonged to them." The *Los Angeles Times* similarly opined that the PMA "has 'bought' its freedom from obsolete and restrictive work practices long used by the union to 'make' jobs for its members." Fairley reported the reaction from the rest of organized labor: "The M.&M. Agreement for the most part was greeted by silence, perhaps a shocked silence reflecting concern that any union should barter away any of its hard-won work rules."[34]

There was little initial comment from liberals and the Left. Not until late 1961 did Harvey Swados, a liberal journalist and novelist, publish "West Coast Waterfront: The End of an Era," in *Dissent*, a small left intellectual journal. After interviewing longshore workers, Swados argued that the M&M meant an end to working conditions that had made "West Coast longshoring the most attractive way of life for a casual laborer in the United States, if not the entire world," a reference to ILWU members' ability to choose which days to work, four on–four off, sling-load limits, and the job security provided by the hiring hall. Finally, Swados claimed that, in private discussions, both parties referred to the $29 million fund as "a bribe to buy back certain working conditions."[35]

Swados and others called it an "old-man's" contract. He noted that the average age in Local 10 was fifty-six and that the average age in Local 13 was thirty-six. Previously, protections had been developed for those whose age made them unfit for hold work, which meant that much of the hold work fell to younger workers, many—perhaps most—of them B men. The B men posed another source of criticism of the M&M. They were not covered by the retirement provisions or work guarantees and not permitted to vote on the contract. The *People's World*, in an article generally positive about the M&M, quoted a B man: "What about us? There's nothing for us."[36]

Some ILWU officials involved in the negotiations concluded later that they may have settled for too little. However, St. Sure's daughter told me that he was replaced as the head of the PMA because some companies felt he had given away too much. Goldblatt later reflected, "Nobody knew whether we got too much out of the agreement or too little; we didn't know whether the employers got the better end of the stick or the short end." Wayne Horvitz told me that the PMA had hired Max Kesaurus, former head of the Bureau of Labor Statistics, to figure out how much the companies would save, but he could not do so, in part because some companies "were not fully honest" about their own financial data. In the end, Horvitz said, St. Sure and the PMA negotiators "took the gamble."

And it paid handsomely. Horvitz said, "In the first year, Matson and I'm sure others too, recovered not only their contribution, but maybe their contribution for a couple, three years." But he was clear: "We knew there was money in them there hills, but we just didn't have an idea how much."[37] By 1962 similar agreements covered the ILWU longshore workers in Hawai'i, Alaska, and British Columbia, none of whom had previously had contracts with the PMA.[38]

Under the M&M, the former limit on sling-load weight was gone, and what replaced it was ambiguous, a requirement that larger loads required either new machines or more men only if the larger load was "onerous" or "unsafe," terms that led to several arbitrations. For break-bulk cargo—still the majority of the work—sling-load weights significantly increased, sometimes to double the previous weight. On the docks, the new loads were often called "Bridges loads." Bridges responded to concerns about the heavier loads in 1963 by saying, "We intend to push to make the addition of machines compulsory. The days of sweating on these loads should be gone. . . . [W]e know that this is literally impossible to achieve but we are working toward it. We want to eliminate hard work by the use of machines." In addition to the cranes and related equipment, other new machines were also being introduced, further reducing the number of longshore workers. Coupled to complaints about heavier loads were complaints about reductions in gang size. Fairley summarized the situation, "At the 1964 and 1965 caucuses, delegates continued to complain bitterly that the Coast Committee [CLRC] had not fought hard enough to protect jobs, but the reductions in manning scales continued unabated."[39]

Throughout the first M&M agreement, some within the ILWU remained critical. In the early 1960s, a Local 13 board member asked Attorney General Robert Kennedy to investigate the implementation of the M&M and "the absolute dictatorial domination of Harry Bridges and his stooges" and of St. Sure and other PMA executives. Though nothing came of those charges, Local 13 continued to lead opposition to the M&M.[40]

Though the M&M confirmed the ILWU's jurisdiction over the new land-based cranes, that provision also presented problems. A minor jurisdictional issue involved the Operating Engineers in Seattle, which was settled to the ILWU's advantage by the NLRB. The major issue was thornier and more long lasting: the steady employment of crane drivers. The new cranes incorporated technology more complex than longshore workers had dealt with before. In the days of break-bulk cargo, new workers learned the skills from more experienced members of their gang, but even then winch drivers were understood to be especially skilled. Operating a crane required special training, either by a company (at first) or by the PMA (later). Certification as a crane driver placed a worker on a special dispatch list. In 1962 the parties negotiated a Crane Supplement to the M&M, permitting employers to employ "steady men" as crane drivers.

In late 1963, the CLRC agreed that "when men are trained by a company, then such men must be made available to that company when needed," a break with the long-standing practice of dispatching the low man first and the equally long-standing right of an ILWU member to decline a job.[41]

In 1965 scheduled negotiations over wages became something else—an effort by the PMA to alter significantly the ability of longshore workers to pick and choose which days they would be available for work. The PMA proposed, essentially, to do away with that long-standing prerogative. The ILWU asked for a significant wage increase. Neither got what they had initially proposed, although the ILWU gained significant improvements for pensioners and pensioners' widows.[42]

Over the course of the first M&M, from 1960 to 1965, there were both anticipated and unanticipated changes in longshoring. The anticipated changes were the significant increase in mechanization, reduction in manning scales, and the resultant increase in productivity. There was also, as anticipated, a wave of retirements by A men. Unanticipated changes were significant increases in total tonnage shipped from Pacific Coast ports, due especially to the military buildup in Southeast Asia. As a result, some anticipated changes failed to materialize, especially the need for a wage guarantee. Greater demand for longshore labor increased the average annual hours worked by A men by about 13 percent from 1960 to 1965, which, coupled with increased wages, meant A men were substantially better off financially. Work hours for B men increased slightly more than those of A men, from 8 percent of all longshore work hours in 1960 to 13 percent in 1965. Increased demand for longshore labor led some locals to promote B men to A status and add new B men.[43]

The first M&M agreement expired in 1966. In retrospect, Bridges called the early 1960s "tough as hell" and "my toughest years." The coast caucus met for eleven days in early April 1966 to discuss concerns and formulate contract demands. Reflecting experience with the M&M's changes in work rules, the caucus called for no decrease in basic gang size, any loads above load agreement to be moved by machines, compulsory use of machines to reduce manhandling of oversize loads, and no oversize loads without machines and additional men. Other demands had to do with wages and benefits, minor adjustments to grievance procedures, and adjustments to the use of the M&M fund for retirements and disability benefits. The caucus also voted to trade the no-layoff guarantee for a wage increase, as a gesture to the B men who were not covered by the no-layoff provision but would benefit from a wage increase.[44]

That caucus also directed the wrap-up of the $13 million fund created by the first M&M for wage guarantees. Wage guarantees had not been needed, but Bridges and the CLRC recommended holding onto the fund against future needs. Instead, the caucus voted to divide it among all A men who had been registered throughout the term of the contract. On December 30, 1966, each got $1,223 (equivalent in purchasing power to nearly $10,600 in mid-2022). A cartoon showed Bridges as Santa delivering checks to longshore workers.[45] That distribution partially undercut the argument that the M&M was an old man's contract but did nothing to address the concerns of B men that the M&M had little or nothing for them.

Negotiations began on May 5, 1966. On June 24, the full coast caucus, ninety-eight members, was called back into session. A major part of the negotiations focused on "skilled men," those with special training on equipment. Agreement was reached on July 6. As submitted to the members, the new contract called for a major wage increase, improvements in benefits, gang bosses to be responsible for preventing such practices as four on–four off, procedures for reducing gang size through machinery, and $34.5 million to be added to the remaining funds from the previous agreement. The agreement specified that employers could employ skilled men as "steady men," permanently assigned to that employer, rather than through dispatch from the hiring hall. The agreement also guaranteed that all dock work belonged to the ILWU. As Bridges put it, "When there is only one man left on the waterfront, pushing buttons, he's going to be ILWU." The second M&M was to run for five years. The members voted to approve by 62 percent, but several large locals produced a majority of no votes, notably 13 (Wilmington), 8 (Portland), 19 (Seattle), and 23 (Tacoma), along with a few smaller ports in the Northwest. Lopsided votes in favor in Local 10 and the clerks' locals overcame those no votes.[46]

The first M&M had been approved by 68 percent, and with less opposition in the large locals. Opposition to the second M&M continued to grow, focusing especially on the steady-man issue and container stuffing and stripping, ultimately producing the longest longshore strike in ILWU history as of this writing. That strike is the topic of chapter 17.

16

Labor Statesman?

1960–1971

In 1960 Einer Mohn commented that Harry Bridges had become "quite a statesman within the community of San Francisco." Mohn was not alone in that judgment. Bridges responded privately: "I cannot say I enjoy the label 'labor statesman,' but at least it is less likely to get me into jail or deported than the earlier label of 'labor agitator.'"[1] During and after the 1960s, labels of both sorts, and many others, were applied to Bridges. Fifty-nine years old in 1960, Bridges remained unchallenged as president of the ILWU and continued as a prominent, and sometimes controversial, public figure. Though he sometimes spoke of his age or retirement, he refused to leave the presidency of the ILWU.

This chapter and the next cover similar time periods. This chapter deals with Bridges and the ILWU in the 1960s except relations with the PMA, which appear in the next chapter.

By the 1960s, the ILWU was generally considered an independent within the house of labor, a status shared at times by the ILA, IBT, UMW, and UAW. After expulsion from the CIO, the ILWU not only held its original Pacific Coast longshore jurisdiction but expanded it. The same was true in Hawaiʻi and for most of its warehouses in the Pacific Coast region. By the mid-1960s, however, the ILWU had lost or transferred all of its midwestern and southern locals. The ILWU also lost most of the locals from its Fishermen's and Shoreworkers' Division, due to changes in the industry and raiding. By the 1960s, Bridges's personal life seemed more stable than it had been for decades. His marriage to Noriko proved to be lasting. Witty and clever, Noriko was highly popular with ILWU members when she accompanied Harry and spoke at union gatherings. Soon after their marriage, they bought a modest middle-class single-family house built in 1949, located on a small cul-de-sac lined by similar single-family homes.

Throughout his presidency, Bridges insisted that international officers' salaries should be no more than that of the best paid ILWU members. Officers' salaries were set, in dollar amounts, in the ILWU constitution, which could be amended only by a majority vote of the convention or a vote of the full membership. Increases to officers' salaries became almost a ritual at conventions, with Bridges always opposed. In 1961 his salary was increased to $260 per week, or $13,520 annually (equivalent to nearly $128,000 in mid-2022). When a delegate pointed out that Bridges's proposed salary was well below that of the best-paid ILWU longshore workers, Bridges replied, "If you want us to get rich on this job, that is your hard luck." In calling for the vote, he quipped, "The recommendation is to increase the Officers' salary and make them rich." In 1969, when Bridges opposed the proposed salary increase, a delegate suggested, "If Harry doesn't want that dough we ought to give it to Nikki." However, another delegate just dismissed Bridges's complaint as a "gimmick."[2] The salary issue was just one source of the growing estrangement between Bridges, on one side, and Louis Goldblatt and Jack Hall, on the other.

Bridges's health was more stable than in the 1950s, with fewer hospitalizations. Even so, he was showing his age. In 1963, while speaking in an ILWU hall in British Columbia, he "blacked out" for nearly five minutes. The attending physician thought that the heat and tobacco smoke in the room together with several glasses of beer during dinner and exhaustion had led to loss of consciousness. His heart rate was normal, but his blood pressure was very low.[3]

In the 1960s, Bridges was smoking four packs a day. In 1969 Herb Caen reported Bridges as saying, "'My doctor . . . ordered me to cut down on booze, sex, and cigarettes.' He paused and set fire to a fresh cigarette off the butt of his old one. 'And naturally,' he said with his crooked Australian grin, 'I do everything he tells me.'" His smoking was no joking matter. His doctor diagnosed him with emphysema and told him, as Bridges put it, "in no uncertain terms that if I did not stop smoking the condition would worsen." He tried to quit in 1971 but quickly resumed. Halfway through the 1975 convention, he stopped, this time for good. He later wrote: "Giving up cigarettes was the hardest thing I ever did."[4]

In the mid-1960s, Harry became dependent on Tuinal, a prescription barbiturate used as a sedative. Noriko became increasingly concerned about Harry's addiction and finally wrote him a letter, pointing out that he was taking five pills each night instead of one and was going to kill himself. Harry stopped taking the pills immediately, even though he was not able to sleep for the next few nights. Noriko also managed to get him to stop drinking, but only for a few months at a time.[5]

One of Bridges's favorite pastimes had long been attending and betting on horse races, usually at Golden Gate Fields, in the east bay. His enjoyment of the horses came together with his well-known commitment to pinching pennies in 1963, when he wrote to the Golden Gate Fields office staff: "I should like to request a pass for the coming meeting at Golden Gate Fields. I am an accredited correspondent of *The Dispatcher*, which is the official trade union newspaper of the International Longshoremen's and Warehousemen's Union."[6]

Bridges now had four children. As of 1960, Jackie was thirty-six, Julie seventeen, Robbie twelve, and Kathy—Katherine—was one, born October 4, 1959, when Harry was fifty-eight. Kathy's childhood included many ILWU events; her favorites were those in Hawai'i. She told me about Harry's evening routine when she was a child: Noriko and Kathy picked him up at ILWU headquarters, they came home, and Harry read the afternoon newspaper, the *San Francisco Examiner*, a Hearst paper. When Kathy asked, "How come you come home and just read the paper and don't pay any attention to me?" Harry replied that it was part of his job to be informed—but also never to trust anything in a Hearst paper![7]

In the late 1950s, Julie and Robbie lived in New York with their mother, Nancy, and attended a private school that Julie described as for "kids that had famous parents." Nancy was an alcoholic, and her family was Julie's major source of stability. Julie attended the University of California, Berkeley, for two years, returned to New York to help her mother, and finished at Hunter College. In 1968 Julie took Nancy to live in Los Angeles. During those years, Julie's relations with Harry were often strained.[8]

Jackie had married Robert Shell, a conservative Mormon, in 1944. They and their three children lived in Hollister, a small town a hundred miles south of San Francisco. She and her husband operated a small trailer court and lived in one of the trailers. Jackie was assisting her mother, Agnes, and her half-brother, Kenneth, both of whom lived in Hollister. Agnes was living on Social Security; she died in 1962. Kenneth had served in the army for seventeen years, including World War II and Korea, where he suffered shell shock and was then unable to work.[9]

As Bridges aged, he stewed about the future of the ILWU. Notes from the late 1960s express his concerns:

> Key issue I am concerned with is where this union is going & how. . . . This could be termed a power struggle. . . . Its [*sic*] happened in other unions. Reuther—one man union. Steel, Murray & Dave McDonald. Dubinsky Hillman & Others. And I have seen it developing here and therefore its [*sic*] probably my fault as well. Bob Robertson stood with me & in the way for years.
>
> You can have a one man union with a program of support the [Vietnam] war, against them reds blacks etc. or one man union with a revolutionary program. Both are one man unions where the job is done from the top, you put over a super duper revolutionary program on paper thru conventions or

committees or hand picked people, strictly from college, research experts, and the one thing you don't do is take the program down below and rassle around with the ranks.

You play around with college professors, intellectuals, architects, liberals and two bit politicians who promise the world and take care of themselves.

And you set up funds, be an expert banker or financier, get into the insurance business or the drug business directly or indirectly, and you are on your way You set up foundations, get on executive jet, take off for other countries with your wife of course and for the good of the union sure.[10]

I assume that many of these concerns, especially in the third and fourth paragraphs, were aimed at Goldblatt and some of his associates. Though Bridges continued to seek nomination after nomination for the presidency, he seems to have seen himself as standing in the way of such a "one man union."

Leadership in the ILWU was never a one-man show, although the press often referred to Bridges and the union as if it were. Bridges was always part of a leadership group, first within Local 38-79, then in the Pacific Coast Branch and the ILWU. By 1960 three of the international officers had served for many years. Bridges and J. R. "Bob" Robertson, first vice president and director of organization, had been ILWU officers since the beginning. Goldblatt became secretary-treasurer in 1943. Germain Bulcke was second vice president from 1947 to 1960. When Bulcke retired, in 1961, the convention eliminated the second vice presidency.[11] The Coast Labor Relations Committee, consisting of Bridges and two members elected by the longshore membership, led the longshore division; it was also quite stable, with Henry Schmidt and Cole Jackman through the 1940s and Howard Bodine and L. G. Thomas during much of the 1950s and early 1960s.

Like Bridges, the longshore division was aging. A study in 1960 indicated that the average age of longshore members was fifty and higher in some locals.[12] The 1960s brought a wave of retirements, especially among the generation of the 1930s. Major changes in leadership also came in the 1960s. Schmidt retired in 1963 after sixteen years on the executive board and other positions. Thomas left the CLRC in 1963. Bodine died in 1966. Robertson retired in 1969. There were similar patterns among the staff. Morris Watson, founding editor of the *Dispatcher*, retired in 1966 and was succeeded by Sidney Roger. Lincoln Fairley became research director in 1946, became an arbitrator in 1967, and then retired in the early 1970s. Jeff Kibre served as the ILWU's Washington representative for fifteen years before retiring in 1967.[13]

Changes in the ILWU leadership overlaid and sometimes resulted from the increasingly visible animosity between Bridges and Goldblatt. Nine years younger than Bridges, Goldblatt was widely seen as Bridges's successor. Among the sources of the breach was Bridges's understanding, and that of others, that

Bridges shared the leadership of the longshore division with the members of the Coast Labor Relations Committee. Otto Hagel took this photo of a CLRC meeting, ca. 1963. Bridges is on the right. Next to him are Howard Bodine and L. B. Thomas, longtime CLRC members. Across the table are the three PMA members of the CLRC. Hagel took a matching photo of the other side of the table, with J. Paul St. Sure opposite Bridges. The CLRC tried to revolve issues of contract interpretation. If they failed, the issue went to the coast arbitrator. (Photo courtesy of Labor Archives and Research Center, San Francisco State University; "Union Management," 1963, by Otto Hagel, © Center for Creative Photography, The University of Arizona Foundation)

the longshore division was the heart of the ILWU and the president should come from longshore—an unwritten consensus that continues through the time of this writing (2021).[14]

When separately interviewed about the split, Bridges, Goldblatt, and Dave Jenkins all pointed to events in Hawai'i, where Goldblatt and Jack Hall had developed a solid working relationship and close friendship. All three cited disagreement between Hall and Bridges over the 1958 sugar strike; Goldblatt described Hall, drunk, having "hard words" with Bridges. Bridges felt that Goldblatt and Hall were too aloof from the rank and file in Hawai'i and too involved in a program to sell insurance to ILWU members there. Robertson's retirement, in 1969, formed another flash point. Goldblatt supported Hall for vice president, but Bridges wanted William Chester, a Black member of Local 10. The situation was resolved by restoring the second vice presidency.[15]

The split extended to nearly every aspect of the two men's working relationship. Jenkins claimed that Goldblatt felt Bridges had become too close to St. Sure and out of touch with the longshore rank and file and that Bridges believed Goldblatt was too much of an intellectual to feel comfortable with workers. Bridges worried that Goldblatt's warehouse agreements with the IBT presented a danger that "we become their [the Teamsters'] prisoners." Goldblatt and Bridges differed over student demonstrations at Berkeley and elsewhere in the 1960s, with Goldblatt supportive and Bridges skeptical that university students could create social change—for him, only workers could accomplish that. By 1970 Bridges and Goldblatt were not speaking to each other except as necessary. Goldblatt said that matters "had reached a stage where if I were in favor of something, he was against it." Bridges publicly stated that he did not want Goldblatt to succeed him.[16]

For Lincoln Fairley, the animosity was so obvious that he avoided becoming too friendly with either because of what happened to staff people who did. "Bill Glazier," Fairley said, "had to work closely with both of them and he . . . finally left because he couldn't take it any longer." After Glazier's departure, there was no administrative assistant for several years, until Joe McCray was hired in 1968. McCray stayed only until 1970, long enough to witness what he called the "awful separation" between Bridges and Goldblatt.[17]

In the early 1960s, creation of the St. Francis Square housing project demonstrated the split between Bridges and Goldblatt, with Goldblatt the major figure and Bridges largely uninvolved. The project grew out of redevelopment in San Francisco's Western Addition, where most housing dated to the late nineteenth century. By the 1920s and 1930s, many one- or two-family buildings had been subdivided into smaller units, and that process accelerated during and after World War II. After the area's large Japanese population was relocated in 1942, the neighborhood became a center of the Black community. In 1948 the Board of Supervisors labeled it "blighted" and endorsed plans to demolish existing buildings and create new neighborhoods. As demolition and redevelopment progressed, James Baldwin toured the site and famously said, "Urban renewal is Negro removal." The motives of those who planned the project cannot be reduced simply to white racism, but the initial result was indeed "Negro removal." Eventually, the Black community joined with others to stop the demolitions, but by then entire city blocks had been leveled.[18]

Initial stages of redevelopment created mostly high-rise upper-income housing. However, redevelopment plans included an area of low-rise garden apartments. After existing buildings there were demolished, the Redevelopment Agency director suggested to Goldblatt that the ILWU undertake that project. Convinced that redevelopment had primarily benefited developers, Goldblatt first secured St. Sure's support, then persuaded the welfare fund trustees to support a housing cooperative for those of low and moderate income. St. Francis Square opened in 1963 with 299 apartments in twelve three-story buildings around landscaped courtyards. Ownership was not limited to ILWU members, but they had priority. In 1970 the project was cited by the American Institute of Architects for "distinguished accomplishment in low and moderate income housing." Throughout its existence, St. Francis Square has housed a racially diverse community.[19]

Bridges mostly stood apart from the St. Francis Square project. Goldblatt described him as "very jaundiced" toward it and thought his reluctance may have stemmed from his view that the union should focus on wages, hours, conditions, and benefits. Bridges did devote an "On the Beam" column to working families' need for moderately priced housing, the failure of redevelopment to meet that need, and the intent of St. Francis Square both to provide such housing and to maintain the area's former ethnic diversity.[20]

In 1963 Bridges was at the center of a major controversy. The PMA insisted that the ILWU, especially Local 10, should add more members because labor shortages were delaying shipping. Bridges announced that the ILWU planned to add 3,000 more longshore members, including 1,000 in Local 10. The process involved adding more B men (probationary members) and advancing existing B men to A status. In October 1963, Local 10 added 714 new B men and advanced some 400 existing B men to the A list. However, the joint ILWU-PMA registration committee voted to deregister 82 B men, rather than advance them, because they had violated work rules. Significant majorities of both those deregistered and those advanced were Black. In April 1964, a lawsuit was filed on behalf of 45 deregistered B men, seeking reinstatement as A men and $600,000 in damages.[21]

Those who supported the lawsuit, soon called the B men's case, charged the union with racial discrimination and claimed the deregistrations were intended to intimidate both the B men who were advanced and those just added. The leading figure in the lawsuit was Stan Weir, white, a Trotskyist, anti-Communist, a member of the SUP during World War II, then an autoworker, who became a B man in 1959. Within Local 10, Weir had been outspoken in confronting Bridges and other ILWU leaders over the M&M. He claimed he had been deregistered because of his criticisms and that others were deregistered because they supported him or had also criticized the leadership. "Bridges fears these young men," Weir claimed. He blamed Bridges personally for the deregistrations and argued that the stated cause—failure to follow work rules—was simply window dressing.[22]

Weir mobilized significant support from the non-CP Left, including journalists, academics, and civil rights leaders, and Bridges personally came under attack in several liberal and left publications. Early in 1964, Weir published "The ILWU: A Case Study in Bureaucracy," in *New Politics*, claiming "a scandalous corruption of internal union democracy and the rigged auctioning of working conditions and job security through collusion between the union's international leadership and the employers." In July in the *New Leader*, Paul Jacobs, the CIO staff member who had organized the expulsion trial of the ILWU, characterized Bridges as a "gag man," controlled by the PMA but posing as "labor's flaming radical." Similar accounts appeared in September and December. Those claims hit the mainstream press in September, when a *Chronicle* article summarized arguments that the deregistrations had resulted from "totalitarian" control of the ILWU by Bridges. Similar articles appeared in the *New York Times* and *Los Angeles Times*.[23]

Although never specifically called a racist, Bridges was especially hurt and angered by the charge of racial discrimination. His first public response was a letter from the Gladstein law firm to the *Chronicle* in October, labeling as "untrue" the claims against Bridges and the ILWU, accusing the paper of libel, and demanding retraction and correction of the article. The *Chronicle* printed the letter in full. Bridges himself said nothing until his "On the Beam" column in December 1964, when he depicted the lawsuit as a threat to the "time-honored low-man-out rules" and dismissed the support committee as "would-be liberals who like to think they know something about the labor movement, and who are self-styled experts on what's wrong." Describing the lawsuits as "built around technicalities" and "filed under the infamous Taft-Hartley law, amended and strengthened against labor by the Kennedy-Landrum-Griffin law," he opined that the lawsuits, if successful, would force the union "to do away completely with the B category." Bridges concluded, "We don't need the help of any courts, any government agencies or any outside experts to figure out the best way to divide the work among our members."[24]

The deregistered B men who appealed to the NLRB lost in late 1965. Other lawsuits wound through the courts for years. Those who filed in federal court lost their final appeal in 1980.[25]

Local 10 was not alone in facing charges of racial discrimination. Local 8, the Portland longshore local, had long been completely white, despite pressure from Bridges and progressives within Local 8. Finally, in 1964, under pressure from Bridges, Goldblatt, and local civil rights organizations, Local 8 admitted forty-six Black B men. In 1968 twenty-six of them filed suit, alleging they had not been advanced to A men due to racial discrimination. The International filed a supporting brief. Local 13, the local for the Ports of Los Angeles and Long Beach, faced a similar lawsuit in the early 1970s.[26]

Though the B men's case brought Bridges criticism from the left, he still attracted denunciation from the right just by his presence, as became apparent in May 1960. A subcommittee of the House Un-American Activities Committee had scheduled three days of hearings in the Supervisors' Chambers of San

Francisco City Hall. HUAC subcommittees had held hearings in San Francisco in 1953, 1956, and 1957. In 1959, facing serious local opposition, HUAC canceled.[27] Announcement of HUAC hearings in San Francisco in 1960 brought renewed opposition. Significant numbers of students mobilized to picket outside city hall and join the audience inside. On May 12, the first day of the hearings, HUAC opponents held a morning rally at Union Square. Among those present was Noriko Bridges with seven-month-old Kathy. Herb Caen reported that Noriko asked Harry for advice about attending and that Harry replied, "Don't drop the baby."[28]

On the next day, student protesters were not admitted inside the Supervisors' Chambers. They began singing and shouting. A bit after one in the afternoon, police turned a fire hose on the demonstrators, soaking them and cascading water down the wide marble steps from the second floor to the main floor. Helmeted police clubbed nonresisting demonstrators and dragged them down the water-slickened steps and into waiting paddy wagons. Sixty-four were arrested. Eventually, all charges were dismissed, and Mayor George Christopher announced that HUAC would no longer be allowed to use city buildings.[29]

Bridges and others were having lunch when Sid Roger arrived and told them what was happening. They went to city hall and arrived as water was being mopped up. Bridges went inside but soon left. Local television stations filmed him leaving. The press quoted Bridges as saying, "This is a hell of a note." In the next day's hearing, the committee asked Police Inspector Michael Maguire if he knew Bridges "came to town" and participated in creating the "riot." Maguire answered no. The subcommittee chair, Edmund Willis (D-LA), subsequently claimed that Bridges was "one of the agitators."[30]

Months later, HUAC released a film and report, *Operation Abolition*, which claimed the "riots" were created by CP agitators and identified Bridges as "an international Communist agent and leader of the International Longshoremen's Union [sic], who recently returned from conferences held with other leaders of Communist-led longshoremen groups." Over the scene of Bridges leaving city hall, the narrator claimed, "Among the Communist leaders who had an active part in the San Francisco 'abolition' campaign and the protest demonstrations was Harry Bridges, whom you see here being escorted out of the building by police officials moments before the rioting broke out." The treatment of Bridges was one of many distortions and falsehoods in the film that was shown across the country to prop up HUAC and keep Americans concerned about the CP, by then a tiny fraction of its former size. Bridges branded HUAC chair Francis Walter "the most consummate liar on the political scene today" and called the film "a hitlerlike [sic] lie."[31]

By the time of the "City Hall swim," Bridges had taken a strong position in the 1960 presidential campaign. In the late 1950s, Bridges and the *Dispatcher* frequently described Senator John F. Kennedy as antilabor, based on his activities on the Senate Select Committee on Labor and Management Practices—the McClellan Committee—which investigated corruption in unions. Robert F. Kennedy, the senator's brother, was the hard-driving chief counsel for the committee; he had previously been staff counsel to Joseph McCarthy's committee. The McClellan Committee's investigations produced the Landrum-Griffin Act of 1959, regulating election and financial procedures of unions. Senator Kennedy was largely responsible for Title I of the act, leading Bridges to refer consistently to the Kennedy-Landrum-Griffin Act. During the 1960 presidential campaign, the ILWU executive board supported neither John Kennedy nor Richard Nixon. Shortly after the executive board action, Kennedy announced, "an effective Attorney General with the present laws" could remove Hoffa and Bridges from office. Soon after, Herb Caen reported that Bridges had "declared all-out war on Jack Kennedy."[32]

Not long after Kennedy's inauguration, Bridges and the ILWU experienced what may have been the Kennedy brothers' well-known commitment to "Don't get mad, get even." Bridges had invited James Healy, head of the Waterside Workers Federation in Australia, to attend the 1961 ILWU biennial convention. The State Department refused to issue Healy a visa. The next year, in 1962, the Federal Housing Administration asked Attorney General Robert Kennedy for information regarding a loan for the St. Francis Square project. Kennedy directed his executive assistant to work with the FBI to secure "information which could be used as a basis for denying the loan."[33] To be certain, such actions against Bridges and the ILWU were nothing compared to Robert Kennedy's zealous pursuit of IBT president James Hoffa, which eventually led to Hoffa's imprisonment.

The Kennedy brothers did not try to remove Bridges. Instead, Robert Kennedy picked an easier target: Archie Brown, an open CP member recently elected to Local 10's executive board. Bridges had announced that the ILWU would not comply with §504 of the Landrum-Griffin Act, which prohibited CP members and convicted felons from holding union office and required unions to submit to the Labor Department a list of officers who had been CP members or convicted criminals. When Robert Kennedy became attorney general, the Justice Department notified Bridges that Brown's election violated §504. Norman Leonard recalled that Bridges responded, "The members of Local 10 had the right to elect anybody they damn-well pleased," and "he didn't have the authority or the power, and if he had it, he wouldn't exercise it any way, to upset a democratic election by the members of Local 10."[34]

Brown was arrested and indicted. Robert Kennedy told the press that Brown was the first to be charged under §504, presumably as a test case. Bridges denounced Brown's arrest and indictment as "a national disgrace" and "a direct attack against the ILWU and other American trade unions which insist upon the rights of its members to elect anyone to office they wish." Local 10's executive board and the ILWU executive board announced support for Brown; the latter specified that its position was in support of ILWU members' "right to be nominated for and be elected to any office."[35]

In court Leonard and Gladstein represented Brown, admitted he was violating §504, but argued that §504 was unconstitutional. Bridges, the first defense witness, denounced §504 as meaning "we could no longer operate as a democratic union. . . . We could no longer elect whom we wanted as officers." The judge found Brown guilty. Gladstein immediately appealed, and the local ACLU submitted an amicus brief. The full Ninth Circuit Court of Appeals, by 5–3, agreed §504 was unconstitutional. Federal attorneys appealed to the Supreme Court. In June 1965, the Supreme Court, by 5–4, declared §504 unconstitutional. Asked for a comment, Bridges described the Landrum-Griffin Act as "one of the phoniest anti-labor laws slipped over on workers by such enemies of labor as Bobby Kennedy."[36]

Sidney Roger later recalled, "Harry's hatred for Kennedy, the detestation he felt for the attorney general, Bobby Kennedy, was incredible." Roger, responsible for the *Dispatcher* on November 22, 1963, recalled that he rushed to confer with Bridges when he learned that President Kennedy had been shot and that Bridges responded, "I hope the son-of-a-bitch croaks." However, Bridges soon realized the enormous effect the assassination was having on ILWU members and Black Americans. On the Pacific Coast docks and in Hawai'i, longshoremen simply closed down and walked away. It happened so spontaneously that few local or international officers were aware of it until it had happened.[37]

Roger described how Bill Chester defended the walkout to Bridges: "Our guys love [Kennedy]. . . . The brothers love that guy." Roger recalled that Bridges initially didn't want anything about Kennedy in the next *Dispatcher*, but when he "saw that the rank and file really totally disagreed with him, he decided to go full blast in the other direction," calling for a photo of Kennedy on the entire first page and directing Roger to write an editorial and "On the Beam" column about the loss of the president.[38]

The 1960 presidential campaign and Bridges's vendetta against the Kennedys were exceptions to the ILWU's usual political preference for liberal Democrats throughout the 1960s and 1970s. In 1964, while asserting "we shall always be independent of any specific political party," the ILWU executive board strongly endorsed Lyndon Johnson over Barry Goldwater, as did the various councils and locals. At the same time, however, the ILWU executive board called for withdrawal of all non-Vietnamese troops from Vietnam and for UN-supervised elections to unite that country. The press reported, "The Johnson-Humphrey ticket may not be everything that Bridges would desire," but he chose not to challenge the "overwhelming ILWU sentiment."[39]

If one were to read only his column in the *Dispatcher*, Bridges seemed indifferent to most presidential campaigns during the 1960s. He always selected the topic for his column and discussed his views with Sid Roger. Roger then drafted the column and returned it to Bridges for his comments and approval. McCray recalled that occasionally the discussions between Bridges and Roger became "fairly contentious." In October 1964, Bridges excoriated Robert Kennedy who was running for the U.S. Senate from New York, calling him a "danger to labor, to civil rights and civil liberties, and maybe even to a peaceful world!" Also that month, his column reflected generally on the importance of voting, but stressed, "The working class still has a much stronger weapon than the ballot box . . . the ability to stop the wheels turning." In 1937 Harry Lundeberg had said almost the same thing in attacking Bridges's insistence on the importance of political action.[40]

Bridges was more forthcoming in private. In early August 1964, before the Democratic National Convention nominated Lyndon Johnson, Bridges explained in a letter that he was delaying endorsement of Johnson because he was concerned the Democrats might nominate Robert Kennedy for vice president. Bridges argued that delaying endorsement strengthened "the hand of our union, working in conjunction with other unions to make sure Kennedy is not on the ticket, and to help bring about a good Democratic Party platform—and further, to make some weight felt against seating the Mississippi delegation at the Convention." The last referred to efforts to seat a racially integrated, politically liberal delegation from Mississippi in place of the official, conservative, segregationist delegation. ILWU members urged convention delegates to support the Mississippi Freedom Democrats; one delegate claimed the ILWU had sent more messages than any other union.[41]

Bridges wrote in a letter late in the 1964 campaign, "I certainly hope for a Johnson victory in November, and, when I say this, I don't necessarily mean a Democratic Party victory." He was opposing both Robert Kennedy in New York and Pierre Salinger in California. Salinger, who had worked for Robert Kennedy on the McClellan Committee and as press secretary for President Kennedy, ran in the California primary against Alan Cranston for the U.S. Senate. Bridges wrote, "It is no accident that labor in California is practically unanimous in its support of Alan Cranston" and that "Salinger has no labor support because he is anti-union and anti-labor." After Salinger won the primary, Bridges wrote, "We see nothing to be gained by our union swinging into line and endorsing Salinger." Nonetheless, the ILWU's two California councils did endorse Salinger, who went down to defeat, the only such Democratic casualty nationwide amid Johnson's landslide victory.[42]

By 1966 antiwar activists were urging that opposition to the war in Vietnam be a major—or *the* major—criterion for supporting candidates. East-bay congressman Jeffrey Cohelan faced a strong primary challenge from Robert Sheer who attacked Cohelan for supporting Johnson's Vietnam policy. The ILWU supported Sheer. Cohelan won. Under pressure from the ILWU to disengage from "the dirty war in Vietnam," Cohelan finally did.[43]

Though the ILWU long opposed U.S. involvement in Vietnam, and Bridges shared that view, he stood back from public antiwar activities. Noriko, however, took a leadership role in the Jeannette Rankin Brigade, an antiwar women's organization. In April 1967, fifty thousand antiwar marchers in San Francisco included Noriko and Kathy, age seven, and a large contingent of ILWU officers and members. Sid Roger recalled that the marchers passed Bridges, who was watching from the sidewalk, and that "people said, 'Harry, come on in. March with us.' He'd make a little gesture. Wave his hand a little in the air. As if to say, 'No. I'm not interested.'" Perhaps Bridges felt that the ILWU had not authorized him to take part. He criticized a Local 6 officer for speaking at the rally without first getting permission from his local.[44]

In 1967 Bridges was in Australia. In one of his letters to Noriko, he expressed dissatisfaction with some opponents of the Vietnam War, especially a prominent figure in the Australian Labor Party. Bridges described him as "really way out" and as wanting "nothing less than the U.S.A. being driven out of Viet Nam in complete defeat and disgrace, humiliated and shamed before the whole world." Bridges continued, "I think this is spelling out what the so called new left program is over there at home, only so far I guess no one dares to spell it out so clearly. And I think its [sic] what Lou [Goldblatt] really means in his draft [of a position for the ILWU] without openly saying so."[45]

By the 1968 election, with the choice between Humphrey and Nixon, neither of whom had taken a strong position against the war in Vietnam, the international executive board, after lengthy discussion between no endorsement and support for Humphrey, voted no endorsement. The California and Oregon ILWU councils also made no endorsement for president, although the Washington council and several ILWU locals in California supported Humphrey. Humphrey lost California and Oregon, but carried Washington. For the U.S. Senate, the ILWU gave strong support to Alan Cranston in California and Wayne Morse (who had become a Democrat in 1955) in Oregon, both critics of the war in Vietnam. Cranston won; Morse lost.[46]

Throughout these years, the ILWU often took strong positions on international peace, the war in Vietnam, and civil rights. The 1961 convention heard from Linus Pauling, a prominent advocate for ending nuclear testing and limiting the spread of nuclear weapons, and the convention passed resolutions calling for those measures as first steps toward nuclear disarmament. The convention also endorsed creation of a National Peace Agency and sent a delegate to the Seventh World Conference against Atomic and Hydrogen Bombs. In 1963 the convention called for an end to the Cold War and for world peace and disarmament. By the mid-1960s, the peace movement had been largely absorbed into opposition to the war in Vietnam. In 1967 the convention bluntly restated the ILWU's position: "We don't belong in Vietnam and should get out." In November 1967, Bridges, Goldblatt, and other ILWU officers participated in the National Labor Leadership Assembly for Peace.[47]

Bridges and the ILWU always opposed discrimination based on race. As efforts to dismantle segregation grew in the late 1950s and early 1960s, resistance by southern whites became more and more violent. In 1963 authorities in Birmingham, Alabama, used fire hoses and police dogs against demonstrations by Black school students, generating a nationwide outcry. George Christopher, mayor of San Francisco, arranged for a Human Rights Day march and rally. Bill Chester, ILWU vice president, was cochair. The *Chronicle* described the twenty thousand marchers as "of all classes, but predominantly labor, and the labor group predominantly longshoremen." Locals 6 and 10 marched behind their banners, and Bridges and Chester were in the first rank of marchers. In July the *Dispatcher* devoted two full pages to Martin Luther King's Letter from Birmingham Jail.[48]

In March 1965, as King and other clergy were trying to march from Selma to Montgomery, Alabama, in support of voting rights, Bridges addressed a large crowd, including many ILWU members, to condemn the violence and threaten a boycott of Alabama. The convention that year unanimously approved Local 10's proposal that ILWU members "refuse to handle any goods or merchandise from Alabama coming across the docks or through the warehouses until the rights of all the people in Alabama are recognized and fully protected."[49]

In 1963 Congressman John F. Shelley ran for mayor. Dave Jenkins became labor director for Shelley's campaign. The ILWU's Joint Legislative Committee strongly supported Shelley. Herb Caen reported that Bridges bet $100 on Shelley to win. He collected. Shelley became the first Democrat to win the mayoralty in fifty-five years, and he repaid labor by appointing union officers, including several ILWU members, to city positions.[50]

In 1967 the city's Democratic power brokers convinced Shelley not to run because they thought he would be a weak candidate against Harold Dobbs, a Republican. The mayoral campaign became a three-way contest among Dobbs; Joseph Alioto, a mainstream Democrat; and Jack Morrison, a progressive Democrat. Chester became cochair of the Labor Committee for Alioto. The ILWU and most other unions also supported Alioto. Jenkins later said that, before the election, he, Chester, and two leaders from Local 6 met with Alioto, and "he agreed to put blacks and trade unionists on every commission." Alioto delivered. One of his first appointments was of Bridges to a new Citizens Charter Revision Commission, along with leaders from the Labor Council and Building Trades Council.[51]

For the CCRC—the sixth such effort since adoption of the charter in 1932—the initial expectation was for a three-year study. In June 1969, the CCRC voted 16–5 to approve recommendations regarding the mayor and supervisors. Bridges was in favor, but the other three labor representatives and two business representatives opposed. In the November election, seven ILWU locals, the Building Trades Council, the League of Women Voters, and many civic groups endorsed the changes, but the Labor Council and most business organizations opposed. The proposals suffered a crushing defeat. The CCRC limped along for several more months, then was dissolved.[52]

Bridges then accepted appointment from Alioto as a commissioner for the Port of San Francisco. In 1969 the state had transferred control of the port to the city, which created the Port Commission to run it. Bridges was sworn in for a four-year term on June 30, 1970. At the swearing in, Alioto cited Bridges for having "brought us social justice where none existed before." Robbie, Noriko, and Kathy were there to watch.[53] Bridges served until 1982. Since then an officer of the ILWU, usually the president, has served on the Port Commission except for nine years when the ILWU president was not a San Francisco resident.

Throughout the 1960s, Bridges continued to defend the Soviet Union, its client states in Eastern Europe, and Cuba; to advocate for opening trade with China and the Soviet Union; and to challenge anti-Communists. His FBI file reported those writings and speeches but nearly always included a statement such as, "Confidential informants . . . could furnish no information concerning CP or related activity on the part of the Subject." One report, in 1964, reported that a "CP official [was] critical of Subject [Bridges] for not paying attention to CP views." Nonetheless, FBI reports on Bridges invariably concluded, "In view of the foregoing, Subject may be expected to commit acts inimical to the U.S. in the event of a national emergency."[54]

In 1968, after Mayors Shelley and Alioto had appointed several former Communists to city positions, Bridges wrote in a letter, "No longer in this country does the accusation of being a communist ruffle anybody's feelings. . . . [T]o be known as a communist these days is to be known as someone who is more in the line of an old-fashioned, Old Left kind of liberal, someone who may be a few degrees to the left of the policies enunciated by Franklin Roosevelt and the New Deal." However, he added, "I still hold to the notion that the one great socialist revolution occurred in 1917." In 1969 at a program in San Francisco celebrating the October Revolution, he said, "The Russian Revolution was my first and favorite revolution."[55]

Bridges's praise for the Soviet Union seems not to have affected the ILWU's working relations with other unions, especially the Teamsters and ILA. There had been a major improvement in relations between the ILWU and IBT after James Hoffa succeeded David Beck as IBT president in 1957. In 1959 the ILWU and IBT worked out a jurisdictional agreement for Hawai'i. In 1967 they conducted a joint three-week strike in support of a common contract for Northern California warehouses and won. The two unions also cooperated in Southern California, although not through joint negotiations.[56]

Bridges developed an acquaintance with Hoffa and seems to have viewed Hoffa's experience as similar to the repeated federal efforts—which Bridges always called "frame-ups"—to remove him from union office. Convicted of jury tampering, Hoffa exhausted his appeals and entered prison in 1967. Shortly after Hoffa entered prison, the ILWU officers' convention report called the jailing of Hoffa "one of the most outrageous frame-ups in the history of the American labor movement" and added, "Whenever a move is made to decapitate any union, by framing its leaders, the target is the entire labor movement," the same argument made against the repeated legal efforts against Bridges. Bridges made a personal and emotional appeal for the delegates to approve a resolution supporting Hoffa, even though "we might not see eye to eye on some of the things that Jimmy does." The resolution passed unanimously. In 1968 Bridges asked Humphrey to commit himself, if elected, to "pardon or parole James Hoffa." I found no response by Humphrey, and Bridges sat out that election.[57]

After his 1959 tour of European ports, Bridges had emphasized that in several places longshore workers were part of unions for all transportation workers. Soon, the press buzzed with speculation regarding a merger or federation involving the IBT, ILWU, and ILA. One result seems to have been that the ILA was invited to rejoin the AFL-CIO, and the AFL-CIO created a Maritime Trades Department, as a way of preventing any such affiliation. Paul Hall, Lundeberg's successor as president of the SIU and head of the new Maritime Trades Department, condemned any initiative that involved Hoffa "and his despicable connections with Harry Bridges."[58]

Nonetheless, in 1966, the *New York Times* claimed, "The International Longshoremen's Association would like to consolidate with the Pacific Coast's International Longshoremen and Warehousemen's Union," citing a comment by ILA president Teddy Gleason to the national convention of the NMU. Bridges used his "On the Beam" column to clarify that Gleason had raised the possibility while the two were talking at a bar in Detroit. Bridges said he had responded that any such possibility should include a discussion with Hoffa who had long been advocating "some type of transport federation." Bridges denied that any negotiations were under way. After Hoffa's successor, Frank Fitzsimmons, addressed the ILWU's 1969 convention, Bridges ruminated about his earlier discussions with Hoffa about a transport federation. "We didn't discuss merger," he specified. "We talked about pooling our strength," and he insisted, "That program is still in the works today." Nothing more ever came of it.[59]

In 1968 the IBT and UAW formed the Alliance for Labor Action (ALA). The UAW had disaffiliated from the AFL-CIO over disagreements with George Meany, and Fitzsimmons had a more liberal political vision than Hoffa. Bridges and Albert Lannon, the ILWU's Washington representative, met with Fitzsimmons to discuss the ALA, and the ILWU executive board discussed the ALA in December 1970 and March 1971. However, the ALA halted operations for lack of funds in mid-1971 and was dissolved in early 1972.[60]

At Bridges's prompting, the ILWU adopted a program for its members to talk with union members elsewhere in the world. Bridges was clear about the purpose: "We don't want to be sending people on junkets. . . . We want to send people over on serious business." He emphasized, "The longshoremen in every country of the world . . . work for the same employer. We all work the same ships and the same cargoes." Approved by a vote of the full membership, the visiting-delegates program—which excluded international officers, board members, and staff—was launched in 1960. Each delegation visited two to four countries in Latin America, Africa, the Middle East, Eastern and Western Europe, and East and South Asia. The delegates were instructed to "talk to all kinds of unions from left to right and get all shades of opinion." After a second group in 1962, the program was amended into the ILWU constitution in 1963. A third group left in 1964, and others followed. Each delegation prepared an extensive report for the *Dispatcher*.[61]

Bridges and the general secretary of the Australian Waterfront Workers Federation, C. H. Fitzgibbon, successor to Jim Healy, continued the previous close contact between Bridges and Healy. Fitzgibbon attended the ILWU's 1963 convention. In 1967 Bridges attended the WWF's conference in Sydney. The Australian labor movement gave Bridges a hero's welcome, and the Australian press treated him like a visiting celebrity. The *Canberra Times* headlined "Return of a Radical," but the Sydney *Tribune*'s opening was "An Old Aussie Comes Home."[62]

Bridges was accompanied by James "Jimmy" Herman, president of Local 34 (San Francisco clerks) on the five-week trip. When his plane arrived, he was greeted by a scrum of reporters, and, as he explained in his next *Dispatcher* column, "My first reaction, as the questions poured in, was that I darned near needed an interpreter after thinking all this time I could speak the language." Asked if he were mellowing, he replied, "I don't like that word. . . . Many of the things I was radical about in my early life are now accepted social standards." For the next several days, he visited the docks, attended the WWF conference (which he likened to an ILWU longshore caucus), and did sightseeing in Sydney.[63]

Given his memories of Australians' anti-Asian sentiments, Bridges decided Noriko should not come along. Writing to her, he indicated he'd changed his mind about not bringing her: "I realize how wonderful it would be if you were along. I have promised them that for sure you will be with me next time." He found Australian dock work "backward": "They work on the docks like we did 20 or more years ago." He was pleased by the reception he'd received: "From what I hear they like my talks & report." Regarding both the docks and the conference, he pointed to a major difference: "Not only in the caucus, but everywhere I have been I have as yet to hear one swear word. Do I have to watch my language?" He closed by saying, "I am taking my pills, working hard, keeping sober and loving you and Kathy all the time. I truly miss you mommie and want to be with you."[64]

After attending to union business in Sydney, Bridges went to Melbourne and reunited with his family and with friends from his youth. He wrote to Noriko: "I saw Mickey Turner. He broke down and cried. Lives half a block from where I was born." One must wonder if Bridges's return to the sites of his childhood led him to reflect on what his life might have been had he remained there. His sisters and brother, he wrote, threw a party for him, and "the Bridges quartet—that includes me—was in fine voice singing our Dad's old songs." And, he complained, "So many nephews, nieces, grand nieces kids etc. dozens of them. I can't keep track."[65]

After Australia Bridges continued to New Zealand, visited the docks, and met officers and members of the New Zealand Waterside Workers' Federation. As he was preparing to leave, he wrote to Noriko: "I am in great shape, altho drinking. Am watching my step plenty. Jim left orders here with the fellows to let me have only two beers and to be in bed by 10:30." He also said that he'd explored his old haunts in Auckland: "Went up the street from the wharf and there was the dancing school I went to years ago. No—not to learn dopey but to meet sheilas [Australian slang for young women]."[66]

Bridges's trip to Australia provided a brief respite from the ILWU's internal tensions. They came out in full in the 1971 convention in Honolulu. Prior to that convention, Bridges wrote out six constitutional amendments he hoped to see approved, including: "1. "International officers shall not be paid a salary greater than any 3% of the highest paid workers the union represents in collective bargaining. . . . [4.] to be eligible to be nominated and elected to International office, a nominee must be a union member for at least 5 years after having worked as a rank-and-file worker under the union's jurisdiction for at least 2 years. . . . 5. Compulsory retirement age for all full-time International Officers to be 60 years of age. . . . 6. As a condition of being nominated a candidate for full-time International office, shall file with the union a copy of his income tax return for the year in which he takes office, including a statement of his financial worth in terms of property, stocks, bonds, etc."[67] These proposals reflected, in part, Bridges's concerns that some unions were dominated by officers with little or no experience as rank-and-file workers, that many union officers' salaries were disconnected from those of the members, and that union officers should have no significant outside income that could create a conflict of interest. Items 4 and 5 were aimed at Goldblatt, who had worked as a warehouseman for less than two years. Bridges was soon to turn seventy. Goldblatt was nine years younger.

Carl Damaso, president of Local 142, the largest ILWU local, opened the convention and said, "I have heard the newspaper gossip about how this Union is going to break apart and how there are disagreements that are slowing this Union down.... [I]t hurts to hear things like that.... This Union is the property of the rank and file, not the officers (loud applause).... If there are misunderstandings or hard feelings among us, we're here to say: 'Cut it out! We've got work to do!'" Damaso was referring, not too subtly, both to the open conflict between Bridges and Goldblatt but also to the proposals that Bridges brought to the convention. None of Bridges's proposed constitutional amendments came out of committee. Harry Bernstein, labor writer for the *Los Angeles Times*, reported that Bridges's "fight with Goldblatt" had caused "acrimony among the delegates." Bernstein quoted one delegate: "It was all so petty.... Harry is the founder of this union, and nobody could defeat him, but when he tried his obvious petty ploys to kill off Goldblatt, he just had to be put down."[68]

In addressing the convention, Bridges referred positively to the ILWU affiliating with the AFL-CIO, but immediately added the qualification that only the members could make such a decision. In conclusion, he quoted "they" as saying, "'Well, isn't it about time that damn Union got itself a new President?'" And he answered, "They might find some agreement right here at the top. I shall leave you guessing on that one."[69]

Shortly before, Jack Hall had died unexpectedly. The executive board had appointed George Martin, from Local 142, as interim vice president for organization, the position Hall had held. In 1969, when Hall became vice president, Martin had succeeded Hall as regional director. At the convention, Martin was nominated for vice president with no opposition.[70]

The conflict between Bridges and Goldblatt brought a reproach from the convention floor. After Bridges, Chester, Martin, and Goldblatt were nominated with no opposition, Harold Shin, Local 142, took the floor and said, "We all talk about achieving unity in all this and that, and I realize that there might be strong personal feelings against certain top leaders of our International Union. But I feel that if they cannot get together, how can they most effectively serve this Union and serve its membership?" He requested that Bridges and Goldblatt shake hands in front of the delegates, which provoked "Loud and standing applause." J. R. Robertson, chairing that part of the proceedings, said, "The orders are to work together. Those are the orders of this group. (Cries of 'Right!')" And the officers shook hands.[71]

Bridges's other defeat in the 1971 convention was over relations with the ILA, but, again, it was never broached in the open meetings. Teddy Gleason, president of the ILA, and six other ILA officials attended the convention as fraternal delegates. One observer thought that the ILA officials looked stiff and out of place in their silk suits as compared to the ILWU delegates in casual Hawaiian shirts. Albert Lannon, then the ILWU's legislative representative in Washington, told me the ILA officers were out of place in another way: "For the first and only time at any ILWU function I was ever at—there were hookers brought in by the ILA gang."[72]

Gleason began his convention address by saying, "We are part of the same industry and our fates in many ways are intertwined." He discussed the ILA's recent experiences and current issues (especially containerization), emphasized that "industrywide bargaining and industrywide contracts are needed for the protection of all," pledged himself "to the goal of industrywide unity and industrywide solidarity," and promised "fraternal solidarity" in the ILWU's current longshore negotiations. He said nothing about a merger. The delegates gave Gleason polite applause.[73]

Bridges then spoke: "I have been asked the question many times, you know, 'When are (we) going to get into the ILA?' Well, it is not going to be ruled out." He rambled through some long tangents before acknowledging that only the members could decide on merger, then pointed to the extensive media comment about the possibility, and said, "When I see so much concern in certain places, whether it be the government, the newspapers, politicians and others, I begin to think: 'Well, maybe there mightn't be too much wrong with it.'" But, after another long tangent, he said, "If you think that I am making a speech supporting this Union affiliating with the ILA, I am not."[74] There was no further discussion, much less a vote, on merger.

In closing his reporting on the convention, Bernstein quoted a delegate: "It was nice to see them [Bridges and Goldblatt] shake hands up on the stage there, . . . but our convention was the end of an era under the unchallenged leadership of Bridges, and it is too early to tell where we are going from here."[75]

By the 1971 convention, Bridges, soon to celebrate his seventieth birthday, was facing serious rank-and-file discontent and complaints over the contract and over his leadership. While he accepted commission appointments from Alioto, criticized student radicals and liberal intellectuals, and mused about mergers, the largest longshore locals were seething over some sections of the second M&M. While convention delegates enjoyed the Hawaiian sun, negotiations with PMA were stalled.

17

The Longest Strike:
Relations with the PMA

1966–1977

Some had speculated in 1960 that the shift to containerization would take a generation, but it came much more quickly, with its greatest initial effect on Locals 10 and 13, sites of the largest container terminals. In the late 1960s, the Port of Oakland (Local 10) briefly became the second-largest container port in the world but was soon surpassed by others, including the Ports of Los Angeles and Long Beach (Local 13, Wilmington). The Port of San Francisco declined as rapidly as the container ports grew. With those developments came changes in the nature of longshore work and the nature of the ILWU Longshore Division. Concerns and anxieties over the M&Ms boiled over in 1971, when the second M&M expired.

By 1971 longshore work had been substantially transformed by mechanization. Concerns that it would produce layoffs faded as trans-Pacific shipping substantially increased, necessitating the promotion of B men to A and the adding of more B men. Ironically, the war in Vietnam, which the ILWU opposed from the beginning, drove some of the increase in shipping and concomitant demand for longshore workers. Implementing the second M&M was much thornier than the first M&M, especially regarding Section 9.43, the "steady man" provision, and the staffing of container freight stations.

From 1934 onward, employers had asked for steady gangs or steady men rather than workers dispatched from the hiring hall, but very few ILWU members were ever designated that way. Section 9.43 read, in part, "Employers shall be entitled to employ steady, skilled mechanical or powered equipment operators without limit as to numbers or length of time in steady employment. . . . The employer shall be entitled to assign and shift such steady men to all equipment for which, in the opinion of the employer, they are qualified." With 9.43 employers quickly sought to extend the steady-man category. Questions immediately arose regarding which skills were covered by 9.43 and the relative significance of seniority in determining which skilled workers could or would become steady. Since some skilled workers continued to be dispatched from the hiring hall, the ILWU's commitment to equalizing earnings raised questions over equalization of pay and work opportunities between the two situations of skilled workers.[1]

Among many ILWU members, concern over 9.43 went much deeper, to the very heart of what it meant to be an ILWU longshore member. Lincoln Fairley quoted one coast caucus delegate in 1967: steady men would no longer be "part of the Union" but would instead be "subservient to the Employer." Fairley summarized those arguments: "Steady men would not need to show up at the hiring hall and, in effect, would become lost to the Union." Bridges tried to counter such arguments, telling the 1966 caucus: "There's nothing wrong with a man working steady. . . . [I]t's just ridiculous for us to have a position where somebody, because they go to work steady at a good wage and good conditions, is ridiculed or castigated in some fashion as not being a good union man." But he failed to persuade all the caucus delegates, even though he returned to that argument in subsequent caucuses.[2]

Disputes over 9.43 were especially prominent in Locals 10 and 13, the two largest ports and the ports where mechanization developed most quickly. In Local 10, a major concern was Matson's shifting of steady men from one type of equipment to another. In response, Local 10 insisted on "one man, one job," that is, one type of equipment for each steady man. Local 13 simply blocked implementation of 9.43.[3]

The other major dispute involved the loading and unloading of containers, called stuffing and stripping. Assembling of cargo into sling loads had been done on the docks or in the hold by ILWU longshore workers, but containers came to the docks fully loaded. Companies, both shipping companies and goods-producing companies, quickly realized that the greatest efficiencies and the least opportunities for pilferage coincided if a container were loaded at the point of production, taken by truck or rail to a port, put on a ship, unloaded from the ship, put on a truck or railroad car, and unloaded at the point where the goods went into a warehouse or directly into a retail establishment. One engineer described to me such an ideal situation: a container is filled with athletic shoes at a factory in Pakistan and unloaded at a big-box store in the Midwest. Such long-haul containers constituted more than 80 percent of all container shipping and were not at issue. At issue were the few containers being stuffed or stripped by workers, often Teamsters, at locations near the docks. Such locations were called container freight stations (CFSs).[4]

Neither M&M negotiation had addressed such containers. A special long-shore caucus tackled the issue in late 1968. The issue was complicated because Sea-Land, a corporation not part of the PMA, had agreed to send such work to the IBT and because in Seattle some CFS work was being done by ILWU warehouse members. After two weeks of heated discussions, the caucus approved a complex proposal intended to satisfy the concerns of different locals. Negotiations over a CFS supplement then dragged on for more than six months. PMA negotiators finally agreed that ILWU members would work any CSF on or near the docks, but the ILWU had to concede that such workers would be steady employees. In September 1969, the CFS supplement was ratified by 78 percent of those voting with all locals in favor. In fact, however, it really only applied to the Port of Oakland, as the situations in Seattle and Los Angeles remained much as before.[5]

The 9.43 issue, the CFS issue, and continuing complaints that the M&Ms were "old-man's contracts" were only the most prominent expressions of dissatisfaction within the ILWU over the M&Ms and with the way containerization in general and the M&Ms in particular were transforming both the nature of longshore work and the longshore division itself.

Many ILWU members were also becoming concerned about declining work opportunities. During the first M&M, the demand for longshore labor had been so brisk that the guaranteed wage provision was omitted from the second M&M. By the late 1960s, however, the dramatic increase in productivity created by mechanization was significantly reducing the demand for labor. Between 1966 and 1970, total tonnage over Pacific Coast docks *increased* by 26 percent, but the average number of work hours *fell* for B men by 36 percent and for A men by nearly 19 percent. Wages fell accordingly.[6]

In preparation for the 1971 negotiations, a special coast caucus met in October 1970. Attending were 105 delegates from all forty longshore and clerks' locals, including Alaska and Hawaii, along with fraternal delegates from ILWU-Canada and the pensioners, and they deliberated on some two hundred resolutions submitted by locals. The caucus also heard from a delegation that had visited eastern container ports and from an ILA vice president about that union's recent contract.[7]

The caucus unanimously rejected continuation of the M&M fund approach and chose instead to seek more wages and benefits, including better pensions. Bridges joined in, saying sarcastically, "Let's not fool around with M.&M. . . . Get rid of that goddam old-man's contract and put that money in pensions! Who is saying that? The younger worker, the rank and file, who plans to stay on the job. . . . That's who wants it. And they are the ones who said 'We are finished with M. & M.'"[8]

The coast caucus met for four weeks, the longest caucus meeting up to that time. Final demands included a contract of not more than two years, wage increases, guaranteed work or pay for all A and B workers, increased pensions, improved medical and dental benefits, a reduced work shift, and ten annual paid holidays. Finally, the caucus selected its usual large negotiating committee. Lincoln Fairley later pointed out, "The parallelism between the [ILWU] caucus demands and what ILA had negotiated for the Port of New York is very clear: sharply increased wages, substantially improved pensions, a guarantee of work or pay and a better method of insuring that containers would be stuffed and unstuffed by longshoremen. . . . For the first time in bargaining history, ILWU longshoremen were following the lead of the ILA rather than setting the pace."[9]

Shortly after the caucus, Bridges wrote in the *Dispatcher*, "The guts of the program is: Job security and a good living for every registered man now in the industry, 'A' or 'B,' young and old." He also said, "Caucus delegates were determined that if it took a good solid strike to convince waterfront employers to accept the union's position—then there would be a strike." Bridges added that "political opportunists" were asking, "What will the union leadership insist we give up?" He replied, "It's not a matter of what we're willing to give up but what the union can hang on to." His frustration with some ILWU members came out when he pointed to the likelihood of "super-duper shen[a]nigans by people who seem to be less interested in getting a good contract than in confusing the rank and file." He argued that the best defense against what he considered disruptive tactics was the new veto formula embedded in voting procedures for a contract: a negative vote in just one of the four major ports, in the smaller ports in a single region, or in all the clerks' locals could defeat the contract even if the coastwise majority voted in favor. He proudly proclaimed, "We're the only union in the country that affords the rank-and-file an opportunity to exercise this much control over what any group of officers or any committee recommends."[10] He later came to regret that procedure.

Bridges's diatribe against "confusing the rank and file" was part of an occasional refrain in his "On the Beam" columns aimed against both his own critics, especially in Local 10, and the emerging rank-and-file movement in several unions, a movement often associated with the campus radicalism of the late 1960s. After approval of the CFS agreement in late 1969, for example, he criticized "the white, so-called radicals and revolutionaries—especially in my home Local 10" who disparaged that agreement. In early 1971, Bridges ramped up those attacks, warning against "these so-called rank-and-file conferences which pretend that all they are trying to do is democratize the labor movement." He was blunt in a personal letter in April: "I think the proposed rank and file union movement is a phoney . . . sheer demagogy."[11]

In 1966, after the second M&M, J. Paul St. Sure had retired—or, as his daughter told me, had been "fired" because "they felt he had betrayed them" and was "in Harry's pocket." He died shortly after. His successor was Edmond Flynn, a graduate of Harvard Law School who had previously served on the NLRB staff, represented the printers' union, and negotiated for Kennicott Copper with its miners' union.[12] For nearly two decades, Bridges and St. Sure had grown comfortable working with each other and had developed a mutual trust. Flynn was new to the PMA and new to the industry. St. Sure's daughter's account suggests that at least some PMA companies were looking to recover lost ground.

The ILWU presented the caucus's demands to PMA negotiators in mid-November 1970. Negotiations broke off when PMA flatly refused to refer several issues to local-level bargaining. Negotiations resumed in early February 1971 with the parties agreeing to set aside those issues for local bargaining and focus instead on coastwise matters. Negotiations recessed in April for the 1971 convention (see previous chapter) and the longshore caucus that followed.[13]

Before the April recess, PMA negotiators offered a guarantee of work or pay for thirty-five hours a week for A men, a modest increase in pay, and a three-year contract. As Bridges put it, the caucus gave that proposal "a resounding deep six." The caucus reaffirmed its October demands, specified there would be no further negotiations unless the PMA were "to come up quickly with a settlement position that can be recommended to the rank and file," directed locals to refuse any container not stuffed in accordance with the Container Freight Station agreement, and began strike preparations. Bridges described the October demands as "a husky bundle of goodies"—likely his way of saying they were unattainable. He explicitly warned, "Longshore strikes can be tough and long" because it "takes two to three months . . . [before] the strike really begins to hurt the employers." He also specified that there would be no strike without an 85 percent vote in favor. "Our program is to avoid a strike," he stressed and described striking as "a last resort when all else fails." "I never did like strikes," he added, "but every now and then comes a time when it seems when if you gotta go, you've just gotta go."[14] Just as the onetime rank-and-file militant had become averse to rank-and-file militancy, so the onetime defiant strike leader had also become reluctant to strike.

Negotiations resumed on May 5, then recessed two days later because ILWU negotiators felt there had been no progress on their key demands: extension of the CFS agreement, guarantee of work or pay for a forty-hour-week for A men and a thirty-two-hour week for B men, and improvements in wages and benefits. Then the PMA refused to enter negotiations because of what it characterized as "wildcat strikes, harassments, sabotage and destruction of cargo-loading equipment" by members of Local 10. In June more than 90 percent of longshore members voted in favor of striking, with even larger margins of approval in the largest locals.[15]

The strike began July 1, 1971. The ILWU exempted all military or emergency federal shipping, all passenger ships, and all perishables. (Doing so not only avoided problems in public relations but also meant there were some jobs for the strikers to rotate through.) Some ships went to ports in Canada or Mexico

This photo of a group of Local 10 pickets in 1971 suggests the diversity of that local, including workers of different races and ages. (Photo courtesy of Anne Rand Library, ILWU)

or to East and Gulf Coast ports, but many dropped anchor to wait. Soon waters near the major ports were filled with ships "in the stream." The strike quickly took a toll on Pacific Coast business. By July 6, firms connected to shipping, related fields, and banking and insurance were laying off or preparing to lay off employees. Five weeks into the strike, California state officials estimated that thirty thousand people other than longshore workers were out of work because of the strike and that the state economy was hemorrhaging $17.5 million per day.[16]

In mid-July, Harry Bernstein of the *Los Angeles Times* claimed that Bridges had opposed striking and "is said to believe that management would have granted most of the union's demands without a strike." Bernstein quoted a "Bridges backer" as saying, "It wouldn't have made a damn bit of difference what management offered. Longshoremen haven't had a real strike since 1948, and the young guys especially had built up a head of steam and wanted to go out."[17] Despite such statements, the overwhelming strike vote makes clear that it was not just "young guys" but nearly all longshore division members who chose to strike.

Sam Kagel, then coast arbitrator whose friendship with Bridges dated to 1934, told me that Bridges had not wanted to strike. And there were, in fact, a significant proportion of younger ILWU members agitating for a strike. Sid Roger, then editor of the *Dispatcher*, dismissed the argument that Bridges had been forced into the strike. Roger described the strike as "inevitable" because "the employers only wanted the status quo" and "were not ready to give up a lot of things that the union felt were absolutely necessary." Roger acknowledged, "Bridges was reluctant, but you could never see it. . . . [W]hatever he had to say publicly was: whichever way the rank and file goes, is the way I will go."[18]

Bridges took no action to reopen negotiations in July. The PMA took out full-page newspaper ads, offering to improve their last offer on wages and benefits if they could return to the bargaining table. Bridges insisted that the PMA had to agree first to continue the existing CFS agreement, but PMA defined that as a jurisdictional issue between the ILWU and IBT. Kagel told me that when he encouraged Bridges to resume negotiations, Bridges spoke disparagingly about the men who had struck against his advice. In public, however, Bridges was consistently supportive of the striking longshore workers. Herb Mills, then an A man in Local 10 and a sharp critic of Bridges, told me that there were rumors among the rank and file that Bridges was punishing them, but Mills concluded that Bridges was punishing the PMA for how little the PMA had been willing to give in negotiations.[19]

During the long recess in negotiations, Bridges spoke to the conventions and leaders of the ILA and IBT. In reporting on those meetings to the ILWU Executive Board, he noted that the ILA contract gave the ILA jurisdiction over container stuffing and stripping within fifty miles of the docks and stated flatly that settlement of the CFS issue was a "prerequisite to settling the strike." He also proposed three possible courses of action: first, "Continue strike in present form . . . despite Teamster threats or opposition"; second, "Explore with Teamsters" a bargain whereby the IBT would agree to having ILWU members work the containers in return for the ILWU agreeing "to recommend to its membership affiliation with IBT"; and third, "Explore with ILA both alliance and affiliation." The executive board rejected both possible affiliations.[20]

In mid-August, six weeks into the strike, President Richard Nixon announced a new federal economic policy, intended to counteract "stagflation"—rising inflation with high unemployment—that had dogged the national economy for the previous year. Nixon ordered a ninety-day freeze on wage, price, and rent increases. He also called for an end to existing strikes—350 separate strikes nationwide involving 150,000 strikers—and for no new strikes during the ninety-day freeze. George Meany, head of the AFL-CIO, and other union leaders immediately rejected both the wage freeze and the strike ban.[21]

On August 19, the *New York Times* front page carried photos of Bridges and Leonard Woodcock, head of the UAW, in its account of union opposition to the Nixon freezes. The day before, Bridges had held a press conference in which he read a telegram to President Nixon presenting ILWU's rejection of the freeze. Asked if he was concerned that labor might be alienating a large segment of the public, Bridges responded simply, "That could be." Asked if he were willing to risk the $5,000 per day fine for not complying with the freeze, Bridges replied,

"One day would take everything I've got."[22] The strike continued. Support rolled in, including substantial financial contributions.[23]

In late August, Harry Bernstein reported in the *Los Angeles Times* that the CFS jurisdictional issue had been discussed in "secret meetings" between Bridges and IBT president Frank Fitzsimmons, but no resolution was in sight. Bernstein specified that Bridges considered the CSF issue crucial because failure to secure those jobs would likely mean membership rejection of any agreement, no matter how good other provisions might be. Bernstein quoted an unnamed ILWU official: "What the hell difference does it make what size of a pay raise we get to do a job if the job itself is taken away from us. . . . If we don't load and unload them [containers], there will be practically no jobs left for us."[24]

On August 25, the ninth week of the strike, negotiations resumed, becoming more intense in mid-September. Nixon sent J. Curtis Counts, director of the Federal Mediation and Conciliation Service, to push the parties toward a settlement. Counts also implied that federal intervention to end the strike might be in the offing. Bridges, in reply, assured Counts that the strike could end only by a vote of ILWU members.[25]

On September 25, in Portland, Nixon met briefly with Bridges and Flynn, then announced that the parties hoped to reach agreement within a week and implied that he would invoke the Taft-Hartley Act if they did not. He did so on October 6, and a federal judge quickly issued an injunction ordering the parties back to work. Though the ILA had struck the East Coast days before, Nixon invoked Taft-Hartley only against the ILWU. The strike-strategy committee recommended complete compliance with the injunction.[26]

ILWU members returned to work for an eighty-day "cooling off" period, during which negotiations were to continue—and strikers could replenish their bank accounts. Negotiations resumed. Late in the eighty days, union members voted on the employers' "final" offer. Following a different strategy than in 1948, when not a single ballot was returned, the ILWU's strike-strategy committee encouraged all members to vote and to vote no. The NLRB announced the result on December 17: 93 percent voted no.[27]

The eighty days expired on December 26, but Bridges announced that the strike would not resume during the holidays. The parties extended the contract to January 17, but made little progress on the most difficult issues. Bridges and the negotiating committee flew to New York on January 5–7 to confer with ILA leaders. The only agreement the two unions reached was that "both coasts would be shut down if the government Pay Board didn't approve settlements negotiated by either union." Bridges also reported that ILA president Teddy Gleason was "not interested in bargaining with ILWU to join ILA" and that Gleason proposed only "to have ILWU rejoin ILA as a completely autonomous West Coast and Hawaii District, as we were in 1934." That is, affiliation with ILA would be completely on the ILA's terms, with no changes in the ILA's constitution. The ILA settled its strike soon after the ILWU committee returned to San Francisco.[28]

While negotiations continued, Bridges met in Washington with IBT president Fitzsimmons to ask Teamster support if the ILWU should strike in support of double-handling of containers worked by IBT—that is, ILWU members would unload and reload any container initially loaded by IBT members. Fitzsimmons responded, "A strike over such an issue cannot succeed." The best solution to the CFS issue, he said, would be a merger of the ILWU with the IBT, and he laid out conditions for merger: the IBT would affiliate the entire ILWU, treat the longshore division as an autonomous division, and convert warehouse locals to IBT locals; affiliation would be completely on the IBT's terms, with no changes in the IBT's constitution.[29] Thus, both IBT and ILA sought to use the stalled strike to maximize their leverage over the ILWU.

ILWU longshore workers returned to the picket lines on January 17. By then the parties were very close: $5.00 per hour for straight time and $5.40 in the second year, thirty-six hours guaranteed work or pay for A men and eighteen hours for B men, most of the improved benefits sought by the ILWU, and expiration on July 1, 1973. PMA agreed to continue the CFS agreement and pay the ILWU $1.00 per ton on containers not in conformance with that agreement, that is, containers not worked by ILWU members. Details remained to be worked out, and there was no agreement on other issues, including paid holidays.[30]

Negotiations resumed on January 31. When negotiations again deadlocked, the parties brought in Kagel as mediator. By then the ILWU was under serious pressure to come to agreement because Congress was considering legislation requiring binding arbitration. Bridges and Flynn testified before Senate and House committees on February 4, with Flynn in favor of legislation and Bridges strongly opposed. In his testimony, Bridges said bluntly that the proposal "won't work to force an end to our strike" and that "it's awfully hard to make [a waterfront worker] work fast and hard." As the proposed legislation moved forward, the ILWU and PMA reached agreement on February 8.[31]

The agreement differed little from what they had agreed to before resumption of the strike. The container provision applied to all containers stuffed or stripped within fifty miles of the docks, and the dollar "tax" per long ton for containers not worked by ILWU members was to be used for the guaranteed wage or pensions. There were no paid holidays. A minor change was made regarding steady men. Remaining details were referred to arbitration. The biggest gain was the guarantee of work or pay for both A men and B men, averaged over twenty-six weeks.[32]

The coast caucus met for four days to consider the proposed settlement. The negotiating committee was divided, with three members opposing acceptance.

The caucus split 99–36 with eleven abstentions to recommend ratifying the agreement. All the largest locals' delegations were divided. Delegates opposed to ratification were given a chance to present their arguments in the *Dispatcher*; several criticized the provisions on CFS, the wage guarantee, and steady men.[33]

The new voting formula gave a veto to each of the four largest locals. The remaining locals were grouped into five units, each with a veto: one unit for the four clerks' locals and one unit each for the small ports in Washington and Oregon, those in Northern California, and those in Southern California. The agreement was approved by all nine units. The overall membership vote was 71 percent in favor. Only two small ports voted against.[34]

Bridges proclaimed victory: "The strike was won, and won hands down!" He described the contract improvements as "solid and substantial gains," and added, "We did not break PMA. . . . We had no plans to do so. . . . PMA had no plans to destroy our union." But, he added, in a comment most likely aimed at some of the loudest strike promoters, the PMA "showed that it was not a pushover or a bunch of pansies or that it was just a matter of talking tough to PMA and that it would cave in." He also said, "We won this one by ourselves as part of the labor movement and with the solid, wholehearted support of all unions and leadership." He specifically acknowledged George Meany of the AFL-CIO, John Henning of the California Labor Federation, Frank Fitzsimmons of the IBT, and the UMW, UAW, and UE. The ILA was conspicuously absent from his list. He complained, "Liberal politicians and liberals generally were just nowhere when we needed a little help," but noted important exceptions: San Francisco mayor Joe Alioto, San Francisco Congress member Phil Burton, and a few other members of Congress.[35]

One obstacle remained: the federal Pay Board, successor to Nixon's freeze on wages and prices. Bridges and the two elected coast committeemen joined PMA representatives in Washington to testify on behalf of the wage increases in the agreement. Pay Board staff presented data on increased productivity as justifying the increases, but the board voted 8–5 to cut the wage increases from 20.9 percent to 14.9 percent. (Inflation from 1966 to 1971 was such that even the 20.9 percent increase would not have restored lost purchasing power.) In protest, four of the five labor representatives on the board resigned, all except Fitzsimmons. In resigning Meany condemned "this system of unfair and unequitable government controls of wages for the benefit of big business" and claimed the board's decision was "political," intended to push the ILWU back on strike as a way of building support in Congress for compulsory arbitration of all labor disputes in transportation. Bridges, Gleason, and Meany then met, and Bridges and Gleason reaffirmed their previous agreement to fight together in the event the Pay Board cut either of their settlements.[36]

On May 8, the revised Pay Board voted 6–1 to cut the ILA's wage increase. Gleason did nothing. On May 14, A. H. Baskin of the *New York Times* concluded that the Pay Board had won its biggest test, the two longshore pay cuts, noting that "the walkout the Administration and the country had really feared—a union-enforced shutdown of all deep-sea ports—did not materialize." The *New York Times* was blunt: Bridges "did not get the support of Thomas W. Gleason." The ILWU accepted the new wage rates. When the ILWU and PMA agreed to put the lost wages into an escrow account, payable at the expiration of the wage freeze, the Pay Board prohibited such arrangements.[37] The ILWU and ILA contract provisions regarding container handling within the fifty-mile limit also came under challenge, first before the NLRB and then in the courts. The ILWU-PMA "tax" on containers not worked by ILWU members was prohibited by the NLRB in 1974.[38]

In 1973 the ILWU and PMA agreed on a two-year contract that made up most of the lost wages from the Pay Board cut and, for the first time, included paid holidays. The ratification vote was more than 79 percent in favor. In early 1975, a proposed new agreement was defeated, despite a vote of nearly two to one in favor, because the majority in Local 13 had opposed, thus defeating the proposal under the ILWU's complex veto provisions. On a second vote, Local 10 joined Local 13 in opposition, although the overall total was still nearly two to one in favor. Negotiations resumed, and a revised agreement was approved with 77.5 percent in favor, including all locals. In addition to wage and benefit increases, the new agreement provided for a total of nine paid holidays and equalization of earnings for steady men and hall men on the same pay scale. It was Bridges's last longshore contract as president.[39]

18

Living Legend
1971–1990

The 1985 ILWU convention adopted a resolution by a unanimous standing vote and with long and sustained applause that called Bridges "rightly known and appreciated worldwide as a 'Living Legend in His Own Time'" and "an active symbol of what has always been great about the ILWU—an independent, militant, rank-and-file democratic union."[1] Though Bridges was accorded the respect of nearly all ILWU members after retiring, his final years as president were not without challenges. And, in the end, both he and Louis Goldblatt were forced to retire. In retirement Bridges's responsibilities as port commissioner continued, and he accepted new responsibilities in organizations devoted to peace.

During Bridges's final years as president, he and Goldblatt continued at loggerheads, affecting nearly everyone and everything in the international offices. In March 1970, Bridges demanded the dismissal of Joe McCray as administrative assistant and Sid Roger as *Dispatcher* editor, although Bridges had second thoughts about Roger. McCray was dismissed, and his replacement, Charles Velson, who had a long history with Bridges and the ILWU, left soon after. In 1972 Bridges pushed Roger to resign. Roger's replacement was Steve Murdock, who also served as administrative assistant to Bridges, but the revolving door for administrative assistants continued. Murdock remained only until May 1975. Harry Bernstein, in the *Los Angeles Times*, noted, "These days, most of his [Bridges's] bitterness seems directed at his former friends and colleagues." Edith Jenkins was more direct: "When Harry stopped having real enemies in the industries, he turned on his closest friends."[2]

Serious discussions of merger ended after January 1973, when the Executive Board considered a proposal from the IBT. All four international officers recommended, "That the matter of a merger between the ILWU and the Teamsters be dropped and considered completely and finally ended and disposed of." In opposing the proposal, Bridges pointed to the IBT's constitutional provision permitting forced merger of locals or bargaining units, jurisdictional problems over containers, and the IBT's requirement to merge the pension funds. Bridges also specified that the IBT had said that any merger with the ILA would be the end of any cooperation with the IBT. The officers' recommendation carried unanimously. Talk about mergers still came up occasionally, but that Executive Board decision was the last serious consideration of a merger.[3]

In 1972 Bridges dismissed Charles Larrowe's *Harry Bridges: The Rise and Fall of Radical Labor in the United States* as "a series of distortions, half-truths, and, in many cases, outright lies," a characterization that Larrowe later added to his introduction. In 1973 the convention discussed Larrowe's book at length, though not by name. Bridges argued that college professors were not qualified to write about labor history, that to write labor history one must "be a working stiff." He further explained that a college professor is unable to understand that "there's no two sides. There's only one side, our side. The boss is always wrong. You can't sell a college professor on that." The 1977 convention called upon all three retiring officers to write an autobiography or memoir.[4] Both Bridges and Goldblatt began soon after retiring.

During Bridges's final years as president, Local 10 continued to pose problems for him. In January 1973, some eleven hundred members of Local 10—more than 40 percent of the total—petitioned the international officers to "investigate the affairs, money and financial situation" of the local. Though provided for by the ILWU constitution, such a request had never previously been made. The Executive Board accepted Bridges's recommendation to take "certain steps" but specified that the officers "do not have authority to make any drastic moves." The international officers appointed J. R. "Bob" Robertson, the widely respected retired vice president, to investigate and develop solutions, which were to be implemented for ninety days before the local could reject or modify them. Most Local 10 members seemed satisfied by Robertson's decisions about budget cutting. The Executive Board agreed, although it had to loan $10,000 to Local 10 to pay its bills. In the 1973 convention, some Local 10 delegates insisted that the convention rule on the constitutionality of the process. After a long discussion, the convention referred the issue to the Executive Board and also adopted a constitutional amendment governing such situations, patterned closely on the actions taken by Bridges and the international officers.[5]

Prior to the 1975 convention, Larry Wing, president of Local 10 and prominent among Bridges's critics, refused to sign credentials for Bridges and Chester as elected delegates. Wing agreed that Bridges and Chester, as international officers, were automatically delegates but argued that the international constitution specified only "elected" delegates could participate in roll-call votes. Carl

Smith, secretary of Local 10, then refused to sign credentials for Wing because Wing, as local president, was also an automatic convention delegate. After a long discussion, the convention accepted the credential committee's report giving full voting rights to all delegates from Local 10, including Bridges, Chester, and Wing. Most understood the dispute as a contest between Bridges's supporters and self-identified "rank and file forces."[6]

Throughout the early 1970s, Bridges and the CP were often in conflict, and the *People's World* frequently criticized Bridges. Bridges, in 1971, accused the paper of "snide cracks, distortions and plain lies about our union, its leadership and activities." In 1974 Albert "Mickie" Lima, head of the Northern California CP, claimed Bridges had "slandered the Party." In 1976 Lima charged Bridges with "opportunism," described the longshore contract as "a typical Social-Democratic diversion from a class struggle policy," and decried "vicious red-baiting, especially by some former Party members." He described the ILWU's "relations with the racist and corrupt Alioto political machine" as "political opportunism." Archie Brown argued that ILWU leaders "followed a policy of 'accommodation' or class collaboration."[7]

Despite such exchanges with Northern California CP leaders, Bridges remained a staunch defender of the Soviet Union in his *Dispatcher* columns and public appearances. Gus Hall, general secretary of the CPUSA, acknowledged both the local CP criticism of Bridges and Bridges's consistent support for the Soviet Union when he wrote to Bridges in 1973: "While we may have our differences on many questions, we are on the same corner, on the same side of the class barricades. There has never been any doubt about that fact in my mind, nor about where Harry Bridges stands."[8]

In April and May 1975, Harry and Noriko spent two weeks in the Soviet Union as guests of the Central Council of Trade Unions and the Sea and River Workers' Union, including a visit to the "rest home" of the Sea and River Workers' Union in Odessa. (Soviet unions maintained such resorts, most on the Black Sea, where union members could take an annual "rest cure," similar to visiting a spa.) Harry and Noriko returned to Moscow for May Day events, and then toured the Leningrad area before returning to Moscow for World War II Victory Day, the thirtieth anniversary of the defeat of Germany. Later, in the *Dispatcher*, Harry acknowledged, "The USSR is not a utopia. Far from it," but nonetheless concluded, "The Soviet people have it made and they know it." A two-page account of their trip, under Harry's byline (but, I suspect, written mostly by Noriko) appeared in the *Dispatcher*, full of praise for the Soviet system.[9]

In October 1976, at the Soviet consulate in San Francisco, the consul presented Bridges with the Soviet Union's Order of Friendship among Peoples. Accompanying Bridges were Noriko, Julie, Robbie, Kathy, and Dave and Edith Jenkins. The Sea and River Workers' Union stated that the award recognized

Bridges's "energetic activities in the trade union movement" and "contribution to strengthening friendship between the people of the USA and the USSR." Bridges accepted on behalf of "the membership of the union I represent and their strong stand over the years for better relations and freer trade between our two countries."[10]

Such support for the Soviet Union kept Bridges on the FBI's watch list, although FBI reports continued to state that informants failed to report "any CP activity" by Bridges. FBI surveillance became minimal, albeit with attention to his foreign travels. When Congress canceled the section of the Subversive Control Act that had sanctioned the FBI's Security Index, the FBI changed its name to the Administrative Index, or ADEX. Bridges was placed in Category I, the most dangerous, "because of his long history of affiliation with the Communist Party and subversive organizations in the United States." The last unredacted report in his file, from July 1976, with a copy to the Secret Service, checked the box that described Bridges as "potentially dangerous because of background, emotional instability or activity in groups engaged in activities inimical to the U.S."[11]

Among the bright spots of Bridges's final years as president must have been the new international headquarters building. The 1967 convention approved assessing locals to fund a new building. The ILWU moved into the four-story building in late 1973; it was renamed the Harry R. Bridges Memorial Building in 1985.[12] Clement Kai-Men Lai claims in his doctoral dissertation, "St. Francis Square and a new ILWU world [sic] headquarters building in the Western Addition were both Redevelopment Agency concessions to the ILWU leadership over SOMA [South of Market Area] displacement," and "the ILWU's leadership . . . was promised a new headquarters building in the Western Addition" as a way "to co-opt labor union leadership." He does not document these assertions, and I found no evidence for his claims. Like the St. Francis Square project, the site for the new headquarters was acquired through open bidding. An even more negative characterization came in a 1974 film, *Redevelopment: A Marxist Analysis*. In the movie, a retired leftist longshoreman asserts that Bridges specifically and unions in general were "bought off" by the Alioto administration through appointments to city commissions and boards, a charge that has since become part of the city's left-wing lore, but never with any evidence.[13]

Another bright spot for Bridges's final years as president was a second trip to Australia. In October 1976, Bridges and Bill Ward, an Executive Board member, attended the Waterside Workers' All-Ports Conference. Harry wrote to Noriko, "I made my speech yesterday. Did pretty well. Made one bloomer [blooper?]. The word 'fuck' slipped out and these Aussies don't like that." He reported that Australian dockworkers faced much the same problems as ILWU members—a serious reduction in jobs due to containerization and jurisdictional issues regarding stuffing and stripping containers.[14]

While in Sydney, Bridges had a brief reunion with Honor Farnham, his first girlfriend. From Sydney, he went to Melbourne, "to see my two sisters and a lot of nieces and nephews to say hello and perhaps good-bye. . . . At my age, I don't know if I'll be able to come back again." In a letter to Noriko, he wrote, "I have had to explain over & over why you are not with me and I must say the mothers understand at once about Kathy." Noriko later described Kathy, then sixteen, as a rebellious teenager who had dropped out of high school.[15]

In the 1975 convention, Local 142, representing a third or more of ILWU members, proposed a constitutional amendment to prohibit anyone beyond age sixty-five from running for an international office. Taken up in executive session, the proposal generated significant opposition and six minority reports. All four international officers—Bridges, Chester, Martin, and Goldblatt—supported the amendment. After extensive discussion and procedural wrangling, delegates took a roll-call vote. Most of Local 6 voted no, but Goldblatt voted yes. Most of Local 10, including Bridges and Chester, voted yes. The minutes do not record the final vote tally, but it was 73–50 in favor before Local 142, the largest local, cast all but one of its votes in favor.[16]

Harry Bernstein, in the *Los Angeles Times*, reported that Bridges "has no serious opposition as president of the international," but added, "Some ILWU members feel he has simply been in too long. Others complain about his pro-Soviet attitude. Still others complain he is too conservative in fighting for more benefits for ILWU members." Over objections from Larry Wing, the convention adopted a resolution to give each retiring international officer $13,000 (equivalent to more than $68,000 in mid-2022).[17] Bridges's, Goldblatt's, and Chester's retirements were now set for 1977. Those two years included several events celebrating their service to the union and wishing them well in retirement.

A dinner in Bridges's honor was held in the Grand Ballroom of the Fairmont Hotel in November 1975. The guests—the *San Francisco Chronicle* called them "glittering people"—included former governor Edmund Brown, Mayor Joseph Alioto, other civic figures, and a host of labor and corporate leaders. The printed program was filled with greetings from politicians, labor leaders, dozens of corporations, and maritime workers' unions from around the world. Guests paid to attend, and additional income came from selling ads in the program, producing two retirement gifts for Harry and Noriko: a new Volvo station wagon and about $20,000. In response to praise from the many speakers, Bridges, as usual, insisted, "I am getting a lot of credit that I don't deserve" and that the real credit belonged to rank-and-file ILWU members and others who supported the union movement.[18]

Other events honoring the retiring officers followed. In May 1976, Local 142 held a potluck picnic for some fifteen hundred ILWU members, pensioners, and their families, to say "aloha" to Bridges and Goldblatt. Harry and Noriko, along with Lou and Terry Goldblatt, were back in Hawaii for the Labor Day weekend and a series of picnics for ILWU members "to say Mahalo and Aloha."[19]

In many ways, the 1977 convention, in Seattle, exemplified the union that Bridges had led and did so much to mold. The *Proceedings* make clear the very personal relationship between Bridges and the delegates, the openness of the floor discussions, the extent to which delegates felt comfortable challenging the leaders, and the commitment of the ILWU to progressive values and internal democracy. As in previous conventions, debates over policy and constitutional issues occupied much of the time. As the *New York Times* reported, "The scrappy independence Mr. Bridges has fostered made name-calling, booing and cheering and emotional rhetoric part of each discussion."[20]

The policy resolutions provide examples of the ILWU's values. A long discussion on the relation between affirmative action, which nearly all favored, and seniority, which nearly all also favored, concluded with a pronouncement against discrimination. Another long discussion of spreading the work through a six-hour day concluded that it was not reasonable to do so without a reduction in pay. Delegates directed that future ILWU contracts allow refusal to handle cargo to or from South Africa and Zimbabwe so long as apartheid continued. Other resolutions reaffirmed opposition to capital punishment and stated that the ILWU would not join "any hysterical reaction" making "alien workers," including undocumented workers, scapegoats for economic problems. Delegates reaffirmed the ILWU's commitment to autonomy, opposed any merger, and supported labor unity. A resolution granting the title *emeritus* to the three retiring officers brought a long round of praise for Bridges, Goldblatt, and Chester.[21]

Before the convention, Bridges professed neutrality regarding his successor, but in the end he was one of many who seconded the nomination of Jimmy Herman, longtime president of Local 34. The elections for president and secretary-treasurer were contested; Herman was elected, and Curtis McClain, Local 6, was elected secretary-treasurer.[22]

The *Seattle Post-Intelligencer* described the final moments of the convention: "Harry Bridges, 75, gaveled his last convention as president of the International Longshoremen's & Warehousemen's Union to a close yesterday and strong men—and women—wept. The impact of that moment swept through the Washington Plaza Hotel ballroom as . . . [Bridges] announced the 22nd biennial convention was over 'sine die.' . . . The end of an era."[23]

In an interview with the *New York Times*, Bridges said that his greatest disappointment "was that the labor movement 'divided and fell apart' after the victorious drive in the mass production industries." Nonetheless, he continued, "I want to put my faith in the labor movement for all its drawbacks and deficiencies of leadership. . . . There is no replacement for it."[24]

Throughout the final years of Bridges's presidency and into his retirement, he remained engaged with politics, repeatedly stressed the importance of politics, but usually remained silent in public regarding elections. Agreement among the labor members of the Pay Board that the board's decision on the ILWU's negotiated wage increase in 1972 was "political" underscored the importance of politics for unions in general and the ILWU in particular. Given the ILWU's long-standing opposition to the war in Vietnam, the escalation of that war by the Nixon administration increased the union's antagonism toward him. During the early months of the 1972 presidential campaign, Bridges used his *Dispatcher* column to encourage ILWU members to remain independent, endorse candidates who supported labor, and not make a candidate's opposition to the war the sole basis for endorsement. The executive board unanimously endorsed George McGovern; there was zero support for Nixon.[25]

In 1974 Joseph Alioto ran for governor of California in the Democratic primary. Bridges changed his voter registration to Democratic so he could vote for Alioto in the primary. The ILWU's primary endorsements that year included Alioto and Wayne Morse for the U.S. Senate in Oregon. Both lost in the Democratic primaries. The ILWU then endorsed the Democratic primary winners for those elections and endorsed mostly Democrats for other positions. Bridges said nothing in the *Dispatcher* about either the primaries or the general election. Bridges also said nothing in his column about the 1976 presidential primaries or the general election, between the incumbent, Gerald Ford, and James Carter of Georgia. The executive board endorsed Carter. The year 1976 was Bridges's last presidential election as ILWU president.[26]

Bridges served on the San Francisco Port Commission from 1970 to 1982. Those years marked significant transitions for the port. By the early 1970s, the rapid advance of containerization had brought a significant expansion of the Port of Oakland, which had easy access to major highways and rail lines and could easily expand into the bay, making space for cranes and a container yard. San Francisco's obsolete finger piers were either abandoned or converted to other uses. The only possibility for container facilities in San Francisco was at the far southern end of the waterfront, but even there the land-transportation possibilities put San Francisco at a serious disadvantage compared to Oakland.[27]

Many in the city's civic leadership had been delighted when the state gave the city control over the waterfront. What they received, however, was obsolete infrastructure that hemorrhaged money. An analysis in 1968 suggested that much of the port acreage be redeveloped for "public open spaces, housing or recreation." Others saw opportunities for developers, but the first such proposals, both very large in scale, were blocked during Bridges's first year on the commission, one in response to environmental concerns and the other due to neighborhood resistance.[28] Later redevelopment proposals for the port were less grandiose.

I found only one press conference that Bridges devoted to Port Commission matters, in September 1974, when questions were being raised about conflicts of interest on the part of port commissioners and Mayor Alioto. Bridges denied any conflict of interest, stating, "I'm the representative of the working people on this commission. If someone thinks that is a conflict of interest, let them take it to a judge and jury." Bridges also criticized the port staff for taking "too much time and energy" in "developing everything but shipping."[29]

Bridges's focus on shipping rather than commercial development sometimes put him at odds with port director Thomas Soules, who, in 1975, bluntly stated, "To bring back shipping from Oakland—it can't be done." Bridges and the two commissioners with whom he often voted were not favorites of Soules, who openly hoped that election of a new mayor in 1975 would give the commission a different majority. He got his wish—Mayor George Moscone appointed four new commissioners, replacing everyone but Bridges. In mid-November 1977, Bridges was part of the unanimous majority that fired Soules.[30]

In 1976 Bridges opposed a proposal by the Maritime Museum, then a private nonprofit corporation, to berth the World War II submarine *Pampanito* at Pier 45B. Bridges opposed partly due to the *Pampanito*'s having sunk a Japanese ship filled with English and Australian prisoners of war. Berthing the *Pampanito* was not approved, but the issue returned in 1981. The 1981 minutes record, "Commissioner Bridges reiterated his statement during the 1976 hearings. . . . [H]e is totally opposed to bringing a weapon of war into San Francisco, a city which is noted as a symbol of peace." He lost, four to one.[31]

When Bridges announced his resignation from the Port Commission in 1982, Herb Caen attributed it to Bridges's "suffering from low blood pressure plus emphysema and what he called 'old age.'" Caen added that Bridges was "now ready to contemplate 'active retirement.'" Mayor Dianne Feinstein chose Jimmy Herman to replace Bridges, establishing the precedent that one seat on that commission belonged to an ILWU officer.[32]

When Bridges left the ILWU presidency in 1977, he planned to write his autobiography, work in the peace movement, and advocate for senior citizens. Within a few years, however, his health imposed more and more limitations on his activities.[33]

One of Bridges's most consistent activities after retiring was attending ILWU pensioners' meetings, conventions, coast caucuses, and sometimes Executive Board meetings. Noriko sometimes attended, especially the conventions and pensioners' meetings. Harry chaired the nominations portion of the ILWU conventions between 1979 and 1985. At each convention, he spoke on world peace and often commented on resolutions. At the 1981 convention, Noriko spoke eloquently in favor of reparations for Japanese Americans sent to relocation camps during World War II and read her poem poignantly expressing her own experiences. The convention in 1985 marked Harry's last appearance.[34]

The 1988 convention considered affiliation with the AFL-CIO. Unable to attend, Bridges announced his full support. The delegates debated the issue at length, some concerned about the role of the AFL-CIO in jurisdictional matters. Others wanted a referendum of all members. The convention finally approved a three-part resolution: recommending affiliation, authorizing the Executive Board to withdraw at any time, and requiring a membership referendum. The membership referendum was three to one in favor.[35] Bridges told me he was very pleased.

As early as his 1959 visit to Moscow, Bridges had been impressed with Soviet medicine as having remedies not available elsewhere. In mid-July 1977, days after he left the ILWU president's office, Harry and Noriko traveled to Romania to spend two weeks in the Sanatoriala Otopeni, run by a geriatrician, Ana Aslan, renowned for treating aging as a preventable disease. The intent was for Harry to get in as good physical and mental shape as possible for his autobiography and work among senior citizens. They both received Aslan's invention, Gerovital, along with vitamins and other treatments. Shortly before, however, the FDA concluded that Gerovital "has not been proven safe and effective."[36]

In January 1978, Harry and Noriko went to Washington, where Harry was the first person honored through a new series of "living self-portraits" at the National Portrait Gallery of the Smithsonian Institution. Each honoree was filmed speaking about his or her life and accomplishments. Bridges's topic was titled "Up from Down Under: Fifty Years of Waterfront Unionism." When asked whom to include in a dinner party, he listed Noriko, the Soviet ambassador, and Katharine Graham, publisher of the *Washington Post* whom he had known as a reporter in San Francisco in the 1930s.[37]

Reporting on his talk, the *New York Times* described Bridges as "whip-thin . . . sharp of eye and disarming of smile . . . the cliche that yesterday's radical is today's prophet of conventional wisdom." He began by describing himself as "a working stiff" who became chair of the strike committee in 1934 "because nobody else wanted the damn thing." He recounted, in his usual rambling style, his life and the history of Pacific Coast waterfront unionism. Of his long battle with federal authorities, he cheerfully acknowledged, "Ninety-five percent of the evidence against me was absolutely true," but insisted that the one thing he didn't do was join the CP. Of the M&M, he said, "In classical Marxist terms . . . it could be called a sellout. There's no class struggle in it. . . . It did lead to certain strains with the Communist Party. In typical ideological terms, of course, they're right. But the union is a bit more practical." With a grin, he called the M&M "a beautiful piece of class collaboration." The closest he came to summing up was to say, "We had a few things to change, and before we got through we changed the darn thing."[38]

On January 17, 1978, the National Portrait Gallery in Washington, DC, honored Bridges with its first "living self-portrait." The *New York Times* called him "dapper" in a blazer and lavender shirt. (Photo courtesy of Labor Archives and Research Center, San Francisco State University, and Smithsonian Institution Archives, image # 78-479-30)

Harry and Noriko found time for the horses. In 1980 they averaged about two trips a month to the racetrack, and Harry usually broke even after expenses. In 1984 he told the Kaiser optician that he needed to have glasses that would assist with "reading, distance vision for driving, watching television, and watching the horses at the race-track."[39]

During the 1977 convention, Harry asked the delegates to approve his appointment as the U.S. vice president of the World Peace Council. He was actually appointed as one of twenty vice presidents of the International Liaison Forum of Peace Forces (ILF), an organization formed in Moscow in 1973 as an outgrowth of peace activities promoted by the Soviet Union and CP members around the world. Its major activity was meetings devoted to peace and disarmament. Bridges attended such meetings in London, Vienna, and Budapest. He wrote to Noriko from Vienna in early 1978 that the conference was keeping him very busy and asked to save the "daily racing papers," so he could catch up with the horses later. In 1984, citing health problems, Bridges submitted his resignation.[40]

Bridges also served on the advisory committee for the National Council of American-Soviet Friendship and described it as having "aims I believe in fiercely," but his health prevented him from attending its meetings. He was a member of the Steering Committee for the U.S. Peace Council but attended few of its meetings. In 1980, citing health reasons, he asked to be moved to the advisory council. He was also the honorary chair of Labor for Peace.[41] Thus, though his name appeared on the letterhead of a number of peace organizations, he took only a limited role in their activities.

Harry and Noriko spent ten days in Cuba in December 1978, and Noriko wrote about their experience. The Cuban CP had invited Harry and others to see the facilities for the elderly. While Noriko's report was generally quite positive, she also noted, "To accept institutionalization is to give up one's privacy." Harry and Noriko had planned to travel to the Soviet Union in 1981, but canceled their trip due to the air controllers' strike. Their invitation was renewed for the following year, and they spent a month in the Soviet Union in 1982.[42]

In retirement Bridges was consulted with some regularity by CP leaders. In June 1979, prior to the CP's national convention, he wrote a long letter commenting on "the main political resolution," emphasizing the need for "one united labor movement." He criticized "the growing social democratic movements," which he labeled "radical chic." He and Noriko declined to attend the convention: "It does not seem politically wise at this time." He also declined to attend the 1983 national convention because it "wouldn't help" his efforts to persuade "union councils and State Federations" to come "into the peace program." He commented, in a letter to Gus Hall regarding the rise to power of Mikhail Gorbachev, "The world is sure getting better all the time." However, he strongly disapproved of the Polish union Solidarity, seeing it as a tool of the Catholic Church.[43]

In his last presidential address, in 1977, Bridges drew attention to the plight of older Americans: "Our culture in the United States is pretty cruel when it comes to the handling of older citizens—and we must find a way to get them organized so that they will pull their weight and have a greater voice in the social life and advancement of our country." Bridges's announcement that he intended to advocate for senior citizens brought a torrent of supportive mail. He soon accepted the vice presidency of the Northern California District of Congress of California Seniors, but he declined renomination in 1981.[44] Aside from lending his name and doing some fund-raising, he seems to have done little in that organization.

Bridges remained on the board of trustees of the Oceanic Society, which he called a "highfalutin environmentalist group." Founded in San Francisco in 1969, the organization advocated for conservation of marine wildlife and habitats.[45]

By the time Harry retired, Noriko was gaining recognition for her writing. In 1977, "To Be or Not to Be; There's No Such Option," her poem about her experience in the internment camp, won first place in a poetry competition, was published in 1978, was subsequently republished in several places, and became assigned reading for ethnic studies and women's studies classes. Her subsequent essays "Memoirs of a Japanese Daughter," in *Ms.* magazine in April 1980, and "Papa Takes a Bride," in *Harper's* in December 1980 and subsequently in *Reader's Digest*, were similarly assigned in many college classes.[46] The 1980 articles were published as by Noriko Sawada. She later explained, "I went back to Noriko Sawada" for writing, "because Nikki Bridges has no ethnicity. . . . I enjoy being 'Nikki Bridges.' However, I need to go back to my roots, to declare that these are my roots." There was another reason: "I wasn't going to share any glory that I got with Harry."[47]

Noriko and Harry planned to write Harry's autobiography during his retirement. They began in 1978 by recording conversations and interviews about Harry's experiences. By late 1980, they had engaged a writer, Charles Einstein, a novelist, journalist, sportswriter, and screenwriter. Einstein recorded more interviews and drafted a manuscript. However, as Harry explained in early 1983, "The manuscript was rejected not only by us but by the publisher as well." In 1984 Harry and Noriko asked a prominent journalist to write his biography, but she declined. In November 1985, Gus Hall offered to have Simon Gerson, longtime editor of the *Daily Worker*, write the book, but Harry and Noriko declined.[48] Years before, in the fall of 1975, Noriko had taken a course on biography in the History Department at San Francisco State University. Ten years later, she asked the instructor, Peter Carroll, if he might be interested in ghostwriting the autobiography. Carroll explained that he had other obligations, persuaded Noriko that what was really needed was a carefully researched academic biography, and recommended me. After meeting with Harry and Noriko in late 1985, I agreed to undertake the project and interviewed Bridges several times between January 1986 and February 1987.

In 1983 Bridges wrote about his family in a letter: Kathy was about to graduate from Humboldt State University with a degree in forestry and had been working for the Colorado Forestry Service; in describing her determination in a letter in 1980, Bridges said, "She is like an armored tank when she makes up her mind." Rob was recently married and working for the Bay Area Rapid Transit system. Harry noted, "I am really pleased with the way Rob has turned out." Julie was working in San Francisco, was married, and had a three-year-old son.[49]

By the early 1980s, Bridges was cutting back on his commitments. In 1982 his Kaiser physician listed his medical conditions: chronic obstructive pulmonary disease, primarily emphysema and intermittent congestive heart failure (causing shortness of breath); orthostatic hypotension (low blood pressure); intermittent angina (occasional chest pain); a compression fracture of the T6 vertebra, in the center of his spine; and a recent fracture of his patella (kneecap). In 1985 Bridges wrote, "My emphysema keeps me down and pretty well chained to the house." He was also suffering from vision problems. In 1987 his ophthalmologist pronounced Bridges legally blind. In September 1988, he fell, broke his right leg, and was in a cast for several months.[50] The last few times I visited, he was bedfast, with a hospital bed in their living room where he could meet and talk with his many visitors. Once during those final years, when he was in Kaiser hospital, I called the hospital and asked to be connected to his room. The receptionist told me that, yes, he was there and that she always remembered when Mr. Bridges was in the hospital because he had the same name as "that famous labor leader."

Harry died at home on March 30, 1990. Noriko and Kevin Fales, Julie's son, were with him. He was eighty-eight. Pacific Coast longshore work stopped when ILWU members learned the news.[51]

San Francisco mayor Art Agnos ordered the city hall flag at half-staff. The *Chronicle* announced his death on the front page and surveyed his career on two more pages with another long article on April 1. Herb Caen observed, "The editorials in both papers extolling Harry Bridges to the skies brought wry smiles to old-timers who remember when these same sheets vilified and crucified him as the devil incarnate."[52]

On April 5, his ashes were scattered in the Pacific Ocean, just outside the Golden Gate, through which he had first entered San Francisco Bay aboard the *Ysabel*, sixty-eight years before. Longshore workers stopped work from the time the ship left until it returned.[53]

Longshore workers again stopped work on April 14 for a memorial service that filled the Local 10 hall. Thousands came, the large majority rank-and-file members of the ILWU and other unions. Noriko, Jackie, Julie, Robbie, and Kathy along with Bridges's nine grandchildren and great-grandchildren sat up front. There were two generations of Hallinans and Aliotos, as well as graying members and former members of the CP. A jazz band played its version of "The Battle Hymn of the Republic." Harry Stamper, a member of Local 12 (North Bend, Oregon) and an accomplished folk singer and songwriter, presented his song about Bridges. Bridges was eulogized by Lieutenant Governor Leo McCarthy, Speaker of the Assembly Willie Brown, Mayor Art Agnos, and former mayor Joseph Alioto; by labor leaders, including Jimmy Herman and John Henning, secretary of the California Labor Federation; by a PMA executive and Sam Kagel, still the coast arbitrator; and by others. But, as the *Examiner* reporter noted,

Harry wasn't there to make his usual complaint that the praise being heaped on him really belonged to the rank and file.[54]

Noriko was the most moving speaker. "It's been my honor and privilege and source of considerable irritation to have shared thirty-one years of Harry's life," she began. She spoke of their difficulty in getting married, of Harry's commitment to improving the lives of ILWU members, and of his commitment to racial and social justice. "There are a lot of things left to be done," she said and cited the need for a national health-care program, housing for the homeless, and better education—all still relevant thirty years later. "I just ask you," she concluded, "don't let him down."[55]

There was another memorial service in Honolulu, on May 1, and again longshore work stopped from 8:00 to 11:00 a.m. The final memorial service was a Mass, at the request of John Henning, on June 2.[56]

Harry's death left a void in Noriko's life, but also opened new opportunities for her, then sixty-seven years old. She told a Hawaiian newspaper in 1990 that she had put her writing on hold for the previous several years to care for Harry. Now, she said, "For the first time in my life, I am truly liberated." She added, with her unique sense of humor, "So now with my newfound wisdom and near-senility . . . I can do what I want."[57] Over the next decade, Noriko's writing and involvement in a variety of organizations continued, as did presentations about the experience of Japanese Americans during the World War II incarceration. She traveled in the United States and Europe. On May 1, 1994, she married Ed Flynn. She explained that, after Harry's death, nearly all of his friends stopped coming to visit, but not Ed. They moved to his home in Pescadero, forty-some miles south of San Francisco. Noriko died in 2003.

Epilogue

So, then, how effective *was* Bridges as a union leader, and how was he effective? Did his relationship with the Communist Party affect his effectiveness as a union leader, and, if so, how?

My answer to the first question, as should be obvious by now, is that Bridges was highly effective as a union leader. His approach to leadership derived in part from his experiences in 1933 and 1934. Unlike some prominent leaders of industrial unionism in the mid-1930s, Bridges came directly off the docks to take leadership of the San Francisco local and then the Pacific Coast District. He came from the rank and file, was of the rank and file, and always held that identity close. David Selvin, whose observation of Bridges began in 1934, said in 1990, "What really angered employers about Bridges [was] his refusal to cut a closed-door deal with them and his insistence that the rank and file ratify everything. . . . The union members' loyalty to Bridges came out of that, too."[1] Warren Hinckle, who wrote for *San Francisco Chronicle*, agreed: "The fusion of leadership with the rank and file was Bridges' genius, and his power."[2]

Beginning before the 1934 strike and continuing long after, Bridges traveled up and down the coast, attending local union meetings, especially the longshore locals, which he always saw as the heart—and muscle—of the union. From 1936 on, the longshore caucus institutionalized the fusion of leadership and membership: frequent meetings of elected delegates from every longshore local to engage in freewheeling discussion of the contract, their concerns, and their goals. The ILWU institutionalized that fusion through large negotiating committees, with representatives from all major locals, and sometimes by "fishbowl" negotiations, with the entire longshore caucus observing and able to raise concerns with the negotiating committee. Bridges always and repeatedly insisted, even to President Nixon in 1971, that it was not he who approved any settlement but the entire membership through a referendum vote—at times by a supermajority. And, in later years, when Bridges was lauded for his accomplishments, his reply was always the same: the credit belongs to rank-and-file ILWU members.

And, as I've tried to make clear, Bridges's leadership was always a shared leadership, from Local 38-79 to the ILA-PCD to the ILWU, Bridges shared leadership with others, as well as sharing decision making with rank-and-file members through such institutions as the longshore caucus and frequent membership referenda. His fear that the ILWU might become a "one-man union," ironically, led him to hold onto the presidency when he might have retired.

Very early Bridges acquired an ideological framework that molded his understanding of labor, unions, and leadership. He drew partly upon his brief experience in the IWW, which emphasized the leadership of the rank and file. He also drew upon a Marxist understanding of class as he developed his approach to collective bargaining: those on the other side of the table were the "class enemy," even though, as was the case after 1948, they might also be personal friends. He put that ideological stamp on his understanding of the M&M when he called it "class collaboration."

In 1934, rebutting charges that Bridges and the ILA-PCD were radicals, Henry Melnikow drew on the work of his mentor, John Commons: "It has been the history of the American labor movement that responsibility made for conservatism."[3] In Bridges's case, responsibility did not produce political conservatism of the sort exhibited by labor leaders from Samuel Gompers to George Meany. When asked by a Senate committee after World War II to define a "left-wing union," Bridges first listed a willingness to arbitrate, something that he had accepted in the mid-1930s as a pragmatic alternative to the syndicalist "quickie strikes" that threatened to undermine the gains made in 1934 but that evolved into a unique instrument through which rank-and-file union members could refuse work they considered unsafe. He quickly added that a left-wing union had "a lot of rank-and-file democracy," with officers who were easy to remove and were paid no more than the highest-paid union members, and that a left-wing union was willing "to stand up and fight" for civil liberties, racial equality, and "things like that."[4]

Others called Bridges a realist. His realism led him to espouse the M&M as the best means to protect the jobs of existing ILWU longshore members, and his bond with the rank and file permitted him to lead his members to accept that pathbreaking agreement. If his first great accomplishment was to lead the 1934 strike that produced the hiring hall, his other great accomplishment was the M&M. As Bridges was facing retirement, A. H. Raskin, longtime and highly respected labor reporter and assistant editor of the *New York Times*, lauded Bridges as "a pattern-setter in a cooperative approach to waterfront automation that reversed the century-old tradition of Luddite resistance by labor generally to technological change." And, Raskin declared, the M&M "pushed other unions into similar accommodations, thus heightening the efficiency of American industry and strengthening its global competitiveness."[5]

For Bridges—the Marxist ideologue and pragmatic realist—his long-term admiration for the Soviet Union was inseparable from his long-term commitment to socialism. Raskin reported that, during a long telephone call in 1977, Bridges "renewed his lifelong call for socializing America." "I'm still for fundamental change," Raskin quoted Bridges as saying, "but it must be democratic, peaceful change. The other is too dangerous."[6]

Raskin also interviewed "a top negotiator for the Pacific Maritime Association," likely Ed Flynn, who said:

I don't think Harry has changed any. . . . He is the friend of the industry not because he has changed but because the industry has changed under his influence. It used to be a terrible industry, accustomed to buying people up, and Harry never believed in that. He taught us that we had to think in terms of human beings. The fact that he often spouted off about how much better they did things in Moscow never altered the fact that he was an innovative guy who could out think anyone else at the table and whose word meant a lot. He comes out of a mold no one else will fit in.[7]

Others described Bridges as honest or, in Herb Caen's words, "dead honest." Raskin noted, "Union leaders who abhorred his political philosophy" privately praised Bridges for "the unrelenting vigil he maintained to bar any spillover in the West Coast piers of the gangsterism that is still rife in Atlantic and Gulf ports."[8]

Any evaluation of Bridges's leadership must include his commitment to a color-blind union, a union with no racial discrimination. He was most successful with his own local in San Francisco, less so with Locals 8 and 13, where his commitment to racial justice ran up against his commitment to local autonomy. Cleophas Williams, one of the first Black officers in Local 10, liked to tell of a meeting where Bridges said, "If things reached a point where only two men were left on the waterfront, if he had anything to say about it, one would be a Black man."[9]

My other question—if Bridges's relationship to the Communist Party affected his effectiveness as a union leader, and, if so, how—is more difficult to answer. There were CP members in the Albion Hall group, and other members of that group were close to the CP if not members. Bridges always acknowledged that he and the San Francisco local had received support and advice from the CP in the mid-1930s. Bridges and the union attracted CP members or sympathizers as union members, staff members, or volunteers, and both the ILWU and the various Bridges defense committees benefited significantly from such capable and committed staff members and volunteers. Although Bridges held CP committee positions in the mid-1930s, I found no evidence that the CP ever *directed* Bridges or the union more generally, much less *controlled* either.[10] In 1934 Bridges sometimes acted contrary to the CP's position, and there were many later instances. His public statements of support for the Soviet Union or the CPUSA's position on domestic or foreign policy were almost always separate from any union action. He failed to persuade the union to follow the CP's lead in opposing Roosevelt in 1939–41. He and the ILWU did follow the CP's lead in verbally opposing the Marshall Plan. He gave a lukewarm endorsement to Wallace in 1948, and other ILWU leaders were more involved in that campaign, which Bridges and CP leaders later acknowledged had been a serious mistake for him, the ILWU, and the Left more generally.

Bridges's effectiveness as a union leader came from his ability to relate to the rank and file, to represent them, to persuade them. That bond derived from Bridges's personality, his experience working on the docks, and his ability not just to express himself but also to express the sentiments and aspirations of the rank and file. Though Bridges's opponents in the 1930s sometimes claimed that it was the CP that elevated him to leadership, the CP could not have created that bond between Bridges and the rank and file. That bond was, as well, fostered in part by the corporate and federal agencies that made him a martyr in the eyes of his members.

There was an obvious downside to Bridges's closeness to the CP and his public sympathy for the Soviet Union, for those positions invited attacks in the press, by business and patriotic organizations, and by the federal government. From 1939 until 1955, significant amounts of the time and funds of the ILWU were spent in defending Bridges. There's no way to know how much of that time and those funds would have gone into organizing if they had not gone into defense activities, nor is it possible to know what difference it would have meant for the ILWU had it been able to focus more on organizing in those years. Similarly, there's no way to know how Bridges's personal trajectory within the CIO might have been different had he distanced himself from the CP. The ILWU was always a relatively small and regional union, and Bridges's national reputation owed more to him personally than to the national prominence of the ILWU.

The memorialization of Harry Bridges that began with the naming of the international headquarters building in 1985 continues. In 1990 Bridges was the only labor leader among twenty San Franciscans identified by Kevin Starr, then dean of California historians, as having contributed significantly to the history of the city; bas-relief sculptures of the twenty were placed over the entrance to 235 Pine Street, a high-rise office building in San Francisco's financial district. Shortly after Bridges's death, ILWU pensioners, mostly in the Northwest, led the way in endowing the Harry Bridges Chair in Labor Studies at the University of Washington; it was inaugurated in 1992 and is now central to the Harry Bridges Center for Labor Studies at UW Seattle. The Harry Bridges Institute in San Pedro was founded in 1993 and led initially by David Arian, Local 13, who served as ILWU international president in the years 1991–94. In 1994 the punk-rock band Rancid released a song about Bridges. Harry Bridges Memorial Park, on the Long Beach waterfront, opened in 1997. In 1997 Bridges was inducted into Labor's International Hall of Fame in Detroit. In 1999 the *California Journal* included Bridges among the thirty men and women who had the greatest influence on California politics and government in the twentieth century. In 2000, Ian Ruskin, a graduate of the Royal Academy of Dramatic Art in London, launched the Harry Bridges Project, in which he has portrayed Bridges to audiences ranging from universities to unions to local historical societies.[11]

Eugene Daub's bust of Harry Bridges was placed on Harbor Boulevard, San Pedro, California, in 2009. (Photo courtesy of Eugene Daub, San Pedro, California)

In 2001 California governor Gray Davis designated Bridges's birthday, July 28, as Harry Bridges Day. That day Nancy Pelosi was among those who gathered on the plaza in front of the San Francisco Ferry Building—once site of the hated shape-up—for its renaming as Harry Bridges Plaza. Plans for a ten-foot-tall statue of Bridges for that site have languished from then to now—2022—due to lack of funds. Busts of Bridges stand in the entry to the international offices and in a park along Harbor Boulevard in San Pedro. A larger-than-life-size bronze statue of Bridges was unveiled in the Local 23 hall (Tacoma) in 2016, and a life-size bronze statue of Bridges was placed outside the Local 13 dispatch hall in Wilmington in 2019. Harry Bridges Boulevard runs along part of the Wilmington waterfront near the Harry Bridges School, a K–8 public school. In Australia the narrow street that runs behind the building on Macauley Road, Kensington, where Bridges was born is now Bridges Lane.

The most powerful monument to Bridges, of course, is the ILWU itself. While facing major challenges, the ILWU remains strong, now claiming some forty-two thousand members in the five Pacific Coast states, thirty-five hundred in the autonomous Inland Boatmen's Union, and fourteen thousand in ILWU-Canada. The union continues to stand on the Left of organized labor in the United States. On May 1, 2008, the longshore division stopped work for eight hours to protest the ongoing war in Afghanistan. In 2016 it was one of only five U.S. unions that endorsed Bernie Sanders in the Democratic primaries. On June 19 (Juneteenth), 2020, all longshore workers stood down and marched to honor Black lives. The ILWU remains highly democratic, including the longshore caucus. In the 2018 election for international officers, all four positions were contested, and the vote for president was decided by 52–48 percent. Its members and officers are diverse by race, ethnicity, and gender. And Bridges continues to be a touchstone for members and officers of the ILWU.[12]

Notes

Abbreviations

See also the list of abbreviations in the front matter.

AA   Australian Archives, Mitchell, ACT, Australia
AAS   Anglo-American Secretariat, also called the Anglo-American
                   Lander Secretariat, the intermediary body between the Eng-
                   lish-speaking Communist Parties and the Executive Com-
                   mittee of the Comintern
b   box
Bridges FBI file   copy in possession of the author, to be transferred to LARC
Bridges INS file   Harry Bridges INS file, National Archives, San Bruno, CA
Bridges Papers   Harry Bridges Papers, Labor Archives and Research Center,
                   San Francisco State University
Butlin Archives   Noel Butlin Archives Centre, Australian National University,
                   Canberra, ACT, Australia
Call-Bulletin   *San Francisco Call-Bulletin*
Chronicle   *San Francisco Chronicle*
Dispatcher   (San Francisco) *Dispatcher*, official newspaper of the ILWU
                   after 1942
Einstein   Charles Einstein interviews of Harry Bridges cited with their
                   number
Examiner   *San Francisco Examiner*
f   file or folder
Gladstein Papers   Harry Renton Bridges Papers, Southern California Library,
                   Los Angeles. These are files given by Richard Gladstein or his
                   heirs. They should properly be called the Gladstein Papers,
                   which is the designation I have used.
illeg.   illegible

ILWU Library	Anne Rand Library, International Longshore and Warehouse Union, San Francisco
interview	one of my interviews with Harry Bridges
LARC	Labor Archives and Research Center, San Francisco State University
LAT	*Los Angeles Times*
LC	Library of Congress
NA	National Archives
News	*San Francisco News*
NSB	Noriko Sawada Bridges interviews of Harry Bridges cited with their number or other distinguishing mark
NSBF Papers	Noriko Sawada Bridges Flynn Papers, LARC
NYT	*New York Times*
PCL	*Pacific Coast Longshoreman* (Tacoma), official newspaper of the ILA Pacific Coast District
PROV	Public Record Office of Victoria, North Melbourne, Victoria, Australia
PW	*People's World* (San Francisco)
RGASPI	*Rossiiskii gosudarstvennyi arkhiv sotsial'no-politicheskoi istorii* (Russian State Archive of Socio-Political History), Moscow
SFLC	San Francisco Labor Council
SLV	State Library of Victoria, Melbourne, Victoria, Australia
Voice	*Voice of the Federation* (San Francisco), official newspaper of the Maritime Federation of the Pacific Coast
WHS	Wisconsin Historical Society

Chapter 1. From Australia to the San Francisco Docks

1. *NYT*, Jan. 18, 1978, A14; *Washington Post*, Jan. 17, 1978, B1, B3. In "Constructing a Radical Identity: History, Memory, and the Seafaring Stories of Harry Bridges," *Pacific Historical Review* 70 (2001): 571–600, I examine Bridges's seafaring stories with the most political content and conclude they never took place. I do not present those stories here. Bridges's situation in 1940, under threat of deportation, may have led him to embellish, combine, or construct stories about his youth that corresponded with his contemporary politics—that is, his account in 1940 of events during his youth may not explain his adult politics, but instead his adult politics as of 1940 may explain his account of events during his youth.

2. Genealogical material, including the marriage registration of Alfred Bridges and Julia Dorgan, are in f1, b1, Harry Bridges Papers, LARC; Dorothy McNaught, interviewed by Robert Cherny, July 2, 1997, hereinafter McNaught interview; *Fitzroy City Press*, May 25, 1894, 2. The Baptism Register of St. Brendan's Church, Kensington, lists his birth date as July 31, 1901, but the official register of births is filled with misinformation. It lists his name as Alfred Renton Byrant [*sic*] Bridges and his date of birth as July 6, 1901. The information was provided by an "authorized agent," who seems to have provided the wrong birth date, added another middle name that does not appear in the christening

record, and provided an erroneous birthplace for the senior Alfred. The birth registration is in f1, b1, Bridges Papers.

3. *Economist*, Mar. 6, 1993, 15; James Grant and Geoffrey Serle, *The Melbourne Scene: 1803–1956* (Melbourne: Melbourne University Press, 1957), esp. 196–198, 202; Russel Ward, *The History of Australia: The Twentieth Century* (New York: Harper & Row, 1977), esp. 12, 18, 20.

4. Much of the information about the Bridges family in this and succeeding chapters comes from three sets of interviews with Harry Bridges. Norika Sawada "Nikki" Bridges, his wife, conducted one set of interviews shortly after Bridges retired from the union presidency; they are designated hereinafter as "NSB" with their number or other distinguishing mark. Shortly after, Charles Einstein conducted a second set of interviews; they are designated as "Einstein" with the number. I conducted the third set, which are described hereinafter as "interview" with the date. Any citation to "interview" without a designation of the interviewee indicates one of my interviews with Harry Bridges. For this information, see NSB HB; interview, Dec. 19, 1985; Einstein 1; and city directory listings.

5. *Fitzroy City Press*, May 25, 1894, 2; *Argus* (Melbourne), June 15, 1901, 9; NSB HB, 1; Einstein 36, 49; McNaught interview; obituary of A. S. [*sic*] Bridges, *Essendon Gazette*, Nov. 21, 1946, 6; City of Melbourne Rate Books, Borough of Flemington and Kensington, 1904–5 and 1905, SLV. The residential address of the Bridges family and the business listings for both Alfred and Julia can be traced in the various city directories.

6. The Bridges Block looks much the same today (2020). McNaught interview. City directories have different addresses for the family nearly every year from 1914 through 1921.

7. NSB 1, HB; Einstein 22, 46; interview, Dec. 19, 1985; McNaught interview; letter, Lucy to Renton and Nikki, Sept. 17, 1964, Bridges Papers, f5, b1; obituary of A. S. [*sic*] Bridges.

8. Interview, Dec. 19, 1985; McNaught interview; Einstein 1; NSB 1; letters, Harry Bridges to Nikki Bridges, Oct. 3, 12, 1967, f3, b2, Bridges Papers.

9. Letter, Harry Bridges to C. H. Fitzgibbon, Dec. 18, 1963, item 98, Waterside Workers Federation of Australia collection, N114, Butlin Archives, Australia National University; interview, Dec. 19, 1985; Einstein 18, 21. For Mannix, see Brenda Niall, *Mannix* (Melbourne: Text, 2015), esp. 68–74; and Colm Kiernan, *Daniel Mannix and Ireland* (Morwell, VIC: Alella Books, 1984), 79, which quotes Mannix as saying that the four years he spent as a parish priest were the happiest of his life.

10. NSB HB and Einstein 1; report on Australian stamps and the postal rate to England, f17, b1, Bridges Papers. Bridges recalled that he was between six and eleven years old at the time; it must have taken place in January 1913, when he was eleven. Given the history of Australian postage stamps, there are several weeks in early January 1913 when conditions corresponded to Bridges's memory. Earlier, his father had run the post office. See Australian Post Office, *Australian Postage Stamps: The Early Commonwealth Period and the Kangaroo and Map Series* (pamphlet, 1968), 9; and Geoff Kellow, *The Stamps of Victoria* (Melbourne: B&K Philatelic, 1990), chap. 16. For the Labour politician's comment, see Brian Lewis, *Our War* (Carlton, VIC: Melbourne University Press, 1980), 2.

11. Einstein 18; NSB 1, HB; interview, Dec. 19, 1985; L. N. Short, "Education," in *The Australian Encyclopedia*, 3rd ed., rev. (Sydney: Grolier Society of Australia, 1979), 2:320; Peter Ling, *Education Policy in Australia, 1880–1914* (Melbourne: Philip Institute of Technology, Centre for Youth and Community Studies, 1984), 167–69.

12. Einstein 1, 4, 18, 46; NSB HB, 1; Register, Christian Brothers' School, St. Mary's, West Melbourne; A. M. Laughton and T. S. Hall, *Handbook to Victoria* (Melbourne: Albert J. Mullett, Government Printer, 1914), 109, 119; B. M. Coldrey, "The Influence of Irish Traditions on the Policies and Professional Training of the Christian Brothers in Victoria, 1868–1930, in the Context of Their Developing Secondary Educational System" (master's thesis, University of Melbourne, 1973), esp. 203–4, 216–18; letters to Bridges from his sisters, f15, b1, Bridges Papers. The name that appears on the Christian Brothers' register is "Bridges Benton A.," but the address, parent's name, and birthday (although not the birth year) are all correct. Bridges always recalled that he had changed his name as a part of confirmation and that he was confirmed under the name Harry Renton Bridges, but there is no record at St. Brendan's of Bridges's confirmation (letter, William A. Jordan, P.P., to Robert Cherny, n.d.). Bridges also recalled that Mannix had something to do with his confirmation, which likely came during the years when Mannix was a parish priest at St. Mary's, raising the possibility that he was confirmed there. See letter, Bridges to C. H. Fitzgibbon, Dec. 18, 1963, unit 98, Waterside Workers Federation Collection, Noel Butlin Archives Center, Australian National University.

13. Einstein 4, 46; NSB 1, HB; city directories; Bridges, Henry Renton Nicholson, file, Personnel Dossiers for 1st Australian Imperial Forces ex-service members, series B2455, World War I Personnel Records Service, AA; John Merritt, *The Making of the AWU* (Melbourne: Oxford University Press, 1986), 341.

14. Interview, Nov. 2, 1986; Einstein 4; copies of letters, Nikki to Dot, Nov. 18, 1980, and Bridges to George, Mar. 30, 1986, f15, b1, Bridges Papers; P. L. Murray, comp., *Official Records of the Australian Military Contingents to the War in South Africa* (Melbourne: Government Printer, 1911).

15. Einstein 4; *Yea Chronicle*, Aug. 24, 1916; Alec H. Chisholm, comp. and ed., *Who's Who in Australia*, 13th ed. (Melbourne: Herald and Weekly Times, 1947), 169.

16. J. T. Sutcliffe, *A History of Trade Unionism in Australia* (Melbourne: Macmillan, 1921), 1; Victor S. Clark, *The Labour Movement in Australasia: A Study in Social-Democracy* (New York: Henry Holt, 1906), 57, 58; Brian Fitzpatrick, *A Short History of the Australian Labor Movement*, rev. ed. (Melbourne: Rawson's Bookshop, 1944), 26; Ian Turner, *Industrial Labour and Politics: The Dynamics of the Labor Movement in Eastern Australia, 1900–1921* (Canberra: Australian National University, 1965), 11–12; Robin Gollan, *Radical and Working Class Politics: A Study of Eastern Australia, 1850–1910* (Parkville, VIC: Melbourne University Press, 1960), 69–72, 78, 80–81.

17. Frank Bongiorno, *The People's Party: Victorian Labor and the Radical Tradition, 1875–1914* (Carlton, VIC: Melbourne University Press, 1996), chaps. 1, 2, 6; Myra Willard, *History of the White Australia Policy to 1920* (Carlton, VIC: Melbourne University Press, 1923), esp. 120–21, 125–26, 132–33; Henry Gyles Turner, *The First Decade of the Australian Commonwealth: A Chronicle of Contemporary Politics, 1901–1910* (Melbourne:

Mason, Firth, and McCutcheon, 1911), 27–33; I. Turner, *Industrial Labour and Politics*, 26, 35–40; R. Noel Ebbels, comp., *The Australian Labor Movement, 1850–1907* (Sydney: Australasian Book Society, 1960), 222–23.

18. Ward, *History of Australia*, 75–82; interview, Dec. 19, 1985.

19. Michael McKernan, *The Australian People and the Great War* (Sydney: William Collins, 1984), 1–2; Stuart Macintyre, *1901–1942: The Succeeding Age*, vol. 4 of *The Oxford History of Australia*, ed. Geoffrey Bolton (Melbourne: Oxford University Press, 1986), chaps. 7–8, esp. 177–82.

20. Alfred E. Bridges, "When Britannia Wants a Soldier" (Melbourne: L. F. Collin, n.d.), Mitchell Library, Sydney; *Theatre Magazine*, Nov. 1, 1915; Einstein 1; interview, Dec. 19, 1985.

21. Australian troops had a casualty rate of 65 percent, compared to 59 percent for New Zealand troops, 50 percent for Canada, and 47 percent for the United Kingdom. L. C. F. Turner, *The Great War, 1914–1918* (Melbourne: F. W. Cheshire, 1971), n.p.; "Our Valiant Dead," *Age* (Melbourne), Apr. 10, 1916, 8; *Yea Chronicle*, Aug. 24, 1916, 3, and Sept. 21, 1916, 3.

22. NSB HB, 1, 7; Einstein 5, 49; McNaught interview; Register, Christian Brothers' School, St. Mary's, West Melbourne; "To Whom It May Concern" from T. S. Burke, secretary, Sands and McDougall, July 21, 1917, f2, b1, Bridges Papers; *Essendon Gazette*, July 5, 1934, 1; letter, Wm. J. Mackay to W. J. Quinn, Feb. 8, 1937, file c-6405274, b6, Bridges INS file; *Graphic of Australia*, Feb. 18, 1916, 2, and Mar. 10, 1917.

23. Interview, Dec. 19, 1985; Einstein 5, 18; NSB 1; *Age* (Melbourne), Sept. 27, 1967, 1.

24. NSB HB; Niall, *Mannix*, 75–79. Mannix's speech was reported in the *Advocate* on May 6, 1916, and reprinted in E. L. Robson, *Australia and the Great War, 1914–1918* (South Melbourne: Macmillan of Australia, 1970), 62–63; Ward, *History of Australia*, 102, 118. Correspondence with the only surviving member of Renton's seven children failed to elicit anything of his mother's or aunts' sentiments toward the war or their Irish nationalism. Letter, Thelma D. Bridges, on behalf of George Bridges, to Robert Cherny, June 16, 1990.

25. Interview, Dec. 19, 1985; Einstein 3, 12; Laurence F. Fitzhardinge, *William Morris Hughes: A Political Biography*, 2 vols. (Sydney: Angus & Robertson, 1979), 2:171–97; McKernan, *Australian People and the Great War*, 7; Ward, *History of Australia*, 111, 113; I. Turner, *Industrial Labour and Politics*, 83–84; Niall, *Mannix*, 85–88; Robson, *Australia and the Great War*, 72–76; Cyril Bryan, *Archbishop Mannix: Champion of Australian Democracy* (Melbourne: Advocate Press, 1918), 61–62.

26. Ward, *History of Australia*, 113–14, 116–17, 121–22; Fitzhardinge, *William Morris Hughes*, 2:213, 225–34; I. Turner, *Industrial Labour and Politics*, 113–16; letter, Thelma D. Bridges, on behalf of George Bridges.

27. Macintyre, *1901–1942*, 163, 169–70; W. Farmer Whyte, *William Morris Hughes: His Life and Times* (Sydney: Angus and Robertson, 1957), 301, 336–40, 348–49.

28. NSB 7; interview, Dec. 19, 1985; Rupert Lockwood, *Ship to Shore: A History of Melbourne's Waterfront and Its Union Struggles* (Sydney: Hale and Iremonger, 1990), 134–46, 151; Macintyre, *1901–1942*, 170; McKernan, *Australian People and the Great War*, 8; Fitzhardinge, *Hughes*, 2:271.

29. Lockwood, *Ship to Shore*, 145–57; *Age* (Melbourne), Aug. 28, 1917, 5, and Aug. 20, 1917, 8; Fitzhardinge, *Hughes*, 2:271, 273–74; Lockwood, *Ship to Shore*, 164–71; Macintyre, *1901–1942*, 171.

30. NSB 1, 9; Einstein 8, 28; *Maritime Worker* (Sydney), Nov. 8, 1967, 2.

31. NSB 9; Einstein 3; Anne Summers, "The Unwritten History of Adela Pankhurst Walsh," *Hecate* 4 (1978): 45; *Argus* (Melbourne), daily from Aug. 16 through Oct. 10, 1917; Macintyre, *1901–1942*, 171–72; Lockwood, *Ship to Shore*, 159–60, 172–78; *Argus* (Melbourne), Oct. 2, 1917, 4; Oct. 12, 1917, 6; Nov. 3, 1917, 22; Nov. 21, 13; Nov. 30, 9; Jan. 22, 1918, 4; Brian Fitzpatrick and Rowan J. Cahill, *The Seamen's Union of Australia: A History* (Sydney: Seamen's Union of Australia, 1981), 50; "Conscription," *Recorder* (Melbourne Branch, Australian Society for the Study of Labour History) 2, no. 4 (1966): 2–4.

32. Brian Lewis, *Our War* (Carlton: Melbourne University Press, 1980), 274; Niall, *Mannix*, 89–96; Bryan, *Mannix*, 128–66, esp. 130, 158, 162; NSB 9; Einstein 3; Robson, *Australia and the Great War*, 98.

33. NSB 9; Einstein 3; "Biographical Notes on Members of the Victorian Socialist Party, Part II," *Recorder* (Melbourne Branch, Australian Society for the Study of Labor History) 82 (June 1976): 7; Fitzpatrick and Cahill, *Seamen's Union of Australia*, 53; Cherny interview, Sept. 2, 1986.

34. Interview, Dec. 19, 1985; NSB 1; Einstein 12; Robson, *Australia and the Great War*, 65; Ernest Scott, *Australia during the War*, vol. 11 of *Official History of Australia in the War of 1914–1918*, ed. Robert O'Neill (St. Lucia, Queensland: University of Queensland Press, 1989), 510–12; Marnie Haig-Muir, "The Economy at War," in *Australia's War, 1914–1918*, ed. Joan Beaumont (St. Leonards, NSW: Allen and Unwin Australia, 1995), 119.

35. McNaught interview; NSB 1; interviews, Dec. 19, 1985, and Nov. 2, 1986; city directories.

36. Interview, Dec. 19, 1985; Einstein 18, 39; Alan Villiers, *The Set of the Sails: The Story of a Cape Horn Seaman* (1949; reprint, Albert Park: Heritage Book Group, 1995), 21–22. The First Victorian Sea Scout Troop was probably the organization that Bridges recalled. See Jill Barnard and Jenny Keating, *People's Playground: A History of the Albert Park* (Burwood, VIC: Chandos, 1996), 101. The Ancient Mariners' Club is mentioned in *Age* (Melbourne), Aug. 20, 1917, 8. The Villiers manuscript collection at the National Library of Australia, Canberra, item 46, b5, includes an envelope from Bridges to Villiers, on the back of which Villiers wrote, "Harry Bridges (Australian 'Red' in S.F., USA) was fellow member of Capt. Suffern's pre-sea training school for boys, Albert Park Lake, Melbourne (which got me to sea)."

37. Einstein 6, 8, 39; NSB HB; interview, Jan. 29, 1986; Agreement and Account of Crew [shipping articles] for the *Daisy Knights*, covering Dec. 7, 1917, through Jan. 4, 1918, Mercantile Marine Office records, Articles of Agreement, VPRS No. 566/P, unit 216, PROV, Laverton. See also Cherny, "Constructing a Radical Identity."

38. Discharge certificate from *Lialeeta*, Jan. 18, 1919, f2, b1, Bridges Papers; office copy, Agreement and Account of Crew, *Lialeeta*, July 5, 1918, VPRS No. 566/P, unit 218, PROV Laverton; NSB HB; interview, Mar. 5, 1986; Einstein 6. For the *Lialeeta*, see Harold Salter, *Bass Strait Ketches* (Hobart: St. David's Park, 1991), 163–64, 246; and Garry Kerr, *The Tasmanian Trading Ketch: An Illustrated Oral History* (Victoria: Mains'l Books, 1987), 17, 21, 37, 87.

39. NSB 5, 6, 20; interviews, Jan. 29 and Mar. 5, 1986; Einstein 6, 8; shipping articles, *Daisy Knights*. When Bridges signed onto the *Daisy Knights* on December 12, 1917, he listed his age correctly as sixteen. Signing on the *Sara Hunter* a month later, he claimed to be eighteen. In July 1918, shortly before his seventeenth birthday, he gave his age as seventeen when signing onto the *Lialeeta*. When signing onto the *Southern Cross* on January 30, 1919, he added a year, listing his age as eighteen. A month later, signing onto the *Valmarie*, he listed his age as nineteen. See shipping articles for *Sara Hunter*, Jan. 7, 1918; *Lialeeta*, July 5, 1918; *Southern Cross*, Jan. 30, 1919; and *Valmarie*, Feb. 28, 1919, all in VPRS no. 566/P, units 215–18, 227, PROV Laverton.

40. Interview, Mar. 5, 1986; NSB 5; Einstein 5, 8.

41. Interview, Mar. 5, 1986; Einstein 4.

42. NSB HB, 9; Einstein 39; interviews Jan. 29, 1986, May 7, 1986; Salter, *Bass Strait Ketches*, 23, 90, 163–64, 246.

43. NSB 5; Einstein 39, 43; discharge certificate, *Valmarie*, Oct. 11, 1919, f2, b1, Bridges Papers; Agreement and Account of Crew for *Valmarie*, Feb. 28, 1919, through Oct. 8, 1919, VPRS No. 566/P, unit 227, PROV Laverton; SUA Contribution books for New South Wales, Victoria, and South Australia, 1912–22, and transfer books for Tasmania, 1916–40, and New Zealand, 1916–22, items 34/3–5, 10, 12, 19, 20, Seamen's Union of Australia collection, Collection E183, Butlin Archives. For the strike, see Fitzpatrick and Cahill, *Seamen's Union of Australia*, 50; and Macintyre, *1901–1942*, 183. Shipping articles had a place to paste in the terms of the most recent arbitration award, but none of the articles for Bridges's vessels carried those provisions.

44. NSB 5; Einstein 39, 43; *Argus* (Melbourne), Oct. 1, 1919, 14; Oct. 2, 1919, 6; Oct. 22, 1919, 12; Oct. 23, 1919, 8; Oct. 25, 1919, 20; Summons to Witness, Oct. 16, 1919, f2, b1, Bridges Papers; Judgment of the Court of Marine Inquiry re No. 222, Stranding of the British Ship *Valmarie*, Melbourne, Oct. 21, 1919; copy of letter, HB to "Skipper," Sept. 1, 1966, f1, b9, Bridges Papers.

45. NSB HB; Einstein 9.

46. NSB 5; Einstein 5, 8, discharge certificate from *Valmarie*, Jan. 1, 1920, f2, b1, Bridges Papers. Bridges may have paid union dues in joining the crew of the *Ysabel* both because it was likely covered by the arbitration award and because he claimed to have been an ASU member shortly after leaving that vessel.

47. Interviews, Jan. 29, 1986 and Mar. 5, 1986; Einstein 5; NSB 5; arrival and departure record for the *Ysabel*, 1920, Marine Exchange Records, J. Porter Shaw Library, National Maritime Museum, San Francisco; statement of George Robert Maynard, Dec. 11, 1940, attached to report of [name redacted], Dec. 22, 1940, file 39-915-705, Bridges FBI file; Application for Certificate of Service as Able Seaman, Apr. 21, 1920; Certificate of Service to Able Seaman, Apr. 21, 1920; Pass to Permit Alien to Land (copy), Apr. 24, Bridges [Gladstein] Papers, Southern California Library. Bridges always remembered that he had transferred his membership from the SUA to the SUP, but his SUP membership card does not indicate that.

48. Interviews, Mar. 5, 1986, and Jan. 29, 1988; Einstein 6; NSB 6; *Delisle* discharge certificate, Sept. 24, 1920, f2, b1, Bridges Papers; testimony of Harry Bridges, Aug. 13, 1934, *Proceedings Before the National Longshoremen's Board, filed as Coast Arbitration Case*, vol. 3, *Transcripts (Bridges)*, 1934 Series, ILWU Library, hereinafter Bridges Testimony,

1934; Marine Exchange records for *Silver Shell*, Maritime Museum Library; for the *Silver Shell* and *Delisle*, see American Bureau of Shipping, *Record of American and Foreign Shipping: 1921* (New York: American Bureau of Shipping, 1921), 264, 818.

49. Interview Jan. 29, 1986; Einstein 18, 21, 22.

50. There is a rich historiography on these topics. On the SUP, see Paul S. Taylor, *The Sailors' Union of the Pacific* (New York: Ronald Press, 1923); Peter B. Gill and Ottilie Dombroff, "History of the Sailors' Union of the Pacific," typed manuscript, ca. 1942, carton 3, Paul Scharrenberg Papers, Bancroft Library, University of California, Berkeley; Paul Scharrenberg, "History of the Sailors' Union of the Pacific," typed manuscript, ca. 1960, carton 3, Scharrenberg Papers; Hyman Weintraub, *Andrew Furuseth: Emancipator of the Seamen* (Berkeley: University of California Press, 1959); and Stephen Schwartz, *Brotherhood of the Sea: A History of the Sailors' Union of the Pacific, 1885–1985* (New Brunswick, NJ: Transaction Books for the SUP, 1986). On the 1901 strike and the ULP, see Robert E. L. Knight, *Industrial Relations in the San Francisco Bay Area, 1900–1918* (Berkeley: University of California Press, 1960); Michael Kazin, *Barons of Labor: The San Francisco Building Trades Council and Union Power in the Progressive Era* (Urbana: University of Chicago Press, 1987); Walton Bean, *Boss Ruef's San Francisco: The Story of the Union Labor Party, Big Business, and the Graft Prosecution* (Berkeley: University of California Press, 1952); Jules Tygiel, "'Where Unionism Holds Undisputed Sway': A Reappraisal of San Francisco's Union Labor Party," *California History* 62 (1983): 196–215; and William Issel and Robert W. Cherny, *San Francisco, 1865–1932: Politics, Power, and Urban Development* (Berkeley: University of California Press, 1986).

51. Robert K. Murray, *Red Scare: A Study of National Hysteria, 1919–1920* (Minneapolis: University of Minnesota Press, 1955).

52. Interview, Mar. 5, 1986; NSB 7; Einstein 7, 8; Marine Exchange Records, Maritime Museum; discharge certificate, Sept. 24, 1920, f2, b1, Bridges Papers; Bridges Testimony, 1934; Taylor, *Sailors' Union of the Pacific*, 102–4.

53. NSB 7, 8; interview, May 7, 1986; Einstein 3; note from Nikki Bridges to author, May 1989; Henry [*sic*] R. Bridges Eastern and Gulf membership card for 1921 (Atlantic No. 4585), f2, b1, Bridges Papers, LARC.

54. Dubofsky, *We Shall Be All: A History of the Industrial Workers of the World* (New York: Quadrangle, 1969).

55. NSB 9.

56. NSB 8; interviews, Mar. 5 and May 7, 1986.

57. NSB 8, 9.

58. Weintraub, *Andrew Furuseth*, 156–58.

59. Bridges Testimony, 1934, 165; *New Orleans Times-Picayune* and *New Orleans States*, May 2–May 26, 1921.

60. Bridges Testimony, 1934, 165; Bridges Testimony, Transcript of Hearing before Charles Sears, in the Matter of Harry Bridges, Immigration and Naturalization Service Case No. 55973/217, vol. 35 (May 29, 1941), 5705. Bridges's union book was stamped by the New Orleans delegate for April, May, and June dues on May 27, 1921 (f2, b1, Bridges Papers). For his arrest, see NSB 9; and interview, May 7, 1986.

61. NSB 8; *New Orleans States*, May 29, 1921, 1, and June 4, 1921, 3; *New Orleans Times-Picayune*, June 1, 1921, 1, and June 2, 1921, 1.

62. Interview, May 7, 1986; *New Orleans States*, June 4, 1921, 3.

63. *New Orleans Times-Picayune*, May 27–June 23, 1921; *New Orleans States*, June 6–15, 1921; Weintraub, *Andrew Furuseth*, 159.

64. Interviews, Jan. 29, 1986, May 7, 1986; NSB 8; Einstein 8, 59. In all these interviews, Bridges recalled his tramping trip to Mexico as after the strike, and I have followed that chronology. His Alien Seaman's Identification Card indicates he was in New Orleans in late May, following the arrival of the *James Timson* (f2, b1, Bridges Papers). Bridges recalled the trip to Mexico as lasting three or four months, but other verified dates for 1921 preclude a trip of that length. The probable date of his arrest is June 11. Thus, the trip to Mexico, return, and hospitalization could not have been more than four weeks. The trip from Bluefields to New Orleans by ship would have taken something less than a week, leaving about three weeks to tramp from New Orleans to Bluefields, a distance of some 2,700 miles or about 130 miles per day. Given his memory of constant travel rather than staying in any one place and of hitching rides on everything from trucks to oxcarts, the itinerary is possible between June 11 and July 13.

65. Copy of Declaration of Intention, f1, b10, Bridges Papers, Southern California Library; Bridges Testimony, 1934, 165–66; letter of recommendation from F. H. Rylander, chief officer of the SS *Lake Falama*, Oct. 7, 1921, f2, b1, Bridges Papers; Bridges Testimony, Sears Hearing, vol. 35 (May 29, 1941), 7383–86; *El Dorado* shipping articles, Aug. 9 and Dec. 2, 1921, SUP Archives; NSB 9.

66. Weintraub, *Andrew Furuseth*, 160–63; Taylor, *Sailors' Union of the Pacific*, 142–46; Schwartz, *Brotherhood of the Sea*, 59; *Labor Clarion*, Sept. 16, 1912, 3, 6; Nov. 11, 1921, 14; Dec. 16, 1921, 16; Mar. 3, 1922, 6. In 1941 Bridges testified that he left the IWW in early 1922, while still on the *El Dorado*; Bridges Testimony, Sears Hearing, vol. 35 (May 29, 1941), 5705. On NSB 11, however, Bridges recollected leaving the IWW as a result of the SUP newspaper's revelations of employer control, but he dated his departure in 1923. See *Industrial Worker* (Chicago), Feb. 17, 1950, 1, 4.

67. NSB 9.

68. NSB 10, 11; discharge certificate, *Eldorado*, Feb. 24, 1922, f2, b1, Bridges Papers; Report of [name redacted], Nov. 29, 1940, 2, 37–58, file 391-515-672, Bridges FBI file.

69. NSB 10, 11; Bridges Testimony, 1934, 166, ILWU Library; certificate of discharge from Marine Hospital No. 19, May 15, 1922, f2, b1, Bridges Papers, LARC; citizenship applications and related papers, f1, b10, and f35, b11, Bridges Papers, Southern California Library. There is extensive information about Agnes, her first child, her first marriage, her second child, and her family in Oregon in report of [name redacted], Nov. 20, 1940, file 301-515-672, 21–27, Bridges FBI file; and Lionel Youst, "Harry and Agnes Bridges: A Couple at Odds, " *Pacific Northwest Quarterly* 106 (2015): 68–83.

70. NSB 10; discharge from the United States Coast and Geodetic Survey, Oct. 4, 1922, f2, b1, Bridges Papers.

Chapter 2. San Francisco Longshoreman

1. For Bridges's work experiences in the 1920s and the nature of longshoring at the time, see his testimony in 1934 before the National Longshoremen's Board: Proceedings of the National Longshoremen's Board, 1934, hearing of August 13, Arbitration

Collection of the Institute of Industrial Relations, University of California, Berkeley, LARC, hereinafter NLB proceedings.

2. Bridges Testimony, NLB proceedings, esp. 187, 230; Charles R. Barnes, *The Longshoremen* (1915; reprint, New York: Arno Press, 1977), chap. 4, esp. 31–33; J. K. Novins, "First in Cargo Handling," *San Francisco Business* 20 (Aug. 13, 1930): 8–10; U.S. Bureau of Labor Statistics, "Longshore Labor Conditions in the United States—Part I," *Monthly Labor Review* 31 (Oct. 1930): 811–30, and "Part II: Longshore Labor Conditions in Major Ports of the United States," *Monthly Labor Review* 31 (Nov. 1930): 1055–69. For a good explanation of the work of the ship clerk, see Don Watson oral history, conducted by Harvey Schwartz, 1994, LARC.

3. Bridges Testimony, NLB proceedings, esp. 178–79.

4. Bureau of Labor Statistics, "Longshore Labor Conditions, Part I," 812; William W. Pilcher, *The Portland Longshoremen: A Dispersed Urban Community* (New York: Holt, Rinehart, and Winston, 1972), 21; Herb Mills, "The San Francisco Waterfront: The Social Consequences of Industrial Modernization, Part One: 'The Good Old Days,'" *Urban Life* 5 (1976): 234.

5. Bridges Testimony, NLB proceedings, 180, 181, 183, 187, 188; Barnes, *The Longshoremen*, 36–40, 53.

6. Wage Scale and Working Rules of the Longshoremen's Association, and Wage Scale and Working Rules of the Riggers' and Stevedores' Union, History file, Local 10 series, ILWU Library; Novins, "First in Cargo Handling," 8, 17.

7. California, Board of State Harbor Commissioners, *Biennial Report: July 1, 1926, to June 30, 1928* (Sacramento: California State Printing Office, 1928), 9; *Report: 1922–1924*, esp. 60–65; *1926–28*, 58–73; San Francisco Chamber of Commerce, "San Francisco," *Crocker-Langley San Francisco City Directory: 1929* (San Francisco: R. L. Polk, 1929), 13; Chamber of Commerce, "San Francisco," *City Directory: 1936*, 12.

8. NSB tape 14; Sanborn Map Company, *Insurance Maps of San Francisco* (New York: Sanborn Map, 1913–14, updated to 1929), vols. 1, 2, 6, and 8, Bancroft Library, University of California, Berkeley (hereinafter Sanborn Maps); Harbor Commissioners, *Report: 1920–22*, esp. the map attached at the end; same, for 1922–24, 69.

9. Sanborn Maps, vols. 1, 2, 6, 8; Harbor Commissioners, *Report: 1920–22*, esp. the map attached at the end; same, for 1922–24, 69.

10. American-Hawaiian Steamship Company Papers, Huntington Library; [Boris Stern], U.S. Department of Labor, Bureau of Labor Statistics, *Bulletin No. 550 (February 1932), Cargo Handling and Longshore Labor Conditions* (Washington, DC: Government Printing Office, 1932), 55, 59.

11. Bridges Testimony, 167, 212, 213, NLB proceedings; Injury Frequency Comparison, Employers' Exhibit No. E, NLB Proceedings; Accidents reported under Longshoremen's and Harbor Workers' Compensation Act during the period from July 1, 1927, to June 30, 1933, File: Coast Arbitration NLB Exhibits—Not Used; Types of Accidents, Employers' Exhibit No. C, NLB proceedings; David F. Selvin, *A Terrible Anger: The 1934 Waterfront and General Strikes in San Francisco* (Detroit: Wayne State University Press, 1996), 41–42; Bridges Testimony, 1939 deportation hearing, 3062. The Longshoremen's and Harbor Workers' Compensation Act of 1927 apparently produced annual reports on claims, but I have not found data on deaths by cause and port.

12. Bridges Testimony, 174–77, NLB proceedings.

13. NSB 21.

14. Robert Coleman Francis, "A History of Labor on the San Francisco Waterfront" (PhD diss., University of California, Berkeley, 1934), 14–17, 32–33, 58, 87, 91. *The Oxford English Dictionary* records the first American usage of *longshoreman* as coming in James Bryce's *American Commonwealth* (1888), in a section dealing with San Francisco in the 1870s.

15. Francis, "History of Labor," 132–35, 144–48, 182–91. Agreement by and between the Members of the Waterfront Employers' Union, Longshoremen's Exhibit No. 61, NLB proceedings; William Issel and Robert W. Cherny, *San Francisco, 1865–1932: Politics, Power, and Urban Development* (Berkeley: University of California Press, 1986), 92–94; Robert Edward Lee Knight, *Industrial Relations in the San Francisco Bay Area, 1900–1918* (Berkeley: University of California Press, 1960), 302–7; R&S Minutes, Jan. 17, 1916, quoted in Mary Renfro, "The Decline and Fall of the Riggers' and Stevedores' Union of San Francisco: A History of the Years 1916 through 1919" (senior honors thesis, San Francisco State University, 1996), 5; Francis, "History of Labor," 159–60. Working Rules that took effect December 1, 1912, specified a minimum of six hold men and a maximum sling weight of twelve hundred pounds; the Working Rules that took effect after the 1916 strike did not specify gang size or load weight. Wage Schedule and Working Rules, Nov. 25, 1912, and Wage Scale and Working Rules, July 1, 1918, History file, Local 10 series, ILWU Library.

16. Renfro, "Riggers and Stevedores," 15–27, esp. 27.

17. Sam Kagel, "A Right Wing Dual Union" (unpublished manuscript, 1930; copy in possession of the author); Renfro, "Riggers and Stevedores."

18. *Labor Clarion*, Aug. 15, 1919.

19. *Labor Clarion*, Aug. 22, 1919, 3, and Sept. 26, 1919, 3; *Chronicle*, Sept. 20, 1919; *Bulletin*, Sept. 25, 1919; Francis, "History of Labor," 159–63; Renfro, "Riggers and Stevedores," 32–38.

20. *Labor Clarion*, Oct. 31, 1919, 6; Nov. 7, 1919, 16; Nov. 14, 1919, 15; Nov. 21, 1919, 10; Renfro, "Riggers and Stevedores," 36–40; Francis, "History of Labor," 173, 174.

21. Francis, "History of Labor," 174–75; Paul Eliel, *Waterfront and General Strikes* (San Francisco: Hooper, 1934), 2; Base Longshoremen'[s] Wages in San Francisco, 1913 to Date, Employers' Exhibit No. S, NLB proceedings; Wage Scale and Working Rates of the Longshoremen's Association, History file, Local 10 Series, ILWU Library; E. Ellison to J. A. O'Connell, Dec. 18, 1919, Waterfront Workers' Federation of the Pacific Coast file, carton 22, Labor Council Records; *Labor Clarion*, Dec. 26, 1919, 12.

22. ILA Local 38-79, *The Truth about the Waterfront: The I.L.A. States Its Case to the Public*, 3rd ed. (pamphlet, San Francisco, ca. 1935), 5–6; *Labor Clarion*, Jan. 30, 1920, 14; July 2, 1920, 10; Aug. 6, 1920, 11; Paul Eliel, "Labor Problems in Our Steamship Business," *Yale Review* 26 (1937): 510–32. In 1930 Sam Kagel, from his perspective on the staff of the Pacific Coast Labor Bureau, called the Blue Book a right-wing dual union; see Kagel, "Right Wing Dual Union."

23. Ottilie Markholt, *Maritime Solidarity: Pacific Coast Unionism, 1929–1938* (Tacoma: Pacific Coast Maritime History Committee, 1998), 20–30.

24. Michael Kazin, *Barons of Labor: The San Francisco Building Trades and Union Power in the Progressive Era* (Urbana: University of Illinois Press, 1987), chaps. 9–10; Issel

and Cherny, *San Francisco, 1865–1932*, 95–98; "Industrial Association" file, carton 10, Labor Council Records; Eric Levy, "The 1926 San Francisco Carpenters' Strike" (master's thesis, San Francisco State University, 1986).

25. Bridges Testimony, 1934, 232, ILWU Library; NSB 10, 11.

26. NSB 14; interview, July 28, 1989.

27. *News*, June 20, 1934, 3; Selvin, *Terrible Anger*, 34–36; Bridges Testimony, NLB proceedings, 219–20; NSB 14; Olson quoted in Bruce Nelson, *Workers on the Waterfront: Seamen, Longshoremen, and Unionism in the 1930s* (Urbana: University of Illinois Press, 1988), 106. The charge that bosses solicited bribes and favors became a staple of union organizing: for example, *Waterfront Worker* 1 (May 1933): 5; or Bridges's speech on June 19, 1934, reported in *News*, June 20, 1934, 3; or ILA Local 38-79, *Truth about the Waterfront*, 6. Bridges told me on March 5, 1986, that they may have exaggerated such charges and that he never personally had to pay a kickback or do favors to get hired.

28. Eliel, "Labor Problems in Our Steamship Business," 515–16.

29. B. B. Jones interviewed by Robert Cherny, Sept. 14, 1986; interview, Mar. 5, 1986. See also [Boris Stern], "Employment Conditions and Unemployment Relief: Longshoremen Labor Conditions and Port Decasualization in the United States," *Monthly Labor Review* 37 (1933): 1301.

30. Bridges Testimony, 219–20, NLB proceedings; NSB tape 14; *Germain Bulcke: Longshore Leader and ILWU-Pacific Maritime Association Arbitrator*, interviewed by Estolv Ethan Ward, 1983 (Regional Oral History Office, Bancroft Library, University of California, Berkeley, 1984), 35 (hereinafter Bulcke oral history).

31. NSB 12; Bridges Testimony, NLB proceedings, 224–26, 264–66; Selvin, *Terrible Anger*, 36–37; Base Longshoremens [*sic*] Wages in San Francisco, 1913 to Date, Coast Arbitration Case files, Employee's Exhibits, ILWU Library. One dollar in mid-1925 had about the same purchasing power as more than $16 in mid-2022; all such equivalents throughout this work were calculated using the online consumer-price-index inflation calculator at https://data.bls.gov/cgi-bin/cpicalc.pl.

32. Bridges Testimony, Bridges deportation hearing, 1939, vol. 16, 2566; NSB tape 14; U.S. Department of Commerce, Bureau of the Census, *Fourteenth Census of the United States Taken in the Year 1920*, vol. 4, *Population: 1920: Occupations* (Washington, DC: Government Printing Office, 1923), 195, 230; *Fifteenth Census of the United States: 1930: Population: Occupations by States* (Washington, DC: Government Printing Office, 1933), 4:177, 208. A sample was drawn from the census schedules for 1920 by examining every fifth page of the enumeration districts considered most likely to include longshoremen. Joshua Sides collected the sample data. The sample located 338, or 14.1 percent of the total, and may be expected to be accurate within ±3.6 percentage points at the 80 percent confidence level, ±4.7 percentage points at 90 percent, and ±5.0 percentage points at 95 percent. A comparison of data on nativity and age between the samples and the published census suggests that the sample is, in fact, quite reliable. In the sample, Irish made up the largest single group, with 25 percent of the total. Those born in the United States with parents born in the United States made up 18 percent, followed closely by Scandinavians at 17 percent and Germans at 14 percent. Other groups included British, 6 percent; Italians, 6 percent; Slavic groups (Slovenes the largest), 5 percent; Spanish as mother tongue, 4 percent; and Portuguese, 3 percent.

33. *Fourteenth Census . . . 1920*, vol. 4, *Population: 1920: Occupations*, 1228; table 12, *Fifteenth Census . . . 1930: Population: Occupations*, 4:177, 208; Francis, "History of Labor," 172, 178–79, 182–83; Bulcke oral history, 38; Constitution By-Laws and Dues Book of the Riggers' and Stevedores' Union [1919], History file, Local 10 series, ILWU Library. For the role of race in San Francisco unions, see Alexander Saxton, *The Indispensable Enemy: Labor and the Anti-Chinese Movement in California* (Berkeley: University of California Press, 1971); Kazin, *Barons of Labor*, chap. 6; Knight, *Industrial Relations in the San Francisco Bay Area*, 213–14; and Francis, "History of Labor," 178, 182–83.

34. Interview, July 28, 1989; Mills, "The San Francisco Waterfront, Part One," 225; Pilcher, *Portland Longshoremen*, 25–29, chap. 10.

35. Pilcher, *Portland Longshoremen*, 103–5, 378–80; Henry Schmidt, *Secondary Leadership in the ILWU, 1933–1966*, interview conducted by Miriam F. Stein and Estolv Ethan Ward (Regional Oral History Office, Bancroft Library, University of California, Berkeley, 1983), 30–31 (hereinafter Schmidt oral history), 50.

36. NSB 11; Pilcher, *Portland Longshoremen*, 32; *Labor Clarion*, Dec. 16, 1921, 16; "Strike Bulletin," IWW Collection, f26-23, b26, Labor Archives, Walter Reuther Library, Wayne State University, Detroit.

37. NSB 11, 12; *Labor Clarion*, Mar. 24, 1922, 11; June 9, 1923; June 20, 1924, 10; Aug. 15, 1924, Sept. 5, 1924, 4; July 3, 1925, 12; July 10, 1925, 5; July 17, 1925, 12; July 24, 1925, 12; July 31, 1925, 12; Sept. 25, 1925, 12; "Stevedores Attention," flyer; open letter from Organization Committee, June 26, 1923; "Longshoremen of San Francisco Harbor," Oct. 9, 1924; pamphlet, *Longshoremen of San Francisco Harbor*, Oct. 9, 1924; unsigned copy of letter from "President" and "Secretary" to "Dear Sirs and Bros.," Oct. 16, 1924, History file, Local 10 Series, ILWU Library; Exhibits 40–64, and Employers' Exhibit No. S, NLB Proceedings; E. G. Stein to Lee J. Holman, May 7, 1924, filed under Attacks, Etc./Lee J. Holman: 1934–36, Local 10 series, ILWU Library.

38. NSB 10. Kenneth's last name appears variously as McClay and McCley. FBI agents determined that Kenneth's father used McLay, but the FBI used McClay for Kenneth. Kenneth eventually switched to Brown, his mother's last name when he was born; report of [name redacted], file 39-915-672, 21–23, 42–57, esp. 44, 54, 55, Bridges FBI file.

39. *Los Angeles Examiner*, Aug. 28, 1945, 7; NSB 10, 11; letter, Alexander Simon, M.D., and H. F. Norman, M.D., Langley Porter Clinic, to Preston Devine, Judge of the Superior Court, Sept. 13, 1949, f18, b1, Bridges Papers. Regarding Agnes's pregnancy, see report of [name redacted], file 39-915-672, 39, Bridges FBI file.

40. NSB 12; report of [name redacted], file 39-915-672, 35, 44, 49, 53, Bridges FBI file.

41. NSB 10; summary of key information and dates in Harry's personal life, f1, b10, Bridges Papers, Southern California Library; "Missing Seaman" (flyer), f14, b1, Bridges Papers, LARC; letter, A. W. Robertson to Alfred E. Bridges, July 10, 1925, f14, b1, Bridges Papers, LARC.

42. NSB 11; Karlson quoted in Charles P. Larrowe, *Harry Bridges: The Rise and Fall of Radical Labor in the United States* (New York: Lawrence Hill, 1972), 11; Selvin, *Terrible Anger*, 37; NSB 13.

43. Bridges Testimony, 1934, 168–70, 173; NSB tapes 11, 12; Schmidt oral history, 30–31; *News*, June 23, 1934, 3. On NSB 11, Bridges states that "we bought the shack" on Alpha Street, where they are recorded in the 1928 city directory; however, San Francisco city

assessor's records, 1914–38, fail to indicate either Harry or Agnes as owners. The 1930 census, accessed through Ancestry.com, confirms that they were renters.

44. Copy of Form 2214, Preliminary Form for Petition for Naturalization; Copy of Declaration of Intention, fl. b10; f35, b11, Bridges Papers, Southern California Library; postcard from Naturalization Service, postmarked July 31, 1928, with appointment date of Aug. 3, f3, b1, Bridges Papers, LARC. FBI interviews with those intended as Bridges's witnesses confirm this account of his failure to complete his citizenship filing; see report of [name redacted], Nov. 29, 1940, file 391-515-672, 61, 71, Bridges FBI file.

45. NSB 11; Bridges Testimony, 166–70, 267, NLB proceedings; Olson quoted in Bruce Nelson, *Workers on the Waterfront: Seamen, Longshoremen, and Unionism in the 1930s* (Urbana: University of Illinois Press, 1988), 106; Bridges Testimony, 1939 deportation hearing, 3068; Bulcke oral history, 35–36.

46. Bulcke oral history, 42–43, 46–48; NSB tape 12; letter, Bridges to George L. Decker, Jan. 20, 1945, Bridges Papers, f10, b5; Pilcher, *Portland Longshoremen*, chap. 10, esp. 103–5, 378–80; Schmidt oral history, 50.

47. Copy of letter, Scharrenberg to Chlopek, June 8, 1926, Paul Scharrenberg Correspondence and Papers, Bancroft Library, University of California, Berkeley (hereinafter Scharrenberg Correspondence), f1, b1.

48. Scharrenberg, "The San Francisco Longshore," Longshoremen file, carton 2, Scharrenberg Correspondence; Rules and Regulations . . . between the Draymen's Association and the Brotherhood of Teamsters, Local No. 85, filed under Teamsters, International Brotherhood of, Local 85 (San Francisco), carton 18, Labor Council Records; letters, Casey to Daniel J. Tobin, May 15, 1916, f 5, b 13, series 1, Casey to Hughes, Sept. 27, 1919, telegram, Casey to Hughes, Oct. 2, 1919, f2, b 14, series 1, Teamsters Papers, WHS; John A. O'Connell, "Transforming a Company Union," *American Federationist* 37 (1930): 61. In 1933 Scharrenberg explicitly raised a concern that he attributed to those in the Blue Book who opposed ILA affiliation: "Will the local union be required to admit certain men who are regarded as reds or general trouble makers along the waterfront?" Copy of letter, Scharrenberg to Ryan, June 30, 1933, f1, b1, Scharrenberg Correspondence.

49. O'Connell, "Transforming a Company Union," 61; copies of letters, Scharrenberg to Chlopek, Dec. 31, 1926, Scharrenberg to Ryan, Nov. 21 and Dec. 24, 1927, Scharrenberg to Stein, Dec. 24, 1927, and Scharrenberg to Ryan, Oct. 9, 1928, and Apr. 8, 1930, f1, b1, Scharrenberg Correspondence; letter, John B. Bryan and E. G. Stein to John A. O'Connell, Nov. 8, 1927; copy of letter, San Francisco Labor Council to Joseph P. Ryan, Nov. 21, 1927; letter, Bryan and Stein to O'Connell, Dec. 23, 1927, filed under Longshoremen's Association, International, Local 38-79 (San Francisco), carton 11, Labor Council Records; NSB 11; Bridges Testimony, 1939 deportation hearing, 3086; *Labor Clarion*, Feb. 15, 1929, 2, 11, 12.

50. NSB 12; Markholt, *Maritime Solidarity*, 50; letter, Ryan to Green, May 1, 1931, attached to copy of letter, Green to Scharrenberg, May 4, 1931; copies, Scharrenberg to Stein, July 1, 1931, and Scharrenberg to Green, telegram, July 10, 1931, f18, b1, Scharrenberg Correspondence; Eliel, *Waterfront and General Strikes*, 3, citing statement by Ryan to Eliel on June 14, 1934; telegrams, Scharrenberg to Green, June 28, 1933; Green to Scharrenberg, June 29, 1933; copies of letters, Scharrenberg to Ryan, June 30, 1933;

Scharrenberg to John B. Bryan, July 1, 1933; and telegram, Scharrenberg to Ryan, July 6, 1933, all in f2, b1, Scharrenberg Correspondence.

51. NSB 12.

52. Bridges Testimony, 169, 177, NLB proceedings; NSB 12; letter, Warren H. Pillsburg, deputy commissioner, U.S. Employees Compensation Commission, June 27, 1929, f6, b3, Bridges Papers, LARC; report of [name redacted], file 39-915-672, 42, Bridges FBI file.

53. Base Longshoremens [sic] Wages in San Francisco, 1913 to Date, Coast Arbitration Case files, Employee's Exhibits, ILWU Library; NSB 12. The city directory lists Harry and Agnes at 3247 Harrison for 1931 and at 3249 1/2 Harrison the next year and in 1933. Interview, July 28, 1989. The 1930 census listing is available through Ancestry.com.

54. NSB 12.

Chapter 3. San Francisco Longshoremen Organize

1. NSB 12, 14; William H. Mullins, *The Depression and the Urban West Coast, 1929–1933: Los Angeles, San Francisco, Seattle, and Portland* (Bloomington: Indiana University Press, 1991), 36–38, 72–75, 102–4; California Board of State Harbor Commissioners, Port of San Francisco, *Biennial Report: 1938–1940* (Sacramento: State Printing Office, 1941), 107; *1928–1930* (1931), 88–97; *1930–1932* (1932), 83–91, 99; *1932–1934* (1936), 82, 91.

2. Harry Bridges Testimony, Aug. 13, 1934, Proceedings before the National Longshoremen's Board, 169–71, 232 (hereinafter Bridges Testimony, NLB), Arbitration Collection of the Institute of Industrial Relations, University of California, Berkeley, LARC, hereinafter NLB proceedings; Report of [name redacted], Nov. 20, 1940, file 391-515-672, 35–36, Bridges FBI file. Bridges's memory of the relief program was accurate. See Mullins, *Depression and the Urban West Coast*, 73.

3. NSB 12; Bridges Testimony, NLB.

4. Several journalists and historians have treated the formation of Local 38-79, the roles of Holman and the CP, and Bridges's involvement. The major accounts, in chronological order, include the following: Mike Quin [Paul William Ryan], *The Big Strike* (Olema, CA: Olema, 1949); Charles P. Larrowe, *Harry Bridges: The Rise and Fall of Radical Labor in the United States* (New York: Lawrence Hill, 1972); Bruce Nelson, *Workers on the Waterfront: Seamen, Longshoremen, and Unionism in the 1930s* (Urbana: University of Illinois Press, 1988); Howard Kimeldorf, *Reds or Rackets? The Making of Radical and Conservative Unions on the Waterfront* (Berkeley: University of California Press, 1988); David Wellman, *The Union Makes Us Strong: Radical Unionism on the San Francisco Waterfront* (Cambridge: Cambridge University Press, 1997); Ottilie Markholt, *Maritime Solidarity: Pacific Coast Unionism, 1929–1938* (Tacoma: Pacific Coast Maritime History Committee, 1998); David Selvin, *A Terrible Anger: The 1934 Maritime and General Strikes in San Francisco* (Detroit: Wayne State University Press, 1998); and Vernon Pedersen, *The Communist Party on the American Waterfront: Revolution, Reform, and the Quest for Power* (Lanham, MD: Lexington Books, 2019). Quin/Ryan's book is the account of a CP journalist; I agree with David Selvin's conclusion (242) that it is more "vivid and dramatic" (Quin's publisher's words) than accurate. I consider Selvin's account the most

balanced and complete. However, of all these, only Pedersen used the CPUSA files at RGASPI. None of them used FBI files and several of the other primary sources cited below. None interviewed Bridges (although Selvin had access to the same interviews I have used), and none interviewed Darcy.

5. Minutes of meeting of Sept. 28, 1931; letter, Holman to John Bjorklund, Mar. 1, 1932, both filed under 1933—Early ILA Organization, 1933–34 series, ILWU Library; Markholt, *Maritime Solidarity*, 34.

6. Harvey Klehr, *The Heyday of American Communism: The Depression Decade* (New York: Basic Books, 1984), 26, 32, 33; letters, William Simons to Earl Browder, Aug. 26, 1930; Secretariat to William Simons, Sept. 9, 1930, Morris Raport to Browder, Nov. 20, 1930; N.H. Allen to CPUSA, Dec. 2, 1930; 515-1-1959, 515-1-1994, RGASPI. For Darcy's initial experience, see letter, sd [Darcy] to Jack Stachel, June 5, 1931, 515-1-2499, RGASPI; Darcy recounted some of these events to me, with additional details, on Aug. 19, 1996, hereinafter Darcy interview, 1996. See also my "Prelude to the Popular Front: The Communist Party in California, 1931–1935," *American Communist History* 1 (2002): 5–37.

7. This summary draws upon many issues of the party's newspapers, the *Daily Worker* and the *Western Worker*, the *Communist* (the party's theoretical journal), the *Communist Organizer* (the party's journal for organizers), J. Peters, *The Communist Party: A Manual on Organization* (San Francisco: Workers Library, 1935), and similar works. On Peters, see Harvey Klehr, John Earl Haynes, and Fridrikh Igorevich Firsov, *The Secret World of American Communism* (New Haven, CT: Yale University Press, 1995), 73–83.

8. These developments can be traced in *Daily Worker* and the *Communist*, esp. Browder, "Why an Open Letter."

9. Interview, May 7, 1986. On the TUUL, see, for example, Klehr, *Heyday of American Communism*, 38–42.

10. Minutes of the founding meeting of MWIU, 515-1-2179; the national secretary's report on the first year of the MWIU, 515-1-1864; Central Committee, RESOLUTIONS ON PARTY WORK, undated, 515-1-2242; letter, Anglo-American Secretariat (AAS), in Russian, with a draft of the document that became "Immediate Tasks of the Trade Union Unity League of the U.S.A."; draft of cover letter dated 26 II 32, final version in English, dated Apr. 28, 1932, 515-1-2977; letter, TO THE CENTRAL COMMITTEE OF THE COMMUNIST PARTY OF USA, typed date of "21.9.32" crossed out in ink, and dated, in German, Aug. 9, 1932, 495-20-508; Darcy, speech at the Seventh Congress of the CI, July 28, 1935, 495-72-287; letter, Hudson to Wellstone and Foster, Mar. 12, 1931, 515-1-2554, all RGASPI; Sam Darcy, "The Great West Coast Maritime Strike," *Communist* 13 (1934): 665. For origins and early history of MWIU, see Nelson, *Workers on the Waterfront*, 78–80; and Pedersen, *Communist Party on the American Waterfront*, chaps. 2–4.

11. Al Richmond, *A Long View from the Left: Memoirs of an American Revolutionary* (New York: Houghton Mifflin, 1972), 206–19; Nelson, *Workers on the Waterfront*, 90; minutes of MWIU National Committee, Oct. 10–11, 1931, 515-1-2554, RGASPI; Samuel Adams Darcy, "The San Francisco General Strike—1934," *Hawsepipe* 1, no. 6 (1982): 1, 7; secretariat meeting minutes, Mar. 15, 1932, 515-1-2910; NSB 12; interview, Nov. 2, 1986; Efim Hanoff, 495-261-883-1, RGASPI; Archie Green interviewed by Robert Cherny, Oct. 12, 1986, hereinafter Green interview; report on Mitchell Slobodek, part of report of

[name redacted], July 30, 1941, file 39-915-1488, esp. 17–23. Bridges FBI file; B. B. Jones interviewed by Robert Cherny, Sept. 14, 1986, hereinafter Jones interview.

12. Letters, DO [District Organizer] Dist. #13 [Darcy] to Org. Dept. C.C. [Central Committee], Apr. 12, 1932, 515-1-2916; letter, George Mink to Browder, July 1, 1932, 515-1-2995; Darcy, speech at the Seventh Congress of the CI, July 28, 1935, 495-72-287; Darcy to Central Committee, Dec. 13, 1933, 515-1-3295; Secretariat [Darcy?] to Browder, Jan. 27, 1933, 515-1-3295, all RGASPI; Darcy, "Great West Coast Maritime Strike," 665; Browder, "Why an Open Letter," 722–23; Klehr, *Heyday of American Communism*, 13.

13. Election results from *San Francisco Examiner*, Nov. 10, 1932, 5; David M. Kennedy, *Freedom from Fear: The American People in Depression and War, 1929–1945* (New York: Oxford University Press, 1999), chaps. 3–5; Frank Freidel, *Franklin D. Roosevelt: Launching the New Deal* (Boston: Little, Brown, 1973), chaps. 1–5, 24–26; Einstein 42.

14. Jones claimed to have been involved; Jones interview. Archie Green told me of Slobodek's involvement; Green interview. Slobodek appears as reporting on the waterfront or as the waterfront section organizer in the district secretariat minutes beginning in January 1933 and concluding in September when he was expelled for "disruptive activities." See, for example, minutes of District Committee meeting of Jan. 28, 1933, 515-1-3293; Sept. 9, 1933, 515-1-3293, RGASPI. The most complete set of the *Waterfront Worker* is at the ILWU Library and is available online at http://archive.ilwu.org/?page_id=1861.

15. *Waterfront Worker;* Green interview. Pedersen, *Communist Party on American Waterfront*, 81–82, claims that the Pan-Pacific Trade Union Secretariat, specifically a functionary code-named Eddy, was centrally important in creating a group of CP members among longshoremen; he cites a letter, "Eddy to Jack, Mar. 10, 1933, 515-1-3350," for his statement that the *Waterfront Worker* "editorial board would consist of longshoremen who were secret members of the Communist Party. . . . For chair of the editorial board Darcy and Eddy chose Harry Bridges." Pederson also cites this letter and Bruce Nelson's book for his statement that "Bridges secretly joined the Communist Party." In my own research, I reviewed that letter, which is unsigned and otherwise not identified as to author, to Jack [I assume Stachel], Mar. 10, 1933, 515-1-3350. Nowhere does the letter refer to "longshoremen who were secret members of the Communist Party," and nowhere does it mention Harry Bridges. Nor does Nelson make that claim. My own research, as cited above, indicates that the early months of the *Waterfront Worker* were prepared by Hynes, Jones, and Slobodek. I deal at more length with the Pan-Pacific Trade Union Secretariat in my forthcoming book on the CP in the San Francisco Bay Area.

16. Letter, Bjorklund to Holman, Mar. 21, 1933; draft of telegram, Holman to Bjorklund, July 3, 1933; telegram, Ryan to Holman, July 8, 1933, all filed under History, Local 10 series, ILWU Library; Clyde W. Deal, "The Tide Turns" (unpublished memoirs), f33, b4, Deal Manuscript Collection, University of Washington Libraries; Deal interview manuscript, Apr. 16, 1971, tape V, University of Washington Libraries; flyer quoted in Robert Coleman Francis, "History of Labor on the San Francisco Waterfront" (PhD diss., University of California, Berkeley, 1934), 188. The Ryan-Scharrenberg exchange includes the following: copy of telegram, Scharrenberg to Ryan, June 30, 1933; copy of letter, Scharrenberg to Ryan, July 6, 1933, copy of letter, Scharrenberg to Ryan, July 7, 1933, filed under California State Federation of Labor, Correspondence, 1930–37,

carton 5; copy of telegram, Ryan to Scharrenberg, July 6, 1933; copy of telegram, Ryan to Scharrenberg, July 8, 1933, filed under Longshoremen's Association, International, Local 38-79 (San Francisco), carton 11; all Labor Council Records filed under History, Local 10 series, ILWU Library.

17. NSB 12; Jones interview; Jones, quoted in Larrowe, *Harry Bridges*, 16. See also the account in Bruce Minton [Richard Bransten] and John Stuart, *Men Who Lead Labor* (New York: Modern Age Books, 1937), 179–80.

18. In a memoir in 1982, Darcy described a Sunday-morning class he presented for twenty-some interested longshoremen. According to Darcy, Bridges participated in the class. When I asked Bridges about this in 1986, he had difficulty remembering any Sunday-morning classes but finally stated, "Could be." See Darcy, "San Francisco General Strike," 7; letter, Darcy to Cherny, Oct. 17, 1986; interview, Nov. 2, 1986; Darcy interviewed by Cherny, Apr. 14, 1994, hereinafter Darcy interview, 1994. I am unable to fit such a class into the chronology that appears from RGASPI documents, other sources, and interviews.

19. Letter, Secretariat to Central Committee, May 17, 1933, 515-1-3295, RGASPI; Richmond, *Long View from the Left*, 217–18; Darcy, "Great West Coast Maritime Strike," 665; "Plan for Work among the Pacific Marine Transport Workers" [unsigned and undated with penciled annotation, "For Earl"], 515-1-3350; minutes of the State Convention of the Trade Union Unity League, Equality Hall, Aug. 6, 1933, 515-1-3345, RGASPI.

20. Richmond, *Long View from the Left*, 162–63; Jackson's transfer to San Francisco, Aug. 11, 1933, 515-1-3146, RGASPI; Jones interview; Green interview; Nelson, *Workers on the Waterfront*, 110–11; Darcy interview, 1996. I deal at length with Harry Gliksohn/Harry Jackson's role in the factional struggles within District 13 in the late 1920s in my forthcoming book on the CP in the San Francisco Bay Area.

21. Earl Browder, "Why an Open Letter to Our Party Membership," *Communist* 12 (1933): 710, 716–17, 730, 732, 748.

22. NSB 13; Darcy, "Great West Coast Maritime Strike," 665–66; Jones interview.

23. Minutes of District 13 Secretariat meeting, June 28, 1933, 515-1-3292, RGASPI.

24. *Waterfront Worker*, July 1933; *Western Worker* (San Francisco), July 10, 1933, 1, 3; minutes, District 13 Secretariat, Sept. 9, 1933, 515-1-3293, RGASPI.

25. Minutes of the District 13 Secretariat meeting, June 28, 1933, 515-1-3292, RGASPI; report, B. K. Sackett to E. J. Connelly, date obscured, file 39-915-379x13, Bridges FBI file.

26. Testimony of Eugene George Dietrich, 1939 deportation hearing, vol. 10 (July 21, 1939), 1454–56; NSB 13, 14. In 1940 FBI agents interviewed many of the members of the Albion Hall group, especially those who later opposed Bridges or the CIO; see Report of E. J. Connelley, 11-29-1940 (some sections are dated as Nov. 20, 1940, and some are corrected by hand to Nov. 20, 1940), file 39-915-614, Bridges FBI file. For general information on Albion Hall, see 538–45 and interviews with individuals; Dietrich, 560–614; Kullberg, 615–24; Henry Morisse, 625–38; John McGuire, 639–43; Robert Boyce, 644–45; McKenna, 646–80; Julius White, 681–89; Schomaker, 1588–1600.

27. Mallen later became president of the Walking Bosses local of the ILWU and was an outspoken opponent of Bridges; McKenna left the Albion Hall group when he realized some of its members were radicals. For Mallen, see memo, William Glazier to Telford

Taylor, June 22, 1955, filed under 1933—Albion Hall and Committee of 500, 1933–34 Series, ILWU Library. Schmidt oral history, 59, 307, 418; memo by Bridges concerning Schomaker testimony, Nov. 28, 1949, f10, b10, Bridges Papers, Southern California Library; Jones interview; NSB tape 13; Dietrich testimony, 1939 deportation hearing, 1458–59. See also the FBI reports on various members of the group.

28. NSB 12; Henry Schmidt, *Secondary Leadership in the ILWU, 1933–1966*, interview conducted by Miriam F. Stein and Estolv Ethan Ward, Regional Oral History Office, Bancroft Library, University of California, Berkeley, 1983, 56–58, 414–15; Dietrich testimony, 1488–89; Bridges testimony, 3070, both 1939 deportation hearing.

29. NSB 12; interview, Mar. 5, 1986; Schmidt oral history, 414–15; Jones interview; Dietrich testimony, 1939 deportation hearing, 1457; clipping, *San Francisco Examiner*, May 14, 1941, file 39-915-A, Bridges FBI file.

30. *Western Worker*, July 17, 1933, 4; July 31, 1933, 2; *Waterfront Worker*, July, esp. 1, 7, Aug. 15, 1; Aug. 19, 1933, 1.

31. Minutes, District 13 Secretariat, Sept. 9, 1933, 515-1-3293, RGASPI. This date corresponds roughly with Bridges's various efforts to place the time when he became involved. In his second INS hearing, before Judge Sears, Bridges dated it in September; see also memorandum by Bridges concerning Schomaker testimony, Nov. 28, 1949, f10, b10, Bridges Papers, Southern California Library. On NSB 19, Bridges dated it in mid-1933 but also at the time of the Matson strike (October 1933); on NSB 17, he seemed to date it in July, August, or September.

32. NSB 13, 19; "Memorandum by Bridges concerning Schomaker testimony," Nov. 28, 1949, f10, b10, Bridges Papers, Southern California Library; Jones interview; Cherny interview with Isaac Zafrani, Apr. 1, 1987; Bridges testimony, 1939 deportation hearing, 3074; Darcy, "Great West Coast Maritime Strike," 665; interview, Mar. 5, 1986. In 1940 FBI agents conducted an extensive investigation around the *Waterfront Worker*, seeking to determine the identity of those who put it out and analyzing every single issue; see report of E. J. Connelly, Nov. 29, 1940, file 39-915-614, Bridges FBI file, 540–44, 690–753.

33. Deal, "Tide Turns," chap. 1, 15–18, and Deal's oral history, 6–8; meeting notice, History file, Local 10 series, ILWU Library.

34. Telegrams, Holman to Green, Ryan, Johnson, and Richberg, July 18, 1933; reports of incidents, filed under Miscellaneous. Disputes: PCLB, Case Reports on, 1933–34 Coastwise Collection, ILWU Library.

35. This issue is dated July 1933, but "July" is crossed out by hand and "August" written in. From the context, this was apparently issued in late July, because it refers to a coming membership meeting "on Thursday," apparently the meeting of July 27. See notice of that meeting, filed under History, Local 10 series, ILWU Library.

36. Schmidt oral history, 53–54. The most complete account of the meeting is in *Western Worker*, Aug. 7, 1933, 1, 3, which incorrectly identifies the date as Friday, July 29, instead of Thursday, July 27. In most particulars, the *Western Worker* version corresponds with Schmidt's memory, except for the initiation, which is not mentioned. There is a brief account on NSB 19.

37. Letter, Bjorklund to Holman, Aug. 21, 1933, filed under History, Local 10 series, ILWU Library; Deal, "Tide Turns," chap. 1, 15–18; Deal's oral history, 6–8.

38. Letter, Deal to Meehan, Sept. 1, 1933, "Marine Council" b9, Local 8 papers; Deal, "Tide Turns," chap. 1, 15–18; Deal's oral history, 6–8; NSB tape 13.

39. *Western Worker*, Sept. 4, 1933, 1, 3; interview, July 28, 1989.

40. Melvyn Dubofsky, *We Shall Be All: A History of the Industrial Workers of the World* (New York: Quadrangle/New York Times Book, 1969), 465.

41. Selvin, *Terrible Anger*, 48; Slate Card Flyer, filed under History, Local 10 series, ILWU Library; letter, Deal to Meehan, Sept. 1, 1933, "Marine Council" file, b9, Local 8 papers; NSB 13, on which Bridges confused some of the chronology and provided relatively little information on the election itself; *Western Worker*, Sept. 18, 1933, 1.

42. Telegram, Morris to Bjorklund, Sept. 7, 1933, file "District Office (Communications) J. C. Bjorklund W. J. Lewis," b 10, Local 8 papers.

43. Melvyn Dubofsky, *The State and Labor in Modern America* (Chapel Hill: University of North Carolina Press, 1994), 115–20; Labor Research Association, *Labor Fact Book II* (New York: International, 1934), 125, 236.

44. Schmidt oral history, 58; minutes of Executive Committee meeting of Sept. 25, 1933; filed under 1933—Basic Demand, July and Nov. Conferences, 1933–34 Coastwise series, ILWU Library. The minutes did not record the number of committee members present or the number of votes that Bridges received, which would have indicated the strength of the Albion Hall caucus on the executive committee.

45. Copy of letter, NRA Board of Adjustment to Joseph C. Sharp, Sept. 2, 1933, filed under 1933—Early ILA Organization, 1933–34 Coastwise series, ILWU Library.

46. *Waterfront Worker*, Sept. 15, 1933; this event was not covered by any of the city's daily papers.

47. NSB 13. Bridges's chronology on this tape is confused; he places the events in June instead of September, but the events he described correspond closely to the *Waterfront Worker*'s description of the September action.

48. Paul Eliel, *The Waterfront and General Strikes: San Francisco, 1934* (San Francisco: Hooper, 1934), 4–5; *Western Worker*, Oct. 30, 1933, 1; copies of telegrams, Holman to Meehan, Oct. 11, 1933; Bjorklund to Holman, Oct. 11, 1933; Bjorklund to Ryan, Oct. 13, 1933; Ryan to Bjorklund, Oct. 13, 1933; minutes of the meeting of ILA Local 38-78 (Portland), Oct. 18,1933; all in file "San Francisco," b20, papers of ILWU Local 8 (Portland).

49. NSB 13.

50. *Waterfront Worker*, Oct. 3, Oct. 7, 1933; Constitution By-Laws and Dues Book of the Riggers' and Stevedores' Union [1919], History file, Local 10 series, ILWU Library; Ron Magden, *Serving Tacoma's Waterfront: One Hundred Years* (n.p.: Print Northwest for ILWU Local 23, 1986), 3, 6, 35. On the long history of racism in California labor, see, for example, Alexander Saxton, *The Indispensable Enemy: Labor and the Anti-Chinese Movement in California* (Berkeley: University of California Press, 1971); and Michael Kazin, *Barons of Labor: The San Francisco Building Trades and Union Power in the Progressive Era* (Urbana: University of Illinois Press, 1987), chap. 6.

51. Executive Committee Minutes, Oct. 9, 1933, filed under ILA 38-79 Executive Board Minutes, Oct. 2, 1923–Jan. 10, 1934, Local 10 Series, ILWU Library. For the CP and race, see, for example, Klehr, *Heyday of American Communism*, chap. 17; for Scottsboro, see Dan T. Carter, *Scottsboro: A Tragedy of the American South*, rev. ed. (Baton Rouge: Louisiana State University Press, 2007).

52. Membership meeting minutes, Feb. 26, 1934, minutes of special membership meeting, Mar. 26, 1934, filed under Minutes of Membership Meetings, Jan. 24, 1934–Jan. 29, 1935, Local 10 series, ILWU Library.

53. Arthur M. Schlesinger Jr., *The Coming of the New Deal* (Boston: Houghton Mifflin, 1959), 111–12, 116; Chamber of Commerce of the United States, Industrial Recovery Act: Synopsis of Codes (bulletin), Aug. 1, 1933–Jan. 20, 1934; Bernard Bellush, *The Failure of the NRA* (New York: W. W. Norton, 1975), 97–98.

54. "Rough Draft of Proposed Code Governing Hours, Wages, and Working Conditions . . . Portland, Ore., July 31, 1934," filed under Misc. Disputes: PCLB, Case Report On, 1933–34 Series, ILWU Library. See also "Origin of Basic Demands in '34 Strike," filed under 1933—Basic Demand, July and Nov. Conferences, 1933–34 Series, ILWU Library. One dollar in mid-1933 would have the same purchasing power as $20.84 in mid-2021.

55. *NYT*, Sept. 8, 1933, 2; Sept. 21, 1933, 41; Sept. 1933, 26, 4; Oct. 30, 1933, 35; *Waterfront Worker*, Oct. 3, 1933. See also executive committee minutes, Sept. 25, 1933, filed under 1933—Basic Demands, July and Nov. Conferences, 1933–34 Coastwise series, ILWU Library.

56. "Unions Use Expert Counselor," *Business Week*, Oct. 9, 1937, 46–48; statement in Henry Melnikow Papers (unprocessed), WHS.

57. U.S. National Recovery Administration, *Hearing on Code of Fair Practices and Competition Presented by the Shipping Industry*, 4 vols. (carbon copy of typed transcript of hearings presented by Waterfront Employers Association of San Francisco, Government Documents Library, University of California, Berkeley), 2:314–72, 394–412, esp. 373, 395; Origin of Basic Demands in '34 Strike, filed under 1933—Basic Demand, July and Nov. Conferences, 1933–34 Series, ILWU Library. Petersen also referred to "racial factors" on 381, again without defining how the Pacific Coast was different from the other three districts or how its differences were relevant for the code.

58. *Hearing on Proposed Shipping Code*, 2:397–412; the same material appears in Boris Stern, "Employment Conditions and Unemployment Relief: Longshore Labor Conditions and Port Decasualization in the United States," *Monthly Labor Review* 37 (Dec. 1933): 1299–1306, esp. 1303–6; Stern, "Employment Conditions," 1304–5; "Statement Accompanying Proposed NRA Code for Shipping," filed under NRA Code Hearings, 1933–34 Series, ILWU Library.

59. Summary of minutes in "Origin of Basic Demands in '34 Strike," filed as 1933—Basic Demand, July and Nov. Conferences, 1933–34 Series, ILWU Library.

60. NSB 12; see also Minutes of General Membership Meeting, Dec. 4, 1933, filed under 1933—Early ILA Organization, 1933–34 Coastwise series, ILWU Library; *Chronicle*, Dec. 19, 1933, 1; *Chronicle*, Dec. 19, 1933, 1; *San Francisco News*, Dec. 19, 1933, 1.

61. *Western Worker*, Dec. 25, 1933, 1; minutes of executive committee meetings, Dec. 20 and Dec. 27, 1933, filed under Executive Board Minutes, Oct. 23, 1923–Jan. 10, 1934, Local 10 series, ILWU Library; *Party Organizer* 6 (Dec. 1933): 21.

62. NSB 13; *Western Worker*, Jan. 15, 1934, 1, 5; Minutes of the Regular [Membership] Meeting, Jan. 16, 1934, f4, b1, ILWU Local 13 Records, Labor and Urban Archives, CSU Northridge.

63. *NYT*, Jan. 10, 10; Jan. 11, 1934, 41; Hearings on Proposed Shipping Code, 3:9–40, esp. 25–28.

64. Hearing on Proposed Shipping Code, 3:319–27, esp. 319–20; *NYT*, Feb. 2, 37; Feb. 4, 1934, 33. For Ryan's use of the shape-up to remain in power, see, for example, Colin Davis, "'All I Got's a Hook': New York Longshoremen and the 1948 Dock Strike," in *Waterfront Workers: New Perspectives on Race and Class*, ed. Calvin Winslow (Urbana: University of Illinois Press, 1998), 132–35.

65. "To Outbreak of Strike" [chronology], ILWU Library.

66. NSB 13, 17.

67. *Western Worker*, Feb. 19, 1; Feb. 26, 1934, 1, 5.

68. *Proceedings of the 27th Annual Convention of the Pacific Coast District, International Longshoremen's Association, . . . 1934*, ILWU Library, esp. 74, 118, 137–38.

69. *Proceedings of the 27th Annual Convention*, esp. 94–95, 150–51.

70. *Proceedings of the 27th Annual Convention*, esp. 119–33; "To Outbreak of Strike" [chronology], ILWU Library. Ryan asked for the delay in the strike in the expectation that the code would be issued on March 22.

71. The late Ron Magdan generously shared his copies of the Seattle employers' association internal communications, establishing that there was frequent communication between the Seattle and San Francisco groups and that San Francisco was expected to take the lead. In 1934 Bridges read a similar letter between the San Francisco and San Pedro employers into the record of the National Longshoremen's Board proceedings: "Memorandum to Senator Boynton from Carmody: Pencil Notes on First Public Session of National Longshoremen's Board . . .," July 10, f3, b9, Institute of Industrial Relations, University of California, Berkeley, Records, LARC.

72. *Chronicle*, Mar. 18, 1934, 3; Mar. 19, 1934, 1; Mar. 20, 1934, 13; Eliel, *Waterfront and General Strikes*, 186–89, esp. 188, 189.

73. Letter, Ryan to Lewis and Bjorklund, Mar. 20, 1934, filed under 1934 Correspondence (Misc.), 1933–34 Series, ILWU Library; letter, Creel to Roosevelt, Mar. 21, 1934, filed under Pacific Longshoremen's Strike—1934, b8, OF 716, Franklin D. Roosevelt Library; *Chronicle*, Mar. 21, 1934, 11.

74. Letter, Roosevelt to Lewis, Mar. 22, 1934, filed under 1933–34/Arbitration Boards—Longshoremen, b12, OF 716b, FDR Library; *Chronicle*, Mar. 23, 1934, 1; Eliel, *Waterfront and General Strikes*, 7.

75. Letter, Bjorklund to all affiliated locals, Mar. 19, f1, b1, William J. Lewis Collection, LARC; *Chronicle*, Mar. 22, 1934, 1; Minutes of Strike Committee, Mar. 22, 1934, file Loc. 10 ILA #38-79 Min., Membership and Comms., 1933, ILWU library.

76. Letter, Casey to D. J. Tobin, Mar. 27, 1934, f6, b16, series 1, International Brotherhood of Teamsters Papers, WHS; letters, Howe to Perkins, Apr. 7, with Tobin to Howe, Apr. 2, attached, filed under White House Correspondence for Mar. and Apr. 1934, b105, General Records of the Department of Labor, Office of the Secretary, Secretary Frances Perkins, General Subject Files, 1933–41, Record Group 174, NA, hereinafter, Perkins Papers, NA; copy of unsigned letter to Ryan, Mar. 28, 1934, filed under General Strike, 1934, carton 31, San Francisco Labor Council Collection, Bancroft Library, University of California, Berkeley.

77. *Chronicle*, Mar. 30, 1934, 1; Eliel, *Waterfront and General Strikes*, 189–92; Henry Grady et al., Statement Issued by President's Special Board on Longshoremen's Strike,

May 28, 1934, f1, b9, Arbitration Collection of the Institute of Industrial Relations, University of California, Berkeley, LARC.

78. Eliel, *Waterfront and General Strikes*, 7–9, 10–11, 183–85, 193, 195–200; *Chronicle*, Apr. 17, 1934, 20; May 8, 1934, 1; *Western Worker*, Apr. 23, 1934, 1, 5; Apr. 30, 1934, 1, 5; May 7, 1934, 1, 5.

79. Letter, Louis J. Oviedo to Whom it may concern, Apr. 12, 1934, filed under Attacks Etc./Lee J. Holman: 1934–36, Local 10 Series; copies of letter, Holman to "May," Oct. 16, 1933; Holman to Bjorklund, Oct. 16, 1933, both filed under History (Including pre-1934 period), Local 10 Series; copies of letters, Holman to Ryan, Mar. 22, 1934, with cover note from Joe [Ryan] to Jack [Bjorklund?]; Holman to Ryan, Apr. 2, 1934, filed under ILWU Case 1934 Correspondence (Misc.), 1933–34 Series, ILWU Library; copy of unsigned letter, probably from O'Connell, to Ryan, Mar. 28, 1934, filed under General Strike, 1934, carton 31, San Francisco Labor Council Collection, Bancroft Library, University of California, Berkeley.

80. Copies of letters, Ivan Cox to Holman, Mar. 28, 1934, filed under ILWU Case 1934, Correspondence (Misc.), 1933–34 Series; Ivan Cox to Anglo California National Bank, Apr. 3, 1934; Holman to Ryan, Apr. 2, 1934; letter, Ryan to Holman, Apr. 12, 1934, all filed under Attacks Etc./Lee J. Holman, 1934–36, Local 10 Series, ILWU Library; clipping, *Call-Bulletin*, Mar. 31, 1934, filed under General Strike, 1934, Newspapers Clippings, carton 31, San Francisco Labor Council Collection, Bancroft Library, University of California, Berkeley.

81. Copy of letter, Cox to Holman, Apr. 10, 1934; letter, Holman to Cox, Apr. 13, 1934;. Minutes of Trial Proceedings of Lee J. Holman, Defendant, Apr. 17, 1934, filed under Attacks Etc./Lee J. Holman: 1934–36, Local 10 Series, ILWU Library; Schmidt oral history, 59.

82. Minutes of Meetings of May 8, 9, 12, June 6, 1934, Strike Committee Minutes, 1933–34 Series, ILWU Library.

83. Schmidt, oral history, 58.

Chapter 4. The Big Strike

1. There are many accounts of the 1934 strikes, including three book-length accounts. In this and the next two chapters, I have attempted to reconstruct events as much as possible from primary sources. I have considered Paul Eliel, *The Waterfront and General Strikes: San Francisco, 1934* (San Francisco: Hooper, 1934), to be more primary source than secondary, in that Eliel was an officer of the Industrial Association, sometimes reported on his own observations of that organization's decision making, and often incorporated primary sources. Mike Quin [Paul William Ryan], *The Big Strike* (1949; reprint, New York: International, 1979), is probably the best known account, but, as correspondence in Darcy's papers makes clear, it was written for a popular audience; Selvin has likened it to a 1930s proletarian novel. I have relied on it only occasionally. Of all the accounts, I find David Selvin's *A Terrible Anger: The 1934 Waterfront and General Strikes in San Francisco* (Detroit: Wayne State University Press, 1996) to be the most consistently reliable.

2. *NYT*, Feb. 11, 1934, 41.

3. U.S. Congress, Subcommittee of the Senate Committee on Education and Labor, *Violations of Free Speech and Rights of Labor: Hearings Pursuant to S. Res. 266* (74th Cong.), 76th Cong., 3rd sess., 1940, pt. 60, 22121–37, 22143–47, 21949, 21965–66, pt. 4, 9, 98, hereinafter *La Follette Committee Hearings*; "Industrial Association" file, carton 10, San Francisco Labor Council Records, Bancroft Library, University of California, Berkeley.

4. Eliel, *Waterfront and General Strikes*, 13–14, 200; *Chronicle*, May 9, 1934, 1, 13; May 10, 1934, 4; May 12, 1934, 2; *NYT*, May 10, 1934, 2; *News*, June 25, 1934, 4; Theodore Durein, "Scabs' Paradise," *Reader's Digest*, Jan. 1937, 19; Sam Darcy, "The Great West Coast Maritime Strike," *Communist* 13 (July 1934): 668; Strike Committee Minutes, May 10, 1933–34 Series, ILWU Library, hereinafter Strike Committee Minutes; *Waterfront Worker*, June 12, 1934, 3; Louis Goldblatt, *Working Class Leader in the ILWU, 1935–1977*, interviewed by Estolv Ethan Ward, 1978, 1979, 2 vols. (Regional Oral History Office, Bancroft Library, University of California, Berkeley, 1980), 1:150.

5. Herbert Resner, *The Law in Action during the San Francisco Longshore and Maritime Strike of 1934* (report, SERA project 3-F2-371, and WPA project 1950, Berkeley, 1936), 9.

6. Eliel, *Waterfront and General Strikes*, 15–18, 201.

7. *Chronicle*, May 13, 1934, 1, 4; *NYT*, May 13, 1934, 1, 34; May 17, 1934, 8; May 18, 1934, 45; May 22, 1934, 45; *Examiner*, May 14, 1934, 8; May 24, 1934, 1, 4; Strike Committee Minutes, May 15, 1934.

8. Durein, "Scab's Paradise," 19, 20; Strike Committee Minutes, June 8, 1934.

9. Eliel, *Waterfront and General Strikes*, 14; undated *Waterfront Worker*; "TO ALL NEGRO PEOPLE," May 16, 1934, filed under Strike Publicity Material and Notes, 1933–34 Series, ILWU Library; Samuel Adams Darcy, "The San Francisco General Strike—1934," *Hawsepipe* 1, no. 6 (1982): 1–7; Darcy, "Great West Coast Maritime Strike," 672. The account of Bridges's visits to churches is from Thomas C. Fleming, "Harry Bridges: An Honest Labor Leader," *Sun Reporter* (San Francisco), Apr. 4, 1990; I found no other account of Bridges's visit to Black churches.

10. *Proceedings of the 27th Annual Convention*, A14; *Waterfront Worker*, n.d; *Examiner*, May 15, 1934, page illeg.; May 16, 1934, 1; May 20, 1934, 4; May 23, 1934, 1,2; *Call-Bulletin*, May 18, 1934, 10; Eliel, *Waterfront and General Strikes*, 16–18, 20, 25, 29; Strike Committee Minutes, May 11, 1934; untitled notice, May 16, 1934, filed under 1934 Correspondence (Misc.); "Conditions upon which Marine Engineers Will Return to Work," May 26, 1934, filed under Coast Arbitration Case Correspondence, both 1933–34 Series, ILWU Library.

11. Strike Committee Minutes, May 8, 10, 11, 1934; Quin, *The Big Strike*, 48; telegram, Casey to Tobin, May 14, 1934, f6, b16, Teamsters Papers, WHS; *Examiner*, May 14, 1934, 1, 8; Eliel, *Waterfront and General Strikes*, 15, 17, 20.

12. *Chronicle*, May 14, 1934, 4; *Examiner*, May 16, 1934, 4; *Call-Bulletin*, May 18, 1934, 10; Eliel, *Waterfront and General Strikes*, 21–24.

13. *Call-Bulletin*, May 18, 1934, 1, 10; *News*, June 30, 1934, 3; Minutes of Special Meeting, May 18, 1934, 1933–34 Series, ILWU Library; Eliel, *Waterfront and General Strikes*, 24–25.

14. Grady et al., Statement by President's Special Board, May 28, 1934; Bulletin, May 19, 1934, 1:30 p.m.; Bulletin, May 19, 1934, 5:30 p.m., filed under Strike Publicity Material

and Notes, 1933–34 Series, ILWU Library; *Examiner*, May 20, 1934, 4; Eliel, *Waterfront and General Strikes*, 204.

15. *Chronicle*, May 21, 1934, 1.

16. J. Mailliard, *Who's Who in Commerce and Industry: 1936* (New York: Institute for Research in Biography, 1936), 602; *National Cyclopaedia of American Biography* (New York: James T. White, 1961), 43:584; *American Plan* (San Francisco) (1922–34); *La Follette Committee Hearings*, pt. 60, 22121; Paul St. Sure, "Some Comments on Employer Organizations and Collective Bargaining in Northern California," an interview by Corinne Glib, 1957, Oral History Project, Institute of Industrial Relations, University of California, Berkeley (hereinafter St. Sure oral history), 373.

17. Eliel, *Waterfront and General Strikes*, 43.

18. *La Follette Committee Hearings*, pt. 4, 120.

19. *Chronicle*, May 21, 1934, 1; *Waterfront Worker*, n.d.

20. Darcy, "Great West Coast Maritime Strike"; Samuel Adams Darcy, "The San Francisco Bay Area General Strike," *Communist* 13 (Oct. 1934): 985–1004, esp. 986, 988, 989; Darcy, "San Francisco General Strike—1934"; Samuel Adams Darcy, "The San Francisco General Strike—1934: Part II," *Hawsepipe* 2 (Nov.–Dec. 1982): 1–2, 4–6; Darcy interviewed by Robert Cherny, Apr. 14, 1994.

21. Bruce Nelson, *Workers on the Waterfront: Seamen, Longshoremen, and Unionism in the 1930s* (Urbana: University of Illinois Press, 1988), 144–45.

22. Strike Committee Minutes, May 13, 23, 1934; see also various issues of the *Western Worker* and the "Baby Western."

23. Strike Committee Minutes, May 9, 13, 14, 30, 31, 1934.

24. Regarding Perry, see "Brief History of Arthur James Kent," Doc. 2123, Leonard Papers; affidavit of Arthur Kent, Los Angeles, Dec. 28, 1937, f2, b3, series 1, Surveillance Papers, LARC; Kent's statement is in report of E. J. Connelley, Nov. 29, 1940, 125, file 38-915-619, Bridges FBI file.

25. *Call-Bulletin*, May 23, 1934, 1, 2; *Examiner*, May 23, 1934, 1, 8; Eliel, *Waterfront and General Strikes*, 28–29.

26. *Examiner*, May 25, 1934, 1, 2; *Chronicle*, May 25, 1934, 1; Eliel, *Waterfront and General Strikes*, 30.

27. Memorandum for the Secretary, May 26, 1934, filed under Conciliation—Strikes/Longshoremen, b42, Perkins Papers, NA; *Examiner*, May 26, 1934, 1, 2; May 27, 1934, 1, 2, 21; Eliel, *Waterfront and General Strikes*, 32.

28. NSB 14.

29. NSB 14; *Chronicle*, May 29, 1934, 1, 3; *Examiner*, May 29, 1934, 1, 3; *News*, May 29, 1934, 1, 4; J. D. Schomaker, untitled report, Oct. 13, 1934, filed under Testimonies from Strike Observers, 1933–34 Series, ILWU Library; Strike Committee Minutes, May 28, 1934; press release: May 28, filed under Strike Publicity Committee Material and Notes, all 1933–34 Series, ILWU Library.

30. *Examiner*, May 29, 1934, 1, 3; *Chronicle*, May 29, 1934, 1, 3; Eliel, *Waterfront and General Strikes*, 33–34, 206–7.

31. Eliel, *Waterfront and General Strikes*, 34–35, with citations to *Oakland Tribune*, May 29, 1934, and *News*, May 29, 1934; Minutes of Special Membership Meeting, May

29, 1933–34 Series, ILWU Library; *News*, May 30, 1934, 1; Strike Committee Minutes, May 29, 1934.

32. *Chronicle*, May 29, 1934, 1, 3; *News*, May 31, 1934, 1–6.

33. Press release, May 30, 1934, filed under Strike Publicity Materials and Notes, 1933–34 Series, ILWU Library; *Chronicle*, June 4, 1934, 1.

34. *News*, May 31, 1934, 3; Schmidt oral history, 85; press release, May 30, filed under Strike Publicity Materials and Notes; unsigned, untitled report on events of May 30, filed under Testimonies of Strike Observers, both 1933–34 Series, ILWU Library; Strike Committee Minutes, May 30, 1934; New Economics Group, "Preliminary Testimony Taken by the San Francisco Committee against Policy Brutality" (mimeographed pamphlet), ILWU Library.

35. Strike Committee Minutes, May 29, June 2, 1934, filed under 1934 Strike Committee Minutes, 1933–34 Series, ILWU Library; *News*, June 4, 1934, 1.

36. *News*, May 30, 1934, 4.

37. *NYT*, 3 June 1934, E6.

38. Anonymous letter to Bridges, postmarked June 6, 1934, f20, b10, Bridges Papers.

39. *Dispatcher*, July 17, 1959, 4; July 6, 1984, A9; State of California, Board of State Harbor Commissioners, Port of San Francisco, *Biennial Report for the Fiscal Years Commencing July 1, 1932, and Ending June 10, 1934* (n.p., 1934), 70; Eliel, *Waterfront and General Strikes*, 50–51; *NYT*, June 3, 1934, 25; June 8, 1934, 43; June 10, 1934, N20. Sources disagree regarding the first name of the man killed in San Pedro who died three years later, some citing him as Tom and some as John; John appears most frequently.

40. Eliel, *Waterfront and General Strikes*, 50–51.

41. Eliel, *Waterfront and General Strikes*, 43–44; Eliel cites Industrial Association files, nearly all of which were later destroyed; Waterfront Employers to McGrady, June 5, 1934, filed under "Conciliation—Strikes/Longshoremen," b42, Perkins Papers, RG 174, NA.

42. Strike Committee Minutes, June 4, 5, 6, 7, 9, 1934; Eliel, *Waterfront and General Strikes*, 44–45.

43. Eliel, *Waterfront and General Strikes*, 44–45; *NYT*, June 17, 1934, E6.

44. Eliel presents the Teamsters' decision alone as marking the end of the first phase of the strike; see *Waterfront and General Strikes*, 45; and *La Follette Committee Hearings*, pt. 4, 124.

45. Copy of letter, Lapham to Farley, executive letter no. 274, June 8, 1934, Lapham Papers, California Historical Society.

46. *News*, June 7, 1934, 1; June 8, 1934, 1; June 9, 1934, 1; July 11, 1934, 1, 5; letter Thomas H. Eliot to Perkins, June 13, 1934, filed under Conciliation—Strikes/Longshoremen, b42, Perkins Papers, NA; Eliel, *Waterfront and General Strikes*, 54, citing *Oakland Tribune*, June 12, 1934; Strike Committee Minutes, June 12 and 13, 1934; press release, June 13, 1934, filed under Strike Publicity Material and Notes, 1933–34 Series,

47. Eliel, *Waterfront and General Strikes*, 53; *News*, June 13, 1934, 1, 3.

48. *News*, June 14, 1934, 8; *Chronicle*, June 14, 1934, 6; *La Follette Committee Hearings*, pt. 4, 120.

49. *News*, June 14, 1934, 1; June 15, 1934, 1, 4; Eliel, *Waterfront and General Strikes*, 58. Eliel cites records of the Industrial Association and his own observations as a participant in the meeting.

50. *News*, June 15, 1934, 1, 4; Strike Committee Minutes, May 29, 1934; *Waterfront Worker*, June 12, 1934, 1, 2, 5; copy of letter, A. Brenner, Secretary, Machinists Lodge 68, to S.F. Labor Council, June 21, 1934, file General Strike, 1934, carton 31, San Francisco Labor Council Collection, Bancroft Library, University of California, Berkeley; Eliel, *Waterfront and General Strikes*, 60–66.

51. *News*, June 16, 1934, 1, 3, 13; *Chronicle*, June 16, 1934, 1, 3; June 17, 1934, 1, 2, 3; *Call-Bulletin*, June 16, 1934, 1, 2; *News*, June 16, 1934, 1, 13; Strike Committee Minutes, June 15, 1934; 1934 Strike Committee Minutes, 1933–34 Series, ILWU Library; Eliel, *Waterfront and General Strikes*, 67–73. The full text of the agreement is in Eliel, *Waterfront and General Strikes*, 218–20. Eliel cites files of the Industrial Association and a statement to him by Boynton regarding Casey's promise to resume work whether the ILA accepted the agreement or not. The photo of the signatures in the *Chronicle*, June 17, 1934, 2, makes clear that only Ryan was expected to sign for the ILA. Finnegan put his signature in the margin; Lewis and Peterson wisely did not do the same.

52. Proceedings of the National Longshoremen's Board, 1934, Testimony of Aug. 22, 733–37, Arbitration Collection, Institute of Industrial Relations Collection, LARC.

53. *San Francisco Chronicle*, June 17, 1934, 3.

54. *News*, June 16, 1934, 1; Eliel, *Waterfront and General Strikes*, 71. Eliel cites no source for his statement that the Industrial Association created the unanimous press response, but his position with the Industrial Association unquestionably put him in a position to know. See also telegram thanking Neylan for his work with the press: Clarence R. Lindner to Neylan, June 16, 1934, f21, series 6, b71, Neylan Papers, Bancroft Library, University of California, Berkeley.

55. Eliel, *Waterfront and General Strikes*, 74–75, citing a statement by Ryan in Mayor Rossi's office on July 18; Strike Committee Minutes, July 17, 1934.

56. Minutes, Special [Local 38-79] Meeting, Strike Committee Minutes, June 17, 1934; Eliel, *Waterfront and General Strikes*, 75–76.

57. *Chronicle*, June 18, 1934, 1, 4; Eliel, *Waterfront and General Strikes*, 76; Kagel interviewed by Robert Cherny, undated, hereinafter Kagel interview; the ten unions forming the Joint Strike Committee were: ILA, MEBA, Machinists, Boilermakers, SUP, MC&S, MFOW, Ships' Clerks, and MM&P.

58. Eliel, *Waterfront and General Strikes*, 76.

59. Eliel, *Waterfront and General Strikes*, 77–78, 220–21.

60. Senate Committee on Education and Labor, *Report*, pt. 4, 121.

61. *NYT*, July 1, 1934, E1; *News*, Aug. 5, 1938, 1.

62. Unidentified newspaper clipping entitled "Arms Invoice!!" with copy of invoice, 1933–34 Series, ILWU Library; memorandum of telephone call with Robert B. Wolf, Longview, Washington, June 19, 1934, file Conciliation—Strikes, Longshoremen, b42, Perkins Papers, NA.

63. Partial transcript of 1934 Strike Mass Meeting, Civic Auditorium; *Chronicle*, June 20, 1934, 1, 2; *Western Worker*, July 2, 1934, 6.

64. Partial transcript of 1934 Strike Mass Meeting, Civic Auditorium; *Chronicle*, June 20, 1934, 1, 2; *Western Worker*, July 2, 1934, 6.

65. Copies of letters, A. Brenner to Officers and Delegates, S.F. Labor Council, June 21, 1934; Vandeleur and O'Connell to Roosevelt, June 21, 1934, both filed under "General

Strike, 1934," carton 31, Labor Council Collection, Bancroft Library, University of California, Berkeley.

66. Eliel, *Waterfront and General Strikes*, 85–87; telegram, Plant to Perkins, June 21, 1934, file Conciliation-Strikes Longshoremen—1934, b35, Perkins Papers, NA.

67. NW Strike Committee Minutes, June 21, 1934; *Chronicle*, June 21, 1934, 2.

68. Eliel, *Waterfront and General Strikes*, 88–89.

69. Memo, Wyzanski to the Secretary of Labor, [ca. 4:00 p.m.,] June 22, 1934, filed under Conciliation—Strikes/Longshoremen—1934, b35, Perkins Papers, NA.

70. "Message from Miss Perkins," June 22, 1934, filed under Strikes—1934, b5; Johnson to Marvin H. McIntyre, June 22, 1934, received 2:39 a.m., apparently June 23, filed under 1934: Pacific Coast Longshoremen's Strike, b11, OF 407b, Franklin D. Roosevelt Papers, Franklin D. Roosevelt Library.

71. *News*, June 23, 1934, 1; Eliel, *Waterfront and General Strikes*, 89–90; letter, Ivan F. Cox to John J. O'Connell, June 26, 1934, filed under Longshoremen's Association, International, Local 38-79 (San Francisco), carton 11, Labor Council Collection, Bancroft Library, University of California, Berkeley.

72. *News*, June 23, 1934, 1, 3; *Chronicle*, June 24, 1934, 1, 5, 9; *NYT*, June 24, 1934, 17.

73. Telegram, Plant to Perkins, June 23, 1934, filed under Conciliation—Strikes/Longshoremen—1934, b35, Perkins Papers, NA; *Chronicle*, June 24, 1934, 1, 5, 9.

74. *News*, June 25, 1934, 1, 3; Strike Committee Minutes, June 25, 1934.

75. *News*, June 26, 1934, 1, 4.

76. *News*, June 26, 1934, 4; June 27, 1934, 1, 4.

77. *News*, June 28, 1934, 1; June 29, 1934, 3; *NYT*, June 27, 1934, 1; Eric Levy, "The 1926 San Francisco Carpenter's Strike" (master's thesis, San Francisco State University, 1986); Melnikow oral history, 201.

78. *News*, June 27, 1934, 1, 4; *NYT*, June 28, 1934, 5; Eliel, *Waterfront and General Strikes*, 96.

79. Press release: Issued by the Joint Marine Strike Committee, June 27, 1934, filed under Strike Publicity Material and Notes, 1933–34 Series, ILWU Library.

80. *News*, June 28, 1934, 1, 4; Melnikow oral history, 195.

81. Bridges to Roosevelt, June 29, 1934, reel 1, Frances Perkins Papers, micro-call no. PS #0472, Columbia University Library; copy filed under Conciliation—Strikes/Longshoremen, b42, Perkins Papers, NA; see also *News*, June 29, 1934, 1.

82. *News*, June 29, 1934, 1, 4.

83. *News*, June 29, 1934, 4; June 30, 1934, 3.

84. *News*, June 30, 1934, 1, 3.

85. Most articles in the Australian press were copied directly from the press release, for example, *Burnie Advocate*, July 2, 1934, 5, or *Hobart Mercury*, July 2, 1934, 3; interview with Dorothy McNaught, July 2, 1997; *Argus* (Melbourne), July 2, 1934, 10; see also *Essendon Gazette and Flemington Spectator*, July 5, 1934, 1.

86. Eliel, *Waterfront and General Strikes*, 102; Minutes of Special Meeting of Local 38-79, July 1, 1934, Local 10 Series, ILWU Library.

87. *News*, July 2, 1934, 1; copy of letter, O'Connell to W. Green, July 2, 1934, file: General Strike 1934, carton 31, San Francisco Labor Council Collection, Bancroft Library, University of California, Berkeley; Eliel, *Waterfront and General Strikes*, 106.

88. NW Strike Committee Minutes, July 5, 1934. The minutes are not clear whether the telegram was sent on July 3 or 5.

89. *News*, July 3, 1934, extra edition, 1, 3.

90. *News*, July 3, 1934, extra edition, 1, 3–5.

91. *News*, July 3, 1934, extra edition, 1, 3–5; testimonies 932 and 1207, testimonies from strike observers, 1933–34 Collection, ILWU Library; Eliel, *Waterfront and General Strikes*, 108–9.

92. Affidavit, Jack MacLalan, June 14, 1939; see also Dietrich testimony (July 21, 1939), Landis hearing, 10:1479, in which Dietrich pooh-poohs the story as designed to enhance Bridges's reputation. A highly dramatized version appears in Estolv Ward, *Harry Bridges on Trial* (New York: Modern Age Books, 1940), 3–7. See also Charles P. Larrowe, "The Great Maritime Strike of '45: Part I—Neither Red nor Dead," *Labor History* 11 (1970): 448.

93. *News*, July 4, 1934, extra edition, 1–3, 7; *Chronicle*, July 4, 1934, 17.

Chapter 5. The Big Strike: Bloody Thursday and After

1. McGrady to Perkins, July 5, 1934, file: Conciliation—Strikes—Longshoremen—1934, b35, Perkins Papers, RG 174, NA.

2. *News*, July 6, 1934, 2, 3; *Chronicle*, July 6, 1934, 1, BC.

3. George Hedley, address, July 19, 1934, f2, b9, Institute of Industrial Relations, University of California, Berkeley, LARC; Isaac Zafrani, untitled report, file: Testimonies from strike observers, ILWU Library.

4. *News*, July 6, 1934, 3; Aug. 5, 1938, 1; *Chronicle*, July 6, 1934, 1, BC; testimonies from Strike Observers, esp. Affidavit of James A. Duggar, Feb. 1937, ILWU Library.

5. T. B. W. Leland, Coroner, Coroner's Inquest upon the body of Howard F. Sperry and Nicholas Bordoise, transcript of testimony, Aug. 2, 1934, b3, ILWU Library; *Chronicle*, July 6, 1934, C; Testimonies from Strike Observers, ILWU Library.

6. *Chronicle*, July 6, 1934, 1; Elaine Black Yoneda oral history, interviewed by Lucy Kendall, California Historical Society, 1976–77, 38; Daniel Frontino Elash, "Greek American Communists and the San Francisco General Strike of 1934," *Journal of the Hellenic Diaspora* 33 (2007): 23–38.

7. Schmidt oral history, 101; Hedley, address.

8. *Chronicle*, July 6, 1934, 1, 2; *Joint Marine Journal* (mimeographed), July 9, 1934, file: ILWU Case Coast 1934 Handbills, 1934 collection, ILWU Library; untitled summary of the victims of 1934, file: Strike Publicity Material and Notes, 1934 collection, ILWU Library.

9. *News*, July 6, 1934, 3; *Chronicle*, July 6, 1934, A2.

10. Copies of telegrams, Joint Maritime Strike Committee to Roosevelt, July 5, 1934, Joint Marine Strike Committee to Green, July 5, 1934, file: ILWU Case 1934, 1933–34 Collections, ILWU Library.

11. *Chronicle*, July 6, 1934, 1, 2; *News*, July 6, 1934, 1, 2.

12. Copy of telegram, Casey to John M. Gillespie, July 6, 1934, series 1, f6, b16, Teamsters Papers, WHS.

13. Telegram, McGrady to Perkins, July 6, 1934, file: Conciliation—Strikes—Longshoremen—1934, b35, Perkins Papers, NA.

14. *News*, July 6, 1934, 3; Strike Committee Minutes, July 8, 1934.

15. Resolution, July 6, 1934, file: General Strike 1934, carton 31, San Francisco Labor Council Collection, Bancroft Library, University of California, Berkeley; David Selvin, *A Terrible Anger: The 1934 Maritime and General Strikes in San Francisco* (Detroit: Wayne State University Press, 1998), 155. For Kidwell, see *Chronicle*, Nov. 25, 1908, 5; and Jan. 17, 1923, 6. Kidwell was registered in the Farmer-Labor Party in the early 1920s but was supported by the Socialists and Communists in 1923. See Ralph E. Shaffer, "Communism in California, 1919–1924: 'Orders from Moscow' or Independent Western Radicalism," *Science & Society* 34 (1970): 418. He was registered as a Republican in the early 1930s but as a Democrat by the mid-1930s; voter registrations from Ancestry.com.

16. Paul Eliel, *The Waterfront and General Strikes: San Francisco, 1934* (San Francisco: Hooper, 1934), 105, 182, 187; Selvin, *Terrible Anger*, 156–57; Kagel interview.

17. Sam Darcy, unpublished memoirs, chap. 8, 351, Darcy Papers, Wagner Library, New York University.

18. *Chronicle*, July 8, 1934, 9.

19. *Chronicle*, July 9, 1934, 1.

20. Eliel, *Waterfront and General Strikes*, 132.

21. *News*, July 9, 1934, 1, 4; *Chronicle*, July 10, 1934, 1, 5; Selvin, *Terrible Anger*, 11–13; Mike Quin [Paul William Ryan], *The Big Strike* (Olema, CA: Olema, 1949), 119–30; Eliel, *Waterfront and General Strikes*, 127–28; Darcy, memoirs, 379–80.

22. Eliel, *Waterfront and General Strikes*, 128.

23. *News*, July 10, 1934, 1–3; July 11, 1934, 7; *Chronicle*, July 11, 1934, 1, 4; Eliel, *Waterfront and General Strikes*, 130.

24. *News*, July 11, 1934, 1; July 12, 1934, 1, 4.

25. *News*, July 12, 1934, 1, 3; letter, Casey to Gillespie, July 12, 1934, Teamsters Papers, WHS.

26. *News*, July 13, 1934, 1, 5.

27. *News*, July 14, 1934, 1, 3; untitled summary of the July 14 meeting, file: Strike Publicity Material and Notes, 1934 collection, ILWU Library.

28. Minutes, special meeting of Local 38-79, July 14, 1934, ILWU Library.

29. Selvin, *Terrible Anger*, 167–68; summary of telephone conversation, July 14, 1934; telegram, Johnson to Ickes, July 15, 1934; file: 1934: Pacific Coast Longshoremen's Strike, b11, OF 407b, Roosevelt Library; Perkins Oral History, bk. 6, 296, Oral History Office, Columbia University; St. Sure oral history, 373.

30. *New York Daily News*, July 19, 1934, 5, 10; for California coverage, see, for example, *Madera Tribune*, July 19, 1934, 1; and *Petaluma Argus-Courier*, July 19, 1934.

31. Memorandum of telephone conversation, July 18, 1934, file: Conciliation— Strikes—Longshoremen—1934, b42, Perkins Papers, NA; Eliel, *Waterfront and General Strikes*, 238–39.

32. Eliel, *Waterfront and General Strikes*, 146, 236–38; telegram, LUHOW [Louis Howe] to the President, July 15, 1934, file: 1934: Pacific Coast Longshoremen's Strike, b11, OF 407b, Roosevelt Library. For examples of *hysteria*, see letter, Harold Mack to Edward Bruce, July 16, 1934, Bruce Papers, Archives of American Art, microfilm reel d87:805–60; or Judge Sylvain Lazarus, *Examiner*, July 24, 1934, 1, 2.

33. Selvin, *Terrible Anger*, 182–85.

34. *Chronicle*, July 16, 1934, 1; *News*, July 16, 1934, 1; *Editor and Publisher*, July 21, 1934, 7.

35. Melnikow oral history, 186–87 (emphasis in the original).

36. *Chronicle*, July 17, 1934, 1; *News*, July 17, 1934, 3; telegrams, McIntyre to the President, July 15, 1934, 12:15 a.m., LUHOW to the President, July 15, 1934, LUHOW to the President, July 16, 1934, Naval Aid to President to RDO Washington, July 16, 1934, file: 1934: Pacific Coast Longshoremen's Strike, b11, OF407b, Roosevelt Library.

37. Telephone call, Williams to Hinckley, July 16, 1934, file: 1934: Pacific Coast Longshoremen's Strike, b11, OF 407b, Roosevelt Library.

38. Herbert Resner, "The Law in Action during the San Francisco Longshore and Maritime Strike of 1934," Project 1950, Works Progress Administration, District No. 8, Official Project 66-3-2858-Symbol 1871, Berkeley, CA, 1936, 47; *News*, July 17, 1934, 1–2; *Chronicle*, July 17, 1934, 1, 2, 4.

39. *Call-Bulletin*, July 17, 1934, 1.

40. Executive committee minutes and General Strike Committee Minutes for July 17, Coast Committee Case Files, b3, 1933–34, ILWU Library, hereinafter GSC.

41. Telegram, Hearst to Neylan, July 18 [1934], f218, series 3, b56, Neylan Papers, Bancroft Library, University of California, Berkeley.

42. Selvin, *Terrible Anger*, 193–94.

43. *News*, July 17, 1934, 1, 4; July 18, 1934, 1, 2; *Chronicle*, July 18, 1934, 1, 4; Robert Cantwell and Evelyn Seely, "War on the West Coast," *New Republic* (Aug. 1, 1934), 308–11.

44. Selvin, *Terrible Anger*, 193–94; Eliel, *Waterfront and General Strikes*, 160; Quin, *Big Strike*, 159–62; *NYT*, July 18, 1934, 3; letter, Winter to Taub and Wirin, July 30, 1934, 515-1-3613, RGASPI; *Nation* 139 (Oct. 10, 1934): 411–13; press release, American Civil Liberties Union, Sept. 23, 1934, file S.F. Waterfront Strike, 1936–37, cartoon 18, Barrows Papers, Bancroft Library, University of California, Berkeley; report of E. J. Connelly, Jan. 20, 1940, 99, file 39-915-558, Bridges FBI file.

45. Selvin, *Terrible Anger*, 193–94. Selvin argues that the close cooperation between the vigilantes and the San Francisco police implies official approval for at least some vigilante actions, approval that may have reached to the mayor's office; I agree.

46. "Meeting on Cadre Question and Political Emigrants," Jan. 28, 1936, 495-14-10, RGASPI.

47. John Kennedy Ohl, *Hugh S. Johnson and the New Deal* (DeKalb: Northern Illinois University Press, 1985), 218, 229, 233.

48. Telegram, McIntyre to the President, July 17, 1934, file: 1934 Pacific Coast Longshoremen's Strike, b11, OF407b, Franklin D. Roosevelt Papers, Franklin D. Roosevelt Library, hereinafter Roosevelt Papers.

49. Copy of letter, Johnson to Kidwell, July 17, 1934, f21, series 6, b71, John Francis Neylan Papers, Bancroft Library, University of California, Berkeley.

50. *News*, July 19, 1934, 1, 4, 5; telegrams, McIntyre to the President, July 17, 1934, and July 18, 1934, file: 1934 Pacific Coast Longshoremen's Strike, b11, OF 407b, Roosevelt Papers.

51. Minutes, July 18, 1934, GSC.

52. Melnikow oral history, 197; minutes, July 19, 1934, GSC. There are two slightly different versions of Vandeleur's comment about the assurances of public officials, one apparently in an earlier and more complete draft of the minutes.

53. *News*, July 19, 1934, 5.

54. Letter, Casey to John M. Gillespie, July 27, 1934, f6, b16, series 1, Teamster Papers, WHS; Neylan oral history, 145; Eliel, *Waterfront and General Strikes*, 172; *News*, July 21, 1934, 1; copy of letter, 42 Steamship Companies to NLB, July 27, 1934, file: Coast Correspondence with NLB, 1934 collection, ILWU Library; St. Sure oral history, 79.

55. Telegram, "Radio Washington" to the President, undated; file: 1934 Pacific Coast Longshoremen's Strike, b11, OF 407b, Roosevelt Papers; *News*, July 18, 1934, 3; July 19, 1934, 4; July 20, 1934, 1, 4; July 21, 1934, 1; letter, Ryan to Bjorklund, July 19, 1934, reproduced in letter from Bjorklund to all affiliated locals, July 21, 1934, file District Office (Communications) J. C. Bjorklund W J. Lewis, bB10 (Vrana), ILWU Local 8 files, Portland, hereinafter Local 8.

56. *News*, July 21, 1934, 1; *Chronicle*, July 22, 1934, 1, 6; handwritten telegram, Thurston to Chas. Peabody, n.d., file: National Longshoremen's Board, bB10 (Vrana), Local 8 papers.

57. *News*, July 23, 1934, 1; *Chronicle*, July 26, 1934, 1; Eliel, *Waterfront and General Strikes*, 175; Proceedings of National Longshoremen's Board, 1934, hearing of Aug. 8, b18, and report of the board to Secretary of Labor Perkins, Feb. 8, 1935, b19-A, Arbitration Collection of the Institute of Industrial Relations, University of California, Berkeley, LARC, hereinafter NLB proceedings.

58. Minutes, Special Meeting of Local 38-79, July 23, 1934, file: ILWU Case Coast 1934, 1934 collection, ILWU Library.

59. Minutes, Special Meeting of Local 38-79, July 24, 1934, file: ILWU Case Coast 1934, 1934 collection; ILA Local 38-79 Strike Bulletin no. 25, July 23, 1934, file: ILWU Case Coast 1934 Handbills, ILWU Library. Morris succeeded Bjorklund as district secretary around this time; Bjorklund had been elected sheriff.

60. *News*, July 24, 1934, 1, 4; July 26, 1934, 1; *News*, July 28, 1934, 1, 2; July 30, 1934, 1, 5.

61. Special Bulletin, file: ILWU Case Coast 1934, 1934 collection, ILWU Library; *News*, July 31, 1934, 1, 16; NLB proceedings, Aug. 22, 1934, esp. 745.

62. Ottilie Markholt, *Maritime Solidarity: Pacific Coast Unionism, 1929–1938* (Tacoma: Pacific Coast Maritime History Committee, 1998), 5–7, 199–201.

63. NLB proceedings, Aug. 16–17, 1934, esp. 163–234.

64. NLB proceedings, Aug. 12–13, 1934, esp. 163–234; Aug. 16 and 17, 1934, special minutes of postsession proceedings both days; Kagel interviewed by Robert Cherny, n.d.; Melnikow oral history, 203–5.

65. NLB proceedings, Aug. 20–21, 1934, esp. 639–40.

66. *Chronicle*, Sept. 16, 1934, 1; Sept 18, 1934, 1; Sept. 21, 1934, 2; Sept. 22, 2, 1934.

67. NLB proceedings, Sept. 24, 1934, esp. 2340–42, 2348–50, 2367.

68. NLB proceedings, Sept. 25, 1934, esp. 2375–77, 2411, 2422–23.

69. Melnikow oral history, 205–6.

70. Report of the NLB to Secretary of Labor Perkins, Feb. 8, 1935, Appendix E, Perkins Papers, NA; *Chronicle*, Oct. 13, 1934, 1, 4; Oct. 14, 1934, 9.

71. Markholt, *Maritime Solidarity*, 216–20.

72. *Chronicle*, Oct. 2, 1934, 4; Oct. 3, 1934, 9; Oct. 16, 1934, 5; memo, Wyzanski to Perkins, Nov. 14, 1934, file Conciliation—Strikes—Longshoremen, b42, Perkins Papers, NA; Melnikow oral history, 214.

73. Memo, McGrady to Perkins, Nov. 16, 1934, file Conciliation—Strikes—Longshoremen, b42, Perkins Papers, NA; *Chronicle*, Nov. 16, 1934, 16; Nov. 18, 1934, 4; Nov 22, 1934, 13; transcript of proceedings before Honorable M. C. Sloss, Arbitrator, Thursday, Jan. 1, 1935, file: Coast Dispatching—Sloss, Jan. 18, 1935, b5, Coast Committee Cases, 1935–36, ILWU Library.

Chapter 6. Pursuing Maritime Unity

1. James MacGregor Burns, *Roosevelt: The Lion and the Fox* (New York: Harcourt, Brace, and World, 1956), 218; Melvyn Dubofsky, *The State and Labor in Modern America* (Chapel Hill: University of North Carolina Press, 1994), 129. Dubofsky disputes those scholars who see the Wagner Act as an effort by capital to discipline labor.

2. *Chronicle*, Oct. 1, 1934, 1, 11; Oct. 2, 1934, 9; Oct. 4, 1934, 8; Oct. 13, 1934, 1; Melvyn Dubofsky and Warren Van Tine, *John L. Lewis: A Biography* (New York: Quadrangle, 1977), 208–11.

3. For the C&H organizing drive, see Harvey Schwartz, *The March Inland: Origins of the ILWU Warehouse Division, 1934–1938* (Los Angeles: Institute of Industrial Relations, University of California, Los Angeles, 1978), 39–45.

4. PolBuro minutes, Oct. 25, 1934, 515-1-3446, RGASPI; Stachel's report was printed as "Our Trade Union Policy," *Communist* 13 (Nov. 1934): 1187–94.

5. Bridges testimony, Aug. 2, 1939, Official Report of Proceedings before the Immigration and Naturalization Service of the Department of Labor, Docket no. 55973-217, in the matter of Harry Bridges—Deportation Hearing, 2606, 2608, 2628; Bridges told me about the Grants Pass meeting during an unrecorded interview in Jan. 1986; letters, S. D. [Darcy] to Comrade Stachel, Nov. 21, 1934, 515-1-3613; M. Raport to Comrade Stachel, Dec. 11, 1934, 515-1-3605; Sam Darcy to Jack [Stachel], Dec. 17, 1934, D[arcy] to Jack [Stachel], Dec. 27, 1934, 515-1-3613; Darcy to Central Committee, Dec. 30, 1934, 515-1-3613; PolBuro minutes, Dec. 20, 1934, 515-1-3447; PolBuro minutes, Feb. 14, 1935, 515-1-3752; PolBuro minutes, Mar. 9, 1935, 515-1-3753, all in RGASPI; *Western Worker*, Nov. 1, 1934, 2; statement of Selim Silver, report of [name redacted], Nov. 29, 1940, file 39-515-672, 185, 187–90, Bridges FBI file

6. Letter, Morris to Lewis, Oct. 30, 1934, f1, b1, William J. Lewis Collection, LARC (hereinafter Lewis Papers, LARC); letter to all maritime unions on the Pacific Coast from Lewis and Morris, Jan. 17, 1935, file Maritime Federation, Jan. 1935–Dec. 31, 1935, b9, ILWU Local 8 records, Portland; Melnikow oral history, 262; unsigned report on West Coast and Denver, July 13, 1935, 496-14-31, RGASPI. See also Proposals for Organizing West Coast Maritime Workers Federation and Establishing United Front Program [undated, but includes references to a Sept. 23 fraction meeting], 515-1-3612, regarding the failed efforts by the CP to take the initiative in forming a federation. See also Vernon Pedersen, *The Communist Party on the American Waterfront: Revolution, Reform, and the Quest for Power* (Lanham, MD: Lexington Books, 2019), 153.

7. *Proceedings of the 28th Annual Convention of the Pacific Coast District, . . . 1935*, b2, Ottilie Markholt Papers; minutes of the originating meeting, f1–2, b1, Maritime Federation of the Pacific Coast Records, LARC (hereinafter MFP Records).

8. *Chronicle*, Mar. 20, 1935, 10; Mar. 30, 1935, 4; Resolution on ILA Local 38-79 letterhead, Mar. 22, 1935, signed by Bridges and Ivan Cox, file: Longshoremen's Association, International, Local 38-79, carton 11, SFLC Collection, Bancroft Library, University of California, Berkeley; *News*, Mar, 23, 1935, clipping in file: Council Elections, 1932–36, carton 23, SFLC Collection, Bancroft, University of California, Berkeley.

9. Ottilie Markholt, *Maritime Solidarity: Pacific Coast Unionism, 1929–1938* (Tacoma: Pacific Coast Maritime History Committee, 1998), 217; Melnikow oral history, 107, 159, 244; Stephen Schwartz, *Brotherhood of the Sea: A History of the Sailor's Union of the Pacific, 1885–1985* (New Brunswick, NJ: Transaction Books/Rutgers—State University for the Sailors' Union of the Pacific, 1986), 112, 113; Bruce Nelson, *Workers on the Waterfront*: Seamen, Longshoremen, and Unionism in the 1930s (Urbana: University of Illinois Press, 1988), 165, 185.

10. Minutes of founding conference, Apr. 15–24, 1935, f3, b1, MFP Records.

11. Minutes of founding conference, Apr. 15–24, 1935, f3, b1, MFP Records. Pedersen, *Communist Party on the American Waterfront*, 153–55, views the convention as a contest between CP and anti-CP groups. I read the minutes as suggesting more complex alignments.

12. *Chronicle*, Apr. 24, 1935, 1; minutes of founding conference, Apr. 25, 1935, f3, b1, MFP Records; *Chronicle*, Apr. 26, 1935, 6; Apr. 28, 1935, 4; Melnikow oral history, 262.

13. The most thorough accounts are in Jane Cassels Record, "Ideologies and Trade Union Leadership: The Case of Harry Bridges and Harry Lundeberg" (PhD diss., University of California, Berkeley, 1954), esp. 39–45; and S. Schwartz, *Brotherhood of the Sea*, 88–90. Bruce Nelson's study *Workers on the Waterfront* presents syndicalism as the central feature of the revival of unionism among maritime workers in the mid-1930s.

14. See, for example, reports by locals, *Proceedings of the 28th Annual Convention*.

15. *Proceedings of the 28th Annual Convention*.

16. NB tape 20; *Chronicle*, May 26, 1935, 1; card from Tom Mooney, Bridges personal papers; Report of E. J. Connelley, Nov. 20, 1940, 22, file 39-915-558; Report of [name redacted], Nov. 29, 1940, file 39-915-672, 38, both Bridges FBI file. For the CP, Bridges's ulcer attack raised several questions, as outlined in a letter by N. S[parks] to Stachel, June 1, 1935, 515-1-3873, RGASPI: "[Bridges] really came within an ace of death and for the first 48 hours after his attack it seemed probable that he would actually die. The Comrades who were in close touch with him told us they knew he had stomach ulcers, but they never thought of raising the question of proper care of his health. I might also say again that the Comrades are still underestimating his importance. . . . [H]is importance is [much greater] than most of the Comrades there seem to realize and [his hospitalization] also raises very sharply the question of secondary cadres."

17. *Chronicle*, June 5, 1935, 1, 3; June 14, 1935, 1; Markholt, *Maritime Solidarity*, 225–26; *NYT*, Aug. 1, 1935, 2; Melnikow oral history, 245. Pedersen, *Communist Party on the American Waterfront*, 155, agrees with Scharrenberg's claim that his expulsion was engineered by the CP. My conclusion is that it was done by Lundeberg, likely as a personal power play; Lundeberg was never directed by the CP.

18. *Chronicle*, June 5, 1935, 1.

19. Trade Union Commission minutes, July 1, 1935, 515-1-3770, RGASPI; *Chronicle*, July 9, 1935, 1, 4; July 11, 1935, 1, 5; July 12, 1, 15, 1935.

20. *NYT*, July 14, 1935, N8; Trade Union Commission minutes, July 13, 1935, 515-1-3754, RGASPI.

21. *Chronicle*, July 14, 1935, 1, 4; *NYT*, July 14, 1935, N8; letter, Morris Raport [Rappaport] to Stachel, July 12: "I do not think that the waterfront employers and the labor fakers are so stupid as to write such a thing. . . . [T]his document stupidly drawn up is used as a guise to hide the real information they are getting" (515-1-13873, RGASPI). I conclude that Rappaport gave the authors of the forgery too much credit for guile.

22. These events are summarized in Markholt, *Maritime Solidarity*, 235–37. Regarding SUP demands to discharge Filipino crew members, see *Chronicle*, Aug. 6, 1935, 5; Aug. 8, 1935, 4. Pedersen, *Communist Party on the American Waterfront*, 155, repeats employers' claims that the embargo was created by "concealed Communists inside the San Francisco ILA." I found no evidence for such a claim. Clearly, by early August if not earlier, Bridges saw the "hot cargo" situation as a serious problem for both the union and him.

23. *Chronicle*, July 6, 1935, 1, 9.

24. *Chronicle*, July 22, 1935, 1; Jan. 21, 1936, 5; [Betty] Jacqueline Bridges Jourdan interviewed by Robert Cherny, Feb, 13, 1993. Her daughter, Marie Shell, has told me that her mother believed it was an assassination attempt, but Ms. Jourdan did not say that explicitly in our interview.

25. Letters, Casey to Tobin, Apr. 23, 1935; Tobin to Casey, Mar. 27, 1935, both in fl, b17, series 1, Teamster Papers, WHS; memo, McGrady to Perkins, Oct. 29, 1935, folder: Maritime Federation of the Pacific Conciliation—Strikes, b40, Perkins Papers, NA; memo, Donoghue to Perkins, Aug. 2, 1935, file Donoghue, PA, b32, Papers, Columbia; letter, Morris to all affiliated [ILA-PCD] locals, Aug. 21, 1935, f3, b1, Markholt Papers.

26. *Pacific Coast Longshoreman* (Seattle; hereinafter *PCL*), Aug. 12, 1935, 6–7; Markholt, *Maritime Solidarity*, 238; Lundeberg, "Report of Harry Lundeberg, during term as president, Maritime Federation of the Pacific, April 30th, 1935 to January 1st, 1936," file Maritime Federation 1936, b2, Markholt Papers. There were no minutes, but Fred Tobin of IBT's Washington office sat in and left a detailed account of what transpired; see letter, Tobin to Michael Casey, Aug. 5 and 6, 1935, fl, b17, series 1, IBT Papers, WHS.

27. Report of the Washington Marine Conference, by P. T., Aug. 8, 1935, 515-1-3915, RGASPI.

28. *Chronicle*, Aug. 9, 1935, 15; May 20, 1936, 7.

29. Anonymous report on the Aug. 11 mass meeting, dated Aug. 12, 1935, file 1934: Pacific Coast Longshoremen's Strike, b11, OF 407b, FDR Papers; *PCL*, Aug. 19, 1935, 2, 3, 5, 6.

30. *PCL*, Sept, 2, 1935, 1.

31. Telegram, Pacific Shipowners and Waterfront Employers to Morris, Aug. 25, 1935, file Correspondence WEA 1935, and separate letters from J. A. Lunny and K. C. Conyers to ILA-PCD District Council, July 30, 1935, letter, H. W. Burchard, to same, July 31, 1935, file Coast ILA-Negotiations, b5, Coast Committee Case Files, ILWU Library.

32. *Chronicle*, Sept. 15, 1935, 3; *PCL*, Sept. 23, 1935, 6.

33. Jack [Johnstone], Report on State Federation of Labor Convention, 515-1-3912, RGASPI; *Chronicle*, Sept. 17, 1935, 3; Sept. 18, 1935, 4; Sept. 19, 1935, 1, 15; Sept. 20, 1935, 1, 2; Sept. 21, 1935, 1, 9.

34. *Chronicle*, Sept. 27, 1935, 1; Sept. 28, 1935, 1, 12; Oct. 1, 1935, 1, 4; Oct. 2, 1935, 1; Oct. 3, 1935, 1, 15; Oct. 4, 1935, 1, 2; Oct. 8, 1935, 1, 1; file: Hot Cargo (Santa Cruz), Sept. 27, 1935, b5, Coast Committee Files, ILWU Library; Markholt, *Maritime Solidarity*, 240–44.

35. Minutes of special MFP convention, Nov. 12–22, 1935, f4, 5, b1, Maritime Federation of the Pacific Coast Records, LARC.

36. *Chronicle*, Jan. 5, 1936, 1; Jan. 12, 1936, 12; Jan. 15, 1936, 15; Jan. 28, 1936, 1, 15; Jan. 29, 1936, 1; Feb. 1, 1936, 3; Apr. 12, 1936, 1, 9; Melnikow oral history, 248.

37. *NYT*, Feb. 14, 1936, E7.

38. Markholt, *Maritime Solidarity*, 258–63; *Chronicle*, Apr. 11, 1936, 1.

39. Markholt, *Maritime Solidarity*, 258–63; *Chronicle*, Apr. 13, 1936, 1, 13; Apr. 14, 1936, 1, 15; *Portland Oregonian*, Apr. 18, 1936, 1; letter, William Fischer to ILA Local 38-78, Portland, et al., Apr. 16, 1936, file Maritime Federation, Jan. 1936–Dec. 31, 1938, b9, Local 8.

40. Telegram, Fischer and F. M. Kelley to Ed Coester, Apr. 15, 1936; letter, Fischer to Local 38-78 and MRP district council secretaries, Apr. 16, 1936, both in file Maritime Federation, Jan. 1936–Dec. 31, 1938, b9, Local 8; *Chronicle*, Apr. 16, 1, 13; Apr. 17, 1936, 1, 10; telegram, Marsh and FitzGerald to McGrady, Apr. 17, 1936, file Longshoremen 1936–1937–1938/Conciliation—Strikes, b38, Perkins Papers, NA; *Call-Bulletin*, Apr. 21, 1936, 1, 2.

41. Kagel interview; *News*, Mar. 23, 1936, clipping in vol. 12, Scharrenberg Scrapbook, Paul Scharrenberg Papers, Bancroft Library, University of California, Berkeley; *Chronicle*, Apr. 18, 1, 13; Apr. 19, 1, 10; Apr. 20, 1, 13, 1936; *Portland Oregonian*, Apr. 20, 1936, 1, 2; Apr. 21 agreement, including Apr. 18 agreement, Sloss's letter of Apr. 20, and transcript of the meeting of Apr. 21, Markholt Papers.

42. Transcript of telephone conversation, E. H. FitzGerald and H. L. Kerwin, Apr. 21, 1936, but apparently misdated since it refers to events of Apr. 20 as coming later that day, Longshoremen 1936–1937–1938/Conciliation—Strikes, b38, Perkins Papers, NA; Apr. 21 Agreement, Markholt Papers; *Chronicle* Apr. 21, 1936, 1, 4, 5; Apr. 22, 1936, 1, 9; unsigned letters, Lundeberg to Dombroff, Apr. 23 and 30, 1936, file Dombroff Personal Correspondence, b3, Markholt Papers. Ottilie Markholt confirmed that the letters were from Lundeberg, and that is also clear from the content and the handwriting.

43. Trade Union Commission to All Marine Fractions and Coastal Districts, Oct. 11, 1935, 515-1-3773, RGASPI; *Chronicle*, Apr. 3, 1936, 13; May 4, 1936, 8; *PCL*, Apr 13, 1936, 7; telegram, Bridges to Perkins, May 1, 1936, copy of telegram, Perkins to Bridges, May 1, 1936; Memorandum, J. R. Steelman to the Secretary, May 1, 1936, all in file Longshoremen 1936–1937–1938/Conciliation—Strikes, b38, Perkins Papers, NA.

44. *Proceedings of the 29th Annual Convention of the Pacific Coast District*, b3, Markholt Papers; *Chronicle*, May 5, 1936, 2; May 20, 1936, 1; July 12, 1936, 3.

45. Copy of letter, Morris to Ryan, June 5, 1936, f2, b1, Lewis Papers, LARC; *Chronicle*, July 12, 1936, 3. CP officials were concerned that Bridges might not be elected; see letters,

N. S[parks] to Earl Browder, Apr. 18, 1935, H. Jackson to Comrade Hudson, Apr. 22, 1935, 515-1-3873, RGASPI.

46. Minutes, second annual convention of the MFP, f1, b2, MFP collection, LARC.

47. *Chronicle*, July 25, 1936, 1; Sept. 11, 1936, 16; Schmidt oral history, 158. The FBI did an extensive interview with Marlowe; see report of [name redacted], Nov. 29, 1940, file 39-515-672, 132–38, Bridges FBI file.

48. Letters, Bridges to Lewis, Sept. 4, 1936, and Lewis to Bridges, Sept. 14, 1936, pt. 1, series 2, microfilm reel 19, CIO Files of John L. Lewis; ILA 38-79 *Bulletin*, Oct. 5, 1936; minutes of reconvened meeting of Local 38-79, Oct 26, 1936, File: Local 10, ILA 38-79 Minutes, Membership Meetings, ILWU Library; John Schomaker, report from Local 38-79, *PCL*, Nov. 2, 1936, 6. For more detail on the 1936 election, see my "Prelude to the Popular Front: The Communist Party in California, 1931–1935," *American Communist History* 1 (2002): 5–37, and my forthcoming book on the CP in the San Francisco Bay Area.

49. *Literary Digest*, Jan. 4, 1936, 9; June 6, 1936, 11; Sept. 5, 1936, 7; Sept. 12, 1936, 5; Oct. 17, 1936, 7; Oct. 31, 1936, 5–6. In late September, Herbert Hoover wrote that he remained hopeful for a Republican victory and thought the *Literary Digest*'s polls might not be reliable; letter, Hoover to Mattei (a shipping executive), Sept. 27, 1936, f335(2), b431, Post Presidential Individual series, Herbert Hoover Papers, Herbert Hoover Presidential Library.

50. Letters, Steelman to Perkins, quoting Bloch, Sept. 8, 1936, reel 13, micro call PS#0472, Perkins Collection, microfilm edition, Columbia; Farley to Perkins, Sept. 14, 1936, file Maritime Situation—Pacific Coast, b38, Perkins Papers, NA; Farley to FDR, Sept. 12, 1936, file Strikes—1936, b5, FDR Papers; and McGrady to FDR, Sept. 20, 1936, reel 10, Perkins Collection, microfilm edition, Columbia (both the Farley letters attached a copy of the McCarthy letter, dated Sept. 9 and sent air mail and special delivery); Casey to J. M. Gilespie, Oct. 30, 1936, f2, b17, series 1, IBT Papers, WHS.

51. Melvyn Dubofsky and Warren Van Tine, *John L. Lewis: A Biography* (New York: Quadrangle/New York Times Book, 1977), 222–44, 250–53; Robert H. Zieger, *The CIO: 1935–1955* (Chapel Hill: University of North Carolina Press, 1995), chaps. 2–4.

52. The letter is a retyped copy with the addressee's name removed and the signatory's name removed, along with other identifiable material, filed under Steelman, John R., and dated Sept. 7, 1936; reel #13, Perkins Papers, Columbia. Some references point to Steelman's letter to Perkins of the previous day.

53. Regarding Perry, see "Brief History of Arthur James Kent," Doc. 2123, Leonard Papers; affidavit of Arthur Kent, Los Angeles, Dec. 28, 1937, f2, b3, series 1, Surveillance Papers, LARC; Estolv E. Ward, *The Gentle Dynamiter: A Biography of Tom Mooney* (Palo Alto, CA: Ramparts Press, 1983), 236–37; S. Schwartz, *Brotherhood of the Sea*, 120–21. Perry interviewed by the FBI, which also collected information about her from other informants. See, for example, report by [name redacted], Nov. 20, 1940, 3–5, file 39-915-571; and esp. report of E. J. Connelley, Nov. 20, 1940, 875–93, 39-915-558, Bridges FBI files.

54. George West, "The Labor Strategist of the Embarcadero," *New York Times Magazine*, Oct. 25, 1935, 7, 17.

55. *Chronicle*, Aug. 1, 1936, 13; Aug. 3, 1936, 4; Aug. 6, 1936, 15; Aug. 20, 1936, 5; Aug. 22, 1936, 5.

56. *Chronicle*, Aug. 25, 1936, 1; Aug. 26, 1936, 3; Aug. 28, 1936, 3, 7; letter, Steelman to Perkins, Sept. 8, 1936, reel 13, micro call PS#0472, Perkins Collection, microfilm edition, Columbia; Melnikow oral history, 166.

57. Letter, Caylor to McGrady, Sept. 1, 1936, file Maritime Situation—Pacific Coast, b38, Perkins Papers, NA; *Chronicle*, Sept. 1, 1936; letter, Steelman to Perkins, Sept. 8, 1936, reel 13, micro call PS#0472, Perkins Collection, microfilm edition, Columbia. The Coast Committee for the Shipowners published an open letter that included copies of all correspondence during the month of August; see file Publicity Employers, series: 1936–37 Maritime Strike, ILWU Library. The September 7 issue of *PCL* has an extensive analysis of the employers' proposals and reasons for rejecting them. See also telegram, Plant to Ryan, Sept. 8, 1936, file correspondence with Joseph P. Ryan, series: 1936–37 Maritime Strike, ILWU Library.

58. *PCL*, Sept. 14, 1936, 8; Sept. 21, 1936, 1, 7.

59. Letters, McGrady to Roosevelt, Sept. 20, 1936, file Pacific Coast Longshoremen's Strike, b11, FDR MS, OF 407b; Plant to Pacific Coast District Local 38, Sept. 23, 1936, ILA-PCD Executive Board to Coast Committee for the Shipowners, Oct. 9, 1936, in file Negotiations; Correspondence with WEA, series: 1935–37, ILWU Library; log of the Joint Negotiating Committee.

60. Log of the Joint Negotiating Committee; *Chronicle*, Oct. 1, 1936, 1, 14; Oct. 3, 1936, 15.

61. Jeffrey L. Stafford, "The Pacific Coast Maritime Strike of 1936: Another View," *Pacific Historical Review* 77 (2008): 589–93; log of the Joint Negotiating Committee.

62. Stafford, "Pacific Coast Maritime Strike of 1936," 593–604; Minutes of the Joint Negotiating Committee, filed as Minutes of Affiliated Unions, Aug. 29, 1936–Feb. 4, 1937, 1936–36 Coastwise Collection, ILWU Library; *Chronicle, October 14, 1936, 1*; letter, Bridges to Ryan, Oct. 15, 1936, file: correspondence with J. Ryan, series: 1936–37 Maritime Strike, ILWU Library. The MFP District Council 2 issued a "Day by Day Report on Pacific Coast situation," on Oct. 18, 1936, file: Press Releases, series: 1936–37 Maritime Strike, ILWU Library

63. *Chronicle*, Oct. 21, 1, A; Melnikow oral history, 277; Stafford, "Pacific Coast Maritime Strike of 1936," 593–604. Stafford presents an argument that the unions backed out on the deal to extend the agreement because Bridges talked on the phone with Perkins who encouraged him to hold out for more. I find my version of the situation more likely, that the union leaders took up the matter with their negotiating committees and were told to ask for more. Further, the MFP unions had agreed that they would go out together and that no union would return until all got a settlement. Thus, Bridges and Lundeberg could not have made commitments for the other MFP unions.

64. Minutes of the Joint Negotiating Committee; Stafford, "Pacific Coast Maritime Strike of 1936," 593–604; *Chronicle*, Oct. 22, 1936, 1, 17; Oct. 23, 1936, 1, 17.

65. Copy of letter, E. T. Ford to Bridges, Oct. 23, 1936, file: Negotiations: Correspondence with WEA, series: 1935–37; ILWU Library; *Chronicle*, Oct. 24, 1936, 1, 15.

66. *Chronicle*, Oct. 25, 1936, 1, 21; Oct. 27, 1936, 1, 15; Oct. 28, 1936, 1, 15.

67. Letter, Plant to Bridges, Oct. 28, 1936, file: Negotiations: Correspondence with WEA, Series: 1935–37, ILWU Library; *Chronicle*, Oct. 29, 1936, 1, 2; Oct. 30, 1936, 1, 17; Minutes of the Joint Negotiating Committee; log of the Joint Negotiating Committee; telegram, McGrady to McIntyre, Oct. 29, 1936, file: 1934: Pacific Coast Longshore Strike, b11, FDR Papers, OF 407b; letter, Casey to Gillespie, Oct. 30, 1036, f2, b17, IBT Papers, WHS. On the failure of negotiations, see telegram, Steelman to Perkins, Oct. 29, 1936, file: Maritime Situation—Pacific Coast, b38, Perkins Papers, NA. For a concise summary of strike events on both coasts, see "The Maritime Strikes of 1936–37," *Monthly Labor Review* 44 (Apr. 1937): 815–27. Melnikow, in his oral history, 277, states that Bridges opposed going on strike.

68. See, for example, report of the Patrol Committee for Nov. 1, 1936; file: Patrol Committee, series: 1936–37 Maritime Strike, ILWU Library; report, Wharton to Charles Martin, Sept. 23, 1936, file Labor, Maritime, 1935–37, Wharton Files, Oregon State Archives.

69. *NYT*, Nov. 1, 1936, 1, 50; Nov. 8, 1936, 1, 39; "Maritime Strikes of 1936–37," 817; telegram, Lawrensen to Bridges, Nov. 11, 1936, file: 1936–27 Maritime Strike East Coast Correspondence, Series 1936–37, ILWU Library.

70. Telegram, Steelman to Perkins, Oct. 29, 1936, file: Maritime Situation—Pacific Coast,; memorandum, McGrady to Perkins, Nov. 5, 1936, b38, Perkins Papers, NA; *Chronicle*, Nov. 7, 1936, 1.

71. Log of the Joint Negotiating Committee.

72. Minutes of the Joint Policy Committee for Nov. 17, Dec. 14, Dec. 21, 1936, file: 1936–7 Maritime Strike Coast Policy Committee Minutes, b6, Coast Committee files, ILWU Library, hereinafter Minutes of the Joint Policy Committee; Melnikow oral history, 278.

73. List of donations, Feb. 20, 1937, file Donations, series: 1936–37 Maritime Strike, ILWU Library. the ILWU Library has letters from waterfront cafés offering special prices to strikers. See file: Joint Relief Committee Correspondence and Misc., series: 1936–37 Maritime Strike, ILWU Library.

74. Letter, Bridges to Ryan, Nov. 29, 1936, file: correspondence with J. Ryan, series: 1936–37 Maritime Strike, ILWU Library.

75. *Chronicle*, Dec. 5, 1936, 4; Dec. 6, 1936, 1.

76. Letter, John Schomaker to K. C. Korlek, Nov. 23, 1936, f2, b4, Francis Murnane Papers, Oregon Historical Society; flyer, Broadcast No. 1 of the Voice of the Maritime Unions, file: Publicity-Radio, series: 1936–37 Maritime Strike, ILWU Library; Dore, transcript of speech, Seattle, Nov. 30 [1936], file: Misc. Speeches by Dore, Lapham, Bridges, series: 1936–37 Maritime Strike, ILWU Library; *PCL*, Nov. 30, 1936, 1; Flyer, "Support the Maritime Workers," and pamphlet, *Negroes and the Maritime Strike*, file: publicity union, series: 1936–37 Maritime Strike, ILWU Library.

77. *Chronicle*, Dec. 9, 1936, 1, 15; Dec. 10, 1936, 10; the *News* presented both Bridges's and Lapham's comments in full, Dec. 9, 1936, 4, 8.

78. Melnikow oral history, 268. Regarding battles over perishable cargoes, see minutes of the Joint Policy Committee for Nov. 11, Dec. 11, 1936; *Chronicle*, Dec. 1, 1936, 9.

79. Clarice Stasz, *Jack London's Women* (Amherst: University of Massachusetts Press, 2003), 282–85.

80. Regarding Mayes, see, for example, copy of letter, Herbert Novoisek to Alameda County Labor Council, Apr. 20, 1936, regarding expulsion of Mayes from the American Federation of Government Employees for "holding secret caucuses"; letters, Bridges to Daniel Tobin, Oct. 1, 1936, and Tobin to Bridges, Oct. 6, 1936, regarding Mayes's role in the 1934 Minneapolis Teamsters' strike; minutes of the *Voice* editorial board for Dec. 9 and 15, 1936; letter from all editorial board members to all members of the MFP, Dec. 16, 1936; all in f56/3, b56, MFP Papers, LARC. Minutes of the Joint Policy Committee, Nov, 5, 6, 10, 1936. The issue was fully aired in the *Voice*: Jan. 7, 1937, 5–8; Jan. 14, 1937, 5–8; Jan. 21, 1937, 5–8; Jan. 28, 1937, 5–8; Feb. 4, 1937, 5.

81. *Chronicle*, Dec. 11, 1936, 6; Dec. 12, 1936, 11; Dec. 13, 1936, 1; Dec. 15, 1936, 5.

82. *Chronicle*, Dec. 16, 1936, 1, 6; Dec. 17, 1936, 1, 10; Dec. 18, 1936, 11; flyers advertising Madison Square Garden meeting, file: Harry Bridges, Material About, and file: 1936–37 Maritime Strike, East Coast Correspondence, series: 1936–37 Strike, ILWU Library; copy of telegram, Lundeberg to Chairman: Seamen's Mass Meeting, Dec. 16, 1936, file: 1936–37 Maritime Strike, East Coast—Correspondence, series: 1936–37 Maritime Strike, ILWU Library, Louis Adamic, "Harry Bridges Comes East," *Nation* (Dec. 26, 1936): 753.

83. *Portland News-Telegram*, Dec. 17, 1936, 1; *Chronicle*, Dec. 18, 1936, 1; Dec. 22, 1936, 6; Dec 23, 1936, 12; press release, ILA-PCD, Dec. 22, 1936, file: press releases, series: 1936–37 Maritime Strike, ILWU Library; telephonic conversation between McGrady and Ella E. Halbig, Dec. 22, 1936; and Steelman, "Pacific Coast Situation," undated but after Dec. 22, file Maritime Strike—Secretary's File, b38, Perkins Papers, NA; letter, Casey to Tobin, Dec. 28, 1936, f2, b17, series 1, IBT Papers, WHS. Pedersen, in *Communist Party on the American Waterfront*, 181, claims Bridges returned from New York "with instructions to undo as much of McGrady's work as possible" and cites McGrady's and Steelman's comments to Perkins and the minutes of the Dec. 17 PolBuro meeting; Bridges does not appear in those minutes either by name or by implication, nor does McGrady or Steelman say anything about Bridges having "instructions" from New York. See the next paragraphs for my understanding of Bridges's actions as well as chapter 8 regarding the PolBuro's views on connections between the East Coast and West Coast strikes.

84. Minutes of the ILA-PCD Executive Board, Dec. 19 and Dec. 23, 1936, f5, b1, Markholt Papers.

85. Minutes of the Joint Policy Committee for Dec. 21, 1936; Local 38-79 Strike Bulletin, undated, ILWU Library.

86. Minutes of the Joint Policy Committee for Dec. 21, 1936.

87. Minutes of Maritime Federation Mass Meeting—Dec. 23, 1936, file: Publicity Union, series: 1936–37 Maritime Strike, ILWU Library.

88. *Chronicle*, Dec. 27, 1936, 1; Dec. 28, 1936, 1, 4; Dec. 30, 1936, 4; LAT, Dec. 28, 1936, 3. The FBI conducted extended interviews with all the witnesses to the accident, all of which corroborated what Bridges told the police and what appeared in the press. See report of [name redacted], Nov. 29, 1940, file 39-515-672, 91–102, Bridges FBI file.

89. *LAT*, Dec. 28, 1936, 1, 3; *Chronicle*, Dec. 28, 1936, 1, 4.

90. *LAT*, Dec. 27, 1936, 3; *Chronicle*, Dec. 24, 1936, 1, 10; copy of letter, [Bob Dombroff] to Friend Harry [Lundeberg], Nov. 13, 1936, file: B. Dombroff—Personal Correspondence, b3, Markholt Papers; summary of telephone conversation with Lundeberg, signed

JRS, Dec. 30, 1936, file: Steelman, John R., Apr 2–Dec 30, 1936, b30, Perkins Papers, Columbia University.

91. Minutes of the Joint Policy Committee for Dec. 29, 30, 1936; telephone conversation between Perkins and McGrady, Dec. 29, 1936, file: Maritime Situation—Pacific Coast, b38, Perkins Papers, NA; *Chronicle*, Jan. 2, 1937, 5; MFP District Council No. 2 to All Trade Unions in San Francisco, Dec. 29, 1936, f6, b2, series 1, Surveillance Papers, LARC; *Chronicle*, Jan. 6, 1937, 1, 4; Jan. 7, 1937, 4.

92. Minutes of the Joint Policy Committee, Jan. 11, 16, 1937.

93. *Chronicle*, Jan. 13, 1937, 1, 4 ; Jan 14, 1937, 1, 4; Jan. 16, 1937, 1; Jan. 17, 1937, 1, 5; Jan. 19, 1937, 1, 4; Jan. 22, 1937, 1, 4; Jan. 24, 1937, 1, 6.

94. Letter, Bridges to all Pacific Coast ILA locals, Jan. 7, 1937, file: Negotiations: Circular Letters to All ILA Locals, series: 1935–37 Maritime Strike, ILWU Library; telephone report from Marsh and FitzGerald to Steelman, Jan. 18, 1937; telephone report from FitzGerald and Marsh to Steelman, Jan. 18, 1937, file: Maritime Situation—Pacific Coast, b38, Perkins Papers, NA; letter, Plant et al. to Bridges, Jan. 25, 1937, file: Negotiations—Correspondence with WEA, Series: 1935–37 Maritime Strike, ILWU Library; minutes of the Joint Policy Committee, Jan. 29, 1937.

95. Minutes of the Joint Policy Committee, Jan. 29, 30 and Feb. 4, 1937; letter, F. M. Kelley to all MFP affiliates, Feb. 5, 1937, file: Balloting Committee, series: 1936–37 Maritime Strike ILWU Library; letter, Perkins to Bridges, Feb. 9, 1937, file: Correspondence with Govt. Representatives, series: 1936–37 Maritime Strike, ILWU Library.

96. Melnikow oral history, 279–80.

97. Letter, Bridges to all Pacific Coast ILA locals, Jan. 30, 1937, file: Negotiations: Circular Letters to all ILA Locals, series: 1935–37 Maritime Strike, ILWU Library; *Voice*, Feb. 4, 1937, 6; Pacific Coast Standard Maximum Sling Loads, Apr. 26, 1937, f8, b1, Markholt Papers. See also Herb Mills and David Wellman, "Contractually Sanctioned Job Action and Workers' Control," *Labor History* 28 (1987): 167–95.

98. *Chronicle*, Oct. 15, 1936, 1; Oct. 16, 1936, 3; Nov. 1, 1936, 6; Nov. 9, 1936, 4; Nov. 13, 1936, 13; Nov. 15, 1936, 8; Nov. 21, 1936, 2; Dec. 1, 1936, 9; Dec. 8, 1936, 1; Dec. 14, 1936, 1, 4; Jan. 4, 1937, 1; Jan. 6, 1937, 1, 5. The full story of the march inland may be found in H. Schwartz, *March Inland*.

99. *Chronicle*, Jan. 10, 1937, 9; Jan. 16, 1937, 10; Jan. 30, 1937, 1; Jan. 31, 1937, 5; Feb. 13, 1937, 14; letter, Casey to Tobin, Jan. 26, 1937, f3, b17, series 1, IBT Papers, WHS.

100. Copy of letter, Green to Tobin, Dec. 14, 1936, attached to letter, Meehan to Bridges, Dec. 23, 1936, file: ILWU Split form ILA, IBT dispute over warehouse jurisdiction, 1937–38, ILWU Library.

101. Copy of letter, Bridges to Craft, Nov. 11, 1936, file: Honolulu Correspondence, series: 1936–37 Maritime Strike, ILWU Library; letters, Ryan to ILA-PCD Executive Board, Nov. 13, 1936, file: Correspondence re: with J. Ryan, series: 1936–37 Maritime Strike, ILWU Library; Craft to Bridges, Nov. 18, 1936, file: Honolulu Correspondence, series: 1936–37 Maritime Strike, ILWU Library; Craft et al. to Ryan, undated but Nov. 1936, ILWU Local 142 Library; copy of telegram from ILA-PCD executive board to Ryan, undated, file: correspondence with J. Ryan, series: 1936–37 Maritime Strike, ILWU Library; letter, Negstad to Keaolka, Mar. 5, 1937, ILWU Local 142 Library.

102. Richard Alan Cushman, "The Communist Party and the Waterfront Strike of 1936–1937: The San Francisco Story" (master's thesis, San Francisco State College, 1970), esp. pt. 1. A search of the *Chronicle* for articles pairing the words *Bridges* and *communist* found none in October 1936 or January 1937. One *Chronicle* editorial did bemoan the tendency to apply the term *communist* to "any one who wants something which might lessen your profits." *Chronicle*, Jan. 4, 1937, 8. Plant did link the two terms in a radio broadcast, summarized by the *Chronicle*, Jan. 17, 1937, 5. Another article referred to a libel suit filed by Melnikow over being called a communist in an employers' pamphlet about the "March Inland." *Chronicle*, Jan. 19, 1936, 4. And see, for example, copy of telegram, American League Against Communism to President Roosevelt, Jan. 6, 1937, file: Correspondence with Govt. Representatives, series: 1936–37 Maritime Strike, ILWU Library.

Chapter 7. Founding the ILWU

1. Robert H. Zieger, *John L. Lewis: Labor Leader* (Boston: Twayne, 1988), 87–88, 92–95; Melvyn Dubofsky and Warren Van Tine, *John L. Lewis: A Biography* (New York: Quadrangle, 1977), 253–79.

2. Meeting of Secretariat of Comrade Marty [Anglo-American Secretariat], Sept. 15, 1936, Speaker: Hathaway, 495-14-16; AAS, "Memorandum on the Most Important Issues Facing the CPUSA," dated Mar. 3, 1937, and stamped Mar. 23, 1937, 515-1-4065, RGASPI.

3. Minutes, AAS Meeting, Apr. 4, 1937, Speaker: Browder, 495-20-521; Decision of the Secretary of the ECCI on the American question, dated in Russian Apr. 4 and 14, 1937, in German May 8, 1937, and in French May 10, 1937, 495-20-509j, all RGASPI.

4. David M. Kennedy, *Freedom from Fear: The American People in Depression and War, 1929–1945* (New York: Oxford University Press, 1999), 332–38; Walter Goodman, *The Committee: The Extraordinary Career of the House Committee on Un-American Activities* (New York: Farrar, Strauss & Giroux, 1968), 13–23.

5. *Voice*, Feb. 25, 1937, 1, 16; *Chronicle*, Mar. 12, 1937, 13; the discharge date of March 6 is based on the FBI's review of Bridges's hospital file, report of [name redacted], Nov. 29, 1940, file 39-515-672, 41, Bridges FBI file.

6. *Chronicle*, Mar. 24, 1937, 29.

7. *Chronicle*, Mar. 26, 1937, 4.

8. *Chronicle*, May 6, 1937, 1, 5; Melnikow oral history, 102, 103, 119, 300; interview, Apr. 29, 1987.

9. *Chronicle*, May 1, 1937, 2; Preliminary Report, Mar. 20, 1937, Markholt Papers (no file or box number).

10. *Voice*, May 6, 1937, 7; *Proceedings of the Thirtieth Annual Convention of the Pacific Coast District No. 38 International Longshoremen's Association*, esp. 195–96, 203–49, b3, Markholt Papers; *Voice*, May 30, 1937, 10.

11. "This World," *Chronicle*, May 9, 1937, 4; May 13, 1937, 6; May 20, 1937, 13; May 21, 1937, 5, 15; May 25, 1937, 4; *Voice*, May 12, 1937, 1, 10; May 20, 1937, 1, 10.

12. *Seattle Post-Intelligencer*, May 15, 1937, 9.

13. Minutes of the Pacific Coast District Executive Board on the Question of Affiliation to the C.I.O., Seattle, July 18, 1937, file: ILA Dist. Exec. Bd. 1937/Seattle/July 18, ILWU Library; press release, May 29, 1937, CIO Files of John L. Lewis (microfilm edition), pt. 1, series 2, reel 18; see also Report of Mervyn Rathborne, Secretary, C.I.O. Maritime Committee, Oct. 11, 1937, CIO Files of John L. Lewis (microfilm edition), pt. 2, reel 21; *Chronicle*, May 30, 1937, 2.

14. PolBuro Minutes, June 3, 1937, 495-14-70, RGASPI.

15. *Chronicle*, June 8, 1937, 1; June 11, 1937, 2, 12; Proceedings of the MFP Convention, file MFP 1937, b2, Markholt Papers.

16. Telegram, Lundeberg to Lewis, June 11, 1937; copy of telegram, Lewis to Lundeberg, June 11, 1937; telegrams, Lundeberg to Lewis, June 16 and June 17, 1937; E. R. Stowell to Lewis, June 22, 1937; letter, Stowell to Lewis, June 22, 1937; copy of letter, Lewis to Stowell, June 23, 1937, all in the CIO Files of John L. Lewis, microfilm edition, pt. 1, reel 7.

17. Proceedings of the MFP Convention.

18. Proceedings of the MFP Convention; clipping *Portland Oregonian*, June 19, 1937, Markholt Papers; *Chronicle*, June 25, 1937, 3; unidentified newspaper clipping, June 25, 1937, Markholt Papers.

19. Proceedings of the MFP Convention; clipping *Oregon Journal* (Portland), July 8,1937, Markholt Papers.

20. Report of E. J. Connelley, Nov. 29, 1940, 6, file 39-915-621, Bridges FBI files.

21. Proceedings of the MFP Convention.

22. Clippings, *Portland News-Telegram*, July 12, 1937, and *Oregon Journal* (Portland), July 7, 1937, Markholt Papers; Proceedings of the MFP Convention; affidavit of James Stewart, Bancroft Library, University of California, Berkeley; Weekly Report of Communist Activities, Portland, July 23, 1937, b9, Van Deman Files, Papers of the U.S. Senate, Committee on the Judiciary, Subcommittee to Investigate the Administration of the Internal Security Act and Other Internal Security Laws, RG 46, NA.

23. Telegram, Bridges to Lewis, June 26, 1937, CIO Files of John L. Lewis (microfilm), pt. 1, series 2, reel 18; *Time*, July 19, 1937, 14–16; Bridges report on the conference, *Voice*, July 22, 1936, 8.

24. *Voice*, July 22, 1936, 8; *Chronicle*, July 11, 11; July 13, 1937, 1; Minutes of the Pacific Coast ILA Executive Board, July 18, 1937, f5, b1, Francis Murnane Papers, Oregon Historical Society.

25. PolBuro Minutes, July 15, 1937, 495-20-71, RGASPI.

26. *NYT*, July 18, 1937, E6; Robert H. Zieger, *The CIO, 1935–1955* (Chapel Hill: University of North Carolina Press, 1955), 73.

27. *Time*, July 19, 1937, 14–16.

28. Minutes of the Pacific Coast District Executive Board on the Question of Affiliation to the C.I.O., Seattle, July 18, 1937; letter, Bridges to "all executive board members," July 20, both in file: ILA Dist. Exec. Bd. 1937/Seattle/July 18, ILWU Library; reports of Bridges and Meehan, *Proceedings of the First Annual Convention of the International Longshoremen's and Warehousemen's Union . . . 1938*, ILWU Library; letters, Vandeleur to Green, Aug. 14, 1937; copy, Green to Vandeleur, Aug. 24, 1937, both in f1, b34, series IIC, AFL Papers, WHS.

29. *LAT*, Sept. 26, 1937, 2; Dec. 9, 1937, 6; Jan. 22, 1938, A3; Feb. 3, 1938, 1; Feb. 11, 1938, 1, 10; Mar. 18, 1938, 6; Mar. 22, 1938, 1; sept. 14, 1938, 1; *Bridges v. California* 314 U.S. 252 (1941). The dissent mentioned that Bridges was an alien and questioned which First Amendment rights were incorporated into the Fourteenth Amendment's protections. The majority opinion did not raise the issue of Bridges's citizenship.

30. *Chronicle*, June 4, 1938, 4.

31. *National Labor Relations Board Decisions and Orders*, 1002–54, copy in file of Coast Longshore Agreements #1, 1934–39, ILWU Library; *Chronicle*, June 23, 1938, 1, 10; memo, Steelman to the Secretary, July 26, 1937, file Steelman, John R., June 4–July 30, 1937, b39, Perkins Papers, Columbia; *Chronicle*, Aug. 1, 1937, "This World" section, 4; Sept. 1, 1937, 1; Sept. 2, 1937, 7.

32. *Chronicle*, Sept. 1, 1937, 1, 6; *Time*, July 19, 1937, 14–16; letter, Bridges to Meehan, Sept. 2, 1937, file ILWU Split form ILA—Bridges/Meehan Correspondence, 1937, ILWU Library; memo, Conciliation Service [apparently Steelman but unsigned] to the Secretary, Sept. 7, 1937; memo, Steelman to the Secretary, Sept. 14, 1937, file: Steelman, J. R., Aug. 6–Sept. 30, 1937, b39, Perkins Papers, Columbia; copy, Huybrecht to E. W. Brown, Nov. 18, 1937, fl, b34, AFL Papers, WHS; Melnikow oral history, 306

33. J. Paul St. Sure, "Some Comments on Employer Organizations and Collective Bargaining in Northern California," interviewed by Corinne Glib, 1957, Oral History Project, Institute of Industrial Relations, University of California, Berkeley, 590.

34. *Chronicle*, Sept. 16, 1937, 1; memo, Steelman to the Secretary, Sept. 15, 1937, file Conciliation—West Coast, 1937, 1938, 1939, b38, Perkins Papers, NA.

35. *Chronicle*, Sept. 26, 1, 1937, 6; Sept. 28, 1937, 7; Sept. 29, 1937, 1, 71; St. Sure oral history, 590–91.

36. Melnikow oral history, 62; letter, Case to Tobin, Oct. 25, 1937, f8, b12, series 1, IBT Papers, WHS.

37. Minutes of executive board meeting of ILWU, San Francisco, Sept. 10–11, 1937, file: ILA Dist.Exec.Bd. 1937/Seattle/July 18; President's Report, Secretary-Treasurer's Report, *Proceedings of the Second Annual Convention of the ILWU . . . 1939*, ILWU Library.

38. *Proceedings of the First Annual Convention*.

39. *Proceedings of the First Annual Convention*.

40. *Proceedings of the First Annual Convention*; *Chronicle*, Apr. 15, 1938, 5; Apr. 16, 1938, 5.

41. *Chronicle*, Apr. 17, 1938, 5; Apr. 19, 1938, 1, 4; Apr. 22, 1938, 6.

42. Memo, Steelman to Perkins, May 10, 1938, file Maritime Situation—Pacific Coast, b39, Perkins Papers, NA.

43. *NYT*, July 23, 1937, 3; Jan. 17, 1938, 6; *Chronicle*, Jan. 8, 1938, 9; Jan. 17, 1938, 11; Jan. 19, 1938, 4; Jan. 20, 1938, 1; Jan 22, 1938, 2, 6; *West Coast Sailors*, June 17, 1938, 1; Aug. 12, 1938, 1; Oct. 14, 1938, 1. Lundeberg had made certain that the SUP's ballots from its 1937 referendum were never counted.

44. *Chronicle*, June 8, 1938, 1, 4; *Voice*, June 9, 1938, 1, 7; June 14, 1941, 1, 2; Aug. 2, 1941, 1, 4; copies, [Lundeberg] to All Branches, Mar. 12, 1938; copy, [Lundeberg] to Secretary, District Council #2, Mar. 15, 1938, both in file [MFP] District Council #2—1938, b4, SUP archives; *West Coast Sailors* (San Francisco), June 17, 1938, 3; letter, Rathborne to Lewis, June 17, 1941, pt. 1, series 2, reel 18, CIO Files of John L. Lewis.

45. Agreement between District No. 1 of the ILWU and the WEA of the Pacific Coast . . . effective Oct. 1, 1938, file: Coast Longshore Agreements, #1, 1934–39, ILWU Library.

46. *Voice*, Mar. 4, 1937, 5; Mar. 11, 1937, 1, 5; *Chronicle*, Mar. 8, 1937, 12; Mar. 10, 1937, 1; Nov. 3, 1937, 2; Kevin Starr, *Endangered Dreams: The Great Depression in California* (New York: Oxford University Press, 1996), 209. See also Robert W. Cherny, "Anticommunist Networks and Labor: The Pacific Coast in the 1930s," in *Labor's Cold War: Local Politics in a Global Context*, ed. Shelton Stromquist (Urbana: University of Illinois Press, 2008), 17–48; Carey McWilliams, *Factories in the Field* (1934; reprint, Santa Barbara: Peregrine, 1971), chap. 14.

47. *PW*, Oct. 17, 1938, 1; Oct. 19, 1938, 1; Oct. 20, 1938, 1; Oct. 31, 1938, 1; Nov. 7, 1938, 1; *Chronicle*, Oct. 18, 1938, 7; *LAT*, Oct. 19, 1938, 6; Oct. 22, 1938, 4. On Patterson, see Harvey Klehr, *The Heyday of American Communism: The Depression Decade* (New York: Basic Books, 1984), 271. On Bulcke, see *Germain Bulcke: Longshore Leader and ILWU-Pacific Maritime Association Arbitrator*, interviewed by Estolv Ethan Ward, 1983, Regional Oral History Office, Bancroft Library, University of California, Berkeley, 1984.

48. Estolv E. Ward, *The Gentle Dynamiter: A Biography of Tom Mooney* (Palo Alto, CA: Ramparts Press, 1983), 244; President's Report, *Proceedings of the Second Annual Convention of the ILWU*, 93–106; see also PolBuro minutes, Nov. 10, 1938, 495-14-99, RGASPI.

49. *PW*, Nov. 21, 1938, 1; Nov 22, 1938, 1; Nov 23, 1938, 1; Jan. 7, 1939, 1; Jan. 9, 1939, 1; *Chronicle*, Jan. 9, 1939, 1, A; William Schneiderman, *Dissent on Trial: The Story of a Political Life* (Minneapolis: MEP, 1983), 63.

50. The *PW* provided coverage of these events in Sacramento in almost every edition from late December through late April.

51. Judy Yung, *Unbound Feet: A Social History of Chinese Women in San Francisco* (Berkeley: University of California Press, 1995), 241–43; *Chronicle*, Feb. 26, 1939, 7; Feb. 27, 1939, 10; Mar. 2, 1939, 4; Mar. 3, 1939, 6; Mar. 6, 1939, 12; Mar. 11, 1939, 4; Mar. 13, 1939, 9; Mar. 17, 1939, 10; July 21, 1939, 3; July 24, 1939, 1; Aug. 30, 1939, 1, 7.

52. *PW*, Mar. 15, 1939, 1; Mar. 29, 1939, 1; Apr. 8, 1939, 1; May 1, 1939, 1; May 12, 1939, 1; June 8, 1939, 1; Aug. 1, 1939, 1; Aug. 23, 1939, 1; Aug 28, 1939, 1.

53. Al Richmond, *A Long View from the Left: Memoirs of an American Revolutionary* (New York: Houghton Mifflin, 1972), 283. Bridges told me about hearing Schneiderman explain the Molotov-Ribbentrop Pact when I was not recording.

54. Robert W. Cherny, "The Communist Party in California, 1935–1940: From the Political Margins to the Mainstream and Back," *American Communist History* 9 (2010): 3–33.

55. Agreement to extend previous agreement, Sept. 30, 1939, Coast Longshore Agreements, File #2, 1940–46, ILWU Library; Bridges's report, *Proceedings of the Third Annual Convention*; ILWU Library; *Chronicle*, Nov. 8, 1939, 18; Nov. 10, 1939, 18; Nov. 11, 1939, 1, 7; Nov. 12, 1939, 1, 5; Jan. 3, 1940, 1, 7.

56. Agreement between District No. 1, ILWU, and WEA of the Pacific Coast . . ., effective Dec. 20, 1940, Coast Longshore Agreements, File #2, 1940–46, ILWU Library; *Chronicle*, June 24, 1942, 7; Kagel, interviewed by Robert Cherny, undated. My own research confirms Kagel's statement. See also Paul Eliel, "Peace in the West Coast Shipping Industry," *Annals of the American Academy of Political and Social Science* 224 (Nov.

1942): 147–51, esp. 148. Eliel described arbitration during 1934–40 as largely a failure but ignores the importance of the 1937 agreement and the constant effort of Bridges after that point to find ways of dealing with job actions. In 1997 I took part in a conference in Amsterdam at which twenty-three researchers surveyed longshoring in twenty ports in fifteen countries on five continents; none of those researchers had encountered anything like the ILWU's system of arbitration. See Sam Davies et al., *Dock Workers: International Explorations in Comparative Labour History, 1790–1970*, 2 vols. (Aldershot, UK: Ashgate, 2000).

57. Note of conversation with Harry Bridges, attached to a confidential letter from the Australian Legation in Washington to the Department of External Affairs in Canberra, Feb. 27, 1941, Series A981, Item MIG 3, Migration Restrictions Deportation of Harry Bridges, Australian Archives.

58. AAS minutes, Sept. 15, 1936, 495-14-16; transcript, meeting of the AAS on the American Question, Apr. 4, 1937, 495-20-521; T. Ryan, report to AAS on "C.I.O. National Conference," Oct. 11–15, 1937, Atlantic City, NJ, Nov. 15, 1937, 495-20-519; minutes, plenary session, CPUSA National Committee, Dec. 3–5, 1938, 495-14-94, RGASPI.

59. Letters, Dalrymple to Murray, July 3, 1938; Dalrymple to Lewis, July 7, 1938; Dalrymple to Bittner, July 25, 1938, all in pt. 1, series 1, reel 13, Lewis CIO Files; *Examiner*, Aug. 4, 1938, 1; *Los Angeles Examiner*, Aug. 5, 1938, 11; Aug. 8, 1938, 1; *Chronicle*, Aug. 9, 1938; *LA Examiner*, Aug. 13, 1938, 5; letter, Scharrenberg to Green, Aug. 19, 1938, fl, b34, series 11C, AFL Papers, WHS.

60. Letter, Francis to Lewis, Sept. 10, 1939, pt. 2, reel 14, Lewis CIO Files.

61. *NYT*, Oct. 17, 1939; Hugh T. Lovin, "The CIO and That 'Damnable Bickering' in the Pacific Northwest, 1937–1941," *Pacific Historian* 23 (1979): 66–79, esp. 72. Lovin provided a good treatment of aspects of the CIO purge of the Left in the Pacific Northwest in 1939–41 but completed his study before important CIO internal correspondence became available to researchers. See also my "Anticommunist Networks and Labor."

62. Letters, Francis to Lewis, Feb. 8, 1941; Francis to Kathryn Lewis, Mar. 22, 1940; Francis to Lewis, Aug. 21, 1940; A. E. Harding to Lewis, Sept. 26, 1940; Francis to Lewis, Feb. 8, 1941; Fremming to Lewis, Mar. 4, 1941, all in pt. 2, reel 14, Lewis CIO Files; Robert C. Cummings, "J. C. Lewis Defends Action of Convention," *Seattle Post-Intelligencer*, Mar. 4, 1941.

63. Letters, Dalrymple to officers and members of all affiliated CIO local unions in the state of Oregon, Aug. 22, 1940; Dalrymple to Haywood, Oct. 10, 1940, with attachment, A. L. Gregg to Dalrymple, Sept. 7, 1940, Dalrymple to Haywood, Feb. 27, 1942, all in pt. 2, reel 13, Lewis CIO Files; *Chronicle*, Oct. 5, 1940, 7; *Business Week*, Oct. 12, 1940, 47.

64. See, for example, almost any issue of *PW* between early April and mid-May 1940; *Longshoremen's Bulletin C.I.O.* (ILWU Local 1-10), no. 52, Sept. 24, 1940; *Proceedings of the Third Annual Convention of the ILWU*, ILWU Library; *Chronicle*, Oct. 26, 1940, 5; Oct. 29, 1940, 12; Nov 2, 1940, 5. See also John Brophy, "Reminiscences of John Brophy, 1955," interviewed by Dean Albertson, Columbia Center for Oral History, Columbia University, 853.

65. *Longshoremen's Bulletin C.I.O.* (ILWU Local 1-10), no. 52, Sept. 24, 1940; *Chronicle*, Jan. 25, 1940; letter, Bridges to Rosco Craycraft, Aug. 17, 1940, Bridges correspondence,

ILWU Library; Brophy Oral History, Columbia University, 853–4; unidentified clipping, dateline Nov. 1, 1940 (AP), file: Harry Bridges, Material about, 1939–43, ILWU History Collection, ILWU Library; *Chronicle*, Nov. 5, 1940; *Business Week*, Nov. 16, 1940, 34; *Longshoremen's Bulletin C.I.O.* (ILWU Local 1-10), no. 2, Oct. 29, 1940.

Chapter 8. Harry Bridges and the Communist Party in the 1930s

1. Estolv E. Ward's *Harry Bridges on Trial* (New York: Modern Age Books, 1940) was subsequently republished several times. On Ward, see *Estolv Ethan Ward: Organizing and Reporting on Labor in the East Bay, California and the West, 1925-1987*, interview by Lisa Ruben, Regional Oral History Office, the Bancroft Library, University of California, Berkeley, 1987. Mike Quin [Paul William Ryan]'s *The Big Strike* (Olema, CA: Olema, 1949) has also been republished several times. He explained what he was trying to accomplish in a letter to Sam Darcy, Nov. 14, 1937; and Darcy to Quin, Oct. 10, 1937, f32, b1, Darcy Papers, NYU.

2. Harvey Schwartz aptly summarizes those references from the post–World War II era in "Harry Bridges and the Scholars: Looking at History's Verdict," *California History* 59 (1980): 71–72.

3. Charles P. Larrowe, *Harry Bridges: The Rise and Fall of Radical Labor in the United States* (1972; reprint, New York: Lawrence Hill, 1979); Frederic Caire Chiles, "War on the Waterfront: The Struggles of the San Francisco Longshoremen, 1851-1934" (PhD diss., University of California, Santa Barbara, 1981); Howard Kimeldorf, *Reds or Rackets? The Making of Radical and Conservative Unions on the Waterfront* (Berkeley: University of California Press, 1988), esp. 163–64; Bruce Nelson, *Workers on the Waterfront: Seamen, Longshoremen, and Unionism in the 1930s* (Urbana: University of Illinois Press, 1988), esp. 270; David Selvin, *A Terrible Anger: The 1934 Waterfront and General Strikes in San Francisco* (Detroit: Wayne State University Press, 1996); Ottilie Markholt, *Maritime Solidarity: Pacific Coast Unionism, 1929-1938* (Tacoma: R-4 Printing, 1998); Stanley I. Kutler, "'If at First . . .': The Trials of Harry Bridges," chap. 5 of *The American Inquisition: Justice and Injustice in the Cold War* (New York: Hill and Wang, 1991); Ann Fagan Ginger, *Carol Weiss King: Human Rights Lawyer, 1895-1952* (Niwot: University Press of Colorado, 1993). David Selvin was there in the 1930s; his book is not a memoir but a carefully researched study. He was a longtime friend. I gave him all the interviews with Bridges that I had available when he was writing, but his book was in press by the time I was in Moscow studying materials at RGASPI. Ottilie Markholt, like Selvin, was there in the 1930s; her husband, Robert Dombroff, was an associate of Lundeberg, but, like Selvin's work, her book is based largely on a careful review of primary sources.

4. The files that exist in RGASPI were either generated by Comintern bodies or were taken to Moscow from CPUSA headquarters in New York. Travel to Moscow became difficult after the outbreak of war in 1939 and even more difficult after the German invasion of the Soviet Union in mid-1941. The Comintern was dissolved in 1943. There are very few documents in the AAS fond after 1938.

5. Harvey Klehr, John Earl Haynes, and Fridrikh Igorevich Firsov, *The Secret World of American Communism* (New Haven, CT: Yale University Press, 1995); Harvey Klehr,

John Earl Haynes, and Kyrill M. Anderson, *The Soviet World of American Communism* (New Haven, CT: Yale University Press, 1998). Klehr and Haynes have also produced a long list of books since 1998, most focused on espionage. The first of these has a good description of the archive and its history.

6. Peter Afrasiabi, *Burning Bridges: America's 20-Year Crusade to Deport Labor Leader Harry Bridges* (Brooklyn: Thirlmere Books, 2016); Colin Wark and John F. Galliher, *Progressive Lawyers under Siege: Moral Panic during the McCarthy Years* (Lanham, MD: Lexington Books, 2015); Amanda Frost, "Suspect Citizen," chap. 7 of *You Are Not American: Citizenship Stripping from Dred Scott to the Dreamers* (Boston: Beacon Press, 2021).

7. Vernon L. Pedersen, *The Communist Party on the American Waterfront: Revolution, Reform, and the Quest for Power* (Lanham, MD: Lexington Books, 2019); Michael John, "Winning for Losing: A New Look at Harry Bridges and the 'Big Strike' of 1934," *American Communist History* (2014): 1–24. I find both works flawed. Neither provide citations that support their conclusions.

8. For the CP line on the six-hour day, see, for example, "Our Tactics in Connection with AFL Appeal on 30 Hours Week," 4.1.33, 515-1-3088, RGASPI.

9. For Hudson's claim, see Hudson to Districts 12 and 13, Jan. 8, 1933 [misdated, actually 1934], 515-1-3340, RGASPI. For similar claims that the February convention was the rank-and-file meeting that the Albion Hall group had advocated, see, for example, Quin, *The Big Strike*, 41; Kimeldorf, *Reds or Rackets?* 89; or Bridges's own claim, which he repeated in several interviews and was published in Harvey Schwartz, ed., *Solidarity Stories: An Oral History of the ILWU* (Seattle: University of Washington Press, 2009), 19.

10. Copy of letter, Darcy to Quin, Oct. 10, 1937, f32, b1; Darcy interviewed by Ron Filipelli, undated (1971?), 69, f32, b3, Darcy Papers, NYU, hereinafter Darcy interview, 1971.

11. Markholt, *Maritime Solidarity*, 81–84.

12. Bridges to Darcy, Dec. 9, 1982, f3, b12, Bridges Papers.

13. "Fisher" [Harrison George] to "E" [Browder], May 26 [1934], 515-1-3613, RGASPI. In my work in progress on the San Francisco CP, I deal at length with George's efforts on behalf of Browder during the late 1920s factional struggles.

14. "Fisher" to "E," May 26 [1934]; letter to "Mr. E." with unsent letter, "Wallace" [George] to District Bureau, Dist. #13, July 17, 1934; Hudson to Earl [Browder], July 12, 1934, 515-1-3613, RGASPI.

15. Browder, in Minutes of PolBuro, July 31, 1934, 515-1-3445; letters, M. Raport [Rappaport] to Central Committee, Sept. 27, 1934; M. Raport to Comrade Stachel, Dec. 11, 1934, both 515-1-3605, RGASPI.

16. TUUL Buro minutes, May 21, 1934, 515-1-3657, RGASPI; Nelson, *Workers on the Waterfront*, 144–45.

17. "Fisher" [George] to "E" [Browder], June 2, 1934; "F" [George] to "E" [Browder], June 9, 1934; "Wallace" [George], addressed to District Bureau, Dist. #13, but sent to "Mr. E" [Browder], July 17, 1934, 515-1-3613, RGASPI.

18. "The Strike of the Longshoremen on the Pacific Coast (Report to PolBuro, June 21, 1934)," apparently by Browder; letter, "F." [George] to "E." [Browder], June 9, 1934, 515-1-3613, RGASPI; Darcy interview, 1996.

19. I have presented some of those analyses in detail in my "Prelude to the Popular Front: The Communist Party in California, 1931–1935," *American Communist History* 1 (2002): 5–37, and I elaborate on that in my forthcoming book on the CP in the San Francisco Bay Area. Here I am limiting my treatment to Bridges.

20. Minutes of the PolBuro, July 31, 1934, 515-1-3445, RGASPI. Chapter 6 and my forthcoming book on the CP in the Bay Area provide more information on the CP's reaction to the strikes.

21. Report approved by B. K. Sackett, Oct. 26, 1940, 8, file 39-915-437, Bridges FBI file; Memorandum, Gerard D. Reilly to the Secretary, Oct. 13, 1937, file Reilly, Gerard D, Oct. 1–Oct. 13, 1937, b38, Perkins Papers, Columbia University; Testimony [of Aaron Sapiro] taken by . . . R. P. Bonham, Nov. 12, 1937, b626–70, House Committee on Internal Security—Files and Reference Section—Cannon HOB—91st Congress, NA; Darcy interview 1971, 68.

22. Joseph Starobin, *American Communism in Crisis, 1943–1957* (Cambridge, MA: Harvard University Press, 1972), 38–42 and esp. 258n51.

23. Minutes of the District Buro, June 16, Aug. 20, Oct. 6, Oct. 13, 1934, 515-1-3609, RGASPI. Bridges told me about being co-opted to serve on party committees on Sept. 2, 1986; it was not in a taped interview, but I made written notes immediately afterward.

24. Minutes of District 13 Buro meetings of Aug. 5, 14, Sept. 5, 10, 24, Oct. 7, Nov. 14, Dec. 25, 1935, 515-1-3874; Jack Johnstone to Jack [Stachel], Sept 24, 1935, 515-1-3875; unsigned Report on West Coast and Denver, dated July 13, 1935, 495-14-31, both RGASPI.

25. Minutes of the Trade Union Commission, July 1, July 15, 1935, 515-1-3770; Roy H. to West Coast Fraction, Sept. 25, 1935, 515-1-3774, RGASPI.

26. Letter, undated but early 1936, from [District 13] District Trade Union Sec. to Trade Union Commission, 495-14-22, RGASPI.

27. PolBuro minutes, Jan. 9, 1936, 515-1-3973; PolBuro minutes, Apr. 23, 1936, 515-1-3974, RGASPI.

28. Trade Union Commission minutes, Apr. 16, 1936, 515-1-3985; PolBuro minutes, Apr. 23, 1936, 515-1-3974, RGASPI.

29. PolBuro minutes, Nov. 5, Dec. 17, 1936, 515-1-3976; PolBuro minutes, Jan. 14, 1937, 495-14-68; "The Strike Movement in the U.S.A./Not for Publication," Mar. 26, 1937, 495-14-22-74, all RGASPI. Pedersen claims without evidence that Bridges was being given directions; see chap. 6.

30. PolBuro minutes, Apr. 22, 1937, 495-14-69, RGASPI.

31. Report on CIO National Conference, Nov. 15, 1937, 495-20-519; "The Situation within the CIO," Mar. 29, 1941, 495-14-139, RGASPI.

32. Minutes of Meeting of the Ninth National Convention of the CPUSA, New York City, June 24–28, 1936, 495-14-37; transcript of meeting, AAS, on the American Question, Apr. 4, 1937, marked confidential, 495-20-521; List of Members and Candidate Members of the U.S. Communist Party Central Committee, Jan. 31, 1938, 495-74-467, RGASPI. The original of this last is in Russian, compiled by an official named Belov, based on reviews provided on Jan. 17, 1938, by Browder, Foster, and Eugene Dennis (then known as Tim Ryan). A copy of the original and a translation was made available to me by John

Haynes, to whom I owe thanks for this and many other forms of assistance in using the Russian archives. That file was closed by the time I was doing research at RGASPI, but it had been open when Haynes did his pioneering trip to RGASPI. This translation was done by Nina Bogdan and differs in minor ways from the translation done for Harvey Klehr and John Haynes.

33. NOTE SUR LES CANDIDATURES AU B.P. DU C.C. DU P.C. DES ETATS-UNIS, 8.2.36, 495-20-515, RGASPI. When Andre Marty was chair of AAS, many of the materials for that secretariat were in French. The handwritten notes, in Darcy's handwriting, are in English. This must be from either August 1936 or February 1937 (with the year mistyped), since Darcy left the AAS in May 1937; I'm guessing it is from August 2, 1936, since it deals with the new PolBuro following the national convention. A third possibility, February 1936, seems unlikely since it was before the 1936 convention.

34. As early as March 1936, before Bridges was elected to the Central Committee, a report of the AAS noted, "There are even several members of the CC who are not citizens. These people are in danger of expulsion if they show the slightest activity," and urged "a campaign . . . among the members of the CP so that they will do everything in their power to become citizens of the USA"; I. Mingulin, "THE CADRE POLICY OF THE CP USA," Mar. 10, 1936, 495-20-515, RGASPI. In 1938 the CPUSA debated whether to require that all members be or become citizens; see Roy Hudson, "The Charter of Party Democracy," *Communist* 17 (1938): 704–10. See also *Chronicle*, May 23, 1941, 3, regarding Elmer Hanoff's termination of party membership as an alien.

35. My research suggests that the concept of party membership was sometimes highly elastic, both among party members and the FBI. Dorothy Ray Healy and Carolyn Decker sometimes went for months without paying dues or attending party meetings, but they considered themselves, and others considered them, to be party members. See Dorothy Ray Healey and Maurice Isserman, *California Red: A Life in the American Communist Party* (Urbana: University of Illinois Press, 1993), 71; and Caroline Decker Gladstein, "Oral History Interview," interviewed by Sue Cobble, Aug.–Nov. 1976, California Histori-cal Society. Miriam Dinkin Johnson resigned from the YCL but, months later, showed up when the Control Commission told her to do so, that is, she accepted party discipline without being a member; Miriam Dinkin Johnson, interviewed by Robert Cherny, Feb. 11 and Mar. 19, 1993. The view of party members as always attending the weekly meeting of their unit, always paying their dues, and unquestionably obeying all party pronounce-ments may have described some, even the majority, but clearly not all. Bruce Hannon assured me that the FBI had persuaded him that he had been a party member because he had attended meetings with CP members, but he also assured me that he had never applied to join, never paid dues, never attended a meeting at which everyone was a party member. Bruce Hannon, interviewed by Robert Cherny, Sept. 27, 1997.

36. PolBuro minutes, Nov. 3, 1938, 495-14-99, RGASPI.

Chapter 9. Deport Bridges!

1. Estolv E. Ward, *Harry Bridges on Trial* (New York: Modern Age Books, 1940); Charles Larrowe, *Harry Bridges: The Rise and Fall of Radical Labor in the United States* (New York: Lawrence Hill, 1972); Stanley I. Kutler, *The American Inquisition: Justice and Injustice in the*

Cold War (New York: Hill and Wang, 1982), chap. 5; Ann Fagan Ginger, *Carol Weiss King: Human Rights Lawyer, 1895–1952* (Niwot: University Press of Colorado, 1993); Peter Afrasiabi, *Burning Bridges: America's 20-Year Crusade to Deport Labor Leader Harry Bridges* (Brooklyn: Thielmere Books, 2016); Amanda Frost, *You Are Not American: Citizenship Stripping from Dred Scott to the Dreamers* (Boston: Beacon Press, 2021). Afrasiabi seems unaware of either Kutler's work or my "Harry Bridges, Labor Radicalism, and the State," Occasional Paper Series, no. 1, Center for Labor Studies, University of Washington, 1994. Colin Wark and John F. Galliher, *Progressive Lawyers under Siege: Moral Panic during the McCarthy Years* (Lanham, MD: Lexington Books, 2015), provide some information about Bridges's lawyers but add nothing new about Bridges or his legal proceedings. Frost's analysis of Bridges's court cases relies largely on secondary works and oral histories.

2. Confidential letter, Turner W. Battle to Marvin H. McIntyre, May 24, 1934, file 1934: Pacific Coast Longshoremen's Strike, b11, Official File 407b, FDR Papers. Battle's letter derives directly from a report by Edwin Haff, INS district director for San Francisco, May 23; folder Conciliation—Strikes—Longshoremen, b42, Perkins Papers, NA. For examples of the calls for deportation of alien radicals in general or Bridges in particular, see Frank E. Merriam to Frances Perkins, July 18, 1934, reel 10, Microfilm PS 0472, Perkins Collection, Columbia; Merriam to the President, July 18, 1934, folder 1934—Pacific Coast Longshoremen's Strike, b11, OF 407b, FDR Papers; Harry L. Harper to Perkins, July 19, 1934, folder Conciliation—Strikes—Longshoremen, b42, Perkins Papers, NA; James B. Holohan to Franklin D. Roosevelt, Aug. 4, 1935, folder Conciliation—Strikes—Longshoremen 1935, b36, Perkins Papers, NA; *Chronicle*, Oct. 9, 1937, 1. See also Frances Perkins Oral History, book 6, 337, 341, 443, Columbia University. See also letters, Roosevelt to Perkins, Aug. 29 and Sept. 18, 1935, OF 1750, FDR Papers.

3. Copies of letters, Knowles to Robert M. Thurston, May 12, 1936, Document 454, and Knowles to Cecile S. Hambleton, Apr. 5, 1938, Document 208, Leonard Papers. Regarding Knowles, see also Official Report of Proceedings before the Immigration and Naturalization Service of the Department of Labor, Docket No. 55973/217, *In the Matter of Harry Bridges—Deportation Hearing*, vol. 19, 3133–3311, esp. 3138, 3159–65, and 3168–73; and FBI report on Knowles, report of E. J. Connelley, Nov. 29, 1940, 1275–78, file 39-915-614, Bridges FBI file. In comparison with the FBI's investigation of others, its investigation of Knowles seems quite cursory.

4. Statement of Ivan Francis Cox, Made on the 31st Day of August 1938, Document 2023, Leonard Papers; letters or copies of letters, Hynes to Frank G. Martin, May 1, 1936, Document 2031; Knowles to C. S. Morrill, Aug. 1, 1936, Document 18; Morrill to Knowles, Aug. 6, 1936, Document 18a; H. M. Niles to Knowles, July 15, 1937, Document 38a; William D. Browne to Knowles, July 25, 1938, Document 58; H. L. Chaillaux to Knowles, Apr. 20, 1936, Document 11; Affidavit of Henry R. Sanborn, *California v. Arthur James Kent*, Doc. 2110, all from Leonard Papers. The FBI, in 1940, interviewed all these figures and included the interviews and conclusions in E. J. Connelley's report of Nov. 29, 1940; for Merriel Bacon, a Portland PD officer, 1238–48; Browne, 1320–22; Sanborn, 1323–27; Hynes, report of E. J. Connelley, Nov. 30, 1940, 31–39, file 39-915-620, Bridges FBI files.

5. For Doyle, see series 1, b3, Surveillance Papers, LARC; letter, Doyle to Wallace Wharton, Jan. 24, 1938, f5, series 1, b3, Surveillance Papers, LARC; Report of E. J. Connelley, Nov. 29, 1940, file 39-915-619, 10, 1250–64, esp. 1252, Bridges FBI file.

6. "Brief History of Arthur James Kent," Doc. 2123, Leonard Papers; affidavit of Arthur Kent, Los Angeles, Dec. 28, 1937; stenographic report, Apr. 11, 1936; Report of Conversation between Arthur Margolis and S. M. Doyle, Apr. 20, 1936; REPORT OF [unidentified contact,] May 8, 1936, and REPORT OF [unidentified contact,] May 15, 1936; affidavit of Arthur Kent, Dec. 28, 1937, all f2, b3, series 1, Surveillance Papers; reports of second meeting, Apr. 13, 1936, Docs. 2237 and Doc. 2239, Leonard Papers. See also the account of Kent in Estolv E. Ward, *The Gentle Dynamiter: A Biography of Tom Mooney* (Palo Alto, CA: Ramparts Press, 1983), 235–37; and report of E. J. Connelley, Nov. 29, 1940, file 39-915-619, Bridges FBI file, includes 212 pages on Kent, 90–302.

7. Report of E. J. Connelley, Nov. 29, 1940, file 39-915-619, 1320, 1322, Bridges FBI file; copy of letter, Stanley M. Doyle to John P. Boyd, Oct. 21, 1949, attached to letter, Stanley M. Doyle to Westbrook Pegler, Oct. 21, 1949, folder Unions, Longshoremen, b91, Westbrook Pegler Papers, Herbert Hoover Presidential Library; Larry to Moke, Monday Midnite, f5, b3, series 1, Surveillance Papers; letter, Gerard Reilly to Frances Perkins, Oct. 13, 1937, folder "Reilly, Gerard D., Oct. 1–Oct. 13, 1937," b38, Perkins Papers, Columbia; John Shomaker told the FBI that Kent (Scott) told him about the microphone in Bridges's hotel room, report of E. J. Connelley, Nov. 29, 1940, file 39-915-619, 243, Bridges FBI file. That report details much of Doyle's activities, 1250–64. See also affidavit of Arthur Kent, Dec. 28, 1937, f2, b3, series 1, Surveillance Papers.

8. *Chronicle*, Aug. 21, 1938, 5; letters, Arthur J. Phelan to R. P. Bonham, July 9, 1938 (two letters of the same date), file 12020/25037, b15, Bridges INS file. The problem with the denomination of the stamps was commented on by James Stewart in his affidavit of June 6, 1950, printed in part in the *Dispatcher*, July 21, 1950, 7, and available in its entirety at the Bancroft Library, University of California, Berkeley, hereinafter Stewart affidavit, 1950; "Surveillance of Harry Bridges," Sept. 18, 1941, file 39-915-1-62; report, E. J. Connelley to Special Agent in Charge (SAC) Cincinnati, Dec. 1, 1940, file 39-915-630, 4; report, E. J. Connelley, Nov. 29, 1940, file 39-915-619, 90–302, esp. 147–48, 1250, both in Bridges FBI file; see unsigned report from Doyle, Sept. 28, 1937, f5, b3, series 1, Surveillance Papers. As late as 1959, the House Un-American Activities Committee called Bridges to testify and began with questions that included reference to "Harry Dorgan" and the membership card; see *NYT*, Apr. 22, 1959, A2.

9. Testimony of Herbert Mills, June 28, 1937, folder "Bridges Case/Miscellaneous Documents, b79, Perkins Papers, Columbia; Statement of Herbert Mills, Dec. 9, 1937, f2, b3, series 1, Surveillance Papers; copy of letter from Doyle, Oct. 17, 1937, f5, b3, series 1, Surveillance Papers. Regarding Keegan, see Report of E. J. Connelley, Nov. 29, 1940, file 39-915-619, 1265–74, Bridges FBI file, which states that, in the 1939 hearing, Keegan apparently "deliberately lied" (1266).

10. Confidential letter, William F. Hynes to Harper Knowles, Aug. 2, 1937, f5, b3, series 1, Surveillance Papers; Statement of John L. Leach [*sic*], Dec. 8, 1937, Surveillance Papers, f2, b3, series 1; see also Deposition of John L. Leach [*sic*], Los Angeles, July 26, 1937, f16, b25, Harry Bridges Papers (actually the case files of Richard Gladstein), Southern California Library. Browder, Foster, and Dennis attributed the name "Rossi" to Bridges in their meeting with the AAS in 1938, see chapter 8.

11. Elinor Kahn Kamath told me on April 8, 1987, of her trip to Britain to secure the affidavit. FBI surveillance of Bridges refers to Kahn's trip; see, for example, memo, Guy

Hottel, SAC Washington, to Director, May 29, 1950, file 39-915-3081; memo, SAC Washington to Director, June 7, 1950, file 39-915-3082; letter, [name redacted] to Director, FBI, June 13, 1950, no file number; copy of memo, Director, FBI, to Assistant Attorney General James McInereny, June 26, 1950, file 39-915-3071; copy of memo, Hoover to Legal Attache, London, Jul [illeg.], 1950, no file number, all Bridges FBI file.

12. Stewart affidavit, 1950.

13. Stewart affidavit, 1950; the initial statement by Ferguson (Stewart) was made in Portland on Dec. 13, 1937, f2, b3, series 1, Surveillance Papers.

14. Complaint for Conspiracy in the Superior Court of the State of California, San Francisco, Ivan Francis Cox, Plaintiff, vs. The Thirteenth District of the Communist Party, et al., Defendants, f4, b3, series 1, Surveillance Papers. On Cox, see statement of William Marlowe, report of [name redacted], Nov. 29, 1940, file 30-515-672, 138, Bridges FBI file.

15. Statement of Ivan Francis Cox, Made On the 31st Day of August 1938, Document 2023, Leonard Papers; see also letter, Cox to Frances Perkins, Sept. 9, 1938, file C-6405274-D [2/2], b2, Bridges INS file; copy of unsigned report, apparently by Doyle, Nov. 24, 1937, f5, b3, series 1, Surveillance Papers.

16. Statement of Ivan Francis Cox; Stewart affidavit; Doyle to Wallace Wharton, Jan. 24, 1938, f5, b3, series 1, Surveillance Papers.; letter, Cox to Perkins, Sept. 9, 1938, f C-6405274-C [1/2], b1, Bridges INS files.

17. Copies of letters, Bonham to Wm. N. Shearer, INS office, Vancouver, BC, Feb. 8, 1938, file 12020/25037, b15, Bridges INS file; Garfield A. King to "Howard," Feb. 10, 1938, document 2116, Leonard Papers; Ward, *Bridges on Trial*, 197–203. For the King-Ramsey-Connor case, see "The Shipboard Murder Case: Labor, Radicalism, and Earl Warren, 1936–1941," and related material, Miriam F. Stein for the Regional Oral History Office, Bancroft Library, University of California, Berkeley, 1976.

18. Copies of reports from Doyle, Sept. 26, 1937; Oct. 17, 1937; Nov. 24, 1937, Feb. 20 and 28, 1938; copy of letter, Doyle to Clifton Watson, Mar. 1, 1938; letter, Doyle to Wharton, Oct. 1, 1937; copy, letter from Doyle, Oct. 17, 1937, f5, b3, series 1, Surveillance Papers; memo, J. D. Swenson to E. J. Connelley, Nov. 27, 19450, file 39-915-603-3, Bridges FBI file. For Mattei's ties to Hoover and the FBI, see f3315, b431, Post-Presidential Individual, Herbert Hoover Papers, Herbert Hoover Presidential Library; and copy of report from Doyle, letter, Hoover to E. J. Connelley, May 7, 1941, file 39-915-1162, Bridges FBI file.

19. Stewart affidavit; Elinor Kahn Kamath told me about her interview with Stewart on Apr. 8, 1987; she was entirely persuaded that Steward was telling the truth, as he had nothing to gain by lying.

20. See, for example, In re: Harry Renton Bridges, File No. 55874/896, folder "Bridges Case/Misc. Documents.," b79, Perkins Papers, Columbia.

21. Perkins Oral History, book 6, 449; Perkins, *The Roosevelt I Knew* (New York: Viking Press, 1946), 317–18. For a different view of FDR's perspective on Bridges, see letters, FDR to Perkins, Aug. 29 and Sept. 18, 1935, OF 1750, FDR Papers.

22. Report, Reilly to the Secretary, Oct. 13, 1937, folder "Reilly, Gerard D., Oct. 1–13, 1937," b38, Perkins Papers, Columbia. Record of Sworn Statement Made Before District Director R. P. Bonham by Major Lawrence A. Milner [Sept. 22, 1937], folder Bridges, Harry, b31, Perkins Papers, Columbia. There are copies of the testimony of Sapiro and

all other potential witnesses as of Mar. 28, 1938, in b626–70, House Committee on Internal Security—Files and Reference Section—Cannon HOB—91st Congress, National Archives. These are the copies provided by Perkins to the Dies Committee.

23. Report, Reilly to the Secretary, Oct. 13, 1937; memo, Hoover to Jackson, May 23, 1940, f Attorney General INS transfer, b90, Robert Jackson Papers, Library of Congress.

24. Report, Reilly to the Secretary, Oct. 13, 1937. On Norma Perry, see Ward, *Gentle Dynamiter*, 235–37.

25. Report, Reilly to the Secretary, Oct. 13, 1937.

26. Examination of Harry Bridges . . ., Oct. 18, 1937, f4, b1, Bridges Papers, Southern California Library.

27. "History of Bridges Case—January 4, 1939," folder "Bridges Case/Misc. Documents," b79, Perkins Papers, Columbia.

28. Letter, Houghteling to the Secretary, Jan. 11, 1938, file Houghteling, James L., b34, Perkins Papers, Columbia; letter, Bridges to Perkins, Feb. 3, 1938, microfilm reel 1, Perkins Papers, Columbia. Perkins's response to Bridges is quoted in 75th Cong., 2nd sess., House of Representatives, Subcommittee of the Special Committee to Investigate Un-American Activities, Nov. 4, 1938, 2082. Neither the Perkins Papers, Columbia, nor the Perkins Papers, NA, nor the Bridges correspondence files in the ILWU Library, San Francisco, include a copy of this letter. A copy of it, indicating that it was dictated by "GDR"—Reilly—is in b626–70, Dies Committee Papers, NA.

29. Perkins oral history, book 6, 445. Charles Wyzanski, years later, recalled that Perkins "detested" Bridges after learning that the tape recording of his Portland hotel room indicated that he had committed adultery with a union member's wife and that Perkins "would have been glad for the sake of womankind he was not on the scene, but she thought there was nothing to the suggestion that he was deportable." Wyzanski quoted in Kirstin Downey, *The Woman behind the New Deal: The Life of Frances Perkins, FDR's Secretary of Labor and His Moral Conscience* (New York: Doubleday, 2009), 272. Other sources also indicate that the recordings made in Portland included evidence of Bridges's adultery. See, for example, Patrick J. Farralley, INS inspector, to District Director, INS, San Francisco, Jan. 25, 1938, file 12020/25037 [1/2], b14, Bridges INS file.

30. Letter, Roger Williamson to Perkins, Jan. 25, 1938, microfilm reel 14, Perkins Papers, Columbia; copy in Papers of the Committee on Commerce from the 75th Congress, file Harry Bridges (confidential), b1, RG 46, NA (hereinafter Copeland Committee files); letters, Perkins to Vandenburg, Jan. 22, 1938, microfilm reel #13, Perkins Papers, Columbia; Copeland to Perkins, Feb. 22, 1938, file Harry Bridges (confidential), b1, Copeland Committee files; statement of Secretary Perkins, Feb. 3, 1938, file Bridges, Harry—correspondence with Labor Department, b2, Copeland Committee files; *NYT*, Feb. 8, 1938, 13; Feb. 10, 1938, 3.

31. Letter, Reilly to Miss Jay, Feb. 10, 1938, folder Reilly, Gerard D., Feb. 10–July 29, 1938, b38, Perkins Papers, Columbia; *NYT*, Feb. 8, 1938, 13; Feb. 9, 1938, 6; Feb. 10, 1938, 1; *Chronicle*, Feb. 8, 1938, 6; Feb 9, 1938, 1, 6; Feb. 10, 13, 1938; *LAT*, Feb. 10, 1938, 1, 3; *NYT*, Feb. 26, 1938, 16; unidentified clipping dated Feb. 21, 1938, file Bridges, Harry (confidential), b1, Copeland Committee Papers, NARA. See also History of the Special Senate Committee to Investigate Labor Conditions in the American Merchant Marine,

file Committee (Special), History of, b2, Copeland Committee files; telegram to Lee Pressman, Feb. 11, 1938, f1, b19, Bridges Papers, Southern California Library; copy of letter, Copeland to Reilly, Mar. 1, 1938, file Bridges, Harry—correspondence with Labor Department by Committee, b2, Copeland Committee Papers, NARA.

32. Aubrey Grossman, one of Bridges's attorneys in the 1930s, told of the cooperative janitor at the American Immigration Lawyers Association meeting, May 15, 1986. What is apparently Knowles's trash constitutes Docs. 7139–97, Leonard Papers. For other material from Knowles's files or the La Follette Committee, see Docs. 1–455 (old series), 2000 et seq., Leonard Papers. Elinor Kahn of the CIO Maritime Committee in Washington sent material to the defense that apparently came from the La Follette investigations, at least in 1941; see Elinor to "Ben" [Margolis?], Apr. 21, 1941, Doc. 2420, Leonard Papers. William "Red" Hynes claimed in 1941 that a La Follette Committee investigator had stolen files from the Los Angeles red squad and that those files were used in Bridges's defense in 1939; see clipping, *Chronicle*, May 15, 1941, file 39-915-A, and report of E. J. Connelley, Nov. 29, 1940, file 39-915-619, 181–82, both in Bridges FBI file.

33. Deposition of John L. Leach [*sic*], Los Angeles, July 26, 1937, f16, b25, Bridges Papers, Southern California Library; for Leech's later claim that he had been forced to make this deposition, see letter, Leech to Keegan, July 26, 1937, Doc. 7299, Leonard Papers. For indications of suborning perjury, see affidavit of Lillian Walker, June 1937, Doc. 2008; statement of Lillian Walker, no date, Doc. 2065; and affidavit by Claude R. Smallman, Doc. 2207, Leonard Papers.

34. Telegram, Bridges to Lee Pressman, Feb. 11, 1938, quoting telegram from Bridges to Perkins, f1, b19, Bridges Papers, Southern California Library. Bridges also told me he had made a similar request to Perkins in person; interview, Apr. 29, 1987.

35. The warrant applied to "Alfred Renton Bryant Bridges alias Harry Renton Bridges alias Harry Dorgan alias Canfield alias Rossi." Copy in James M. Landis Papers, folder Special Correspondence, 1938–41, b72, LC; letter, Lee Pressman to Aubrey Grossman, Apr. 1, 1938, f1, b19, Bridges Papers, Southern California Library. For King signing as Mother or Grandma, see her letters of Dec. 3, 1941, f4, b19; or Sept. 2 and 3, 1943, f13, b8, Bridges Papers, Southern California Library. For Gladstein and Grossman, see Colin Wark and John F. Galliher, *Progressive Lawyers under Siege: Moral Panic during the McCarthy Years* (Lanham, MD: Lexington Books, 2015). For King, see Ginger, *Carol Weiss King*.

36. Kutler, *American Inquisition*, 126–27; Keegan to Sapiro, Apr. 20, 1938, Doc. 2267, Leonard Papers; Joseph K. Carson Jr. to Secretary of Labor, Apr. 25, 1938, reel 1, Perkins Papers, Columbia; *Chronicle*, May 7, 1938, 2; *NYT*, May 23, 1938, 20.

37. 75th Cong., 3rd sess., House of Representatives, Special Committee on Un-American Activities, Public Hearings, Aug. 12, 13, 1938, esp. 104, 106, 107; *NYT*, Aug. 14, 1938, 1; Aug. 15, 1938, 1; Aug. 17, 1938, 1; *Chronicle*, Aug. 31, 1938, 5.

38. *NYT*, Sept. 1, 1938, 1; *Chronicle*, Sept. 1, 1938, 7.

39. 75th Cong., 3rd sess., House of Representatives, Special Committee on Un-American Activities, Public Hearings, 2075–83, esp. 2081, 2909–19.

40. Memos, Reilly to Houghteling, Oct. 6, 1937; Reilly to the Secretary, Oct. 13, 1937, folder "Reilly, Gerard D., Oct. 1–Oct. 13, 1937"; Reilly to the Secretary, Dec. 20, 1938,

folder "Reilly, Gerard D., Dec. 6–20, 1938," b38, Perkins Papers, Columbia; History of the Bridges Case—Jan. 4, 1939, op. cit.; Knowles testimony, 3219;

41. Ickes Diaries, microfilm reel 3, page 3149–50, LC.

42. George Martin, *Madame Secretary, Frances Perkins* (Boston: Houghton Mifflin, 1976), 411, 415; Drew Pearson and Robert S. Allen, "Washington Merry-Go-Round," *Washington Post*, Jan. 31, 1939, clipping, and *NYT*, Mar. 25, 1939, clipping, folder "Impeachment Proceedings," b94, Perkins Papers, Columbia; Downey, *Woman behind the New Deal*, chap. 27; Report No. 311, 76th Cong., 1st sess., House of Representatives, f5, b1, Bridges Papers, Southern California Library.

43. Interview, Jan. 20, 1988; Ickes Diaries, reel 3, 3444; letter, Reilly to the Secretary, Mar. 10, 1939, folder "Reilly, Gerard D., Feb.–Apr. 1939," b38, Perkins Papers, Columbia.

44. Grossman to Edward W. Cahill, Mar. 31, 1938; memo, Bonham to T. B. Shoemaker, Mar. 29, 1938, f C-6405274-B, b1, Bridges INS File; Aubrey Grossman, American Immigration Lawyers Association meeting, May 15, 1986. These files and the card index, with additions from succeeding proceedings lasting until 1955, now constitute the Bridges Case Files of the Leonard Papers. Not all the materials are identified as to the date they were received. Regarding Agnes FBI investigators later determined that Bridges had apparently not lived with Agnes and Betty in 1938 and 1939. Report of E. J. Connelley, Nov. 20, 1940, 23, 24, file 39-915-558, Bridges FBI file.

45. The hearing is summarized in Ward, *Bridges on Trial*; Larrowe, *Bridges*, 151–216; Kutler, *American Inquisition*, 131–33; Afrasiabi, *Burning Bridges*, chap. 3; Ginger, *Carol Weiss King*, chap. 19. Unless otherwise noted, the following summary is based on those sources or on the transcript of the hearing. See also Estolv Ethan Ward, *Organizing and Reporting on Labor in the East Bay, California and the West, 1925–1987*, interviewed by Lisa Rubens, 1987, Regional Oral History Office, Bancroft Library, University of California, Berkeley, 95–99; and *Law and Social Conscience*, Ben Margolis interviewed by Michael S. Balter, Department of Special Collections, University of California, Los Angeles, 1985, tape 3, side 2. All San Francisco newspapers carried daily coverage.

46. Stewart affidavit; "Brief History of Arthur James Kent"; report of E. J. Connelly, Nov. 29, 1940, 183, 276, file 39-915-619, Bridges FBI file.

47. Copy of report by Doyle, Nov. 24, 1937; 75th Cong., 3rd sess., House of Representatives, Special Committee on Un-American Activities, Public Hearings, Nov. 4, 1938, 2081, quoting Bonham; interview, Jan. 20, 1988; telephone interview with Aubrey Grossman, Jan. 19, 1988.

48. Memo re Ferguson, Doc. 7133, Leonard Papers.

49. Re: Harry Bridges, Doc. 2236, Leonard Papers.

50. Docs. 2082–84, Leonard Papers.

51. "SUMMARY OF INFORMATION RECEIVED FROM ANONYMOUS TELEPHONE INFORMANT," Doc. 2251, Leonard Papers; conversation with Caroline Decker Gladstein, Feb. 11, 1986.

52. F2–6, b5, James M. Landis Papers, Harvard Law Library; HR 9766 (Allen, LA), 77th Cong., 1st sess. For the floor debate and vote, see *Congressional Record—House*, June 13, 1940, 12380–12407; memorandum for the President from James H. Rowe Jr., Aug. 13, 1940, with notation by Roosevelt dated Aug. 15, 1940, OF 1750, FDR Papers; and Russell to J. W. Bailey, Sept. 10, 1938, b2, Copeland Committee Records.

53. Kutler, *American Inquisition*, 135. The FBI was critical of the amateurish activities of the American Legion and similar groups, as well as army and navy intelligence activities within the United States in the late 1930s and gained major new authority for internal security. See Joan M. Jensen, *Army Intelligence in America, 1775–1980* (New Haven, CT: Yale University Press, 1991), 211, 213–14, 264; and Roy Talbert Jr., *Negative Intelligence: The Army and the American Left, 1917–1941* (Jackson: University Press of Mississippi, 1991), 234, 256–59. See also Richard Gid Powers, *Secrecy and Power: The Life of J. Edgar Hoover* (New York: Free Press, 1987), 231, 256, 281. For the American Legion, see William Pencak, *For God & Country: The American Legion, 1919–1941* (Boston: Northeastern University Press, 1989), 312–14; and memos, A. H. Belmont to D. M. Ladd, Oct. 2, 1952; and Belmont to Ladd, July 31, 1950; FBI American Legion Contact Information [microfilm edition of FBI file] (Wilmington, DE: Scholarly Resources, 1984).

Chapter 10. If at First You Don't Succeed: Deportation

1. *Reminiscences of Robert Houghwout Jackson: Oral History, 1952*, Columbia University, 304, 314 (hereinafter Jackson oral history).

2. Curt Gentry, *J. Edgar Hoover: The Man and His Secrets* (New York: W. W. Norton, 1991), 607; Matthew F. Maguire, Memorandum for Mr. Hoover, Aug. 27, 1940, file 39-915-90, Bridges FBI file. Jackson's account of his conversation with FDR regarding moving the INS from Labor to Justice contains no mention of Bridges but notes that Jackson was not in favor of the move; f Attorney General INS transfer, b90, Robert Jackson Papers, Library of Congress. Hoover stated in late 1938 that "no investigation" of Bridges had been conducted by the FBI; memo, Hoover to Jackson, Dec. 9, 1940, f Attorney General—HUAC 2, b89, Jackson Papers, LC.

3. Clippings covering Hoover's visit to San Francisco, file 39-915–Sub A, Bridges FBI file; memo, Hoover to SAC, all field offices, Sept. 26, 1940, file 39-915-204, Bridges FBI file.

4. Connelley, Memo for the Director, Sept. 5, 1940, file 39-915-[illeg.]71; Connelly to Director, Oct. 21, 1940, file 39-915-390, Bridges FBI file.

5. Connelley, Report, Nov. 29, 1940, file 39-915-614, Bridges FBI file.

6. Connelley, teletype to all FBI offices, Sept. 17, 1940; see, for example, Percy Wyly II to Connelly, Sept. 18, 1940, file 39-215-[illeg.]; Connelley to Special Agent in Charge All Bureau Offices, Sept. 18, 1940, file 39-915-164, Bridges FBI file. All responses appear in the Bridges FBI file. The initial request was followed by specific requests to individual field offices about particular visits by Bridges; see, for example, report regarding visits by Bridges to New York City and continuing efforts to determine if he had attended the 1936 and 1938 CP national conventions, New York City field office, Sept. 20, 1940, file 39-915-112, Bridges FBI file.

7. Memo, Connelley to Director, Oct. 8, 1940; copy, Attorney General to Secretary of the Treasury, Oct. 14, 1940, file 39-215-273, Bridges FBI file. The tax returns are not in the file provided to me, and they were not used in the legal proceedings.

8. Memo, B. K. Sackett to Connelley, Oct. 16 1940, file 39-915-39[illeg.]; report to Sackett, Oct. 25, 1940, file 39-915-403, Bridges FBI file.

9. Report, [name redacted], Nov. 14, 1940, file 39-915-526; report of [name redacted], Nov. 29, 1940, file 39-915-672, 139–55, esp. 155, 166–79, 178, 180–83, 184–90, Bridges FBI file.

10. Memos, Connelly to Director, Oct. 13, 1940, file 39-915-419; Connelly to Director, Oct. 31, 1940, file 39-915-482; E. A. Tamm to Director, Nov. 29, 1940, file 39-915-623, esp. 3, 4, 7, Bridges FBI file; Clarence N. Goodwin, "Personal Memorandum for the Attorney General in re Harry R. Bridges," Feb. 24, 1941, file Legal File Attorney General, Bridges, Harry—Deportation, of—2, b86, Robert H. Jackson Papers, LC. Goodwin provides the citation to 39–30, 3, 8; the copy of the Bridges FBI file provided to me did not include those sections of his file or else they were among the many redactions.

11. Reports, Connelley, "Part I: Harry Bridges' Membership in and/or Affiliation with the Communist Party of the United States of America," esp. 3, Nov. 20, 1940, noted as received by the Department of Justice on Nov. 22, file 39-915-558; a brief version, dated Dec. 4, 1940, is file 39-915-639; "Part II Communist Party of the United States of America: *Illegal Status*," esp. 3, date illeg., file 39-915-592-595; report, [name redacted], approved by Connelley, Nov. 29, 1940, file 39-915-617; memo, Connelley to Director, Dec. 6, 1940, file 39-915-645; memo, Hoover to Attorney General, Dec. 5, 1940, file 39-915-640, all Bridges FBI file.

12. Goodwin, "Personal Memorandum for the Attorney General"; Goodwin obituary, *NYT*, Sept. 23, 1956, 84.

13. *NYT*, Dec. 17, 1940, 1, 16; Jan. 29, 1941, 13; Feb. 13, 1941, 1, 15; Memo, Alexander Holtzoff to Attorney General, Feb. 6, 1941, file Legal File Attorney General, Bridges, Harry—Deportation, of—2, b86, Jackson Papers, LC.

14. Memo, Connelley to Director, Mar. 8, 1941, file 39-915-936; on Hannon, see Connelley to Director, Apr. 8, 1941, file 39-915-1003, Bridges FBI file.

15. *NYT*, Mar. 7, 1941, 15. The hearing was covered in detail by the San Francisco daily papers and is summarized in Charles Larrowe, *Harry Bridges: The Rise and Fall of Radical Labor in the United States*, 2nd ed. (New York: Lawrence Hill, 1979), 226–32; Stanley I. Kutler, *The American Inquisition: Justice and Injustice in the Cold War* (New York: Hill and Wang, 1982), 136–38; Ann Fagan Ginger, *Carol Weiss King: Human Rights Lawyer, 1895–1952* (Niwot: University Press of Colorado, 1993), chap. 22; Peter Afrasiabi, *Burning Bridges: America's 20-Year Crusade to Deport Labor Leader Harry Bridges* (Brooklyn: Thirlmere Books, 2016), chap. 4. If not otherwise cited, information on the hearing comes from these four sources. For Del Guercio's delight in accusing Bridges's attorneys of being Communists, see Del Guercio to T. S. Shoemaker, Apr. 8, 1941, file 284-P-28152, pt. 1, June 26, 1939, to June 2, 1942 [2/2] b18, Bridges INS file; *Chronicle*, Apr. 1, 1941, 1; clipping, *San Francisco Examiner*, date illeg. but May 1941, file 39-915-A; memo P. E. Foxworth to Director, Apr. 25, 1941, file 39-915-1097, Bridges FBI file.

16. Report, [name redacted], Nov. 15, 1940, esp. 1, 10, file 39-915-531; teletype, Hoover to SAC New York City [Sackett], Nov. 15, 1940, file 39-915-542; memo, Connelley to SAC New York City, Oct. 19, 1940, file 39F-915-[illeg.] but between 407x and 407x2; memo, H. H. Clegg to Director, Nov. 18, 1940, file 39-915-628x, all Bridges FBI files; memo, I. F. Wixon to Schofield, Apr. 4, 1941, file C-6405274-D [2/2], b2, Bridges INS file; *Chronicle*, Apr. 3, 1941, 8. Hoover specified that no money was to be advanced to

Gitlow "in connection with this case, which might place the Bureau in the position of financing these witnesses." [Name redacted] memo for Mr. Foxworth, Mar. 21, 1941, file 39-915-967, Bridges FBI file.

17. Memo, B. E. Sackett to SAC San Francisco, Feb. 17, 1941, file 39-915-793; memo, Hoover to Mr. Tolson et al., Apr. 3, 1941, file 39-915-1020; memo to Mr. Tolson et al., Apr. 9, 1941, file 39-915, 1071, Bridges FBI file.

18. Memo, Hoover to Tolson, Tamm, and Foxworth, May 13, 1941, file 39F-915-1261, Bridges FBI file.

19. Clippings, *News*, May 7; *Chronicle*, May 21; *NYT*, May 21, 24; *Call-Bulletin*, May 27; Herb Caen's column, paper illeg., June 28, all 1941, all file 39-915-A, Bridges FBI file; *Chronicle*, Sept. 30, 1941, 1, 6, 14.

20. Report, Connelley, "Part I: Harry Bridges' Membership," 822–56, esp. 822, 833–34, Nov. 20, 1940, file 39-915-558; copy of memo, Foxworth apparently to Director, Aug. 19, 1941, file 39-915-1564X, Bridges FBI file; memo, Hoover to Attorney General, May 2, 1941, file: Bridges, Harry—Deportation of [2], b86, Jackson Papers, LC; *Chronicle*, Apr. 27, 26; Apr. 29, 1941, 1, 8; memo, Del Guercio to Schofield, Apr. 28, 1941, file 284-P-28152, pt. 1, June 26, 1939, to June 2, 1942 [1/2], b18, Bridges INS file.

21. Report, [name redacted], approved by Connelley, May 11, 1941, file 39-915-1204; letter, Connelley to Hoover, May 12, 1941, file 39-915-1205; copy of letter, Maguire to Schofield, May 21, 1941, attached memo, Maguire to Hoover, May 22, 1942, file 39-915-1269; memos, Tamm to Director, May 26, 1941, file 39-915-1268; Tam to Director, May 27, 1941, file 39-915-134[last digit illeg.]; [name redacted] to [name redacted], May 27, 1943, file 13-915-134[last digit illeg.]; report, [name redacted], signed by Connelley, June 9, 1941, file 39-915-1343; letter to Director, no signature page, Mar. 5, 1942, file 39-915-1854; report titled James D. O'Neil, Dec. 5, 1941, file illeg. but likely 39-915-1850, all Bridges FBI file; *Chronicle*, Apr. 29, 1941, 1, 8; May 1, 1941, 8; June 27, 1941, 7; Oct. 9, 1941, 1; Oct. 12, 1941, 1; Oct. 26, 1941, 1. In late April or early May, an FBI agent interviewed Arthur Kent seeking to verify portions of O'Neil's original statements, but Kent could not do so for several of the most crucial; report, [name redacted], May 15, 1941, covering Apr. 30, 1941, through May 5, 1941, esp. 5, file 39-915-1215, Bridges FBI file.

22. *Chronicle*, June 7, 1940, 12; report, Connelley, "Part I: Harry Bridges' Membership," 884, 894, 895, 897, Nov. 20, 1940, file 39-915-558, Bridges FBI file. A similar account of Lundeberg's position that Bridges was a CP member but that he had no evidence for that claim is in the affidavit of J. H. Prevost, a close associate of Lundeberg in 1939–42, f21, b7, Bridges Papers, Southern California Library.

23. T. S. Shoemaker to Schofield, Apr. 18, 1941, file 284-P-28152 pt. 1, b18, Bridges INS file; *Chronicle*, June 11, 1941, 8; clipping, *Examiner*, June 11, 1941, file 39-915-A, Bridges FBI file; memo, Hoover to Attorney General, June 10, 1941, file 39-915-134[last digit probably 8]; Bridges FBI file.

24. For Darcy's departure and Johnstone's appointment to replace him temporarily, see correspondence for District 13 in 515-1-3875, RGASPI. The last correspondence from Darcy in San Francisco is from May 21, 1935, and Johnson arrived in late August or September. In June Darcy applied for a passport in New York City. See *Chronicle*, Aug. 1, 1935, 5; and July 30, 1941, 13. For the failed meeting in late May, see N. S. to Stachel,

June 1, 1935, 515-1-3873, RGASPI. In an affidavit in 1945, Agnes Bridges claimed the meeting of Lundeberg, Bridges, and Darcy in the Bridges home took place the night before Bridges went to the hospital, but this affidavit was produced under the guidance of A. L. Crawford, part of the Knowles-Doyle operation to attack Bridges, and it conflicts with evidence that Bridges was taken ill in a meeting at the apartment of Norma Perry the night before he was supposed to meet with Lundeberg. See chapters 6 and 9.

25. *Chronicle*, May 28, 1941, 14; 75th Cong., 1st sess., House of Representatives, *Investigation of Un-American Propaganda Activities*, 14:8036.

26. *Chronicle*, June 13, 1941, 1, 14; letter, Connelley to Director, July 30, 1941, file 39-915-1511, esp. 2, Bridges FBI file.

27. See handwritten notes on clipping from *Sunday Worker*, July 12, 1942; also clippings, some with handwritten notes, from *PW*, Mar. 4, 1942, 2; *New York Herald Tribune*, Mar. 17, 1943, 11; *Daily Worker*, May 22, 1943, 5, all in file 39-915-A, Bridges FBI file. The FBI added those names to its index. Clipping, *NYT*, Apr. 29, 1941; May 25, 1941, file 39-915-A; memo, Connelley to Director, Apr. 3, 1941, file 39-915-977; report on Bridges's defense committees, first page redacted, stamped Sept. 30, 1943, esp. 9, 16, file 39-915-2381; memo, SAC San Francisco to Hoover, July 20, 1945, file 39-915-2565; report, [name redacted], San Francisco field office, June 1, 1945, esp. 49, file 39-915-2560; Bridges FBI files; George Wilson to Robert G. Folkoff, f3, b9, Bridges Papers, Southern California Library; NSB tapes 17–18, side 18; memo, Hoover to Matthew Maguire, June 6, 941, file 39-915-1207, Bridges FBI file; clippings, *Chronicle*, May 17, 1941, and *News*, May 17, 1941, file 39-915-A, Bridges FBI file; letter, Wilson to Gardner, Mar. 18, 1941; CIO press release, Mar. 18, 1941; Harry Bridges Defense Committee, Analysis of Cash Receipts and Disbursements, Feb. 1, 1941, to Oct. 31, 1941; all in f4, b5, Bridges Papers, Southern California Library. See also CIO Executive Board Minutes for Mar. 10–12, 1945, 456–64, esp. 461, Archives of Labor History and Urban Affairs, Wayne State University, which note that the CIO national officers carefully checked all expenses to be certain they were legitimate. In mid-December 1940, the FBI arranged with "the telegraph company" to receive copies of correspondence between the Washington and San Francisco offices of the defense committee; memo for E. A. Tamm from [name redacted], Dec. 27, 1940, file 39-915-691, Bridges FBI file.

28. Information on the original recording is online at http://www.woodyguthrie .de/k304.html. See also the summary of interview with Pete Seeger by Ian Ruskin, undated, online at http://www.theharrybridgesproject.org/peteseeger.html. As of this writing, the original was available at https://www.youtube.com/watch?v=Pqk6ij924vw. Woody Guthrie wrote a different song about Bridges, apparently just after the Angel Island trial, but it was not recorded at that time; see https://socialconcerns.nd.edu /labor-song-month#Current%20Song.

29. Pieper to Director, Aug. 16, 1941, file 39-915-1552, and Foxworth to Director, Nov. 6, 1941, file 39-915-1733, both Bridges FBI file.

30. Huberman obituary, *NYT*, Nov. 10, 1968, 88; Trumbo obituary, *NYT*, Sept. 11, 1976, 17; memo, Connelley to Director, Mar. 29, 1941, file 39-915-971, Bridges FBI file.

31. Clipping, *Chronicle*, June 18, 1941, file 39-915-A, Bridges FBI file.

32. Memoranda for the File, Aug. 25, 1941, file 39-915-68, Bridges FBI file; *PM*, Aug. 25, 1941, 13–15; Aug. 26, 1941, 19; Aug. 28, 1941, 11; Aug. 29, 1941, 19; Sept. 3, 1941, page obscured; Sept. 4, 1941, 2; Sept. 8, 1941, page obscured; Sept. 10, 1941, page obscured;

"A Reporter at Large: Some Fun with the F.B.I.," *New Yorker*, Oct. 11, 1941, 53–57; letter, Kammet to Wilson, Aug. 26, 1941; Gardner, Report on the Illegal Tapping of Harry Bridges' Telephone by FBI, Sept. 12, 1941; and King to Wilson, Aug. 22, 1941, all in f6, b6, Bridges Papers, Southern California Library.

33. Memoranda for the File, Aug. 25, 1941, file 39-915-68, Bridges FBI file. Regarding the food cart, reportedly placed by an FBI agent, see *Washington Post*, Sept. 11, 1941, 15.

34. Memo, Foxworth to Director, Sept. 18, 1941, file 39-915-1-62, Bridges FBI file. For Hoover, see Richard Gid Powers, *Secrecy and Power: The Life of J. Edgar Hoover* (New York: Free Press, 1987), 214; and Gentry, *J. Edgar Hoover*, 245–46.

35. Unsigned, undated document entitled Re: Virginia Gardner, file 39-915-1613, Bridges FBI file; copies of affidavits of Bridges et al. are in f6, b4, Bridges Papers, Southern California Library; *PM*, Aug. 29, 1941, 19; *NYT*, Sept. 4, 1941, 9; clipping *P.M.*, Sept. 10, 1941, file 39-915–Sub A; memo, to Director, Sept. 30, 1941, 1, file 39-915-1633; Bridges FBI file. I found no evidence of such surveillance in all the thousands of pages of FBI reports covering the period before June 21; there is substantial evidence later. Wire tapping was illegal; see f Attorney General—Wire Tapping, b. 94, Jackson Papers, LC.

36. Memo, Strickland to Ladd, Nov. 13, 1941, file 39-915-1748; Bridges's index card is file 39-915-1763; memo, Hoover to Edward J. Ennis, Jan. 9, 1942, file 39-915-1788; Bridges FBI file; Athan G. Theoharis and John Stuart Cox, *The Boss: J. Edgar Hoover and the Great American Inquisition* (Philadelphia: Temple University Press, 1988), 171–74.

37. Memos, Hoover to SAC San Francisco, June 2, 1942, file 39-915-illeg. but likely 1933; Hoover to SAC San Francisco, Aug. 25, 1942, file 39-915-2041; Hoover to SAC San Francisco, Aug. 29, 1942, file 39-915-2953, Bridges FBI files.

38. In re: Harry Renton Bridges, Before the Board of Immigration Appeals in DEPOR-TATION Proceedings, Jan. 3, 1942, 55973-217–San Francisco, Bridges INS file; *NYT*, Sept. 30, 1941, 1, 13; Jan. 6, 1942, 1; memo, Pieper to Director, Nov. 5, 1941, file 39-915-1695; memo, Ladd to Director, Oct. 5, 1942, file 39-915-1096; Washington City News Service, Jan. 5, 1942, file 39-915-A; memo, Schofield to Attorney General, Jan. 14, 1942, f 39-915-1795; Bridges FBI file.

39. Copy, memo, Schofield to Attorney General, Jan. 14, 1942, file: Bridges, Harry—Deportation of [2], b86, Jackson Papers, LC; Opening Brief on Behalf of Bridges, 112, copy in possession of author; Washington City News Service, May 28, 1942, file 39-915-A, Bridges FBI file.

40. Clipping, Frank Kent, "The Great Game of Politics," *Washington Star*, June 1, 1942, file 39-915-A, Bridges FBI file; Harold Ickes Diaries, July 5, 1942, microfilm reel 5, June 26, 1045, reel 7, LC.

41. Washington City News Service, May 28, 1942, file 39-915-A, Bridges FBI file; James M. Landis oral history, 50, 60, Columbia University; Francis Biddle, *In Brief Author-ity: From the Years with Roosevelt to the Nürnberg Trial* (Garden City, NY: Doubleday, 1962), 302.

42. For the defense committees' financial problems, see, for example, letters and copies of letters, Carol [King] to Richie [Gladstein], Jan. 21, 1942, f2, b27; Gladstein to Margolis, Apr. 27, 1943, f9, b8; Gladstein to Wilson, Apr. 30, 1943; Wilson to Gladstein, May 7, 1943, f4, b5, all Bridges Papers, Southern California Library. For Kahn's report on inactivity, see copy of report, Kahn to Bridges et al., June 30, 1942, f1, b20, Bridges

Papers, Southern California Library. For Crum, Willkie, and the others, see letters and copies of letters, Gladstein to King, June 26, 1942; Crum to Grossman, July 15, 1942, both in f1, b20; Grossman to Kenny, Aug. 4, 1942, Baldwin to Bridges, Aug. 17, 1942, f2, b20, Bridges Papers, Southern California Library. The King-Willkie correspondence is in Bridges FBI file, file 39-915-1-95, consisting of letters surreptitiously copied by the FBI during a break-in to King's office. For Bridges's claim about Willkie, see *Proceedings of the Seventh Biennial Convention*, 82, ILWU Library.

43. *Chronicle*, Sept. 30, 1941, 1, 6; *NYT*, Feb. 9, 1943, 1, 13; June 27, 1944, 21. On Pressman's role, see, for example, letter, Carol [King] to Richie [Gladstein], Apr. 30, 1943, f13, b8, Bridges Papers, Southern California Library, wherein King complains, "THIS BRIEF BORES ME." On Hoover's view that the case would go to Supreme Court, see 5 of Hoover memo with missing first page, likely June 10, 1941, file number likely 39-915-1344, Bridges FBI file.

44. Intercepted phone call to Curran, Dec. 27, 1944, file 39-915-2493, Bridges FBI file; copy of letter, Gladstein to King, Jan. 12, 1945, f3, b9, Bridges Papers, Southern California Library; Foxworth to Director, Jan. 4, 1942, with attachment dated Dec. 28, 1942, file 39-915-2221, Bridges FBI file.

45. Mimeographed letters, Dorothy Ann Schumacher to All Affiliates of California CIO Council, Jan. 17, 1945; Schumacher to All ILWU Locals, Jan. 19, 1945; AFL Bridges Committee to President Roosevelt, Feb. 25, 1945; [Elinor Kahn] press release, Mar. 30, 1945; all in f6, b9, Bridges Papers, Southern California Library; letter, William C. Malone to President Roosevelt, Mar. 17, 1945, f6, b11, Bridges Papers, Southern California Library; J. F. B., memo for the President, Mar. 14, 1945, OF 1750, FDR Papers; report of [name redacted], Washington FBI office, May 2, 1945, file 39-915-2567; the many direct appeals to FDR are recorded in clippings dated between Feb. and Apr. 1945, file 39-915-A, Bridges FBI file.

46. Copy of letter, Gladstein to King, Feb. 6, 1945, f3, b9, Bridges Papers, Southern California Library. Pressman, King, and Gladstein, in that order, appeared as counsel on the brief, with Greene and Grossman as of counsel.

47. Brief for Harry Bridges; Brief of American Civil Liberties Union as *Amicus Curiae*; Brief for the American Committee for the Protection of the Foreign Born *Amicus Curiae*, all in possession of the author.

48. For more extensive treatment of the Supreme Court appeal, see Larrowe, *Harry Bridges*, 238–47; Kutler, *American Inquisition*, 138–42; Ginger, *Carol Weiss King*, chaps. 23, 27; Afrasiabi, *Burning Bridges*, chap. 5; and *Bridges v. Wixon*, 326 U.S. 135 (1945), 65 S.Ct. 1443, 89 L.Ed. 2103. Douglas's notes on the case indicate that, for him, the issue of affiliation was central; see f788, Bridges v. Wixon O.T. 1944, b120, William O. Douglas Papers, LC; Ladd immediately provided an analysis for Hoover; see memo, Ladd to Hoover, June 19, 1945, file 39-915-2558, Bridges FBI file.

49. Ickes diaries, May 26, 1945, reel 7.

50. Laura Robertson, press release, June 18, 1945, f6, b9, Bridges Papers, Southern California Library.

51. Clipping, *Chronicle*, June 19, 1945; *Time*, July 2, 1945, both in f7, b9, Bridges Papers, Southern California Library; clipping, *Chronicle*, July 18, 1940, file Harry Bridges, Material about, 1939–43, series ILWU History, ILWU Library.

52. Report of [name redacted], approved by Connelley, July 5, 1941, file 39-915-1449; copy of letter, Hoover to SAC San Francisco, Aug. 12, 1941, file 39-915-1530; letters, Wendell Berge to Director, Aug. 78, 1941, file 39-915-1531; Matthew McGuire to Hoover, Aug. 9, 1941, file 39-915-1532; copy of letter, Hoover to Connelley, Aug. 18, 1941, file 39-915-1562; report of [name redacted], July 13, 1941, file 39-915-1454; report of [name redacted], July 24, 1941, file 39-915-1474; [name redacted] memo for Mr. Kimball, Sept. 4, 1941, and copy of letter, Foxworth to Director, Sept. 4, 1941, file 39-915-1591; report of [name redacted], Sept. 9, 1941, file 39-915-1619; report of [name redacted], Nov. 27, 1941, file 39-915-1747, all Bridges FBI file.

53. Memo, Tamm to Ladd, May 14, 1942, file 39-915-1-84; for telephone surveillance, see, for example, E. E. Conroy to Director, Feb. 19, 1943, file 39-915-1-99; or Pieper to Director, Nov. 27, 1944, file 39-915-1-106; Conroy to Director, Dec. 1, 1943, file 39-915-2399; summaries of phone calls by Bridges, Nov. 14, 15, 1944, file 39-915-2472, all Bridges FBI file.

54. For material copied from King's office and cover memos from Ladd of Mar. 23, May 12, and Oct. 5, 1942, see files 39-015-1-81, 39-915-1-86, 39-915-1-94, 39-915-1-96, Bridges FBI file. The material that the FBI collected was used to create files on some of King's correspondents, see Athan G. Theoharis and John Stuart Cox, *The Boss: J. Edgar Hoover and the Great American Inquisition* (Philadelphia: Temple University Press, 1988), 13–14.

55. Report of [name redacted], signed and approved by Pieper, July 26, 1945, file 39-915-2566, Bridges FBI file.

56. See, for example, interview with Bridges's father in *Canberra Times*, Apr. 7, 1941, 4. Bridges once told me, at a time when I was not recording, that he was not especially worried about being sent to Australia, as he could rejoin his father's firm and work with his brother.

57. *Melbourne Argus*, May 30, 1942, 3; cablegram to Australian Minister, Washington, June 25, 1942, with copies to P.M. and Minister E.A. (External Affairs, that is, the foreign ministry), June 26, 1942; cablegram, Dixon, Australian Legation, Washington, to External Affairs, June 20, 1942, refers to Evatt's recent meeting with Cordell Hull, both in series A981, item MIG 3, Title Migration Restrictions: Deportation of Harry R. Bridges, Department of External Affairs, AA. I've been unable determine if Hull shared Evatt's statement with others.

58. Clipping, illeg. source; clipping from *San Francisco Examiner*, May 22, 1941, file 39-915-A, Bridges FBI file; clipping, *New York Herald-Tribune*, Apr. 9, 1950, in Miscellaneous: Enquiry re Mr. Harry Bridges, file marked secret, External Affairs, Series/Accession Number A1838/2, item number 1461/131, AA. On May 2, 1941, Connelley sent Hoover an eighteen-page list of people who had been ordered deported but had been refused entrance by their country of origin. See Connelley to Director, file 39-915-11[illeg.], Bridges FBI file.

59. *Chronicle*, Oct. 7, 1941, 12; clipping, *New York Herald Tribune*, Oct. 30, 1941, file 39-915-A, Bridges FBI file.

Chapter 11. World War, Labor Peace

1. Maurice Isserman, *Which Side Were You On? The American Communist Party during the Second World War* (Middletown, CT: Wesleyan University Press, 1982), 84; clipping,

Call-Bulletin, stamped Jan. 28, 1941, file 39-915-A, Bridges FBI file; memo, N. J. L. Pieper to Director, Jan. 27, 1941, file 39-915-777, Bridges FBI file.

2. Robert H. Zieger, *The CIO, 1935–1955* (Chapel Hill: University of North Carolina Press, 1995), 108–10; memo, Hoover to Attorney General, Dec. 23, 1940, file 39-915-708; memo, B. E. Sackett to Director, Dec. 13, 1940, file 39-915-712, both Bridges FBI file; interview, May 7, 1986.

3. Robert Jackson oral history, 311, Columbia University.

4. *Chronicle*, June 12, 1941, 1, 12. After Frankensteen's testimony, Hoover quickly informed the attorney general that Connelley had advised the INS not to call Frankensteen as a witness because he was connected with the CIO and "all officials of the CIO" were "against the current hearing of Harry Bridges." Memo, Hoover to Attorney General, June 11, 1941, file 39-915-1336, Bridges FBI file.

5. The ILA Pacific Coast District claimed three longshore locals in Puget Sound and a few other locals there and in Alaska Territory. *Chronicle*, Oct. 22, 1940, 12; Jan. 10, 1941, 11; Feb. 12, 1941, 7; Feb. 13, 1941, 5; June 10, 1941, 9; July 3, 1941, 9; Nov. 25, 1941, 7; telegram, Bridges to Lewis, Sept. 13, 1940; letters, Bridges to Lewis, Sept. 20 and Nov. 7, 1940; Bridges to Sidney Hillman, Nov. 7, 1940; all pt. 1, series 2, reel 18, CIO Files of John L. Lewis.

6. *Proceedings Fourth Annual Convention*, esp. 17–19, 26–27, 35–37, 46, 59–61, 63–64, 67, 85–87; clippings, *Washington Post*, Apr. 10, 8, Apr. 11; *Washington Star*, Apr. 10, A7; *New York Post*, Apr. 10, all 1941, all in file 39-915-A, Bridges FBI file; *Voice*, June 7, 1940, 2.

7. Clipping, *Washington Star*, dateline June 25, file 39-915-A, Bridges FBI file. For CPUSA policy making in the absence of communication with Moscow, see John Earl Haynes and Harvey Klehr, "The 'Mental Comintern' and the CPUSA's Self-Destruction, 1944–1958" (keynote address, "One Hundred Years of Communism in the USA," conference at Williams College, Nov. 9–10, 2018); Isserman, *Which Side Were You On?* 104–7, 272n15.

8. *NYT*, June 27, 1941, 12; clipping, *Detroit Times*, June 27, 1941, file 39-915-A, Bridges FBI file. Bridges's travels and meetings during June 25–Aug. 20, 1941, are summarized in memo for the director, Aug. 27, 1941, file 39-915-68, Bridges FBI file. Similar logs of his travels and meetings appear in other places in his file, esp. report, [name redacted], July 10, 1941, covering July 1–2 through July 7–9, 1941, file 39-915-1435.

9. *NYT*, July 11, 1941, 11. Bridges's speech to the NMU was reported in detail by an FBI agent; see report, [name redacted], July 20, 1941, Cleveland, OH, file 39-915-1489, Bridges FBI file.

10. Clippings, *P.M.*, July 17, 1941; *NYT*, July 17, 1949, file 39-915-Sub. A, Bridges FBI file.

11. Hudson, in the *Daily Worker*, July 20, 1941, 1, quoted in Isserman, *Which Side Are You On?* 113; *Chronicle*, Oct. 5, 1941, 1; Pearson and Allen, column for Oct. 18, 1941, American University digital archive. The full text of Bridges's October speech promising full support of FDR appeared in the *Daily Worker*, date unclear, file 39-915–Sub A, Bridges FBI file.

12. James B. Atleson, *Labor and the Wartime State: Labor Relations and Law during World War II* (Urbana: University of Illinois Press, 1998), 44–45; James B. Atleson, "The Law of Collective Bargaining and Wartime Labor Relations," in *American Labor in the*

Era of World War II, ed. Sally M. Miller and Daniel A. Cornford (Westport, CT: Praeger, 1995), 46, 140–50; Statement of the Trade Union Committee to Defend America, Dec. 12, 1941, file Bridges Plan, b1, series ILWU History—World War II, ILWU Library; *Chronicle*, Jan. 11, 1942, 15; *Dispatcher*, May 7, 1943, 1, 4, 5; May 21, 1943, 1, 3; May 5, 1944, 1, 2; *Proceedings Fifth Biennial Convention*, 24, 26, 298; telegram, Lundeberg to Lewis, May 4, 1943, pt. 1, series II, reel 22, CIO Files of John L. Lewis. On the Little Steel formula and the coal strike, see Robert H. Zieger, *John L. Lewis: Labor Leader* (Boston: Twayne, 1988), chap. 6; Melvyn Dubofsky and Warren R. Van Tine, *John L. Lewis: A Biography* (New York: Quadrangle, 1977), chaps. 17, 18. See also Bridges's comments on Lewis in *PW*, May 24, 1943, 3; May 27, 1943, 1.

13. Atleson, *Labor and the Wartime State*, 140–50; George Lipsitz, *Rainbow at Midnight: Labor and Culture in the 1940s* (Urbana: University of Illinois Press, 1994), chap. 3; Richard P. Boyden, "The West Coast Longshoremen, the Communist Party, and the Second World War" (unpublished paper, 1967).

14. Data for California are specific, but those for Oregon and Washington are for all "nonwhite"; table 13, https://www.census.gov/library/publications/1953/dec/population-vol-02.html.

15. Goldblatt oral history, 286–87; Jenkins oral history, 152.

16. *Dispatcher*, Dec. 18, 1942, 1–3, 7.

17. *Dispatcher*, July 2, 1943, 1, 2; Dec. 3, 1943, 6, 8; Apr. 7, 1944, 5, 9; Dec. 15, 1944, 2; Apr. 20, 1945, 14; July 13, 1945, 16; esp. June 1, 1945, 8–9; *Proceedings of the Sixth Biennial Convention*, 46–47; Harvey Schwartz, "A Union Combats Racism: The ILWU's Japanese-American 'Stockton Incident' of 1945," *Southern California Quarterly* 62 (1980): 164–65.

18. Robert W. Cherny, "Longshoremen of San Francisco Bay, 1848–1960," in *Dock Workers: International Explorations in Comparative Labor History, 1790–1970*, ed. Sam Davies et al., 2 vols. (Aldershot, Hampshire: Ashgate, 2000), 1:137, 138; Bureau of the Census, *1940 Census*, vol. 3, Population, pt. 2, table 13, 233; *1950 Census*, vol. 2, Population, pt. 5, table 76, 5-315, 5-318. The 1950 federal census grouped all nonwhites, so those figures likely include a small number of Asian Americans and American Indians, but not Latinos. For the increase in Latinos in San Pedro, see Harvey Schwartz, *Solidarity Stories: An Oral History of the ILWU* (Seattle: University of Washington Press, 2009), 78–79.

19. Nancy Quam Wickham, "Who Controls the Hiring Hall? The Struggle for Job Control in the ILWU during World War II," originally published in Steve Rosswurm, ed., *The CIO's Left-Led Unions* (New Brunswick, NJ: Rutgers University Press, 1992), and reprinted in Sally M. Miller and Daniel A. Conford, eds., *American Labor in the Era of World War II* (Westport, CT: Praeger, 1995), 132–37, esp. 136, 137; my page citations here and later are to the latter version.

20. Wickham, "Who Controls the Hiring Hall?" 137–38.

21. Statement of Paul Eliel, Aug. 17, 1943, hearing before the subcommittee of the Senate Committee on Military Affairs, Sheridan Downey, chair, b3, series ILWU History—World War II, ILWU Library; letter, Pieper to Director, Dec. 23, 1942, file 39-915-2236; memo, Hoover to Attorney General, Jan. 11, 1943, file 39-915-2228, Bridges FBI file.

22. Albert Vetere Lannon, "World War II and the Struggle for Solidarity with New Union Members: San Francisco Longshoremen and the Newcomers," file General, b1, series ILWU History—World War II, ILWU Library.

23. Lannon, "World War II and the Struggle for Solidarity"; Hoover to SAC San Francisco, Sept. 23, 1944, file 39-915-2463, Bridges FBI file. On Kearney and the ACTU in Local 10, see William Issel, *Church and State in the City: Catholics and Politics in Twentieth-Century San Francisco* (Philadelphia: Temple University Press, 2013), 86–87.

24. Clipping, *Washington Post*, July 15, 1942, file 39-915-A, Bridges FBI file.

25. Memo, Hoover to Attorney General, Oct. 3, 1942, file 39-915-2098; memo, executive assistant to the attorney general to Hoover, Oct. 9, 1942, file 39-915-2124, both Bridges FBI file.

26. *PW*, July 31, 1942, 2; *NYT*, Aug. 5, 1942, 11; *Labor Herald* (San Francisco), Oct. 16, 1942, 1; Washington City News Service, Aug. 4, 1942, file 39-915-A, Bridges FBI file.

27. *PW*, July 8, 1942, 1, 3; July 27, 1942, 1; *NYT*, July 29, 1942, 8; see also additional clippings and applications, file Longshore Battalions, b1, series ILWU History World War II, ILWU Library; memos, R.R. Roach to Ladd, July 3, 1942, file 39-915-2000; memo, Pieper to Director, Aug. 7, 1942, file 39-915-2948; Hoover to Attorney General, Feb. 23, 1943, file 39-915-2270; report, [name redacted], signed and approved by Pieper, July 26, 1945, 4, file 39-915-2566; Bridges FBI file.

28. Nelson Lichtenstein, *Labor's War at Home: The CIO in World War II* (New York: Cambridge University Press, 1982); Atleson, *Labor and the Wartime State*; Lipsitz, *Rainbow at Midnight*. Miller and Cornford, introduction to *American Labor in the Era of World War II*, 1–25, surveys relevant works.

29. *Chronicle*, Oct. 5, 1941, 1, 17; Nov. 19, 1941, 4; clipping, *Washington Times-Herald*, Oct. 18, 1941, file 39-915–Sub A, Bridges FBI file; *NYT*, Nov. 23, 1941, 42; Bridges, Memorandum re Developments in Negotiations with Maritime Commission and West Coast Ship Operators re Plan to Increase Productivity in Longshore Industry, undated but after Dec. 19, 1941, file Bridges Plan, b1, series ILWU History World War II, ILWU Library.

30. Conference to Determine Policy, U.S. Maritime Commission, Dec. 19, 1941, file Bridges Plan, b1, series ILWU History World War II, ILWU Library.

31. SK [Kagel], Confidential Report on Longshore Production Plan, Feb. 20, 1942, file Bridges Plan, b1, series ILWU History World War II, ILWU Library; Oral History Interview with Emory Scott Land, 1963, by John T. Mason, 150, 191, Center for Oral History, Columbia University.

32. *NYT*, Mar. 14, 1942, S6; *NYT*, June 8, 1943, 43; *Proceedings Fifth Biennial Convention*, 49; *PW*, July 12, 1943, 4; clipping, *Examiner*, June 8, 1943, Peglar Papers—Subj. Unions, Longshoremen, b90, Herbert Hoover Presidential Library.

33. Michael Torigian, "National Unity on the Waterfront: Communist Politics and the ILWU during the Second World War," *Labor History* 30 (1989): 409–32, esp. 413, 414; Boyden, "The West Coast Longshoremen"; Wickham, "Who Controls the Hiring Hall?"; Howard Kimeldorf, "World War II and the Deradicalization of American Labor: The ILWU as a Deviant Case," *Labor History* 33 (1992): 248–78. I had already drawn very similar conclusions to those of Kimeldorf before I found his article.

34. Letter, copied for FBI by U.S. Office of Censorship, Bridges to Gordon McKay, Oct. 31, 1942, file 39-915-2203, Bridges FBI file; mimeographed letter, Bridges to All Longshore, Shipclerks, and Bosses Locals, Sept. 19, 1950, file General, b1, series ILWU History—World War II, ILWU Library (emphasis in the original).

35. Hearing, Senate Manpower Subcommittee on Military Affairs, Sheridan Downey chair, San Francisco, Aug. 17, 1943, 33, 20, 22, b3, series ILWU History—World War II, ILWU Library; see also *Chronicle*, Jan. 14, 1942, 21; *Chronicle*, Jan. 11, 1942, 15; *Dispatcher*, May 7, 1943, 2; mimeographed letter, Bridges to All Longshore, Shipclerks, and Bosses Locals, Sept. 19, 1950, file General, b1, series ILWU History—World War ii, ILWU Library

36. *Wartime Shipping: A Plan and a Memorandum Prepared and Submitted by Maritime Unions Affiliated with the Congress of Industrial Organizations*, Feb. 1943, b3, series ILWU History—World War II, ILWU Library.

37. *Chronicle*, July 15, 1942, 5; F. P. Foisie to Paul Eliel, Sept. 29, 1942; Statement of Chairman, Feb. 4, 1943, attached to Foisie to [WEA] Members, Feb. 5, 1943, both in Pegler Papers—Subj., Unions, Longshoremen, b90, Herbert Hoover Presidential Library; *Daily Worker*, Apr. 24, 1943, 5.

38. Statement of Paul Eliel, Hearing, Senate Manpower Subcommittee on Military Affairs, Sheridan Downey chair, San Francisco, Aug. 17, 1943, 33, 20, 22, b3, series ILWU History—World War II, ILWU Library; *Dispatcher*, Oct. 20, 1944, 7.

39. Statement of the Waterfront Employers Association of the Pacific Coast before the Senate Sub-Committee on Military Affairs, SF, Aug. 12, 1943, esp. 58, 77, 80, 82, 85, 87, 91, 100, 103, b3, series ILWU History—World War II, ILWU Library; Wickham, "Who Controls the Hiring Hall?" 127; *Dispatcher*, Oct. 22, 1944, 7.

40. Partial Findings of Subcommittee, Aug. 18, 1943, Peglar Papers—Subj. Unions, Longshoremen, b90, Herbert Hoover Presidential Library.

41. Memo, Guy Hottel to Director, Apr. 10, 1942, file 39-915-1-104, Bridges FBI file.

42. Press release, May 26 [1944], file "No Strike Pledge," b2, series ILWU History, World War II—1940–45, ILWU Library. Joseph Starobin, *American Communism in Crisis, 1943-1957* (Cambridge: Harvard University Press, 1972), notes: "Bridges went far beyond Party policy. . . . Only those who simplify the relation between left wing labor leaders such as Bridges and the Party itself will be surprised" (269n17). For Starobin's account of internal CP discussions, see 59, 77.

43. Clippings, *PM*, May 29, 3, and June 19, 1944, 14, file "No Strike Pledge." b2, series ILWU History, World War II—1940–45, ILWU Library.

44. Telegram, Bridges to the *Times*, Chicago, May 27, 1944: Bridges, statement to *St. Louis Post Dispatch*, July 9, 1944, file "No Strike Pledge," b2, series ILWU History, World War II—1940–45, ILWU Library. "Teheran" was the usual spelling at that time.

45. Isserman, *Which Side Are You On?* 188–91; Browder, *Teheran: Our Path in War and Peace* (New York: International, 1944).

46. *Fortune*, Feb. 1945, 228, 230; see, for example, Starobin, *American Communism in Crisis*, 59, which refers to Bridges's proposal as "an absolute no-strike policy."

47. Zieger, *The CIO, 1935–1955*, 216.

48. *Dispatcher*, June 2, 1944, 3.

49. *Dispatcher*, Aug. 11, 1944, 1, 4–6; June 15, 1944, 1, 4; June 21, 1944, 1–11; *Business Week*, Aug. 5, 1944, 108; Bruce Dancis, "San Francisco Employers and Longshore Labor Relations, 1934–1949" (1974), 41–43, ILWU Library.

50. *Chronicle*, June 1, 1942, 7; Nov. 5, 1942, 1, 6, 8, 9; *PW*, June 1, 1942, 1; *Labor Herald* (San Francisco), Sept. 18, 1942, 1; *PW*, Oct. 24, 1942, 1; Oct. 26, 1942, 3; Oct. 28, 1942, 3;

Oct. 30, 1942, 1; transcript of call, Bridges to Huberman, Sept. 3, 1943, file 39-915-2370, Bridges FBI file; *Dispatcher*, Oct. 8, 1943, esp. 5; Oct. 22, 1943, 1, same, Local 6 edition, A; *Chronicle*, Nov. 3, 1943, 1.

51. For example, *Dispatcher*, Local 6 edition, Apr. 21, 1944, A; Oct. 20, 1944, throughout; Nov. 3, 1944, throughout; intercepted phone calls, Bridges to Frederick Myers, Nov. 8, 1944; Bridges to Curran, same date, file 39-915-2487.

52. *Chronicle*, Apr. 21, 1945, 4; Apr. 24, 1945, 11; Apr. 25, 1945, 13; Apr. 27, 1945, 9; Apr. 29, 1945, 11; May 2, 1945, 9, 3H; May 3, 1945, 10; *Dispatcher*, May 4, 1945, 1, 11; May 18, 1945, 3, 10; see also WFTU records, Cornell University, http://rmc.library.cornell.edu /EAD/htmldocs/KCL05595.html.

53. *Dispatcher*, May 4, 1945, 11; May 18, 1945, 1; *Chronicle*, May 12, 1945, 9; *People's World*, May 11, 1945, 1. Memo, SAC San Francisco to Director, May 9, 1945, 39-915-2569, Bridges FBI file. Bridges's FBI file, file 39-915-2552, has a clipping from the *Chronicle* for May 8, no page number, with the photo, but that photo and article do not appear in the digitized version of the *Chronicle*, apparently pushed off the page in the later edition by breaking news of V-E day. The *Chronicle*, May 10, 11, also reported that Murray and at least one local AFL leader had been at the same reception.

54. *Dispatcher*, June 4, 1943, 1; Goldblatt oral history, passim esp. 1, 54, 69, 94–99, 106; 125, 242.

55. *Proceedings of the Sixth Biennial Convention*, 28, 31–33.

56. Melnikow oral history, 222, 228–29, 239–41; Archie Green interviewed by Robert Cherny, Oct. 12, 1986.

57. Goldblatt oral history, 419–22.

58. *Proceedings of the Sixth Biennial Convention*, 25–27

59. *Proceedings of the Sixth Biennial Convention*, 327–30; "Alexander Marsden Kidd," *California Law Review* 48 (1960): 188.

60. *Proceedings Fourth Annual Convention*, 3–5, 113, 212–13, 220–21; *Proceedings of the Sixth Biennial Convention*, 28, 29, 153, 218; *Dispatcher*, June 1, 1945, 10.

61. *Dispatcher*, June 15, 1945, 11. It is not possible here to provide a thorough history of the ILWU in Hawai'i. The most important treatment is Sanford Zalburg, *A Spark Is Struck! Jack Hall & the ILWU in Hawaii* (Honolulu: University Press of Hawaii, 1979). Useful oral histories are in Harvey Schwartz, *Solidarity Stories: An Oral History of the ILWU* (Seattle: University of Washington Press, 2009), chap. 5. Other works include Curtis C. Aller, "The Evolution of Hawaiian Labor Relations: From Benevolent Paternalism to Mature Collective Bargaining" (PhD diss., Harvard University, 1958); Edward D. Beechert, *Working in Hawaii: A Labor History* (Honolulu: University of Hawaii Press, 1985), chaps. 14, 15; Gerald Horne, *Fighting in Paradise: Labor Unions, Racism, and Communists in the Making of Modern Hawai'i* (Honolulu: University of Hawai'i Press, 2011); Bernard W. Stern, *Rutledge Unionism: Labor Relations in the Honolulu Transit Industry* (Honolulu: University of Hawaii, Center for Labor Education and Research, 1986); and Bernard W. Stern, *The Aloha Trade: Labor Relations in Hawaii's Hotel Industry, 1941–1987* (Honolulu: University of Hawaii, Center for Labor Education and Research, 1988). An FBI agent in Honolulu (name redacted) filed a heavily redacted, eighteen-page report on ILWU activities in Hawai'i on Aug. 19, 1941, file 39-915-1571, Bridges FBI file.

62. In addition to the works previously cited, see my "San Francisco Labor and the Hawaiian Sugar Industry," paper, Economic History Association annual meeting, 1987.

63. Copy of letter, Neylan to Hearst, Jan. 30, 1934, folder 14, series 5, b65, John Francis Neylan Papers, Bancroft Library, University of California, Berkeley.

64. Zalburg, *Spark Is Struck!*, chaps. 10–15, esp. 85, 86; cable intercepted by Office of Censorship, Bridges and Paton to Kawano, Feb. 13, 1943, file 39-915-2301, Bridges FBI file; Hall oral history, in Schwartz, *Solidarity Stories*, 226–31; Goldblatt oral history, 303–10, esp. 305; *Proceedings of the Seventh Biennial Convention*, 172.

65. Zalburg, *Spark Is Struck!*, chaps. 10–15; *Dispatcher*, Nov. 3, 1944. 3; *Proceedings of the Sixth Biennial Convention*, 206–7.

66. *Dispatcher*, June 1, 1945, 1, 13; *Chronicle*, May 24, 1945, 8; *Chronicle This World*, May 26, 1945, 4, Schwartz, " Union Combats Racism," 161–76, esp. 169.

67. *Dispatcher*, May 18, 1945, 11; June 1, 1945, 1; letter, King to Grossman, Jan, 30, 1941, file 3, b19, Bridges Papers, Southern California Library.

68. Dale Curran, "Bunk in San Francisco," *Jazz Record* (Mar. 1945): 6, 7, 14, 15; *PW*, July 13, 1943, 5; *Chronicle*, July 5, 1943, 14; July 10, 1943, "This World" section, 10; July 12, 1943, 4; Sept. 18, 1943, 8; Nov. 6, 1943, 6; May 13, 1944, 8; June 10, 1944, 19; July 1, 1944, 8. See also photos of the performances on the website the Swedish Bunk Johnson Society, at http://www.fellers.se/Bunk/1943_West-coast.html.

69. FBI agents tracked the living arrangements of Harry and Agnes from their arrival in San Francisco to 1940; report of [name redacted], Nov. 29, 1940, file 39-515-672, Bridges FBI file; Resner, interviewed by Robert Cherny, Dec. 18, 1992, and Jan. 23, 1993.

70. Lionel Youst, "Harry and Agnes Bridges: A Couple at Odds," *Pacific Northwest Quarterly* (Spring 2015): 76; letters, Pieper to Director, Nov. 16 1942, file 39-915-2167; same, Nov. 27, 1942, file 39-915-2180; Hoover to SAC New York, Jan. 9, 1943, file 39-915-2229; Hoover to Communications Section, Jan. 9, 1943, file 39-915-2226; memos, Pieper to Director, Jan. 9, 1943, file 39-915-2227; Hoover to SAC San Francisco, Feb. 19, 1943, file 39-915-2265; E. G. Fitch to Ladd, Feb. 24, 1943, file 39-915-2269; memo, E. G. Fitch to Ladd, Apr. 13, 1943, file 39-915-2366, Bridges FBI file. The Bridges FBI file includes transcripts of several of Nancy's phone calls; see, for example, call from Leo Huberman, Apr. 3, 1943, file 39-915-2336, Bridges FBI file.

71. *Chronicle*, Dec. 30, 1944, 1, 7; Mar. 21, 1945, 3; Apr. 26, 1945, 3H; *Dispatcher*, Aug. 6, 1948, 5. Regarding Crawford's work with INS officials in 1941, see letter, Connelley to Hoover, Nov. 23, 1941, file 39-915-1726; memo, Pieper to Director, Feb. 13, 1945, file 30-915-2530; memo, Pieper to Director, Feb. 9, 1945, file 39-915-2533; letter to Director, signature page missing, Feb. 26, 1945, file 39-915-2539, Bridges FBI file.

72. *Dispatcher*, June 15, 1945, 3; H [Bridges] to Dearest [Nancy], undated, f19, b10, Bridges Papers.

73. Memo, SAC San Francisco to Director, Apr. 6, 1945, file 39-915-2550, Bridges FBI file; *Chronicle* June 10, 1945, 1; Aug. 23, 1945, 1, 7; Aug. 28, 1945, 5; Aug. 29, 1945, 9; Sept. 1, 1945, 1, 7; *Dispatcher*, Aug. 6, 1948, 5.

74. *Chronicle*, Sept. 4, 1945, 1, 10.

75. Memo, L. H. Garner to J. J. Hart, Sept. 17, 1945, f C-6405274-f[1/2], b2, Bridges INS File. There are several other memos in that file relating to the citizenship hearing

and also the affidavit by Agnes Bridges; *Chronicle*, Sept. 18, 1945, 1, 8; Sept. 28, 1946, 3; memo signed Montequila, copy from INS files provided by Stanley Kutler.

Chapter 12. Cold War, Labor War

1. Joseph R. Starobin, *American Communism in Crisis, 1943–1957* (Cambridge, MA: Harvard University Press, 1972), 45, 232; John Earl Haynes and Harvey Klehr, "The 'Mental Comintern' and the Self-Destructive Tactics of the CPUSA, 1944–8," chap. 1 of *Post–Cold War Revelations and the American Communist Party: Citizens, Revolutionaries, and Spies*, ed. Vernon L. Pedersen, James G. Ryan, and Katherine A. S. Sibley (London and New York: Bloomsbury Academic, 2021), 18, 21, 22, 24–25; Duclos's article, in English, is online at http://www.marxists.org/history/usa/parties/cpusa/1945/04/0400-duclos -ondissolution.pdf.

2. Maurice Isserman, *Which Side Are You On? The American Communist Party during the Second World War* (Middletown, CT: Wesleyan University Press, 1982) 218–33; Edward P. Johanningsmeier, *Forging American Communism: The Life of William Z. Foster* (Princeton, NJ: Princeton University Press, 1994), 304–13; *PW*, May 28, 1945, 1; May 31, 1945, 2; June 4, 1945, 1; June 6, 1945, 1; June 13, 1945, 1; July 19, 1945, 3; July 31, 1945, 3; Aug. 1, 1945, 3; Dave Jenkins, interviewed by Robert Cherny, Dec. 3, 1992.

3. *NYT*, Jan. 11, 1943, 6; memo, Pieper to Director, Aug. 29, 1944, file 39-915-2461; memo, E. E. Conroy to Director, Sept. 2, 1944, with transcript of phone call between Bridges and Goldblatt on Aug. 23, 1944, file 39-915-2462; clipping, *Guild Reporter*, Feb. 15, 1945, 3, file 39-915-2515; Bridges FBI file.

4. Teletype, Conroy to Director, Feb. 5, 1943, citing a confidential informant, file 39-915-2252; memo, Guy Hottel, SAC Washington field office, to Director, Apr. 21, 1943, with transcript of phone call between Bridges and Goldblatt, Apr. 13, 1943, file 39-915- 2334; memo, Conroy to Director, Feb. 4, 1944, with transcript of phone call between Curran and Saul Mills, Feb. 1, 1944, file 39-015-2414, Bridges FBI File.

5. Copy of letter, James Thimmes et al. to Murray, June 8, 1946, f3–35; undated statement from California CIO Council Executive Board, f3–26; telegram, Bill Gillespie to Murray, July 16, 1946, f3–29; all in b3, series II Irwin DeShetler Papers, Archives of Labor History and Urban Affairs, Wayne State University; *NYT*, July 19, 1946, 3.

6. Letters, DeShetler to Haywood, Dec. 18, 1946, f2–1; DeShetler to Haywood, Feb. 11, 1947, f2–2; b2, series II, DeShetler Papers.

7. *NYT*, Nov. 19, 1946, 1; Robert H. Zieger, *The CIO, 1935–1955* (Chapel Hill: University of North Carolina Press, 1995), 213; Dubofsky, *State and Labor*, 193.

8. *Dispatcher*, Aug. 24, 1945, 1; Sept. 28, 1945, throughout, esp. 8; Oct. 5, 1945, 5.

9. Report approved by SAC San Francisco, Dec. 20, 1946, 11, file 39-915-2601; memo, SAC Seattle to Director, Jan. 7, 1946, file 39-915-2584, Bridges FBI file; *Dispatcher*, Feb. 22, 1946, 1, 2, 3, 10; Apr. 5, 1946, 1–3, 5.

10. *Chronicle*, May 6, 1946, 1; May 7, 1946, 1, 7; May 8, 1946, 1; May 9, 1946, 1, 6; May 10, 1946, 6; May 11, 1946, 8; May 12, 1946, 1, 13.

11. Letter, Hoover to Vaughn, May 15, 1946, file FBI, Maritime, b168, President's Secretary's Files, Harry S. Truman Library; Report of [name redacted] approved by SAC San Francisco, Dec. 20, 1946, 13, 14, file 39-915-2601, Bridges FBI file.

12. *Chronicle*, May 23, 1946, 24; May 29, 1946, 5; June 1, 1946, 1, 4; June 2, 1946, 1, 6; June 3, 1946, 1, 10; June 1946, 4, 5; June 7, 1946, 1; June 8, 1946, 1, 7; June 9, 1946, 1; June 11, 1946, 7; *NYT*, Feb. 8, 1946, 1, 2, 3.

13. James Carey, Memo on 1946 Maritime Question within the WFTU, Apr. 20, 1949, folder WFTUERP—Misc. Material, b122, CIO Secretary Treasurer Collection, Archives of Labor History and Urban Affairs, Wayne State University.

14. *Chronicle*, June 12, 1946, 1; June 13, 1946, 1, 7; June 14, 1946, 1; June 16, 1946, 8; *NYT*, June 13, 1946, 1, 10; June 15, 1946, 1, 10; transcript of telephone call from Bridges to Robertson, June 14, 1946, b15, Coast Committee files, ILWU Library; Report of the Officers, *Proceedings of the Seventh Biennial Convention*, 21.

15. *Dispatcher*, June 18, 1946, 1, 9; July 12, 1946, 1.

16. Clark Kerr, *The Gold and the Blue: A Personal Memoir of the University of California, 1949–1967*, vol. 1, *Academic Triumphs* (Berkeley: University of California Press, 2001), 137; *Dispatcher*, Aug. 9, 1946, 1; Aug. 23, 1946, 1, 5; Sept. 6, 1946, 10; Sept. 20, 1946, 1, 9.

17. *Dispatcher*, Oct. 4, 1946, 1, 4; *Chronicle*, Oct. 1, 1946, 1; Oct. 2, 1946, 1, 3; Oct. 3, 1946, 1; Oct. 4, 1946, 1, 3; Oct. 6, 1946, "This World" section, 4; Oct. 8, 1946, 1; Oct. 25, 1946, 9; Oct. 27, 1946, 1, 9; Oct. 28, 1946, 1, 2; Oct. 29, 1946, 1; Oct. 30, 1946, 1, 2; Nov. 14, 1946, 1; *Dispatcher*, Nov. 15, 1946, 1, 10; Nov. 16, 1946, 3; Nov. 18, 1946, 1, 3; Nov. 19, 1946, 1; letter, Harriet Bouslag to Cole Jackman, Aug. 6, 1946, file: Coast 1945–46 Nego. of June 14; Feinsinger Correspondence, b15, Coast Committee, ILWU Library.

18. Sanford Zalburg, *A Spark Is Struck! Jack Hall & the ILWU in Hawaii* (Honolulu: University Press of Hawaii, 1979), chaps. 25–29 esp. 150.

19. *NYT*, Nov. 19, 1946, 1; *Chronicle*, Nov. 19, 1946, 2. Neither Zieger, *The CIO, 1935–1955*, chap. 9; nor Bert Cochran, *Labor and Communism: The Conflict That Shaped American Unions* (Princeton, NJ: Princeton University Press, 1977), chap. 10, mentions the 1946 convention resolution.

20. *Chronicle*, Dec. 21, 1946, 8; Dec. 25, 1946, 1; *NYT*, Dec. 25, 1946, 40; Jan. 5, 1947, 10; Feb. 10, 1947, 43; Mar. 2, 1947, 118; *NYT*, Feb. 12, 1947, 51.

21. Report of the Officers, *Proceedings of the Seventh Biennial Convention*, 32, 304.

22. *Chronicle*, June 1, 1947, 2.

23. Zalburg, *Spark Is Struck!*, chaps. 31–32; *Chronicle*, July 12, 1947, 1; July 13, 1947, 8; July 17, 1947, 1; July 31, 1947, 8.

24. *Chronicle*, June 1, 1947, 2; memorandum of Agreement, June 6, 1947; untitled addendum to agreement of June 6, 1947, both in file 1946 strike—1948, series Coast Longshore Agreement #3, ILWU Library; *Chronicle*, June 10, 1947, n.p.; *Chronicle*, June 22, 1947, "This World" section, 4.

25. *NYT*, Apr. 18, 1947, 6; May 14, 1947, 1, 3; June 21, 1947, 1, 3; June 24, 1947, 1; Truman's veto message is online at https://millercenter.org/the-presidency/presidential-speeches/june-20-1947-veto-taft-hartley-bill.

26. *Washington Post*, June 24, 1947, 1; Taft and the Senate report are quoted in Jerome D. Fenton, "The Taft-Hartley Act and Union Control of Hiring: A Critical Examination," *Villanova Law Review* 4 (1959): 348; *Chronicle*, June 24, 1947, 4.

27. *Chronicle*, June 24, 1947, 4; *Dispatcher*, June 27, 1947, 9; July 11, 1947, 1, 2.

28. *NYT*, Oct. 12, 1947, 1; Oct. 16, 1947, 1; Oct. 18, 1947, 1; Nov. 10, 1947, 1; Nov. 13, 1947, 1; Nov. 16, 1947, E10; *Chronicle*, Oct. 26, 1947, "This World" section, 7.

29. See, for example, Starobin, *American Communism in Crisis*, 14–19, chaps. 6, 7; Cochran, *Labor and Communism*, chap. 10; Harvey Klehr and John Earl Haynes, *The American Communist Movement: Storming Heaven Itself* (New York: Twayne, 1992), 103–13.

30. *Dispatcher*, July 11, 1947, 5; Sept. 5, 1947, 5; Nov. 14, 1947, 2; Dec. 12, 1947, 2; Dec. 26, 1947, 1–3; Mar. 5, 1948, 5, 8; Mar. 19, 1948, 5; Apr. 2, 1948, 7; Apr. 16, 1948, 5; Dennis quoted in Starobin, *American Communism in Crisis*, 17.

31. My timing of the CP decision is based on Starobin, *American Communism in Crisis*, 172–77.

32. *Dispatcher*, July 25, 1947, 1, 12; Aug. 8, 1947, 1; Sept. 2, 1947, 2; Oct. 3, 1947, 3; Oct. 17, 1947, 5; Oct. 31, 1947, 1.

33. *Dispatcher*, Nov. 28, 1947, 1; Dec. 12, 1947, 6; Dec. 26, 1947, 1.

34. CIO Executive Committee minutes for Jan. 22–23, 1948, esp. 116–18, 270, 306–41, box Jan. 22–23, 1948, CIO Executive Committee Minutes, Archives of Labor History and Urban Affairs, Wayne State University; *Labor Herald* (San Francisco), Feb. 2, 1948, 6.

35. Memo, Director to Attorney General, Feb. 12, 1948, f1, b21, Confidential Files, Papers of Harry Truman, Harry S. Truman Library; *Dispatcher*, Dec. 12, 1948, 8; Dec. 26, 1948, 1–3; Jan. 8, 1948, 8; *People's World*, Dec. 31, 1947, 1; Curtis D. MacDougall, *Gideon's Army* (New York: Marzani & Munsell, 1965), 2:320; press release, National Wallace for President Committee, Apr. 6, 1948, folder Wallace, Henry, b47, CIO Secretary Treasurer Collection, Archives of Labor History and Urban Affairs, Wayne State University.

36. *Labor Herald*, Mar. 23, 1948, 6; Apr. 13, 1948, 1, 8; Apr. 20, 1948, 4; *PW*, Apr. 29, 1948, 1; press release, Progressive Party, New York, Aug. 30, 1948, file Wallace, Henry, b47, CIO Secretary Treasurer Collection, Archives of Labor History and Urban Affairs, Wayne State University.

37. *Labor Herald*, Sept. 6, 1948, 4; Oct. 5, 1948, 1; *PW*, May 14, 1948, 1.

38. MacDougall, *Gideon's Army*, 1:291. Wikipedia has county-by-county election returns for each state.

39. Kenny, quoted in Janet Stevenson, *The Undiminished Man: A Political Biography of Robert Wallace Kenny* (Novato, CA: Chandler & Sharp, 1980), esp. 168, 170–71; Dennis quoted in Starobin, *American Communism in Crisis*, 16–17; letter, Darcy to Bridges, Oct. 19, 1964; copy of letter, Bridges to Darcy, Oct. 30, 1964, f3, b12, Bridge Papers, LARC. See also Edward L. and Frederick H. Schapsmeier, *Prophet in Politics: Henry A. Wallace and the War Years, 1940–1965* (Ames: Iowa State University Press, 1970), esp. 181; Karl M. Schmidt, *Henry A. Wallace: Quixotic Crusade 1948* (Syracuse, NY: Syracuse University Press, 1960), esp. 258–59.

40. Political Action Policy Statement, San Francisco CIO Council, undated but apparently Feb. 1948, file Corr. 1948, Jan.–Mar., b11, Adolph German Papers, WHS; copy, C. V. O'Halloran et al. to Murray, Feb. 6, 1948, folder 1948, CIO California, bA5–13, John Brophy Papers, Department of Archives, Catholic University; *Chronicle*, Feb. 11, 1948, 1; Feb. 12, 1948, 1; *NYT*, Feb. 11, 1948, 1; Feb. 15, 1948, 15.

41. *Chronicle*, Feb. 12, 1948, 13.

42. *Chronicle*, Feb. 13, 1948, 2; press release—California CIO Council—Feb. 15, 1948, folder California CIO, box A5–13, Brophy Papers; letter, Zusman to Brophy, Feb. 19, 1948,

folder California CIO 1948, box A5–13, Brophy Papers; Haywood to Bridges, Feb. 18, 1948, file "Natl CIO Policy," collection "Harry Bridges Material About," ILWU Library; copies f2–4, b2, series II, DeShetler Papers; file Corr. 1948, Jan.–Mar., b11, Germer Papers; *LAT*, Feb. 21, 1948, 1; *Chronicle*, Feb. 21, 1948, 1, 8; *NYT*, Feb. 21, 1948, 11.

43. Copies of letters, Bridges to Haywood, Feb. 26, 1948; Bridges to Kroll, Mar. 1, 1948; all in file National CIO Policy, series Harry Bridges Material About, ILWU Library.

44. Copy of letter, Haywood to Bridges, Mar. 5, 1948, file National CIO Policy, series Harry Bridges Material About, ILWU Library; *Chronicle*, Mar. 5, 1948, 1; Mar, 6, 1948, 1; untitled press release, Mar. 8, National CIO Policy, series "Harry Bridges Material About," ILWU Library; letter, Murray to Germer, Mar. 20, 1948, file Corr. 1948, Jan.–Mar., b11, Germer Papers.

45. *Chronicle*, Mar. 6, 1948, 1. The INS launched its investigation the month before. John Boyd of the INS explained to J. Edgar Hoover that the INS was "determining whether any action should be taken looking to the cancellation of his [Bridges's] naturalization," a necessary precursor to deportation; copy of letter, Boyd to Hoover, Feb. 26, 1948, file 39-915-2624, Bridges FBI file; memo, Boyd to Wm. A. Carmichael, Feb. 24, 1948, Bridges INS file, Kutler copies. Stanley Kutler sent me copies of the material he had copied from Bridges INS file when it was still in the possession of the INS and before it had been reviewed for redactions. I cite these materials as "Bridges INS file, Kutler copies" because they lack the file numbers assigned in the Bridges INS file at the National Archives branch. *My file of these will be given to LARC.*

46. Mimeographed letter, Brophy to all industrial union councils, Mar. 8, 1948, file Corr. 1948, Jan.–Mar., b11, Germer Papers; Brophy to Zusman and Posner, Apr. 7, 1948, folder PAC 1948, b85, CIO Secretary Treasurer Collection; copy, Haywood to Daugherty and Halling, Aug. 2, 1948, f2–4, b2, series II, DeShetler Papers; memo, Bauer to Carey, Aug. 18, 1948, folder IU Councils California, b105, CIO Secretary Treasurer collection; telegram, Lunceford to DeShetler, July 9, 1948, folder Corres., 1948, b20, series I, DeShetler Papers, all in Archives of Labor History and Urban Affairs, Wayne State University.

47. *Labor Herald*, June 22, 1948, 1, 3–5; July 13, 1948, 1; *PW*, Mar. 24, 1948, 1; Apr. 29, 1948, 1.

48. *Chronicle*, Aug. 15, 1947, 2; *Dispatcher*, Aug. 22, 1947, 4; Apr. 16, 1948, 7; May 14, 1948, 7; May 28, 1948, 5; Nov. 26, 1948, 3; *Labor Herald*, Dec. 16, 1947, 1; letters, Haywood to Bridges, July 28, 1948, folder ILWU, series National and International Unions, CIO Papers, Catholic University; DeShetler to Adolph Germer, Aug. 26, 1948, file Corr. 1948, July–Aug., b11, German Papers.

49. Report of the Officers, *Proceedings of the Eighth Biennial Convention*, 14. Of the various accounts of the 1948 longshore strike, I prefer Betty V. H. Schneider and Abraham Siegel, *Industrial Relations in the Pacific Coast Longshore Industry* (Berkeley: Institute of Industrial Relations, University of California, Berkeley, 1956), and have generally followed their analysis.

50. Schneider and Siegel, *Industrial Relations*, 64–66; *Dispatcher*, Apr. 16, 1948, 1; Apr. 30, 1948, 1, 8; May 14, 1948, 1; May 28, 1948, 1.

51. Schneider and Siegel, *Industrial Relations*, 65–66; carbon copy of charge by WEA against ILWU, filed with NLRB on Aug. 20, 1948, file: ILWU—Referendum—ER Offer—TH Compliance, b20, Coast Committee Case—1948, ILWU Library.

52. Clipping, Arthur Caylor, SF News, July 10, 1948, file: publicity newspaper clippings, b22, Coast Committee Case—1948, ILWU Library.

53. *Chronicle*, Aug. 22, 1948, 1; Aug. 30, 1948, 2; Sept. 8, 1948, 1.

54. Schneider and Siegel, *Industrial Relations*, 66–69; *Chronicle*, Sept. 2, 1948, 1, 2.

55. Schneider and Siegel, *Industrial Relations*, 69; *Chronicle*, Sept. 3, 1948, 1, 14; St. Sure oral history, 594–98; *Chronicle*, Sept. 8, 1948, 1, 12.

56. Summary of vote, file: ILWU—Referendum—ER Offer—TH Compliance, b20, Coast Committee Case—1948, ILWU Library; *Dispatcher*, Sept. 17, 1948, 3; *Chronicle*, Aug. 6, 1948, 16; Aug. 19, 1948, 1.

57. Schneider and Siegel, *Industrial Relations*, 70; *Chronicle*, Sept. 4, 1948, 1.

58. *Chronicle*, Oct. 1, 1948, 1; Oct. 5, 1948, 2; *News*, Sept. 27, 1948, 1; *NYT*, Oct. 2, 1948.

59. Report of R. J. Thomas, undated but after Apr. 1949, file ILWU, Series National and International Unions, b27, Records of the CIO, Catholic University; *Chronicle*, Oct. 9, 1948, 1, 3; Oct. 10, 1948, 9; Oct. 13, 1948, 15; Oct. 14, 1948, 1; Oct. 15, 1948, 1, 14.

60. *Chronicle*, Oct. 17, 1948, 1; Oct. 17, 1948, "This World" section, 4; brochure, file: "Nailing the Shipowners Lies," b22, Coast Committee Case—1948, ILWU Library; Thomas, undated report, 2–3; press release, Federated Press, Oct. 20, 1948, file, publicity newspaper clippings, b22, Coast Committee Case—1948, ILWU Library.

61. St. Sure oral history, 603–5; interview of Sevier by Larrowe, quoted in Larrowe, *Bridges*, 298.

62. Thomas, undated report, includes the full text of the agreements, 3–10.

63. *Chronicle*, Nov. 8, 1948, 1, 2; Nov. 12, 1948, 1; Nov. 26, 1948, 10; St. Sure oral history, 98, 606; Schneider and Siegel, *Industrial Relations*, 74. For the Employers' Council, see George O. Bahrs, *The San Francisco Employers Council* (Philadelphia: University of Pennsylvania Press, 1948).

64. *Dispatcher*, Nov. 26, 1948, 1; *Chronicle*, Nov. 28, 1948, 1, 12; Dec. 5, 1948, "This World" section, 2; Schneider and Siegel, *Industrial Relations*, 74–76; Clark Kerr and Lloyd Fisher, "Conflict on the Waterfront," *Atlantic Monthly*, Sept. 1949, 17–23, esp. 18.

65. *Dispatcher*, Nov. 26, 1948, 1, 8; Dec. 10, 1948, 1, 8; Dec. 24, 1948, A–D; Schneider and Siegel, *Industrial Relations*, 73.

66. *Chronicle*, Nov. 26, 1948, 10; Nov. 27, 1948, 1; Nov. 28, 1948, 1, 12; Dec. 4, 1948, 1, 12; Dec. 6, 1948, 1.

67. *Dispatcher*, Dec. 24, 1948, 1, 8; *Chronicle*, June 10, 2007, 29.

68. Schneider and Siegel, *Industrial Relations*, 79; Kerr and Lloyd, "Conflict on the Waterfront," 20.

69. Thomas, undated report, 12; *Dispatcher*, Nov. 12, 1948, 8.

70. Unidentified clipping, Nov. 21, 1946, Bridges personal papers; letter, Charles Bridges to Harry Bridges, Aug. 5, 1947, f15, b1; Alexander Simon, MD, and H. F. Norman, MD, Langley Porter Clinic, to Hon. Preston Devine, Judge of the Superior Court, Sept. 13, 1949, f18, b1, Bridges Papers, LARC.

71. *Chronicle*, Mar. 14, 1948, "This World" section, 3.

72. Herb Caen, *Baghdad-by-the-Bay* (Garden City, NY: Doubleday, 1949), 41–42.

73. Letter, Goldblatt to Edward Barsky, Mar. 13, 1947, f12, b5; multiple telegrams from J. R. Robertson, Feb. 16, 1949; f1, b6; Bridges Papers, LARC; interview, Feb. 4, 1987.

Chapter 13. Try, Try, Again: Deportation and Expulsion

1. David Jenkins, interviewed by Robert Cherny, May 8, 1987, hereinafter Jenkins interview. By the time I interviewed Dave and Edith, his wife, who was sometimes present and commented during the interviews, they were quite critical of the party and sometimes quite critical of Bridges.

2. Goldblatt oral history, 419–21; Jenkins interview, May 8, 1987; Joseph Starobin, *American Communism in Crisis, 1943–1957* (Cambridge, MA: Harvard University Press, 1972), 38–42 and esp. 258n51.

3. Memos, Ladd to Director, Sept. 14, 1945, file 39-915-2574; SAC San Francisco to Director, Sept. 20, 1945, file 39-915-2578; SAC San Francisco to Director, Sept. 24, 1945, file 39-915-2579; copy of memo, Director to SAC San Francisco, July 25, 1946, file 39-915-2593; report of [name redacted], approved by SAC San Francisco, Dec. 20, 1945, 19, file 39-915-26[redacted]; undated document, file 39-915-2665; copy of memo, Director to SAC San Francisco, Oct. 10, 1947, file 39-915-2611; memo, SAC San Francisco to Director FBI, Nov. 18, 1949, file 39-915-[remainder illeg.], Bridges FBI file. For the DETCOM and similar programs, see Athan Theoharis, "The Truman Administration and the Decline of Civil Liberties: The FBI's Success in Securing Authorization for a Preventative Detention Program," *Journal of American History* 64 (Mar. 1978): 1010–30.

4. John P. Boyd to Director, June 24, 1948, file 39-915-2651, Bridges FBI file; copy, with fewer redactions, file C-6405274-F, b2, Bridges INS file; copy of memo, Director to Boyd, July 23, 1948, with various attachments dated July 21, 1948, file 39-915-2656; copy, Director to Attorney General with cc. Commissioner INS, Sept. 7, 1948, file 39-915-2659, Bridges FBI file; copy of memo, W. F. Miller, re telephone call, May 29, 1949, file 0606-36231, b12; copy of letter, Norene to Doyle, July 25, 1949; David Caldwell and Howard Fenn to Norene, Oct. 6, 1949; file memo, R. J. Norene, July 13, 1949, all in file 1200-25566, b8, Bridges INS file.

5. Summary of interview with Rathborne, June 22, 1949; memos, Bruce Barber to Boyd, Sept. 21, 1948; Boyd to Peyton Ford, Sept. 20, 1948; copy of memo, Barber to Boyd, Oct. 26, 1948, all Bridges INS file, Kutler copies.

6. Memo, John McGowan to Boyd, Oct. 13, 1948; letter, Robert Hitchcock to John Boyd, Oct. 13, 1948; copy of letter, Boyd to Hitchcock, Oct. 22, 1948, all Bridges INS file, Kutler copies.

7. *NYT*, Mar. 2, 1950, 37; *LAT*, Mar. 10, 1950, 16; *Dispatcher*, July 3, 1949, 4; for Clark's comment, see *Milwaukee Journal*, June 27, 1949, copy in file 39-915-2782, Bridges FBI file.

8. *Chronicle*, May 26, 1949, 1, 5, 17; *NYT*, May 26, 1, 17; May 28, 1949, 4. There are several academic studies of the trial, including Stanley I. Kutler, *The American Inquisition: Justice and Injustice in the Cold War* (New York: Hill and Wang, 1982), 145–48; and James P. Walsh, *San Francisco's Hallinan: Toughest Lawyer in Town* (Novato, CA: Presidio Press, 1982), chap. 8. See also Peter Afrasiabi, *Burning Bridges: America's 20-Year Crusade to Deport Labor Leader Harry Bridges* (Brooklyn: Thirlmere Books, 2016), chaps. 6, 7; Vince Hallinan, *A Lion in Court* (New York: G. P. Putnam's Sons, 1963), chaps. 13, 14.

9. A memo, Donohue to Clark, received June 20, 1949, had to do with a call from Murray's office to set up a meeting between Arthur Goldberg, CIO General Counsel,

and Clark, June 23, 1949, file Attorney General Correspondence, 1945–49, Bricker-Brim, b23, Papers of Tom C. Clark, Truman Presidential Library. Apparently in response, Murray sent Arthur Goldberg to talk with Clark. I received the letter from Goldberg, July 31, 1987, in response to my question as to whether the CIO had any involvement in the case.

10. *NYT*, Sept. 2, 1949, 12; Sept. 23, 1949, 15; Oct. 5, 1949, 25; Oct. 6, 1949, 23; Oct. 13, 1949, 22; Oct. 25, 1949, 17; Oct. 29, 1949, 8; Resner confirmed his and Anderson's CP membership when I interviewed him on Dec. 18, 1992, and Jan. 23, 1993; Norman Leonard, *Life of a Leftist Labor Lawyer*, oral history conducted by Estolv Ethan Ward, 1985, 51–55 (hereinafter, Leonard oral history); memos, Guy Hottel to Director, Sept. 28, 1949, and Director to Attorney General, Oct. 5, 1949, file 39-915-28[illeg.], Bridges FBI file; *Reminiscences of James M. Landis*, Oral History Research Office, Columbia University, 1964, 60. For Leonard, see also Colin Wark and John F. Galliher, *Progressive Lawyers under Siege: Moral Panic during the McCarthy Years* (Lanham, MD: Lexington Books, 2015).

11. *Chronicle*, Mar. 8, 1949, 28; Mar. 18, 1949, 1; Mar. 23, 1949, 14; Apr. 1, 1949, 16; Apr. 4, 1949, 15.

12. *Proceedings of the Eighth Biennial Convention*, 271–84, 355; *Dispatcher*, June 10, 1949, 1, 6, 7.

13. *LAT*, July 7, 1949, 15; *Chronicle*, Aug. 9, 1949, 4; clipping, *Washington News*, Sept. 14, 1949, file 39-915-A, Bridges FBI file; *LAT*, Oct. 5, 1949, 1; Resolution, California State Council, folder IU Council, Calif., b105, CIO Secretary Treasurer Collection, Archives of Labor History and Urban Affairs, Wayne State University.

14. *LAT*, Nov. 2, 1949, 17; *Washington Post*, Nov. 2, 1949, 4; *NYT*, Nov. 4, 1949, 3; Daily Proceedings of the Eleventh Constitutional Convention of the CIO, b67, Murray Papers, Catholic University. Re the MFW, see *Dispatcher*, Aug. 5, 1949, 1, 2, 3, 6, 7, 12; *NYT*, July 7, 1949, 16; July 20, 1949, 15; Aug. 1, 1949, 33; report of [name redacted], Mar. 4, 1954, file 39-915-3244, Bridges FBI file. See also Robert H. Zieger, *The CIO, 1935–1955* (Chapel Hill: University of North Carolina Press, 1995), 286–87.

15. *NYT*, Nov. 5, 1949, 1, 6; *LAT*, Nov. 5, 1949, 4. See also Bert Cochran, *Labor and Communism: The Conflict That Shaped American Unions* (Princeton, NJ: Princeton University Press, 1977), 304–8.

16. *Dispatcher*, Mar. 3, 1950, 3; copies of memos, Director to SAC San Francisco, Mar. 16, 1950, file 39-915-3042; Director to SAC San Francisco, Sept. 26, 1950, file 122-234-7; report of [name redacted], July 24, 1951, file 122-234-13; report of [name redacted], Mar. 25, 1953, file 122-234-33, Bridges FBI file. The 122-234 file sequence was for the investigation into a possible criminal case involving the Taft-Hartley affidavit. The former, deportation, case continued with the 39-915 file sequence.

17. *NYT*, Nov. 6, 1949, 24; Nov. 12, 1949, 2.

18. For the Smith Act trial and Gladstein's conviction for contempt of court, see, for example, Kutler, *American Inquisition*, chap. 6; Hallinan, *Lion in the Court*, chap. 13; Walsh, *Hallinan*, 163; and Hallinan interviewed by Robert Cherny, Feb. 11, 1987; for Hallinan's previous involvement in Left activities, see memo, SAC San Francisco to Director, Nov. 7, 1949, file 39-915-2882, Bridges FBI file.

19. Copy of memo, Director to Payton Ford, Oct. 26, 1949, file 39-915-2858; report of [name redacted], approved by Henry M. Kimball, SAC San Francisco, Nov. 10, 1949, file 39-915-2887; memo, Ladd to Director, Nov. 22, 1949, file 39-915-2930, Bridges FBI file; Harold Lipset obituary, *Chronicle*, Dec. 6, 1997, A17; memo, SAC San Francisco to Director, Nov. 7, 1949, file 39-915-2882, Bridges FBI file.

20. *Chronicle*, Nov. 15, 1949, 1, 9; Walsh, *Hallinan*, 171–72.

21. *Chronicle*, Nov. 19, 1949, 1, 2; Nov. 22, 1949, 1, 6; Nov. 23, 1949, 1, 5; Hallinan, *Lion in the Court*, 247–50; Walsh, *Hallinan*, 173–75; Hallinan interview.

22. *Chronicle*, Nov. 24, 1949, 1, 4; Dec. 1, 1949, 1, 7; Dec. 2, 1949, 1, 6; Dec. 7, 1949, 1, 6; Dec. 8, 1949, 1, 6; Dec. 9, 1949, 1, 7; Dec. 10, 1949, 1, 4; Dec. 14, 1949, 1, 6; Walsh, *Hallinan*, 175–78; Hallinan, *Lion in the Court*, 252–53. Schomaker told the FBI in 1940 that he had joined in 1934 or 1935 and said nothing about recruiting Bridges, see Report of E. J. Connelley, Nov. 29, 1940, 1588–1600, file 39-915-614, Bridges FBI file.

23. *Chronicle*, Dec. 15, 1949, 1, 13; Dec. 16, 1949, 1, 8; Dec. 17, 1949, 1, 2; Dec. 20, 1949, 1, 9; Dec. 21, 1949, 1, 4; Dec. 22, 1949, 1, 6; Walsh, *Hallinan*, 178–83; *NYT*, Dec. 14, 1949, 1; Dec. 17, 1949, 11; Dec. 21, 1949, 36; *LAT*, Dec. 21, 1949, 18; Leonard oral history, 56–59; Hallinan, *Lion in the Court*, 253–59; memo, Howard Penn to Norene, Jan. 28, 1950, file 1200-25566, b9, Bridges INS file; Bruce Barber to District Director, Chicago, Jan. 30, 1950, file 0901/12228, b10, Bridges INS file; memo, Barber to Boyd, Nov. 15, 1948, Bridges INS file, Kutler copies.

24. Copy of memo, Director to Commissioner INS, Nov. 25, 1949, file 39-915-[illeg.]; memo, SAC Miami to Director, Jan. 12, 1950, file 39-915-[remainder obscured by redaction but likely 2997], Bridges FBI file.

25. *NYT*, Jan. 5, 1950, 5; Jan. 7, 1850, 8; *LAT*, Jan. 10, 1950, 10; Jan. 11, 1950, 17; memo, Ladd to Director, Jan. 10, 1950, file 31-915-2992, Bridges FBI file; Leonard oral history, 59–61.

26. Jan. 14, 1950, 6; Walsh, *Hallinan*, 183–85.

27. *NYT*, Jan. 15, 1950, E13; Jan. 25, 1950, 8; Jan. 28, 1950, 6; Feb. 1950, 7, 16; Feb. 10, 1950, 7; Feb. 17, 1950, 19; Feb. 18, 1950, 6; Feb. 26, 1950, E6; *LAT*, Jan. 17, 1950, 16; Jan. 24, 1950, 6; Jan. 26, 1950, 15; Jan. 27, 1950, 6; Feb. 1, 1950, 17; Feb. 3, 1950, 19; Feb. 7, 1950, 18; Feb. 8, 1950, 13; Feb. 9, 1950, 19; Feb. 15, 1950, 14; Feb. 21, 1950, 6; Feb. 28, 1950, 7; Mar. 1, 1950, 23; memo, Norene to the file, Mar. 2, 1950, file 1200-25566, b9, Bridges INS file.

28. Copy of memo, Donohue to Ford, May 26, 1949, Bridges INS file, Kutler copies; *NYT*, Mar. 2, 1950, 37; *LAT*, Mar. 10, 1950, 16; memo, SAC New York to Director, Sept. 19, 1949, file 39-915-2805; copy of memo, Director to SAC, New York, Oct. 27, 1949, file 39-915-2867, Bridges FBI files.

29. *LAT*, Mar. 17, 1959, 19; Apr. 1, 1959, 2; Apr. 5, 1959, 1, 10, 12; Apr. 11, 1959, 1; June 17, 1959, 1; *NYT*, Mar. 17, 1950, 10; Mar. 21, 1950, 23; Apr. 1, 1950, 1, 6; Apr. 5, 1950, 1, 10; Apr. 9, 1950, 5; teletype, Kimball to Director, Apr. 4, 1950, file 39-915-[illeg.], Bridges FBI file; Hallinan, *Lion in the Court*, 276–77; Walsh, *San Francisco's Hallinan*, 187, 189.

30. Memo, SAC San Francisco to Director, Mar. 10, 1949, file 39-915-3039; copy of memo, Director to SAC San Francisco, Apr. 26, 1959, file 39-915-[remainder illeg. but likely 3038]; clipping, *Examiner*, Apr. 5, 1950, file 39-915-3058; SAC San Francisco to Director, July 20, 1950, file 39-915-310[remainder illeg.], Bridges FBI file.

31. *Washington Post*, Apr. 5, 1950, 2; clipping, *Examiner*, Apr. 5, 1950, file 39-915-3058, Bridges FBI file; *Melbourne Argus*, June 19, 1950, 4; *Sydney Morning Herald*, June 20, 1950, 3; *Canberra Times*, June 21, 1950, 2. The Menzies government closely followed the Bridges trial and appeals. External Affairs had a file on Bridges, marked "Secret," that began with newspaper clippings on the trial. A memo from O. L. Davis, first secretary of the Australian Embassy in Washington, to the secretary of External Affairs, on December 14, 1949, discussed the trial in progress and, in a confidential memorandum five months later, offered the information that the British consul general in Los Angeles had learned from "a source which he is not in position to quote" that Bridges was really named Rosenstein and had been born in Poland! Davis asked about following up on the information that Bridges was really Polish and asked whether it could be done informally through the FBI. See Memo, O. L. Davis to Secretary, Department of External Affairs, Dec. 14, 1949; Confidential Memo, Davis to the Secretary, May 24, 1950, 1950s External Affairs file on Bridges.

32. Healy to Bridges, May 8, 1958, series: ILWU history, file: Trade Unions Relations/Foreign—Australia, ILWU Library (hereinafter ILWU Library); Ray Markey and Stuart Svensen, "James (Jim) Healy," *Australian Dictionary of Biography*, http://adb.anu.edu.au/biography/healy-james-jim-10470; *Maritime Worker*, June 1, 1938, 2; July 1, 1938, 2.

33. Zieger, *The CIO, 1935–1955*, 286–89, esp. 289.

34. The full transcript is in b1, ILWU History Files, CIO—Expulsion Trial, 1950, ILWU Library; see esp. 2-748; *Dispatcher*, May 26, 1, 3, 5; June 9, 12; copy of memo, Guy Hottel, SAC Washington, to Director, May 29, 1950, file 39-915-[illeg. but probably 3005], Bridges FBI file; see also Paul Jacobs, "The Due Processing of Harry Bridges," *Reporter*, Mar. 8, 1956, 36, 38, 39.

35. Transcript of the hearing, esp. 749–920; *Dispatcher*, June 23, 1950, 3.

36. Jenkins oral history, 79; Jenkins interview, May 8, 1987.

37. *Chronicle*, July 11, 1950, 4; July 13, 1950, 6; *Dispatcher*, July 7, 1950, 1, 12; see also the six-page report by an FBI informant present at the Local 10 meeting, summarized in copy of memo, Director to Ford, July 13, 1950, 39-915-30[illeg.], Bridges FBI file.

38. *NYT*, July 13, 1950, 22; *Chronicle*, July 19, 1950, 1, 9; July 21, 1950, 7; 1950, file 39-915-[final digits not recorded but likely 3057 or 3058]; teletype, Kimball to Director, July 20, 1950, file 39-915-3097, Bridges FBI file.

39. *Chronicle*, July 21, 1950, 7; *NYT*, July 26, 1950, 18; Hoover, handwritten comment on Washington City News Service teletype, July 13, file 39-915-[illeg.]; teletype, Kimball to Director, July 13, 1950, file 39-915-[illeg.]; memos, Ladd to Director, July 12, 1950, file 39-915-39[illeg.]; Ladd to Director, July 14, 1950, file 39-915-3101; Ladd to Director, July 18, 1950, file 39-915-[illeg.]; Ladd to Belmont, July 26, 1950, file 39-915-[illeg.], Bridges FBI file.

40. Teletype, Kimball to Director and Ladd, July 26, 1950, file 39-915-3095, Bridges FBI file; *Chronicle*, Aug. 1, 1950, 1, 12; *Chronicle*, Aug. 1, 1950, 1, 12; Aug. 3, 1950, 1, 6; Aug. 4, 1950, 1, 12; Aug. 6, 1950, 1, 14; *LAT*, Aug. 4, 1950, 20; Aug. 6, 1950, 1; *Dispatcher*, Aug. 11, 1950, 3.

41. *Chronicle*, Aug. 7, 1950, 26; Aug. 10, 1950, 1; Aug. 25, 1950, 1, 7; *Washington Post*, Aug. 9, 1950, 1; *LAT*, Aug. 25, 1950 1; *Dispatcher*, Sept. 1, 1950, 1, 4; the Circuit Court

opinion is in file 39-915-3114, Bridges FBI file, esp. 8, 11; Leonard oral history, 66–69. Harry and Nikki Bridges told me about Harry's organizing of the deputy sheriffs on more than one occasion, but I cannot find it any of my interview transcripts.

42. *Dispatcher*, Sept. 1, 1950, 5; clipping, *Oregon Journal*, Oct. 17, 1950, file Harry Bridges—Material About, 1944–51, History Collection, ILWU Library.

43. *NYT*, Aug. 30, 1950, 25; Brophy oral history, 948–49; Minutes of the CIO Executive Board for Aug. 29, 1950, CIO Executive Board Minutes, Archives of Labor History and Urban Affairs, Wayne State University.

44. *Dispatcher*, June 3, 1951, 1, 3–5; report of [name redacted], signed by Harry Kimball, San Francisco SAC, Apr. 23, 1951, 11, file 39-915-3156, Bridges FBI file.

45. *Chronicle*, July 17, 1951, 4; *Bridges et al. v. United States*, 199 F.2d 811 (1952).

46. Letter, Goldblatt to Taylor, Oct. 24, 1952, f134, b11, subseries 1, series 7, Telford Taylor Papers, Arthur W. Diamond Law Library, Columbia University, hereinafter Taylor Papers; teletype, SAC San Francisco to Director, Jan. 27, 1953, file 39-915-3211; copy of memo, Director to Attorney General, Feb. 6, 1953, file 39-915-3212, Bridges FBI file.

47. Interview with Telford Taylor by Robert Cherny, June 18, 1987; for Taylor's participation in the Americans for Democratic Action and views on foreign policy, see, for example, *NYT*, Apr. 1, 1950, 8, and Sept. 17, 1951, 29; copy of memo, Director to Assistant Attorney General, Criminal Division, Jan. 23, 1953, file 39-915–[illeg., probably 3210]; copy of memo, Director to Attorney General, Feb. 6, 1953, file 39-915-3212, Bridges FBI file.

48. Letter, Taylor to Leonard, Dec. 2, 1952, f134, b11, subseries 1, series 7, Taylor Papers. For the many examples of the close working relationship between Taylor and Leonard, see f134–37, b11, and f151–55, b22, subseries 1, series 7, Taylor Papers.

49. Taylor interview; *Bridges v. United States*, 346 U.S. 209 (1953).

50. Jenkins oral history, 71, 76, 79–81, 175–76; copy of memo, Hoover to James McInerney, May 25, 1950, file 39-915-3068; memo, from [name obscured] to Director, May 22, 1950, file number obscured; report of [name redacted], signed by Kimball, San Francisco SAC, Apr. 23, 1951, file 39-915-356, Bridges FBI file; Hallinan, *Lion in the Court*, 279.

51. *Dispatcher*, Oct. 28, 1949, 9; Sept. 29, 1950, 3; Sept. 28, 1951, 1, 6; June 22, 1951, 1; Oct. 13, 1951, 4, 5; *Business Week*, Nov. 21, 1953, 176–77.

52. Rickey Hendricks, *A Model for National Health Care: The History of Kaiser Permanente* (New Brunswick, NJ: Rutgers University Press, 1993), esp. 70–75.

53. *Dispatcher*, May 26, 1951, 1; May 12, 1951, 1, 4; June 9, 1950, 4; June 3, 1951, 3; *Chronicle*, Feb. 6, 1950, 2; Feb. 14, 1950, 1; Feb. 19, 1950, "This World" section, 2; Mar. 15, 1950, 17; *Einar Mohn, Teamster Leader: An Oral History*, interviewed by Corinne Lathrop Gilb, for University of California Institute of Industrial Relations, 1970, b8, Corrine Gilb Collection, LARC, 363–74.

54. *Chronicle*, July 25, 1950, 5; *Dispatcher*, Aug. 4, 1950, 1, 5; Sept. 1, 1950, 5

55. For examples of individuals, see Bill Bailey with Lynn Damme, *The Kid from Hoboken: An Autobiography* (San Francisco: Circus Lithographic Prepress, 1993); Bailey interviewed by Robert Cherny, Mar. 16, 1993; Pat Tobin, interviewed by Robert Cherny, Feb. 9 and 25, 1987; *Dispatcher*, Oct. 17, 1995, 5; James Herman interviewed by Robert Cherny, July 30, 1993; *Dispatcher*, Mar. 1998, unnumbered insert. For organizations, see

Dispatcher June 9, 1950, 1; June 23, 1950, 2; Micah Ellison, "The Local 7/Local 37 Story: Filipino American Cannery Unionism in Seattle, 1940–1959," *Seattle Civil Rights & Labor History Project*, online at https://depts.washington.edu/civilr/local_7.htm.

56. Unless otherwise indicated, this summary and those paragraphs that follow are drawn from Sanford Zalburg, *A Spark Is Struck! Jack Hall & the ILWU in Hawaii* (Honolulu: University Press of Hawaii, 1979), chaps. 41–49. Cover letter, J. Shannon to Mr. Stowe, June 9, 1949, f407-B, Honolulu Strike, b182, President's Secretary's Files, Harry S. Truman Library; 81st Cong., 1st sess., Senate Committee on Labor and Public Welfare, *Hawaiian Labor Situation:* Hearing, July 12, 1949, esp. 98ff.

57. Clippings, *Honolulu Advertiser*, Aug. 16, 17, 1949, Local 142 library; letter, Stainback to Oscar L. Chapman, Stainback file, b30, Chapman Papers, Truman Library.

58. Zalburg, *Spark Is Struck!*, chap. 48.

59. Letter with attached report, Hoover to Donald S. Dawson, Feb. 21, 1950; copy, letter, Stainback to Louis Johnson, Feb. 20, 1950, both in file Justice Dept. f1, b21, Confidential Files, Papers of Harry S Truman; Zalburg, *Spark Is Struck!*, chap. 39.

60. *Dispatcher*, June 3, 1951, 5, 6; Jun 22, 1951, 4; *Business Week*, Apr. 21, 1951, 41–43; *Proceedings of the Ninth Biennial Convention . . . 1951*, ILWU Library.

61. *Business Week*, Apr. 15, 1950, 120, 123; Zalburg, *Spark Is Struck!*, chap. 52.

62. Zalburg, *Spark Is Struck!*, chaps. 49–52, 53–59.

63. Zalburg, *Spark Is Struck!*, chaps. 53–59.

64. *International Longshoremen's and Warehousemen's Union v. Juneau Spruce*, 189 F.2d 177 (9th Cir. 1951); same, 342 U.S. 237; *Proceedings of the Ninth Biennial Convention . . . 1951*, ILWU Library, 45–46; *Dispatcher*, Jan. 18, 1952, 1, 7.

65. Court cases previously cited; Goldblatt oral history, 409–15; Zalburg, *Spark Is Struck!*, 384; *Honolulu Star Bulletin*, Mar. 6, 1954, 18; *Business Week*, Feb. 6, 1954, 113; Feb. 12, 1955, 138.

66. Goldblatt oral history, 415–19; *Maneja v. Waialua Agricultural Co.*, 349 U.S. 254 (1955); *Chronicle*, June 3, 1955, 2; *Honolulu Advertiser*, Sept. 22, 1955, 1, 5; Minutes of the 1955 biennial convention, Local 142 Library, Honolulu. The records of the company can be found in the Spruce Corporation Records, Alaska State Library. The ILWU's practice of not owning real estate continues to the present. The current ILWU headquarters building, the Harry Bridges Memorial Building, is owned by the Pacific Longshoremen's Memorial Association, and the Local 10 hall is owned by the Bay Area Longshoremen's Memorial Association. Both memorial associations are legally defined as nonprofit foundations.

67. *People's World*, Oct. 20, 1950, 7; Oct. 21, 1950, 2; Oct. 27, 1950, "Out Times" insert, 4; Nov. 9, 1950, 1950, 1, 2; Oct. 23, 1950, 2; Oct. 29, 1950, 1; Oct. 31, 1950, 7; Nov. 6, 1952, 1; *Dispatcher*, Oct. 13, 1950, 2; Oct. 27, 1950, 5, 7; Oct. 10, 1950, 2; Oct. 24, 1950, 2.

68. *Proceedings of the Tenth Biennial Convention . . . 1953*, ILWU Library, esp. 119, 405–14, 535–37.

69. Jenkins interviews; *Dispatcher*, 1949–53. The FBI's estimate of party membership showed 60,000–65,000 nationwide during most of World War II and 23,800 in 1953; see FBI Central Research Section, Membership of the Communist Party, USA, May 1955; FBI estimates of CP member by states, 1947 and 1952, online at https://archive.org/details/ernie1241_cpusa.

70. Resner interviews; telegram, Nancy Bridges to Phil Whykes, Jan. 14, 1952, f15, b1, Bridges Papers, LARC. Confirmation that the law firm paid for the house can be found in the sale of the house of 1955, when Anderson placed a lien on the house to protect a loan he had made to Bridges; see *Chronicle*, Feb. 28, 1956, 3.

71. Memo, SAC Los Angeles to Director, Jan. 2, 1953, file 39-915–320[illeg., perhaps 6], Bridges FBI file.

72. *Proceedings of the Tenth Biennial Convention . . . 1953*, 3–4, 547, and see the current version on the union's website, https://www.ilwu.org/about/ten-guiding-principles/.

Chapter 14. The Last Deportation Trial and New Beginnings

1. Memo, SAC San Francisco to Director, June 29, 1953, file 39-915-[illeg.], Bridges FBI file; *Chronicle*, June 8, 1954, 1, 8; July 3, 1954, 7; Aug. 13, 1954, 1, 8; Dec. 30, 1954, 3. For summaries of the trial, see Stanley I. Kutler, *The American Inquisition: Justice and Injustice in the Cold War* (New York: Hill and Wang, 1983), 148–49; and Peter Afrasiabi, *Burning Bridges: America's 20-Year Crusade to Deport Labor Leader Harry Bridges* (Brooklyn: Thirlmere Books, 2016), chap. 8.

2. Regarding Taylor and McCarthy, see, for example, *NYT*, Jan. 20, 1954, 10; Jan. 31, 1954, 57; Apr. 8, 1954, 15; May 17, 1954, 6, 15; Taylor interviewed by Robert Cherny, June 18, 1987, hereinafter Taylor interview; letter, Taylor to Goldblatt, June 7, 1955, 7-1-13-165, Telford Taylor Papers, Arthur W. Diamond Law Library, Columbia University, hereinafter Taylor Papers; *Norman Leonard: Life of a Leftist Labor Lawyer*, interviewed by Estolv Ethan Ward, 1985, Regional Oral History Office, Bancroft Library, University of California, Berkeley, 1986, 65, hereinafter Leonard oral history.

3. Taylor interview; telegram, Taylor to Leonard, July 5, 1955, 7-1-13-165, Taylor Papers.

4. Letter, Taylor to Bridges, Aug. 16, 1954; letter, Taylor to Leonard, June 29, 1955, 7-1-13-165, Taylor Papers; Taylor interview.

5. *Chronicle*, June 10, 1955, 7; June 21, 1955, 1, 10; June 22, 1955, 1, 9; June 23, 1955, 1, 18; June 24, 1955, 1, 9; June 25, 1955, 1, 6; June 28, 1955, 1, 4; July 23, 1955, 4.

6. Copy of memo, SAC San Francisco to Director, Mar. 8, 1954, file number not recorded but between 39-915-3244 and 39-915-3245, Bridges FBI file; interview with Bruce and Ted (son of Bruce) Hannon by Robert Cherny, Sept. 27, 1997.

7. *Chronicle*, July 12, 1955, 1, 2; July 14, 1955, 2; July 15, 1955, 14; July 16, 1955, 4; July 20, 1955, 11; July 21, 1955, 18. The INS and FBI files differ regarding the reason that Rathborne was not called; see memo, Warren Olney III to Commissioner INS, July 19, 1955, file C-640574, pt. 7, b7, Bridges INS file; copy of memo, Director to Commissioner INS, Apr. 15, 1955, file 39-915-3284, Bridges FBI file.

8. Teletype, FBI San Francisco to Director FBI, July 18, 1955, file 39-915-3308; memo to Mr. Boardman from [redacted], July 19, 1955, file 39-915-3309; teletype, FBI San Francisco to Director, July 19, 1955, file 39-915-3310; teletype, FBI San Francisco to Director, July 20, 1955, file 39-915-3312; teletype, FBI San Francisco to Director, July 19, 1955, file 39-915-3313, all Bridges FBI file. Jones's testimony generated a three-page report to [Louis B.] Nichols, number-three person at the FBI, from C. D. DeLoach, Aug. 25, 1955, file 39-915-3326, Bridges FBI file.

9. *Chronicle*, July 30, 1955, 1, 4; Goodman's entire opinion, ten pages plus eleven pages of appendices, is in Bridges's FBI file, attached to memo SAC San Francisco to Director, July 29, 1955, file 39-915-3316.

10. Taylor interview; *NYT*, Oct. 1, 1955, 22; memo, regional counsel, Southwest Region, to General Counsel, Central Office, Aug. 2, 1955; copy of memo, Warren Olney III to Solicitor General, Sept. 21, 1955, both file C-6405274, pt. 7, b7, Bridges INS file.

11. Maurice Zalburg, *A Spark Is Struck! Jack Hall & the ILWU in Hawaii* (Honolulu: University Press of Hawaii, 1979), chaps. 53–59, 64; Taylor interview; *Yates v. United States*, 354 U.S. 298 (1957); *Fujimoto et al. v. United States*, 251 F.2d 342 (1958). *Dispatcher*, Jan. 31, 1958, 6–8, featured a three-page spread on the Hall case.

12. Copies of letters, Glazier to Richard Lynden, Mar. 21, 1958; Goldblatt to Meehan, Mar. 27, 1958, f7, b11, Bridges Papers, LARC; *Dispatcher*, Mar. 10, 1961, 3; *Chronicle*, Mar. 7, 1961, 2; *Proceedings of the Fourteenth Biennial Convention . . . 1961*, 415–19; Schmidt oral history, 331.

13. *Chronicle*, Nov. 4, 1955, 12.

14. Malcolm Johnson, *"On the Waterfront": The Pulitzer Prize–Winning Articles That Inspired the Classic Movie and Transformed the New York Harbor* (New York: Chamberlain Bros., 2005). See also William J. Mello, *New York Longshoremen: Class and Power on the Docks* (Gainesville: University Press of Florida, 2010), esp. chaps. 2, 3; Philip Taft, *Corruption and Racketeering in the Labor Movement*, 2nd ed. (Ithaca: New York State School of Industrial and Labor Relations, Cornell University, 1970), esp. 31–35, 54; Howard Kimeldorf, *Reds or Rackets? The Making of Radical and Conservative Unions on the Waterfront* (Berkeley: University of California Press, 1988); and Charles P. Larrowe, *Shape-Up and Hiring Hall: A Comparison of Hiring Methods and Labor Relations on the New York and Seattle Waterfronts*, 2nd ed. (Westport, CT: Greenwood Press, 1976).

15. U.S. Senate, 83rd Cong., 1st sess., *Waterfront Investigation: Hearings before a Subcommittee of the Committee on Interstate and Foreign Commerce*, pt. 1, New York–New Jersey Waterfront (Washington, DC: Government Printing Office, 1953), esp. 433–51, 469–79; *NYT*, Oct. 28, 1951, 128; Dec. 11, 1951, 54; Aug. 4, 1953, 22; Sept. 21, 1953, 1, 28; Sept. 23, 1953, 1; Sept. 26, 1953, 31; Oct. 15, 1953, 1; Nov. 19, 1953, 1.

16. *NYT*, May 6, 1954, 67; May 23, 1954, 1, 85; Aug. 28, 1954, 1; *Dispatcher*, May 14, 1954, 2; May 28, 1954, 1.

17. *Proceedings of the Eleventh Biennial Convention . . . 1955*, 9–10, 41, 414; *Proceedings of the Twelfth Biennial Convention . . . 1957*, 46–54; *Proceedings of the Thirteenth Convention . . . 1959*, 9, 23; *Dispatcher*, Feb. 14, 1958, 1, 7; Feb. 28, 1958, 1, 8.

18. *Dispatcher*, Feb. 3, 1954, 3; Jan. 3, 1958, 5.

19. "Einar Mohn, Teamster Leader: An Oral History," interviewed by Corinne Lathrop Gilb, for the University of California Institute of Industrial Relations, 1970, 373–75, 575, 623–25, b8, Corrine Gilb Collection, LARC (hereinafter Mohn oral history); *Dispatcher*, June 20, 1958, 1; July 4, 1958, 1, 5.

20. *Proceedings of the Thirteenth Biennial Convention . . . 1959*, 107–8; Zalburg, *Spark Is Struck!*, 483.

21. *Chronicle*, Apr. 15, 1953, 2; *Dispatcher*, May 1, 1953, 1; Sept. 4, 1953, 1, 5; Sept. 18, 1953, 1.

22. *Chronicle*, Oct. 25, 1953, 1; May 18, 1954, 1, 2; Oct. 28, 1954, 18; Dec. 18, 1954, 1, 2; Apr. 8, 1955, 1, 2; *Dispatcher*, May 28, 1954, 1, 3; Dec. 10, 1954, 1, 4, A–D, 7.

23. *LAT*, Nov. 2, 1954, 2; Nov. 19, 1954, 27; *Chronicle*, Nov. 18, 1954, 1, 10; Nov. 19, 1954, 1, 3; Nov. 30, 1954, 1, 4.

24. *LAT*, Nov. 19, 1954, 27; Nov. 21, 1954, S11; *Dispatcher*, Nov. 26, 1954, 1, 8; *Chronicle*, Dec. 1, 1954, 1, 19; Dec. 2, 1954, 1, 4; Dec. 4, 1954, 1, 2; copies of letters, St. Sure to Lundeberg, Nov. 30, 1954; Bridges to PMA, Dec. 1, 1954; Lundeberg to St. Sure, Dec. 3, 1954; letter, H. D. Huxler to Secretary of Labor, Jan. 12, 1955, all in file: 1955 arbitration case—SUP—PMA, b100, James Mitchell Papers, Eisenhower Presidential Library.

25. *LAT*, Dec, 7, 1954, 19; Dec. 9, 1954, 16; Dec. 23, 1954, 8; Dec. 30, 1954, 21; *Dispatcher*, Dec. 10, 1954, 1, 7; *Chronicle*, Dec. 8, 1954, 1, 2; Dec. 9, 1954, 44; Dec. 23, 1954, 1 11; Jan. 1, 1955, 3; Jan. 26, 1955, 1; *NYT*, Feb. 2, 1955, 53; memo of call, Mitchell to Glenn Brockway, Dec. 22, file: 1955 arbitration case—SUP—PMA, b100, Mitchell Papers.

26. *Dispatcher*, Apr. 1, 1955, 3; Apr. 29, 1955, 6; *LAT*, Apr. 16, 1955, 12.

27. *Chronicle*, Apr. 28, 1955, 18.

28. St. Sure oral history, 607–8; *Chronicle*, Dec. 14, 1954, 1.

29. *Chronicle*, Nov. 13, 1956, 3; July 15, 1959, 38.

30. *Chronicle*, Aug. 28, 1956, 6; Sept. 22, 1956, 1, 4; Sept. 23, 1956, 5; Sept. 25, 1956, 3; Oct. 9, 1956, 2; Oct. 12, 1956, 1, 5; Oct. 13, 1956, 59; Oct. 14, 1956, "This World" section, 4, 6; memo, Moore to Gladstein, Sept. 21, 1956, file: Harry Bridges, Material About—Sausalito Assault, History Collection, ILWU Library; copy of memo, SAC Los Angeles to Director, Sept. 27, 1956, file 39-915–[illeg., perhaps 3343], Bridges FBI file.

31. *Chronicle*, Jan. 29, 1957, 1, 6; Feb. 3, 1957, 5; Feb. 8, 1957, 32; Feb. 12, 1957, 1, 11; clippings, San Rafael *Independent-Journal*, Feb. 8 and Feb. 26, 1957, file Harry Bridges Material About—Sausalito Assault, History Collection, ILWU Library.

32. The ILWU Library in San Francisco contains a thick file of correspondence between Bridges and Healy, and between the ILWU and WWF, as well as other Australian unions, file Trade Unions Relations/Foreign—Australia, ILWU Library. See also my "Harry Bridges's Australia, Australia's Harry Bridges," in *Frontiers of Labor: Comparative Histories of the United States and Australia*, ed. Greg Passmore and Shelton Stromquist (Urbana: University of Illinois Press, 2018), 338–40.

33. *Dispatcher*, Jan. 2, 1959, 1; Jan. 16, 1959, 1, 2; Jan. 30, 1959, 1, 2, 3; Feb. 13, 1959, 1, 2, 3; Feb. 27, 1959, 1, 2, 3; Mar. 13, 1959, 1, 2, 3; Mar. 27, 1959, 1, 2, 3; *Chronicle*, Feb. 27, 1959, 8; Mar. 3, 1959, 6. Bridges's application for a passport generated a large number of reports by the FBI, beginning in July 1958 and continuing until his return in early 1959, including alerting FBI agents in all the relevant embassies; the reports are so heavily redacted as to be meaningless. See files 39-915-3414 through 3472. The FBI identified Glazier as "a dues-paying member of the CP" in Washington and San Francisco; see unsigned, undated report titled "William Henry Glazier," file 39-915-3435, Bridges FBI file.

34. *Proceedings of the Thirteenth Biennial Convention . . . 1959*, 72–100; *Dispatcher*, Apr. 24, 1959, 3; May 8, 1959, 1; May 22, 1959, 1, 7; memo, F. J. Baumgardner to A. H. Belmont, Apr. 21, 1959, file 39-915-3501, Bridges FBI file. On efforts to create a pan-Pacific meeting of dockworkers' unions, see, for example, letter, Healy to Bridges, Jan. 20, 1940; copies

of letters, Bridges to Healey, May 2, 1940; Bridges to WATFED, Jan. 25, 1946; Bridges to Healy, Nov. 14 1951; Bridges to Healy, Nov. 25, 1952; Bridges to Healy, Apr. 16, 1958; Bridges to Healy, Sept. 18, 1958, file Trade Unions Relations/Foreign—Australia, ILWU Library; see also cable, Healy to Bridges, Nov. 30, 1942, file 39-915-2246, Bridges FBI file. The ILWU Library has a large file on the Tokyo conference.

35. *Chronicle*, Sept. 21, 1959, 1, 4, 9. The Soviet version of Khrushchev's visit to San Francisco appears in A. Jubel et al., *Face to Face with America: The Story of N. S. Khrushchev's Visit to the U.S.A.* (n.p.: n.p., n.d.), 252–86. On the new Local 10 hall opened the previous February, see *Business Week*, Mar. 14, 1959, 116–19.

36. *Chronicle*, Sept. 22, 1959, 1A; *Dispatcher*, Sept. 25, 1959, 1, 3; *News Call-Bulletin*, Sept. 21, 1959, 1, 4; clipping, *Oakland Tribune*, Oct. 5, 1959, file Harry Bridges Material About, 1959–60, History Collection, ILWU Library; Jubel, *Face to Face*, 283–86.

37. *Chronicle*, Sept. 25, 1959, 21.

38. *Chronicle*, Sept. 21, 1956, 8; Sept. 23, 1956, 69; Feb. 3, 1957, 59; *Dispatcher*, Oct. 26 1956, 2. Later Bridges offered additional reasons: "I switched . . . to try and demonstrate that there was little difference or meaning to party labels. Truman was a murderous war hawk, and the Demo's were the war party. Also, the Democratic party led by Hubert Humphrey, passed the Communist Control Act, going further than McCarthy." Copy of letter, Bridges to Gus Rystad, Jan. 18, 1977, f6, b12, Bridges Papers, LARC.

39. *Dispatcher*, Oct. 29, 1954, 3; Oct. 26, 1956, 2.

40. *Dispatcher*, Oct. 24, 1958, 1, 8; *Chronicle*, Nov. 7, 1958, 12.

41. Jenkins oral history, 171–74; Nathan Godfried, "'Voice of the People': Sidney Roger, the Labor/Left, and Broadcasting in San Francisco, 1945–1950," *American Communist History* 18 (2019): 56–57; California Un-American Activities Committee Papers, b35, California State Archives, hereinafter CUAC Papers; California Legislature, *Third Report: Joint Fact-Finding Committee on Un-American Activities in California: 1947*, 77–94; b45 and b52c, CUAC Papers; the reduction in course offerings and programs can be traced through f1–9, b1, CLS Collection, LARC; Skovgaard, "California Labor School," 17; Jenkins interviews; Holland Roberts memoirs, f1/21, b1, Roberts Papers, LARC; flyer, "How to Padlock a School," f4, b5, CLS Collection, LARC; Al Richmond, *A Long View from the Left: Memoirs of an American Revolutionary* (New York: Delta, 1975), esp. 300, 298ff, 382; reports of William B. Dillon, Oct. 28, 1954, Mar. 1, 1955, 3:14–27, 54–78, esp. 16, 59–60; reports of Max H. Fischer, Oct. 20, 1957, 4:26–36, esp. 29, Victor Arnautoff FBI file, NA.

42. Jenkins oral history, 188–89, 194; Bill Bailey with Lynn Damme, *The Kid from Hoboken: An Autobiography* (San Francisco: Circus Lithographic Prepress, 1993), 419–20; copy of letter, Bill Sennett et al. to National Committee, Mar. 26, 1958, attached to *Oral History: Louise Todd Lambert*, interviewed by Lucy Kendall, May–Aug. 1976, transcript at California Historical Society, following 295; Harvey Klehr and John Earl Haynes, *The American Communist Movement: Storming Heaven Itself* (New York: Twayne, 1992), 108, 137, 147.

43. Report of [name redacted], Dec. 30, 1954, file 39-915-32668; memo, SAC San Francisco to Director, June 10, 1955, file 39-915-3302; memo, SAC San Francisco to Director, Feb. 17, 1955; memo, SAC San Francisco to Director, Feb. 18, 1955, but stamped

Mar. 16, 1955, both file 39-915-3278; memo SAC San Francisco to Director, Apr. 2, 1956, file 39-915-3337, Bridges FBI file.

44. Copy of report on Bridges sent to the State Department, other federal officials, and FBI agents abroad, attached to copy of memo, Hoover to C. Tomlin Bailey, July 28, 1958, file 39-915-3414, Bridges FBI file; *Dispatcher*, Nov. 23, 1956, 2; Roger oral history, 607; clipping, Herb Caen's column, *Examiner*, Aug. 1957, file Harry Bridges Material About, 1957–58, History Collection, ILWU Library.

45. Bridges's FBI file contains long summaries and sometimes copies of his various columns and speeches; see, for example, SAC San Francisco to Director, June 10, 1955, file 39-915-3302, Bridges FBI file. The same terminology was used following Goodman's decision in the trial; see report of [redacted], Jan. 11 1956, file 39-915-13336 [*sic*; should be 3336], Bridges FBI file. Regarding surveillance, see, for example, report of [redacted], Aug. 11, 1959, file 39-915-3518, Bridges FBI file, which attributes information regarding Bridges's current address to observation by special agents of the FBI.

46. Memo, Nichols to Toland, Aug. 15, 1957, file 39-915-3359, Bridges FBI file; Roger oral history, 513–18. A transcript of much of the interview is part of report of [redacted], Nov. 15, 1957, file 39-915-3362, Bridges FBI file. The full transcript of interview is in *Dispatcher*, Aug. 30, 1957, 3–6.

47. *Dispatcher*, Aug. 30, 1957, 3–6; Roger oral history, 517–18.

48. Memo, M. A. Jones to Nichols, Aug. 19, 1957, file 39-915-3361; report of [redacted], Nov. 16, 1957, file 39-915-3362; SAC San Francisco to Director FBI, Nov. 15, 1957, file 39-915-3363, all Bridges FBI file.

49. Copy of letter, DeLoach to Tolson, Feb. 27, 1959, file 39-915-3476; memo, DeLoach to Tolson, Mar. 19, 1959, with attached blind memorandum on Bridges, file 39-915-3491; copy of letter, DeLoach to Tolson, Apr. 1, 1959, with handwritten response by Tolson, file 39-915-3493, Bridges FBI file.

50. U.S. House of Representatives, 86th Cong., 1st sess., Committee on Un-American Activities, Hearings, Passport Security, pt. 1, Testimony of Harry R. Bridges, Apr. 21, 1959 (Washington: U.S. Government Printing Office, 1959), copy attached to memo SAC WFO to Director, July 30, 1959, file not recorded, Bridges FBI file.

51. Bridges testimony; memo, SAC San Francisco to Director, Sept. 17, 1959, file 39-915-3519.

52. Memo for Tolson, Belmont, and DeLoach from Hoover, Apr. 23, 1959, file 39-915-3500, Bridges FBI file.

53. *Chronicle*, Jan. 21, 1955, 1; Feb. 3, 1955, 3; Oct. 5, 1956, 3; teletype, FBI San Francisco to Director, Aug. 27, 1954, file 39-915–325[illeg., likely 5]; report by [name redacted], Dec. 30, 1954, file 39-915-3268; report by SA [redacted], June 29, 1955, file 39-915-3304, which summarizes the Nevada court records; memo, SAC San Francisco to Director, Nov. 16, 1959, file 39-915-3526, all Bridges FBI file; Jenkins interviews; Theodora Kreps interviewed by Robert Cherny, Apr. 16, 1987; Robert Bridges interviewed by Robert Cherny, July 14, 1987.

54. Hospitalizations appear on Bridges's tax returns, f8–10, b2, Bridges Papers, LARC; and in his FBI file, teletype, FBI San Francisco to Director, Aug. 27, 1954, file 39-915–325[illeg., likely 5]; report by [name redacted], Dec. 30, 1954, file 39-915-3268; report of

SA [redacted], Jan. 16, 1957, file 39-915-3352; *Chronicle*, July 4, 1957, 3; clipping, paper, and date illeg. but Dec. 1958, file Harry Bridges Material About, 1957–58, History Collection, ILWU Library; Noriko Sawada Bridges, interviewed by Robert Cherny, July 23 and 25, 1990, hereinafter NS Bridges interview.

55. Jenkins oral history, 72–73; Roger oral history, 595–96. Although I remember Bridges telling me about his problems with alcohol, I cannot find it in any of the transcriptions of my interviews with him.

56. NS Bridges interview; *Chronicle*, Feb. 9, 2003. My reading of materials in the Noriko Sawada Bridges Flynn (NSBF) Papers, LARC, indicates a fairly consistent use of Noriko rather than Nikki with much of her correspondence and nearly all of her published writing. Nikki appears in correspondence with close friends. I have therefore used Noriko in most places throughout this chapter.

57. NS Bridges interview; *Chronicle*, Dec. 9, 1958, 1, 2.

58. NS Bridges interview; *Chronicle*, Dec. 10, 1958, 1, 17; *Chronicle*, Dec. 11, 1958, 1, 10; *Dispatcher*, Dec. 19, 1958, 3.

Chapter 15. Transforming Longshoring: The M&Ms

1. For announcements of benefits increases, see, for example, *Dispatcher*, Sept. 4, 1953, 2, 6–7, 10, 11; June 11, 1954, 1; July 18, 1958, 1, A–D; *Business Week*, July 30, 1955, 78. The most complete account of the ILWU's response to the challenges of new technology in the 1950s and 1960s is Lincoln Fairley's *Facing Mechanization: The West Coast Longshore Plan* (Los Angeles: Institute of Industrial Relations, University of California, Los Angeles, 1979), written after Fairley had retired as ILWU research director, but with the benefit of his work as research director throughout all the events through 1967 and his close observation of those events as an arbitrator through 1971. See also Paul T. Hartman, *Collective Bargaining and Productivity: The Longshore Mechanization Agreement* (Berkeley: University of California Press, 1969), which covers the first M&M with extensive statistical data. Fairley's work followed that of Hartman and drew upon it in places.

2. On the problems created by the four on–four off practice for local officers, see, for example, *George Kuvakus, Sr., Oral History Interview*, by Tony Salcido, 1992, Urban Archives Center, California State University, Northridge, hereinafter Kuvakus oral history. Herbert Mills also told me of abuse of the practice in 1993. Bridges quoted in Fairley, *Facing Mechanization*, 40, 47; *Dispatcher*, Aug. 3, 1956, 6.

3. Ronald E. Magden, *The Working Longshoreman* (Tacoma, WA: R-4 Typographers, n.d.), chap. 11.

4. *Proceedings of the First Annual Convention*, 300–301; 1938 agreement, file Coast Longshore Agreements, 1934–39; *Proceedings of the Fourth Annual Convention . . . 1940*, 167–68; *Proceedings of the Sixth Biennial Convention*, 34, all ILWU Library.

5. *Proceedings of the Ninth Biennial Convention*, 259–61, ILWU Library; Fairley, *Facing Mechanization*, 55–57.

6. *Proceedings of the Twelfth Biennial Convention*, 73–74.

7. *Proceedings of the Twelfth Biennial Convention*, 140–54, esp. 151–52.

8. Fairley, *Facing Mechanization*, 69–74.

9. Fairley, *Facing Mechanization*, 74–77; *Dispatcher*, 1, 4, 5, 8, 9.

10. Marc Levinson, *The Box: How the Shipping Container Made the World Smaller and the World Economy Bigger* (Princeton, NJ: Princeton University Press, 2006).

11. Levinson, *Box*, 36–59.

12. Levinson, *Box*, 60–65; interview with Guido Bart by Robert Cherny, May 3, 2000; interview with Lloyd Yates by Robert Cherny, June 30, 2000.

13. *Dispatcher*, Aug. 15, 1958, 1; Sept. 12, 1958, 1, 3; *NYT*, Feb. 5, 1959, 62.

14. Fairley, *Facing Mechanization*, 83.

15. *Dispatcher*, Sept. 28, 1958, 6, 7.

16. *Dispatcher*, Apr. 24, 1959, 3.

17. *LAT*, Nov. 13, 1958, 13; Dec. 6, 1958, 6; *Dispatcher*, Sept. 26, 1958, 1; Oct. 10, 1958, 1, 8; Oct. 24, 1958, 1; Nov. 7, 1958, 6;

18. *Proceedings of the Thirteenth Biennial Convention*, 125–37.

19. *Proceedings of the Thirteenth Biennial Convention*, 39, 54, 67, 117, 371–72.

20. *Dispatcher*, Apr. 24, 1959, 3; Fairley, *Facing Mechanization*, 99–102.

21. Interview, Sept. 2, 1986.

22. Ellen St. Sure Lifschutz, interviewed by Robert Cherny, Jan. 22, 1993.

23. *Dispatcher*, July 31, 1, A–D, 8; Aug 14, 1959, 1, 8; Fairley, *Facing Mechanization*, 103–11.

24. Hartman, *Collective Bargaining and Productivity*, 36; Fairley, *Facing Mechanization*, 85.

25. *Dispatcher*, Mar. 11, 1960, 2.

26. *Dispatcher*, Apr. 8, 1960, 1, 4; Apr. 22, 1960, 1, 7, 8; May 6, 1960, 7; Fairley, *Facing Mechanization*, 112–17.

27. *Dispatcher*, May 20, 1960, 4; June 3, 1960, 1, 3; July 1, 1960, 1; July 29, 1960, 1; Aug. 28, 1960, 6.

28. *Dispatcher*, Oct. 7, 1960, 1; Wayne Horvitz, interviewed by Robert Cherny, Dec. 12, 1992; Fairley, *Facing Mechanization*, chaps. 5, 6.

29. Fairley, *Facing Mechanization*, 141–44.

30. Horvitz interview.

31. Fairley, *Facing Mechanization*, 142, 161, 163.

32. *Dispatcher*, Oct. 21, 1960, 1, 2, 4–7.

33. *LAT*, Oct. 23, 1960, H11; Nov. 2, 1960, B7; Dec. 23, 1960, 2; *Dispatcher*, Dec. 2, 1960, 3, 9; Jan. 13, 1961, 1, 5; Kuvakus oral history.

34. *Chronicle*, Oct. 20, 1960, 36; *NYT*, Oct. 21, 1960, 32; *Wall Street Journal*, Oct. 21, 1960, 14; *Dispatcher*, Nov. 4, 1960, 4; *Time*, Dec. 27, 1963, 19; Fairley, *Facing Mechanization*, 169.

35. Harvey Swados, "West-Coast Waterfront—The End of an Era," *Dissent* 8 (Autumn 1961): 448–60; see also the reply by Lincoln Fairley, "The West Coast Longshore Contract," *Dissent* 9 (Spring 1962): 86–190, and the reply to that by Swados in the same issue, 190–93.

36. *PW*, Nov. 5, 1960, 4; Fairley, *Facing Mechanization*, 154.

37. Roger oral history, 623; Ellen St. Sure Lifschutz interview; Goldblatt oral history, 835; Horvitz interview.

38. Fairley, *Facing Mechanization*, 175–77.

39. Fairley, *Facing Mechanization*, 196–200, 206, 211–21, esp. 219; Roger oral history, 616.

40. Undated clipping, *Los Angeles Herald Examiner*, file ILWU History, Harry Bridges, Material About, 1962–63; ILWU Library; *LAT*, June 7, 1964, B9.

41. Fairley, *Facing Mechanization*, 183–90. Herb Mills was among those who argued that crane operation was not complex as to require a separate category of longshore worker; Mills, "The Container Revolution," unpublished ms. in possession of author.

42. Fairley, *Facing Mechanization*, 190–92; *Dispatcher*, June 11, 1965, 1, 7, 8.

43. Fairley, *Facing Mechanization*, 222–32, esp. 227, 228.

44. Fairley, *Facing Mechanization*, 219, 236–37; *Dispatcher*, Apr. 29, 1966, 1, 6.

45. Fairley, *Facing Mechanization*, 232; *Dispatcher*, Dec. 23, 1966, 8.

46. *Dispatcher*, June 24, 1966, 1; July 8, 1966, 1, 2, 4–7; Aug. 5, 1966, 8; Fairley, *Facing Mechanization*, chap. 9, esp. 242, 251.

Chapter 16. Labor Statesman?

1. Mohn oral history, 625; copy of letter, Bridges to Frank O. Porter, Dec. 11, 1963, f3, b8, Bridges Papers, LARC.

2. *Proceedings of the Fourteenth Biennial Convention*, 390–93; *Proceedings of the Eighteenth Biennial Convention*, 303–13.

3. State Compensation Insurance Fund, Employer's Report of Industrial Injury, Mar. 10, 1963; report of Douglas J. Clifford, MB, ChB, Mar. 7, 1963, both in f3, b8, Bridges Papers, LARC; clipping, Richmond, CA, *Independent* June 7, 1962, file ILWU History Collection, Harry Bridges Material About, 1962–63, ILWU Library.

4. Joe McCray interviewed by Robert Cherny, Mar. 23, 1993; copy of letter, Bridges to Bob, Sept. 7, 1979, f6, b13, Bridges Papers, LARC; *Chronicle*, Feb. 20, 1969, 28.

5. Noriko Sawada Bridges, interviewed by Robert Cherny, July 25, 1990, hereinafter NS Bridges interview.

6. Copy of letter, Bridges to Golden Gate Fields, attn. Mrs. Dorn, Oct. 17, 1963, f3, b8, Bridges Papers, LARC.

7. Katherine Bridges, interviewed by Robert Cherny, Apr. 14, 1987.

8. Julie Fales, interviewed by Robert Cherny, June 29, 1987; obituaries for Julie Bridges, *Chronicle*, Sept. 16, 1991, B6; *Dispatcher*, Oct. 22, 1991, 6.

9. Letter, M. C. to Harry, Aug. 14, 1961, f1, b8, Bridges Papers, LARC.

10. Untitled, undated notes in Bridges's handwriting, f26, b10, Bridges Papers, LARC.

11. *Proceedings of the Fourteenth Biennial Convention*, 82.

12. Lincoln Fairley, *Facing Mechanization: The West Coast Longshore Plan* (Los Angeles: Institute of Industrial Relations, University of California, Los Angeles, 1979), 154, 397. The 1960 census data for the San Francisco–Oakland metropolitan area indicated that 35 percent were over the age of fifty-five and another 31 percent between forty-five and fifty-five. See Cherny, "Longshoremen of San Francisco Bay, 1848–1960."

13. These changes can be tracked in *Dispatcher*, esp. Apr. 18, 1969, 1, 10; July 1, 1969, 1, 6, 7.

14. Roger oral history, 626.

15. NS Bridges interview, July 27, 1990; interview, Sept. 2, 1986; Goldblatt oral history, 879–87, 920–27, 1012–15; Jenkins oral history, 85–91; Roger oral history, 727.

16. Goldblatt oral history, 879–87, 920–27, 1012–15; Jenkins oral history, 85–91.

17. Lincoln Fairley interviewed by Robert Cherny, Sept. 8, 1986; McCray interview.

18. For an overview of Western Addition redevelopment, see William Issel, *Church and State in the City: Catholics and Politics in Twentieth-Century San Francisco* (Philadelphia: Temple University Press, 2013), chap. 8. Other treatments include Rachel Brahinsky, "Fillmore Revisited: How Redevelopment Tore Through the Western Addition" (2019), https://sfpublicpress.org/news/2019–09/fillmore-revisited-how-redevelopment-tore -through-the-western-addition; and Jordan Klein, "A Community Lost: Urban Renewal and Displacement in San Francisco's Western Addition District" (unpublished, 2008, online at http://jordanklein.us/files/WA_Paper.pdf). Of these, only Issel mentions the role of the ILWU in opposing redevelopment of St. Francis Square.

19. Goldblatt oral history, 791–800; *Dispatcher*, July 1, 1960, 1, 5; Dec. 30, 1960, 7; Nov. 1, 1963, 6; Dec. 18, 1970, 8. For more information on St. Francis Square, see Hilary Botein, "Labor Unions and Race-conscious Housing in the Postwar Bay Area: Housing Projects of the International Longshoremen's and Warehousemen's Union and the United Automobile Workers," *Journal of Planning History* 15 (2016): 210–29; and Carol Cuenod, "Redevelopment A-1 and Origin of St. Francis Square," http://www.foundsf .org/index.php?title=Redevelopment_A-1_and_Origin_of_St. Francis_Square. Clement Kai-Men Lai, "Between 'Blight' and a New World: Urban Renewal, Political Mobilization, and the Production of Spatial Scale in San Francisco, 1940–1980" (PhD diss., University of California, Berkeley, 2006), suggests, "St. Francisco Square and a new ILWU world headquarters building in the Western Addition were both Redevelopment Agency concessions to the ILWU leadership over SOMA [South of Market Area] displacement" (140). I found no evidence for such a claim.

20. *Dispatcher*, June 17, 1960, 2; Goldblatt oral history, 799–800.

21. Clippings, *Examiner*, July 31; *News Call Bulletin*, July 30; *Chronicle*, Aug. 2; (Honolulu) *Advertiser*, Aug. 7; *Examiner*, Aug. 14, all 1963, all in file HB, Material About, 1962–63, ILWU Library; *Dispatcher*, July 26, 1963, 2; *Chronicle*, Oct. 2, 1963, 4; *Dispatcher*, Oct. 4, 1963, 1; *Chronicle*, Apr. 16, 1964, 2; *George R. Williams et al., Plaintiffs-Appellants, v. Pacific Maritime Association et al., Defendants-Appellees*, 617 F.2d 1321 (9th Cir. 1980). Seonghee Lim, "Automation and San Francisco Class 'B' Longshoremen: Power, Race, and Workplace Democracy, 1958–1981" (PhD diss., University of California, Santa Barbara, 2015), chaps. 3–4, summarizes the origins of the classification into A and B and also presents information on the experience of B men in the early 1960s.

22. Stan Weir, "B Men and Automation" (1967), reproduced at http://www.foundsf .org/index.php?title=B_Men_and_Automation; Norman Diamond, "In Memoriam: Stan Weir, 1921–2001" (2001), https://libcom.org/library/memoriam-stan-weir-1921–2001; Stan Weir, interviewed by Robert Cherny, Oct. 28, 1990. Lim, "Automation," presents a detailed account of Weir's experiences. Although Sidney Roger, in his oral history, said, "I really believe on the basis of all kinds of things that I've heard and seen that some evidence was doctored" (703, 718–20), he also said that "most were de-registered for legitimate reasons" (709, 710).

23. Stanley Weir, "The ILWU: A Case Study in Bureaucracy," *New Politics* (Winter 1964): 23–28; Paul Jacobs, "Harry, the Gag Man," *New Leader*, July 6, 1964, 12–13; Herman Benson, "Harry Bridges Own Witch-Hunt" *Union Democracy in Action*, Sept. 30, 1964, 4–5; Michael Munk, "ILWU Leadership Being Attacked over Firings," *National Guardian*, Dec. 26, 1964, 5; *Chronicle*, Sept. 17, 1964, 1, 17; *NYT*, Nov. 22, 1964, S22; *LAT*, Dec. 6, 1964, C9.

24. Roger oral history, 712, 716; *Chronicle*, Oct. 23, 1964, 46; Dec. 14, 1964, 6; *Dispatcher*, Dec. 11, 1964, 2.

25. *Dispatcher*, Dec. 10, 1965, 1, 7; clipping, Honolulu *Star-Bulletin & Advertiser*, Feb. 13, 1966, file ILWU History—B-Men De-registration Suit (Local 10) Publicity Clippings, ILWU Library; *Williams et al., Plaintiffs-Appellants, v. Pacific Maritime Association* (9th Cir. 1980). The same file in the ILWU Library contains a wealth of other material on the case. Lim, "Automation," presents a detailed account of the court case, including interviews with several of the plaintiffs in addition to Weir.

26. A full account of the racial issues in Local 8 and 13 is beyond the scope of this work. For more information, see Bruce Nelson, "The 'Lords of the Docks' Reconsidered: Race Relations among West Coast Longshoremen, 1933–61," in *Waterfront Workers: New Perspectives on Race and Class*, ed. Calvin Winslow (Urbana: University of Illinois Press, 1998), 155–92; Jake Alimahomed-Wilson, "Black Longshoremen and the Fight for Equality in an 'Anti-racist' Union," *Race and Class* 53 (2012): 39–53, and *Solidarity Forever? Race, Gender, and Unionism in the Ports of Southern California* (Lanham, MD: Lexington Books, 2016); Sandy Polishuk, "'They Can't Come in the Front Door Because You Guys Won't Let Them': An Oral History of the Struggle to Admit African Americans into ILWU Local 8," *Oregon Historical Quarterly* 120 (2019): 546–61.

27. *Chronicle*, Dec. 12, 1956, 1, 2; June 21, 1957, 1, 4; June 22, 1957, 1, 4; June 6, 1959, 1; June 12, 1959, 7, 32; Aug. 12, 1959, 36; Aug. 13, 1959, 7; Aug. 22, 1959, 1, 10; *Dispatcher*, Aug. 28, 1959, 5. An excellent overview is Joshua Paddison's "Summers of Worry, Summers of Defiance: San Franciscans for Academic Freedom and Education and the Bay Area Opposition to HUAC, 1959–1960," *California History* 78 (1999): 188–201, 219–21.

28. Paddison, "Summers of Worry"; *Chronicle*, May 12, 1960, 7; May 13, 1960, 1, 5; May 16, 1960, 21; NSB interview, July 25, 1990.

29. *Chronicle*, May 14, 1960, A, B.

30. *Dispatcher*, May 20, 1960, 5; *Chronicle*, May 14, 1960, 2. Much the same version of Bridges's activities appears in a copy of a letter by William Glazier to Walter Atkinson, July 10, 1961, f1, b8, Bridges Papers, LARC; Sidney Roger oral history, 667–69; interview, Sept. 2, 1986. See also the account in the Richmond *Independent*, May 14, 1960, clipping in file ILWU History, Harry Bridges, Material About, 1959–61, ILWU Library.

31. Memo, M. A. Jones to Mr. Nease, May 2, 1958, with attached HUAC report, *Operation Abolition* (Washington, DC: Government Printing Office, 1957), file 61-7582-3769, FBI files online at (https://sites.google.com/site/ernie124102/home); press release, Feb. 1, 1961, file ILWU History, Harry Bridges, Material About, 1961, ILWU Library. *Operation Abolition* is online at https://blogs.princeton.edu/reelmudd/2010/10/operation-abolition -and-operation-correction/. *Operation Correction*, on the same website, was created by the San Francisco ACLU to point out and refute the many distortions in the HUAC film.

Quotations are from the printed report: U.S. House of Representatives, 86th Cong., 2nd sess., *The Communist-Led Riots against the House Committee on Un-American Activities in San Francisco, Calif., May 12–14, 1960, Report by the Committee on Un-American Activities* (Washington, DC: U.S. Government Printing Office, 1960), 7, 8.

32. *Dispatcher*, Sept. 23, 1960, 1; Remarks of Senator John F. Kennedy at Mormon Tabernacle, Salt Lake City, UT, Sept. 23, 1960, John F. Kennedy Presidential Library, https://www.jfklibrary.org/archives/other-resources/john-f-kennedy-speeches/salt-lake -city-ut-19600923-mormon-tabernacle; copy of letter, Bridges to Gus Rystad, Jan. 18, 1977, f6, b12, Bridges Papers, LARC; *Chronicle*, Sept. 29, 1960, 17.

33. *The Yale Book of Quotations*, ed. Fred R. Shapiro (New Haven, CT: Yale University Press, 2006), 423; letter, Healy to Bridges, May 22, 1961, file Trade Unions Relations/ Foreign—Australia, ILWU History series, ILWU Library; copy of memo, F. J. Baumgardner to W. C. Sullivan, Jan. 25, 1962, file 39-915-3553, Bridges FBI file.

34. *Chronicle*, Oct. 21, 1959, 1, 14; Nov. 17, 1959, 10; Leonard oral history, 161–62.

35. *NYT*, May 25, 1961, C27; *LAT*, May 25, 1961, 4; *Dispatcher*, June 2, 1961, 1, 3; June 30, 1961, 1.

36. Leonard oral history, 162–63; *Dispatcher*, Dec. 1, 1961, 12; Nov. 15, 1963, 3; June 26, 1964, 1, 8; June 11, 1965, 1, 8; *Chronicle*, Mar. 31, 1962, 2; Apr. 4, 1962, 2; Apr. 5, 1962, 32; May 5, 1962, 1, 16; June 28, 1964, "This World" section, 5; June 8, 1965, 1, 10; *Archie Brown, Appellant, v. United States of America, Appellee*, 334 F2d 488 (9th Cir. 1964); *U.S. v. Brown*, 381 U.S. 437 (1965).

37. Roger oral history, 680–84; *Dispatcher*, Nov. 29, 1963, 3.

38. Roger oral history, 680–84; *Dispatcher*, Nov. 29, 1963, 1–3.

39. *Dispatcher*, Oct. 2, 1964, 1, 4, 5, 8; Oct. 16, 1964, 9–11; clipping, *Los Angeles Herald Examiner*, Aug. 31, 1964, file ILWU History, Harry Bridges, Material About, 1964, ILWU Library.

40. McCray interview. McCray characterized Bridges as "a terrible writer . . . who could speak easily and eloquently. . . . Harry's syntax when he was writing was terrible . . . and Sid would get it all fixed up." *Dispatcher*, Oct. 16, 1964, 2; Oct. 30, 1964, 2; Oct. 11, 1968, 2; *Chronicle*, June 25, 1937, 3.

41. Copy of letter, Bridges to Mike Johnson, Aug. 3, 1964, f4, b8, Bridges Papers, LARC; *Dispatcher*, Sept. 4, 1964, 3. In searching major newspapers, I found neither any report of union efforts to block the nomination of Kennedy for vice president nor any indication Johnson had such a concern. Most press accounts of Johnson's decision eliminating Kennedy from consideration focused on Johnson's concern with Kennedy's close association with civil rights issues. See, for example, Tom Wicker, "Rights Role Hurt Kennedy Chances," *NYT*, Aug. 1, 1964, 6; William S. White, "Kennedy Bar a Blow to Goldwater," *LAT*, Aug. 6, 1964, A5; and Robert J. Donovan, "An Era Comes to End in Act of Realism," *Washington Post*, Aug. 1, 1964, A4.

42. Copies of letters, Bridges to Steve Allen, Apr. 22, 1964; Mike Johnson, Aug. 3, 1964; Charles Walters, Oct. 9, 1964; f4, b8, Bridges Papers, LARC; *Dispatcher*, Oct. 16, 1964, 10.

43. Copy of letter, Bridges to Scheer, July 28, 1966, f1, b9, Bridges Papers, LARC; *Dispatcher*, Sept. 30, 1966, 1, 3, 4; Oct. 14, 1966, 3; Oct. 28, 1966, 4–5; *Proceedings of the Sixteenth Biennial Convention . . . 1967*, 377.

44. *Chronicle*, Apr. 16, 1967, 1, B, 3; Roger oral history, 747; Katherine Bridges interviewed by Robert Cherny, Apr. 14, 1987.

45. Letter, unsigned but from Bridges to "My darling" (Noriko), Sept. 16, 1967, f3, b2, Bridges Papers, LARC.

46. *Dispatcher*, Oct. 25, 1968, 4, 6, 7.

47. *Proceedings of the Fourteenth Biennial Convention*, 496–97, 504, 509; *Proceedings of the Fifteenth Biennial Convention*, 521, 522; *Proceedings of the Seventeenth Biennial Convention*, 458; *Proceedings of the Eighteenth Biennial Convention*, 23, 439–40.

48. *Chronicle*, May 27, 1963, 1, 5; *Dispatcher*, June 2, 1961, 10; May 31, 1963, 1, 4, 5; July 12, 1963, 4–5.

49. *Chronicle*, Mar. 11, 1965, 10; *Proceedings of the Sixteenth Biennial Convention*, 492; *Dispatcher*, Sept. 29, 1967, 1, 8.

50. *Chronicle*, Oct. 4, 1963, 29; *Dispatcher*, Nov. 1, 1963, 8; Jenkins oral history, 223.

51. *Chronicle*, Feb. 28, 1968, 57, 60. Quentin Kopp told me of the pressure on Shelley not to run in a phone call on Dec. 15, 2019.

52. *Chronicle*, Aug. 22, 1968, 43; Sept. 10, 1968, 2; Sept. 18, 1968, 6; Oct. 20, 1968, 4; Dec. 19, 1968, 7; June 17, 1969, 1, 18; June 23, 1969, 4; June 27, 1969, 41; July 18, 1969, 3; July 25, 1969, 52; Aug. 21, 1969, 41; Sept. 24, 1969, 4; Oct. 27, 1969, 38; Nov. 5, 1969, 1, 22. The work of the revision commission is summarized in Frederick M. Wirt, *Power in the City: Decision Making in San Francisco* (Berkeley: University of California Press, 1974), 142–50. Quentin Kopp, a member of the CCRC, discussed his memory of those events in a phone call on Dec. 15, 2019; he did not remember Bridges taking an active part in discussions.

53. *Chronicle*, June 2, 1, 20; July 1, 1970, 5; *Dispatcher*, Oct. 13, 1967, 6; Jenkins oral history, 89, 215, 216, 233.

54. For examples, see report of [redacted], San Francisco FBI field office, Aug. 5, 1964, file 39-915-3574; copy of letter, Hoover to Director of Secret Service, Aug. 15, 1966, file 39-915-3585, Bridges FBI file.

55. Copy of letter, Bridges to R. Palme Dutt, Dec. 12, 1968, f3, b9, Bridges Papers, LARC; *PW*, Nov. 15, 1969, 2; report of [name redacted] of the FBI's San Francisco field office, Feb. 26, 1970, file 39-915-3608, Bridges FBI file.

56. *Dispatcher*, July 17, 1959, 3; July 31, 1959, 8; Oct. 20, 1961, 1, 2, 4; *NYT*, July 7, 1959, 66; *LAT*, July 7, 1959, 1; Jan. 4, 1968, 4.

57. *Dispatcher*, Oct. 19, 1962, 3; Sept. 4, 1964, 1, 7;. *Proceedings of the Seventeenth Biennial Convention*, 17–21, 41, 253–62, 453–53; copies of letters, Bridges to Humphrey, Nov. 9, 1964, f4 b8; Bridges to Humphrey, July 30, 1968, f2, b9, Bridges Papers, LARC. On Hoffa, see Arthur A. Sloane, *Hoffa* (Cambridge, MA: MIT Press, 1992); and Thaddeus Russell, *Out of the Jungle: Jimmy Hoffa and the Remaking of the American Working Class* (Philadelphia: Temple University Press, 2003).

58. *NYT*, July 16, 1959, 52; July 17, 1959, 42; Sept. 25, 1959, 2; Apr. 20, 1960, 77; Apr. 25, 1960, 58; *Proceedings of the Fifteenth Biennial Convention*, 286, 519.

59. *Proceedings of the Eleventh Biennial Convention*, 414; *NYT*, Oct. 5, 1966, 93; *Dispatcher*, Oct. 14, 1966, 2; *Proceedings of the Eighteenth Biennial Convention*, 228–34.

60. Email from Albert Lannon to Robert Cherny, Feb. 21, 2020; *Dispatcher*, Dec. 15, 1970, 3; Mar. 5, 1971, 8;

61. *Proceedings of the Thirteenth Biennial Convention*, 168, 169; *Dispatcher*, July 29, 1960, 1, 2, 5; Oct. 19, 1962, 1, 5; July 19, 1964, 1, 4.

62. *Dispatcher*, Sept. 29, 1967, 2; *Canberra Times*, Sept. 7, 1967, 3; *Sydney Tribune*, Sept. 13, 1967, 1; *Melbourne Age*, Sept. 27, 1967, 1.

63. *Dispatcher*, Sept. 29, 1967, 2, 3. I had a similar reaction when with a large group of Australians all speaking quickly and at the same time.

64. Letters, Harry to Noriko, Sept. 19 and 21, 1967, f3, b2, Bridges Papers, LARC.

65. Letters, Harry to Noriko, n.d., Sept. 28, Oct. 12, 1967, f3, b2, Bridges Papers, LARC.

66. Letter, Harry to Noriko, Oct. 16, 1967, f3, b2, Bridges Papers, LARC.

67. Unsigned, undated page headed "Constitutional Amendments" f6, b9, Bridges Papers, LARC.

68. *LAT*, Apr. 18, 1971, D16; *LAT*, Apr. 29, 1971, A1, 6; *Proceedings of the Nineteenth Biennial Convention*, 79–81; Goldblatt oral history, 920–21.

69. *Proceedings of the Nineteenth Biennial Convention*, 81–92, esp. 92.

70. *Chronicle*, Mar. 9, 1971, 2.

71. *Proceedings of the Nineteenth Biennial Convention*, 384–85; Roger oral history, 890, 908.

72. *Proceedings of the Nineteenth Biennial Convention*, 121–34; Larrowe, *Harry Bridges*, 380; email, from Albert Lannon to Robert Cherny, Nov. 19, 2019.

73. *Proceedings of the Nineteenth Biennial Convention*, 129–35; *LAT*, Apr. 21, 1971, 8.

74. *Proceedings of the Nineteenth Biennial Convention*, 135–43. See also *LAT*, Apr. 21, 1971, 8.

75. *LAT*, Apr. 21, 1971, 8.

Chapter 17. The Longest Strike: Relations with the PMA

1. The steady-man issue is well summarized in Lincoln Fairley, *Facing Mechanization: The West Coast Longshore Plan* (Los Angeles: Institute of Industrial Relations, University of California, Los Angeles, 1979), chap. 10.

2. Fairley, *Facing Mechanization*, 263–64.

3. Fairley, *Facing Mechanization*, 258, 262.

4. Fairley, *Facing Mechanization*, chap. 11.

5. Fairley, *Facing Mechanization*, 271–93; *Dispatcher*, Oct. 11, 1968, 1, 2; Oct. 25, 1968, 1, 8; Nov. 8, 1968, 1, 4; Apr. 4, 1969,1, 8; Sept. 9, 1969,1, 8; Oct. 1, 1969, 1, 3.

6. Fairley, *Facing Mechanization*, appendix tables 1, 3, 395, 398.

7. *Dispatcher*, Oct. 9, 1970, 1, 8; Oct. 23, 1970, 1, 8. .

8. Quoted in Fairley, *Facing Mechanization*, 311.

9. *Dispatcher*, Nov. 6, 1970, 1, 2, 6–10; Fairley, *Facing Mechanization*, 312–14.

10. *Dispatcher*, Nov. 6, 1970, 1; Nov. 20, 1970, 2.

11. *Dispatcher*, Oct. 1, 1969, 2; Jan. 8, 1971, 2; Feb. 10, 1971, 2 (emphasis in the original); Mar. 5, 1971, 2; letter, Bridges to George Morris, Apr. 6, 1971, f6, b9, Bridges Papers, LARC. Albert Vetere Lannon has described the disruption of Local 6 by such rank-and-file caucuses in the 1970s in "Angela's Children: How the Communist Legacy Turned against Itself in ILWU Local 6," *Historia Actual On-Line* 6 (2005): 7–13.

12. *Dispatcher*, Sept. 30, 1966, 2; *Chronicle*, Jan. 18, 1969, 7; Feb. 16, 2006, B7. I received conflicting views on St. Sure's retirement from Wayne Horvitz, whom I interviewed on Dec. 12, 1992, and from Ellen St. Sure Lifschutz, St. Sure's daughter, whom I interviewed on Jan. 22, 1993. Horvitz said St. Sure retired at an appropriate time in his career, at age sixty-five. St. Sure Lifschutz insisted that he had been fired.

13. *Dispatcher*, Dec. 18, 1970, 1; Feb. 1971, 5, 1; Apr. 16, 1971, 2.

14. *Dispatcher*, Mar. 5, 1971, 2; May 7, 1971, 1, 2, 8; May 21, 1971, 1, 2.

15. *Dispatcher*, June 17, 1971, 1, 8; *Chronicle*, June 16, 1971, 6; *LAT*, May 5, 1971, 1; June 17, 1971, 1; June 26, 1971, A1.

16. *Chronicle*, July 1, 1971, 1, 30; *LAT*, July 4, 1971, B5; July 6, 1971, C11; *Wall Street Journal*, Aug. 9, 1971, 4.

17. *LAT*, July 13, 1971, 3, 17; *Washington Post*, Aug. 16, 1971, A1, A4. See also Marion Mauk, "Harry Bridges: New Look at an Old Radical," *Southland Sunday* (Long Beach), Dec. 17, 1972, 12–14, 16, 18, esp. 14.

18. Roger oral history, 897–900, 914; Kagel, interviewed by Robert Cherny, n.d.

19. *Chronicle*, Aug. 7, 1971, 2; *LAT*, July 29, 1971, 1, 27; Aug. 12, 1971, A1, 23; *Wall Street Journal*, Aug. 9, 1971, 4; Kagel interview; Herb Mills, interviewed by Robert Cherny, Mar. 9, 1993.

20. *Dispatcher*, July 30, 1971, 1, 2, 8.

21. *LAT*, Aug. 16, 1971, A1, 13; *NYT*, Aug 17, 1971, 21; Aug. 18, 1971, 1, 20; Aug. 19, 1971, 1, 22.

22. *NYT*, Aug. 19, 1971, 1; *Dispatcher*, Aug. 27, 1971, 1, 2, 4, 5, 8.

23. *Dispatcher*, Sept. 10, 1971, 1; Oct. 8, 1971, 3; Oct. 22, 1971, 7.

24. *LAT*, Aug 24, 1971, A3; Aug. 28, 1971, B12.

25. *Dispatcher*, Sept. 24, 1971, 1, 2.

26. *San Francisco Examiner*, Sept. 26, 1971, 1, 12; *LAT*, Sept. 26, 1971, 1, 19; *Chronicle*, Oct. 7, 1971, 1, 30; *Dispatcher*, Oct. 8, 1971, 1, 2, 8.

27. *Dispatcher*, Oct. 22, 1971, 1, 2, 8; Dec. 22, 1971, 1, 3.

28. *Dispatcher*, Jan. 14, 1972, 1.

29. *Dispatcher*, Jan. 28, 1972, 8.

30. *Dispatcher*, Jan. 28, 1972, 7.

31. *NYT*, Feb. 5, 1972, 1, 57; Feb. 6, 1972, 60; Feb. 9, 1972, 1, 78; *Dispatcher*, Feb. 11, 1972, 1, 2.

32. *Dispatcher*, Feb. 11, 1972, 1, 2, 4, 5, 8.

33. *Dispatcher*, Feb. 11, 1972, 5; Feb. 24, 1972, 4, 5.

34. *Dispatcher*, Feb. 24, 1972, 8.

35. *Dispatcher*, Feb. 11, 1972, 2.

36. *Dispatcher*, Mar. 10, 1972, 1; Mar. 24, 1972, 1, 8; *NYT*, Mar. 17, 1972, 1; Mar. 21, 1972, 82; Mar. 23, 1972, 34; Apr. 15, 1972, 36.

37. *NYT*, May 9, 1972, 1; May 14, 1972, E2; May 16, 1972, 9; *Dispatcher*, Apr. 14, 1972, 1, 8; May 12, 1972, 1, 8.

38. Norman Leonard, *Life of a Leftist Labor Lawyer*, interview by Estolv Ethan Ward, 1985, Regional Oral History Office, Bancroft Library, University of California, Berkeley, 189–90.

39. *Dispatcher*, July 20, 1973, 1, 3; July 25, 1975, 1; Aug. 8, 1975, 7.

Chapter 18. Living Legend

1. *Proceedings of the Twenty-Sixth Biennial Convention*, 254–55.

2. Copies of memos, Harry to Bill, Jack, Lou, Mar. 24, 1970; Harry to Sid, Mar. 26, 1970, both in f5, b9; copy of letter, Bridges to Steve Murdock, May 16, 1972, f6, b9, Bridges Papers, LARC; Roger oral history, 821, 846, 852; *LAT*, May 21, 1972, H3; *Dispatcher*, Feb. 9, 1973, 8; Feb. 20, 1976, 3; May 11, 1973, 8; Mar. 19, 1975, 4; Jenkins oral history, 90.

3. Minutes of the International Executive Board for Jan. 30–31, 1973, 5, 6, and attachments 5, 6, ILWU Library.

4. Charles Larrowe, *Harry Bridges: The Rise and Fall of Radical Labor in the United States* (New York: Lawrence Hill, 1972), esp. vi, vii; *Proceedings of the Twentieth Biennial Convention*, 332–35; *Proceedings of the Twenty-Second Biennial Convention, 1977*, 412–13. Larrowe told me that the subtitle had been added at the insistence of his publisher. His book is limited in several ways, but nothing in it justifies Bridges's characterization. In my conversations with Bridges, I never fully understood his animosity toward Larrowe's book. Of course, Larrowe was a professor of economics and therefore an intellectual by definition.

5. *Chronicle*, Feb. 24, 1973, 3; Mar. 2, 1973, 3; *PW*, Apr. 14, 1973, 4; Minutes of International Executive Board meeting of Jan. 30–31, 1973, 12; meeting of Aug. 2, 1973, 9, ILWU Library; *Proceedings of the Twentieth Biennial Convention*, 227, 230, 231, 233–35, 376.

6. *Proceedings of the Twenty-First Biennial Convention*, 145–153; *Dispatcher*, May 11, 1973, 5; *Chronicle*, Sept. 13, 1975, 4; Sept. 17, 1975, 13; *PW*, Apr. 24, 1976, 2.

7. *LAT*, Mar. 18, 1971, C8; see also copy of letter, Gus Rystad to *PW* editor, Mar. 17, 1971, f6, b12, Bridges Papers, LARC; *PW*, Mar. 13, 1971, 6, 12; copy of letter, Bridges to *People's World*, not for publication, Mar. 15, 1974, f9, b9; letter, Albert J. Lima to Nils Lange, Nov. 18, 1974, f5, b12, both Bridges Papers, LARC; flyer, "A Communist Viewpoint Waterfront Situation," f1, b12; "An Estimation of the ILWU Today," by ML [Mickie Lima], "The Pacific Coast Longshore Situation," by A.B. [Archie Brown], part of materials sent to CP District Committee Members, Apr. 6 1976, f2, b12, Bridges Papers, LARC.

8. See, for example, *Dispatcher*, Jan. 22, 1971, 2; May 12, 1972, 2; Nov. 22, 1974, 2; letter, Hall to Bridges, Apr. 5, 1973, file 4, box 12, Bridges Papers, LARC.

9. Interview with Noriko Sawada Bridges by Robert Cherny, Aug. 3, 1990, hereinafter NS Bridges interview; *Dispatcher*, May 16, 1975, 2; June 13, 1975, 4, 5.

10. *Chronicle*, Oct. 27, 1976, 5; *Dispatcher*, Nov. 5, 1976, 1; Dec. 17, 1976, 6; email from Robert Bridges to Robert Cherny, Jan. 18, 2021. See also the file of congratulatory messages from Soviet unions and the WFTU, f11, b9, Bridges Papers, LARC.

11. Michael Newton, *The FBI Encyclopedia* (Jefferson, NC: McFarland, 2003), 9; memo, SAC San Francisco to Director FBI, Dec. 30, 1971, file 39–915-[illeg.]; memo, SAC San Francisco to Director, FBI, Oct. 4, 1972, file 39–915-[illeg.]; Report by [name redacted], Aug. 27, 1974, file 39–915-[illeg]; report of [name redacted], July 4, 1976, with copy to Secret Service, no file number, Bridges FBI file. The final six pages in his FBI file, dated 1981 and 1982, were completely redacted in the interest of national defense or foreign policy.

12. *Proceedings of the Seventeenth Biennial Convention*, 70, 476; *Dispatcher*, Sept. 9, 1969, 3; Dec. 16, 1974, 4; Jan. 11, 1974, 4–5; *Proceedings of the Twenty-Sixth Biennial Convention*, 253–55.

13. Clement Kai-Men Lai, "Between 'Blight' and a New World: Urban Renewal, Political Mobilization, and the Production of Spatial Scale in San Francisco, 1940–1980" (PhD diss., University of California, Berkeley, 2006), 140, 201–2; *Redevelopment: A Marxist Analysis*, https://archive.org/details/Redevelopment_A_Marxist_Analysis.

14. *Dispatcher*, Nov. 19, 1976, 4, 5; Dec. 3, 1976, 5; letter, Harry to Noriko, Sept. 23, 1976, f24, b1, NSBF Papers, LARC.

15. Letter, Honor [Farnam] Crush, May 26, 1977, f16, b1; unidentified clippings from Australian newspapers, f1, b10; clipping, *Advocate* (Tasmania), Oct. 7, 1976, 3, f1, b10, Bridges Papers, LARC; letter, Harry to Noriko, Sept. 23, 1976, f24, b1; Noriko Bridges, interviewed by Colleen Fong, Sept. 16, 1986, f4, b1, both NSBF Papers, LARC. Unfortunately, TROVE, the online collection of digitized Australian newspapers, does not include the major Sydney or Melbourne dailies for 1976.

16. Copy of letter, Bridges to Newton Miyagi, Dec. 8, 1976, f11, b9, Bridges Papers, LARC; *Proceedings of the Twenty-First Biennial Convention*, 417–18. The convention's deliberations on the constitutional amendment were held in executive session and not recorded in the *Proceedings*. The minutes of the executive session do not include the official vote tally, only the record of how individual locals and delegates voted; the minutes of the executive session were made available to me with permission of the international officers. Local 142 seems to have had 43 votes (88–89); if so, the total would have been 125–51.

17. *Chronicle*, Apr. 10, 1975, 19; *Proceedings of the Twenty-First Biennial Convention*, 375–82, 416. Wing objected not to the substance but the process.

18. *Chronicle*, Nov. 30, 1975, 11; Dec. 4, 1975, 25; *Dispatcher*, Dec. 12, 1975, 1, 2. There are six folders of material related to the testimonial dinner, files 8–13; some $36,000 was raised from sale of ads in the program, f13, all in b12, Bridges Papers, LARC. Such testimonials for labor leaders were fairly standard affairs by that time, although many were designed to raise funds for some charitable purpose.

19. *Dispatcher*, June 11, 1976, 4; Sept. 26, 1976, 8. *Mahalo* is an expression of gratitude.

20. *Proceedings of the Twenty-Second Biennial Convention . . . 1977*; *NYT*, Apr. 24, 1977, 27.

21. *Proceedings of the Twenty-Second Biennial Convention*, 248–59, 262–66, 338–64, 415–16, 522–23, 534, 516 (on affirmative action), 315–35 (on the six-hour day), 497–98, 502 (South Africa), 527 (capital punishment), 515 (alien workers), 518 (no mergers, labor unity). For later actions on South Africa, see Peter Cole, *Dockworker Power: Race and Activism in Durban and the San Francisco Bay Area* (Urbana: University of Illinois Press, 2018).

22. *LAT*, Apr. 13, 1977, OC1, 2; *Proceedings of the Twenty-Second Biennial Convention*, 445; *Dispatcher*, June 24, 1977, 6.

23. *Seattle Post-Intelligencer*, Apr. 24, 1977, A 3.

24. *NYT*, Apr. 23, 1977, 8.

25. *Dispatcher*, Oct. 27, 1972, 1, 2, 7, 8, A20.

26. *Dispatcher*, May 10, 1974, 2, 8; May 24, 1974, 2, 8; Oct. 11, 1974, 2, 6; Oct. 25, 1974, 2, 8; Nov. 22, 1974, 2; May 14, 1976, 8; May 28, 1976, 8; Oct. 22, 1976, 1, 7, 8; copy of letter, Bridges to Gus Rystad, Jan. 18, 1977, f6, b12, Bridges Papers, LARC; Noriko Bridges to Hamilton Jordan, Oct. 8, 1976, f24, b1, NSBF, LARC.

27. *Chronicle*, Sept. 9, 1974, 3. For a thorough history of the evolution of the port in the late twentieth century, see Jasper Rubin *A Negotiated Landscape: The Transformation of San Francisco's Waterfront since 1950*, 2nd ed. (Pittsburgh: University of Pittsburgh Press, 2016),

28. Report, "The San Francisco Port: Asset or Liability" (San Francisco: San Francisco Planning and Urban Renewal Association, 1968), 8; Rubin, *Negotiated Landscape*, 146–59; T. H. Watkins and R. R. Olmsted, "The Times They Were a'Changing," *San Francisco Sunday Examiner and Chronicle, California Living Magazine*, Nov. 14, 1976, 26, 28, 30–32.

29. *Chronicle*, Sept. 12, 1974, 2.

30. *Chronicle*, Jan. 16, 1975, 3; Sept. 8, 1976, 4; Feb 28, 1976, 2; Dec. 7, 1976, 17; Nov. 28, 1977, 23; Jan. 17, 1978, 3; Rubin, *Negotiated Landscape*, 168–69.

31. *Chronicle*, July 1, 1976, 47; July 18, 1976, A20; Port Commission minutes, Oct. 8, 1980, 2; May 13, 1981, 1; June 10, 1981, 1. Port Commission minutes are available at the Internet Archive, https://archive.org.

32. *Chronicle*, Mar. 12, 1982, 41; Nov. 10, 1982, 24; San Francisco Port Commission Minutes, Dec. 16, 1982,

33. *Chronicle*, May 18, 1973, A24; copy of letter, Bridges to Bob, Sept. 7, 1979, f6, b13, Bridges Papers, LARC.

34. *Proceedings of the Twenty-Third Biennial Convention*, 359–68, 551; *Proceedings of the Twenty-Fourth Biennial Convention*, 493–96; *Proceedings of the Twenty-Fifth Biennial Convention*, 532–64; *Proceedings of the Twenty-Sixth Biennial Convention*, 335–53. For Bridges's involvement with the ILWU pensioners, see, for example, f15, b14, Bridges Papers, LARC.

35. *Proceedings of the Twenty-Seventh Triennial Convention*, 56–57, 152–218, esp. 210; *Dispatcher*, July 8, 1988, 8; Sept. 14, 1988, 1.

36. Case reports for Harry Bridges and Mariko [*sic*] Bridges, both dated July 30, 1977; copy of letter, Nikki Bridges to Mrs. Smith, Nov. 9, 1977, both f3, b3, Bridges Papers, LARC; *NYT*, May 8, 1977, 87; copies of letters, Nikki Bridges to Mrs. Smith, Nov. 9, 1977; to Mr. and Mrs. Subbert, Feb. 15, 1979; to Charles Gherman, Oct. 15, 1979, f3, b3, Bridges Papers, LARC. In late October 1977, Harry had minor surgery, probably for benign prostrate hyperplasia at Kaiser hospital in Oakland; admission and release forms, Kaiser hospital, Oakland, Oct. 31, 1977, f6, b3, Bridges Papers, LARC.

37. Letters, Marvin Sadik to Bridges, Dec. 6, 1977, f1, b15, Bridges Papers, LARC; letter, Harry to Nikki, undated, f24, b1, NSBF Papers, LARC.

38. *NYT*, Jan. 18, 1978, A14; *Washington Post*, Jan. 17, 1978, B1, B3. Given Bridges's dislike of Charles Larrowe's biography, it is somewhat ironic that Bridges chose, for his title, the same title that Larrowe used for his first chapter.

39. Copy of letter, Nikki to Harriet [Bouslog] and Steve [Sawyer], Apr. 21, 1980, f7, b15; report of optical services, Aug. 8, 1984; memo, August Colenbrander to William B. Shekter, Nov. 30, 1987, f4, b3, Bridges Papers, LARC.

40. *Proceedings of the Twenty-First Biennial Convention*, 420–22; *Proceedings of the Twenty-Second Biennial Convention*, 363–64; letter, Harry to Nikki, Feb. 8–17 [?], 1978, f31, b1, NSBF Papers, LARC. There are extensive materials about Bridges's participation in the ILF in f8, b14, Bridges Papers, LARC. The U.S. State Department labeled the

World Peace Council and, by implication, the ILF as "financed and controlled by the U.S.S.R.," said it attracted "prestigious noncommunist figures—literary, humanitarian, scientific—who are motivated by a genuine concern for peace," and claimed it "swarmed with KGB officers." U.S. Department of State, *Foreign Affairs Note: Soviet Active Measures: The World Peace Council*, Apr. 1985.

41. See, for example, Alan Thomson to Bridges, Mar. 16, 1984; Bridges to Thompson, Apr. 13, 1984, f1, b14, Bridges Papers, LARC. There are extensive files of the National Council of American Soviet Friendship at the Tamiment Library and Robert F. Wagner Labor Archives, New York University. There are extensive materials about the U.S. Peace Council in f9, 10, b14, Bridges Papers, LARC. See, esp., copy of letter, Bridges to Mike Myerson, July 20, 1980.

42. Letter, Harry to Noriko, probably Nov. 26, 1978, f4, b2; unidentified clipping (*Political Affairs?*), Noriko and Harry Bridges, "Cuba: A Young Society Which Cares for the Old," f13, b15; copy of letter, Bridges to Debkumar Ganguli, Aug. 28, 1981; letter, Evelyn Velson to Nikki Bridges, n.d., f9, b15; other travel materials, f10, b15, Bridges Papers, LARC; untitled twenty-five-page typed report, f10, b5, NSB Papers, LARC; NS Bridges interview, July 27, 1990.

43. Copies of letters, Bridges to George Meyers, June 7 and Aug. 6, 1979; Bridges to Hall, Oct. 31, 1983; and Mar. 13, 1986, f4, b12, Bridges Papers, LARC. Bridges's characterization of Solidarity came from my conversations with Harry and Noriko at the time.

44. *Proceedings of the Twenty-Second Biennial Convention*, 59–60. For the response to his intent to organize seniors, see f12, 13, b14, Bridges Papers, LARC. Materials regarding Bridges's role in the Congress of California Seniors are in f14, 15, b14, Bridges Papers, LARC.

45. See various material regarding the society, f3, b14 Bridges Papers, LARC.

46. Noriko Bridges to Nora Lupton, Jan. 9, 1981, f17, b1, NSBF Papers, LARC.

47. Acceptance speech, f26, b6; clipping from *Hawaii Herald*, June 15, 1990, A6, A7, f8, b1, NSBF Papers, LARC.

48. *Chronicle*, obituary for Charles Einstein, Mar. 11, 2007, B6; *Chronicle*, Nov. 4, 1981, 39; copy of letter, Nikki to Dot, Nov. 2, 1980, f15, b1; Bridges to Katharine Graham, June 29, 1983, f8, b13, Bridges Papers, LARC. The Einstein manuscript is in f12, b3. The tapes of the interviews by Noriko Bridges and Einstein will be deposited at LARC. Copies of letters, Bridges to Alexander, Oct. 10, 1984; Bridges to Hall, Nov. 29, 1985, both in f 9, b3, Bridges Papers, LARC. This file contains a good deal of other correspondence regarding the biography.

49. Copies of letters, Bridges to Jack, July 28, 1983, f8, b13; Bridges to Lucy, Jan. 11, 1980, f15, b1, both Bridges Papers, LARC.

50. Letter, Charles Gherman to Bridges, May 6, 1982, f9, b15; copy of letter, Bridges to Jack and Mitsy, Aug. 19, 1985, f15, b1; report of optical services, Aug. 8, 1984; memo, August Colenbrander to William B. Shekter, Nov. 30, 1987, f4, b3; ambulance response record, Nov. 2, 1988, f6, b3, all Bridges Papers, LARC; copy of letter, Noriko to Aunt Setsuko, Kazuyuki, and Hisako, Mar. 12,1987, f18, b2; Noriko to Jude Pauline Eberhard, Nov. 1988, f20, b2, NSBF Papers, LARC. My thanks to my daughter, Sarah Cherny, MD, for her assistance in understanding these diagnoses.

51. Noriko Bridges to Si [Gerson], June 9, 1990, f22, b2, NSBF Papers, LARC; phone call with Kevin Fales, Mar. 27, 2020.

52. *Chronicle*, Mar. 31, 1990, 1, 4, 5; Apr. 8, 1990, "Sunday Punch" section, 1.

53. Noriko Bridges to Si [Gerson], June 9, 1990, f22, b2, NSBF Papers, LARC.

54. *Examiner*, Apr. 15, 1990, B1, B4; Noriko Bridges to Si [Gerson], June 9, 1990, f22, b2, NSBF Papers, LARC; my own memories of the event.

55. *Examiner*, Apr. 15, 1990, B4.

56. Noriko Bridges to Si [Gerson], June 9, 1990, f22, b2, NSBF Papers, LARC.

57. Clipping from *Hawaii Herald*, June 15, 1990, A6, A7, f8, b1, NSBF Papers, LARC. Noriko wrote movingly about missing Harry, but their daughter denied permission to quote from those letters; see copies of letters, Noriko Bridges to Lois and Jack, Nov. 21, 1990; to Hon Brown, Dec. 2, 1990, both f21, b2, NSBF Papers, LARC.

Epilogue

1. *Chronicle*, Apr. 1, 1990, B7.

2. *Chronicle*, Apr. 1, 1990, p B7.

3. NLB proceedings, Sept. 24, 1934, esp. 2340–42, 2348–50, 2367, b18.

4. 81st Cong., 1st sess., Senate Committee on Labor and Public Welfare, *Hawaiian Labor Situation: Hearing*, July 12, 1949, esp. 131–32.

5. Harry Bernstein, *LAT*, Apr. 24 1977, A3; *NYT*, Apr. 23, 1977, 8.

6. *NYT*, Apr. 23, 1977, 8.

7. *NYT*, Apr. 23, 1977, 8.

8. *Sunday Examiner and Chronicle*, Apr. 8, 1990, "Sunday Punch" section, 1; *NYT*, Apr. 23, 1977, 8.

9. Williams quoted in Harvey Schwartz, *Solidarity Stories: An Oral History of the ILWU* (Seattle: University of Washington Press, 2009), 48. I never found that comment in my research. Herb Mills told me that Williams's comment reflected a more general attitude among Black Local 10 members; Mills remembered a slightly different comment, that if the waterfront became so mechanized that only one worker was needed, it would be an ILWU member who would push the button; Mills interview, Mar. 15, 1993.

10. I therefore disagree fundamentally with Vernon Pedersen's implied conclusion that the CP ever controlled the San Francisco waterfront in *The Communist Party on the American Waterfront: Revolution, Reform, and the Quest for Power* (Lanham, MD: Lexington Books, 2019), for example, 71, where he speaks of "the triumph" of the CP.

11. Thomas Marsh to Harry Bridges, Mar. 13, 1990, f22, b2, NSBF Papers, LARC. Regarding Bridges's induction into Labor's Hall of Fame, now called Labor's International Hall of Fame, see f14, b16, Bridge Papers, LARC. See also Robert W. Cherny, "Harry Bridges," *California Journal* 30 (Nov. 1999): 18–19; and the Harry Bridges Project, https://www.imdb.com/name/nm0750823/bio?ref_=nm_ov_bio_sm.

12. On Bridges as a touchstone, see, for example, William (Willie) E. Adams, interviewed by Harvey Schwartz, May 15, 2018, copy provided by Schwartz; membership data from ILWU, *How the Union Works*, https://www.ilwu.org/wp-content/uploads/2010/12/how-the-union-works.pdf.

Selected Bibliography

A Note on Sources

The endnotes provide the most complete list of sources. Repeating all of them here would add many more pages to what is already an overly long book. This selected bibliography, therefore, identifies only the most significant. For secondary works, I have listed only works that deal with Bridges or the ILWU in a central way. I plan to file a more complete bibliography with my papers at the Labor Archives and Research Center.

Archival Materials

The two most significant archives are the Anne Rand Library, Harry R. Bridges Memorial Building, San Francisco (ILWU Library), and the Labor Archives and Research Center, Leonard Library, San Francisco State University. At LARC, the most significant collections have been the Harry Bridges Papers and the Noriko Sawada Bridges Flynn Papers. In the notes, I sometimes refer to Harry Bridges Personal Papers to designate items that were loaned to me by Bridges and that I have not located in this archival collection. LARC also has the Proceedings of the National Longshoremen's Board, 1934; the proceedings of meetings of the Maritime Federation of the Pacific; the oral histories by Corinne Gilb, listed below; and a complete file of the *People's World*. I plan to deposit Bridges's FBI file and my own research files at LARC.

The most significant collections of papers in federal archives have been the Bridges FBI file, 39-915, still held by the FBI; the Bridges INS file, National Archives, San Bruno, California; and the files of Secretary of Labor Frances Perkins, Record Group 174.3.1, National Archives. I found relevant material in every presidential library from Hoover through Johnson and in the Nixon papers that were then at the National Archives.

The papers of Bridges's lawyers have been significant. They are as follows: Richard Gladstein Papers, listed as Harry Renton Bridges Papers, Southern California Library, Los Angeles; Harry Bridges legal case files, part of the Norman Leonard Records, LARC; and Telford Taylor Papers, Arthur W. Diamond Law Library, Columbia University, New York.

Other important archival material is in the Frances Perkins Papers, Columbia University, and collections at the Archives of Labor and Urban Affairs, Walter Reuther Library, Wayne State University, Detroit; University Archives, Catholic University, Washington, DC; Tamiment Library, New York University; Bancroft Library, University of California, Berkeley; the University of Washington, Seattle; Harvard Law Library, Harvard University, Cambridge, MA; the National Archives; and the Library of Congress. Outside the United States, the most important materials were at the Russian State Archive of Social and Political History, Moscow; the State Library of Victoria, Melbourne, Australia; and the Public Record Office of Victoria, North Melbourne, Australia. For the 1930s, I made extensive use of the papers of Ottilie Markholt, which were then in her apartment in Tacoma; my citations to those papers are based on my research at that time. Those papers are now at the University of Washington, Seattle, and likely have different file and box numbers.

Oral Histories

A rich collection of oral histories related to the ILWU exists, many of which are now online, notably the following:

Bulcke, Germain. *Germain Bulcke: Longshore Leader and ILWU-Pacific Maritime Association Arbitrator*. Interviewed by Estolv Ethan Ward, 1983. Regional Oral History Office, Bancroft Library, University of California, Berkeley, 1984.

Goldblatt, Louis. *Working Class Leader in the ILWU, 1935–1977*. Interviewed by Estolv Ethan Ward, 1978, 1979. 2 vols. Regional Oral History Office, Bancroft Library, University of California, Berkeley, 1980.

Jenkins, David. *David Jenkins: The Union Movement, the California Labor School, and San Francisco Politics, 1926–1988*. Interviewed by Lisa Rubens, 1987–88. Oral History Center, Bancroft Library, University of California, Berkeley, 1993.

Melnikow, Henry. "Henry Melnikow and the National Labor Bureau: An Oral History." Interviewed by Corinne Lathrop Gilb. Institute of Industrial Relations, University of California, Berkeley, 1959.

Mohn, Einar. "Einar Mohn, Teamster Leader: An Oral History." Interviewed by Corinne Lathrop Gilb. Institute of Industrial Relations, University of California, Berkeley, 1970.

Roger, Sidney. *Sidney Roger, a Liberal Journalist on the Air and on the Waterfront: Labor and Political Issues, 1932–1990*. Interviewed by Julie Shearer, 1989–90. 2 vols. Oral History Center, Bancroft Library, University of California, Berkeley, 1998.

Schmidt, Henry. *Secondary Leadership in the ILWU, 1933–1966*. Interviewed by Miriam F. Stein and Estolv Ethan Ward. Regional Oral History Office, Bancroft Library, University of California, Berkeley, 1983.

St. Sure, J. Paul. "Some Comments on Employer Organizations and Collective Bargaining in Northern California." Interviewed by Corinne Glib, 1957. Oral History Project, Institute of Industrial Relations, University of California, Berkeley.

Watson, Don. Interviewed by Harvey Schwartz, 1994. Labor Archives and Research Center, San Francisco State University.

See also the published collection of interviews by Harvey Schwartz, *Solidarity Stories: An Oral History of the ILWU*. Seattle: University of Washington Press, 2009.

Interviews

I interviewed seventy-some people and had access to several recorded interviews done by others. All my interviews will go to LARC.

Newspapers

The most important newspapers are those published by the ILWU and other maritime unions, notably the *Dispatcher* (San Francisco), the *Voice of the Federation* (San Francisco), and *Pacific Coast Longshoreman* (Tacoma); the first two are available online, through the ILWU Library. Communist publications are also useful: *Western Worker* (San Francisco) and *People's World*; the first is available online. The *San Francisco Chronicle* and *Los Angeles Times*, both available online, are other important sources. For the 1930s, the *San Francisco News* provides an important alternative perspective to the city's other three daily newspapers.

Works Dealing Centrally with Bridges or the ILWU

This list is incomplete but includes major academic works of which I am aware as well as significant nonacademic works. I have not included works where Bridges or the ILWU are mentioned but are not prominent.

Afrasiabi, Peter. *Burning Bridges: America's 20-Year Crusade to Deport Labor Leader Harry Bridges*. Brooklyn: Thirlmere Books, 2016.

Alimahomed-Wilson, Jake. "Black Longshoremen and the Fight for Equality in an 'Antiracist' Union." *Race and Class* 53 (2012): 39–53.

———. *Solidarity Forever? Race, Gender, and Unionism in the Ports of Southern California*. Lanham, MD: Lexington, 2016.

Botein, Hilary. "Labor Unions and Race-Conscious Housing in the Postwar Bay Area: Housing Projects of the International Longshoremen's and Warehousemen's Union and the United Automobile Workers." *Journal of Planning History* 15 (2016): 210–29.

Boyden, Richard P. "The West Coast Longshoremen, the Communist Party, and the Second World War." Unpublished paper, 1967.

Buchanan, Roger. *Dock Strike: History of the 1934 Waterfront Strike in Portland, Oregon*. Everett, WA: Working Press, 1975.

Cherny, Robert W. "Anticommunist Networks and Labor: The Pacific Coast in the 1930s." In *Labor's Cold War: Local Politics in a Global Context*, edited by Shelton Stromquist. Urbana: University of Illinois Press, 2008.

———. "The Communist Party in California, 1935–1940: From the Political Margins to the Mainstream and Back." *American Communist History* 9 (2010): 3–33.

———. "Constructing a Radical Identity: History, Memory, and the Seafaring Stories of Harry Bridges." *Pacific Historical Review* 70 (2001): 571–600.

———. "Harry Bridges." *California Journal* 30 (November 1999): 18–19.

———. "Harry Bridges, Labor Radicalism, and the State." Occasional Paper Series, no. 1, Center for Labor Studies, University of Washington, 1994.

———. "Harry Bridges's Australia, Australia's Harry Bridges." In *Frontiers of Labor: Comparative Histories of the United States and Australia*, edited by Greg Passmore and Shelton Stromquist. Urbana: University of Illinois Press, 2018.

———. "The Longshoremen of San Francisco: An Exception in the American Labor Movement?" In *Environnements Portuaires/Port Environments*, edited by John Barzman and Eric Barré. Dieppe: Publications des Universités de Rouen et du Havre, 2003.

———. "Longshoremen of San Francisco Bay, 1849–1960." In *Dock Workers: International Explorations in Comparative Labor History, 1790–1970*, edited by Sam Davies et al. 2 vols. Aldershot, Hampshire: Ashgate, 2000.

———. "The Making of a Labor Radical: Harry Bridges, 1901–1934." *Pacific Historical Review* 64 (1995): 363–88.

———. "Prelude to the Popular Front: The Communist Party in California, 1931–1935." *American Communist History* 1 (2002): 5–37.

Chiles, Frederic Caire. "War on the Waterfront: The Struggles of the San Francisco Longshoremen, 1851–1934." PhD diss., University of California, Santa Barbara, 1981.

Cole, Peter. *Dockworker Power: Race and Activism in Durban and the San Francisco Bay Area*. Urbana: University of Illinois Press, 2018.

Cushman, Richard Alan. "The Communist Party and the Waterfront Strike of 1936–1937: The San Francisco Story." Master's thesis, San Francisco State College, 1970.

Dancis, Bruce. "San Francisco Employers and Longshore Labor Relations, 1934–1949." Unpublished paper, 1974, ILWU Library.

Darcy, Samuel Adams. "The Great West Coast Maritime Strike." *Communist* 13 (July 1934): 664–86.

———. "The San Francisco Bay Area General Strike." *Communist* 13 (October 1934): 985–1004.

———. "The San Francisco General Strike—1934." *Hawsepipe* 1 (September–October 1982): 1, 7.

———. "The San Francisco General Strike—1934: Part II." *Hawsepipe* 2 (November–December 1982): 1–2, 4–6.

Eliel, Paul. "Labor Problems in Our Steamship Business." *Yale Review* 26 (1937): 510–32.

———. "Peace in the West Coast Shipping Industry." *Annals of the American Academy of Political and Social Science* 224 (November 1942): 147–51.

———. *The Waterfront and General Strikes: San Francisco, 1934*. San Francisco: Hooper Printing, 1934.

Fairley, Lincoln. *Facing Mechanization: The West Coast Longshore Plan*. Los Angeles: Institute of Industrial Relations, University of California, Los Angeles, 1979.

Finlay, William. *Work on the Waterfront: Worker Power and Technological Change in a West Coast Port*. Philadelphia: Temple University Press, 1988.

Francis, Robert Coleman. "A History of Labor on the San Francisco Waterfront." PhD diss., University of California, Berkeley, 1934.

Frost, Amanda. *You Are Not American: Citizenship Stripping from "Dred Scott" to the Dreamers*. Boston: Beacon Press, 2021.

Ginger, Ann Fagan. *Carol Weiss King: Human Rights Lawyer, 1895–1952*. Niwot: University Press of Colorado, 1993.

Hartman, Paul T. *Collective Bargaining and Productivity: The Longshore Mechanization Agreement*. Berkeley: University of California Press, 1969.

Horne, Gerald. *Fighting in Paradise: Labor Unions, Racism, and Communists in the Making of Modern Hawai'i*. Honolulu: University of Hawai'i Press, 2011.

John, Michael. "Winning for Losing: A New Look at Harry Bridges and the 'Big Strike' of 1934." *American Communist History* (2014): 1–24.

Johnson, Victoria. *How Many Machine Guns Does It Take to Cook One Meal? The Seattle and San Francisco General Strikes*. Seattle: University of Washington Press, 2008.

Kagel, Sam. "A Right Wing Dual Union." Unpublished paper, 1930.

Kerr, Clark, and Lloyd Fisher. "Conflict on the Waterfront." *Atlantic Monthly*, September 1949, 17–23.

Kimeldorf, Howard. *Reds or Rackets? The Making of Radical and Conservative Unions on the Waterfront*. Berkeley: University of California Press, 1988.

———. "World War II and the Deradicalization of American Labor: The ILWU as a Deviant Case." *Labor History* 33 (1992): 248–78.

Kutler, Stanley I. *The American Inquisition: Justice and Injustice in the Cold War*. New York: Hill and Wang, 1982.

Lannon, Albert Vetere. "World War II and the Struggle for Solidarity with New Union Members: San Francisco Longshoremen and the Newcomers." Seminar paper, San Francisco State University, 1995, ILWU Library.

Larrowe, Charles. "Did the Old Left Get Due Process? The Case of Harry Bridges." *California Law Review* 60 (1972): 39–83.

———. "The Great Maritime Strike of '34." *Labor History* 11 (1970): 403–31.

———. *Harry Bridges: The Rise and Fall of Radical Labor in the United States*. 2nd ed. New York: Lawrence Hill, 1979.

———. *Shape-Up and Hiring Hall: A Comparison of Hiring Methods and Labor Relations on the New York and Seattle Waterfronts*. Westport, CT: Greenwood Press, 1955.

Lim, Seonghee. "Automation and San Francisco Class 'B' Longshoremen: Power, Race, and Workplace Democracy, 1958–1981." PhD diss., University of California, Santa Barbara, 2015.

Magden, Ronald. *A History of Seattle Waterfront Workers, 1884–1934*. Seattle: Trade Printery, 1991.

———. *Serving Tacoma's Waterfront: One Hundred Years*. Tacoma: Print Northwest, 1986.

———. *The Working Longshoreman*. Tacoma: R-4 Typographers, n.d.

Magden, Ronald, and A. D. Martinson. *The Working Waterfront: The Story of Tacoma's Ships and Men*. Tacoma: ILWU Local 23 and Port of Tacoma, 1982.

Markholt, Ottilie. *Maritime Solidarity: Pacific Coast Unionism, 1929–1938*. Tacoma: Pacific Coast Maritime History Committee, 1998.

Mills, Herb. "The San Francisco Waterfront: The Social Consequences of Industrial Modernization, Part One: 'The Good Old Days.'" *Urban Life* 5 (1976): 221–50.

———. "The San Francisco Waterfront: The Social Consequences of Industrial Modernization, Part Two: The Modern Longshore Operations." *Urban Life* 6 (1977): 3–32.

Nelson, Bruce. "Class and Race in the Crescent City: The ILWU from San Francisco to New Orleans." In *The CIO's Left-Led Unions*, edited by Steve Rosswurm. New Brunswick, NJ: Rutgers University Press, 1992.

———. *Divided We Stand: American Workers and the Struggle for Black Equality*. Princeton, NJ: Princeton University Press, 2002.

———. "The 'Lords of the Docks' Reconsidered: Race Relations among West Coast Longshoremen, 1933–61." In *Waterfront Workers: New Perspectives on Race and Class*, edited by Calvin Winslow. Urbana: University of Illinois Press, 1998.

———. *Workers on the Waterfront: Seamen, Longshoremen, and Unionism in the 1930s*. Urbana: University of Illinois Press, 1988.

Pedersen, Vernon. *The Communist Party on the American Waterfront: Revolution, Reform, and the Quest for Power*. Lanham, MD: Lexington Books, 2019.

Pilcher, William W. *The Portland Longshoremen: A Dispersed Urban Community*. New York: Holt, Rinehart, and Winston, 1972.

Polishuk, Sandy. "'They Can't Come in the Front Door Because You Guys Won't Let Them': An Oral History of the Struggle to Admit African Americans into ILWU Local 8." *Oregon Historical Quarterly* 120 (2019): 546–61.

Quam-Wickham, Nancy. "Who Controls the Hiring Hall? The Struggle for Job Control in the ILWU during World War II." In *The CIO's Left-Led Unions*, edited by Steve Rosswurm. New Brunswick, NJ: Rutgers University Press, 1992.

Quin, Mike [Paul William Ryan]. *The Big Strike*. Olema, CA: Olema, 1949.

Record, Jane Cassels. "Ideologies and Trade Union Leadership: The Case of Harry Bridges and Harry Lundeberg." PhD diss., University of California, Berkeley, 1954.

Renfro, Mary. "The Decline and Fall of the Riggers' and Stevedores' Union of San Francisco: A History of the Years 1916 through 1919." Senior honors thesis, San Francisco State University, 1996.

Resner, Herbert. *The Law in Action during the San Francisco Longshore and Maritime Strike of 1934*. Project No. 1950, Works Progress Administration, District No. 8, Official Project No. 66-3-2858–Symbol 1871, Berkeley, CA, 1936.

Schneider, Betty V. H., and Abraham Siegel. *Industrial Relations in the Pacific Coast Longshore Industry*. Berkeley: Institute of Industrial Relations, University of California, Berkeley, 1956.

Schwartz, Harvey. "Harry Bridges and the Scholars: Looking at History's Verdict." *California History* 59 (1980): 71–72.

———. *The March Inland: Origins of the ILWU Warehouse Division, 1937–1938*. Los Angeles: Institute of Industrial Relations, University of California, Los Angeles, 1978.

Selvin, David. *A Terrible Anger: The 1934 Maritime and General Strikes in San Francisco*. Detroit: Wayne State University Press, 1998.

Stafford, Jeffrey L. "The Pacific Coast Maritime Strike of 1936: Another View." *Pacific Historical Review* 77 (2008): 589–93.

Torigian, Michael. "National Unity on the Waterfront: Communist Politics and the ILWU during the Second World War." *Labor History* 30 (1989): 409–32.

Ward, Estolv. *Harry Bridges on Trial*. New York: Modern Age Books, 1940.

Wark, Colin, and John F. Galliher. *Progressive Lawyers under Siege: Moral Panic during the McCarthy Years*. Lanham, MD: Lexington Books, 2015.

Wellman, David. *The Union Makes Us Strong: Radical Unionism on the San Francisco Waterfront*. Cambridge: Cambridge University Press, 1997.

Youst, Lionel. "Harry and Agnes Bridges: A Couple at Odds." *Pacific Northwest Quarterly* 106 (Spring 2015): 68–83.

Zalburg, Sanford. *A Spark Is Struck! Jack Hall and the ILWU in Hawaii*. Honolulu: University Press of Hawai'i, 1979.

Index

Page references in *italics* refer to illustrations

ment, 347n10; relationship with wife, 8; union activism of, 3–4; "When Britannia Wants a Soldier," 4–5; on World War I, 4–5

Bridges, Alice (Alice Whykes), 1, 259

Bridges, Betty Jacqueline (Jackie), 30, 35, *179*, 400n44; and Bridges's citizenship, 220; at Bridges's 1939 INS hearing, 178; marriage of, 296; psychiatric care, 238; on robbery attempt, 113–14, 379n24

Bridges, Charles, 4

Bridges, George, 6

Bridges, Harry (Alfred Renton Bridges), 1; in Albion Hall group, 42–44; antidiscrimination activism and beliefs, 15, 49, 204–5, 217–18, 271; death, 337; deportation proceedings, eligibility for, 166; during Great Depression, 35, 38; on FBI Administrative Index, 328; FBI files on, 155, 167, 181, 184, 191, 308, 396n11, 429n45; hearings and trials (*see* trials, hearings, and appeals, of Bridges); importance for war effort, 194; induction into Labor International Hall of Fame, 343; INS investigations of, 154–56, 166–70, 172, 174, 180, 184, 188, 220, 232, 240–42, 417n45; IWW membership, 14, 15, 17, 340, 353n66; love of horse racing, 3, 295–96, 334, 335; meeting with Nixon, 259–60; in New Orleans, 15–17, 40; radicalism charges against, 340; Republican Party registration, 270–71, 428n38; robbery/assassination attempt on, 113–14, 379n24; Sailors' Union of the Pacific membership, 12, 13; in San Francisco work-relief program, 38; and St. Francis Square project, 300; support for East Coast strikers, 129; Supreme Court appeals (1937), 142, 196, 388n29; Supreme Court appeals (1945), 194–96; Supreme Court appeals (1949), 252–53, 262; trials (*see* trials, hearings, and appeals, of Bridges); unemployment experiences, 14, 35

—character: analytical abilities, 58; foibles, ix; honesty, 341; iconic status of, x, 294, 344, 443n12; intelligence, 121; pragmatism, 222, 341; realism, 340; thrift, 296; writing skills, 58, 435n40. *See also* Bridges, Harry (Alfred Renton Bridges): leadership

—CIO regional directorship, 134, 140, 152; firing from, 232, 233, 239; replacements for, 233; on voting policy, 231

—citizenship: attainment of, 219–20; declaration of, 17, 358n44; hearing for, 413n75; immigrant status of, 28; missed deadlines for, 114–15; retention of, 264; revocation of, 248. *See also* Bridges, Harry (Alfred Renton Bridges): deportation proceedings; Immigration and Naturalization Service

—civil denaturalization trial (1955), 262–65; Bridges's testimony in, 263, 264; defense for,

264; judge in, 263, 264–65, 426n9; verdict in, 264; witnesses, 264, 425n8

—Communist Party relationship, ix, 36, 80, 93, 112, 154–66; Central Committee membership, 165–66, 394n4; CIO and, 149; committee positions held, 342; conflict in, 327; cooperation with Party, 162; denials of, 159, 166, 174, 242, 263; effect on his leadership, 341; as "fellow traveler," 155; historiography of, 154–56, 391n2; as "influential," 162, 164–66; as national security risk, 250, 251; in 1950s, 259; Party committee service, 162–63, 165–66, 393n23, 394n4; Party's advice to, 341; Party's lack of control over, 166; Party support for, 178, 341–42; *People's World*'s criticism, 327; Plant on, 386n102; PolBuro meeting, 113; during retirement, 335; RGASPI files on, 155, 159, 162; "Rossi" pseudonym, 165, 169, 170, 174, 246, 396n10; signing of Taft-Hartley affidavit, 248; support for Popular Front, 153. *See also* Bridges, Harry (Alfred Renton Bridges): deportation proceedings; FBI, investigations of Bridges

—conflicts: Goldblatt, 295, 297–300, 311–12; Lundeberg, 107, 109–10, 118–21, 123, 139, 141, 267–69, 380n42; Murray, 222, 228; Ryan, 65, 71, 73, 74, 79–80, 112, 126, 128, 133, 140, 176, 266

—criminal conspiracy trial (1949–50), 242–55; attorneys, 242–43, 246; Australian information on, 422n31; bail for, 248, 250, 251, 255; defense for, 245–46; duration of, 249; FBI in, 246–47; fund-raising for, 254; ILWU's payment for, 253–54; INS role in, 232–33, 240–42, 245, 247, 417n45; jail term, 251–52; judge, 245; perjury charges in, 242, 246; press coverage of, 247, 248; prosecution of, 242, 245, 247–48; res judicata argument in, 253; Supreme Court appeal, 252–53, 262; as union busting, 242; verdict in, 248; witnesses in, 246–47

—deportation proceedings (1939–40), 166–72, *179*, 196, 346n1, 394n35; attorneys for, 175–78, 180; Bridges's testimony in, 178–79, 181; Cox's lawsuit on, 170–71, 219; decision in, 181; demands for, 167–68, 174; denunciation of Dies Committee, 176; duration of hearing, 178; enemies' accusations, 167–74; evidence in, 168–74, 177, 180–81, 183, 396nn7–8; FBI file in, 167; historiography of, 167; INS hearing, 154, 168, 174–82, 184, 363n31; lack of corroboration for, 175; location for, 177–78; perjury in, 167, 170, 175, 181, 183; press coverage of, 400n45; prosecutor's case in, 173; "Re: Harry Bridges" memo, 180–81; Roosevelt and, 177, 181; Senate committees on, 174–75; testimony in, 171–75, 180–81, 184; warrant for, 175, 399n35; wiretapping in, 169, 245, 396n7, 398n39. *See also* FBI, investigations of Bridges

Bridges, Harry (*continued*)

—views (*continued*): one-man unions, 296–97, 340; party politics, 259, 305; pilfering, 32; Polish Solidarity, 335; presidential campaign of 1960, 302–3; racial discrimination, 49, 204–5, 217–18, 271; on racism, 49; on representation, 52; retirement age, 329; return to Australia, 407n56; right to strike, 210; Russian Revolution, 308; Soviet medicine, 333; Soviet Union, x, 201, 272–73, 308, 327–28, 341, 342; student demonstrations, 299; support for Roosevelt, 176, 202, 212, 221, 308, 342; syndicalism, 121, 155; Taft-Hartley, 227, 234; technological progress, 279–81; third party movement, 230, 231, 232; union busting, 210, 211; union democracy, 121; unions' political action, 137, 212, 305; Vietnam War, 306; Wobblies, 29

Bridges, Henry Renton: Boer War stories, 3; death of, 5; union activism, 3–4, 14, 58

Bridges, Julia Dorgan, 1; anticonscription views, 7; business interests of, 2, 8; Catholicism of, 30; Irish nationalism of, 2–3, 5, 349n24; news of son, 80; relationship with husband, 8

Bridges, Julie, 239, *260*, 264, 275; during Bridges's civil denaturalization trial (1955), 264; college education, 296; marriage of, 336; relations with Harry, 296

Bridges, Katherine, *276*, 296, 302; in Colorado Forestry Service, 336; high school years, 329

Bridges, Lucy, 1, 5

Bridges, Nancy Berdecio: alcoholism, 296; during Bridges's criminal conspiracy trial (1949–50), 248; Bridges's relationship with, 197; divorce from Harry, 275; marriage to Harry, 220

Bridges, Noriko "Nikki" Sawada, *276*, 310, 347n4, 423n41; and Bridges's health, 295; at Bridges's retirement celebrations, 329–30; death of, 338; eulogy for Bridges, 338; on HUAC protest, 302; on Japanese American reparations, 332–33; in Jeannette Rankin Brigade, 306; on loss of Bridges, 443n57; love of racing, 334; marriage to Bridges, 275–77, 294; "To Be or Not to Be; There's No Such Option," 336; travels, 335; travel to Romania, 333; wartime internment of, 277, 336; writings, 336, 338

Bridges, Robert Alfred Renton, 239, *260*, 275, 296; marriage of, 336

Bridges, Thomas Lester, 1

Bridges-Robertson-Schmidt trial. *See* Bridges, Harry (Alfred Renton Bridges): criminal conspiracy trial

Bridges v. California (1937), 142, 196, 388n29

Brophy, John, 138, 233

Brost, John, 139

Browder, Earl, 41, 97, 393n32; AAS and, 135, 151; on Bridges, 189; expulsion from Communist

Party, 222; H. George and, 159, 161; on MFW leadership, 165; presidential candidacy, 119; release from prison, 193–94; report to Polburo, 161; on Teheran Conference, 210, 211, 221

Brown, Archie: indictment under Landrum-Griffin Act, 303–4

Browne, William, 168

Brudge, Elmer, 118

Bryson, Hugh, 229, 255, 267

Budge, Alexander, 255

Bulcke, Germain, 147, 148; on coast caucus negotiating committee, 284, 285; ILWU service, 243, 297

Bureau of Labor Statistics, on longshore workers, 21

Burton, Harold: in Bridges's Supreme Court appeal, 253

Burton, Philip, 323

Caen, Herb, 191, 231, 239, 302, 303, 337; on Bridges's health, 332; on Bridges's relationship to communism, 272; on Khrushchev's visit, 270; on Shelley, 307

California: general elections, 71, 147, 212; labor-Left culture of, 271; New Deal Democrats of, 148; right-to-work proposition, 271

California Board of State Harbor Commissioners, on San Francisco waterfront, 21–22; appointment to, 148

California Journal, honoring of Bridges, 343

California Labor Federation: annual convention (1937), 144; CP and, 115–16

California Labor School (CLS), 271

Callaghan, Martin, 280

Cannery and Agricultural Workers' International Union, 36

capitalism, Third Period, 36

Carey, James, 224, 242

cargo, break-bulk: 281; loading and unloading of, 21–22, *22*; sling-loads of, 291, 315; traditional transfer methods, 279, 281. *See also* containerization

cargo, hot: boycotts of, 113, 114, 116; in 1946, 224; and renewal of ILA agreement, 114; in strike of 1936–37, 131

Carroll, Peter, 336

Casey, Joe, 144

Casey, Michael: and Bloody Thursday, 88, 89, 93; on Blue Book affiliation, 32, 33; on control of union members, 161; death of, 136, 143; on general strike, 92; Industrial Association communications, 70; in 1934 strike, 61–62; opinion of NLB, 79; on strikebreakers, 114; in strike negotiations, 72, 73, 74, 371n51; and strike of 1936–37, 125; Teamsters leadership, 13; on WEU negotiation, 56

Congress of Industrial Organizations (CIO) (*continued*): communism stances, 134–35, 137–38, 149, 151, 164, 226, 243; conflict with AFL, 108, 134–37, 144, 146; conflict with WFTU, 224; CP in, 135, 149, 151–53, 154, 164, 222; demand for second front, 206; denunciation as communist, 140, 176; effect of IPP on, 231; in election of 1948, 229; endorsement of Marshall Plan, 229–30; expulsion of Communists, 151–53, 154; expulsion of ILWU, 240, 252, 259, 262, 294; expulsion of Left Unions, 252; expulsion of NUMCS, 267; expulsion of unions, 243–44; formation of, 134; honoring of Bridges, 211; ILA-PCD affiliation for, 138–39; ILA-PCD support for, 135, 136; Left-Right divide in, 228; maritime unions of, 223, 234; merger with AFL, 262; national conference (1937), 164; national convention (1946), 226, 249; national convention (1949), 243; and no-strike pledges, 202, 211; political action by, 213; raids on ILWU, 233; red-baiting by, 211; strike of 1945–46, 223; and strike of 1948, 236, 237; trial of ILWU, 249–50, 252; West Coast regional directors, 152; during World War II, 199. *See also* AFL-CIO

Congress of Industrial Organizations (CIO) California Industrial Union Council: on Bridges's trial, 242; election endorsements (1948), 230; Left control of, 233; loss of charter, 243; Political Action Committee, 233

Congress of Industrial Organizations (CIO) Maritime Committee, *Wartime Shipping: A Plan and Memorandum*, 208

Congress of Industrial Organizations (CIO) San Francisco Industrial Union Council, endorsement of Havenner, 230

Connelley, E. H., 193; in FBI investigation of Bridges, 184–88, 408n4; on INS, 184

Connor, Frank, 171

container freight stations (CFSs), 315–16; ILWU agreement on, 317, 318, 320, 324

containerization: development of, 279; double handling of, 322; effect on locals, 314; Matson's use of, 281–82; pilferage from, 315; at Port of Oakland, 314, 331; stuffing and stripping, 293, 315–16, 318, 322. *See also* mechanization; technology

contracts. *See* bargaining

Coos Bay (Oregon), mapping survey of, 18–19

Copeland, Royal: on Bridges's deportation, 175, 180

Couderakis, George (Nicholas Bordoise), death and funeral of, 86, 90

Cowan, Claire, 187, 189

Cox, Ivan, 58, 115; ILA-PCD service, 119; lawsuit against Bridges, 170–71, 219

Craft, William, 133

cranes: Matson's use of, 282; operating permits for, 291–92, 321n41. *See also* mechanization

Cranston, Alan, 305, 306

Crawford, A. L.: in Cox lawsuit, 170, 171, 219; representation of Agnes, 219

Creel, George, 48–50; on WEU negotiations, 55

Crocker, William H.: on 1934 strikes, 94–95

Crouch, Paul, 246–47

Crum, Bartley, 194

Cuba, Bridges's travel to, 335

Cummings, Homer, 94

Curran, Joe, 125, 130, 226; in CMU, 224; conflict with Bridges, 223; leadership of East Coast seamen, 135; meeting with Ryan, 140

Curtin, John: on Bridges's deportation, 198

Curtis, Harry, 47; at NLB hearings, 103

Cushing, Oscar K., 105; NLB service, 78–79, 96, 103

Cutright, Charles, 74, 80, 81, 158

Daffron, Shelby, 81

Daily Worker, coverage of Duclos, 221

Daisy Knights (ketch), Bridges on, 8–9, 12, 251n39

Dalrymple, William, 151; anti-communism of, 152

Damaso, Carl, 312

Darcy, Samuel Adams, 38, 241; AAS service, 165, 394n33; at Bloody Thursday funerals, 91; on Bridges as communist, 154, 162; dissolution of MWIU, 108; expulsion from CP, 157; in general strike of 1934, 159, 160; Hynes and, 39; on Jackson, 41; meeting with Lundeberg, 186, 193; as issue in 1941 INS hearing, 188, 404n24; in 1934 strikes, 61, 64; organizing by, 37–38; on vigilante raids, 98; on Wallace campaign, 231; waterfront organizing by, 36, 37, 38

Daub, Eugene: bust of Bridges, *343*, 344

Davis, Gray, 344

Davis, O. L., 422n31

Deal, Clyde, 39; on Holman, 44, 45

decasualization: ILA-PCD on, 52; ILWU resolution on, 270

Decker, Carolyn, 181, 394n35

Del Guercio, Albert: Board of Immigration presentation, 193; prosecution of Bridges, 186, 187, 402n15

Delisle (steamship), Bridges on, 12, 13, 14

DeLoach, C. D., 273, 274

Democratic Party: Bridges on, 271, 305; Bridges's harm to, 177; Bridges's support for, 221; of California, 147; CP and, 210–11, 256; in elections of 1946, 226; in Hawai'i, 256; ILWU endorsement of, 271; IPP and, 230; Wallace campaign and, 231. *See also* New Deal

Dennis, Eugene, 393n32, 396n8

DeShetler, Irwin, 223
Dies, Martin, 176. *See also* House Committee on
Un-American Activities
Dietrich, Eugene "Dutch," 42–43, 373n92; con-
servatism of, 52; militancy of, 158; visit to
Northwest locals, 52
Dispatcher, The (ILWU newspaper): on afford-
able housing, 300; antidiscrimination views,
203; on Bridges's international tour, 269; on
containerization, 282, 283; "For a People's
Victory and a People's Peace!" slogan, 212;
Fortune ranking of, 226; on ILWU-Teamster
Unity, 266; on international longshore meet-
ings, 310; on John L. Lewis, 202; on Korean
War, 250; on Marshall Plan, 229; on mechani-
zation, 282; on M&M agreement, 288–89; "On
the Beam" column, 203, 212, 300, 301, 304,
309, 317, 327, 331; on presidential campaign of
1960, 302–3; promotion of Wallace, 230; pub-
lication of Martin Luther King, 307; on strike
of 1971, 323; on Truman administration, 258
Distributors' Association of Northern California
(DANC), 266
Dombroff, Bob, 138
Donoghue, Patrick, 114
Donohue, F. Joseph "Jiggs," 251; on Bridges's bail,
255; prosecution of Bridges, 242, 245, 247–48
Dore, John F., 127, 136
Dorgan, Beatrice, 2, 5
Dorgan, Ellen, 2, 5, 6, 7; boardinghouse of, 8
Dorgan, Harry (alleged pseudonym), 274; forged
membership book of, 169, 172, 175, 176, 396n8
Douglas, Helen Gahagan: CIO endorsement of,
230
Douglas, William O.: in Bridges decision, 196
Downey, Sheridan, 147, 148, 212; Senate Man-
power Subcommittee of, 209
Doyle, Stanley "Larry," 241; accusations against
Bridges, 168–72, 174–76, 178, 179, 181
Dreyfus, Barney, 275
Dubofsky, Melvyn, 377n1
Duclos, Jacques: on American CP, 221–22

Easter Rising (Ireland), 5
Eastland, James O., 271
Eddy (Pan-Pacific Trade Union Secretariat),
361n15
Eggleston, Arthur, 140
Einstein, Charles, 336, 345, 347n4, 442n48
Eisenhower, Dwight, 271; election as president,
259
El Dorado (ship), Bridges on, 17, 353n66
Eliel, Paul, 25–26; on arbitration of 1934–40,
389n50; on Bloody Thursday funerals, 91; on
Blue Book, 26; on Bridges, 92; on Industrial
Association, 370n49, 371n51, 371n54; on 1934

strike, 69–70; PCMIB chair, 207–8; at Stanford
Business School, 208; on striker communism,
70; on vigilante violence, 98; *The Waterfront
and General Strikes*, 367n1
Engstrom, James, 139, 178
Evatt, H. V., 198

Fairley, Lincoln, 281, 282, 284; on Bridges-
Goldblatt animosity, 299; in CLRC/PMA
negotiations, 287, 290; *Facing Mechanization*,
430n1, 437n1; on ILWU caucus demands, 317;
ILWU research directorship, 430n1; on steady
men, 315
Fales, Kevin, 337
Farm Equipment Union, expulsion from CIO,
244
Farmer-Labor Party, MFP endorsement of, 119
Farnham, Honor, 9, 329
FBI: Administrative Index (ADEX), 328;
authority for internal security, 401n53;
bribery accusation against, 264; in Bridges's
criminal conspiracy trial (1949–50), 246–47;
on Bridges-Wallace interview, 273; on communist espionage, 162; on CP membership,
394n35; Custodial Detention Index, 192; DET-
COM program, 241, 248, 419n3; estimate of
CP membership, 424n69; files on Bridges, 155,
167, 181, 184, 191, 308, 396n11, 429n45, 439n11;
investigation of Knowles, 395n2; report on
Taylor, 253; Security Index, 328; surveillance
of Bridges, 201, 230–32, 272, 328; surveillance
of King, 197
—investigation of Bridges, 155; following
Supreme Court decision, 197; in 1948, 241;
wartime surveillance, 201
—investigation of Bridges (1939–40), 167, 181,
396n11; wiretapping in, 169, 396n7, 398n39
—investigations of Bridges (1940–45), 183–98,
401nn6–7, 402n10; burglary in, 183; CP status
in, 185; report to Jackson, 185; *Waterfront
Worker* in, 184; wiretapping in, 183, 191–93,
197, 209–10, 405n35. *See also* Bridges, Harry
(Alfred Renton Bridges): Communist Party
relationship; Bridges, Harry (Alfred Renton
Bridges): deportation proceedings
FBI Special Agent in Charge of an FBI field office
(SAC, Miami), reports on Bridges, 246–47
FBI Special Agent in Charge of an FBI field office
(SAC, San Francisco), 206; surveillance of
Bridges, 197, 241, 248, 251
featherbedding, 278–79, 281; in CLRC/PMA
negotiations, 288
Federal Maritime Commission, 123–24, 207; on
pay increases, 124
Federal Mediation and Conciliation Service
(FMCS), 233–34

HUAC testimony, 257; and ILWU Hawai'i strike, 225–26; relationship with Goldblatt, 298; Smith Act conviction, 257, 262, 265

Hall, Paul, 309

Hallinan, Vincent: fund-raising for Bridges, 254; prison sentence of, 245, 248; representation of Bridges, 244–47

Halling, Bjorne, 42, 47, 53, 55, 207

Hamlet, Harry: as Federal Maritime Commission advisor, 123–24

Hanna, Edward J.: NLB service, 78–79, 104

Hannon, Bruce, 186, 394n35; in Bridges's civil denaturalization trial (1955), 263–64

Hanoff, Elmer (Efrim) "Pop": CP organizing by, 37

Hansen, Donald: assault on Bridges, 269

Harris, Charles: misconduct charges against, 10

Harris, George: in Bridges criminal conspiracy trial, 245–46, 251–52

Harrison, Gregory, 235

Harry Bridges Center for Labor Studies (University of Washington, Seattle), 343

Harry Bridges Chair in Labor Studies (University of Washington), 343

Harry Bridges Institute (San Pedro), 343

Harry Bridges Memorial Park (Long Beach), 343

Harry Bridges Plaza (San Francisco), 344

Harry R. Bridges Memorial Building, 324n66, 328

Hartman, Paul T.: Collective Bargaining and Productivity, 430n1

Hathaway, Clarence, 151, 237

Havenner, Frank, 212, 213; CIO endorsement of, 230

Hawai'i: Big Five factors, 216–17, 255, 256; Dock Seizure Act, 256; ILWU/IBT agreement on, 308; ILWU in, ix–x, 216–18, 277, 412n61; ILWU strike (1946), 225–26; longshore organizing in, 133; pineapple industry, 227, 257, 280; Smith Act proceedings, 259, 262, 265, 1951; sugar industry, 217, 218, 225–26, 256, 280

Hawaiian Employers' Council (HEC), 226

Haynes, John, 155, 392n5, 393n32

Hays, Lee: "Song for Bridges," 190–91

Haywood, Allan, 227, 233; firing of Bridges, 232; INS testimony of, 241; and strike of 1948, 236

Healy, Dorothy Ray, 394n35

Healy, James, 192, 248–49; meeting with Bridges, 270; relationship with Bridges, 269, 310, 427n32

Hearst, William Randolph: anti-communism of, 97; on general strike, 97

Hearst papers, Bridges on, 296

Hedley, George, 85, 86

Henning, John, 323, 338

Herman, James "Jimmy," 310; Port Commission service, 332

Hillman, Sidney, 151

Hinckle, Warren, 339

Hinckley, Robert, 96

hiring halls: in general strike of 1934, 99, 101, 102, 104, 340; ILA Local 38–79 on, 117; ILA-PCD on, 92; ILA supervision of, 105; in ILA-WEA bargaining, 122; ILWU stance on, 204, 205; NMU's, 137; postwar challenges to, 228; steady men dispatched from, 314–15; in strike of 1934, 59, 65–67, 69, 71, 72, 76, 79, 84; in strike of 1948, 237; in strikes of 1936–37, 130; under Taft-Hartley Act, 233–34; WEA's proposals for, 209

Hockensmith, Lynn Harvey, 47

Hoffa, James: IBT presidency, 308; imprisonment of, 309; RFK's pursuit of, 303

Holifield, Chet: CIO endorsement of, 230

Holman, Lee: Blue Book inaction, 45; ILA leadership, 43–46, 47; ILA organizing, 36, 39; insubordination charges against, 57; and Matson campaign, 48, 56; opponents of, 42; red-baiting by, 57; removal from ILA presidency, 56–58

Holt, Harold, 248

Holt, Victoria, 256

Hoover, Herbert, 38, 381n49

Hoover, J. Edgar, 172; and Bridges investigation, 183–84, 192, 401n2, 402n16, 408n4; on Bridges's bail, 251; on Bridges's communism, 186, 241; on Bridges's HUAC subpoena, 274; Custodial Detention Index of, 192; on Hawaiian Democratic Party, 256; on Local 10 communism, 206; on maritime union convention, 224

Horvitz, Wayne, 287, 288; on M&M agreement, 290–91; on St. Sure, 438n12

Hot Jazz Society (San Francisco), 218

Houghteling, James L., 174, 188

House Committee on Un-American Activities (HUAC), 162, 171, 240; in AAS files, 166; on Bridges, 179–80; Bridges's denunciation of, 176; Bridges's subpoena from, 273–74; Bridges's testimony before, 396n8; demonstration against, 302; Hawai'i case, 257, 258; Operation Abolition (film and report), 302; on Ross, 247; San Francisco hearings, 301–2

House Immigration Committee, on Allen bill, 186

Howe, Louis, 96

Huberman, Leo: Storm over Bridges, 191

Hudson, Roy, 39, 42; on Bridges's wartime stance, 201; on Communist Party espionage, 160; on communist waterfront influence, 156; MWIU secretaryship, 161; reports to PolBuro, 163, 164

Hughes, William Morris, 4; endorsement of conscription, 5

of 1953, 259; of 1955, 266; of 1959, 270, 284; of 1961, 306, 311–13; of 1963, 307; of 1973, 326; of 1975, 329; of 1977, 326, 330, 440n16; of 1983, 335; of 1985, 325; of 1988, 333
—locals: alignment with Bridges, 205–6; Gulf of Mexico, 204; ILA-PCD, 145–46; membership meetings, 284; national, 145; racial discrimination in, 204; raids on, 233; revolt against ILWU, 243; segregated, 204; strike (1939), 149–50; Walking Bosses, 362n27. *See also names of specific locals*
—positions taken: affirmative action, 330; Afghanistan War, 344; anti-apartheid, 330; antidiscrimination, 145, 203, 204, 217–18, 330, 341; civil rights, 306–7; Democratic Party endorsement, 271; equalized earnings, 315; hiring halls, 204; Hoffa, 309; labor-saving devices, 145; Landrum-Griffin Act compliance, 303; loyalty to Bridges, 339; Marshall Plan, 228–30, 239, 240; NMU gains, 224; nuclear disarmament, 306–7; opposition to Vietnam War, 306–7, 331; right to decline jobs, 292; Roosevelt, 153; Taft-Hartley affidavits, 227, 233, 244; third party endorsement, 229, 230; War Shipping Administration, 208; world trade, 285
—postwar era, 199; bargaining proposal, 211–12; membership growth, 226; no-strike pledge, 210–12, 411n42; presidential campaign (1968), 306, 309; reorganization, 213–15
—relationships: AFL-CIO, 144, 262, 312, 333; HEC, 226; IBL, 266; ILA, 265–66, 269, 312–13, 317, 321; international unions, 277, 310; other unions, 262, 308–9; SUP, 144, 146, 266–69; Teamster merger (proposed), 325–26
—retirement, 285; among officers, 297; pensioners, 342–43
—voting: procedures, 317, 323; strike votes, 225, 234
—World War II, during, 199, 202–18; staffing, 214–16; work stoppages, 202–3
International Longshore and Warehouse Union (ILWU) Canada, 266, 344
International Longshore and Warehouse Union coast caucuses: endorsement of CLRC proposal, 287; meetings (1959), 286–87; meetings (1971), 316–17, 318, 322–23; negotiating committees, 284, 285, 332, 339; on second M&M agreement, 292
International Longshore and Warehouse Union (ILWU) Local 6, 102, 211; CP members, 210; opposition to Bridges, 254; racial discrimination in, 217–18
International Longshore and Warehouse Union (ILWU) Local 8, racial issues in, 301, 341, 434n26

International Longshore and Warehouse Union (ILWU) Local 10, 153, 204; Black members, 205, 443n9; in B men's lawsuit, 300–301; civil rights activism, 307; effect of containerization on, 314; integration efforts, 205; Khrushchev's visit to, 270–71, 428n35; memorialization of Bridges, 337; M&M disputes in, 315; on no-strike pledge, 212; opposition to Lend-Lease, 199; opposition to strike settlement (1972), 324; picket (1971), *319*; PMA on, 318; racial discrimination in, 205, 301; strike committee, 236; telegrams to FDR, 208; violence at, 250; Wallace candidacy referendum, 230, 240, 243
International Longshore and Warehouse Union (ILWU) Local 13 (San Pedro): average age of, 290; and CLRC/PMA negotiations, 288, 289; effect of containerization on, 314; ethnic composition of, 204; on gang size, 287; M&M disputes in, 315; opposition to strike settlement (1972), 324; in *Pacificus* dispute, 268; racial issues in, 205, 341, 434n26; revolt of, 243; stop-work meeting (1958), 284
International Longshore and Warehouse Union (ILWU) Local 16: in Juneau collective bargaining, 257; wildcat strike (1948), 258
International Longshore and Warehouse Union (ILWU) Local 34, 149, 215
International Longshore and Warehouse Union (ILWU) Local 37, 217
International Longshore and Warehouse Union (ILWU) Local 91, opposition to Bridges, 250–51
International Longshore and Warehouse Union (ILWU) Local 142, ix; disaffiliation of, 258; merger of Hawaiian locals, 266; retirement age amendment, 329, 440n16
International Longshore and Warehouse Union longshore caucuses: on CFS issue, 315–16; in CLRC/PMA negotiations, 287; leadership/membership fusion of, 339; on mechanization, 280–81
International Longshore and Warehouse Union (ILWU)- PMA: registration committee, 300–301; Trust/Welfare Funds, 254, 278
International Longshoremen's Association (ILA), 13; AFL chartering of, 24; and Blue Book affiliation, 33, 358n48; 115, 116; corruption in, 265; districts of, 51; Eastern Seaboard agreement, 72; Holman's organizing for, 36; national convention (1935), 111–12; on NLRB election, 200; Portland strike (1922), 29; relations with ILWU, 265–66, 269, 312–13, 317, 321; revocation of charter, 265. *See also* strike(s), longshore; International Longshoremen's Association Pacific Coast District
International Longshoremen's Association (ILA) Local 38–44, 132

International Longshoremen's Association (ILA) Local 38-72, bank account dispute, 141–42

International Longshoremen's Association (ILA) Local 38-79: under award of 1934, 118; at Bloody Thursday funerals, 91; censure of Ryan, 71; charges of radicalism against, 74, 104; charter of, 42; convention of 1934, 53–54, 157; Defense Committee, 64–65; direct action by, 111; disavowal of arbitration, 157; elections, 45–48, 115; executive committee, 47–48, 53; factions in, 47; formation of, 359n4; on gangs, 102–3, 111; hiring hall issues, 117; Holman's presidency of, 47, 56–68; on its conservatism, 63–64; Matson campaign, 48–50; membership meetings (1934), 74, 80, 94, 101, 102; and MFP founding, 110; militancy of, 49, 157; and NRA codes, 47, 50; opposition to Blue Book, 47; Publicity Committee, 63, 64, 65; racial issues in, 49–50; in *Santa Rosa* action, 117–18; shipping companies' offer to, 124; solidarity with seamen, 74; Strike Committee, 61, 62, 63, 64, 68, 70–71, 73, 76, 80, 158, 160; in strike of 1936–37, 125–33; union buttons of, 48, 49; unity of, 49; in WEU negotiations, 55–58

International Longshoremen's Association Pacific Coast District (ILA-PCD), 24; allegations of communism against, 56, 63; annual conventions, 111–12, 118–19, 136–37; approach to mechanization, 282; award of 1934, 114, 115, 131; bargaining with WEA, 122–25; belief in unity, 47; Bridges's meeting with, 48; and British Columbia strike, 113–15; charges of radicalism against, 340; CIO relations, 134, 135, 138–41, 164; coastwise contract demand, 54–55; conflict with SUP, 133; on contract expiration, 123; on contract extensions, 124; creation of locals, 108; on decasualization, 52; democratic organization of, 45; dispatcher membership in, 81; on dispatching, 51; District Convention (1937), 164; East Coast strike (1936), 124, 128, 129, 130; employers' recognition for, 72, 81; executive board meeting (1937), 141; federal intervention for, 200; in general strike arbitration, 92, 101, 102; general strike victory, 105; on hiring halls, 92, 102, 103, 104; hiring hall supervision for, 105; and hot cargo boycotts, 115, 116; locals of, 408n5; at NLB hearings, 103; in 1934 strike, 65, 67; NLRB representation and, 142; on NRA codes, 50–51; organizing efforts of, 39; peace pact with WEA, 118; as sole longshore representative, 56; in strike of 1936–37, 126–31; support for CIO, 136; in Tacoma, 26; tension with IBT, 137; wage demands of, 50; WEU and, 53–58. *See also* bargaining

International Organization of Masters, Mates, and Pilots (MM&P), 51, 109, 128; in strike of 1936–37, 125

International Seamen's Union of America (ISU), 13; charter of, 116; "fink book" for, 102; hiring hall issues, 110; membership drive, 17; national leadership of, 116; in 1934 strike, 102; shipowners' demands on, 15, 16; strikes of, 61, 108, 125

International Woodworkers of America, contract with Juneau Spruce, 257–58

Jackman, Cole, 297

Jackson, Harry, 52, 76; in factional struggles, 362n20; and MWIU, 40–41, 108

Jackson, Robert, 181; and Bridges's Supreme Court appeal, 253; investigation of Bridges, 183, 185–86, 188, 196, 401n2; and Murray, 200; opposition to Allen bill, 183

Jacobs, Paul, 249; accusations against Bridges, 301

James Timson (ship), Bridges on, 16, 353n64

Japanese Americans: ILWU support for, 203, 217–18; reparations for, 332–33; wartime relocation of, 203

Jeannette Rankin Brigade, Noriko Bridges in, 306

Jenkins, David: on Bridges-Goldblatt animosity, 299; on Bridges's communism, 250; on Duclos, 221–22; friendship with Bridges, 240, 419n1; resignation from CP, 272; in Shelley campaign, 307

Jenkins, Edith, 272, 419n1

John, Michael: *American Communist History* (journal), 156

Johnson, Hiram, 77, 94

Johnson, Hugh, 98–100

Johnson, Joseph, 57, 68, 104, 158

Johnson, Lyndon, 304–5

Johnson, Malcolm: exposé of waterfront corruption, 265

Johnson, Manning, 246

Johnson, Michael, 215–16

Johnson, Miriam Dinkin, 394n35

Johnson, William "Bunk," 218

Johnstone, Jack, 188–89, 403n24; on communist longshore workers, 163; CP organizing, 115

Joint Maritime Strike Committee (1934), 74, 75, 79, 102; Bloody Thursday resolution, 88; Bridges on, 86–87, 99, 103, 160; creation of, 107; on general strike proposal, 82, 89; Vandeleur and, 92

Joint Policy Committee (1936), 126–27, 129–31

Jones, Bruce R. "Ben," "B. B.," 37, 361n14; on Bridges, 39; in criminal conspiracy trial, 247; in civil denaturalization trial (1955), 264, 425n8; on Jackson, 41; *Waterfront Worker* participation, 43

anti-Bridges sentiment in, 139–40; anti-communism in, 139; Bridges's district presidency
in, 110; creation of, 107, 109; District Council,
163; districts of, 110, 165; on Farmer-Labor
Party, 119; on hot-cargo issues, 116; in ILWU/
SUP conflict, 146; Joint Negotiating Committee, 123–24, 126; Joint Policy Committee, 126–
27, 129–31; left-wing members, 139; Resolution
47, 116, 163; in strike of 1936–37, 125–31, 164
Maritime Federation of the World (MFW):
Bridges's presidency of, 244, 251; opposition
to Korean War, 251maritime unity convention
(San Francisco, 1946), 223–24
Maritime Worker (Melbourne), 249
Markholt, Ottilie, 380n42, 391n3; *Maritime Soli-
darity*, 155
Marlowe, William, 119
Marsh, F. P., 117, 118, 123; Joint Policy Committee
meeting, 130; in strike of 1936–37, 124, 129–30
Marshall Plan: Bridges's opposition to, 228–30,
239, 240, 342; CIO endorsement of, 229–30;
CP attack on, 228, 240, 241; the *Dispatcher* 's
promotion of, 230; ILWU condemnation of,
228–30, 239, 240
Martin, George, 312, 329
Marty, Andre, 394n33
Marx, Karl, 8
Matson Navigation (firm): 19, 21, 22, 26, 60, 82,
126, 190, in Blue Book dispute, 45, 48; and
containerization, 280–82, *283*, 291; dock (San
Francisco), *22*; Hawaiian shipping, 216; ILA
strike against (1933), 48–50, 53, 56, 58; M&M
agreement and, 291; in 1934 longshore strike,
60, 62, 84; in 1936–37 longshore strike, 120; in
1948 longshore strike, 236–37; in 1949 Hawai-
ian longshore strike, 256; reduction of fleet,
282
Mattei, A. C., 172, 181
Mayes, Barney, 127–28; in Minneapolis Teamsters' strike, 384n80
Maynard, George, 12–13
McCarthy, Bill, 120
McCarthy, Joseph, 162, 240
McChrystal, A. J., 206
McClain, Curtis, 330
McClay, Kenneth: birth of, 19; in Bridges household, 30, 34; names used by, 357n38; shell
shock, 296
McClung, Ray, 96
McCray, Joe, 299, 435n40
McGrady, Edward F., 67, 105; on Bridges, 117;
on communist influences, 71; on failed
mediation, 84; hiring-hall proposal, 79; on
ILA-WEA bargaining, 123–24; on maritime
unions, 120; in 1936–37 longshore strike, 124,
126, 130; NLB service, 78–79, 104; request

for presidential intervention, 72; role in 1934
strikes, 62, 63, 65, 78; on strike settlement, 92;
WEU and, 69–70, 88
McIntyre, Marvin, 99
McKenna, Roger "Fats," 362n27
McLaughlin, John, 185; in general strike, 92, 93;
in 1934 longshore strike negotiations, 72, 73;
on 1937 Teamster embargo, 144
McLean, Malcolm: container design of, 281
McWilliams, Brian, x
Meany, George, 262, 309; conservatism of, 340;
support for strike of 1971, 323
mechanization, 226–27; CLRC proposal on, 285;
reduction in workforce through, 278, 280, 314.
See also Modernization and Mechanization
(M&M) agreements; technology
Meehan, Matt, 118, 119, 145
Melbourne (Australia): 1–14, 30; Bridges family residences in suburbs of, 347n5; Bridges's
visits to, 311, 329Melbourne Waterside Workers, in World War I, 6
Melnikow, Henry, 50, 88–89, 93, 110, 112, 163,
214–15, 340; Bridges's work with, 136, 163, 207,
215, 340; on collective bargaining, 215; Kagel's
work for, 50, 238; on labor conservatism, 104,
105, 340; on MFP planning, 109; in 1933 code
hearings, 50, 51, 53; 1934 general strike statement of purpose by, 96; on 1937 Teamster
embargo, 143; in NLB hearings, 103–5; in
strike of 1936–37, 122, 124, 126, 127, 131
Menzies, Robert: on Bridges's deportation, 248,
422n31
Merriam, Frank, 75, 78, 178; gubernatorial candidacy in 1938, 147; use of National Guard,
87, 97
Military Intelligence, 168, 171, 182
Miller, Joe, 82
Mills, Herbert, 21, 178, 344n9; deposition against
Bridges, 169–70, 173, 174, 176; on PMA negotiations, 320
Milner, Lawrence: at INS hearing, 178; perjury
by, 181; testimony against Bridges, 173
Minott-Weinacht Productions, Bridges documentary, x
Mitchell, James: in *Pacificus* dispute, 267–68, 289
Modernization and Mechanization (M&M)
agreements, 277, 278–93, 300, 313–16, 317, 340;
benefits under, 430n1; Bridges on, as "class
collaboration," 333, 340; effect on American
industry, 341
—first (1960), 278, 288–92; effect on longshore
work, 290, 292; expiration of, 292; Matson
and, 291; opposition to, 289; press coverage
of, 288–89, 290; productivity increases under,
292; stop-work meetings on, 289; wage guarantees, 292

Modernization and Mechanization (M&M) agreements (*continued*)
—second (1966), 278, 292; duration of, 293; expiration of, 314; ILWU dissatisfaction with, 316; negotiations for, 313; opposition to, 293; section 9.43, 314–15, 316; steady man provision of, 314

Mohn, Einer, 254–55, 266; on Bridges's statesmanship, 294

Molony, Guy, 16

Molotov, Vyacheslav: appearance with Bridges, 213, *214*

Molotov-Ribbentrop Pact (1939), 149, 152, 153; CPUSA on, 199

Mooney, Tom, 39, 90, 147–48, 171

Moore, Pete, 269

Moore, Walter, 19

Morris, W. T. "Paddy," 47, 53, 102, 103, 112, 114, 115, 126, 157; in MFP planning, 109; and gang steward issue, 103; militancy of, 158; on 1935 award extension, 115; refuses to seek reelection, 1936, 118, 119

Morrison, Jack, 307

Morse, Wayne, 148, 187, 202, 207, 213 262; ILWU support for, 306; NWLB service, 208, 216; opposition to Taft-Hartley, 227; senatorial campaign, 306, 331

Moscone, George, 332

Munro, Phil, 2, 8

Murdock, Steve, 325

Murphy, Dan, 96

Murphy, Frank, 196

Murray, Philip, 151, 190, 202, 223, 236; Bridges on, 296; on Bridges's trial (1948), 242, 248; "charter" with U.S. Chamber of Commerce, 211; as CIO president, 199–200, 244; firing of Bridges, 231–33; on ILWU expulsion, 252; on Marshall Plan, 228–30; "Murray Plan," 207; in 1948 strike, 234, 236; and no-strike pledges, 202, 210; opposition to CP, 222, 226; relations with Bridges, 200, 222, 228; revocation of California Industrial Union Council charter, 243

Myers, Frederick "Blackie," 199

National Association for the Advancement of Colored People, support for Bridges, 195

National Council of American-Soviet Friendship, 442n41; Bridges's service on, 335

National Guard: 59, 147, 173; anti-communism of, 182; in 1934 strike, 62, 75, 78, 87–88, 94, 96, 97, 158

National Labor Leadership Assembly for Peace, 307

National Labor Relations Board (NLRB), 107, 114, 143–45, 153, 171, 234, 255, 265; and Marine Cooks and Stewards, 267; ILWU support for, 153; in M&M agreement, 291; in 1948 strike, 234; no-picketing warehouse agreement (1950), 254; on Pacific Coast longshore representation, 142, 200; under Taft-Hartley Act, 227

National Longshoremen's Board (NLB), 78–81, 88, 92, 99, 101–105; hiring hall ruling, 102; ILA-PCD witnesses at, 103

National Maritime Union (NMU), 199, 225, 249, 309; Bridges's 1941 address to, 201; and CIO, 138, 140; in Committee for Maritime Unity, 224, 226; CP interests in, 226; expulsion of CP members, 255; jurisdictional conflict with SUP, 145–46; 1942 address to, 206; in 1946 strike, 223, 225; in 1946 unity convention, 223–24; organized, 137

National Portrait Gallery, Bridges's "living self-portrait" at, 333, *334*

National Recovery Administration (NRA), 38; Board of Adjustment, 48

National Recovery Administration (NRA) codes, 41, 48; hearings (1934), 50–51, 53; ILA and, 47, 50–51

National Union of Marine Cooks and Stewards, CIO (NUMCS): 227, 229, 255; bankruptcy and dissolution, 267; expulsion from CIO, 244, 252; in 1946 strike, 223, 225; in 1946 unity convention, 223–24; in 1948 strike, 235, 238;

National War Labor Board: "Little Steel formula," 202; Morse on, 208; union representation on, 202; wage increases under, 212

negotiations. *See* bargaining

Negroes and the Maritime Strike (1936), 127

Nelson, Bruce, 155; *Workers on the Waterfront*, 378n13

Neutrality Act of 1935, scrap iron provision, 118

Nevada, miscegenation law in, 277

New Deal, 38, 308; Bridges's support for, 176; general strike of 1934 and, 96; ILWU support for, 153; unraveling of, 135. *See also* Democratic Party

New Orleans: Bridges in, 15–17; waterfront strike in, 14–17

New York City, seamen's strike (1936), 125

New Yorker, "Some Fun with the F.B.I.," 192

New Zealand, Bridges's visit to, 311

Neylan, John Francis, 73, 82, 99; general strike meeting of, 100–101; on Hawaiian Big Five, 216; on Hugh Johnson, 98; on ILWU/IBU dispute, 144; use of press in 1934, 95–96

Niles, Harry M., 168

Nixon, Richard M.: Bridges and, 259–60, 271, 339; wage freeze of, 320–21

Norene, Roy, 169, 241

North American Aviation, UAW strike at, 200

Northern California District of Congress of California Seniors, Bridges's vice presidency of, 335

Oakland: labor conference (1945), 213; strike violence at, 60; Teamsters of, 76, 93, 144
Oakland Police Department, raid on CP, 97
O'Connell, John, 32–33, 57, 109, 132; on general strike prospect, 81; in 1934 strike, 76; on 1934 Strike Strategy Committee, 88
O'Connor, T. V., 32
Olsen, Carl, 85, 86, 87
Olsen, F., 8–9
Olsen, John, 26
Olson, Culbert, 147, 148, 212
O'Meara, John, 98
O'Neil, James, 139, 193; contempt of court imprisonment, 188; FBI interviews with, 187–88, 403n21
Organized Labor Democratic Committee, 147
Owens, John R., 51; on longshore work week, 52

Pacific American Shipowners Association (PASA): merger with WEA, 238; in strike of 1948, 235
Pacific Coast: changing demographics of, during World War II, 203; wartime development of, 203
Pacific Coast Maritime Industrial Board (PCMIB), 207–8, 212
Pacific Longshoremen's Memorial Association, 424n66
Pacific Maritime Association (PMA), 238; contracts with ILWU, 254; on four on-four off practice, 278; on gang size, 278, 279; "hard-timing" by SUP, 267–68; ILWU-PMA Welfare Fund, 254, 278; on local-level bargaining, 318; mechanization and, 281, 287; meeting with Khrushchev, 270; negotiations with CLRC, 1957ff., 280–82; on productivity, 286–87; technological training by, 282. See also bargaining, longshore contracts, 1948
Pacific Steamship Company, 22; and 1934 strike, 62
Pacific Union Club, 63
Pacificus (steam schooner) dispute, 267–69Paddison, Joshua: "Summers of Worry, Summers of Defiance," 433n27
Pampanito (submarine), at San Francisco Maritime Museum, 332
Pankhurst, Adela: Communism of, 8; meeting with Bridges, 7, 14
Paton, Eugene: ILWU service, 201; military service of, 213
Patri, Giacomo, 191
Patterson, Ellis, 147

Pauling, Linus, 306
Pay Board, federal, in strike of 1971, 321, 324; wage data of, 323, 331
Pearson, Drew, 202
Pedersen, Vernon, 393n29, 443n10; The Communist Party on the American Waterfront, 156, 378n11, 378n17, 379n22, 384n83
Pelosi, Nancy, 344
People's Front (Popular Front), 149; Bridges's support for, 153; during World War II, 201, 210
People's World (PW): on Bridges trial (1948), 242; on California legislature, 389n50; criticism of Bridges, 327; loss of subscribers, 271; on Soviet-Hitler pact, 149
Perkins, Frances: appointment of arbitrators, 105; and Bridges deportation efforts, 167, 171, 173, 174–75, 177, 181, 187; on Bridges's adultery, 398n39; Bridges's correspondence with, 174; and general strike of 1934, 95, 96, 100, 105; and hot cargo boycotts, 114; impeachment threat against, 177; on INS, 172–73; role in 1934 strike, 65, 72, 76, 77; role in strikes of 1936–37, 130; and WEU, 78, 88
Perry, Norma, 65, 112, 141; and Bridges as communist, 184; expulsion from CP, 121; as issue in 1941 INS hearing, 188, 404n24; ties to Industrial Association, 176–77; Voice of the Federation work, 127
Petersen, A. H., 51, 365n57; NLB testimony, 92; during 1934 strike, 63; in strike negotiations, 73
Pfleger, Herman, 105; during NLB hearings, 103–4; representation of shipping companies, 100–101
Pilcher, William, 28–29
pineapple industry, Hawaiian: ILWU and, 227, 257; technological innovation in, 280
Plant, Thomas G., 72; accusations against ILA, 74; on Bridges's communism, 386n102; on 1934 strike arbitration, 99; and 1934 strike negotiations, 73, 76; NLB testimony, 92; representation of WEA, 122; retirement, 237; in strike of 1936–37, 130; in WEA-ILA bargaining, 123; WEU presidency, 53, 55
PM (newspaper), on Bridges's wiretapping, 191, 192
Polish Solidarity Union, 335
Port Labor Relations Committees, in 1937 contract, 131–32
Portland, INS investigation in, 169–70, 172, 174–76, 178, 180, 183, 241, 245
Portland Police Department Red Squad, 139–40, 170, 174, 241; Teamsters' payments to, 172
Port of Oakland, containerization, 314, 331
Powell, Adam Clayton, 128
Prevost, J. H., 403n22

25; in 1921 strike, 18; and NLRB, 145, 153; racial exclusion by, 15, 113; relations with Blue Book union, 32; relations with ILWU, 144, 146, 266–69; in strike of 1936–37, 123, 125–31

Salinger, Pierre, 305

Sanatoriala Otopeni clinic (Romania), Bridges at, 333

Sanborn, Henry, 178; in Bridges's deportation procedure, 168, 169–71, 175, 176

Sanders, Bernie: ILWU endorsement of, 344

Sandin, Philip, 250

San Francisco: antipicketing ordinances, 146–47; antiunion organization in, 26; Black community of, 299; Bridges's arrival in, 12–13; in census of 1960, 432n12; China Basin, 23; Chinatown pickets, 148; class tensions in, 83; commerce of, 21–23; Embarcadero, 22–23, 60, 66, 84–85, 102; Ferry Building, 22, 26; Fort Mason, 23; jazz in, 218; labor politics of, 12–13; Maritime Museum, 332; 1934 strike, 59–83; 1934 general strike, 76, 88–100; rail yards of, 23; streetcar lines, 95; Union Iron Works, 23; V-E Day celebration, 213; Western Addition, 299, 328. *See also* International Longshoremen's Association Local 38–79; longshore workers (San Francisco); waterfront (San Francisco)

San Francisco Building Trades Council, strikes of, 26, 67

San Francisco Chamber of Commerce: during Bloody Thursday, 90; on force against strikers, 91

San Francisco Chinese Society, support for Bridges, 195

San Francisco Employers Council, 151; dealings with IBT, 266; and strike of 1948, 236, 237

San Francisco General Strike, 1934, 88–89, 92–100. *See also* strikes, longshore and maritime (1934)

San Francisco Industrial Association: bloodshed threats from, 87; and Bloody Thursday, 85, 87, 88, 90; destruction of records, 59, 370n41; employers' empowerment of, 83; on force against strikers, 91; Impartial Wage Boards of, 79; on labor leaders, 63; in 1934 strike, 59–61, 69–72; origin, 26; on port opening, 79; public relations efforts, 63, 74–75; rejection of strike agreements, 74–76; use of nonunion labor, 72; and vigilante raids, 98; waterfront employers and, 70

San Francisco Labor Council, 75; arbitration efforts, 94; Blue Book affiliation, 32, 33; Bridges's service on, 132, 161; on communism, 77; elections of 1936, 132; general strike goals, 99; in general strike of 1934, 88, 89, 92–100; during 1934 strike, 52, 56, 67, 76, 77, 80, 81, 84, 88–100; on strike of 1919, 25; support for Bridges, 117–18

San Francisco Police Department: Anti-radical and Crime Prevention Bureau (Red Squad), 96–96, 98; in 1934 strike, 60, 66–67, 68, 75, 76

San Francisco Port Commission, Bridges's service on, 308, 325, 332

San Pedro: Latino population of, 409n18; strike fatalities in, 69, 370n39. *See also* International Longshore and Warehouse Union (ILWU) Local 13

Santa Rosa (liner), ILA Local 38–79 action, 117

Sapiro, Aaron, 116, 121; on Bridges as communist, 161–62, 166; in Bridges's deportation action, 170, 173, 174; federal conviction of, 174; at INS hearing, 178

Sara Hunter (ship), Bridges on, 351n39

Scharrenberg, Paul, 32, 358n48; on Blue Book, 33, 39; call for war, 109; expulsion from SUP, 112, 378n17; on hiring halls, 110

Schmidt, Henry, 45, 47, 53, 54, 58, 115, 132, *143*; on Albion Hall group, 42, 43, 47; and Bloody Thursday, 86, 88; CLRC service, 297; criminal conspiracy trial (1949–50), 242–55; at ILA-PCD annual convention (1934), 54; ILA Local 38–79 presidency, 119; at NLB hearings, 103; opposition to Lend-Lease, 199; retirement of, 297; strike participation, 62, 74, 131; support for CIO affiliation, 141; testimony on Bridges, 197; *Waterfront Worker* participation, 43; on working conditions, 31

Schneiderman, William, 148, 170, 240, 241; in Bridges's deportation action, 169; on union amalgamation, 224

Schofield, Lemuel, 188

Schomaker, John, 42, 115, 119, 264, 396n7; as informant, 241, 421n22; picketing by, 66–67; testimony against Bridges, 246, 263; *Waterfront Worker* participation, 43

Schrimpf, Henry, 115, 119, 139, 246

Schwartz, Harvey, 391n2; on Bridges's relation to communism, 155

Schwellenbach, Lewis, 224

Scottsboro Action Committee, 61

scrap iron: ILWU picketing of, 118, 148; national export embargo on, 148; in Neutrality Act of 1935, 118

Sea and River Workers' Union (USSR), 327–28

Seafarers International Union (SIU), 146; AFL chartering of, 146; work stoppage (1954), 267

Seamen's Defense Committee, 125

Seamen's Union of Australia (SUA), strike by, 10; Bridges's claim to membership in, 10, 351nn46–47

Sears, Charles: hearing on Bridges's deportation, 186, 187, 189, 193, 197, 200, 219

Sea Thrush (Shepard Line ship), SUP picketing of, 145–46

ROBERT W. CHERNY is a professor emeritus of history
at San Francisco State University. His many books
include *Victor Arnautoff and the Politics of Art*.

The Working Class in American History

The University of Illinois Press
is a founding member of the
Association of University Presses.

University of Illinois Press
1325 South Oak Street
Champaign, IL 61820-6903
www.press.uillinois.edu